Black America

Black America

A State-by-State
Historical Encyclopedia

Volume I: A–M

Alton Hornsby, Jr., Editor

 GREENWOOD

AN IMPRINT OF ABC-CLIO, LLC
Santa Barbara, California • Denver, Colorado • Oxford, England

Copyright 2011 by Alton Hornsby, Jr.

All rights reserved. No part of this publication may be reproduced, stored in a retrieval
system, or transmitted, in any form or by any means, electronic, mechanical,
photocopying, recording, or otherwise, except for the inclusion of brief quotations in a
review, without prior permission in writing from the publisher.

Library of Congress Cataloging-in-Publication Data

Black America : a state-by-state historical encyclopedia / edited by Alton Hornsby, Jr.
   p. cm.
Includes bibliographical references and index.
ISBN 978–0–313–34112–0 (hardcopy (set) : acid-free paper) — ISBN 978–1–57356–976–7 (ebook (set))
— ISBN 978–0–313–34113–7 (hardcopy (vol. 1) : acid-free paper) — ISBN 978–1–57356–977–4 (ebook
(vol. 1)) — ISBN 978–0–313–34114–4 (hardcopy (vol. 2) : acid-free paper) — ISBN 978–1–57356–978–1
(ebook (vol. 2))
1. African Americans—History—Encyclopedias. 2. African Americans—Biography—Encyclopedias.
I. Hornsby, Alton.
   E185.B537   2011
   973'.0496073—dc22   2010045519

ISBN: 978–0–313–34112–0
EISBN: 978–1–57356–976–7

15 14 13 12 11   1 2 3 4 5

This book is also available on the World Wide Web as an eBook.
Visit www.abc-clio.com for details.

Greenwood
An Imprint of ABC-CLIO, LLC

ABC-CLIO, LLC
130 Cremona Drive, P.O. Box 1911
Santa Barbara, California 93116-1911

This book is printed on acid-free paper ∞

Manufactured in the United States of America

To Family and Friends
Thanks for always being there!

Contents

Volume 2

Preface

In its two volumes, *Black America: A State-by-State Historical Encyclopedia* provides a concise reference of African American history from the origins of slavery in the American colonies to present times. It begins with an introduction that traces the historiography, or writing, of African American history from its beginnings in the nineteenth century to the current debates on the meanings of the black experience. Each of the 50 states and the District of Columbia has a separate chapter written by contributors with expertise in African American history. Each chapter includes the following sections:

- Chronology—showing at a glance the major events and figures in African American history in the state

- Historical Overview—tracing in more detail the history of African Americans in the state from settlement to the present day

- Notable African Americans—providing brief biographical sketches of important African Americans in many fields who were born or were active in the state

- Cultural Contributions—describing cultural events and activities in the state that contributed to the black experience in America

- Bibliography—offering a select list of print and electronic information resources on the black history of the state

The encyclopedia shows the similarities of experiences, values, and cultural heritage and outlook of African Americans regardless of the state in which they live. For example, African Americans, North and South, East and West, have lived with racial discrimination, both overt and subtle. Fundamental to their values has been a messianic Christianity and a zeal for education as a pathway to success. Yet within these commonalities there have been exceptions. In some of the smaller states, such as Vermont in New England, it has been difficult to establish black churches in which to worship in the evangelistic expressive style (involving active emotional participation whether through shouting or call and response) that characterizes most black services elsewhere.

The evolution of the value of education among African Americans began in bondage when, even though education of slaves was prohibited by the southern states, clandestine schools were established. In other parts of the country, there was little or no segregation in schools—although some states resegregated from time to time—while in the South the schools were born segregated, with the exception of parts of Louisiana, which experienced a pattern of resegregation like some of the northern states.

The separate schooling in the South led to the founding of unique institutions of higher education that would have a monumental and fundamental impact on African American culture while, with few exceptions, these schools did not exist elsewhere. Hence, blacks outside the South who sought a unique cultural experience would have to attend southern black colleges.

Much like religion, music became a basic feature of African American culture. Black musical expression has had both commonalities and differences in different states, from the spirituals dating from the period of enslavement to the Mississippi Delta or St. Louis or Memphis blues, and from New Orleans or Chicago jazz to gospel and to rap—either northern style or "Dirty South" style.

While racism and legalized or de facto segregation and discrimination have existed everywhere, all the northern states ended slavery before the beginning of the Civil War, while it took that war to end it in most of the South. Similarly, de jure or legal racial discrimination persisted in the South until well into the twentieth century. Once it was ended, southern African Americans, for the most part, entered into a de facto pattern of race relations like that which has prevailed in other parts of the country. Yet even the dismantling of de jure segregation and discrimination took different courses in different states and even within different cities within a state. Because of the style of race relations that had been established in Atlanta after blacks became a political force there, the desegregation process was much smoother than in Birmingham or for that matter in all of Alabama. Desegregation in Oklahoma occurred earlier and with less overt strife than in many other places; still there were race riots in Oklahoma's history as there were in Georgia's.

These volumes, then, using a mosaic compiled in the separate histories in the 50 states and the District of Columbia, capture the totality of the black experience in the United States. In content and perspectives as well as readability, this encyclopedia will appeal to students and scholars at all levels as well as to a general audience.

Acknowledgments

Several individuals have assisted in the preparation of this encyclopedia and I hereby wish to express my deep appreciation. They include, of course, the contributors who made this an outstanding work; archivists and librarians at the Robert W. Woodruff Atlanta University Center Library, the Auburn Avenue Research Library on African American History and Culture, and the Robert W. Woodruff Library of Emory University. Also my research assistants Jason Ruiz and Augustus Wood III; Nyla Dixon and Bettye Spicer who typed various parts of the manuscript; and Lindsay Claire, John Wagner, and Wendi Schnaufer, my editors at Greenwood ABC-CLIO.

Introduction

The earliest writers of African American history were black men who wanted to tell of the achievements and contributions of people of African descent to the world generally, and to the making of the United States specifically. These writers, known as contributionists because of their emphasis on black contributions to both world and American history, believed deeply in the fundamental American Creed of Christianity and Democracy. Indeed, historian Dickson Bruce Jr. asserts that they were more faithful to it than much of white America. Thus he writes of an ironic conception of American history (Bruce, 53–62).

By the end of the nineteenth century, African American historians, while still not scientifically trained in historical method, were better educated than their predecessors. The most educated of this group were William Wells Brown, who was also a novelist, and George Washington Williams, who had been a soldier in the Civil War. Despite being better educated than previous chroniclers of African American history, this new group still adhered to contributionism and hoped to reach white as well as black audiences. But they were either ignored or ridiculed by the white intellectual establishment and were irrelevant to the majority of other white Americans.

Because he was academically trained, W. E. B. Du Bois was a major exception among African American historians of the early twentieth century. In 1896, Du Bois was just beginning his academic career after publishing his dissertation, "The Suppression of the African Slave Trade to America 1638–1870." Although Du Bois's writings represented a real breakthrough in African American historiography, his socialistic or Marxist analyses "tainted" his work in the eyes of many of his contemporaries, both black and white. It was then left to Carter G. Woodson, also a scientifically trained African American historian, to return to the basics of contributionism. Woodson believed it was critical that African and African American stories be researched in a scholarly manner and then told to the world. Failure to do so would leave the African race as "a negligible factor" in the history of mankind (Hornsby, "Changing Vicissitudes," 1–11).

Woodson and his adherents set up an organizational structure, the Association for the Study of Negro Life and History (ASNLH), and established two major publications, the *Journal of Negro History* and the *Negro History Bulletin*, to carry out their agenda. The *Journal of Negro History* was to be a scholarly periodical, while the *Negro History Bulletin* was to appeal to a more popular audience. They also established a Negro History Week to fall between the birthdays of Abraham Lincoln and Frederick Douglass in February of each year. All people, from grade-school children to elderly men and women, in or out of school, could participate in these observances of the achievements and contributions of African Americans.

There developed around Woodson and the ASNLH a group of young, university-trained scholars, including Lorenzo Johnson Greene of Missouri, Luther Porter Jackson of Virginia, Earle E. Thorpe and Helen Edmonds of North Carolina, and Clarence Bacote of Georgia, who published extensively in articles, essays, and books the results of their original research. A few white scholars also wrote African American history, including Melville J. Herskovitz, Herbert Aptheker, August Meier, and Elliott

Rudwick, all Jews, and Richard Hofstadter and the Swedish sociologist Gunnar Myrdal. Some of these scholars had been interested in the black experience for some time, but they had had difficulty getting their works accepted by the mainstream profession. Aptheker also bore the double burden of being a Marxist. Although the outpourings of scholarship from the Woodson school reached some readers, particularly in the nation's black colleges, even in some of these schools, and certainly in the larger world, most people got little more of the African American experience than what they heard or read during Negro History Week in February.

A major breakthrough in the evolving academic acceptance of black history occurred in 1947 when John Hope Franklin published the first edition of *From Slavery to Freedom*. Both the scholarly world and many general readers were impressed with the thoroughness of his research, the clarity of his writing, and the rather dispassionate way in which he approached painful subjects, such as slavery and racial violence, in his analyses. He soon became the preeminent African American historian.

But it took the Civil Rights Movement of the 1960s and 1970s to usher in a New Black History—an enterprise that would win wide acceptance by white academia and lead to new schools of historiography among blacks. The New Black History Movement was a part of the Civil Rights Movement for inclusion of the Black Power Movement programs of separation and self-sufficiency. Adherents of both philosophies embraced the demand for a Black Studies curriculum in all of the nation's institutions of higher education. The Civil Righters wanted Black Studies infused into the whole of the university while the Black Powerites wanted black control of black institutions and black control of black studies programs at white institutions. At the core of the matter, for both groups, was a new black history. All seemed to agree that heretofore black history had not been written or taught well, if at all, by whites as well as by many blacks. The Black Powerites went one step further and accused the contributionists of teaching a white man's black history. They contended that the contributionists were assimilationists who were slaves to the American Creed. Their philosophy deemed the American Creed corrupt, racist, and imperialist; they believed that African American history should begin with the history, cultures, and values of Africa rather than that of the English colonists in America and "the founding fathers." They called themselves Afro-centrists, since Africa was at the heart of their writings and teachings. While some white scholars like Herbert Aptheker, Melville Hervozitz, and Howard Zinn felt comfortable with Afro-centrism, the majority of white academia was ill at ease or downright opposed. Nevertheless, in the mode of traditional American historiography, many more white scholars began to teach and write African American history.

The more vocal opponents of Afro-centrism pointed to what they called "sugar coating"—embellishments and exaggerations in the work of the Afro-centrists. Scholars, including Arthur Schlesinger, who compared Afro-centrism to the Ku Klux Klan, Mary Lefkowitz, and Clarence E. Walker, ridiculed the Afro-centrists' exclusivism. That exclusivism seemed to suggest that Westerners were ethically bankrupt and that Africa was the origin and center of world culture and its most humane values, while Europe and the West were backward except for what they borrowed or stole from Africa.

Despite the prevalence of these warring schools of thought, the New Black History became the most attractive field of study in the profession, and it soon led to a New Women's History as well as to new treatments of the experiences of other groups, including gays, lesbians, bisexuals, and transgender people. Indeed, in the women's history movement, the distinct experiences of black women, including the double burdens of racism and sexism, became one of the most attractive fields. The demand for distinct portrayals of racial, ethnic, and gender groups has led some scholars to characterize the developments as "every group its own historian."

While the New Black History, even Afro-centrism, borrowed from the contributionists in emphasizing black achievements and contributions, it is more complex, going far beyond a few great men and women to explore the daily lives and circumstances of ordinary men and women and "forgotten communities." In that exploration, it has found that even in the most tragic and oppressive eras of black life and history, African Americans have shown aggressiveness and independence and have built parallel institutions to the larger society where social formation could occur, where they could make a living, and where they could participate in political action. This approach also supplemented African American religiosity by making spirituals and the blues sources of psychological solace during times of oppression. In a larger sense, the New Black History was part of an emerging New Social History where laborers assumed an importance besides kings and presidents—studying and writing and teaching history from the bottom up.

Marxists and other nontraditional scholars, such as Eugene Genovese, gained prominence for the new social history by emphasizing issues of a class struggle. African American historians, such as Nell Painter and Robin Kelley, while not Marxists, added African American communists, socialists, and working-class radicals to the historical matrix. And new data and interpretations came forward on the origins and meanings of whiteness and ethnicity.

Even before the emergence of the New Black History, historians and other scholars had begun to find decreasing favor with wide, sweeping narratives of a nation's or a group's history. Thus, case studies appeared that examined smaller or micro bits of the story to better explain larger or macro developments and trends. Such is the approach of this two-volume *Black America: A State-by-State Historical Encyclopedia*, which shows how the black experience in each of the 50 states and the District of Columbia renders many similarities on the one hand, but several differences on the other. These volumes also demonstrate what most scholars now agree on—the strength of the black family, although many dysfunctions persist into present times. Yet each state illustrates certain unique experiences—for example, the Creole and Voodoo cultures and the jazz scene of Louisiana and the effects of the world's largest center of African American higher education and the eminence of Martin Luther King Jr. in Georgia. The sea has been an important contributor to the economic life of blacks in New England and the soil to African Americans in the South and Midwest. White resistance to black civil and political rights in parts of the South and to economic opportunities in the North have been important influences on the development of black communities. And recent occurrences, including the election of President Barack Obama, the first African American to hold the office, and a deep economic recession in which African Americans are hardest hit, show that much of black America, state by state, still has some steep hills to climb socially and economically.

Bibliography

Asante, Molefi Kente. *Kemet, Afrocentricity, and Knowledge*. Trenton, NJ: Africa World Press, 1990.

Bernal, Martin. *Black Athena: The Afroasiatic Roots of Classical Culture*. Rutgers, NJ: Rutgers University Press, 1987.

Bruce, Dickson D., Jr. "The Ironic Conception of American History: The Early Black Historians, 1883–1915." *Journal of Negro History* 69, no. 2 (Spring 1984): 53–62.

Hornsby, Alton, Jr. "The Black Revolution, Black History and Professor Franklin." In Alton Hornsby Jr. *Essays in African American Historiography and Methodology*. Acton, MA: Copley Publishing Group, 2004, 71–78.

Hornsby, Alton, Jr. "The Changing Vicissitudes of Black Historiography." In Alton Hornsby Jr. *Southerners Too: Essays on the Black South, 1733–1990*. Lanham, MD: University Press of America, 2004, 1–11.

Lefkowitz, Mary. *Not Out of Africa: How Afrocentrism Became an Excuse to Teach Myth as History*. New York: Basic Books, 1996.

Novick, Peter. *That Noble Dream: The Objectivity Question and the American Historical Profession*. Cambridge: Cambridge University Press, 1988.

Schlesinger, Arthur M., Jr. *The Disuniting of America: Reflections on a Multicultural Society*. New York: Norton, 1991.

Walker, Clarence E. *We Can't Go Home Again*. Oxford: Oxford University Press, 2000.

ALABAMA

Lisa N. Nealy

Chronology

1721	The ship *African* sails into Mobile harbor with a cargo of over 100 slaves.
1724	The French *Code Noir* (Black Code), which regulates slavery in the French West Indies, is extended to France's North American colonies and thus institutionalizes slavery among the settlers in the Mobile area.
1763	France cedes present-day Alabama to Great Britain.
1780	Spain seizes Mobile from Great Britain.
1783	Great Britain gives the northern and central regions of present-day Alabama to the United States and the Mobile region to Spain.
1798	The Mississippi Territory, which includes present-day Alabama, is organized.
1813	The United States seizes control of the Mobile area from Spain.
1817	*(March 3)* The U.S. Congress establishes the Alabama Territory.
1819	*(December 14)* Alabama enters the Union as the 22nd state.
1820	Over 47,000 black slaves and 633 free blacks live in Alabama.
1830	Over 117,000 black slaves and 1,572 free blacks live in Alabama; the state's slave population has more than doubled in a decade.
1854	Alabama establishes its public school system.
1861	*(January 11)* Alabama becomes the fourth state to secede from the Union.
1861	*(February–May)* Montgomery serves as the capital of the Confederate States of America.
1861	*(February 4)* Representatives from Alabama and the five other states that had seceded from the Union meet in Montgomery to form the Confederate States of America.
1861	*(February 18)* Jefferson Davis of Mississippi is sworn in as president of the Confederacy on the portico of the Alabama Capitol in Montgomery.
1864	Union forces win the Battle of Mobile Bay.
1865	*(December 2)* Alabama ratifies the Thirteenth Amendment to the U.S. Constitution abolishing slavery.
1866	Lincoln Normal School, a private educational institution for African Americans, is founded at Marion; the school relocates to Montgomery in 1887 and eventually becomes Alabama State University.
1868	*(July 13)* Alabama ratifies the Fourteenth Amendment to the U.S. Constitution, which extends citizenship to African Americans.

1868	(*July 13*) Alabama rejoins the Union after the state adopts a constitution that allows African Americans to vote.
1869	(*November 16*) Alabama ratifies the Fifteenth Amendment to the U.S. Constitution, which extends the vote to African Americans.
1870	African Americans make up nearly 48 percent of Alabama's population.
1870	Benjamin S. Turner, a Republican, is the first African American elected to the U.S. House of Representatives from Alabama.
1871	The city of Birmingham is founded.
1872	James T. Rapier of Lauderdale County, a black Republican, is elected to the U.S. House of Representatives from Alabama during Reconstruction.
1874	Jeremiah Haralson, who was born a slave on a plantation near Columbus, is elected to the U.S. House of Representatives from Alabama.
1880	The African American National Baptist Convention is organized in Montgomery.
1881	(*February 10*) The Alabama legislature establishes Tuskegee Institute as a normal school for the education of African American teachers; graduates must agree to teach for two years in Alabama.
1881	(*June*) Booker T. Washington arrives in Alabama to become superintendent of the Tuskegee Institute.
1896	(*October 8*) George Washington Carver arrives in Alabama to direct the Agricultural School of Tuskegee Institute.
1896	The U.S. Supreme Court affirms the constitutionality of the "separate but equal" doctrine in regard to race relations in its *Plessy v. Ferguson* decision.
1900	The Federal Census records 827,307 blacks living in Alabama, about 45 percent of the state's population.
1901	Alabama adopts a new state constitution, which disfranchises substantial numbers of black voters.
1913	The first Alabama chapter of the National Association for the Advancement of Colored People (NAACP) is established.
1931	Nine black youths are arrested in Paint Rock and accused of raping two white women on a freight train. Held in the Jackson County jail in Scottsboro, the nine are soon known as the "Scottsboro Boys." Eight of the nine are convicted by all-white juries and sentenced to death, but the questionable evidence presented at the trials causes widespread outrage and the U.S. Supreme Court twice overturns the convictions.
1933	The federal government creates the Tennessee Valley Authority (TVA).

1936	(*August 3*) Alabama native Jesse Owens wins the first of his four gold medals at the Olympics in Berlin.
1941	A squadron of African American fighter pilots, which later distinguishes itself in air combat during World War II, begins training at Tuskegee and at Maxwell Army Airfield in Montgomery, eventually becoming famous as the "Tuskegee Airmen." Four hundred fifty of the airmen served overseas in World War II and were cited for outstanding combat service.
1954	(*October 31*) Dr. Martin Luther King Jr. becomes pastor of Montgomery's Dexter Avenue Baptist Church.
1955	(*December 1*) Rosa Parks, an African American woman, refuses to give up her seat on a bus to a white passenger as required by a Montgomery ordinance and thereby sparks a bus boycott in Montgomery.
1955–1956	Dr. Martin Luther King Jr. leads the Montgomery Bus Boycott.
1956	(*January 30*) Segregationists bomb the Montgomery home of bus boycott spokesman Dr. Martin Luther King Jr.; the home is damaged, but no one is hurt.
1956	(*December 21*) The U.S. Supreme Court orders the desegregation of Montgomery's buses, thus ending the Montgomery Bus Boycott.
1956	Autherine Lucy tries unsuccessfully to desegregate the University of Alabama.
1958	(*June 30*) In its decision in the case of *National Association for the Advancement of Colored People (NAACP) v. Alabama*, the U.S. Supreme Court ends the state's attempt to prevent the NAACP from conducting business in Alabama.
1961	(*May 1*) Harper Lee of Monroeville wins the Pulitzer Prize for her first and only novel, *To Kill a Mockingbird*, which portrays race relations in 1930s' Alabama.
1961	(*May 20*) The "Freedom Riders" bus is attacked by an angry mob when it arrives in Montgomery; attempting to test the 1960 Supreme Court decision desegregating bus and train terminals, the Freedom Riders had earlier experienced similar hostile receptions at Anniston and Birmingham.
1963	Alabama Governor George Wallace fails to stop racial integration at the University of Alabama.
1963	(*May 19*) Dr. Martin Luther King's "Letter from Birmingham Jail," where he was being held for participation in Birmingham civil rights demonstrations, is issued, becoming a seminal text of the Civil Rights Movement.
1963	(*September 15*) Birmingham's 16th Street Baptist Church is bombed, killing four African American girls—11-year-old Denise McNair and 14-year-olds Carole Robertson, Cynthia Wesley, and Addie Mae Collins.
1963	The Southern Christian Leadership Conference (SCLC) offices in Birmingham and the Birmingham home of A.D. King, Martin Luther King's brother, are bombed by segregationists.

1965	*(March 7)* Civil rights demonstrators attempting to march from Selma to Montgomery to demand the end of voting restrictions on blacks are attacked by state and local law enforcement officers as they cross Selma's Edmund Pettus Bridge; the scene is broadcast on national television, winning the demonstrators much support.
1965	*(March 21)* Martin Luther King Jr. leads over 3,200 civil rights demonstrators on a march from Selma to Montgomery after two previous attempts had failed.
1970	The Alabama Space and Rocket Center opens in Huntsville.
1982	*(November)* Oscar Adams wins election to the Alabama Supreme Court, becoming the first African American elected to statewide constitutional office in the state.
1987	Guy Hunt becomes the first Republican governor of Alabama since 1874.
1992	Astronaut Mae Jemison becomes the first African American woman in space.
1992	The Birmingham Civil Rights Institute opens.
1995	Alabama celebrates the 30th anniversary of the civil rights march from Selma to Montgomery.
1998	Dr. David Satcher of Anniston is appointed surgeon general of the United States by President Bill Clinton.
2000	The 2000 Census puts the number of African Americans living in Alabama at over 1.1 million persons, approximately a quarter of the state's population.
2000	*(August)* Rosa Parks is inducted into the Alabama Academy of Honor.
2002	Vonetta Flowers of Birmingham wins a gold medal in bobsledding at the Salt Lake City Winter Olympics, thus becoming the first African American to win gold at a Winter Olympics.
2002	*(May 22)* Bobby Frank Cherry, the last surviving suspect, is convicted of murder in the 1963 bombing of the 16th Street Baptist Church in Birmingham, which killed four black girls.
2002	Alabama ratifies the Twenty-fourth Amendment to the U.S. Constitution, which abolishes the poll tax; the amendment had gone into effect 38 years earlier in 1964.
2005	*(January)* Condoleezza Rice, an Alabama native, is appointed secretary of state by President George W. Bush, becoming the first African American woman to hold the office.
2005	*(October)* Death of Rosa Parks, whose refusal to give up her seat sparked the Montgomery Bus Boycott.
2006	*(January)* Death of Coretta Scott King, an Alabama native and widow of Dr. Martin Luther King Jr., who led the Montgomery Bus Boycott in the 1950s.

Historical Overview

The Nineteenth Century

In the early part of the nineteenth century, Mobile became a principal slave trading post. As a result Alabama's black population increased from about 42,000 in 1820 to more than 342,000 by 1850. The Alabama Constitution of 1819 had, for the times, a liberal provision protecting slaves from abuse. But slaves could not enter into contracts, lend money, rent housing, own horses or dogs, buy liquor, or leave the plantation without a pass. They could not be taught to read or write. Inciting slaves to rebel was considered the most serious crime. Rape of black women by white men or black men was not considered a crime.

During early statehood and until antebellum times, African American slaves worked principally on cotton plantations and as domestic servants. Semiskilled and skilled blacks were employed as blacksmiths, carpenters, and brick masons. The other class of African Americans in early Alabama were the so-called free blacks. This group was always small, yet they were viewed as a dangerous segment of the population. Thus, steps were taken to keep them away from slaves as much as possible. They were denied the right to vote. Mobile County had the largest number of free blacks before the Civil War. Many of them were mulattos with French and Spanish heritage. These Creoles, as they were called, were often well educated and prosperous, owning their own businesses and working as barbers, blacksmiths, carpenters, coach-draymen, and draymen. Prominent free blacks during this period included Pierre Chestang, who ferried supplies for Andrew Jackson in the War of 1812, Solmon Perteal, a merchant, and Horace King, a contractor who helped construct the state capitol in Montgomery in 1850–1851. Both free blacks and slaves, while being Americanized, continued to retain and practice significant elements of their African culture.

Between 1830 and 1860, the enslaved population in Alabama increased by more than 270 percent, while the white population grew by only 171 percent. On the eve of the Civil War, 33,700 enslavers held more than 430,000 bondspersons. Meanwhile, the issue of the expansion or the restriction of slavery in the western territories of the United States was being debated in the nation's capital at Washington. By the end of 1860, tensions had reached a boiling point. South Carolina seceded from the Union and attacked the U.S. arsenal at Fort Sumter, South Carolina. On January 11, 1861, by a vote of 61 to 39, Alabama voted to secede. Soon 11 southern states had seceded and formed the Confederate States of America. President Abraham Lincoln had earlier called for 75,000 volunteers to "defend the Union." The Civil War had begun.

As the war progressed, Union armies occupied north Alabama. More than 10,000 slaves left the plantations and joined the Union forces. On the other hand, many slaves were ordered to assist the Confederacy as warriors in servant and supply positions and in construction and repair of bridges and railroads.

At the close of the Civil War, after the Republican-controlled Congress finally reached agreement on a Reconstruction plan, the rebellious South was subjected to military rule, pending the organizations of new governments. At the same time the federal government sought to provide, in connection with northern-based missionary groups, basic necessities and a rudimentary education to the freedpersons. But continuing their prewar opposition to black education, whites attacked and burned many of the early schools.

The history of black higher education in Alabama dates back to 1867, when two former bondspersons, with the help of the American Missionary Association and the Freedmen's Bureau, founded Talladega College. Then in 1908, Miles College was founded in Birmingham by the Alabama Conference of the Colored

Methodist Episcopal Church. But the premier African American college in the state, and indeed one of the best known in the nation, was the Tuskegee Institute.

Tuskegee was a product of biracial efforts on the part of black and white citizens and the state of Alabama. Its early mission was to educate teachers for Alabama's black schools. But under its first principal, Booker T. Washington, who arrived in 1881, the school became known for its agricultural-industrial focus. Nevertheless, it continued to produce more teachers than mechanics. With both northern and southern philanthropic and governmental assistance, the campus grew in acreage, buildings, students, and faculty to become one of the larger black colleges. Among the early faculty was George Washington Carver, who arrived on the campus in 1896 as director of the Agricultural School. He added to the institution's reputation by establishing a scientific laboratory, where he helped to revolutionize agricultural production and the variety of products that could be offshoots of produce, including peanuts and potatoes.

Under the new constitution adopted under military or "radical reconstruction," African Americans were allowed to vote and to hold office. Among those elected were Congressman Benjamin S. Turner (1871–1873), James T. Rapier (1873–1875), who had also been nominated for secretary of state, and Jeremiah Haralson (1875–1877). No other African Americans were elected to the Congress until 1993, when Earl Hilliard took office. He served until 2003. In that year Arthur Davis, who still serves, was also elected. In 2010, Davis became a candidate for governor of Alabama. Since the passage of the Voting Rights Act of 1965, hundreds of blacks have been elected to state, county, and municipal offices in Alabama.

But black participation in Alabama government was to be short-lived. Almost immediately white

extremists, centered in the notorious Ku Klux Klan, set out to intimidate, frighten, and even murder black voters and their white Republican allies. As these campaigns of terror continued, white Democrats were maneuvering to retake the state government. In 1875, they won approval for a new constitutional convention and in short order restored the old, white Democratic leadership to power in Alabama.

The new government moved quickly to mandate racial segregation in the schools. Then, once radical reconstruction was ended throughout the South in 1877, Alabama joined the rest of the southern states in passing laws segregating the races in almost all spheres of public life. The state also enacted measures to disfranchise most black voters. It would take considerable bloodshed and the Civil Rights Act of 1965 to restore black voting rights in Alabama.

The Twentieth Century

As to segregated public facilities and public accommodations, African Americans, as they did in the case of voting rights, took the lead in dismantling Jim Crow. A year and a half after the Supreme Court struck down school segregation in *Brown v. Board of Education* (1954), Montgomery blacks began the first direct action protests in the state.

On December 1, 1955, African American seamstress Rosa Parks refused a traditional order on southern buses to give up her seat to a white passenger. After her arrest for violating state and local segregation laws, blacks organized a boycott of the city's buses. An organizational structure was established under the name of the Montgomery Improvement Association. A young African American minister, who had recently arrived in the city from doctoral studies in theology at Boston University, Martin Luther King Jr. was elected president of the association.

Rosa Parks is fingerprinted in Montgomery, Alabama. Parks' arrest for refusing to give up her seat on a bus to a white man on December 1, 1955, inspired the Montgomery Bus Boycott, a prolonged action against the segregated Montgomery, Alabama, bus system by African American riders and their white supporters. (Library of Congress)

The King-led boycott, marked by bombings and other forms of intimidation and police harassment, lasted until December 1956, when the U.S. Supreme Court ruled segregation on Montgomery buses unconstitutional. The Montgomery Bus Boycott is generally regarded as the beginning of the direct action phase of the modern Civil Rights Movement.

Seven years later, in response to an appeal from local civil rights leaders, King, now president of a regional civil rights organization called the Southern Christian Leadership Conference (SCLC), led nonviolent demonstrations in Birmingham, Alabama. The demonstrations virtually paralyzed much of downtown Birmingham during the spring and summer of 1963. At one point during the protest, young school children walked out of classrooms and joined the demonstrations. The city officials in Birmingham, led by police commissioner Eugene "Bull" Connor, took a hard line against the demonstrators. Hundreds, including Martin Luther King Jr. and his chief assistant, Ralph David Abernathy, were arrested. High-powered water hoses were turned on the protesters and vicious dogs were ordered to snarl and bite them.

The pictures of the attempted repression of the demonstrators through the violent means employed by the police provoked a negative backlash in public opinion across the nation. The presidential administration of John F. Kennedy

The scene outside of the 16th Street Baptist Church in Birmingham, Alabama, on September 15, 1963, after members of the Ku Klux Klan bombed the building. Four young African American girls were killed in the racist attack. (Bettmann/Corbis)

Sunday, the 15th. Four little black girls in a Sunday school class were killed. The church was allegedly targeted because it had been a major meeting site for civil rights leaders and their followers. The child murders were a serious test of the King philosophy of nonviolent resistance. But he persisted in persuading his followers not to retaliate but to continue to practice nonviolence. In later times, three Ku Klux Klansmen were charged with the murders.

Two years after Birmingham, the focus of the movement shifted to Selma and away from public accommodations to voting rights. At this time, Selma had acquired a notorious reputation for denying African Americans the right to vote. In January 1965, civil rights forces led by Martin Luther King Jr. opened a voter registration drive in Selma. Dr. King was attacked as he registered at a formerly all-white Selma hotel but was not seriously injured. On January 19, Dallas County law enforcement officers began arresting blacks who wanted to register to vote. On January 23, a federal judge issued an order prohibiting interference with those seeking to register to vote.

By February 1, the drive to register black voters in Selma had developed into a nationwide protest movement as local whites in Dallas County stiffened their resistance and civil rights leaders intensified their efforts. More than 700 blacks, including Martin Luther King Jr., were arrested on February 1. On February 26, a black demonstrator, Jimmie L. Johnson, was killed by state police in Marion, Alabama. Three white men killed a white protester, the Reverend James Reeb, near Selma on March 11.

On March 7, state police routed several hundred protesters attempting to march across the Edmund Pettus Bridge in Selma en route to the state capitol in Montgomery. The police used billy clubs and cattle prods to break up the march. Several blacks, including future Congressman John Lewis, were severely beaten. On March 17, a federal judge prohibited Alabama officials from

condemned the tactics in a speech the president made in June 1963. He concluded by announcing that he would now push for a civil rights bill. With the boycotts, demonstrations, and violence seriously hurting white businesses in the city, and the negative press which the city was facing, Birmingham's white leaders finally agreed to the desegregation of public accommodations in the fall of 1963. Another major result of the Birmingham protest was a letter that King wrote while incarcerated to ministers who had felt that the demonstration was unwise. King's letter justifying the demonstrations, "A Letter from the Birmingham Jail," has become a literary classic.

The civil rights victories in Birmingham were tempered in September 1963 when a bomb exploded at the 16th Street Baptist Church on interfering with the proposed march from Selma to Montgomery. President Lyndon B. Johnson then ordered federal troops to protect the protesters on their 50-mile trek to Montgomery. The march occurred from March 21 to 25. Fifty thousand people met the marchers on March 25 at the state capitol in Montgomery, where Martin Luther King Jr. and others denounced Alabama leaders, including Governor George C. Wallace, for attempting to deny blacks their constitutional right to vote. That night, a white demonstrator, Viola Liuzzo, was murdered.

Meanwhile, on February 3, 1956, Governor Wallace's defiance of a school desegregation order ended when a black coed, Autherine Lucy, enrolled at the University of Alabama under court order. It should be stressed that even in the eras of segregation, blatant discrimination, and disfranchisement, blacks developed significant parallel institutions for their spiritual and social welfare and for a total community life. Foremost among these institutions were churches and schools.

In the post-emancipation period, crudely constructed churches were established in rural communities. By the twentieth century, as the black population became largely an urban one, huge mega churches were constructed throughout the state. The Dexter Avenue Baptist Church in Montgomery—whose pastors included a fiery leader of the pre–civil rights era, the Reverend Vernon Johns, and civil rights leader Martin Luther King Jr.—and the 16th Street Baptist Church in Birmingham are among the state's oldest and most historic black churches. Up until about 1920, most black schools in Alabama were poorly constructed one- or two-room structures with poor ventilation. Then, from the 1920s through the pre–civil rights era, attractive school buildings appeared. The Fairfield High School outside of Birmingham and the Parker High School in Birmingham were among the oldest and most important of these structures.

During the transition from slavery to freedom, black Alabamians were generally poor, ill housed, poorly educated, and ill cared for physically and mentally. They worked in the most menial jobs—unskilled labor and domestic service. But there were always notable exceptions. Blue-collar blacks who worked in coal mills, iron works, and steel mills earned good wages and lived comfortable middle-class lives. Then there were business and professional people—doctors, lawyers, teachers—and property owners. Some, like A. G. Gaston of Birmingham, became millionaires. As the Civil Rights Movement expanded economic opportunities, the black middle class grew significantly.

Notable African Americans

Aaron, Henry Louis (Hank) (1934–)

Henry Louis Aaron was born in Mobile, Alabama, on February 5, 1934. Aaron is a retired African American baseball player and member of the Baseball Hall of Fame. In 1974, he broke the major league record for home runs previously held by Babe Ruth; he finished his career with 755 home runs and held the record until 2007. Aaron holds the major league record in each of the following categories: career runs batted in (2,297); career extra hits (1,477); and career total bases (6,856). He is the only player to have 17 seasons with more than 150 hits. He won one World Series ring with the Milwaukee Braves in 1957 and the National League Most Valuable Player (MVP) Award the same year. He also earned three Gold Glove Awards and made 24 All-Star appearances.

On August 1, 1982, Aaron was inducted into the Hall of Fame and received votes on 97.8 percent of the ballots, second to only Ty Cobb, who received votes on 98.2 percent of the ballots in the inaugural 1936 Hall of Fame election. Aaron was then named the Braves' vice president and director of player development. This made him one of the first minorities in major league baseball upper-level management.

Abernathy, Ralph David (1926–1990)

Ralph David Abernathy was an African American civil rights leader. Abernathy was born the son of a farmer in Linden, Alabama. After serving in the army during World War II, he enrolled at Alabama State University in Montgomery, graduating with a degree in mathematics in 1950. His involvement in political activism began in college while he led demonstrations protesting the lack of heat and hot water in his dormitory and the dreadful food served in the cafeteria. In 1951, he earned a master of arts degree in sociology from Atlanta University (later Clark-Atlanta University). He became pastor of the First Baptist Church in Montgomery. While living in Montgomery he formed a close and enduring partnership with Dr. Martin Luther King Jr.

In 1955, when Rosa Parks refused to move to the back of the bus, Abernathy and King organized the bus boycott in Montgomery. After a year of the boycott it finally ended when the U.S. Supreme Court affirmed the U.S. District Court's ruling that segregation on buses was unconstitutional. Abernathy was King's number two man in the SCLC, in which he held the official title of secretary-treasurer. Abernathy was with Martin Luther King Jr. in Memphis when King was assassinated. Abernathy assumed the presidency of the SCLC after King's death. Less than a week after the assassination, Abernathy led a march to support striking sanitation workers in Memphis, Tennessee.

In May 1968, Abernathy and others including the Reverend Jesse Jackson organized a Poor People's Campaign march on Washington. The two-week protest event included setting up a shantytown named "Resurrection City," though Abernathy himself slept in a hotel during the campaign. On June 19, he delivered a speech at the Lincoln Memorial in front of tens of thousands of black and white citizens. However, the campaign ended in failure on June 24, when the federal government intervened, using force to disband the protesters. Abernathy was jailed for nearly three weeks following the collapse of the campaign. Abernathy was active in the American Freedom Coalition in the 1980s and served as vice president of the American Freedom Coalition until his death in 1990.

Adams, Oscar William, Jr. (1925–1997)

Born in Birmingham, Oscar William Adams Jr. was the first African American to serve on the Alabama Supreme Court and the first African American elected to statewide office in Alabama. In 1967, he partnered with a white attorney to form the first integrated legal office in the state. Appointed as justice of the state Supreme Court by the governor in 1980, he won election to the office in 1982 and 1988 and retired in 1993.

Amerson, Lucius Davenport (1933–1994)

In January 1967, Lucius Davenport Amerson became the first southern black sheriff in the twentieth century when he was elected as sheriff of Macon County, of which Tuskegee is the county seat.

Arrington, Richard, Jr. (1934–)

Richard Arrington Jr. was the first African American elected as mayor of Birmingham, Alabama. He served four terms as mayor from 1980 to 1999.

Barkley, Charles Wade (1953–)

Charles Barkley was a star player in the National Basketball Association from 1984 to 2000. He was named MVP in the 1991 and 1993 NBA All-Star Game and was a member of the U.S. team at the 1992 Olympics. After retiring from professional basketball, he became a sports commentator for network television.

Barrow, Joe Louis (1914–1981)

Born in Chambers County, Joe Louis Barrow, who fought under the name Joe Louis, began his boxing career in 1932. Known as "the Brown Bomber," Louis became world heavyweight champion in 1937 and held the title until 1949, when he retired. He is famous for his two bouts with the German former champion Max Schmeling, to whom he suffered his first defeat in 1936 and whom he defeated easily in defense of his title in 1938. In 2005, the International Boxing Research Organization named Louis the greatest heavyweight fighter of all time.

Carver, George Washington (1864–1943)

George Washington Carver became one of the world's greatest scientists. He was an African American botanical researcher and agronomy educator who worked in the agricultural extension at Tuskegee Institute in Tuskegee, Alabama, teaching former slaves farming techniques for self sufficiency. Carver derived over 300 different products from various plants; from the sweet potato alone, he derived 118 products.

Carver confronted an increasingly marginal southern economy devastated by war, poor family, malnutrition, and ignorance. Carver was able to improve the health and agricultural output of both black and white southern farmers, developing hundreds of uses for a monocrop economy.

He was the first black to attend Iowa State University. He graduated in 1894 with a bachelor's degree in botany and agriculture. Additionally, he spent two more years at Iowa State to complete a master's degree, studying agricultural chemistry, bacteriology, zoology, and entomology. Carver became passionate about botany and managed the university's greenhouse, where he quietly conducted experiments on plants and taught other undergraduate students.

In 1896, Washington invited Carver to head the agriculture department at the Tuskegee Normal and Industrial Institute in Alabama. Carver transformed the department: Tuskegee's first laboratory was built with bottles, old fruit jars, and other objects. Along with peanut butter, Carver made adhesives, axle grease, bleach, buttermilk, chili sauce, fuel briquettes, instant coffee, linoleum, mayonnaise, meat tenderizer, metal polish, paper, plastic, shaving cream, shoe polish, and synthetic rubber.

Carver helped the United Peanuts Growers Association persuade Congress to pass a bill calling for a protective tariff on imported peanuts in 1921. By 1938, one year after the film of his life called *The Life of George Washington Carver* opened in Hollywood, peanuts were a $200 million industry and the number one product in Alabama. Carver died in 1946. He donated his entire savings—$30,000—for the study of soil fertilizing and continued creation of useful products from waste materials. In his entire working life, Carver only patented three of his 500 agriculture-based inventions.

Clarke, John Henrik (1915–1998)

Born in Union Springs, John Henrik Clarke was an author, educator, and historian. He became a respected authority in African and African American studies. Among his major works were *Malcolm X: The Man and His Times* (1969) and *Dimensions of the Struggle Against Apartheid: A Tribute to Paul Robeson* (1979).

Cole, Nat King (1919–1965)

Nat King Cole was an African American jazz singer, pianist, and songwriter born Nathaniel Adam Coles in Montgomery, Alabama. His birth date, according to the *World Almanac*, was on St. Patrick's Day in 1919. Other sources place his birthdate in 1917. His father was a butcher and a deacon in the Baptist Church. His family moved to Chicago while he was still a child. There, his father became a minister; Cole's mother Perlina was the church organist. Cole learned to play the organ from his mother. He learned not only jazz and gospel music, but also European classical music.

When the family lived in the Bronzeville neighborhood of Chicago, Nat would sneak out of the house and hang around outside the clubs, listening to artists such as Louis Armstrong, Earl "Fatla" Hines, and Jimmie Noon. He participated in Walter Dyett's renowned music program at Dusable High School. Inspired by the playing of Earl Hines, Cole began his performing career in the mid-1930s while he was still a teenager and adopted the name "Nat Cole." His older brother, Eddie Coles, a bass player, soon joined Cole's band, and they first recorded in 1936 under Eddie's name. They also performed at clubs. Cole got his nickname "King" performing at one jazz club, a nickname presumably reinforced by the otherwise unrelated nursery rhyme about "Old King Cole." He was also a pianist in a national touring revival of ragtime and Broadway theater legend Eubie Blake's review, "Shuffle Along"; when the review ended suddenly in Long Beach, California, Cole decided to remain there.

Cole and three other musicians formed the "King Cole Swingers" in Long Beach and played in a number of local bars before getting a gig on the Long Beach Pike for $90 per week. Cole married a dancer, Nadine Robinson, who was also with "Shuffle Along," and moved to Los Angeles where he formed the Nat King Cole Trio. The trio consisted of Cole on piano, Oscar Moore on guitar, and Wesley Prince on double bass. The trio played in Los Angeles throughout the late 1930s and recorded many radio transcriptions. Cole did not achieve widespread popularity until "Sweet Lorraine" in 1940. Although he sang ballads with the trio, he was shy about his voice, though he prided himself on his diction. But he never considered himself a strong singer. His subdued style, however, contrasted well with the belting approach of most jazz singers.

On August 23, 1956, Cole spoke at the Republican National Convention in the Cow Palace in San Francisco. He was also present at the Democratic National Convention in 1960, to throw his support behind presidential candidate John F. Kennedy. Cole was also among the dozens of entertainers recruited by Frank Sinatra to perform at the Kennedy Inaugural Gala in 1961. Cole frequently consulted with President Kennedy and later President Johnson on the issue of civil rights. Yet he was dogged by critics, who felt he shied away from controversy when it came to the civil rights issue. Among the most notable was Supreme Court Justice Thurgood Marshall, who was disappointed that Cole did not take stronger action after being attacked on stage by white supremacists.

Cole's first mainstream vocal hit was his 1943 recording of one of his compositions, "Straighten Up and Fly Right," based on a black folktale that his father had used. Johnny Mercer invited him to record it for Capitol Records. It sold over 500,000 copies and proved that folk-based material could appeal to a wide audience. Although Cole would never be considered a rocker, the song can be seen as anticipating the first rock-and-roll records. Bo Diddley, who performed similar adaptations of folk material, was one influence on Cole. Cole learned and recorded songs in different languages. In 1958, Cole went to Havana, Cuba, to record *Cole Espanol*, an album sung in Spanish. The album was popular in Latin America as well as in the United States. In 1990, Cole was awarded the Grammy Lifetime Achievement Award.

He married singer Maria Hawkins Ellington—no relation to the famous Duke Ellington. They had five children, including singer Natalie Cole. Cole was a heavy smoker of Kool Menthol cigarettes, smoking three packs a day. He believed smoking kept his voice low. He smoked several cigarettes in quick succession before a recording for this very purpose.

Davis, Angela Yvonne (1944–)

Angela Yvonne Davis is an activist and scholar born on January 26, 1944, in Birmingham, Alabama, during the midst of the Jim Crow laws. Davis' father was a graduate of St. Augustine's College, a historically black college in Raleigh, North Carolina, and taught history there. After leaving teaching due to its low salary, he owned and operated a service station in the black section of Birmingham. Davis' mother, also college educated, was an elementary school teacher with a history of political activism.

During her childhood, Davis experienced the humiliations of racial segregation. She was bright and begged to enter school early, attending Carrie A. Tuggle School, a black elementary school in dilapidated facilities, and later Parker Annex, a similarly dilapidated annex of Parker High School devoted to middle-school education. Davis read voraciously. By her junior year, at 14, she applied for and was accepted to a program of the American Friends Service Committee that placed black students from the South in integrated schools in the North.

She chose to attend high school at Irwin High School in Greenwich Village, New York, a small private school favored by the radical community. Davis became acquainted with socialism and communism, and she was recruited to the communist youth group Advance. Davis also became familiar with children of the leaders of the Communist Party, including her lifelong friend Bettina Aptheker.

Upon graduation from high school, Davis was awarded a full scholarship to Brandeis University in Waltham, Massachusetts. She was one of three black students in her freshman class. Davis majored in French and studied Sartre. She was accepted for the Hamilton College Junior Year in France Program. Nearing completion of her degree in French language, she realized her major interest was philosophy. Davis became interested in the ideas of Herbert Marcus.

Civil rights activist and communist Angela Davis addresses the press at the University of California, Berkeley, where she received a standing ovation following her first class, October 6, 1969. University regents had banned her employment, but she had support from the school's chancellor and faculty. (AP/ Wide World Photos)

Davis attended the University of Frankfurt for graduate work in philosophy. In 1965, she graduated magna cum laude and a member of Phi Beta Kappa. And in 1969, she worked as an assistant acting professor in the Philosophy Department at the University of California, Los Angeles. She was also a radical feminist, an active member of the Communist Party U.S.A., and associated with the Black Panther Party. In a controversial decision, the board of regents of the University of California urged then–California Governor Ronald Reagan to fire Davis in 1969 due to communist affiliation. Davis was later rehired after a community uproar over the decision.

Davis first achieved national attention in 1970 on August 18, when she was linked to the murder of Judge Harold Haley. During an attempted Black Panther prison break, Davis fled and was the subject of an intense manhunt. After 18 months as a fugitive, she was captured, arrested, tried, and eventually acquitted in one of the most famous trials in recent U.S. history. Davis later became professor of the history of consciousness at the University of California and chair of the department at the University of California, Santa Cruz. She works for racial and gender equality and for prison reform. She is also the founder of Critical Resistance, a national organization opposed to the expansion of the prison-industrial complex.

Gaston, Arthur G. (A. G.) (1892–1996)

Arthur G. Gaston was a wealthy businessman in Birmingham. His economic enterprises included a motel that housed civil rights leaders and was a place where the leaders planned strategies for the 1963 demonstrations in Birmingham.

Gomillion, Charles Goode (C. G.) (1900–1995)

Charles Goode Gomillion was an educator and civil rights leader. A long-time teacher and administrator at Tuskegee Institute, he founded the Tuskegee Civic Association. He led the movement for black voting rights in Tuskegee and Marion County for more than 25 years. He was the lead plaintiff in the case of *Gomillion v. Lightfoot* (1960), in which the Supreme Court overturned an act by Alabama officials to gerrymander black citizens in Tuskegee, restricting their voting rights.

Gray, Fred D. (David) (1930–)

Fred D. Gray was an attorney and civil rights leader in Montgomery and Tuskegee. He defended the National Association for the Advancement of Colored People (NAACP) and other civil rights organizations in Alabama as well as Martin Luther King Jr. and Rosa Parks. In 1970, he was elected to the Alabama legislature from Marion County.

Hall, Ethel (1928–)

Ethel Hall was an educator and the first African American woman to sit on the Alabama State Board of Education.

Handy, William Christopher (W. C.) (1873–1958)

Born in Florence, William Christopher Handy was an influential blues composer and musician who achieved success as a musician with such compositions as "Memphis Blues" and "St. Louis Blues." Known as the "Father of the Blues," he was deeply influenced by folk music, which he incorporated into his own blues compositions.

Herman, Alexis M. (1946–)

Raised in Mobile, Alexis M. Herman founded A. M. Herman & Associates, a consulting firm, in 1981. Active in Democratic politics, Herman became vice chair of the Democratic National Committee and was responsible for organizing the 1992 Democratic National Convention. She became deputy director of President-Elect Bill Clinton's Transition Office after the 1992 election and then was appointed head of the White House Office of Public Liaison, where she was responsible for the Clinton administration's interactions with interest groups. She became secretary of labor in 1997, the first African American nominated to the position, which she held until 2001. In the aftermath of the disputed 2000 presidential election, Herman was a member of the Gore transition team and a likely White House chief of staff in a Gore administration. With the election of George W. Bush, Herman left government service and became a member of the Democratic National Committee.

Holmes, Alvin A. (1939–)

Alvin A. Holmes was an educator, civil rights leader, and member of the Alabama legislature. In the Alabama House he sponsored legislation to name a portion of Interstate Highway 85 in Alabama for Martin Luther King Jr. and to have the state declare an official holiday for King's birthday. He is credited with securing more positions for blacks in Alabama government than any other legislator.

Jackson, Vincent Edward ("Bo") (1962–)

Vincent Edward "Bo" Jackson was a National Football League player with the Tampa Bay Buccaneers and Oakland Raiders in the 1980s. He also played professional baseball for the Kansas City Royals. Before entering the pros, Jackson was a star running back at Auburn University, where he won a Heisman Trophy.

Jemison, Mae Carol (1956–)

Dr. Mae Carol Jemison became the first African American woman to travel in space when she went into orbit aboard the Space Shuttle *Endeavour* on September 12, 1992. Born on October 17, 1956, in Decatur, Alabama, Jemison was the youngest child of Dorothy Jemison, an elementary school teacher and Charlie Jemison, a roofer and carpenter.

The family moved to Chicago, Illinois, when Jemison was three to take advantage of better educational opportunities there. She graduated from Morgan Park High School in 1973 and entered Stanford University on a National Achievement Scholarship. Jemison graduated from Stanford in 1977, receiving a B.S. degree in chemical engineering and having fulfilled the requirements for a B.A. degree in African and Afro-American studies. When she obtained her M.D. degree in 1981, she interned at Los Angeles County–USC Medical Center and later worked as a general practitioner. Her published works include *Seeing the Future: Science, Engineering and Education* (2000). She has also appeared in films, including *Star Trek: The Next Generation* (1993). Dr. Jemison has received numerous awards. *Ebony* magazines named her among the "50 Most Influential Women" in 1993.

King, Coretta Scott (1927–2006)

Coretta Scott King, the wife of assassinated civil rights activist Martin Luther King Jr. was born on April 27, 1927, in Heiberger, Alabama. King was the second of three children born to Obadiah Scott and Bernice McMury. She had an older sister, Edythe, born 1925, and a younger brother, Obadiah Leonard, usually called Obie, born in 1930. She attended Lincoln High School in Marion, which she described as a "unique educational institution." She graduated at the top of her class in 1945 and went on to attend Antioch College in Yellow Springs, Ohio. Coretta Scott followed her sister's lead. As part of a racial integration program that Antioch College instituted in 1943, Edythe was admitted with a full scholarship. She studied music with Walter Anderson, the first black department chair in a college that was not historically black.

While in college, she became politically active largely due to her experience of racial discrimination by the local school board. The board denied her request to perform two years of required practice teaching at Yellow Springs public schools for her teaching certificate (she completed the requirement at a private school run by Antioch College instead). She was very active in the Ohio Progressive Party and attended her first national political convention in 1948 as a student delegate. After matriculating from the college, Scott won a scholarship to the New England Conservatory of Music to study vocal performance at the New England Conservatory in Boston, where she met Martin Luther King Jr.

She married King on June 18, 1953, on the lawn of her parents' house. The ceremony was performed by King's father. The Kings had four children: Yolanda Denise, Martin Luther III, Dexter Scott, and Bernice Albertine. Coretta King received honorary degrees from many institutions including Preston University, Duke University, and Bates College. She was a member of Alpha Kappa Alpha, an African American sorority.

After her husband was assassinated in 1968, King attended commemorative services at Ebenezer Baptist Church in Atlanta to mark her husband's birth every January 15, and fought for years to make it a national holiday. King's quest was realized in 1986, when the first Martin Luther King Day was celebrated. During the 1980s, King affirmed her long-standing opposition to apartheid, participating in a series of sit-in protests in Washington, D.C. This prompted nationwide demonstrations against South African racial policies. In 1986, she traveled to South Africa and met with Winnie Mandela, while Mandela's husband Nelson Mandela was still a political prisoner on Robben Island.

King was also a long-time advocate for world peace. In 1957, King was the founder of the Committee for a Sane Nuclear Policy. She was also vocal in her opposition to capital punishment and the 2003 invasion of Iraq. King was an advocate of women's rights, lesbian and gay rights, and HIV/AIDS prevention.

Mays, Willie Howard (1931–)

Willie Howard Mays was a National Baseball League player. He starred with the New York Giants, San Francisco Giants, and New York Mets from 1951 to 1973. In 1951, he was named National League Rookie of the year, and MVP in 1954 and 1965. The "Say Hey Kid," as he was called, won accolades not only for his batting, but also for his acrobatic "basket" catches in the outfield.

Moton, Robert Russa (1867–1940)

Robert Russa Moton was Booker T. Washington's successor at Tuskegee Institute. Moton continued both the educational and racial policies and practices of Washington, but fought for black participation in World War II. In recognition of his racial leadership he was awarded the NAACP's Spingarn Medal in 1931.

Nixon, Edgar Daniel (E. D.) (1889–1987)

Edgar Daniel Nixon was a fearless civil and human rights leader in Montgomery and was instrumental in organizing the Montgomery Bus Boycott in 1955–1956. Nixon bailed Rosa Parks out of jail after her arrest for refusing to give up her bus seat to a white passenger, and he helped find an attorney to represent her. In February 1956, a bomb exploded outside Nixon's Montgomery home. Nixon led the Montgomery branch of the Pullman Porters Union and was president of the local chapter of the NAACP, the Montgomery Welfare League, and the Montgomery Voters League.

Owens, James Cleveland (Jesse) Owens (1913–1980)

Born in Oakville, James Cleveland Owens won four gold medals at the 1936 Summer Olympics in Berlin, where he embarrassed the German dictator Adolph Hitler, who had contended that his "Aryan race" was mentally and physically superior to all other races. Owens, who had attended Ohio State University, won medals for the 100-meter race, the 200-meter race, the long jump, and as part of the 100-meter relay team.

Paige, Leroy (Satchel) (1906–1982)

Born in Mobile, Satchel Paige was a major league baseball player with a penchant for witticisms. A right-handed pitcher, Paige played professional baseball from 1926 to the 1960s, mostly in the

Negro leagues. In 1948, at the age of 42, he made his major league debut with the Cleveland Indians, becoming the oldest player ever to debut in the major leagues. He joined the St. Louis Browns in 1952 and played in the All-Star Game in 1952 and 1953. In 1971, he was elected to a separate division of the Baseball Hall of Fame for players from the old segregated Negro leagues.

Parks, Rosa (1913–2005)

Rosa Parks was born in Tuskegee, Alabama, on February 4, 1913. Parks entered school in Montgomery, Alabama, in 1924. She left school in 1929 to care for her grandmother. In 1932, Parks married Aarand Parks in Pine Level, Alabama. By 1934, Parks received her high-school diploma. In 1943, Parks became secretary of the Montgomery chapter of the NAACP. During that year, Parks tried to register to vote and was denied. Also, in that same year, Parks was forced off the bus for not entering at the back door.

In 1944, Parks was denied the opportunity to register to vote once again. However, in 1945, Parks finally received a certificate for voting. By 1949, Parks became an advisor to the NAACP Youth Council and met Martin Luther King Jr., in 1955. She was also arrested in the same year on December 1 for not yielding her seat to a white man on a Montgomery bus, where Parks stood trial and was found guilty on December 5. And thus the Montgomery Bus Boycott began.

In 1963, Parks attended the civil rights march on Washington. She also participated in the Selma-to-Montgomery civil rights march and worked for Congressman John Conyers in Detroit. And in 1987, she cofounded the Rosa and Raymond Parks Institute for Self-Development with Elaine Steele. The institute helped Detroit youth pursue their education and create a promising future for themselves.

A bust of Parks was unveiled at the Smithsonian Institution in Washington, D.C., in 1991.

Rosa Parks refused to give up her bus seat to a white man. This act of resistance set off a boycott of the Montgomery, Alabama, bus system, which in turn activated the larger movement against segregation throughout the country. (AP/Wide World Photos)

In 1992, Parks published her first book, *Rosa Parks: My Story*, with Jim Askins. President Bill Clinton awarded her the Presidential Medal of Freedom in 1996. She was also awarded the Rosa Parks Peace Prize during a trip to Stockholm, Sweden.

Pitts, Lucius H. (1914–1974)

Lucius H. Pitts was president of Miles College from 1960 to 1971. He helped build the academic reputation of the college. He showed unusual leadership and courage when he joined his students during the Birmingham civil rights demonstrations in the 1960s.

U.S. Secretary of State Condoleezza Rice addresses the media following a meeting at the U.S. Embassy in Baghdad, Iraq, April 2006. Rice was secretary of state in the George W. Bush administration during 2005–2009. (U.S. Department of Defense)

Reed, Thomas (1927–1997)

Thomas Reed was an attorney, civil rights leader, and state legislator. As a lawyer and civil rights leader, he helped desegregate the Alabama state troopers.

Rice, Condoleezza (1954–)

Condoleezza Rice became the first African American woman to be appointed as national security advisor (2001) and secretary of state (2005), serving in both capacities under President George W. Bush. Rice was born in Birmingham, Alabama, on November 14, 1954. Her mother, a pianist and organist, named Condoleezza from an Italian term "con dolcozza" which instructs the performer to play "with sweetness." Her parents, John and Angelena Rice, raised Condoleezza to pursue excellence in education.

Rice was from a deeply religious family who stressed education. Condoleezza was her parents' only child. She learned to read music before learning to read books. Rice came from four generations of college-educated family members (great-great-grandparents, great-grandparents, her parents, and her aunt). She started playing the piano at the age of three, taught by her grandmother.

In 1965, Rice became the first black student to attend music classes at Birmingham Southern Conservatory of Music. She moved to Denver, Colorado, in 1969 to attend an integrated school for the first time. By 1971, Rice had graduated from high school. In 1974, she graduated cum laude from the University of Denver and received an M.A. in government from Notre Dame University. In 1981, Rice received her Ph.D. in international studies from the University of Denver.

Rice's first book was *The Soviet Union and the Czechoslovak Army, 1948–1983: Uncertain Allegiance*. In 1986, she published her second book, *The Gorbachev Era*, in collaboration with Alexander Dallin. She was also appointed special assistant to the director of the joint chief of staff at the Pentagon through a Council on Foreign Relations Fellowship. By 1987, Rice was promoted to associate professor of political science at Stanford University. Between 1989 and 1991, Rice served in President George Herbert Walker Bush's administration as director of Soviet and East European affairs and special assistant to the president for national security affairs, and senior director for Soviet affairs at the National Security Council.

By May 1993, Rice was promoted to full professor at Stanford and in the same year named provost of Stanford. In 1994, she was elected to the board of trustees at the University of Notre Dame and, by 1995, had published another book, entitled *Germany Unified and Europe Transformed: A Study in Statecraft*. Rice became policy advisor to George W. Bush's presidential campaign in 1999. Rice delivered an address at the Republican

National Convention in 2000. She was named national security advisor by President-Elect George W. Bush and was sworn in on January 20, 2001. She succeeded Colin Powell as secretary of state in January 2005 and served until the end of the Bush administration in 2009.

Shores, Arthur D. (Davis) (1904–1996)

Arthur D. Shores was an attorney and civil rights leader in Birmingham. He defended civil rights leaders and their followers during the 1963 racial protests in Birmingham. He also represented the first black students to enter the University of Alabama. Although his efforts led to two bombings of his home in the 1960s, in 1975 he was awarded an honorary degree by the University of Alabama.

Shuttlesworth, Fred L. (Lee) (1922–)

Fred Shuttlesworth was a clergyman and civil rights leader in Birmingham. In the late 1950s he led attempts to desegregate schools in the city. After becoming pastor of Birmingham's Bethel Baptist Church in 1963, Shuttlesworth was well established as the principal civil rights leader in the city. He cofounded the Alabama Christian Movement for Human Rights, which became one of the foremost civil rights organizations in the state after the NAACP was banned. He was also a cofounder of the SCLC, which he served as secretary from 1958 to 1970 and president for a brief period in 2004. Although he was beaten and jailed several times and his home was bombed, Shuttlesworth continued to be a crusader against racial injustices. He led protests against discrimination in employment and public accommodations. As the latter demonstrations progressed, in 1963 he invited Martin Luther King Jr. and his leadership cadre to become directly involved in the Birmingham movement. The campaign that followed has been called the climactic struggle of the Civil Rights Movement.

Thomas, Louphena (1918–)

Louphena Thomas was an educator and politician. In 1977, she became the first African American female to serve in the Alabama legislature.

Washington, Booker Taliaferro (1858–1915)

Booker Taliaferro Washington was one of the most controversial African American leaders of the nineteenth century. He founded Tuskegee Institute in Tuskegee, Alabama. Washington was born in 1856, seven years before the Emancipation Proclamation, on a slave plantation in Franklin County, Virginia. Washington had no schooling when he was a slave, but had a childhood hunger for education. After Washington was freed, he began teaching himself with a used copy of Noah Webster's elementary spelling book. He attended a makeshift school, while laboring at a West Virginia salt furnace and later a coal mine. Washington left home in 1872 to attend Hampton Normal and Agricultural Institute, where he earned admittance by the vigor with which he cleaned classrooms. He paid his way primarily through janitorial work, and graduated with honors in 1895.

In 1881, Washington was recommended by General Samuel Chapman Armstrong to start a school in Tuskegee, Alabama. The mission of the Tuskegee Normal and Industrial Institute was to train school teachers and masters of various crafts and trades.

Washington worked tirelessly, ceaselessly, and with great success to procure white patronage and protection for his school, becoming known as "the sage of Tuskegee." Washington's implicit and explicit advocacy of the social philosophy of "accommodation" earned him high praise from white Americans. On September 18, 1895, the opening day of the Cotton States and International Exposition in Atlanta, Georgia, before an interracial audience, Washington delivered the address now known as the "Atlanta Compromise." In this speech, Washington denounced the black emigration movement in general and the movement of blacks from the South in particular. He also angered many civil rights activists of the period by supporting segregation of the races.

Washington went on to become the most prominent and powerful black man in pre–World War I America. Many urged Washington to write his autobiography, among them Walter Hines Page of the Boston publisher Houghton Mifflin. Many of the black intelligentsia deemed *Up from Slavery* a disservice to the race. Leading the vanguard among the black intelligentsia as an anti-Washington faction were William Monroe Trotter and W. E. B. Du Bois. Du Bois took Washington to task for soft-pedaling the horrors of slavery, for promoting stereotypes about blacks, and for being less than honest about the racism he had encountered.

Washington dined at the White House with President Theodore Roosevelt six months after the publication of *Up from Slavery*, on October 16, 1901. This visit increased Washington's fame and power that helped him expand his network, dubbed "the Tuskegee Machine" by Du Bois. Washington served as advisor to President William Howard Taft and secured political appointments for black men loyal to his philosophy, as well as determined the fate of a few white men seeking office. Washington served as a trustee of both Fisk and Howard universities and helped both connect with major philanthropists. Many activists were furious with Washington for not speaking out vociferously against white mob violence, Jim Crow, and other injustices.

Young, Coleman Alexander (1918–1997)

Born in Tuscaloosa, Coleman Alexander Young moved with his family to Detroit in 1923. He was elected to the Michigan State Senate in 1964 and was elected as the first African American

mayor of Detroit in 1973, narrowing defeating a white police commissioner. He was reelected four times by wide margins, serving as mayor for 20 years and retiring in 1993.

Cultural Contributions

In addition to such world-renowned musicians and composers as Nat King Cole, Erskine Hawkins, Lionel Ritchie and the Commodores, Odetta, Eddie Kendricks of the Temptations, Wilson Pickett, Martha Reeves, Joe Ligon, Percy Sledge, Willie "Big Mama" Thornton and the Mighty Clouds of Joy, and literary and artistic figures like Albert Murray, Sonia Sanchez, and Bill Traylor, Alabama's African American communities have contributed many exhibits, festivals, museums, and institutes to our nation's cultural treasure. These include the Scottsboro Museum and Cultural Center, located in the Joyce Chapel, one of the oldest African American churches in the state (c. 1876). The museum focuses on the famous Scottsboro Boys case but also has exhibits on other aspects of black history. The Alabama Blues Project, in partnership with the University of Alabama, has historic markers and sponsors exhibits on Alabama bluesmen and blueswomen. The project has also promoted the Music City Blues Society Festival in Birmingham and the Freedom Creek Festival. Montgomery is home for the National Center for the Study of Civil Rights and African American Culture.

Montgomery has a Civil Rights Trail, which includes the National Center for the Study of Civil Rights and African American Culture. In addition to its archives, the facility features artwork, sculptures, and artifacts. The six-block Civil Rights District in Birmingham honors the Civil Rights Movement and pays tribute to the clergy who contributed to the movement. Another site along the Civil Rights Trail is the Kelly Ingram Park, where civil rights demonstrators massed in 1963. The park contains sculptures which depict attacks on the protesters and jailed children. Also on the trail is the Fourth Avenue Business District, the major black business area in the city from the early 1900s to the 1960s. It was also a social and cultural center for Birmingham's blacks. Tuxedo Junction, named for the street car crossing at Tuxedo Park, received national notoriety from the 1939 hit song by Erskine Hawkins called "Tuxedo Junction." The Nixon Building Dance Hall (c. 1922) is also there. It was the social hall for black Birmingham in the 1920s and 1930s. Another historic cultural site is the marker noting the location of the Smithfield neighborhood. Smithfield was one of the oldest middle-class black subdivisions in the Birmingham area, dating from the early 1900s. The city's first African American high school is also located there.

The most visited cultural facility in Birmingham is the Birmingham Civil Rights Institute. Housed in a domelike structure, it features several galleries and has exhibits on both the Civil Rights Movement and global human rights movements. It sponsors lectures and other cultural programs throughout the year.

Tuskegee boasts the George Washington Carver Museum, The Oaks (Booker T. Washington's home), and the Daniel "Chappie" James Center for Aerospace Science and Health Education.

Bibliography

Badger, R. Reid, and Lawrence A. Clayton, eds. *Alabama and the Borderlands: From Prehistory to Statehood*. Tuscaloosa: University of Alabama Press, 2003.

Bailey, Richard, *They Too Call Alabama Home: Alabama Profiles, 1800–1999*. Montgomery, AL: Pyramid Publishing, 1999.

Barnard, William D. *Dixiecrats and Democrats: Alabama Politics, 1942–1950*. Tuscaloosa: University of Alabama Press, 1985.

Carter, Dan T. *Scottsboro. A Tragedy of the American South*. Baton Rouge: Louisiana State University Press, 1969.

Davis, Angela. *An Autobiography*. New York: International Publishers, 1989.

Dorman, Lewy. *Party Politics in Alabama from 1850 through 1860*. Tuscaloosa: University of Alabama Press, 1995.

Felix, Antonia. *Condi: The Condoleezza Rice Story*. New York: New Publishers, 2000.

Flynt, Wayne. "Alabama's Shame: The Historical Origins of the 1901 Constitution." *Alabama Law Review* 53 (2001): 67–76.

Flynt, Wayne. *Alabama in the Twentieth Century*. Tuscaloosa: University of Alabama Press. 2004.

Gregory, Read. *Quiet Strength: The Faith, the Hope, and the Heart of a Woman Who Changed a Nation*. Grand Rapids, MI: HarperCollins Publishers, 1994.

Hornsby, Alton, Jr. *A Biographical History of African Americans*. Montgomery: E- Book Time Books, 2005.

Jackson, Harvey H. *Inside Alabama: A Personal History of My State*. Tuscaloosa: University of Alabama Press, 2004.

Lofton, J. Mack. *Voices from Alabama: A Twentieth-Century Mosaic*. Tuscaloosa: University of Alabama Press, 1993.

Marks, Henry S., and Marsha Marks. *Alabama Past Leaders*. Huntsville, AL: Strode, 1981.

Novkov, Julie. *Racial Union: Law, Intimacy, and the White State in Alabama, 1865–1954*. Ann Arbor: University of Michigan Press, 2008.

Permaloff, Anne, and Carl Grafton. *Political Power in Alabama: The More Things Change....* Athens: University of Georgia Press, 1995.

Rogers, William Warren, Robert David Ward, Leah Rawls Atkins, and Wayne Flynt. *Alabama: The History of a Deep South State.* Tuscaloosa: University of Alabama Press, 1994.

Van Der Veer Hamilton, Virginia. *Alabama: A History.* New York: W. W. Norton, 1984.

Washington, Booker T. *Up From Slavery: An Autobiography (New Edition).* Boston: Houghton Mifflin Co., 1981. Originally published 1901.

ALASKA

Anne Hornsby

Chronology

1741	Russia lays claim to Alaska.
1867	The United States purchases Alaska from Russia.
1869	A few blacks begin to arrive in Alaska.
1886	African American Captain Michael Healy is given command of the *Bear*, the largest cutter in the U.S. Revenue Cutter Service in Alaskan waters.
1890s	The Alaskan gold rush brings many African American miners into the territory.
1896	Captain Michael Healey is found guilty of mistreating his crew.
1912	Alaska becomes a U.S. territory.
1941–1945	Largest migration of blacks into Alaska begins as blacks work on the ALCAN Highway and are assigned to military bases throughout Alaska and the Aleutians.
1942–1943	Over 10,000 U.S. soldiers build the ALCAN Highway; 3,695 of these soldiers are black.
1959	*(January 3)* Alaska enters the Union as the 49th state.
1963	*(February 11)* Alaska ratifies the Twenty-fourth Amendment to the U.S. Constitution abolishing poll taxes.
1970s	Construction of the Trans-Alaska oil pipeline (completed in 1977) brings many African American works into the state.
1984	Maryline Blackburn, a European-born African American singer, represents Alaska in the Miss America pageant.
1991	James C. Hayes elected as the first black mayor of Fairbanks, and the first African American mayor in the state.
1993	The National Association for the Advancement of Colored People (NAACP) investigates complaints of discrimination at Alaskan military bases.
1993	*(March 26)* The Alaska legislature votes to rename the bridge over the Gestle River as the "Black Veterans Recognition Bridge," in commemoration of the service of the African Americans who helped build the ALCAN Highway.
1994	The African American Historical Society of Alaska is founded.
1995	The Blacks in Alaska History Project is incorporated.
2000	African Americans comprise 3.5 percent of Alaska's population.
2007	Blacks comprise 3.8 percent of the state's population.

2008	Controversy erupts in the state's black community over Governor Sarah Palin's failure to recognize the state's Juneteenth celebration.
2008	Former Fairbanks Mayor James C. Hayes and his spouse are convicted of fraud.
2010	Census estimates put blacks at about 4 percent of the state's population.

Historical Overview

The Alaskan territory, rich in natural resources such as gold, salmon, copper, and, most recently, petroleum, was invaded by Russia in 1741 and subsequently purchased by the United States in 1867. The area became a territory of the United States in 1912 and gained statehood in January 1959. The territory experienced a colonial relationship with both Russia and the United States in which its natural resources were exploited by absentee capital investment. From the perspective of the United States, the Land Ordinances of 1785 and 1787 facilitated this exploitation because, among other provisions, they established purchasing rights to land in the northwest territory that would be advantageous to some groups. Thus land in the Alaskan territory was sold at favorable rates to white male citizens, while at the same time, citizenship was denied to the indigenous people of the area.

The state of Alaska, though the largest state in terms of land area in the United States, is the fourth-smallest in population, with only North Dakota, Vermont, and Wyoming trailing behind. According to the 2005 Census, the racial and ethnic composition of the state is 67.6 percent white, 15.6 percent native, 4.1 percent Hispanic, 4 percent Asian, 3.5 percent black, and 5.4 percent mixed race. In 2010, the percentage of blacks had risen slightly to 4 percent. Of approximately 627,000 people living in the state, some 70 percent live in urban areas, with 265,000 or a quarter-million residing in Anchorage or its suburban environs. If one adds the 50,000 living in Matanuska Valley, a bedroom community of Anchorage, the population of the two areas comprises one-half the population of the state. In addition, some 80,000 live in Fairbanks and surrounding areas. The African American population is centered in the cities of Fairbanks (11 percent) and Anchorage (6 percent).

The African American presence in Alaska began shortly after the Civil War. In the post-bellum period, some black seamen who migrated to the North Pacific to work in the whaling and fur trade remained and took up residence in the area. The discovery of gold in 1880 on the coast along Gastineau Channel saw more African Americans moving to Alaska. However, the big influx of African Americans into the territory occurred during World War II, when blacks were stationed in various military bases and decided to stay and take up permanent residence. Most of the current black population of the state lives in Anchorage and Fairbanks, where military bases are established (Fort Richardson, Elmendorf Air Force Base, Fort Wainwright, and Eielson Air Force Base). There are also a smaller number of African Americans living in Big Delta (Delta Junction) near Fort Greely and in Juneau, Ketchikan, and Kodiak near sites of Coast Guard activity.

In spite of enduring social and economic constraints imposed by the larger society, African Americans, with some occasional shortcomings, have made many significant contributions to the state. These range from the construction of the ALCAN Highway, holding political office, serving in the Revenue Cutter Service, winning the Miss Alaska Pageant, and operating an array of businesses.

The ALCAN Highway

African American military regiments were instrumental in the construction of the ALCAN

African American road workers march back to camp for a meal along a two-day-old section of the Alaska-Canada Defense Highway, 1942. The crew is helping to construct the Alaska Highway, which will stretch from Dawson Creek, British Columbia, Canada, to Fairbanks, Alaska. (AP/Wide World Photos)

Japan's attack on Pearl Harbor led to American fears that sea routes to Alaska could be cut off, posing a threat to the security of the Pacific Northwest and the entire country. Thus, there was a need for an overland route to get people and military supplies to Alaska. The 1,500-mile-long ALCAN Highway was constructed by U.S. Army engineers in 8 months and 12 days, from March to November 1942 (the harsh winter climate prompting the urgency). It covers the Canadian Yukon and Alaska and starts at Dawson Creek in British Columbia and ends in Fairbanks, Alaska.

Among the regiments involved in the construction of the highway were the African American 93rd, 95th, and 97th Corps of Engineers. The 93rd General Service Regiment was deployed to Skagway, the 95th to Dawson Creek, and the 97th disembarked at Valdez and worked the northern interior. The African American regiments were joined by four white regiments of the 18th, 35th, 340th, and 341st. Because the military was segregated at the time, all the commanding officers of the regiments were white; only black chaplains and doctors were commissioned officers in the northwest military units.

There was initial disagreement among military commands about the advisability of deploying black troops to work on the highway because of preconceived notions about blacks. Some army commanders thought blacks did not possess the necessary skills to operate the equipment and that they were unable to function efficiently in extreme cold environments. The U.S. Army commander for Alaska, General Simon Buckner Jr., was concerned that black soldiers would cohabit with indigenous Alaskans and produce a "mongrel race." However, due to the shortage of troops, the army deployed 3,695 black men of the 93rd, 95th, and 97th regiments to help with the construction. The number of black engineers represented one-third of the total 10,607 engineers who worked on the highway.

Highway (Alaska-Canada Highway), now known as the Alaska Highway. Though the immediate urgency of building this highway was as a security measure precipitated by Japan's attack on Pearl Harbor in December 1941, talk of such construction began as early as 1929 between the United State and Canada. Prior to the construction of the ALCAN Highway, there were only some 2,500 miles of roads in Alaska and only one main highway, which was the Richardson between Valdez and Fairbanks. The territory's link to the United States consisted of ship traffic from Pacific Northwest ports and a small number of Pan American Airways Clipper flights. Thus, there was a desire to build a highway through Canada that would connect Alaska with the lower 48 states to stimulate economic activity in the area.

Though all troops endured the harsh climate, the 97th labored in the interior, northern region and worked under the most extreme conditions of any of the regiments. These troops encountered the largest snowfall and widest swings in temperature of -80 degrees F to +90 degrees F and have been said to have carved the most miles in the final stretch. Upon completion of the ALCAN Highway, little if any local or public recognition was bestowed upon the black regiments for their contribution to the project. However, Brigadier General James A. O'Connor stated: "Some day the accomplishment of these colored soldiers' achievements accomplished far from their homes will occupy a major place in the lore of the North country." Froelich Rainey, a reporter for the *National Geographic* magazine, wrote the following in 1943: "If I were asked to design a monument commemorating the construction of the Alcan [Alaska-Canada] Highway, . . . I would model a 20-ton caterpillar tractor driven by two soldiers, one negro and one white, but so greasy and grimy that the difference in color would be practically imperceptible."

Today, the work of these black troops has received more widespread acclaim. In 1993, the State of Alaska passed a bill, signed by Governor Walter Hickel, renaming the bridge over the Gerstle River the Black Veterans Recognition Bridge, and in 2002, Governor Fran Ulmer recognized the efforts of the black soldiers of the 93rd, 95th, and 97th as being instrumental in building the Alaska Highway by stating: "If you've ever driven the Alaska Highway, you might remember a bridge just south of Delta on the way to Tok, that spans the Gerstle River. There's a sign on both ends displaying its name—Black Veterans Memorial Bridge. It is a small gesture to name a bridge, but I hope that by doing so we will be reminded of the significance of the contributions of the regiments and of every black soldier since . . . without the black soldiers, the Alcan would likely never have been built in such a short time."

Captain Michael Healy

Michael Healy was an African American who served the state and won great acclaim in his career, but left in disrepute. Healy was captain of Alaska's Revenue Cutter Service, which was reorganized in 1915 as the Coast Guard. Michael Healy was born in 1893 on a Georgia plantation to the white owner, Michael Morris Healy, and former domestic slave, Mary Eliza Clark. Michael Morris purchased Mary Eliza in 1829 and took her as his common-law wife, since, at the time, state law would not recognize a civil marital union between whites and blacks. The couple had 10 children who were light in complexion and identified themselves as white. Michael Healy married a white woman, Mary Jane Roach. The children were sent north for their education, some to a Quaker school in New York and some to Holy Cross College in Massachusetts. Michael attended Holy Cross and, in 1854, was sent to school in France to quell his high spirits. However, he soon left the school to become a seaman, sailing to Calcutta on a British ship in July 1855. He later joined the Revenue Cutter Service and quickly rose through the ranks, being commissioned as third lieutenant in 1865 and promoted to captain in March 1883. In 1886, Michael was given command of the largest cutter in the Arctic, the *Bear*. The *Bear* has been described as the "prime symbol of American sovereignty in Alaska." The *New York Sun* referred to the powers given to Captain Healy for his various patrols as those which made him "a good deal more distinguished person in the waters of the far Northwest than any President of the United States, or any potentate in Europe . . . ask anyone in the arctic, 'Who is the greatest man in America?' and the reply would invariably be 'Why, Mike Healy.' "

Starting his service on the East Coast, by the mid-1870s, Michael was based in San Francisco Bay, where the cutters traveled north each spring and patrolled the Alaskan coast and Bering Sea from a base at Unalaska. Initially, the main duties of the cutters involved the protection of seals from poachers (their numbers were becoming extinct) and providing assistance to the whaling fleet. Not only were the seals in danger of extinction, but the onrush of white settlers to the state, disrupting the traditional, stable economic and social patterns of the natives whose economic way of life was that of herders, resulted in depletion of the stocks of wildlife in general. This situation wreaked havoc for the native inhabitants of the state in the various villages as the food supply declined. There was need of a reliable source of food.

Michael joined ranks with Dr. Sheldon Jackson, a Presbyterian minister from New York, to solve the food supply problem. On one of his voyages to the Siberian coast, Captain Healy observed the Chukchi people sustaining themselves by raising reindeer. With this knowledge and the fundraising ability of Dr. Jackson, the two began to import reindeer to Alaska. There were enough lichens and tundra vegetation in the interior of Alaska to serve as food for the reindeer. In addition, reindeer reproduced quickly, and the native herders could use their meat for food and their skins for clothing. The project was a success, if for a short time, due to lack of congressional support in later years.

Captain Healy's aggressive personality and quick and violent temper, both traits exacerbated by his weakness for alcohol, led to his decline in the Revenue Cutter Service. He was known as a strict disciplinarian and meted out harsh treatment for perceived misdeeds of his crew. Captain Healy stood trial for court-martial twice, in 1890 and 1895–1896, for mistreatment of his crew. He was acquitted in the 1890 trial. Of the 19 counts against him in the trial beginning in January 1896, Captain Healy was found guilty of 16, not guilty on two, and one not proven. Captain Healy's sentence was light when the judges took into consideration his "creditable and valuable service." Therefore, he was suspended from active duty for four years and placed in the indeterminate status of "waiting orders." He was placed on the bottom of the captains list of the Revenue Cutter Service and "his condemnation would be read out at a full muster on every ship in the fleet." The sentence was carried out and the case closed in June 1896.

In 1900, Michael was given command of a new ship, the *McCulloch*, which he sailed to Alaska in the summer. However, he soon became depressed and was diagnosed with "melancholia with suicidal tendency." Toward the end of his career, he supervised repairs in dry dock and sailed twice to Alaska in 1902 and 1903, after which he retired after 40 years in the service. In honor of his service, the Coast Guard named a Polar-Class icebreaker after him. This 420-foot, 16,300-ton *Healy* is one of three other icebreakers in the Coast Guard fleet. The *Healy* is designed to carry a crew of 75, with accommodation and facilities for 50 scientists.

Modern Alaska

The easing of racial relationships in the state in modern times was exemplified by the election of a fiscally conservative and socially moderate Democrat, James C. Hayes, as the first black mayor of Fairbanks in 1991. His victory occurred in a city where the black population was only 12 percent, many of whom were stationed in the local military bases. Hayes, who rose through the political ranks from a seat on the local school board and city council, served three terms as mayor (1992–2001). Though Hayes, who initially ran unopposed, admitted that there were still undercurrents of racial tension in the city as evidenced by the local chapter of the NAACP investigating civilian black complaints of racial discrimination and harassment at Fort Wainwright Army and Elison Air Force bases, he also said that in Fairbanks "people tend to accept you as you are . . . they just want to hear your platform and hear what you believe in, and then see you go out and work really hard. That's been the key to my success."

In addition to his duties as mayor, Hayes was also associated with the Lily of the Valley Church of God in Christ, where he served as assistant pastor and eventually pastor. (The church was founded by his in-laws, LeeRoy and Mazie Parham, where his father-in-law was pastor.) In 2000, just before leaving the mayor's office, Hayes was involved in the establishment of Love Social Services Center, a tax-exempt organization that provided tutoring and social programs for low-income and disadvantaged youth in the South Fairbanks area and at the state's youth jail as well as operating a summer camp and a computer lab at the center. His wife, Chris Hayes, served as the center's executive director and other officers of the organization included family members and Lily of the Valley Church of God in Christ deacons and members. Since its inception, Love Social Services has received $2.9 million in federal grants through the efforts of Republican U.S. Senator Ted Stevens of Alaska.

However, in 2008, Hayes and his wife were found guilty of 16 counts of conspiracy, theft from a program receiving federal funds, money laundering, and filing false tax returns. They were also found guilty of using government funds earmarked for Love Social Services for their personal use and to help pay for construction and furnishing of a new Lily of the Valley Church of God in Christ building. Hayes was also accused of using the federal funds to pay for personal expenditures such as a plasma television, a family wedding reception, and credit card bills. Chris Hayes was accused of writing checks to cash on Love Social Services Center's account and converting the cash to money orders and cashier's checks to pay for personal items. According to the indictment, over $450,000 of federal funds were illegally diverted or used. Hayes was sentenced to 5½ years in prison and his wife, Chris, was sentenced to 3 years. Though Jim Hayes is appealing his case, they both reported to prison on June 11, 2008.

In the area of entertainment, in 1984, Maryline Blackburn, who grew up in Fairbanks, became the first African American representative to the Miss America pageant from Alaska. First runner-up in the Alaska pageant was Sarah Palin, nee Heath, who later became governor of the state and the 2008 Republican vice-presidential candidate. Blackburn, now in the music and entertainment business, recalls a note Sarah Palin wrote her saying, "I do love you. You're more admired than even you know. And please keep God number One. He's got great things for you, baby. Love, Sarah Heath."

African Americans, small in number in a thinly populated state, have made notable contributions to the state of Alaska. Beginning shortly after the Civil War until the present, blacks began to infiltrate the state, where they were involved in working in the maritime trade, seeking their fortune in the gold rush, serving with segregated military regiments that helped build the ALCAN Highway during World War II, serving in the military, constructing the Trans-Alaska Pipeline, and building businesses and careers throughout the state.

During the 2008 presidential campaign, African Americans showed little enthusiasm for the vice presidential campaign of their governor Sarah Palin. Earlier that year, controversies had arisen over the exclusion of black businesspeople from the Alaskan oil and gas pipeline board, the lack of minorities on the governor's staff, and the governor's failure to issue a proclamation recognizing the Juneteenth celebration, a holiday recognizing the arrival of news of emancipation of slaves in Texas and the Southwest.

Notable African Americans

Alexander, Gwendolyn (dates unknown)

Gwendolyn Alexander is president of the African American Historical Society of Alaska. In 2008, she strongly criticized Alaska Governor and Republican vice presidential candidate Sarah Palin for her failure to participate in or support the state's Juneteenth celebrations as previous governors had done.

Davis, Bettye (1938–)

Born in Louisiana, Bettye Davis was elected to the Alaska House of Representatives in 1990 as a Democrat from Anchorage. She was reelected in 1992 and 1994, but defeated in 1996. In 2000, Davis was elected to the Alaska State Senate. She is a member of the League of Woman Voters and of the Anchorage chapter of the NAACP, and a former treasurer of the National Organization of Black Elected Legislative (NOBEL) Women.

Democratic Senator Bettye Davis rises in support of a bill on the Senate floor, in Juneau, Alaska, April 10, 2008. (AP/Wide World Photos)

Harper, George T. (1930–2004)

Born in Atlanta, George Harper served in the U.S. Navy in the late 1940s and then earned a B.S. degree from Chase College in 1960. He first visited Alaska in 1980, and moved to Anchorage in 1981. He worked as a computer programmer for the Bureau of Land Management until 1992. He also taught computer classes at the University of Alaska–Anchorage. In 1992, Harper created a Black History Month exhibit honoring black U.S. Army engineers who constructed the Alaska Highway during World War II. Harper was also a cofounder of the Blacks in Alaska History Project, which was incorporated as a nonprofit organization in 1995. The purpose of the project is to build and maintain a collection of information and historical photographs documenting the presence and contributions of African Americans in Alaska. The project also produces exhibits and lectures publicizing these historical resources.

Cultural Contributions

The major cultural activities in Alaska, other than those sponsored by the church, are centered around the African American Historical Society. This group, founded in 1994, specializes in the history of slavery and the history of Juneteenth, Martin Luther King Jr. teaching tolerance to youth, African Americans and the ALCAN Highway, the Million Father March, and various youth events and activities. Its major community-wide festival is the Juneteenth celebration. This festival began as a loosely organized event in the 1980s. In 1994, the historical society assumed sponsorship of the event. It receives financial support from the Alaskan African American Business Council and other organizations. During the festival various foods, African American photographs, and other items are sold.

Bibliography

Alaska History and Cultural Studies. www.akhistorycourse.org.

Borneman, Walter R. *Alaska: A Narrative History*. New York: Harper-Collins, 2003.

Ebony, October 1998.

Haycock, Stephen. *Alaska: An American Colony*. Seattle: University of Washington Press, 2002.

Juneteenth Celebration in Alaska. www.juneteenthalaska.com.

Lundberg, Murray. "Captain Michael Healy, Revenue Cutter Service." http://polarcircle.tripod.com.

Naske, Claus-M., and Herman E. Slotnick. *Alaska: A History of the 49th State*. Norman: University of Oklahoma Press, 2003.

O'Toole, James M. *Passing for White*. Boston: University of Massachusetts Press, 2002.

ARIZONA

Jamane Yeager

Chronology

1539	Estevanico, a Moroccan slave, leads the expedition of Fray Marcos De Niza in search of the Seven Golden Cities of Cibola; the expedition crosses the region that will become Arizona.
1752	Four soldiers of African descent are stationed at the newly established Tubac presidio, the first Spanish colonial garrison and first European community in what will become Arizona.
1776	A Spanish presidio is established at Tucson in south-central Arizona.
1821	Mexico, of which the Arizona region is a part, gains its independence from Spain.
1824	African American mountain men enter Arizona, including Jim Beckwourth, Edward Rose, and Moses "Black" Harris.
1848	(February) The Treaty of Guadalupe Hidalgo ends the Mexican-American War; Arizona is part of a vast stretch of Mexican territory ceded to the United States.
1850	The Compromise of 1850 establishes the Territory of New Mexico, which includes Arizona.
1850	The daughter of Wiley Box, a stagecoach driver, marries a black Indian named Curly Neale, who owns a hotel in Oracle, near Tucson.
1858	The Butterfield Stage Company employs African American women as cooks at stage stops across Arizona.
1860	The 1860 Census records a black man named Charley Embers as living near the Vulture Mine near Wickenburg; other blacks include Charles Cooper and the Isaiah Bell family, residents of Tucson.
1863	The Territory of Arizona is established.
1863	Ben McClendon, a runaway slave, finds gold deposits near Wickenburg.
1866	Charley Embers begins working as a cook in a mining camp at Ajo, south of Tucson.
1868	A domestic named Mary Green and her two children become the first African American residents of Phoenix.
1870	Moses Green becomes the first African American born in Arizona.
1870	Harvey Merchant, a black cowboy, is rescued from Indians by soldiers.
1876	The Southern Pacific Railroad enters Arizona from California.
1876	Nat Love, a black cowboy and writer known as "Deadwood Dick," resides in Arizona; William Curly Neal works as a freight driver in Oracle, Arizona.
1877	Silver is discovered near Tombstone.

1880	The Census shows 155 African Americans living in the Arizona Territory.
1881	The city of Phoenix incorporates; the Southern Pacific Railroad crosses Arizona.
1881	Henry Ransom, former 10th Cavalryman, becomes the first driver for the Tucson Transfer Company.
1881	The Gunfight at O.K. Corral takes place at Tombstone in southeastern Arizona.
1883	The Atlantic & Pacific (Santa Fe) Railroad crosses northern Arizona.
1884	Jim Young, "The Giant," fights with the well-known boxer John L. Sullivan in Tucson.
1885	The black "buffalo soldiers" of the 10th Cavalry are dispatched to Arizona to fight the Apache leaders Marqus and Geronimo.
1886	Geronimo surrenders to General Nelson Miles; the Indian fighting in Arizona ends.
1889	Frank Shirley opens a barber shop in Phoenix.
1891	Henry O. Flipper, the first black graduate of West Point, lives in Nogales and Tucson; Charley Williams, popularly known as "Banjo Dick," moves to Nogales after the failure of the "Banjo Dick Mine," the first all-black mining company in Arizona.
1892	The 24th Regiment of all-black soldiers is sent to Fort Huachuca to help guard the Mexican border.
1892	Julia Thomas opens an oyster parlor and confectionary in Phoenix.
1893	1,357 African Americans reside in the Arizona Territory; Richard Rosser and his family arrive in Phoenix to operate a truck farm.
1897	William Powaton Crump comes to Arizona from West Virginia and runs a statewide fruit-and-produce business.
1899	A black fraternal lodge, Alpha Lodge No. 17, is formed in Tucson with 14 Master Masons present; Tanner Chapel African Methodist Episcopal (AME) Church is founded in Phoenix.
1900	Compass Lodge No. 18 opens in Clifton, and Maricopa Lodge No. 16 is formed with 20 Master Masons in Phoenix.
1900	Mt. Calvary Missionary Baptist Church is founded in Tucson.
1902	Cotton cultivation is introduced into Arizona.
1905	Arizona Territory is the top copper producer in the United States.
1905	Henry O. Flipper works for the Col. Green Mining Company in southern Arizona; the Prince Chapel AME Church is founded in Tucson.
1909	Segregation is made legal in the Arizona Territory and Arizona school districts are segregated.

1912	*(February)* Arizona becomes the 48th state.
1912	Arizona grants women the right to vote but forbids racially mixed marriages.
1912	J.W. Miller's Afro Mining Company fails.
1913	More all-black units are stationed at Fort Huachuca in southern Arizona.
1919	The Phoenix Advancement League is formed.
1921	Booker T. Washington Memorial Hospital is founded in Phoenix.
1921	Death of the well-known African American cowboy of Tombstone, "Old Bat" Baptiste.
1926	Phoenix Union Colored High School opens, becoming the first segregated high school in Arizona.
1931	*The Gleam*, a black-owned newspaper, is founded.
1933	Walter Yancy of Waco, Texas, attends the University of Arizona and begins recording local history.
1933	The black-owned *Phoenix Tribune* is founded; another black-owned newspaper, the *Phoenix Index*, is founded in 1936.
1938	An African American cowboy named Nathan Hall works at the 3C (Old Hugget) Ranch in Oracle, near Tucson.
1942	Three African American soldiers are killed in Phoenix during the Thanksgiving Day Riot.
1942	14,000 African American soldiers of the 93rd Infantry Division and 32nd and 33rd companies of the Woman's Auxiliary Army Corps are stationed at Fort Huachuca for training.
1942–1962	The *Arizona Sun* newspaper is edited by Doc Benson.
1945	Phoenix Union Colored High School is renamed George Washington Carver High School.
1947	The Greater Phoenix Council for Civic Unity formed.
1950	*The Leader* newspaper is operated by David Solomon.
1950	Hayzel B. Daniels and Carl Sims become the first African American legislators in Arizona.
1953	Segregation ends in the Phoenix Union High School District, a year before legal segregation ends nationally.
1960	The Phoenix National Association for the Advancement of Colored People (NAACP) Youth Council stages sit-ins in four downtown coffee shops and lunch counters.

1964	The Phoenix City Council adopts a public accommodations ordinance.
1966	Dr. Morrison F. Warren is the first African American appointed to the Phoenix City Council.
1971	The *Arizona Informant* newspaper is founded by brothers Cloves C. Campbell Sr. and Dr. Charles R. Campbell.
1972	Cloves Campbell Sr. becomes the first African American elected to the Arizona State Senate.
1972	Calvin Goode becomes the second African American to serve on the Phoenix City Council; he serves for 22 years.
1992	Establishment of a Martin Luther King Jr./Civil Rights Day passes the Arizona legislature.
1998	Leah Landrum Taylor, an African American woman, is elected to the Arizona House of Representatives as a Democrat.
2000	Roosevelt Elementary School District is renamed in honor of Cloves C. Campbell Sr.
2006	The Arizona Commission on African American Affairs (ACAAA) is created to establish more effective communication between the Arizona legislature and the state's African American community.
2006	Leah Landrum Taylor is elected to the Arizona State Senate.
2006	Cloves Campbell Jr. wins a seat in the Arizona House of Representatives.
2008	Vernon Parker, a Republican, is sworn in as the first African American mayor of Paradise Valley.
2009	Mayor Vernon Parker of Paradise Valley announces his candidacy for the 3rd District U.S. House seat in Arizona.

Historical Overview

Prehistory to Territorial Status in 1863

Prior to the arrival of the Spanish in Arizona during the sixteenth century, the land was occupied by natives that the former called Indians. It was a black Moroccan slave, Esteban (variously known as Esteven, Estevanico, or Little Stephen), who led the Spaniards from Mexico through Arizona and into New Mexico in 1539 as they searched for illusive cities of gold. Esteban became the guide to Fray Marcos de Niza and, upon discovering the cities of Cibola in Zuni, New Mexico, was killed by Indians. He is believed to be the first non-Native American to set foot in Arizona. The next significant encounter with Arizona occurred in the 1690s when the Jesuit, Padre Francisco Kino, began establishing missions in southern Arizona.

These missions were followed with the building of presidios to protect missionaries and explorers. The first presidio was located at Tubac in 1752 and was moved to Tucson in 1776. According to Dobyns (1976), four soldiers with varying degrees of African ancestry and shades of hue transferred to Tucson with the presidio. It was difficult to identify blacks during the Spanish period because of the rigid caste classification system that the Spanish had, with whites coming from Spain being at the top of the hierarchy, Africans at the bottom, and numerous designations in between.

Although probably many more blacks accompanied every expeditionary force following de Niza's return, all but Esteban have been lost to posterity. The only evidence of a prolonged stay by any black is found in the reports of Jaramillo, a lieutenant under the command of Coronado. He reports that two black families were constantly in touch with Friar Louis de Escalon. From 1542 to about 1650, the Sebastian and Melchor Perey families and their descendants were settled somewhere between the Arizona and New Mexico border near present-day Greenlee. After 1650, there is no further mention of the two families.

The arrival of African Americans in Arizona from other parts of the United States in significant numbers did not occur until after 1850. After the conclusion of the Mexican War, African Americans came in increasing numbers. In 1850, there were only 21 known blacks in the entire territory, which included New Mexico and Arizona. In 1860, 85 "free" blacks were known to have been in the territory, with 21 residing in the future territory of Arizona. By 1870, the number had climbed to 26.

Mining was a chief motivation behind most immigration to Arizona prior to the Civil War. Not only were the hillsides and mountains of Arizona thought to be filled with gold, but the rich fields of California's north were said to contain "enough gold to make every man in this country rich." Since the major southern routes leading to California passed through Arizona, from 1848 to the end of the California rush, the future territory became spotted with settlements involved in on way or another with gold. Gila, Tubac, and Tucson became leading communities almost overnight. John, an African American

from Kentucky, was among those black pioneers who ventured into Arizona because of his white employer, as well as the California gold rush. He was a member of the famous Duval party, which crossed through Arizona on the way to California in 1849. John had been employed as a barber and cook in El Paso, Texas, and when the family decided to move west, he accompanied them since he was the sole servant. The Butterfield stage company employed a number of African American women as cooks at various stage stops across Arizona.

Mining in Arizona began in earnest after the Gadsden Purchase was completed in 1854. The Arivac Mining Company employed a number of blacks as miners, cooks, and teamsters. In 1856, Charles D. Poston purchased the Arivac works, retaining all the black employees. Poston became fond of one of the African American cooks at the Arivac site, a Jim Berry, and a warm friendship between the two men developed. As the Civil War became a reality, Poston and his close friend, Professor Raphael Pumpbelly, decided to leave the territory. Berry volunteered to accompany the two men, acting as scout, cook, and protector. Upon reaching the Colorado River, however, the black man left the two men for reasons that have not been explained, returned to his wife and home in Sonora, Mexico, and was never heard of again.

From Territory to Statehood (1863–1912)

On June 25, 1863, Pauline or Paulino Weaver, Henry Wickenburg, Charles Genung, another famous explorer, and two Mexicans formed the Weaver Mining District as the result of a large discovery of gold deposits near the town site by their companion Ben McClendon. McClendon was the first African American to reside in Wickenburg. He came by way of Yuma in 1861, admitted to being a runaway slave, and was accepted by the community. The party of six soon discovered an extensive gold mine they called

"Rich Hill," north of the town of Wickenburg. According to accounts, the claimed yielded $2,765 worth of gold daily.

Despite the presence of African American miners in the territory, the largest numbers of blacks employed in the mining companies were hired as common laborers, cooks, servants, and teamsters. Mining interests played an indirect role in motivating many African Americans to move to the territory; the newspaper campaign waged by Arizona's journalists influenced both whites and blacks to make the journey. Charley Embers came to Arizona in 1866. He worked as a cook at the Ajo Mining Camp for 10 years. In 1876, Embers was hired as a surveyor by A. W. Maxten and made his home in Tucson, where he lived until 1933. A few adventurous black men established their own mining works. Charley Williams, popularly known as "Banjo Dick," came to Arizona in 1871 and worked for L.A. Smith and his family as a cook and general housekeeper. In the mid-1880s, Banjo Dick obtained loans from Mrs. Wiley Box and William Neal to open a small mining operation near Tucson, known as the Banjo Dick Mine. This was the first all-black mining company to be established in Arizona. It was owned, financed, operated, and worked exclusively by African Americans for African Americans.

The Banjo Dick Mine existed for only a few years. In 1891 the ore ran out and Banjo Dick reluctantly moved to Nogales, where he earned a living by shining shoes and playing his banjo for private parties and community events. The failure of Banjo Dick did not end black capitalism. Mrs. Wiley Box continued to finance mining companies and staked a few claims of her own. One claim which blossomed into an extremely profitable project was the Afro Mining Company, which was owned and operated by J.W. Miller. Miller came to Tucson in the early 1900s and worked for two years as a cook. Around 1910 or 1912, he staked a claim in the Camobabi Mountains near Tucson. After securing capital investments from

Mrs. Box and William Neal, he opened the mine for operation and extracted several thousand dollars' worth of gold. In 1923 the company faced bankruptcy; finally in 1928 the mine was closed for lack of ore, not money.

Not only did African Americans finance mining enterprises with their own capital as well as that obtained from other sources, but a few inherited mines and mining claims. Elize A. Allen and "Minnie J." inherited the claims of Milton B. Duffield, Arizona's first U.S. marshal.

Cattle raising and the ranching industry also imported or influenced African Americans to come to Arizona. Like the mines, Arizona's cattle industry was backed heavily by outside investment. Most of the ranchers and investors were white, but there is at least one exception. C. B. Martin, an African American, owned and operated a cattle ranch near Dos Cabezas. Many African Americans were employed by ranchers as cooks, laborers, and cowboys. From 1850 to the end of the frontier era, several hundred African American cowboys found their way into the territory. Some were hired to make the trek, some were brought by whites, and still others came on their own in pursuit of personal ambitions. Three such individuals, Jim Younger, John "Old Bat" Baptists, and "Nigger John" were employed by one of Tombstone's more famous lawmen, John Slaughter. All three men had worked for Slaughter in Texas and accompanied him on his journey to Arizona. "Nigger John" was originally one of Slaughter's "hundred slaves." He rode with Slaughter and his hired hands on numerous cattle drives, serving the entire caravan as cook, barber, laundryman, and body servant. John remained in Slaughter's service for almost 25 years before retiring.

Jim Younger worked for Slaughter in Texas, and during that time became an accomplished cowboy and gunman. After reaching Arizona, Jim continued working for Slaughter and eventually saved enough money to purchase several mining claims. In the 1880s, Jim received momentary recognition when he fought the famous John L. Sullivan. Jim lost the fight but won the $500 prize money offered because he knocked Sullivan down in the first round. Perhaps the most famous of Slaughter's black cowboys was "Old Bat." He had been one of Slaughter's slaves, but after coming to Arizona Slaughter added him to the payroll, primarily because Old Bat saved the wagons from total destruction as the Slaughters crossed the Rio Grande en route to Arizona. He knew a great deal about mining and was also the chief accountant and bookkeeper for the many Slaughter enterprises. He worked for Slaughter for 74 years. There were other black cowboys who also rode across Arizona's rangeland: Harvey Merchant, who hired out to the ranchers of Tucson and the surrounding area; William C. Phillips, who was involved in the first fatal shooting in the town of Williams; and the renowned Nat Love, also known as "Deadwood Dick," who not only was a cowboy but was an accomplished writer as well.

Besides the military, mining, and cattle industries, the lumber industry also played an important role in the growth of Arizona, including the importation of African Americans to the territory. Lumbering in Arizona was slower in developing than either mining or ranching; nevertheless it was an essential element in Arizona's economic growth. Unlike the mining and cattle businesses, however, lumber companies are known to have imported African Americans to the territory through direct and formal channels. Most, if not all of the African Americans who were employed by Arizona's lumber industry came to the territory by "signing up" with representatives of the various companies. A majority of those who were brought to Arizona were imported as a cheap, but highly skilled, labor supply. The main employers of African American lumbermen in Arizona were the Ayer Lumber Company (later known as Arizona Lumber and Timber Company) located in northern Arizona at Flagstaff, and the Camps Up Canyon Timber Company of southern Arizona. Little is known about the "Camps Up" operation except that

in 1880 two African Americans, Carter Crone and Samuel Moor, had at some previous point been brought to the camp from Arkansas. According to Joseph C. Dolan, owner of the Arizona Lumber and Timber Company after 1933, E. E. Ayer, a prominent Chicago lumberman, was responsible for establishing the first extensive sawmill operation in northern Arizona, and transported 10 or 20 blacks from Louisiana and Arkansas to the Flagstaff area during the late 1880s to work at various skilled jobs for the Ayer Lumber Company.

After 1890, and continuing throughout the twentieth century, more African Americans were brought in, usually a dozen at a time. Cady Lumber Company brought African Americans to Arizona from McNary, Louisiana, in 1924. A special fleet of trains transporting approximately 700 lumbermill hands and their families arrived in a town in northern Arizona, which the company would call McNary. Those black lumbermill families were beholden to Cady Lumber Company, whose lands were denuded of trees after years of being overworked. It was said that the company owner, A. Cady, had too much respect and faith in his black employees to leave them suffering in the barren southern site. The families brought all their possessions, including fowl, pigs, cattle, and pets. Housed in segregated, framed houses and having virtually all their needs available, nonetheless some were unable to get acclimated to the harsh mountain winters. As some left for warmer climates, they were quickly replaced by other workers from Texas, Oklahoma, and Arkansas, thankful to escape oppression as well as the coming Depression. The company had built and owned its own vegetable and produce stores, health facilities, and schools—the latter separate. During the Depression, no one had to rely on welfare aid, which was the case of millions across the country. Afterwards, as some families managed to improve their financial status, they migrated to Phoenix, Tucson, and other urban towns.

The military, by necessity, was also an important element in this early period of American

Two African American workers pole logs onto the bull chain, a hooked conveyor that carries the logs into the sawmill for processing into lumber, Flagstaff, Arizona, 1957. (AP/Wide World Photos)

settlement. The United States had inherited the Indian problem from the Mexicans following the war of 1848. To increase the population of Arizona, in 1863, Congress passed an act creating the Territory of Arizona. Despite earlier failures, the presence of the military helped to further populate and settle the territory. Businessmen, traders, farmers, and ranchers followed, if not accompanied the military as they established posts near Tucson, Tubac, Gila, Yuma, and a number of other advantageous sites throughout Arizona. Accompanying the military on their journeys to and through the territory were a number of African American cooks, servants, and teamsters. Captain R. S. Ewell, the commander of Fort Buchanan, employed a black woman named Nancy, who had been with his family for years. She served the captain as cook, servant, and housekeeper and was "famous throughout Arizona for her cooking and humanness."

Jim Young came west with the regular army as a cook. Before joining up with the army, Jim led a harsh life as a Mississippi slave, but had somehow escaped the plantation and the South shortly before 1840. His life with the army was not an easy one and was filled with more hazards than even those of his white comrades, since African Americans were not allowed to handle weapons prior to 1863. African Americans are also known to have been attached to the garrison at Fort Defiance, in the northern region of the territory. Besides protecting the territory's population from hostile Indians, the military was also responsible for furthering scientific exploration of the territory.

Ab Reading, a native of Chester, Pennsylvania, was a cook and body servant to three civilians with the famous Beale and Ives expedition of 1857. By emphasizing the territory's natural beauty and resources, and with the help of the federal government and the territory's leading newspapers campaigning for easterners to invest capital in Arizona's leading industries, cattle and mining, the population began to increase.

When the Civil War ended in 1865, African American soldiers more than adequately had shown their courage in battle. In the years following the Civil War, although there was no longer any question about their courage, prejudice against African American soldiers remained strong. In spite of the insults, the men still wanted to serve in the army. The military life, even with its inequities, was better than the life they had previously known; it provided a measure of dignity, education, and opportunity to exercise leadership. In 1866, the U.S. government turned its attention to preventing conflicts that arose in the western territories between Native Americans and settlers and among the settlers themselves. In the same year Congress authorized the establishment of African American regiments. To forestall objections of white citizens to having black soldiers stationed nearby in the developed communities, the army sent the men to remote sites. These were places that were considered undesirable because of the rugged, undeveloped land or because the climate routinely was freezing cold or miserably hot. This is the climate that the 9th and 10th Cavalry and the 24th and 25th Infantry, also known as "buffalo soldiers," were sent to establish order on the frontier. They were to guard telegraph and supply lines and to protect settlers in sparsely settled territories.

Upon learning of the "buffalo soldiers," General George Crook, commander of the Arizona theater of operations, petitioned Washington for use of the 9th and 10th cavalries in Arizona. Finally in March 1885, the 10th was dispatched to Arizona with orders to capture Geronimo and other marauding Apache war chiefs. Buffalo soldiers were sent to Arizona, where Fort Huachuca had been built to provide protection against Apache Indians. After Geronimo's surrender in 1886 and after the battles with Native Americans diminished in intensity, the fort remained to provide protection from bandits who frequented the territory and who freely crossed the borders between the United States and Mexico. In this tense situation, all-black divisions stationed at Fort Huachuca guarded the U.S.-Mexico border from the late 1890s through 1931. From 1870 to 1910, the 9th and 10th were commended for their excellence in physical fitness, marksmanship, battle tactics, bravery, and sacrifice. Despite the existence of outspoken antagonism against African American military men, many soldiers remained in Arizona after their discharge from the army. Regardless of the reasons, the fact remains that many African American soldiers became residents of the territory and attempted to find their "pots of gold" somewhere within the boundaries of Arizona.

Two men who remained were William Neal and Emmet "Dick" Woodly. Neal came to Arizona in 1878 with a detachment of the 9th Cavalry. After his discharge he returned to Tucson, where he worked as a cook for the owner of the Maison Dore. Upon receiving his discharge from the army in 1869, Emmet "Dick" Woodly came to Tucson and began working for M. E. N. Fish as a common laborer at his flour mill. He later worked for Fish at his home as a cook, housekeeper, and general handyman around the house. He married a Mexican girl and lived in Tucson until the late 1880s. Lieutenant Henry O. Flipper, West Point's first black graduate, spent much of the 1890s in southern Arizona after being discharged from the military, where he surveyed the Nogales townsite, briefly edited a local newspaper, and defended the community in an important land grant case.

From Statehood through World War II
(1912–1950)

Arizona gained statehood on February 14, 1912, and with the adoption of the new state constitution Arizona's African American population faced total segregation. Consequently African Americans had to restructure their existence and organize to meet their own needs and aspirations. For example, the "Colored Pioneers Association" with branches in Phoenix, Tucson, Flagstaff, Safford, and Fort Huachuca was organized in response to the white Pioneers Association sponsored by the Phoenix newspaper for citizens born in the territory prior to 1890. (Records show that Moses Green born in 1879 was the first African American born in Arizona.) At that time many African Americans were property owners, but they had to depend on businesses operated by Anglos. The church had traditionally served both as places of worship and community togetherness, so through these networks of race-controlled institutions, they sought to strengthen race pride.

In Tucson, the Prince Chapel AME Church was organized in 1906, Mount Cavalry Baptist Church was established in 1907, and Phillips Chapel Colored AME Church was organized in 1925. In Phoenix, Tanner Chapel AME Church and the First Colored Baptist Church were centers of vitality in the African American community. In 1915, the "Phoenix Colored Director" listed the following enterprises: shoemaker, printer, blacksmith, embalmer, two hotel-owners, beauticians, a hospital, and barbers. Many black barbers had all-white clientele, including the exclusive Hotel Adams, which always maintained an African American–operated shop. Even though many services were available within the African American community, jobs were not. After 1910, the African American population had quadrupled from the previous 10-year period. Most migrants came mainly from Oklahoma, Texas, Louisiana, and Arkansas.

The most prideful institution of Arizona blacks at the time was the Booker T. Washington Memorial Hospital, organized by Dr. Winston C. Hackett in 1921. It served all races, including patients from Tucson. Almost simultaneously in Tucson, Creed Taylor, an engineer from Chicago, began services at the private Desert Sanitarium. By 1920, the population had increased 76 percent, many spreading out to smaller towns—Flagstaff, Clifton, Douglas, Prescott, Yuma, and Globe. Wages were low and living conditions were deplorable. While African Americans were organizing on various fronts to defend their human rights, the Ku Klux Klan was beginning to infiltrate Arizona around 1916–1917. Chapters sprung up in Phoenix, Glendale, Flagstaff, and some rural areas.

In 1919, the Phoenix Advancement League was formed in opposition to segregation in Phoenix. Its purpose was to fight segregation and bigotry perpetuated by state laws. Headed by Samuel Bayless and C. Credille, both merchants, this organization was forerunner to the local NAACP branch. By 1922, other branches were active in Tucson, Flagstaff, Bisbee and Yuma. The African American population growth slowed in the 1920–1930 decade (8,000 to 10,749), yet business activities continued to thrive. Black-owned newspapers appeared during this decade. The *Gleam*, founded and edited by Mrs. Winston Hackett; the *Phoenix Tribune*, published by Arthur R. Smith, a Texas-born English teacher; and the *Index*, locally edited by Reverend W. Gray; all kept the community informed of what their contemporaries were doing nationally.

In the 1930s when the Depression struck Arizona, African Americans were seriously affected. Many moved from the rural areas into the urban cities, such as Phoenix and Tucson, seeking relief and shelter. In Phoenix the city established the Community Welfare Council, a conglomerate of 22 agencies; African Americans were ignored in the handouts. In an effort to circumvent these tactics, African American leaders in Tucson and Phoenix formed the Colored Businessmen's Association, so the business and employment needs of the people would be met by the group raising and appropriating funds. The black Masons, the black Elks, and members of other black fraternal lodges made an effort to take care of their own jobless members and friends. All of these organizations demanded and succeeded in getting an "all Negro Division" of the Phoenix Community Chest during the 1930s, and they also welcomed the arrival of federal funds and programs designed to help all Phoenicians in need of aid. Black voters, like the majority of white voters, were grateful, and throughout the decade, they supported Franklin D. Roosevelt and his New Deal.

The 1940s pre- and post-war were times of influx and ferment. Jobs were generally plentiful, the national Federal Employment Practices Committee (FEPC) made it possible for African Americans to work in places where they previously had been barred, except in menial positions. The Air Force bases—Luke and Williams near Phoenix; Davis-Monthan at Tucson; and Yuma Proving Grounds—were a few examples where hiring had to be nondiscriminatory, according to Executive Order 8802, which inserted a nondiscrimination clause into government defense contracts. As a result more jobs became available to African Americans, and they came out of World War II determined to achieve first-class citizenship. African American veterans, like others, benefited from the G.I. Bill and other postwar opportunities. Winston Hackett, Wade Hammond, Augustus Shaw, Lincoln Ragsdale, and other black leaders joined with Father McLaughlin and other white supporters to reorganize the Phoenix Urban League in 1945. The League grew increasingly concerned with racial discrimination in employment, housing, and education, as did the local branch of the NAACP. The Urban League, the NAACP, and other groups worked hard to facilitate change, but it was always a struggle.

1950 to the Present

During the 1950s civic leadership concerns swung back to schools, plus a growing interest in local politics. As for the school system, it was historically nonpolitical, with its board members making policy decisions independent of municipal or county governments. Since African Americans accounted for 2 to 3 percent of any school district, it was all but impossible to elect one of its own to the policy-setting body. African Americans were unable to exert any political muscle to push for any sort of reforms. However, neither did Mexican Americans or American Indians, the other "minority" groups who accounted for approximately 40 percent of Arizona residents in 1940. Not until the municipal and state elections for the 1950 term did African Americans become sufficiently organized to select and support visible candidates to represent their interests on governing bodies. Sylvanus "Breezy" Boyer, a contractor and popular fraternal leader, established a precedent by running for a seat on the Phoenix City Council. He was opposing, as an independent, the Charter Government ticket that included Barry Goldwater, the latter's first try at public office. The Charter ticket candidate enjoyed the advantages of good coverage from the local daily newspapers, plus radio. Boyer had to appease himself to campaigning in lodge halls, churches, and at Eastlake Park. He did not win, but he tried anyway. Arizona's first two African American legislators, Hayzel B. Daniels and Carl Sims, both representing predominantly African American Phoenix neighborhoods, "worked their hearts out" to help enlist the aid of white colleagues to rid the state of mandatory segregation.

William P. Mahoney Jr. and other Phoenix liberals pressured influential legislators to obtain passage of the law. Tucson and several smaller communities soon desegregated their schools, but Phoenix refused. Clovis Campbell, a college-educated civic activist, was the first elected black state senator for the 1970–1972 term. By the 1960s, the antipoverty programs of President Johnson's "Great Society" narrowed the breach between African Americans and Hispanics. Many of the programs were designed towards community involvement and reforms in housing, health, education and youth, the two divergent ethnic groups generally worked cooperatively for the good of their communities, forgetting real or imagined differences. As promising "grassroots" leaders developed knowledge of how the political system operated, they appeared before authorities, unintimidated, to press their cases for community betterment. Many African Americans and Mexican Americans were elected to city councils of Tucson, Flagstaff, Parker, and Chandler, but the Phoenix council candidates were handpicked by Charter Government kingmakers.

In 1966, the body tapped its first African American candidate, Dr. Morrison F. Warren. He was the director of the Payne Laboratory of Multicultural Education at Arizona State University. His credentials virtually assured citywide support in the election. At his own choosing he served only one term. In the 1971 elections, the Charter ticket tapped as its next African American candidate Calvin Goode, a Phoenix Union High counselor and an accountant. A hardworking, reliable lawmaker, he was always most accessible to African Americans and Hispanics, mainly because he was the only councilman from their jurisdiction. He consistently fought and voted for the interests of minority neighborhoods, and particularly that of youth. After two terms, the Charter people abandoned Goode, who decided to run as an independent, eventually coming off as the top vote-getter in the election. Goode served for 22 years. In 1962, the U.S. Civil Rights Commission listened to testimony in Phoenix from African American leaders that included representatives of the local Urban League, the NAACP, and other organizations. African American leaders testified that black unemployment and underemployment in the private and public sectors far exceeded that of whites.

The socioeconomic system in Arizona remained basically the same as in the early days of statehood.

The changes emphasized three main categories: employment, housing, and education. African Americans, Hispanics, and American Indians were all being discriminated against in these areas. In the fall of 1963, a new faction of aggressive leadership sprang up in Phoenix. Lincoln Ragsdale and the Reverend George Brooks were not the basic firebrand radicals; they were mature, responsible citizens who could mesh with the younger activists straining at the leash for head-on confirmation with the establishment. Ragsdale, an ex-pilot in the famous all-black 99th Fighters Squadron in World War II, was now a successful businessman, owner of a mortuary and an insurance agency. Reverend Brooks was a Presbyterian minister with excellent communications among the white clergy. They challenged the power structure without fear of economic reprisal, a factor which—real or imagined—had in the past thrown fear in some African Americans who might have otherwise stepped forth. The two leaders of the reinvigorated Phoenix NAACP teamed up with the local chapter of the Congress of Racial Equality (CORE) and its leaders, Jim Williams and Austin Coleman. When Anglo churchmen joined in, the campaign for legalized civil rights for all was in high gear. In January 1965, Democratic governor Sam Goddard pledged the enactment of civil rights legislation during his inauguration address. Four months later, Arizona had its long-awaited equal rights law, even though it was not as strong as African Americans and their white allies would have desired.

Out of the 1960s emerged a resurgence of African American benevolence and pride. The Urban League, NAACP, CORE, OIC, and other African American–led organizations provided leadership and inspiration and offered economic and legal assistance. Much-needed social services and cultural offering came into being. Prominent black artist Eugene Grigsby taught many Phoenix youth the beauty of African art, while members of the Richard H. Hamilton American Legion Post 65 (named after a Phoenix World War II black

Daryl McCullick, left, Ivan Pena, center, and Tariq Sabur perform Capoeira Angola, an African Brazilian martial art, at the annual Juneteenth festival in Phoenix, June 17, 2006. Juneteenth is the traditional celebration of the announcement in Texas in 1865 that slavery was ended. (AP/Wide World Photos)

serviceman) taught them about the patriotism and valor of African American servicemen past and present. Civil rights advances and a new appreciation of black history gave new importance to Juneteenth and other traditional holidays. During the 1980s, the African American population remained at 5 percent of the total Phoenix population. The number of African Americans reached 51,053 in 1990, up from 37,672 in 1980 and 27,896 in 1970. At the same time, more African Americans, many of them professional and business people, moved into the middle class. The positive effects of civil rights awareness and of economic growth and prosperity made it easier for individual African Americans to benefit from new economic and political opportunities, but progress for them as a group within the larger Phoenix population was slow. Educational and employment gains for individuals were noted

during the decade, and structural changes in the city's political system allowed for more minority group representation.

Starting in 1982, legislation was repeatedly introduced to establish some form of official state observance in honor of Reverend Martin Luther King Jr., but the Arizona legislature repeatedly defeated these efforts. Although the city of Phoenix quickly joined other cities, states, and the national government in establishing a paid King Holiday, Arizona in 1991 remained the only state without any form of such a holiday. In 1992, the Martin Luther King Jr. Civil Rights Day on the third Monday of January passed the Arizona legislature. Problems continued to persist into the 1990s, but concerned observers also continued to be hopeful that the African American experience in Phoenix and Arizona would remain largely an advancing one.

Notable African Americans

Banks, Laura Nobles (dates unknown)

Dr. Laura Nobles Banks was an educator in the Tucson school district. Dr. Banks attended Dunbar School through junior high, where she was salutatorian for her ninth-grade class. In 1936, Banks advanced to partially segregated Tucson High. She found herself in an environment where all the teachers were white, just the opposite of Dunbar, where they were all African American. Unlike the caring, nurturing, and helpful teachers at Dunbar, the dispensers of knowledge and privilege at the high school were less giving; some were indifferent; and others openly showed discriminatory behavior.

In 1939, Dr. Banks matriculated to Tucson High's cousin, the University of Arizona. Here the students were mostly white with a few African Americans. Though the university has never been officially off limits to people of color, they felt unwelcome. Dr. Banks graduated from the university in 1943 and returned to her first school to teach fourth grade under Morgan Maxwell Sr. She remained there until school integration came in 1951. She completed her master's degree at the University of Arizona in 1968 and she was the first to receive an education specialist degree in 1970. She returned to the university and was awarded her doctorate in 1980, and was elevated to assistant superintendent for Region Four in 1980.

She retired 2 years later, after 39 years as a teacher and administrator. Dr. Banks did not just fight discrimination within Tucson Unified School District Number One. She did it as president of the NAACP (1960–62) and as board president of the Tucson Urban League (1974–75). She was the first female to be president of the League's board. In 1950, Dr. Banks and her husband, Jack opened Jack's Barbecue. By 1993, Jack's Barbecue had become Tucson's longest, continuously running African American business (43 years) and the largest black-owned restaurant. On February 1, 2003, several hundred well wishers gathered for the dedication of the Laura Nobles Banks Elementary School, a new school in the Tucson Unified School District (TUSD), which was only the fourth school named after an African American in the entire school district.

Crump, William P. (dates unknown)

William P. Crump migrated to Phoenix from West Virginia in 1897. After a stint as a waiter at the Ford Hotel, he made a name for himself among both black and white communities by becoming the owner of a successful fruit and produce enterprise and actively supporting the Republican Party, as most blacks did at the time. He was one of the leaders who filed a legal challenge against the local school board in 1910. Crump took what he believed to be his responsibility to the less fortunate in the African American community seriously. He spoke out against injustices perpetrated against black Phoenicians and was thought of by many members of the white community as a leader in the African American community. Crump crusaded against the sale and consumption of alcohol on Sundays, and he believed it was his responsibility as one of the "chosen" to champion the masses while keeping them on the "straight and narrow."

Daniels, Hayzel B. (1913–1992)

Hayzel B. Daniels was the first African American to graduate from the University of Arizona Law School and be admitted to the Arizona State Bar in 1948. Daniels earned his B.S. in social sciences in 1939 and an M.A. in education in 1941 from the University of Arizona. He taught at Fort Huachuca, Arizona, where his father was stationed with the 10th Cavalry. Daniels also served in the army during World War II. Daniels opened a law office in Phoenix and became involved in politics and the NAACP. In 1950, he and Carl Sims were the first African Americans elected to the Arizona legislature. As a lawmaker and an attorney, Daniels fought against school desegregation.

In June 1952, he argued successfully against school segregation in *Phillips et al. v. Phoenix Union High School District*. In November 1953, Daniels argued successfully against segregation in the (Phoenix) Wilson Elementary School District in *Heard et al. v. Davis et al.* Judge Charles C. Bernstein ruled in this case that segregation in public schools was an unconstitutional violation of the Fourteenth Amendment. The U.S. Supreme Court used Bernstein's ruling to inform its landmark 1954 *Brown v. Board of Education* decision. Daniels went on to serve as the first African American assistant state attorney general and was appointed Phoenix City Court judge in 1965, becoming the first African American judge in Arizona.

Daniels belonged to many organizations, including the Arizona Black Lawyers Association, which changed its name to the Hayzel B. Daniels Bar Association in 1993.

Goode, Calvin (1927–)

Calvin Goode served 11 terms, or 22 years, as a Phoenix city councilman. Goode's family came to Arizona to work in the agricultural fields when he was a baby. He graduated from eighth grade in Gila Bend, but he could not attend the high school there because he was of African descent. So the Goode family moved to Prescott, where their children were allowed to attend the schools. Goode attended high school in Prescott until his junior year when he became ill. The doctor thought he had a heart condition and that he would only live another year. His family decided to send him to Phoenix for his health. He enrolled at Carver High School, the only high school in Arizona built

exclusively for African American students. Goode graduated from Carver in 1945 and went to Phoenix College for two years. He earned both a business degree and an M.A. degree in education from Arizona State.

In 1955, Goode returned to Carver High School as an accountant. He also began a tax accounting business, called Calvin Goode & Associates. When the schools were integrated in 1954, Carver High was closed and he worked other jobs in the Phoenix Union High School District (PUHSD). In 1971, Goode was persuaded to run for a seat on the Phoenix City Council. He was elected and served for a total of 11 terms. Goode was often called the "conscience of the council" because he used his voice to raise questions and push for neglected parts of the community. To commemorate his years of service to the city, the Phoenix Municipal Building was named in his honor.

Grigsby, Jefferson Eugene (1918–)

Jefferson Eugene Grigsby, celebrated artist, writer, and educator, was born in Greensboro, North Carolina. Grigsby discovered his love of art after his family moved to Winston-Salem, North Carolina, when he was nine years old. He obtained his B.A. degree from Morehouse College, his M.A. degree in art from Ohio State University, and his Ph.D. from New York University. At Morehouse College he met his longtime mentor, Hale Woodruff.

In 1942, Grigsby served in World War II as a master sergeant of the 573rd Ordinance Ammunition Company. In 1943, he married Rosalyn Thomasena Marshall, a high-school biology teacher and social activist. Three years later at the invitation of the school's principal, W. A. Robinson, Grigsby began working at Carver High School as an art teacher. After the school closed in 1954, Grigsby worked at Phoenix Union High School until 1966. Grigsby began teaching at the university

A 1974 photo of jazz musician Charles Mingus. (AP/ Wide World Photos)

level in 1966, working at the School of Art at Arizona State University until 1988. During this time, Grigsby published *Art and Ethics: Background for Teaching Youth in a Pluralistic Society*, the first book ever written for art teachers by an African American artist and author.

Mingus, Charles (1922–1979)

Charles Mingus, also known as Charlie Mingus, was an American jazz bassist, composer, bandleader, and occasional pianist. He was also known for his activism against racial injustice. Mingus was born in Nogales, Arizona, where his father was stationed as a U.S. Army sergeant. He was raised largely in the Watts area of Los Angeles, California. In the 1950s Mingus settled in New York, after touring in the 1940s with the bands of Louis Armstrong

and Lionel Hampton. He founded his own recording and publishing companies to protect the growing body of his original work.

Mingus recorded over 100 albums, composed over 30 musical scores, and toured on four continents. A devotee of Duke Ellington, his musical compositions formed a bridge between the big band/swing and bebop eras; he had blues and gospel roots as well. During the early 1960s Mingus experimented with free form jazz and also wrote some of his most richly textured, rhythmically complex music, including such pieces as "The Black Saint and the Sinner Lady." Mingus grappled with deep-seated psychological problems and dropped out of the music scene in the mid-1960s to concentrate on writing an autobiography.

In 1968, he was evicted from his New York City apartment, and much of his written music was lost in that episode. When Mingus finally returned to music, and the bass, in June 1969, he was motivated by economic pressures. To his surprise he found himself accorded the status of an elder statesman. His autobiography, *Beneath the Underdog*, was published in 1971, the same year he received a Guggenheim fellowship for composition. In 1974, Mingus organized what Leroy Ostransky, author of the *Understanding Jazz*, deemed the "greatest jam session since the expression was coined," which was recorded and released as *Mingus at Carnegie Hall*. The Charles Mingus collection is in the Library of Congress.

Ragsdale, Eleanor (1926–1998)

Eleanor Dickey Ragsdale was born in Collingdale, Pennsylvania. She graduated from high school in Darby, Pennsylvania, in 1943 and enrolled in Cheyney University of Pennsylvania, whose main mission was to cultivate African American teachers who would become leaders in their local communities. Eleanor graduated from Cheyney in 1947, and relocated to Phoenix, to pursue a career in teaching at Dunbar Elementary School.

In 1947 she met Lincoln Ragsdale and was married in 1949. She immediately became involved in the Civil Rights Movement in Phoenix. She was a charter member of the local NAACP, Phoenix Urban League, and the Greater Phoenix Council for Civic Unity (GPCCU). By the second year of their marriage, Lincoln asked Eleanor to work with him in the mortuary and insurance businesses they had. She continued to teach until the end of 1950. She obtained her insurance license and became involved in every aspect of the Ragsdale Realty and Insurance Agency. Between 1951 and 1957, the Ragsdales had four children. In addition to working in the family businesses, she devoted a great deal of her time negotiating political partnerships with their clients and associates, black churches in Phoenix and across the country, and most importantly, black women's clubs and voluntary associations.

In 1953, Eleanor desegregated Phoenix's all-white Encanto–Palm Croft residential neighborhood.

When Eleanor and her husband were not permitted to purchase their home, they circumvented the restrictive covenant that barred them. Eleanor had a white friend purchase the house, and when the contract was still in escrow the friend transferred the title to the Ragsdales. Although they had acquired the house, their problems were far from over. One morning the family awoke to find the word "nigger" spray-painted on their white block home in "two-foot-high black letters." The Ragsdales left the racial epithet on the wall for the neighbors to see.

Ragsdale, Lincoln (1926–1995)

Lincoln Ragsdale was born in Ardmore, Oklahoma, and was reared in a family of morticians who owned several mortuaries throughout Oklahoma. After completing high school in 1944, Lincoln joined the Air Force and was relocated to Tuskegee, Alabama, where he became a cadet at the celebrated Tuskegee Flying School. Tuskegee, a racially segregated institution, trained almost one thousand African American pilots for missions in Europe during World War II. After completing his training at Tuskegee, Ragsdale was stationed at Luke Air Force Base in Litchfield Park, Arizona. He was the first African American pilot to serve at the installation. After his military service ended, Lincoln settled in Phoenix.

Like most African Americans who served in the military during World War II, Lincoln Ragsdale emerged from the war with a renewed determination to secure more socioeconomic opportunities and liberty for African Americans. He, with his wife, Eleanor, became members of the local chapter of the NAACP and the Phoenix Urban League. In 1953, Ragsdale and his wife helped desegregate the predominately white neighborhood near Phoenix's Encanto Park. Ragsdale also helped desegregate Phoenix's most influential corporations as early as 1962, including Motorola, General Electric, and Sperry Rand. In 1963, Ragsdale joined with six other local leaders to form the Phoenix Action Committee (ACT) political campaign. ACT sought the election of its members to the Phoenix City Council. They erected a platform calling for a public accommodations bill, open housing, and job opportunities for minorities.

Although Lincoln was not elected, he helped bring the issue of minority political participation to the front pages of local news. He also brought these issues to the attention of local conservative political power brokers such as the Charter Government Committee. Between 1963 and 1992, he fought for diversity in Phoenix's public and private sectors and for entrepreneurial opportunities for people of color in Arizona. Ragsdale played a major role in the Martin Luther King Jr. Holiday movement in Arizona. Ragsdale and his fellow insurgents dealt racism and discrimination serious blows, and in the years that followed, they continued to fight racial inequality. Lincoln Ragsdale died June 9, 1995, in Phoenix.

Rosser, Richard (dates unknown)

Richard Rosser arrived in Phoenix from Georgia in 1893 with his family of 11. He bought a small farm on the city's outskirts and soon owned a truck farm. He bought property and thrived financially. A religious man, Rosser bequeathed a portion of his family's land bordering their home in 1905 to his congregation, in an effort to erect the Second Colored Baptist Church at Fifth and Jefferson Streets in 1908. Ultimately this church became the First Institutional Baptist, becoming the largest black congregation.

Shirley, Frank (dates unknown)

Frank Shirley arrived in Phoenix in 1887. He opened the Fashion Square Barber Shop, which provided service to both black and white communities. Active in the community, Shirley founded the Afro-American Society, a leading social group, in 1893. Shirley and business partner John E. Lewis also led The Good Citizens League. The organization's goal was to "better the conditions of the colored race in the city, both material and moral, and restrain influences for their undoing, whether fostered by whites or blacks." The Good Citizens League was nonpolitical, unless the candidate appeared to be adverse to their material interests. The Good Citizens League also encouraged African American participation in parades, celebrations, and other community activities.

Cultural Contributions

By 1910, African Americans in Phoenix had established and maintained a myriad of clubs, businesses, and religious associations. The Colored Masons, the Colored Odd Fellows, and the Colored Knights of the Pythias were but a few organizations that provided cultural camaraderie as well as civic activism. In addition, African Americans participated in the Colored Republican Club (CRC). It was one of the most desirable clubs to belong to, as many of the city's leading black residents were members of the CRC, including Shirley, Rosser, Crump, and a host of others. Always nearby to capture many of the events in the African American community was the black press. In Phoenix, the *Arizona Gleam*, which was the first black newspaper in Arizona—followed by the *Phoenix Index*, the *Arizona Leader*, and the *Arizona Tribune*—preceded the current black periodical, the *Black Informant*, which was founded in 1971 by two brothers, Cloves C. Campbell Sr. and Dr. Charles R. Campbell.

Many African Americans of the Southwest and elsewhere celebrate Kwanzaa. In the Southwest, the celebration involves commemorating ancestors, acknowledging deceased loved ones, participating in African naming ceremonies, communal feasting, the sharing of family mementos, and interfaith religious observances that include African and African American icons, foods, and beliefs. Juneteenth—contraction of June nineteenth—is a uniquely Southern holiday that commemorates the emancipation of African slaves on June 19, 1865. The festivities included athletic contests, gospel singing, barbecue feasts, and art exhibitions. The interest petered out sometime during the heightened migrations of blacks from the East and Midwest; however, the Phoenix revival of Juneteenth stemmed from the ghetto sections in 1968, especially around the Matthew Henson Housing Project, where the guiding spirit was Vernel Coleman, a lady highly respected by city officials and beloved in the black communities. Though severely crippled with arthritis, she helped pull in other neighborhoods and factions to spark the cultural renaissance. Juneteenth is celebrated in most communities in Arizona.

This "Black-but-Proud" movement, demonstrating itself through drama, art, creative writing, and scholarship funding, eventually came under the sponsorship of various civic organizations, social agencies, churches, and private individuals.

These activities continued year-round, rather than just on June 19 and Black History Month. The "Black Theatre Troupe," the brainchild of Helen Mason, city Recreation Department supervisor, who was also the granddaughter of the city's first black citizen, Mary Green, gained national recognition. In Tucson, the "Ododo Players" were brought together and directed by Bill Lewis, a Pima College instructor who later transferred to Cleveland's illustrious Karamu House. One of the truly versatile precursors of the state cultural movements was none other than Eugene Grigsby, a distinguished artist of national acclaim. He was the founder of "Artists of the Black Community in Arizona" that gives encouragement and exposure to practitioners of the craft.

African American history and tradition also inspired the development of an African American cultural center in Phoenix, housed in the former all-black Carver High School. The George Washington Carver Museum and Cultural Center archives the cultural heritage and experience of the early pioneers who made significant impacts on the development of the African American community. The Arizona African American Art Museum features rare artifacts from all over the African continent from the mid 1800s to the early 1900s. Begun as a community outreach program, it went to schools from primary to university level, introducing students to the variety of cultural artifacts that represent African culture. The African American Multicultural Museum opened in November 2005 in Scottsdale. The mission is "Fellowship through Education."

Bibliography

Allmendinger, Blake. *Imagining the African American West*. Lincoln: University of Nebraska Press, 2005.

Billington, Monroe Lee, and Roger D. Hardaway. *African Americans on the Western Frontier*. Boulder: University Press of Colorado, 1998.

Harris, Richard E. *Black Heritage in Arizona*. Phoenix: Phoenix Urban League, 1977.

Harris, Richard E. *The First Hundred Years: A History of Arizona Blacks*. Arizona: Relmo Publishers, 1983.

The HistoryMakers. PoliticalMakers: www.thehistorymakers.com/biography.

Junne, George H. *Blacks in the American West and Beyond—America, Canada, and Mexico: A Selectively Annotated Bibliography*. Westport, CT: Greenwood Publishing Group, 2000.

Kenner, Charles L. *Buffalo Soldiers and Officers of the Ninth Cavalry, 1867–1898, Black and White Together*. Norman: University of Oklahoma Press, 1999.

Lawson, Harry. *The History of African Americans in Tucson: An Afrocentric Perspective*. Tucson, AZ: Lawson's Psychological Services, 1996.

Long Island University. African Americans and the Old West: www.liunet.edu/cwis/CWP/library/african/west/west.htm.

Luckingham, Bradford. *Minorities in Phoenix*. Tucson: University of Arizona Press, 1994.

Nimmons, Robert Kim. *Arizona's Forgotten Past: The Negro in Arizona, 1539–1965*. Flagstaff: Northern Arizona University, 1971.

Ravage, John W. *Black Pioneers: Images of the Black Experience on the North American Frontier*. Salt Lake City: University of Utah Press, 1997.

Smith, Gloria L. *Black Americans in Arizona*. With 1992 Supplement: *African-Americana in Arizona*. Tucson: G. L. Smith, 1992.

Smith, Gloria L. *Black Heritage Trails and Tales of Tucson and Old Fort Huachuca Near Sierra Vista, Arizona*. Tucson: G. L. Smith, 1985.

Smith, Gloria L. *African Americans and Arizona's Three C's: Cotton, Copper, Cattle*. 1992 Supplement to *Black Heritage Trails and Tales of Tucson and Old Fort Huachuca*. Tucson: G. L. Smith, 1992.

University of Washington. BlackPast.org: www.blackpast.org.

Whitaker, Matthew C. *Race Work: The Rise of Civil Rights in the Urban West*. Lincoln: University of Nebraska Press, 2005.

Whitaker, Matthew C. "Creative Conflict: Lincoln and Eleanor Ragsdale, Collaboration, and Community Activism in Phoenix, 1953–1965." *Western Historical Quarterly* 34 (2003): 165–191.

Whitaker, Matthew C. "Shooting Down Racism: Lincoln and Eleanor Ragsdale and Residential Desegregation in Phoenix, 1947–1953. " *Journal of the West* 44 (2005): 34–43.

Yancy, James Walter. The Negro of Tucson, Past and Present. In the Steps of Esteban: Tucson's African American Heritage: http://parentseyes .arizona.edu/esteban/specialtopics.html.

ARKANSAS

Shirley Waters-White and Gladys L. Knight

Chronology

1723	*(February 18)* A census conducted by French colonial officials finds six black slaves living in the French settlement near the mouth of the Arkansas River.
1798	A census conducted by Spanish colonial officials finds 56 black slaves, out of a total population of 393, living in the Arkansas region.
1803	Arkansas comes into the possession of the United States as part of the Louisiana Purchase from France.
1819	*(March 2)* Congress organizes the Arkansas Territory.
1820	The population of Arkansas Territory is over 14,000, including 1,617 slaves and 59 free blacks.
1820	The passage of the Missouri Compromise ensures Arkansas Territory will become a slave state and greatly encourages slaveholders to bring their property into the territory.
1825	Arkansas Territory institutes slave patrols to prevent enslaved blacks from leaving their farms and plantations.
1836	*(June 15)* Arkansas enters the Union as the 25th state.
1837	The General Assembly enacts an Anti-Miscegenation law declaring all marriages between blacks and whites or between mulattos and whites to be "illegal and void."
1842	The Arkansas General Assembly prohibits the immigration of free blacks into the state after March 1, 1843.
1859	The General Assembly expels from the state all free blacks over the age 21, with any remaining after January 1, 1860, subject to enslavement.
1860	The U.S. Census finds 111,115 slaves living in Arkansas, and, despite recent laws ordering their expulsion, 144 free blacks.
1861	*(May 6)* Arkansas secedes from the Union and joins the Confederacy.
1863	*(May 1)* The first regiment of black troops from Arkansas is mustered into service as the First Arkansas Volunteers of African Descent. The regiment is one of four African American regiments raised at Helena in Phillips County.
1863	General Patrick Cleburne, the Confederate commander in Arkansas, recommends that slaves be recruited in the army in return for freedom at the war's end; however, strong opposition to arming slaves led to the rejection of this proposal and damage to Cleburne's career.
1864	*(May 11)* The First Arkansas Volunteers of African Descent are designated as the 46th Regiment U.S. Colored Troops.

1865	*(April 14)* Arkansas ratifies the Thirteenth Amendment to the U.S. Constitution abolishing slavery.
1866	The Kiblah School for free blacks is founded in Miller County.
1866	The new "Rebel legislature" refuses to ratify the Fourteenth Amendment granting citizenship to former slaves and attempts to enact a new Black Code limiting the rights of African Americans.
1868	*(April 6)* Arkansas ratifies the Fourteenth Amendment to the U.S. Constitution extending citizenship to African Americans.
1868	*(June 22)* Arkansas is readmitted to the Union.
1868	Eight black men serve as delegates to the convention charged with drafting a new state constitution.
1868	Under a new Reconstruction government, the Arkansas General Assembly passes a state law protecting the civil rights of African Americans.
1869	*(March 15)* Arkansas ratifies the Fifteenth Amendment to the U.S. Constitution granting voting rights to African Americans.
1872	William H. Grey, from Washington, D.C., becomes the first African American to hold a high state post in Arkansas when he becomes commissioner of immigration and state lands.
1873	Joseph C. Corbin becomes the state's first black superintendant of public instruction.
1873	Under the Reconstruction government, 20 black men serve in the Arkansas General Assembly.
1873	A second state civil rights act is passed; under the new law, business owners providing public accommodation, transportation, or entertainment must give equal service to all.
1873	Branch Normal College, now the University of Arkansas at Pine Bluff, is established as the first state-supported institution of higher education for blacks.
1874	Eight African Americans attend a new constitutional convention, which results in a new state constitution that guarantees African Americans voting and other civil rights and sets up a new black school system.
Mid-1870s	The practice of creating "fusion tickets," in which white Democrats and black Republicans divide up local offices and do not run against each other for the offices given to the other party, allows blacks to hold state and local offices and sit in the state legislature until the 1890s, when the fusion principle breaks down and Jim Crow laws severely restrict political participation by blacks.
1877	Philander Smith College is founded to provide higher education to blacks.
1882	The Mosaic Templars of America (MTA), a black insurance and fraternal organization, is founded in Little Rock.

1884	Arkansas Baptist College is founded in Little Rock by the Colored Baptists of the State of Arkansas.
1884	A new Anti-Miscegenation law reinforcing the still-valid 1837 statute is enacted.
1886	Shorter College is founded by the African Methodist Episcopal Church in Little Rock.
Late 1880s– early 1890s	Arkansas Democratic Party officials, alarmed at defections from the party to independent agrarian third parties by white farmers angry over their declining economic fortunes, seek to distract white voters with more appeals to racism and more proposed Jim Crow legislation.
1891	The General Assembly passes a Jim Crow law requiring separation of the races on trains and in train station waiting rooms; 11 of the 12 African Americans in the Assembly vote against the measure.
1891	Arkansas enacts an annual poll tax of $1 per year and appoints officials to county boards who are empowered to prevent illiterate persons from voting. These two measures significantly reduce African American voting in the state.
1895	Elias Camp Morris, an African American minister from Helena, is elected president of the National Baptist Convention.
1900	African Americans comprise 38 percent of the population of Little Rock.
1903	The Streetcar Segregation Act establishes the "separate but equal" rule on streetcars and leads to a boycott in three cities, which causes a 90 percent drop in black ridership, but Jim Crow restrictions on public transit last another 60 years.
1905	John E. Bush, a cofounder of the Mosaic Templars of America (MTA), allies with white planters, who fear disruption of their black tenant labor force, to defeat a plan for black public education to be supported only by taxes collected from black taxpayers.
1906	(*October*) The Argenta Race Riot leads to lynching of black restaurateur Homer G. Blackman, who was not accused of any crime.
1906	Arkansas adopts a "white primary" rule preventing blacks from voting in the state's Democratic Party primaries, where most state officials were then elected.
1919	A bloody race riot resulting from attempts by local black sharecroppers to unionize erupts in Elaine in Phillips County. The violence, which did not end until the arrival of federal troops, left 5 whites and over 200 blacks dead.
1921	The Arkansas legislature prohibits the cohabitation of blacks and whites.
1928	Dr. John Marshall Robinson, a black Little Rock physician, founds the Arkansas Negro Democratic Association to protest the Arkansas rule banning blacks from voting in Democratic primaries, which, given the weakness of the Republican Party in Arkansas since the end of Reconstruction, are the only meaningful elections in the state.

1930	Arkansas spends twice as much per year to educate a white student as it does to educate a black student.
1937	The General Assembly mandates segregation for all race tracks and gambling establishments.
1944	In *Smith v. Allwright*, the U.S. Supreme Court declares "white primaries," which Arkansas has had since 1906, to be unconstitutional.
1947	The General Assembly upholds and strengthens various Jim Crow statutes passed since the 1890s mandating separation of the races, including an outright ban on integrated schools.
1954	(*July 27*) The school board in Charleston, Arkansas, quietly votes to integrate all grade and high schools; it is the first school board in a former Confederate state to do so.
1955	One of the first chapters of the Southern Christian Leadership Conference (SCLC) is established in Little Rock.
1955	Segregationist groups, such as the White Citizens Council, initiate campaigns of "massive resistance" to implementation in Arkansas of the *Brown v. Board of Education* Supreme Court decision calling for integration of public schools.
1955	The Hoxie School Board in Lawrence County admits black students, but the intimidation tactics of white supremacists lead the board to obtain a federal-court restraining order to allow integration of local schools to continue.
1956	Arkansas voters approve an "interposition" amendment to the state constitution and a pupil assignment measure, both of which are aimed at hampering school integration.
1957	The Arkansas General Assembly enacts four new segregation laws.
1957	(*September 2*) Governor Orval E. Faubus surrounds Central High School in Little Rock with units of the Arkansas National Guard to prevent nine black students from integrating the school; the Little Rock Nine are finally admitted under the protection of federal troops sent by President Dwight Eisenhower.
1958–1959	Segregationists controlling the Little Rock School Board close Little Rock public schools during this academic year, known as the "Lost Year," to prevent integration.
1959	(*August*) Organized by the newly formed Women's Emergency Committee to Open Our Schools (WEC), moderate white voters join with black voters to elect a new school board that reopens Little Rock schools and allows integration to move forward.
1961	Barbara Williams Dotson and Joe Ferguson become the first two black graduates of Charleston High School.
1964	(*January 23*) The Twenty-fourth Amendment to the U.S. Constitution abolishing the poll tax takes effect; Arkansas has never ratified this amendment.

1964	Arkansas voters accept an amendment to the state constitution replacing the poll tax with a voter registration system.
1970–2000	White student enrollment in Little Rock public schools declines by 53 percent, thus maintaining de facto segregation in many schools.
1978	Moderate Democrat Bill Clinton is elected governor of Arkansas.
1992	Former Arkansas Governor Bill Clinton is elected president of the United States.
2000	Author E. Lynn Harris is inducted into the Arkansas Black Hall of Fame.
2000	About 48 percent of white K–12 students in Little Rock attend private schools, while only about 4 percent of black students attend such schools.
2000	According to the U.S. Census, African Americans comprise 15.7 percent of the Arkansas population and 23.3 percent of black households in Arkansas are single parent.
2006	The estimated median annual household income of African Americans in Arkansas is just over $23,000, while that for whites in the state is over $40,000.
2007	African American unemployment in Arkansas is 11.4 percent, while white unemployment in the state is only 4.4 percent.

Historical Overview

Organized as a territory on March 2, 1819, Arkansas gets its name from a Quapaw Indian word. "The Natural State," as it is nicknamed, entered the Union as the 25th state on June 15, 1836. Its present constitution was adopted in 1874. The 2005 population of Arkansas was estimated at 2,779,154, of which approximately 15.7 percent, or 418,950, are African Americans. The 2005 figures represent a drop in the African American population of Arkansas, which accounted for 20 percent of the state's total population in 1990.

Arkansas has not been known as a leader in the fight for black equality in the United States. The state has always had a relatively small African American population, but as one of the former Confederate states, Arkansas has a long history of oppression and discrimination directed toward its black citizens. In the period leading up to the Civil War, only 3 percent of the black population was

free. The population of enslaved Africans at statehood was approximately 28,000. By 1860, there were over 111,000 black slaves in the state, but, thanks to the recent passage of laws expelling them from Arkansas, only 144 free blacks.

In 1900, 35 years after emancipation, the first Jim Crow laws were established in Arkansas to mandate segregation. Arkansas was one of the 44 states in the Union in which dozens of its citizens were murdered by lynch mobs. Between 1889 and 1918, nearly 250 people were lynched by white mobs. Of that number, approximately 80 percent were African American. Conversely, however, Arkansas was one of Marcus Garvey's greatest supporters—in 1924, there were 39 divisions of Garvey's Universal Negro Improvement Association (UNIA) in Arkansas. In addition, one of the first SCLC chapters in the United States was established in Little Rock in the 1950s.

Many Americans are probably most familiar with the capital of Arkansas, Little Rock; it was the site of the infamous school integration event at Central

High School. After the U.S. Supreme Court ruled that segregation of public schools was unconstitutional, nine black students enrolled at the formerly segregated Central High School. When they attempted to attend classes, however, they were barred from doing so by the governor of the state, who, armed with a weapon, actually stood in the doorway of the school to prevent their entering. It was only with the assistance—and protection—of federal troops sent by President Dwight D. Eisenhower that the students were able to attend classes. Eight of the nine went on to complete the school year.

Arkansas holds another claim to fame, as well. In July 1954, the school board of tiny Charleston, Arkansas, which is located about 20 miles east of Fort Smith in western Arkansas, quietly voted unanimously to integrate grades 1–12 in its schools. Although considered by some scholars to reflect an economic rather than a moral decision, nevertheless, in the fall of 1954, the "colored school" did not open, and all African American children were integrated into the elementary and high schools of Charleston. In recognition of this action, Charleston, Arkansas, was named a National Commemorative Site.

School integration was an enormous gain for civil rights in the state. But the struggle did not end there. In the wake of the famous sit-in that was staged by five African American college students on February 1, 1960, at a Woolworth's store in Greensboro, North Carolina, black youth and young adults launched a sit-in movement throughout the nation. (Sit-in demonstrators protested segregated lunch counters and white businesses that barred black patrons.) Activists in Little Rock staged the state's first sit-in in March at a local Woolworth's. Five demonstrators were jailed, and their bail was posted by the National Association for the Advancement of Colored People (NAACP). Between 1961 and 1962, the local Student Nonviolent Coordinating Committee (SNCC) conducted more demonstrations. Businesses struggled as a result

of the negative attention and the loss of business. In 1963, businesses desegregated their lunch counters. However, the private club located inside the state capitol was not desegregated until 1965.

Arkansas was the setting for other civil rights demonstrations. The Freedom Riders, a demonstration in which black and white activists challenged segregated public transportation and facilities, made stops in Arkansas en route to the Deep South. Freedom Riders did not experience violence in Arkansas. However, demonstrators were subjected to violence and intimidation at bus terminals in the Deep South in states including Alabama and Mississippi. Other civil rights demonstrations occurred in Pine Bluff. The Pine Bluff Movement consisted of college and high-school students who demonstrated at segregated hotels and theaters and discriminatory schools. Between 1960 and 1967, SNCC played an enormous role in civil rights activism in the state.

For all the activism that took place in Arkansas, progress was slow in coming. In the 1970s and beyond, racism and discrimination were still evident. After the triumphant desegregation of Central High School in Little Rock, numerous white parents took their children out of public schools and enrolled them in private schools. Arkansas public schools remain largely racially divided to this day.

Among the other problems that persisted long after the landmark Civil Rights Act of 1964 was the lack of black representation in leadership positions in the state. The election of Arkansas Governor William "Bill" Clinton in 1978, however, was meaningful for African Americans in the state. During Clinton's terms, between 1978 and 1992, he addressed racial issues, poverty, and appointed blacks in key positions. After becoming President of the United States in 1992, Clinton appointed Rodney Slater, from Marianna, the secretary of transportation and Dr. Jocelyn Elders, from Little Rock, the surgeon general. Elders was the first African American U.S. surgeon general.

African American students Elizabeth Eckford (l) and Jefferson Thomas and others walk away from Central High School in Little Rock, Arkansas, after class, 1959. (Library of Congress)

In the 1980s onward, black Arkansans have experienced highs and lows. Despite the growth of the black middle class throughout the nation, 36 percent of African Americans in the state were below the poverty line in 1980. Gang violence and crime were largely concentrated in impoverished black communities. Blacks were frequently subjected to racial discrimination and injustice in the judicial system. On a progressive note, the state made efforts, beginning in the 1990s, to address discrimination in the courts. In 1997, Arkansas paused to commemorate the 40th anniversary of the integration of Central High School. This time, the occasion was one of merriment for blacks and whites alike. In 2005, a civil rights monument, statues of the Little Rock Nine, was commemorated at the state capitol.

Life for blacks has changed significantly since the desegregation of Arkansas schools and other public places. In the new millennium, more institutions have become increasingly diversified. Younger generations of blacks have no recollection of what life was like when blacks were openly discriminated against. Nonetheless, challenges remain. In 2000, 23.3 percent of black households in the state were single-parent families. In 2006, the estimated median annual household income of African Americans in the state was just over $23,000, while whites made over $40,000. In 2007, African American unemployment was 11.4 percent, and white unemployment was 4.4 percent.

Notable African Americans

Angelou, Maya (1928–)

Poet, author, and performer Maya Angelou was born Marguerite Annie Johnson in Memphis, Tennessee, on April 4, 1928. She made her home in Stamps, Arkansas, from the age of 3, when she was sent to live with her grandmother after her parents were divorced. Maya's name came from the diminutive form used by her brother, who could not pronounce "Marguerite." After being abused by her mother's boyfriend some years later, Maya stopped talking, doing all her communicating by written word. This was the beginning of a prolific writing career, which continued even after she again found her physical voice. Her career has included a wide variety of endeavors, from nightclub singer to actor to dancer, singer, poet, and author. She has penned songs recorded by legendary blues singer B. B. King. In addition, Angelou has won the Tony Award for her performance in *Look Away* on Broadway and the Emmy for the television miniseries *Roots*.

Maya Angelou was honored by President-Elect William Jefferson Clinton when she was asked to write the inaugural poem in 1993. Her poem was titled "On the Pulse of the Morning." The recurring theme of her writing is the individual's struggle to exist and thrive in a hostile world. Maya Angelou was named the Reynolds Professor of American Studies Chair at Wake Forest University in Winston-Salem, North Carolina, in 1981.

Bates, Daisy (1913–1999)

Daisy Bates was born in 1913. After her mother was murdered by three white men and her father mysteriously disappeared, she was raised by foster parents in Arkansas. She became nationally famous as the primary counselor and mentor of the nine young people who became known as the Little Rock Nine, the group of nine African American students who were enrolled in segregated Little Rock High School in 1957. As a young married woman, Daisy and her husband, C. L. Bates, started the *Arkansas State Press* in 1941. She served as city editor for the newspaper beginning in 1954. The paper was forced to close in 1959 after continued intimidation by news

distributors and an advertising boycott by white business owners, most likely in retaliation for Bates' activism.

Bates was active in the Little Rock NAACP, where she was chosen president of the Arkansas Conference of Branches in 1952. As such, she was the principal spokesperson for the integration case that gained national attention in 1957–1958. She remained active in the desegregation movement in Arkansas until 1960, when she moved to New York. She continued to work in the NAACP in New York, where she served on the National Board until 1970.

Beals, Melba Portillo (1941–)

Melba Portillo Beals was the first of the Little Rock Nine who published a memoir of that traumatic time. She is the author of *Warriors Don't Cry: A Searing Memoir of the Battle to Desegregate Little Rock's Central High School* (1995). Melba Portillo was born on December 7, 1941, in Little Rock. She came from a middle-class family: her mother was one of the first black graduates of the University of Arkansas and a high-school English teacher. Her brother worked as a U.S. Marshal in Little Rock.

In her book, Beals recounts the daily harassment and intimidation and threats endured by the nine students who integrated Central High School in Little Rock. When Little Rock's public schools were closed in 1958 to put an end to the desegregation attempt, she went to California to finish her senior year. The Little Rock Nine and Daisy Bates received the Springer Medal from the NAACP in 1958 in recognition of their singular contribution to the Civil Rights Movement. In 1999, the group was awarded the Congressional Medal of Honor by President Bill Clinton.

Melba Portillo Beals received her Bachelor of Arts degree from San Francisco State University and a Master of Arts degree from Columbia University in New York, both in journalism. Her

Eldridge Cleaver led a life of transformations: youthful years of crime and imprisonment; a decade as a famous African American activist and writer; a period of exile; and recent years as an outspoken and conservative Christian. (Library of Congress)

career included reporting for public television and employment at the NBC affiliate in the San Francisco Bay area. In 1999, a sequel to her memoirs titled *White Is a State of Mind*, which chronicles her senior year in California and her college and family life experiences, was published.

Cleaver, Leroy Eldridge (1935–1998)

Born on August 31, 1935, Eldridge Cleaver was a native of Wabbaseka, Arkansas. The former Black Panther leader was raised in Los Angeles, California, beginning in 1946. A series of encounters with the law resulted in his serving several terms in the California penal system, including Soledad for possession of marijuana, and San Quentin and Folsom for assault. Cleaver converted to Islam in the 1960s, only to denounce the faith after the assassination of Malcolm X. Nonetheless, he was determined to follow Malcolm's dream of an Organization of African Unity.

As a staff member of *Ramparts Magazine*, he met the leaders of the new Black Panther Party for Self-Defense and joined the organization soon thereafter. He rose to the position of minister of defense. When Huey Newton, leader of the Panthers, was arrested in Oakland in March 1967, Cleaver led a "free Huey" movement on his behalf. A year later, in April 1968, Cleaver was wounded in a shootout with police. Although arrested and convicted, he spent only two months behind bars before a judge ordered his release.

Following this period, Cleaver became a lecturer at the University of California at Berkeley. He also became politically active within the system, running for president on the Peace and Freedom ticket. When he engaged in a verbal sparring match with Ronald Reagan, whom he accused of trying to prevent his speaking at Berkeley, Cleaver's parole was revoked and he was ordered back to prison. To avoid being incarcerated once again, Cleaver and his wife Kathleen fled into exile in Cuba on November 24, 1968. The couple was granted asylum in Algeria, where they remained until 1972, when they moved to Paris.

Eldridge Cleaver converted to Christianity while in Paris, and decided to return to the United States in 1975. He subsequently served eight months in jail plus community service in order to clear his legal debt from 1968. His dramatic turnabout extended to his joining the Republican Party in 1980, throwing his support to an endorsement of Ronald Reagan in 1984. Between 1984 and 1992, Cleaver, who had run for the U.S. Senate as a Democrat in 1968, sought public office as a Republican. Cleaver's publications include his iconic *Soul on Ice* (1968), *Soul on Fire* (1978), *Eldridge Cleaver: Post-Prison Writings and*

Throughout her political career, Elders was beset by criticism from the conservatives in government. Despite the fact that 20 percent of all births in Arkansas were to teen mothers by the 1980s, her recommended solution of contraceptives for public school students drew a firestorm of criticism and hostility as she was attacked by conservatives for her views. Her 1993 appointment as surgeon general of the United States also drew negative reactions and caused problems for the Clinton administration, but she was confirmed by the Senate on September 7, 1993. The conservative attacks continued, however, and her views on such issues as drugs and sex education continued to draw fire on an already-beleaguered Clinton. Under attack on nearly all his programs and policies, President Clinton finally asked for her resignation.

In 1994, Elders joined the University of Arkansas for Medical Sciences as a faculty researcher. She retired from medicine in 1999 and returned to live in Little Rock. Her autobiography is titled *Jocelyn Elders, M.D.: From Sharecropper's Daughter to Surgeon General of the United States* (1996).

Jocelyn Elders was the first African American and only the second female to fill the position of surgeon general. She was appointed by President Bill Clinton in 1993. (National Institutes of Health)

Speeches (1969), and *Eldridge Cleaver's Black Papers* (1969).

Elders, Jocelyn (1933–)

Jocelyn Elders was named Minnie Lee Jones at her birth in Schaal, Arkansas, on August 13, 1933. She later changed her name to Jocelyn while in college. In 1949, Elders attended Philander Smith College in Little Rock on a scholarship. After graduation in 1952, she entered the U.S. Army's Medical Specialist Corps and, in 1956, enrolled at the University of Arkansas Medical School on the G.I. Bill. During her residency in Little Rock, Dr. Elders was appointed chief pediatric resident. Her early public service employment was as director of the Arkansas Department of Health, appointed by Arkansas Governor Bill Clinton. Elders became a black national icon when President Bill Clinton appointed her surgeon general of the United States.

Green, Al (1946–)

Al Green was born on April 13, 1946, in Forrest City, Arkansas. He began singing as a youth; his group, Al Green and the Soul Mates, rose to number 5 on the R&B charts with "Back Up Train" in 1967. Green is possibly best known for his 1971 hit "I'm So Tired of Being Alone," which hit number 11 on the R & B charts, and "Let's Stay Together," his number one hit later that year. Beginning in 1979, Al Green professed he "was saved" and began to record and perform only gospel music. In 1995, however, he was inducted into the Rock and Roll Hall of Fame, and later released his first secular album in many years. In 2000, he was inducted into the Gospel Music Hall of Fame. Green returned to recording and performing popular music in 2001 and released "I Can't Stop" in 2002 and "Everything's OK" in

Al Green discusses his new CD, *I Can't Stop*, in Memphis, Tennessee, 2003. (AP/Wide World Photos)

2005. He has continued to record both secular and gospel music in recent years. The nine-time Grammy winner also pastors in Memphis, Tennessee.

Harris, E. Lynn (1957–)

Novelist E. Lynn Harris was born on June 20, 1957, in Flint, Michigan. Like many other well-known Arkansans, he moved to Arkansas, in this case to Little Rock, in his youth and was raised in Arkansas. He attended the University of Arkansas in Fayetteville and graduated with honors in 1977, earning a bachelor of arts in journalism.

Harris has become a well-known and popular writer with his focus on the fictional lives of gay and bisexual men. His first book, *Invisible Life*, was self-published. Its focus was on his personal struggle to come to terms with his homosexuality. His subsequent novels, often dealing with men who experience what popular culture has come to know as "living on the down-low," made him

a popular author. He was awarded Novel of the Year by Blackboard African-American Bestsellers in 1997 and later won the James Baldwin Award for Literary Excellence. Harris was inducted into the Arkansas Black Hall of Fame in 2000.

John, William Edgar "Little Willie" (1937–1966)

Blues aficionados recognize the name given to William Edgar John, born on November 15, 1937, in Cullendale, Arkansas. John began his singing career as a member of a family gospel quartet in the 1940s. He gained public acclaim as a soloist at amateur shows while still in his teens, and received his first recording contract at the age of 17 in 1955. His debut record, "All around the World," went to number five on the charts in 1955. His next two records debuted at number five and number six on the charts. Little Willie John died in Walla Walla State Penitentiary on July 6, 1966, while serving 8 to 20 years for manslaughter.

Johnson, (Johnny) John H. (1918–2005)

The publishing company started by John H. Johnson is the largest African American–owned and -operated company in the world. Born in Arkansas City on January 19, 1918, Johnson's parents moved the family to Chicago to give the children a better educational opportunity. While a student at DuSable High School, Johnny changed his name to make it sound more "mature" on the advice of a teacher. He attended the University of Chicago while working at the Liberty Life Insurance Company. There he became editor of the company newsletter.

His experience there led him to look at publishing as a career, and in 1942 he started *Negro Digest*, the first publication by Johnson Publishing Company. In 1945, *Ebony* magazine debuted, and in 1951, he began publication of *Jet*. *Ebony* magazine, with 2.5 million readers each month, is the number one African American magazine in the world; *Jet* magazine is the number two newsweekly magazine with a circulation of 9 million. Johnson and his wife Eunice also produced the Ebony Fashion Show, started in 1958, which has raised over $50 million for various charities and led to a cosmetics company aimed at producing products for women of color.

John H. Johnson was one of the Forbes 400 richest Americans, served on the board of several Fortune 500 corporations, and was special U.S. ambassador for Presidents John F. Kennedy and Lyndon Baines Johnson. He accompanied Vice President Richard Nixon to Africa and Europe in 1957 and 1959. Johnson received the Presidential Medal of Freedom from President Bill Clinton in 1996 on the 50th anniversary of *Ebony* magazine.

Joplin, Scott (c. 1867–1917)

Known as the "Father of American Ragtime," Scott Joplin was born near Marshall, Texas, to a formerly enslaved father and a free mother in about 1867. His family moved to Texarkana while he was very young. It was in Arkansas that young Joplin began to play piano, practicing in homes where there was a piano where his mother worked as a domestic. At the age of 17, Joplin left Texarkana, joining a ragtime competition in St. Louis, Missouri, in 1885. He later attended George R. Smith College in Sedalia, Arkansas, where he studied music theory. Among his early teachers was Julius Weiss, a German immigrant who taught Joplin piano technique and introduced him to the European operas that influenced his later work.

Beginning in 1901, Joplin began to compose operas and ballets. By 1909, he had completed more than 40 piano ragtime pieces and published a sheet music booklet titled *School of Ragtime*. Unfortunately, he was unable to find support for his opera, *Treemonisha*, although he continued to have his ragtime ("Maple Leaf Rag" and other works) published by John Stark. Joplin himself mounted an unstaged version of *Treemonisha*

without costumes or a full orchestra in 1915 at the Harlem Lincoln Theatre. He died two years later before seeing it fully staged. Joplin's "The Entertainer" became one of his best-known songs when it was used in the film *The Sting* in 1973. Scott Joplin died on April 1, 1917. He was posthumously awarded the Pulitzer Prize for his contributions to American music.

Liston, Charles "Sonny" (c. 1932–1970)

Sonny Liston was heavyweight boxing champion of the world from 1962 to 1964. Liston was born in rural St. Francis County in about 1932. His parents were sharecroppers and his family was large; Liston may have had as many as 20 siblings. At age 13, Liston ran away from home, joining his mother, who had earlier fled the family farm, in St. Louis. Liston then turned to a life of petty crime, committing various robberies and assaults. He was convicted of first-degree robbery and larceny in 1950 and sent to the Missouri State Penitentiary for five years. While in prison, Liston took up boxing, and upon his parole in 1952 he launched an amateur career that earned him several Golden Gloves championships. He turned professional in 1953 and had much success in the ring, but continued to get into trouble with the law. He was arrested 14 times between 1953 and 1958 and was convicted for assaulting a police officer in 1956. In 1958, he moved to Philadelphia and in 1960 was questioned by a congressional committee regarding possible mob connections.

A series of impressive victories over top heavyweight contenders earned Liston a title shot. He knocked out heavyweight champion Floyd Patterson in the first round in Chicago on September 25, 1962. Because of his prison history, many in the African American community were unhappy with Liston being the heavyweight champ. In July 1963 in Las Vegas, Liston again defeated Patterson with a first-round knockout. On February 25, 1964, in Miami Beach, a heavily favored Liston lost his title to Cassius Clay, when Liston, claiming injury, did not answer the bell in the seventh round. A second bout with Clay (now Muhammad Ali), in Lewiston, Maine, on May 25, 1965, resulted in another defeat and another controversy, when Liston went down on a questionable punch. Liston continued to box until 1970, but never got another shot at the title. He died under mysterious circumstances in Las Vegas in December 1970.

Pippen, Scottie (1965–)

Scottie Pippen was born in Hamburg, Arkansas, on September 25, 1965. He attended the University of Central Arkansas, where he played basketball for all four years. The Seattle Supersonics selected him as the fifth overall pick in 1987, but then traded him to the Chicago Bulls. During his first stint with Chicago from 1987 to 1998, he played with Michael Jordan and was part of six NBA championship teams, including the 1995–1996 team that won an NBA-record 72 games. Pippen was traded to the Houston Rockets in 1998 and to the Portland Trailblazers in 1999 before returning to the Chicago Bulls in 2003. He retired from the NBA in 2004.

Pippen played in seven NBA All-Star games (1990, 1992–1997) and was named the All-Star Game Most Valuable Player in 1994. He was a three-time NBA First Team selection (1994–1996) and an eight-time NBA All-Defensive First Team selection (1992–1999). In 2005, the Bulls retired Pippen's Number 33 jersey. Pippen was also a member of the original "Dream Team" that won a gold medal at the Barcelona Olympics in 1992.

Still, William Grant (1895–1978)

Pop and symphonic composer William Grant Still was born on May 11, 1895, in Woodville, Mississippi. He was raised from infancy in Little Rock, Arkansas. Still studied violin with William Price. Graduating as his high-school valedictorian, he went on to attend Wilberforce University. Leaving Wilberforce in 1915 before earning his diploma, he chose to pursue music in bands and orchestras. Still worked as arranger and performer with W. C. Handy in 1916. In 1917, however, he returned to formal studies at the Oberlin Conservatory, but his studies there were interrupted by service in the U.S. Navy during World War I. In 1919, he moved to Harlem, where he continued his studies with George Whitefield Chadwick, the director of the New England Conservatory of Music, and Edward Varies, French modernist.

Still's best-known composition is the *Afro-American Symphony*, performed in 1931 by the Rochester Philharmonic Orchestra under conductor Howard Hanson. It was the first African American symphony performed by a major orchestra. Hanson conducted many of Still's compositions in the United States and Europe. Major orchestras in some of the great cities of the United States have performed his compositions, among them the Chicago Symphony Orchestra, the New York Philharmonic, the Philadelphia Symphony, the Cleveland Orchestra, the Cincinnati Symphony Orchestra, and the New York City Opera Company. Still was a prolific composer of operas, symphonies, ballets, chamber music, and works for solo instruments, writing over 200 pieces in his lifetime.

Cultural Contributions

Although Arkansas is not identified with any particular music form or cultural movement, African American popular culture can be found wherever blacks live, and Arkansas is steeped in rich African American cultural traditions. Indeed, Arkansas produced many black Arkansans who attained fame by popularizing African American culture, music, art, and literature. Ragtime was one of the popular music forms that was created by blacks in the late nineteenth century. Scott Joplin, who was born near Texarkana and studied music in Arkansas, is one of the most celebrated ragtime players.

William Grant Still, who grew up in Little Rock, melded the African American spiritual into mainstream classical music and helped spark a new appreciation for traditional black music. Inspired by the popular blues musicians and singers who traveled throughout the South, Arkansas-born William Edgar John pursued a career in the blues industry. Al Green, an Arkansas native and popular soul music entertainer and gospel singer, is a household name among African Americans. His music helped define the black consciousness era of the late 1960s and 1970s.

Music was not the only cultural contribution made by African Americans. Arkansas natives Eldridge Cleaver and Maya Angelou popularized Afro-centric fashion and literature. John H. Johnson created a medium, *Ebony* magazine, from which black culture and traditions could be celebrated and shared. Cultural attractions in Arkansas offer locals an intimate way to appreciate and enjoy black culture. Such cultural attractions include the Ozark Folk Festival, which is the oldest folk festival west of the Mississippi. Arkansas also hosts the King Biscuit Blues Festival in Helena, which is one of the largest festivals in the South. Fans travel to Arkansas from around the world for this event.

Bibliography

Altman, Linda Jacobs. *Celebrate the States: Arkansas.* New York: Benchmark Books, 2000.

Barnes, Kenneth C. *Journey of Hope: The Back-to-Africa Movement in Arkansas in the Late 1800s.* Chapel Hill: University of North Carolina Press, 2004.

Bates, Daisy. *The Long Shadow of Little Rock: A Memoir.* Fayetteville: University of Arkansas Press, 1987.

Beals, Melba Pattillo. *Warriors Don't Cry: A Searing Memoir of the Battle to Integrate Little Rock's Central High.* New York: Washington Square Press, 1994.

Bolton, S. Charles. *Arkansas, 1800–1860: Remote and Restless.* Fayetteville: University of Arkansas Press, 1998.

Bush, A. E., and P. L. Dorman, eds. *History of the Mosaic Templars of America: Its Founders and Officials.* With an introduction by John William Graves. Fayetteville: University of Arkansas Press, 2008.

Carmichael, Maude. "Federal Experiments with Negro Labor on Abandoned Plantations in Arkansas: 1862–1865." *Arkansas Historical Quarterly* 6 (June 1942): 101–116.

Dillard, Tom W. "To the Back of the Elephant: Racial Conflict in the Arkansas Republican Party." *Arkansas Historical Quarterly* 33 (Spring 1974): 3–15.

The Encyclopedia of Arkansas History and Culture: www.encyclopediaofarkansas.net.

Finley, Randy. *From Slavery to Uncertain Freedom: The Freedmen's Bureau in Arkansas, 1865–1869.* Fayetteville: University of Arkansas Press, 1996.

Freyer, Tony. *The Little Rock Crisis: A Constitutional Interpretation.* Westport, CT: Greenwood Press, 1984.

Gordon, Fon Louise. *Caste and Class: The Black Experience in Arkansas, 1880–1920.* Athens: University of Georgia Press, 1995.

Graves, John William. "The Arkansas Separate Coach Law of 1891." *Arkansas Historical Quarterly* 32 (Summer 1973): 148–165.

Graves, John William. "Jim Crow in Arkansas: A Reconsideration of Urban Race Relations in the Post-Reconstruction South." *Journal of Southern History* 55 (August 1989): 421–448.

Graves, John William. "Negro Disfranchisement in Arkansas." *Arkansas Historical Quarterly* 26 (Autumn 1967): 199–225.

Graves, John William. *Town and Country: Race Relations in an Urban-Rural Context, Arkansas, 1865–1905.* Fayetteville: University of Arkansas Press, 1990.

Higgins, Billy D. *Peter Caulder: Free Black Frontiersman in Antebellum Arkansas.* Fayetteville: University of Arkansas Press, 2005.

Huckaby, Elizabeth. *Crisis at Central High, Little Rock, 1957–58.* Baton Rouge: Louisiana State University Press, 1980.

Jackson, Ronald V., David Schaefer-Meyer, and Gary R. Teeples. *Arkansas 1850 Census Index.* Bountiful, UT: Accelerated Indexing Systems, Inc., 1976.

Jacoway, Elizabeth. *Turn Away Thy Son: Little Rock, the Crisis That Shocked the Nation.* New York: Free Press, 2007.

Kirk, John A. *Redefining the Color Line: Black Activism in Little Rock, Arkansas, 1940–1970.* Gainesville: University Press of Florida, 2002.

Kirk, John A. *Beyond Little Rock: The Origins and Legacies of the Central High Crisis.* Fayetteville: University of Arkansas Press, 2007.

Kirkpatrick, Judith. *There When We Needed Him: Wiley Branton, Civil Rights Warrior.* Fayetteville: University of Arkansas Press, 2007.

Lankford, George E., ed. *Bearing Witness: Memories of Arkansas Slavery, Narratives from the 1930s WPA Collections.* 2nd ed. Fayetteville: University of Arkansas Press, 2006.

Lewis, Catherine M., and J. Richard Lewis, eds. *Race, Politics, and Memory: A Documentary History of the Little Rock School Crisis.* Fayetteville: University of Arkansas Press, 2007.

Lewis, Todd E. "Mob Justice in the American Congo: Judge Lynch in Arkansas in the Decade after World War I." *Arkansas Historical Quarterly* 52 (Summer 1993): 156–184.

"The Little Rock Crisis: A Fiftieth Anniversary Retrospective." Special issue, *Arkansas Historical Quarterly* 66 (Summer 2007).

Love, Berna J. *End of the Line: A History of Little Rock's West Ninth Street.* Little Rock: Center for Arkansas Studies, University of Arkansas at Little Rock, 2003.

McNeilly, Donald P. *The Old South Frontier: Cotton Plantations and the Formation of Arkansas Society, 1819–1861.* Fayetteville: University of Arkansas Press, 2000.

Murphy, Sara Alderman. *Breaking the Silence: Little Rock's Women's Emergency Committee to Open Our Schools, 1958–1963.* Fayetteville: University of Arkansas Press, 1997.

Patterson, Ruth Polk. *The Seed of Sally Goodin: A Black Family of Arkansas, 1833–1953.* Lexington: University of Kentucky Press, 1985.

Presley, Leister. *Arkansas Territory: Census.* Washington, DC: Federal Population Schedules, 1830.

Rothrock, Thomas. "Joseph Carter Corbin and Negro Education in the University of Arkansas." *Arkansas Historical Quarterly* 30 (Winter 1971): 277–314.

Shinn, Josiah H. *Pioneers and Makers of Arkansas.* Baltimore: Generalized Publishing Company, 1967.

Smith, C. Calvin, ed. "The Elaine, Arkansas, Race Riots, 1919." Special Issue. *Arkansas Review: A Journal of Delta Studies* 32 (August 2001).

Smith, C. Calvin, and Linda W. Joshua, eds. *Educating the Masses: The Unfolding History of Black School Administrators in Arkansas, 1900–2000.* Fayetteville: University of Arkansas Press, 2000.

Smith, Jessie Carney. *Black Firsts: 4,000 Groundbreaking and Pioneering Historical Events.* Detroit, MI: Visible Ink, 2003.

Stockley, Grif. *Blood in Their Eyes: The Elaine Race Massacres of 1919.* Fayetteville: University of Arkansas Press, 2001.

Stockley, Grif. *Daisy Bates: Civil Rights Crusader from Arkansas.* Oxford: University Press of Mississippi, 2005.

Stockley, Grif. *Race Relations in the Natural State.* Little Rock: Butler Center for Arkansas Studies, 2007.

Stockley, Grif. *Ruled by Race: Black/White Relations in Arkansas from Slavery to the Present.* Fayetteville: University of Arkansas Press, 2008.

Taylor, Orville W. *Negro Slavery in Arkansas.* Durham, NC: Duke University Press, 1958. Reprinted by the University of Arkansas Press, 2000.

Urwin, Gregory J. W. " 'We Cannot Treat Negroes . . . as Prisoners of War': Racial Atrocities and Reprisals in Civil War Arkansas." In Anne Bailey and Daniel E. Sutherland, eds. *Civil War Arkansas: Beyond Battles and Leaders.* Fayetteville: University of Arkansas Press, 2000.

Whayne, Jeannie M., ed. Special issue on slavery in Arkansas. *Arkansas Historical Quarterly* 58 (Spring 1999).

CALIFORNIA

Randal Beeman

Chronology

1780s–1790s	The Pico and Tapia families, many members of whom have partial African ancestry, are among the founders of Los Angeles.
1830s–1840s	Spanish-speaking blacks or persons of mixed racial heritage are settlers and cowboys, or vaqueros, in Mexican California.
1848–1850	Many blacks are among those who come to Gold Rush California seeking to get rich in the mines, but often finding employment in other areas.
1850	(*September 9*) California enters the Union as the 31st state; it is admitted as a free state as part of the Compromise of 1850.
1855–1857	Black leaders in the state hold three "Colored Conventions" to seek equal rights and the right to testify in court cases for blacks.
1865	(*December 19*) California ratifies the Thirteenth Amendment to the U.S. Constitution, which bars slavery. California's ratification comes two weeks after the amendment takes effect.
1870	(*January 28*) California rejects the Fifteenth Amendment to the U.S. Constitution guaranteeing the vote to African Americans.
1879	Publication of the *California Eagle* (originally *The Owl*) begins in Los Angeles; it will become the leading black newspaper in the state of California.
1908	Lt. Col. Allen Allensworth founds the black farming colony of Allensworth in Tulare County.
1910s	California chapters of the Afro-American Protective Association are organized.
1910	California's black population reaches approximately 22,000.
1913	California Afro-American Protective Association chapters host a visit by W. E. B. Du Bois to Los Angeles.
1918	Election of Frederick M. Roberts to the State Assembly; he is the first African American to hold office at the state level in California.
1920s	Restrictive housing covenants and Jim Crow–type laws are enacted in the state.
1920	California's black population reaches approximately 39,000.
1928	Los Angeles elects a Ku Klux Klan member as mayor in 1928.
1930s	"Okie" migration from the Midwest and South to California includes many black migrants.
1930	California's black population reaches approximately 81,000.

1938	The election of Democrat Augustus Hawkins to the State Assembly over Frederick Roberts indicates the shifting of black political allegiance from the Republican Party to the Democratic Party in the state.
1940s	The number of African Americans coming to California to work in West Coast ship-yards and other wartime industries surges.
1944	One-quarter of American blacks live west of the Mississippi River and California's black population has more than doubled since the start of World War II.
1944	Discriminatory hiring practices in California are challenged by Tarea Hall Pittman, Charlotta Bass, and other black leaders in the state.
1948	W. Byron Rumford is elected to the State Assembly; several other African American legislators are later elected at the state level in the 1950s and early 1960s.
1959	California ratifies the Fourteenth Amendment to the U.S. Constitution, guarantee-ing full civil rights to African Americans; the state's ratification comes 91 years after the amendment took effect.
1962	*(April 3)* California ratifies the Fifteenth Amendment to the U.S. Constitution, 92 years after the amendment took effect.
1962	Augustus Hawkins becomes the first African American elected to Congress from California.
1963	*(February 7)* California ratifies the Twenty-fourth Amendment to the U.S. Constitution abolishing the poll tax.
1963	The California legislature passes the Rumford Fair Housing Statute (originally intro-duced by Augustus Hawkins) outlawing racial discrimination in real estate transac-tions; the statute is repealed by the initiative process in 1964.
1964	African American politician Willie Brown is elected to the California State Assembly, eventually becoming one of the most powerful politicians in state history; he later serves two terms as the mayor of San Francisco.
1965	Race riots in Watts become the symbol of racial rioting in the 1960s with 34 people killed, 1,000 injured, and 4,000 arrested.
1966	A race riot erupts in San Francisco as a result of a police shooting.
1966	Founding of the militant Black Panther Party in Oakland.
1966	Kwanzaa first celebrated in California after being created by UCLA graduate Ron Maluana Karenga.
1973	Tom Bradley is elected mayor of Los Angeles, the first African American to hold the office; he serves until 1993.

1982	Mayor Tom Bradley of Los Angeles becomes the first African American to run for governor in California; although news organizations project Bradley as the winner, he loses narrowly to Republican George Deukmejian, giving rise to the term "Bradley effect" to describe the tendency of voters to tell pollsters they will vote for a black candidate but then actually voting for his/her white opponent.
1986	Mayor Tom Bradley of Los Angeles fails in his second attempt to become governor of California, losing to incumbent governor Deukmejian by a wide margin.
1991	Black motorist Rodney King is beaten by several members of the Los Angeles Police Department; the incident is caught on videotape and replayed frequently on television.
1992	Four police officers indicted in the Rodney King case are acquitted by an all-white jury; the verdict sparks six days of rioting in which 58 people are killed, 2,500 injured, and 16,000 arrested.
1995	Former USC and NFL football star O. J. Simpson is acquitted of murdering his ex-wife Nicole Brown Simpson; reaction to case reveals a continued racial divide in California.
1995	Willie Brown is elected the first African American mayor of San Francisco; he is reelected in 1999.
2008	Karen Bass is elected as speaker of the California State Assembly, the first African American woman to hold that position.
2008	(*November 4*) Democrat Barack Obama, the first African American nominee for president of a major party, carries California with about 61 percent of the vote.

Historical Overview

From the commencement of non-Indian settlement in the late 1760s, there has been a continual presence of persons of African ancestry in the state. The experience of black California is incredibly variegated—with episodes of oppression interspersed with a general prosperity that has often been greater than what black people have experienced in the rest of the United States. African Americans have raised cattle, mined for gold, opened retail businesses and newspapers, designed buildings, and fought for civil rights and racial equality.

The Spanish and Mexican Period

Though the first European explorers came to California in 1542, the Spanish claim to California was not backed up with actual settlers until the first of 21 missions were established by the Franciscans beginning in 1769. Among the first towns, or pueblos, built in California was Los Angeles, whose 46 original settlers in 1781 included 26 persons of partial African descent. Mulatto Francisco Reyes became the first leader of the tiny pueblo, though many of the city's top residents would eventually attempt to downplay their black heritage. Racial identity in Spanish and Mexican California was complex and often changing, but it is clear that a number of Californios, as the region's residents became known, had varying degrees of African ancestry. Among these early part-black families to settle Los Angeles were the Picos and the Tapias, whose descendants would become prominent in the social and political life of Mexican-era California (1821–1846).

Most of the Californios were involved in small-scale industry or in the raising of cattle for the hide and tallow trade, exporting beef hides and beef fat to merchants and manufacturers from England and the United States. Outsiders would frequently comment on the horsemanship skills of the vaqueros, some of whom were Spanish-speaking blacks.

The first Americans to see California were sailors, primarily from New England, including free blacks such as Allen Light (1804–1850s?), whose ship the *Pilgrim* was involved in the hide and tallow trade. Like many Americans, Light abandoned ship and became an active participant in Californio society. Other Americans reached California via the system of trails developed by mountain men and explorers of the American West, whose ranks included the famous mulatto James Beckwourth (1798–1866), and the black trapper Peter Ranne, who came to California with the Jedediah Smith expedition of 1826.

An African American miner with a shovel in Auburn Ravine during the Gold Rush, California, 1852. (Hulton Archive/Getty)

Beckwourth had a storied career living among the Indians, stealing horses from Mexican settlers, and leading '49ers across the Sierra, where a pass through the mountains now bears his name.

The Gold Rush and Early Statehood Period

Although a few black settlers came before the Gold Rush of 1848–1849, the gold strike quickly increased the black population of California. Free blacks came from the northeastern United States, the Caribbean, and from countries in the former Spanish empire, while others came as slaves from the American South. There were 2,000 African Americans in the state by 1852, and over 4,000 by 1860. Though some blacks worked the mines as both laborers and independent miners, discriminatory conditions kept many blacks out of the mines. Those excluded from mining often did well working as cooks and other service jobs at a time when common laborers were doing quite well in the inflated gold rush economy. Peter Lester (1814–188?) was a Gold Rush bootblack and shoe repairman who became a successful businessman in San Francisco, devoting his free time to fighting against proslavery forces in California. He also promoted desegregated educational facilities and opposed attempts to ban black immigration to the state.

Slavery was still legal during the initial stages of the Gold Rush, and many slave owners from the American South brought their slaves to California. The prevailing doctrine of "free labor" in the gold fields meant that '49ers viewed black slavery as an unacceptable institution, and slavery was banned in California in 1849. The Compromise of 1850 ensured that California would remain a free state, but the agreement that let California into the Union required the state to enforce the Fugitive Slave Act. Often considered the "Mother of Civil Rights in California," Mary Ellen "Mammy" Pleasant (1814–1904) used her considerable financial resources to help operate the Underground Railroad in California. She later provided assistance to John Brown in the buildup to the Harper's Ferry attack in 1859.

Several important cases regarding the Fugitive Slave Act were fought over during the 1850s in California, including the cases of Bridget "Biddy" Mason (1818–1891) and Archy Lee (1840–1872). Mason was born into slavery in the Deep South, and her owner Robert Smith had moved to California to become part of the Mormon Colony in Riverside. When Smith attempted to leave California with his slaves in 1851 and remove them to Texas, Mason fought her removal in court with the help of family and friends such as the Robert Owens family. (Owens was a former slave who earned enough money in California to purchase his and his family's freedom.) When Smith failed to show up in court, the judge granted Mason her freedom. She became well known as a nurse, midwife, and real estate investor after earning substantial wealth in the Los Angeles real estate market in the 1870s and 1880s. Through parsimonious living and her investments, Mason became a major property owner in the bustling city of Los Angeles. "Grandma Mason" ministered to the needy and used her financial clout to establish the Los Angeles branch of the African Methodist Episcopalian Church in 1872. She died in 1891, remembered for her business acumen and her philanthropic endeavors.

In another case, Archy Lee, a slave from the South, claimed that his time in the Free State of California in the 1850s had made him a free man. When his master attempted to take Lee back to Mississippi with him in 1857, Lee looked to the courts for relief, even though blacks were not allowed to testify against whites in courts of law during this period. After an initial setback where a local judge ruled Lee would be returned to bondage, others testified on his behalf and Lee won his freedom in 1858. He soon moved to Canada to avoid any potential legal setback that would place him back into slavery. Throughout the 1850s, the Democratic Party in California was divided over

slavery and the prosecution of the Fugitive Slave Act. The proslavery Democrats (known as "Chivalry Democrats") were eventually defeated by the antislavery factions, ensuring California's support for the Union during the Civil War. Nonetheless, Lee and hundreds of other California blacks left California for places such as Canada in order to ensure their newly won freedom.

During the 1850s, African American leaders, many of whom had been free blacks from New England, held three "Colored Conventions" in 1855, 1856, and 1857 to lobby for suffrage, citizenship rights, and expanded educational opportunities. Though blacks were not admitted to California's public high schools until the 1890s (exceptions included San Francisco, which officially integrated its school system in 1875), the black community and white reformers such as John Swett established several parochial schools for blacks in this period in Sacramento, Stockton, and other cities. In addition to demands for suffrage and for the education of black youth, a major issue during this time was to establish the right of black people to testify in court cases against whites, which was prohibited by state law.

Black Migration to California, 1880s–1930s

Prior to the 1880s, the majority of the African American population in California lived either in San Francisco or the Gold Rush counties. Many blacks became farmers and ranchers in the San Francisco Bay area, while others worked in the service industries as cooks, domestics, and common laborers. Eventually more blacks would move into Southern California due to the demand for agricultural labor, from the promotional appeals of real estate investors (including the appeal of a temperate climate), and for the purpose of establishing black colonies in the state. From 1860 to 1910, the black population of Los Angeles grew from approximately 4,000 to

21,000. By 1910, Los Angeles had the largest concentration of African Americans west of Texas.

The most famous agricultural settlement in California was the community established by Lieutenant Colonel Allen Allensworth (1842–1914). A former self-educated slave and Civil War veteran, Allensworth enjoyed a long career as a chaplain in the U.S. Army. In 1908, he founded an agricultural colony north of Bakersfield. Prior to 1900, state law forbade blacks to homestead in California, and thus most of the higher-quality land in the region had been previously homesteaded by white farmers. Colonization schemes prior to Allensworth included attempts to form black farming colonies near Victorville, San Bernardino, and in Lucerne, northeast of Los Angeles.

Allensworth was the most notable of the attempts to create black agricultural colonies in California. Allensworth envisioned the settlement as a place for retired black soldiers to homestead at the termination of their military careers. In the years around World War I, Allensworth briefly thrived, though the community met resistance from some urban blacks in the state who saw the idea of African Americans engaged in agriculture as a backwards step for blacks in a state where the black experience was, from the onset, an urban experience.

Allensworth first settled in Los Angeles in 1906, where he cultivated his desire to build a community for black settlers that would allow them to escape the growing harshness of post-Reconstruction-period America. After establishing his settlement, hundreds of blacks moved to Allensworth to start farms and business enterprises along streets named for famous abolitionists such as Frederick Douglass. Social institutions such as a churches, clubs, and societies for community and self-improvement also emerged in the bustling town.

Allensworth favored the philosophy of Booker T. Washington, and his new settlement borrowed heavily from black educational institutions such as the Tuskegee Institute and Fisk University. Problems with the harsh desert environment, the development of a safe and dependable water supply, and the untimely death of Allensworth in a car accident in 1914 led to the colony's demise in the 1920s.

Demand for agricultural labor was tremendous in California from the 1870s through the 1920s, and many blacks were lured to the state to work in the fields in places such as Fresno and the Imperial Valley along the Mexican border. Soon growers found that Mexican laborers and other nationalities were willing to work for less than blacks. Many African Americans left the agriculture industry and were caught up in the real estate–driven boom of Los Angeles after 1880.

As mentioned earlier, Bridget "Biddy" Mason's real estate holdings soon became the center of African American residential and cultural life in Los Angeles. Her grandson, Robert Owens, was hailed as one of the wealthiest black persons in the American West. As thousands of blacks migrated to the state, they extolled the virtues of California's prosperity, its relative lack of severe Jim Crow conditions, and the wonder of the great weather to relatives back home, many of whom joined their exodus.

Community boosters such as Jefferson Lewis Edmonds, an iconoclastic publisher and promoter, led the campaign for California that reached black communities all over the United States and the world. African Americans arrived in droves, and many formed chapters of the Colored Peoples' League, the Urban League, the United Negro Improvement Association (UNIA), and various fraternal organizations, literary societies, and women's social clubs. They also created the San Francisco Drama Club and other progressive institutions, including the first California chapter of the National Association for the Advancement of Colored People (NAACP) in 1913. Soon there were chapters in cities across the state.

Some of the new Californians were acquiring lifestyles prosperous enough to garner the praise of W. E. B. Du Bois, who pronounced that Los Angeles was a haven for black people after his visit to the area in 1913. Golden State Mutual Life Insurance, headquartered in Los Angeles, was the most valuable black-owned business west of the Mississippi. In 1918, publisher and mortician Frederick Roberts, a Republican from Berkeley, was the first African American elected to the California State Assembly. Many middle-class and working-class blacks moved to the Watts area south of downtown Los Angeles (annexed by the city in 1926), while others gravitated to the area around Central Avenue and the area around Little Tokyo, particularly after thousands of black workers were brought to the area to break a railroad strike in 1903. After the San Francisco earthquake of 1906, blacks in the Bay Area tended to concentrate around the port city of Oakland, which offered more job opportunities and less expensive housing. While many blacks were relegated to service jobs and menial labor positions, others began to find a relative affluence in California that was rarely seen in the rest of the United States.

During 1926, a number of prominent African American leaders in Orange County, south of Huntington Beach, broke ground for the Pacific Beach Club, intended to be the first all-black social club on the segregated beaches of Southern California. Plans called for an elaborate Egyptian Revival clubhouse and a large auditorium and dance hall, with the entire facility to be staffed by black workers. While some whites in the area supported the club, other local whites resisted its opening, and the club was eventually torched by arsonists before it could officially open in 1926. It soon fell into foreclosure. Even though many black people were finding new prosperity and new adventures in California, they also found the same discrimination that had plagued them "back home."

Even with a growing institutional racism in the 1920s, the African American community of California produced an assortment of talented people in this period, including noted architect Paul Williams (1894–1980), editor and activist Charlotta Bass, scholar and activist Tarea Hall Pittman (1903–1991), diplomat and academician Ralph Bunche, and athlete turned civil rights icon Jackie Robinson.

While most Americans are at least vaguely familiar with the mass migration of impoverished people to California in the 1930s due to the persistent popularity of the John Steinbeck novel *The Grapes of Wrath*, few are aware that this exodus also involved blacks from the Depression-ravaged South. Blacks came from Oklahoma, Texas, and other parts of the "Dust Bowl" to seek jobs in the fields of California. Settling primarily in the Central Valley, the "Black Okies" faced competition from poor whites and Mexicans, as well as more severe forms of racism. Many moved to the small cities and towns in areas dominated by agriculture, such as Arvin, Bakersfield, and Tulare. In time they often drifted away from agriculture to work in the construction industry or manufacturing during World War II. Depression conditions hit the poor the hardest, yet blacks in California had more success in joining various New Deal Relief agencies, such as the National Youth Administration and the Works Progress Administration, than their black counterparts in the American South.

World War II and Afterward

World War II was an important catalyst for the growth of California, and the war brought hundreds of thousands of African Americans to the state. This wave of black migrants from Texas, Louisiana, and other parts of the South mirrored the previous "great migration" of blacks to the Northern cities. Blacks represented only about 1.7 percent of the California population prior to 1940, but by 1950 they would comprise about 4.7 percent of the state's citizens. Roughly 124,000 blacks lived in California in 1940, as compared to 462,000 in 1950. By 1944, Los Angeles alone would he home to over one-quarter of African Americans living west of the Mississippi River. By the early 1950s, over 1,000 blacks were moving to Los Angeles per month, and the flow of people would also dramatically change the Bay Area's ethnic mix, with blacks primarily locating in Oakland and Richmond to work in the shipyards. The newly arrived would find poor housing prospects, vitriolic racism, and severe economic and social problems after the war years ended. Nonetheless, the lure of California seemed to overwhelm any difficulties that emerged.

California had a small yet vibrant black presence prior to World War II, but from 1942 onward, a flood of African Americans came to the state, with tens of thousands of new arrivals per month in 1943. They came to work in the aircraft plants and the other emerging defense industries. Though many employers welcomed the new additions to the employment pool, especially after the displacement of many Japanese workers after the internment of Japanese began on the West Coast in 1942, other employers and unions attempted to relegate blacks to menial jobs and "auxiliary" unions that kept workers' dues but did not enforce key working rights for blacks.

Discrimination against African American workers met with national protests from leaders such as A. Phillip Randolph and his National Association of Sleeping Car Porters. African Americans in the state also participated in the noted "Double V" campaign that equated "Victory Overseas" with "Victory at Home" for black Americans during the conflict. Black leaders in California railed against blacks being denied union jobs, equal pay, and opportunities for advancement. Newspapers such as the *California Eagle* and the *Los Angeles Sentinel* decried unfair employment practices in the state's war industries. Charlotta Bass, Tarea Hall Pittman, a graduate of UCLA and longtime advocate for minority rights, and a Howard and University of California–Berkeley graduate, Frances Albrier, worked with

the League of Women Voters and an assortment of civil rights and left-wing organizations to demand better treatment of blacks in the California workplace. In the Bay Area, alliances between the Urban League, progressive union leaders, and groups such as the Committee against Segregation and Discrimination and the Congress of Industrial Organizations challenged employers and unions to give blacks equal access to jobs and contracts.

President Franklin D. Roosevelt issued Executive Order 8802 in June 1941 establishing a Fair Employment Practices Commission (FEPC) to oversee and adjudicate discriminatory practices in the war industries. The FEPC banned any discrimination based on national origin, color, creed, or race, and it had the power to charge violators with misdemeanor and to restore workers to their jobs or lost promotions. Slowly yet imperfectly, blacks began to get hired in the shipyards and aircraft assembly plants. And though they would face continued slights and overt racism, the situation did get better as the war progressed. In the case of *James v. Marinship* (1944), Joseph James successfully sued his employer, Marinship, on behalf of over 100 other workers for the right to belong to the International Brotherhood of Boilermakers, Iron Shipbuilders, and Helpers as full members with the same rights and benefits of others in the union.

During the war tens of thousands of black soldiers and sailors trained in the state and shipped out to overseas combat theaters from California. A lively music and nightlife scene catered to all service members, though blacks tended to have their own segregated and self-segregated entertainment haunts. Tensions between white service personnel and Mexican American youth in Los Angeles led to the bloody "Zoot Suit Riots" of June 1943, and evidence suggests that blacks passively (and sometimes openly) sided with the Mexican Americans in this struggle. Sadly, the Zoot Suit riots would be eclipsed in the American memory by future riots in Watts (1965) and

Los Angeles (1992) that would have blacks at the center of the storm.

The armed forces of the United States were officially segregated until 1948, and though black combat units would eventually take part in heavy fighting, blacks in the navy were primarily assigned below-deck jobs as stewards, laundrymen, and cooks, or as stevedores (dock loaders), while based on shore. On July 17, 1944, a ship named the *Quintalt Victory* exploded at Mare Island in the San Francisco Bay killing 320 people, including 202 black sailors. Later that month, black sailors from nearby Port Chicago were ordered to load additional ships, even though safety conditions had not improved from the time of the explosion. Over 250 sailors refused to load the ships until safety conditions were improved and other grievances addressed. (Few black sailors had been allowed to testify at the inquiry over the explosion, and survivors had not been granted the traditional leave expected in such cases.) Eventually 50 black sailors were charged with mutiny, convicted, and sentenced to long jail terms. Though they were let out of prison in 1946, the Port Chicago "mutineers" would not officially have their records cleared until the 1990s, when only a handful of the black sailors still survived.

California State Assemblyman Augustus Hawkins (elected as a Democrat in 1934, after defeating Frederick Roberts for his seat) proposed a State Fair Employment Practices Commission in 1946, modeled after the federal agency of the same name. He met with resistance in the state legislature, and the California FEPC did not get passed into law until 1959. Hawkins understood that the law would only serve as a tool to fight discrimination, but it would not end the problems that seemed to worsen in the years after the war.

Blacks moving to California in wartime found that the state had a series of restrictive housing laws that dated back to the 1910s and 1920s,

after the first major wave of black migration to the state. African Americans and those of Asian and Mexican ancestry found themselves locked out of vast areas of the California housing market by rules passed by various housing associations. Along with the migration of blacks to California, numerous whites from the Midwest and South came to the state in the first decades of the twentieth century. Previously held racial attitudes prevailed in the multicultural society of California. The Ku Klux Klan was active in the state in the 1920s, controlling the political apparatus in several counties. Indeed, some of the early black and Latino gangs in California were formed as defense mechanisms against marauding gangs of white toughs parading through minority neighborhoods hurling racial epithets and other taunts.

Chester Himes (1900–1984) came to California to work in the war industries, and even though he found good pay and even some authority, the pervasive racism of California was more degrading than the racism he had encountered in other parts of the country. An educated person, Himes had struggled greatly before coming to California, and had once served a lengthy prison sentence. His experience in the California workplace inspired his highly regarded first novel, *If He Hollers Let Him Go* (1945). Though Himes would later move back East and write commercially successful detective stories, his somber assessment of racism in California seemed to be affirmed in the years after the war.

As blacks arrived in a state where large swaths were inaccessible to them for housing (along with swimming pools, movie theaters, and the like), African Americans concentrated in segregated areas with subpar housing and other amenities. Though some of their communities were relatively nice (Watts would be described as a "palm tree ghetto"), restrictive housing covenants and economic setbacks challenged many blacks in California in the years after World War II.

The 1960s "Civil Rights Revolution" in California

The civil rights revolution that occurred in the United States in the 1950s, and particularly the 1960s, was experienced in a dramatic fashion in California. Building upon the southern civil rights crusade in the late 1950s, there were several successful campaigns to limit segregation and increase opportunities for black and other ethnic groups in America's most multicultural society. The anger and frustration that resulted in the politics of confrontation reached their utmost expression in California, as did some of the most intense expressions of the Black Power Movement of the period.

After World War II, the major black communities of California, both in South Los Angeles and the Oakland area, experienced an economic stagnation. California's economy grew rapidly after World War II, and many blacks would find steady work in government agencies such as the U.S. Post Office, or on military bases, as teachers, or in the service industries. However, upward mobility was not available to many African Americans in California due to the removal of manufacturing jobs to the suburbs, which were mostly off limits to blacks due to restrictive housing covenants barring blacks from the suburbs. Regional transportation systems built after World War II (such as the Bay Area Regional Transit system in the San Francisco area) often

African American demonstrators climb on a squad car after rioting erupted in the Los Angeles neighborhood of Watts on August 11, 1965. Triggered by the arrest and beating of a young African American man suspected of drunk driving, the riots lasted for more than a week, ending with 34 people killed and over 1,000 injured. (AP/ Wide World Photos)

ran directly through black neighborhoods, which displaced many middle-class blacks while furthering economic decline in what became known as the "inner city." As whites left what had been mixed-race neighborhoods, tax dollars and political attention went to the suburbs. New housing in the black neighborhoods often focused upon large public housing projects that would eventually become overcrowded and plagued by crime. By the middle of the 1950s, as many as one-third of Oakland's black residents were unemployed.

The fight against racially restrictive housing laws was a decades-old story in California in the 1950s. By the 1920s, it was a common practice to require whites to sign an agreement not to sell their homes to blacks, Latinos, and Asians. In a few cases black homeowners owned their right to live where they wished, including Booker T. Washington Jr., who successfully won his battle to live in the San Fernando Valley in the 1920s. Henry (187?–1967) and Texanna (1886–1987) Laws came to California from Texas in 1910, and saved enough money to buy property in Watts in the early 1920s. Watts was then a white community, but blacks were moving in on the edges of the community, and in the 1940s, the Laws family was finally able to build a small home on the property they had owned for years in an all-white neighborhood. In 1944, the Laws were thrown out of their home by local authorities for violating housing restrictions, even though two of their sons were fighting for the United States in the Pacific theater. The Superior Court judge ruled, as was the tradition, that the Laws could own the property yet not live there. Charlotta Bass, celebrities such as Paul Robeson and Lena Horne, the NAACP, and other civil rights groups all supported the Laws in their struggle. In May 1948, the U.S. Supreme Court ruled in the case of *Shelley v. Kramer* that restrictive racial covenants were unenforceable. The Laws were able to move back into their home, and within a few years blacks were the majority in Watts.

With their growing numbers in California, blacks were gaining ground in the electoral process in the late 1950s and early 1960s. Augustus Hawkins had introduced numerous bills intending to discard housing restrictions in the state in the 1940s and 1950s. In 1963, W. Byron Rumford (who had been elected to the State Assembly in 1948) was able to gather a coalition to finally pass what became known as the Rumford Fair Housing Statute. While Hawkins went on to become the first black U.S. Representative from California in 1962, F. Douglas Ferrell and Mervyn Dymally were also elected to the State Assembly that year, followed by the indefatigable Willie Brown's election to the Assembly in 1964. Yet as swiftly as blacks seemed to be achieving political success in the state, an undercurrent of anger and neglect began to spill out of California's black ghettos in 1964 and 1965.

In 1964, California voters overturned the Rumford Fair Housing Statute via the ballot initiative process. Known as Proposition 18, and labeled the "Property Rights Initiative" by supporters, white voters followed the lead of the real estate industry and an aspiring politician named Ronald Reagan. White voters were, in effect, blatantly saying they had the right to sell their homes to whomever they pleased. Proposition 18 was overturned by the State Supreme Court in 1967. Though civil rights coalitions in the state were making gains in banning segregation and opening access to employment in the years after World War II (such as the victory to open San Francisco's hotel to black workers in the early 1960s), political anger and economic frustration erupted in 1965 in Watts.

Watts became the symbolic race riot site of the 1960s, which is in some ways ironic as African Americans in Watts were in some respects better off than many blacks in other areas of the United States. A major flash point between the black citizens of Los Angeles and their government was in the area of police-community relations.

Buildings on fire along Avalon Boulevard during riots in Watts, California, 1965. (Library of Congress)

Los Angeles Police Chief William Parker was notorious for recruiting white police from the American South. Parker's "law and order" image resulted in part from the Los Angeles Police Department's (LAPD) strategy of cruising large geographic areas in police cars, and usually responding only to crisis situations more like an invading army than a protective force. Tensions between the police and the black community, which had been smoldering for decades, erupted on August 11, 1965, when motorist Marquette Frye was pulled over on Avalon Boulevard near 166th Street. Angry citizens surrounded the scene, and the ensuing six-day orgy of violence and destruction began.

Watts was not the first, and certainly not the last, of the violent racial riot spots in the United States during the 1960s. It was the worst, and it caused people to ponder a new direction for blacks in California. Some chose to work with the growing coalition of other minority group activists, such as the United Farm Workers Movement of César Chavez, as well as white-led groups such as Students for a Democratic Society, while others embraced the militant black nationalism of the 1960s.

Los Angeles became a major power center for the Nation of Islam, and for Malcolm X when he broke away from the Black Muslims. Malcolm X inspired UCLA student Ronald McKinley Everett (1941–) to change his name to Ron Maulana Karenga. Karenga formed the radical group United Slaves (US) and preached a return to African values and principles in the black movement. Karenga is responsible for the introduction of Kwanzaa, an alternative holiday for American blacks, in 1966. Karenga was at the forefront of a Pan Africanism that harkened back to the days of Marcus Garvey, with the addition of the militant leftist politics of the 1960s. Karenga's group was controversial, occasionally violent, and often at odds with other black organizations.

Among Karenga's enemies was the most widely known of the 1960s black nationalist organizations in California, the Black Panther Party for Self-Defense (BPP). Huey P. Newton and Bobby Seale met at Oakland City College in the early 1960s, and by 1966 the events of the period spurred them to form the BPP. Seale and Newton drew up a 10-point platform that included higher concepts, such as not requiring blacks to register for the military draft, educational goals, and most notably, local concerns such as protecting the black community from police violence and police brutality. Schooled in the California Penal Code, the fledgling BPP made a name for itself by confronting police during car stops and arrests. BPP members carried guns, law books, tape recorders, and other (then legal) apparatus to "patrol the police." In early 1967, the BPP even entered the state capitol building in Sacramento with their guns as a symbolic protest.

The organization grew rapidly and soon had chapters across the United States and much interest from both local law enforcement and the Federal Bureau of Investigation, who would openly war with BPP. While many historians dismiss the BPP as an exaggeration of the period's militant nature, the BPP did instill a sense of pride and resistance among many young blacks nationally, and the BPP organizational efforts made it an effective force in Oakland and Bay Area politics through the 1970s. Though implicated in violent activities, radicals, such as Karenga, communist professor Angela Davis, and BPP member Eldridge Cleaver, all gained appointments to academic positions in the state. Black nationalism was a confrontational force in California life, but the movement hastened the end of overt racism in California and ushered in a plethora of black studies programs and other curriculum changes at the universities and colleges in the state.

Since 1970—Tragedy and Triumph

By the 1970s, California society was increasingly divided economically, and black California reflected this trend. More and more middle-class blacks sought jobs, educational opportunities, and freedom from inner-city decay in the decades after the 1960s. The flight of middle-class blacks from urban neighborhoods added to problems already inherent with lower tax bases and higher levels of crime and poverty. California's black urban enclaves became notorious for gang-related behaviors that most often victimized blacks and other minorities living in the inner cities. Job programs from the 1960s and 1970s, which often failed to bring any real long-term economic reform, dried up in the more conservative California of the 1980s and 1990s. Just as the gangs of California, such as the "Crips" and the "Bloods," became household names around the country, the names of California's prisons were also well known and associated with housing a disproportionate number of black inmates.

In the 1980s, the national crack epidemic spread out from Los Angeles along with the region's gang culture, replete with ugly stereotypes that were exacerbated by the popularity of West Coast "gangsta rap" music and Hollywood films that glorified the violence and pointlessness of criminal life. Citizens in the state demanded a "get tough" attitude in response to the bloody crack and gang epidemics, responding with tough laws to lengthen criminal sentences, limit parole opportunities, and require judges to sentence offenders to mandatory minimum terms. Politicians and judges expanded the power of police to enforce the laws, as many voters demanded harsher treatment of criminals. This crackdown often focused on minority neighborhoods, and these efforts often brought up old antagonisms

Looters run with stolen shoes in Los Angeles on April 30, 1992. The worst riots in modern U.S. history began the day before when outnumbered police were faced down by a crowd angered by the acquittals of four white police officers accused in the videotaped beating of African American motorist Rodney King. (AP/Wide World Photos)

between the police and mostly black and (increasingly) Latino neighborhoods.

In 1992, these tensions blew up once again over the fate of motorist Rodney King, who was pulled out of his car and savagely beaten by numerous LAPD officers. The incident, caught on videotape, was replayed countless times on the television news. The four officers on trial for the King beating had their trial moved to a predominantly white area in neighboring Ventura County, and the all-white jury found them not guilty of the charges. On April 29, 1992, spontaneous demonstrations broke out around the city, focused in the mostly black area of south-central Los Angeles. Over the next four days, at least 58 were killed, thousands more injured and arrested, with billions of dollars of damage resulting from looting and fires. Less than half of those arrested during the 1992 riots were African Americans,

yet the national media portrayed the event as a mostly black-versus-white confrontation.

Since the 1960s, blacks have slipped to the third-largest "minority" in California, outnumbered by Latinos and Asians respectively. A number of female African American politicians earned power and respect in state and national politics, such as Karen Bass, Yvonne Bratwaithe Burke, and Maxine Waters. Other black political leaders such as Tom Bradley, Willie Brown, and Ron Dellums represented California at the city, state, and national levels, but black voting blocs in California's cities often found them locked out or forced to assume secondary roles as newer ethnic groups took center stage on the political scene. Ethnic rivalries over such issues as college admissions created tensions between African Americans and Asians in the state, while black-Latino rivalries played out in the streets, high schools, and job sites of California. Reflecting a broader national trend, a nascent middle class emerged in the black community in California after the 1960s, and a substantial percentage of blacks in the state made their way to the suburbs such as Inglewood and Palmdale. Traditional black areas such as Compton and Watts are now majority Latino demographically. In the 1990s, California was the first state where whites were no longer a majority, and the state leads the nation in mixed-ethnicity marriages. In spite of these interethnic tensions, over the years numerous coalitions among ethnic groups fought against discrimination, gangs, poverty, and the disproportionate incarceration of minorities in California's prison sprawling prison system.

Notable African Americans

Allensworth, Allen (1842–1914)

Allen Allensworth was the most notable of those who attempted to create black agricultural colonies in California. Formed in 1908, Colonel Allensworth envisioned the settlement as a place for retired black soldiers to homestead at the termination of their military careers. In the years around the First World War, Allensworth briefly thrived, though the community met resistance from some urban blacks in the state who saw the idea of African Americans engaged in agriculture as a backwards step for blacks in a state where the black experience was, from the onset, an urban experience.

Allensworth first settled in Los Angeles in 1906, where he cultivated his desire to build a community for black settlers that would allow them to escape the growing harshness of post-Reconstruction-period America. After establishing his settlement, hundreds of blacks moved to Allensworth to start farms and business enterprises along streets named for famous abolitionists such as Frederick Douglas. Social institutions such as a church, clubs, and societies for community and self-improvement also emerged in the bustling town.

Allensworth favored the philosophy of Booker T. Washington, and his new settlement borrowed heavily from black educational institutions such as the Tuskegee Institute and Fisk University. Problems with the harsh desert environment, the development of a safe and dependable water supply, and the untimely death of Allensworth in a car accident in 1914 led to the colony's demise in the 1920s.

Bass, Charlotta (1874–1969)

Charlotta Bass served as the managing editor for the *California Eagle* newspaper (founded 1879) from 1912 to 1951. Bass was an important and vocal civic leader who also was involved in politics. Born in South Carolina, Charlotta Spears came to California for health reasons like so many others at the time. She began to work at the newspaper, then called *The Owl*, and hired her eventual husband J. B. Bass to help her run the enterprise after the original owner passed away. The paper had a circulation of over 60,000 readers in the mid-1920s, making it the most widely read black newspaper on the West Coast. Bass worked for decades to end discriminatory hiring practices, and she also served as the co-president for the Los Angeles chapter of Marcus Garvey's UNIA. Bass ran for several political offices and served as the Progressive Party's vice presidential nominee in 1952.

Bradley, Tom (1917–1998)

Tom Bradley was elected as the first African American mayor of Los Angeles in 1973, serving the nation's second-largest city for 20 years until his retirement in 1993. Bradley was the grandson of slaves and the son of Texas sharecroppers who came to Los Angeles in 1924. Bradley's parents divorced while he was young, and his mother struggled to raise the family. Bradley was highly successful academically and received a track-and-field scholarship at UCLA. Scoring high on the police exam, Bradley dropped out of UCLA and

A 1973 photo of former Los Angeles Mayor Tom Bradley campaigning. (AP/Wide World Photos)

joined the LAPD in 1940. He eventually became a lieutenant and earned a law degree, and he served on the Los Angeles City Council in the tumultuous 1960s. He first ran for mayor in 1969, and after his election in 1973 his tenure was generally characterized as innovative. He successfully hosted the 1984 Olympics, though he did face the turmoil of the 1992 race riot. Bradley made two unsuccessful campaigns for the governorship, and he spent his later years practicing law at a prestigious firm in downtown Los Angeles.

Bunche, Ralph (1903–1971)

Ralph Bunche was born in Detroit, Michigan, but was raised by his grandmother in Los Angeles. He attended Jefferson High School and then went on to the University of California, Los Angeles, where he graduated with honors in 1927. Bunche then matriculated to Harvard University and would spend his academic career outside of California as a professor and administrator at both Howard University and at Harvard. He also worked for the State Department in World War II, and he eventually won the Nobel Peace Prize in 1950 for his work with the United Nations over the Palestinian-Israeli question.

Burke, Yvonne Brathwaite (1932–)

Yvonne Burke retired in 2008 after a long stint (1992–2008) as a powerful and connected Los Angeles City Supervisor. Educated at UCLA, Burke (originally Perle Yvonne Watson) attended law school at USC and begin working as an attorney in 1956. Active in political and social circles (her husband William Burke is a wealthy Los Angeleno), Burke was elected to the

California State Assembly in 1967, serving until her election to the U.S. House of Representatives in 1973, where she served until 1979.

Mason, Bridget "Biddy" (d. 1891)

Bridget "Biddy" Mason was born into slavery in the Deep South, and her owner Robert Smith had moved to California to become part of the Mormon Colony in Riverside. When Smith attempted to leave California with his slaves in 1851 and remove them to Texas, Mason fought her removal in court with the help of family and friends such as the Robert Owens family. (Owens was a former slave who earned enough money in California to purchase his and his family's freedom.) When Smith failed to show up in court the judge granted Mason her freedom. She became well known as a nurse, midwife, and real estate investor after earning substantial wealth in the Los Angeles real estate market in the 1870s and 1880s. Through parsimonious living and her investment in the Los Angeles real estate market, Mason became a major property owner in the bustling city of Los Angeles. "Grandma Mason" ministered to the needy and used her financial clout to establish the Los Angeles branch of the African Methodist Episcopalian Church in 1872. She died in 1891, and was known for her business acumen and for her philanthropic endeavors.

Pittman, Tarea Hall (d. 1991)

Tarea Hall Pittman was born in Bakersfield, but eventually moved to the San Francisco Bay Area with her family in the 1930s. She graduated form USC in the 1920s and was married to Dr. William Pittman, a dentist forced into menial low-paying jobs during the Great Depression. Among other activities, Pittman served as the West Coast director of the NAACP and an organizer of the National Negro Congress of 1936. During World War II, she led the fight in the Bay Area for equal pay, access to housing, and civil rights for the burgeoning black population during and after World War II.

Robinson, Jack Roosevelt "Jackie" (1919–1972)

Jackie Robinson was raised by a single mother who had brought the one-year-old Jackie to Pasadena in 1920. Education and athletic prowess allowed Robinson to rise above his humble circumstances. In high school he was a star in multiple sports. He attended Pasadena City College, and then became a four-sport star at the University of California, Los Angeles. After serving in the U.S. Army, where he had protested discrimination to the point of being declared insubordinate, Robinson went on to play for the Kansas City Monarchs of the Negro League, until the Brooklyn Dodgers made him the first black player in the major leagues in 1948. His stellar play and quiet dignity made him popular with fans, and his post-baseball career included service on the national board of the NAACP and numerous business ventures, including a construction firm dedicated to building low-income housing.

Williams, Paul (1894–1930)

Paul Williams lost his parents at the tender age of four, yet he managed to obtain an education at the Los Angeles School of Art and Design, and later at the University of Southern California (USC). In 1921, he became the first certified black architect in the American West and soon began a productive career that would result in his being the first African American member of the American Architectural Institute. He served on numerous commissions, including the Los Angeles Planning Commission, wrote numerous texts, and designed some of the signature buildings of Los Angeles, including the Beverly Hills

Hotel. He designed homes for movie stars, the local business elite, and for common people as well. He received numerous honorary doctorate degrees in his lifetime, and his reputation has continued to grow even after his death in 1980.

Cultural Contributions

African Americans in California have enjoyed a rich cultural life, and their cultural contribution in a divergent range of areas has reached far beyond the borders of the state to influence American and world culture. Black California produced a strong literary tradition, a vibrant church culture, notable artists and architects, fabled actors and musicians, and champion athletes.

Since publication of *The Owl* (later the *California Eagle*) began in 1879, black newspapers have helped cultivate African American culture in California. Black newspapers have served as community forums to address civil rights and other community concerns. Black churches have also enjoyed a sustained and powerful impact over black communities in the state as well as the larger community as a whole. The pulpits of California's black churches have been used to attack racism, promote cultural strength, and minister to the religious sentiments of the communities they have served.

As they have throughout American history, African Americans created lasting artistic expressions in California, from architects such as Paul Williams to popular hip-hop artists who help define cultural trends for the rest of the planet. African Americans began coming to Hollywood from 1910 onward, seeking fame and fortune in the film industry. Though blacks were often stereotyped into demeaning roles such as Hattie McDaniel's noted portrayal of a Southern "mammy" in *Gone with the Wind* (1939), numerous black performers became wealthy, using their newly won power and money to fight for black rights in the state. Lighter-skinned black actresses such as Dorothy Dandridge and Nellie Conley often portrayed seductresses,

while black males in the early movies often played subservient and comical characters, sometimes in black face. Among the more noted actors in this genre were David "Pigmeat" Markham (1904–1981) and Stepin Fechit, the stage name for Lincoln Theodore Monroe Andrew Perry (1902–1985).

In roles often directed exclusively at black audiences, jazz musicians such as Lena Horne, Cab Calloway, and Louis Armstrong often played themselves in movie roles. Their presence on the West Coast led to a thriving music scene in Los Angeles that was highly developed by the 1930s. Though music and dance clubs could be found in every black community of size throughout California, the center of the West Coast African American renaissance was Central Avenue in Los Angeles, which had been the heart of black Los Angeles for decades. Jazz clubs on Central Avenue were frequented by people of all races until downtown Los Angeles gradually declined as a cultural center after World War II.

After World War II, black Californians continued to make rich contributions to the cultural life of the Golden State. The West Coast jazz scene became highly recognized and regarded around the world, and writers such as Chester Himes, Eldridge Cleaver, and prison author George Jackson continued to record the unpleasant side of race relations in California. Black musical artists continued to set national music and fashion styles well into the 1990s, with groups such as NWA and performers such as Too Short and Xhibit embodying the hardest (and most controversial) edges of black urban life.

In the realm of athletics, African Americans in California continued to excel. UCLA graduate Jackie Robinson became the first black player in the integrated major leagues in 1947, a step that is now hailed as a major moment in the early Civil Rights Movement. Kingsburg resident Rafer Johnson won the Olympic decathlon in 1960, and other black athletes such as Florence Griffith Joyner continued this record of athletic achievement.

Bibliography

Allen, Robert. *The Port Chicago Mutiny: The Story of the Largest Mass Mutiny Trial in U.S. Naval History*. New York: Warner Books, 1989.

Bunche, Lonnie G., III. *Black Angelenos: The Afro-American in Los Angeles, 1850–1950*. Los Angeles: California Afro-American Museum, 1988.

De Graff, Lawrence B., Kevin Mulroy, and Quintard Taylor, eds. *Seeking El Dorado: African Americans in California*. Los Angeles: Autry Museum of Western History, 2001.

Flamming, Douglas. *Bound for Freedom: Black Los Angeles in Jim Crow America*. Berkeley: University of California Press, 2006.

Foner, Eri, ed. *The Black Panthers Speak*. New York: Da Capo Press, 1995.

Hilliard, David. *Huey: Spirit of the Panther*. New York: Thunder Mouth Press, 2006.

Hudson, Karen E. *The Will and the Way: Paul R. Williams, Architect*. New York: Rizzoli, 1994.

Johnson, Marilyn S. *The Second Gold Rush: Oakland and the East Bay in World War II*. Berkeley: University of California Press, 1993.

Margolies, Edward, and Michel Faber. *The Several Lives of Chester Himes*. Jackson: University of Mississippi Press, 1997.

Mungen, Donna. *The Life and Times of Biddy Mason: From Slavery to Wealthy California Land Owner*. Lewisville, TX: MC Printing, 1976.

Radcliffe, Evelyn. *Out of Darkness: The Story of Allen Allensworth*. Menlo Park, CA: Inkling Press, 1998.

Smith, R. J. *The Great Black Way: L.A. in the 1940s and the Lost African American Renaissance*. New York: Public Affairs, 2006.

Taylor, Quintard. *In Search of the Racial Frontier: African Americans in the West 1580–1990*. New York: W. W. Norton, 1999.

Taylor, Quintard. *African American Women Confront the West, 1600–2000*. Norman: University of Oklahoma Press, 2003.

Tolbert, Emory J. *The UNIA and Black Los Angeles: Ideology and Community in the American Garvey Movement*. Los Angeles: UCLA Center for Afro-American Studies, 1980.

Urquart, Brian. *Ralph Bunche: An American Life*. New York: W. W. Norton, 1993.

Wheeler, Gordon B. *Black California: The History of African Americans in the Golden State*. New York: Hippocrene Books, 1993.

COLORADO

Ronald J. Stephens

Chronology

1859	Clara Brown, a former slave freed in 1856, arrives in Cherry Creek from Kansas as cook for a group of prospectors heading to Pike's Peak. At Cherry Creek, she works as a nurse, cook, and laundress.
1860	Barney Lancelot Ford, an escaped slave, comes to Colorado, where he fights against statehood until African Americans are permitted the right to vote.
1864	Black Mountain Man James Beckwourth kills William Paine, who has terrorized Colorado residents, in a gunfight.
1865	Denver City becomes the territorial capital, and shortens its name to Denver.
1868	Shorter African Methodist Episcopal (AME) Church of Denver is the first African American Church established in Colorado; its founder is Bishop Thomas M. D. Ward, a pioneer of African Methodism in the West, who fulfills multiple needs of African Americans of the Five Points area.
1876	(*August 1*) Colorado enters the Union as the 38th state.
1881	The *Colorado Statesman* and the *Denver Weekly Star* are founded; both Colorado black newspapers encouraged change and promoted civil rights issues. Joseph D. D. Rivers, editor of the *Colorado Statesman* and close friend of Booker T. Washington, encourages blacks to come west, invest in real estate, and establish businesses. J. R. Smith and Lewis Price use the *Denver Weekly Star* for similar purposes.
1890	Approximately 6,000 African Americans live in Colorado, with about 5,000 owning property. Of those 6,000, 3,254 live in Denver.
1893	Denver's Fire Station Number 3, which is located in the heart of the Five Points Neighborhood, becomes the first all-black fire station in the city.
1896	The Bonita Silver and Gold Mining Company is founded and managed by two African American women: Mary E. Phelps, president, and Mrs. L. K. Daniels, secretary.
1900	Denver's restrictive housing covenants and Jim Crow segregation force the majority of the city's African Americans to live in the Five Points Neighborhood.
1904	The Scott Methodist congregation is established as Denver's only United Methodist denomination to welcome African Americans.
1920	Five Points becomes the heart of the black community and plays an important role in the social, political, and economic history of Denver's African Americans. This period is also marked by a number of changes and challenges for the Five Points Neighborhood as the black business sector of the community matures into a significant force.
1921	Racial segregation is pervasive in Denver, as is the Ku Klux Klan. Some Klan members even become elected officials, such as Colorado's Governor Clarence Morley, who

serves from 1925 to 1927, and Denver's Mayor Benjamin Stapleton, who serves from 1923 to 1931.

1922   *(May 23)* Marcus Garvey arrives in Colorado Springs. After leaving Colorado Springs, he travels to Denver where he delivers two addresses on behalf of the Denver Division of the Universal Negro Improvement Association (UNIA).

1924   *(October 5)* Marcus Garvey speaks to the Denver Division of the UNIA at Fern Hall.

1924   *(October 13)* Amy Jacques speaks to the Colorado Springs Division of the UNIA at People's Methodist Episcopal Church.

1925   Gilpin County's Lincoln Hills is an African American mountain resort community. Parcels of land are sold to African Americans throughout the United States for $5 down and $5 a month until a total of $50 is accrued.

1925   Winks Lodge is purchased and restored by the James P. Beckwourth Mountain Club.

1935   Colorado passes a Civil Rights Statute on equality of privileges for all persons, stating that "all persons within the jurisdiction of said state shall be entitled to the full and equal enjoyment of the accommodations, advantages, facilities, and privileges of inns, restaurants, eating houses, barber shops, public conveyances on land or water, theatres, and all other places of public accommodation and amusement, subject only to the conditions and limitations established by law and applicable alike to all citizens."

1942   World War II brings wartime industry to Denver. President Franklin Roosevelt's Executive Order 8802, issued in response to A. Philip Randolph's threatened 1941 "March on Washington," means that black men and women in Denver are hired in defense industry plants and other firms with defense contracts, such as Denver's military installations. Fitzsimmons Army Hospital, Fort Logan, Lowry Air Base, and Buckley Naval Air Station all employed a sizeable number of civilian workers in the Remington Arms of Denver's Ordinance Plant, Kaiser Company, and the Rocky Mountain Arsenal.

1947   Denver's first African American Rodeo is organized. The cowboy Willie "Smokey" Lornes sponsors the rodeo "to help some of the colored cowboys get a start and prove that the white people weren't the only ones to be able to successfully put on a show."

1950   Elvin R. Caldwell is elected to the Colorado state legislature. Caldwell is the first black Denver city councilman. He serves as council president three times. Charles Cousins and Caldwell open the historic Club 715 Restaurant and the Minute Spot. Caldwell later buys the Rossonian Hotel and Lounge.

1963   *(February 21)* Colorado ratifies the Twenty-fourth Amendment to the U.S. Constitution abolishing the poll tax.

1971   Paul W. Stewart founds the Black American West Museum (BAWM). The museum is dedicated to African American men, women, and children who ventured westward. BAWM's

1971 (*cont.*)	exhibitions cover photos, artifacts, black pioneers, buffalo soldiers, mountain men, homesteaders, cowboys, and military heroes.
1972	Wellington Webb is elected to the Colorado legislature.
1978	King Trimble, who was appointed to fill the unexpired seat of Wellington Webb in 1977, is elected to a full term in the Colorado legislature in his own right.
1980	Wilma Webb is appointed to the Colorado legislature to finish the unexpired term of Representative King Trimble.
1981	The Negro Historical Association of Colorado Springs (NHACS) is founded as a nonprofit, tax=exempt organization. Its mission is to ensure that black people are included as an integral part of the history of the Pikes Peak region. One of the original organizers of the organization is Lu Lu Pollard.
1984	The Colorado legislature approves a bill making Martin Luther King Jr. Day a legal holiday in Colorado.
1985	NHACS is instrumental in having the site of Payne Chapel AME Church on the corner of Pueblo Avenue and Weber Street designated a historic site by the State of Colorado. The church was first built in 1884 for black people in Colorado Springs.
1991	Wellington Webb becomes the first African American mayor of Denver. During the campaign, Webb pledged to walk the entire city. He walked more than 300 miles across Denver, including during the city's annual Juneteenth parade in northeast Denver. Over 39 consecutive days he walked more than 300 mile and lost 25 pounds, not once going home or getting into a car.
1998	Republican Joe Rodgers is elected as Colorado's first black lieutenant governor.
1998	NHACS selects William Seymour as a suitable Colorado Springs resident to memorialize. A statute is unveiled in 2002 of Seymour on the grounds of the Colorado Springs Pioneers Museum as a symbol of a black pioneer.
2001	The first African American Republican Leadership Summit is held at the Keystone Resort in Colorado hosted by Colorado's black Lieutenant Governor Joe Rodgers.
2003	The Blair Caldwell African American Research Library is dedicated to Omar Blair and Elvin Caldwell.
2003	The Denver Public Library's Blair-Caldwell African American Library is dedicated at 14th and Welton Streets in the Five Points area of Denver.
2008	(*January*) Peter C. Groff becomes president of the Colorado State Senate, the first African American to lead either chamber of the Colorado legislature.
2008	The Democratic National Convention is held in Denver, when Barack Obama becomes the first African American to receive the presidential nomination of a major party.

2008   Democrat Barack Obama, the first African American presidential nominee of a major party, carries Colorado with about 54 percent of the vote.

2009   (*May*) Peter C. Groff, president of the Colorado State Senate, is appointed by President Barack Obama to head the faith-based initiatives center in the U.S. Department of Education.

Historical Overview

After the Civil War, many African Americans migrated to Colorado from the South to find work laying track for the railroads, the expansion of which made Denver one of the chief trade centers of the American West. Black workers and professionals, and their families, also relocated to the Denver, Colorado Springs, and Pikes Peak areas because Colorado was considered a place where they could escape the Jim Crow segregation and racial discrimination of the South.

From the Civil War, President Abraham Lincoln's signing of the Emancipation Proclamation, Reconstruction, the black migration to Kansas, World War I, and numerous other events of the late nineteenth and early twentieth centuries sprang a combination of social factors that influenced waves of former slave and free black families to migrate to Colorado. The first of these factors involves the southern black collective response to white supremacy to escape racial discrimination and Jim Crow segregation practices in the South. A second set of reasons concerns the black man and woman's search for creative entrepreneurial and meaningful employment opportunities, and finally their search for better schools for their children and housing for their families influenced movement patterns. According to the Negro Historical Association of Colorado Springs, in the decade before the Civil War, many pioneering black families originally bound for California found Colorado an ideal location to resettle. And during the years following the Civil War, many African American servants settled in Colorado with their masters.

Three decades before the turn of the century brought respectability and the wealth of the mountains poured revenues into Colorado parks, fountains, statues, tree-lined streets, and elaborate mansions, African American migrants had been rushing to Denver to find work or silver and gold. In 1858, Denver was founded during the Pikes Peak Gold Rush in the Kansas Territory. On November 22, 1858, General William Larimer, a land speculator from eastern Kansas, placed cottonwood logs to stake a claim on the hill overlooking the confluence of the South Platte River and Cherry Creek, across the creek from the existing mining settlement of Auraria. Larimer named the town site Denver City after the Kansas Territorial Governor James W. Denver. At first Denver was a mining settlement where prospectors panned gold from the sands of nearby Cherry Creek and the South Platte River. The prospectors discovered that the gold deposits in these streams were quickly exhausted. It appeared that Denver City might become an instant ghost town, but discoveries by George A. Jackson and John H. Gregory of rich gold deposits in the mountains west of Denver in early 1859 assured Denver's future as a supply hub for the new mines in the mountains.

Prior to arriving in Denver, black men during Reconstruction (1864–1896) made numerous attempts to vote and to hold office as though they lived in a democracy, even though the principles of democracy were severely limited for them. After Reconstruction, African Americans created and planted the seeds of growth well into the late 1890s and early twentieth century. Historian Nell Painter stated after the Civil War, the promise of black freedom and civil rights quickly ended after southern and border-states and localities enacted policies that effectively disfranchised them. As a consequence, newly freed African Americans rushed west to find their destiny. Gold, silver, land, and a chance of self-sufficiency drew all ethnic and economic backgrounds west. The post–Civil War era may have severely limited African Americans from initially taking advantage of opportunities due to racial laws and norms, but western territories placed fewer restrictions on African Americans and offered a chance of self-determination and a way out from the persecution.

African Americans moved to Colorado as fur traders, mountain men, guides, miners, buffalo soldiers, pioneers, cowboys, farmers, entrepreneurs, doctors, lawyers, and businesspeople. They migrated west utilizing all forms of transportation such as wagon trains, railroad, stagecoaches, handcarts, and horseback, and many walked. Many lived in tents, sod houses, log cabins, caves, tarpaper shacks, and clapboard homes. In 1856, for example, Clara Brown, after a lifetime of servitude, was freed in her owner's will, and made her way first to Kansas and by 1859 was hired by a group of prospectors heading to Pike's Peak as a cook. Eight weeks later, she arrived at Cherry Creek, where she worked as a nurse, cook, and laundress. Another example was Frank Loper, a former slave born in Mississippi, on the plantation of Confederate President Jefferson Davis. Loper migrated to Colorado Springs in 1886 after his overseer left Mississippi. The African American population size in Colorado by the early 1920s increased, as a small, yet distinguished number of black professionals and their families discovered Denver, the site of the largest concentration of black Coloradans, and Colorado Springs, the site of the second-largest concentration of African Americans in the state.

At first Denver's African American community was scattered throughout the city, which included the Cherry Creek area. In the pursuit of achieving the American dream, they created

black colonies while working jobs in Denver during the week and farming their homesteads in towns like Dearfield on the weekends. They spent their holidays at Winks Lodge in Lincoln Hills and their summers at Camp Nizhone. Lincoln Hills was an all–African American mountain resort community that was founded by Windell "Wink" Hamlet in 1910. Parcels of land were sold to African Americans from all over Colorado, especially from Denver, for $5 down and $5 a month until a total of $50 was accrued. Windell built Winks Lodge at Lincoln Hills, where he hosted many African American celebrities vacationing in the mountains. Five Points residents would take the train from Moffat Depot in downtown Denver.

The Five Points community offered easy access from the city via the railroad as well as a beautiful mountain view and a river running through the property. Denver City was across the South Platte River from the site of seasonal encampments of the Cheyenne and Arapaho. Denver City was a frontier town, with an economy based on servicing local miners with gambling, saloons, livestock, and goods trading. E. J. Sanderlin came to Colorado in 1859 and opened one of the first barbershops and restaurants in Denver. Barney Lancelot Ford, an escaped slave, arrived in Colorado in 1860. Barney Ford fought against Colorado statehood until African Americans were given the right to vote. In 1865, Denver City became the territorial capital, and shortened its name to just Denver. On August 1, 1876, Denver became the state capital as Colorado was admitted to the Union. The completion of the Denver Pacific and Kansas Pacific rail lines in 1870 facilitated the success of Denver becoming a major trade center for the West. This small dusty town along the Platte River rapidly became the third-largest city in the West. By 1890, Denver had a population of 106,713. The population was smaller than San Francisco and Omaha, but larger than Los Angeles, Seattle, Phoenix, or any town in Texas. In 1890, the U.S. Census reported that about 6,000 African Americans lived in Colorado, with about 5,000 owning property. Of those 6,000, 3,254 lived in Denver.

Curtis Park had been one of Denver's first subdivided parcels. German, Irish, and Jewish immigrants and African Americans of wealth quickly moved outside the city. Many escaped the crowded congestion of Denver to the carefully manicured suburbs. By 1881, the area of Five Points was named for the five-way intersection of Welton Street, 27th Avenue, Washington Street, and 26th Street. During the late 1890s, Curtis Park was considered the most elegant streetcar suburb in Denver. As other suburbs were being built, the wealthy moved away to more prominent neighborhoods such as Capitol Hill. By the late 1890s, African Americans began to move in larger numbers to Five Points. In 1893, Fire Station Number 3, which was located in the heart of the Five Points neighborhood, became the first all–African American fire station in Denver. During the early 1900s, restrictive housing covenants and Jim Crow segregation forced the majority of Africans Americans to live in the Five Points neighborhood, while others settled in neighborhoods scattered throughout the Denver metropolitan area. The politics in Colorado during the Progressive Era left African Americans with no choice but to create internal opportunities, which resulted in a number of progressive black thinkers.

The African American community in Denver thrived at the time. The pioneering efforts of Ernest McClain, who became Colorado's first African American licensed dentist, and Lewis Douglass and Frederick Douglass Jr., sons of the famous abolitionist Frederick Douglass, served as several of the signers of the famous "100" Blacks Petition for the right to vote for African Americans. This helped in the creation of the first black school in the city. Walker Anderson's family migrated to Denver in the 1870s, and he became a pioneer builder and miner, participating

in the construction of the Central City Opera House, the Antler's Building, the Denver Courthouse, Daniels and Fisher's Tower, the state capitol, and the Rio Grande Building. And J. R. Smith and Lewis Price founded the all-black newspaper, the *Denver Weekly Star*, in 1881. Francis T. Bruce was listed on the Denver police roster in the 1890s, and helped to organize the Black Masonic Lodge.

As Denver's overall population continued to grow, the area identified as Five Points was quickly becoming the heart of the African American community. Denver's small African American community continued to grow during the early part of the twentieth century, and the Five Points area played an important role in African American social, political, and economic history. The first two decades of the twentieth century represented a period of profound social, political, cultural, religious, and economic changes and challenges for African Americans in communities in Colorado. This ultimately fostered a sense of community and identity, as Five Points was quickly maturing into a significant black business sector of the city. What influenced these developments? In an editorial published in the *Colorado Statesman* on July 17, 1920, the editor, Joseph D. D. Rivers, encouraged black migration to Colorado, stating:

We note with extreme satisfaction and pride that countless numbers of prominent, Well-to-do colored citizens in many of the Southern states are leaving the Southland and migrating to the North and West because of the vicious and inhuman conditions that prevail in the South. Under the present democratic administration the Negro in the South, regardless of his wealth and standing, has suffered untold barbarities and unspeakable, inhumane treatment. The proper school facilities and advantages have even been denied them, they are robbed of their reward for honest toil, and a scandalous systematic propaganda is carried on in the South against the Negro to create the impression generally that he is a rapist and a criminal as a justification in the eyes of the world for the wholesale lynchings, that take place in the South almost daily. No justice in the courts, poor housing conditions for the Negro labors, peonage, lack of protection to the Negro under the laws of the South—all these things and many more are breaking the back of the camel and he is becoming restless and dissatisfied, and hence the Great Exodus.

Government statistics report that upwards of 300,000 Negroes have left the South in the past four years and settled in the North and West. These immigrants are composed of all classes—the poor, the well-to-do, the professional man, the common laborer and the bad, along with the good.

Many excellent families have left, looking and hoping for better school advantages for their children and stronger protection for themselves and their families under the laws of the states wherever they may cast their lot. Yet in the face of this great exodus and the cry of alarm sent out by the white man of the South because of the exodus of thousands of Negroes, they do not pretend in the least to adjust or ameliorate the intolerable conditions that exist in the South in so far as the Negro is concerned. Can you blame the Negro for moving? No, not for one moment. Any other race of people would have gone long, long ago, rather than to live under such intolerable conditions and unjust laws.

The editorial also outlined reasons why black families should consider Colorado as their new place of residence. These included wonderful climate and scenery; expanding mining, agricultural, and stock-raising industries; thousands of acres of vacant land for settlement; and laws that afford equal protection regardless of race. For established black farmers and professional men and women leaving the South, the *Statesman*'s

editorial essentially painted a picture of an oasis in the West, highlighting profitable advantages in acquiring land in Colorado and the beauty of the state. The editorial framed these advantages in comparative terms as a means to entice potential hard-working and respectable business leaders, workers, and homeowners to take notice of the profits they could earn from their investments.

The present indications this year for the production of corn and wheat in Colorado show that the crops will be the greatest in the history of the state. The Colorado Crop Reporting Service estimates a crop of 24,498,000 bushels of wheat, compared with 17,645,000 last year; 15,203,000 bushels of corn, compared with 11,205,000 bushels last year. The production of potatoes for this year is estimated at 13,072,000 bushels, compared with 11,040,000 bushels last year. So we see that there is an increase each year both in crops and in the acreage. The Colorado Statesman advises and urges the settlement of honest, upright, sturdy and industrious farmers from the South into Colorado.

In 1910, Oliver T. Jackson founded the African American farming community of Dearfield, Colorado. Jackson believed it was important for "all of our people to get back to the land, where we naturally belong, and to work out their own salvation from the land up." Jackson was a messenger at the Colorado state capitol, serving five governors, including Govenor John Shafroth, who helped him realized his dream of Dearfield. The 1920 U.S. Census indicated a total of 6,075 African American residents in the Mile High City, an increase of 649, or 12 percent, from 1910.

The Five Points area essentially played an important role in African American social, political, and economic history. The Five Points neighborhood matured into a significant black business sector of the city during the 1920s. The 1920 Census had also indicated a total of 6,075 African American residents in Denver, an increase of 649, or 12 percent, from 1910. From all indications this black migration initiative created the political, economic, and cultural basis for a number of businesses in the Five Points area, which were operated by black attorneys, physicians, surgeons, and embalmers. The establishments of Douglass' Undertaking, the Rossonian Hotel, and the only white-owned Atlas Drug Store, which was built in 1911, proved to be successful. Denver's Five Points neighborhood was also home to two black-owned newspapers, both of which had been founded during the late nineteenth century. Both the *Colorado Statesman* and the *Denver Star* promoted civil rights, black migration, and black economic development. Joseph D. D. Rivers, editor of the *Colorado Statesman* and a close friend of Booker T. Washington, told blacks to settle in the West to find work and establish businesses.

Welton Street, from 22nd to 29th Streets, was the "main street" of the African American community in Denver from the 1920s to the early 1970s. The Welton Street business district of Five Points during the 1920s not only attracted many kinds of businesses—for example, restaurants, bars, physicians, real estate agencies, and insurance companies—but also served as an important resource site for residents in the community. Successful businesses and businesspeople provided stability and leadership for local communities. Businesses became meeting places to discuss important local issues and business owners supplied credit and other financial assistance to help people when times were difficult.

However, the most enduring institution that was responsible for gluing the community together was the black church. The churches in the Five Points neighborhood similarly played a pivotal role in the lives of community residents. Serving both social and charitable needs, black churches offered incoming migrants

and permanent residents a place they could call home away from home. As in other states throughout the country, black churches functioned as houses of worship, providing both members and visitors opportunities for Christian fellowship, meaningful sermons from their distinguished pastors and invited guest speakers, and as first-rate sacred and secular sites for community networking. Shorter AME Church, for example, was the first African American Church organized in Denver in 1868 by Bishop Thomas M. D. Ward, a pioneer of African Methodism in the West. Shorter AME with its rich history in the Five Points community fulfilled multiple needs of black residents of the area. Scott Methodist Church, which traces its roots to 1904, was founded as Denver's only United Methodist denomination to serve blacks at the time. Scott Methodist purchased the building that originally belonged to the Christ Church congregation on 22nd and Ogden Streets. Racial residential segregation was pervasive in Denver. So too was the Ku Klux Klan. Born alongside D. W. Griffith's film, *Birth of a Nation*, the Klan in Denver, which was organized during the early 1920s, sought not only to discriminate against African Americans, but also against Jews, Roman Catholics, and any other groups that were perceived as social or political threats to white, Protestant society.

The fear of change and cultural difference were the driving force that inspired the Klan. The changing demographic face of residential life and to some extent employment dynamics in Denver accelerated racial and religious tensions in the city. The Klan used violence and harassment against African Americans and other groups. Car caravans of Klansmen honking horns and shouting insults drove through Jewish neighborhoods, the local chapter of the National Association for the Advancement of Colored People (NAACP) received numerous threats, and one black man was driven out of town for not following the Klan's idea of proper contact between the races.

Klan participation in Denver reached its peak during the 1920s, when over 50,000 Coloradans joined the organization, making the state second behind Indiana in Klan membership. Some Klan members were even elected officials such as Governor Clarence Morley, who served the state from 1925 to 1927, and Denver Mayor Benjamin Stapleton, who served the city from 1923 to 1931. Five Points witnessed the formation of neighborhood improvement associations in surrounding white communities. These associations drafted covenants that prevented residents from selling property to nonwhites. The political climate in Colorado during the Progressive Era left African Americans with no choice but to create internal opportunities, which developed as a result of a series of progressive New Negro thinkers such as Garvey, W. E. B. Du Bois, and James Weldon Johnson, who spoke to Five Points residents. Garvey and his organization, the Universal Negro Improvement Association and African Communities League (UNIA-ACL), offered an abundance of hope to hundreds of black Coloradans.

The two Colorado divisions of the UNIA illustrated how collective and individual confidence, faith, and pride can achieve African Redemption. Marcus and Amy Jacques Garvey's thundering voices during their visits to Denver and Colorado Springs were not only spellbinding, persuasive, and inspiring to residents, but also pragmatic in constructing and promoting a human civilization of racial equality. Garvey's slogan "Africa for the Africans" at home and abroad situated the African predicament on the same continuum as other global liberation movements struggling in a white supremacist world. In effect Garvey rallied them to make the mental shift from a race of an inferior people to a race of superiority, a people who embraced their cultural dignity, identity, independence, and ethnic heritage. At the time the aims and objectives of the organization had not become widely known to the Colorado Springs and Denver African

American communities. This did not occur until shortly after the opening of the first International Convention of the UNIA-ACL on August 1, 1920. It was this UNIA convention that elected Garvey a world leader and Negro leader of 12,000,000 people of the United States, and as the provisional president of Africa. Convention delegates also drafted and adopted the UNIA's constitution and bill of rights.

World War II brought wartime industry to Denver. President Franklin D. Roosevelt's Executive Order 8802, issued in response to A. Philip Randolph's threatened "March on Washington" in 1941, meant that black men and women in Denver would be hired in defense industry plants and other firms with defense contracts. Denver's military installations—Fitzsimmons Army Hospital, Fort Logan, Lowry Air Base, and Buckley Naval Air Station—employed a sizeable number of civilian workers, as did the Remington Arms Ordnance Plant in Denver, the Kaiser Company, and the Rocky Mountain Arsenal.

The events and circumstances later surrounding the Civil Rights Movement in Colorado also significantly influenced social change in the state. Rachel Bassette Noel, a local civil rights leader, activist, educator, and humanitarian, led the fight to achieve integration in the public school system in Denver. In 1965, Noel was elected the first African American to serve on the Denver Public Schools Board of Education. Noel, who had been exposed to civil rights and the fight for equality from observing her father, attorney A. W. E. Bassette Jr., authored the Noel Resolution in 1968, which called for desegregation in the Denver public school system. The Noel Resolution became the foundational guidelines for desegregation of Denver public schools, covering student ratio imbalances and racial balance of administrative employees and teachers. It was upheld by the Colorado Supreme Court.

At a time when racially bigoted action was the norm of society, the Noel Resolution served as a model to the entire country and helped to create equal educational opportunities for all students. Other events and circumstances emanating out of the Civil Rights Movement in Colorado highlight the copious triumphs of the Denver chapter of the Black Panther Party for Self-Defense, which was led by Lauren Watson. Watson searched for an improved life in Denver, having been convinced that African Americans, more often than not, would succeed despite poor community-police relations and charges of police brutality aimed at African Americans in the Five Points neighborhood and Denver public schools.

Following the Black Power phase of the Civil Rights Movement, Wellington Webb became the first African American mayor of Denver, Colorado. Webb's track record paved the way for his successful and historic mayoral bid in 1991. Webb pledged to walk the entire city and the Denver media followed. In his three terms as mayor of Denver, Webb focused on four major areas: parks and open space, public safety, economic development, and children. Webb was president of the Democratic Mayors and the past president of the U.S. Conference of Mayors and National Conference of Black Mayors.

As Webb served Denver, the 2004 U.S. Census reported that the African American population in all of Colorado was composed of 178,731 persons residing primarily in eight counties along the Front Range. The largest concentration of African Americans live in two counties: Denver with 10.7 percent of the population, followed immediately by Arapahoe County with 10.2 percent. This represented a considerable shift from the 2000 U.S. Census, where 11.1 percent of African Americans resided in Denver and 7.7 percent in Arapahoe. Other counties with significant numbers of African Americans in the state include El Paso with 6.8 percent (2004); Adams with 3.2 percent (2004); Pueblo with 1.9 percent (2000); Boulder, 0.9 percent (2000); Fremont, 5.3 percent (2000); and Douglas with 1.0 percent (2000).

With respect to health outcomes, African Americans suffer the greatest degree of health disparities both nationally and in Colorado. According to *Racial and Ethnic Health Disparities in Colorado 2005*, a report by the Colorado Department of Public Health and the Environment Office of Health Disparities, African Americans have the highest overall death rate and shortest life expectancy in the state. Additionally, the African American community has the highest mortality and morbidity rates when compared to other ethnic and racial groups, specifically in the areas of chronic disease, communicable disease, injury, maternal health, and child health.

A 2002 *Statewide Needs Assessment: Report on African American Populations in Colorado* submitted by the Colorado Minority Health Forum and authored by Carla King & Associates, Inc., further detailed that in 2000, the median income for all African Americans in Colorado was $37,798, while for Colorado residents, the median income was $40,853. The report noted that for all Colorado residents, the poverty rate was 8 percent and for black Colorado residents it was 28 percent. In 2003, the high-school graduation rate was 49 percent. Poverty and low socioeconomic status have burdened the African American population with a historical disadvantage of unequally distributed risks and opportunities that largely contribute to health disparities.

Notable African Americans

Ayers, Perry (dates unknown)

Perry Ayers, his brother Oye Oginga, and a small contingent of artists and art lovers created and developed the Denver Black Arts Festival in 1986. The first festival occurred in 1987. It rained for two days straight. By 1990, the crowd reached 60,000. In 1991, more than 100,000 people attended. It is one of the premier festivals in the nation.

Beckwourth, James (1798–1866)

Born in 1798, James Beckwourth was a mountain man, fur trapper, explorer, frontiersman, army scout, Crow chief, and cofounder of the city of Pueblo, Colorado. He discovered Beckwourth Pass in California, was a scout for the Union Army, and later a storekeeper in Denver. In 1864, Beckwourth was a guide for John M. Chivington during the Sand Creek Massacre and testified against him.

Brown, Clara (1803–1885)

Born in Tennessee in 1803, Clara Brown was sold and separated from her family at age 35. Freed in 1859, Brown moved to Denver, then to Central City. By 1866, she had saved $10,000, and searched for her family. A stained-glass window in the capitol and a chair in the Central City Opera House commemorate Brown's life.

Douglass, Frederick, Jr. (1842–1892) and Douglass, Lewis H. (1840–1908)

Lewis H. Douglass and Frederick Douglass Jr., sons of the famous abolitionist Frederick Douglass, served as sergeant majors in the Civil War before migrating to Denver. The Douglass Undertaking Company, located at 2745 Welton Street, was known as "The Old Reliable." The Douglass brothers also created the first black school in Denver and ran a restaurant on California Street.

Fard, Jeff S. (1965–)

Jeff S. Fard, a.k.a. Brother Jeff, is a writer, poet, cultural critic, community organizer, and entrepreneur. In demand on the national lecture circuit, Brother Jeff speaks to youth, students, community organizations, and healthcare professionals about cultural identity, history, diversity, self-empowerment, community building, economic development, health disparities, and the arts.

Ford, Barney Lancelot (1822–1902)

Barney Lancelot Ford was born in 1822. After escaping to Chicago via the Underground Railroad, Ford married Julia Lyoni, and the couple arrived in Colorado during the gold rush. In Denver, Ford set up a barbershop. He also fought against Colorado statehood until African Americans gained the right to vote, and served with William N. Byers and John Evans on the board of the Dime Savings Bank.

Groff, Peter C. (1963–)

Peter C. Groff is the first African American state Senate president in Colorado history and only the third in U.S. history. Senator Groff is the highest-ranking African American official in Colorado. He is the founder and executive director of the University of Denver Center for African American Policy. Groff became Colorado's sixth African American state senator when he was appointed to the Colorado State Senate on February 10, 2003.

Hackley, Edwin H. (1859–1940)

Edwin H. Hackley graduated law school at Michigan in 1883. After moving to Denver in 1884, he passed the Colorado Bar, becoming one of Colorado's first lawyers. Hackley organized the *Colorado Statesman* but sold his interests to G. F. Franklin. His wife Azalia was the first African American graduate from the College of Music, University of Denver, in 1899. She was also a playwright, poet, and musician.

Harris, Rosalind "Bee" (1950–)

Rosalind "Bee" Harris is the founder, publisher, owner, and art director of the Denver *Urban Spectrum* newspaper. In providing a voice for the community, the *Urban Spectrum* has been "spreading the news about people of color" for more than

20 years, attracting 60,000 readers every month. Bee Harris is an active member in the community, with memberships and organizational affiliations.

Jackson, Oliver Toussaint (1862–1948)

Born in 1862 in Ohio, Oliver Toussaint Jackson, who was inspired by Booker T. Washington's *Up from Slavery*, founded and established the black town of Dearfield on May 5, 1910. The first winter in Dearfield, only two of the seven families had wooden houses and the suffering was intense.

Love, Nat (1854–1921)

Cowboy Nat Love earned the title "Deadwood Dick" after winning a riding, roping, and shooting contest in Deadwood, South Dakota, on July 4, 1876. Love moved to Denver, marrying his second wife on August 22, 1889. One year later, he became a Pullman porter for the Denver and Rio Grande Railroad. In 1907, Love published his autobiography, *The Life and Adventures of Nat Love.*

McClain, Thomas Ernest (1876–1949)

Dr. Thomas Ernest McClain was Colorado's first African American licensed dentist. After attending dental school at Meharry Medical College of Walden University in Nashville, Tennessee, he moved to Denver in 1907 with his wife Lafayette L. Stewart McClain. He was a member of Zion Baptist Church, Masons, and the Mountain Lodge No. 39 of Denver.

McDaniel, Hattie (1895–1952)

Hattie McDaniel lived in Denver, attended East High School, and toured with her family's traveling Baptist tent show. By the 1920s, she joined Morrison's Orchestra, toured the Pantages and Orpheum vaudeville circuit, and performed with the Melony Hounds on Denver's radio station KOA. She was the first African American to win an Academy Award in 1939 for best supporting actress for her portrayal of Mammy in *Gone with the Wind.*

Noel, Rachel B. (1918–2008)

Rachel B. Noel was the first African American woman to serve in public office in Colorado, elected to the seven-member school board of the Denver public schools. Noel introduced the Noel Resolution, requiring total integration by December 1968. Public opposition did not discourage her. Although the new school board overturned the resolution in 1969, the suit to integrate Denver schools was eventually upheld by the U.S. Supreme Court. Noel was an associate professor at Metropolitan State College of Denver from 1969 to 1980, and the first female department chair of the African and African American

Actress Hattie McDaniel seated at a piano, 1952. (Library of Congress)

Studies Department from 1971 to 1980, when she retired.

Robinson, Cleo Parker (c. 1948–)

Cleo Parker Robinson, the executive artistic director of the Cleo Parker Robinson Dance Ensemble, is a Denver native and renowned choreographer. Overcoming nephritis, kidney failure, a heart attack, and ulcers in childhood, Robinson received formal dance training at Colorado Women's College, performed with the Alvin Ailey Dance Center, Arthur Mitchell's Dance Theatre of Harlem, and established the Cleo Parker Robinson Dance Ensemble in 1970.

Stewart, Paul W. (1925–)

Paul W. Stewart founded the Black American West Museum. As a child, Paul W. Stewart loved to watch westerns and play cowboys and Indians, always playing the Indian because he was told, "There is no such thing as a Black cowboy." It was not until the early 1960s while visiting a cousin in Colorado, that Stewart saw a black cowboy. Stewart moved to Denver and practiced his trade as a barber. His clients shared stories of their lives as African American miners, cowboys, homesteaders, fur traders, and pioneers as he cut their hair.

Vason, Lu (1937–)

Lu Vason is president and producer of the Bill Pickett Invitational Rodeo, the only traveling black rodeo in the country. After attending the Grand Daddy of Rodeos in Cheyenne, Vason thought rodeo "was exciting but lacked one thing, black cowboys." He organized the first Bill Pickett Invitational Rodeo in 1984 in Denver. Today, nine rodeos are held in city arenas and fairgrounds across the country.

Webb, Wellington E. (1941–)

President Jimmy Carter appointed Wellington E. Webb as Region Eight director for the U.S.

Former Mayor Wellington E. Webb delivers his inauguration speech after being sworn in for his third term as Denver mayor, July 19, 1999, in Civic Center Park. (AP/Wide World Photos)

Department of Health and Human Services in 1977. In 1981, Colorado Governor Richard Lamm appointed Webb to his cabinet as executive director of the Department of Regulatory Agencies. By 1987, Webb was elected Denver city auditor, where his track record paved the way for his successful and historic mayoral bid in 1991.

Webb, Wilma (1943–)

Wilma Webb was elected Democratic committeewoman in 1970. By 1980, she finished State

Representative King Trimble's term in House District 8, introducing a controversial bill to establish a statewide holiday on Martin Luther King Jr.'s birthday, which was approved in 1984. Wilma Webb coined the term "Marade" in 1986 after Governor Lamm signed House Bill 1201 making Martin Luther King Jr.'s birthday a legal holiday in Colorado. The term "Marade" is composed of two words: March means demonstrate and Parade means celebrate. The Marade gathers at the Dr. Martin Luther King Jr.'s I Have A Dream Monument in Denver's City Park and ends at the capitol. Wilma Webb is married to former Denver Mayor Wellington Webb. She is the mother of four, including Denver's Clerk and Recorder Stephanie O'Malley.

Cultural Contributions

The cultural character of black Colorado from the first arrival of African Americans to the present has always been embodied in the pioneering spirit and rich traditions of African American culture. In creating a unique cultural identity following the exodus to Nicodemus, Kansas, African Americans who migrated further west, particularly to Colorado, validated their culture as a response to oppression through creativity. This in turn helped to secure their place and participation in American history. These acts of empowering and reaffirming their cultural identity were manifested through their cultural contributions in the making of the West. The gold rush attracted a varied and experienced African American population.

Northerners, southerners, easterners, free and enslaved men, women and children who migrated as janitors, porters, store clerks, barbers, drivers, intellectuals, hotel owners, barbers, cooks, cowboys, nurses, laundresses, and educated and uneducated made Denver their home and created self-help and cultural organizations. They often sought city jobs, since wages were high and the work was more dependable than prospecting.

Although they were part of the mining rush to Colorado, most were employed in towns. Black men and women took whatever jobs were available. The Denver Horse Railroad Company, in 1871, for instance, was the first to make connection to the Five Points area, where the majority of African Americans resided. The neighborhood was Denver's first streetcar suburb with connection from Auraria, through downtown, to the final destination of Five Points. By 1881, the Five Points name came to be used because the signs on the front of the streetcars were not big enough to hold all of the street names. The intersection brought together 27th Street, Washington Street, East 26th Avenue, and Welton Street. Welton Center was tried as an alternative name, but Five Points just seemed to stick. By 1886, Denver's first electric rail line was opened. The 15th Street line, which was closed in 1888, ran in downtown Denver between Larimer and Tremont streets.

Although short-lived, this line set the stage for a trolley system that would consist of 156 miles of electric track by 1900. African Americans played a pivotal role in the development of this project. In addition African Americans were lured by success stories, where few prospectors found instant wealth and the glamour of the gold fields. Early laws of the Colorado Territory dictated that African Americans would not be permitted to stake mining claims. However, African Americans would hire white lawyers to make their claims, usually for a 20 percent commission. This was later reversed after the area became a state in 1876. Adventurous African American frontier women emigrated to the West and helped "civilize" the Wild West by creating churches, social groups, and schools and providing community services.

They also supplied the needed skills as cooks, nannies, housekeepers, nursemaids, laundresses, and shopkeepers. These skills helped to ensure that an African American culture was forming as

African American women followed their husbands and fathers out west to work side by side with them as miners, farmers, and cowhands. A final set of cultural contributions made by African Americans of Colorado, in both Colorado Springs and Denver, unfolded through their religious and secular practices.

A number of church organizations were founded by African Americans in both cities, as many of them expected to attend religious services, a fundamental belief system in African culture. The same holds true for African American entertainers who were either Colorado-born or who frequented and showcased their skills as cultural creators in many of the venues made available to them and/or they created.

Bibliography

Abbott, Carl, Stephen Leonard, and David McComb. *Colorado: A History of the Centennial State.* Niwot: University Press of Colorado, 1994.

Armitage, Susan. " 'The Mountains Were Free and We Loved Them': Dr. Ruth Flowers of Boulder, Colorado." In Quintard Taylor and Shirley Ann Wilson Moore, eds., *African American Women Confront the West: 1600–2000.* Norman: University of Oklahoma Press, 2003, pp. 165–177.

Baker, Roger. *Clara: An Ex-Slave in Gold Rush Colorado.* Central City: Black Hawk Publishing, 2003.

Ball, Wilbur. *Black Pioneers of the Prairie.* Eaton, CO: W. P. Ball, 1988.

Barefield, Ollie Solomon. *Negro Pioneers in Colorado.* Greeley: Colorado State College, 1966.

Beckwourth, James Pierson. *The Life and Adventures of James P. Beckwourth as Told to Thomas D. Bonner.* Lincoln: University of Nebraska Press, 1972. Reprint of 1856 edition.

Berwanger, Eugene H. "William J. Harding: Colorado Spokesman for Racial Justice, 1863–1873. " *Colorado Magazine* 52, no. 1 (Winter 1975): 52–65.

Berwanger, Eugene H. *The Frontier against Slavery: Western Anti-Negro Prejudice and the Slavery Extension Controversy.* Urbana: University of Illinois Press, 1967.

Billington, Monroe Lee, and Roger D. Hardaway, eds. *African Americans on the Western Frontier.* Niwot: University Press of Colorado, 1998.

Bond, Anne Wainstein. "Buffalo Soldiers at Fort Garland." *Colorado Heritage* (Spring 1996): 28–29.

Bruyn, Kathleen. *"Aunt" Clara Brown: Story of a Black Pioneer.* Boulder, CO: Pruett, 1970.

Colorado Department of Public Health and Environment, Health Statistics Section, Colorado Health Information Dataset: *Leading Causes of Death, Death Rates and Age-Adjusted Death Rates, Colorado 2002.* www.cdphe.state.co.us/cohid/deathgeo.html.

Colorado Department of Public Health and Environment, Health Statistics Section, Colorado Vital Statistics Dataset: *Life Expectancy by Race/Ethnicity and Gender, Colorado 2002.* www.cdphe.state.co.us/cohid/deathgeo.html.

Dickson, Lynda F. "Lifting as We Climb: African American Women's Clubs in Denver, 1880–1925." *Essays in Colorado History*, no. 13 (1992): 69–98.

Gwaltney, William W. "The Making of Buffalo Soldiers West." *Colorado Heritage* (Spring 1996): 45–48.

Gwaltney, William W., and Thomas Welle. "By Force of Arms: The Buffalo Soldiers of Colorado." *Colorado Heritage* (Spring 1996): 30–34.

Holley, John Stokes. *The Invisible People of the Pikes Peak Region: An Afro-American Chronicle.* Colorado Springs: The Friends of the Pikes Peak Library and the Friends of the Colorado Springs Pioneers Museum, 1990.

How Minority Youth Are Being Left Behind by the Graduation Rate Crisis. A Report of the Civil Rights Project at Harvard University. Cambridge, MA: Harvard University Press, 2004.

Katz, William Loren. *The Black West: A Documentary and Pictorial History of the African American Role in the Westward Expansion of the United States.* New York: Harlem Moon, 2005.

Leckie, William H. *Buffalo Soldiers: A Narrative of the Black Cavalry in the West.* Norman: University of Oklahoma Press, 1967.

Lohse, J. B. *Justina Ford: Medical Pioneer.* Palmer Lake, CO: Filter Press, 2004.

Love, Nat. *The Life and Adventure of Nat Love.* Lincoln: University of Nebraska Press, 1995.

Mauck, Laura. *Five Points Neighborhood of Denver.* Chicago: Arcadia Publishing, 2001.

McGue, D. B. "John Taylor—Slave-Born Colorado Pioneer." *Colorado Magazine* 18 (September 1941): 161–168.

Negro Historical Association of Colorado Springs. *Black Settlers of the Pikes Peak Region, 1850–1999.* Colorado Springs: Colorado Springs Historical Society, 2000.

Noel, T. J. *Denver Landmarks and Historic District: A Pictorial Guide.* Boulder: University Press of Colorado, 1996.

Painter, Nell. *Creating Black Americans: African American History and Its Meanings, 1619 to the Present.* New York: Oxford University Press, 2007.

Purdue, Fray Marcos, and Paul W. Stewart, eds. *Westward Soul.* Denver, CO: Black American West Museum, Inc., 1982.

Simmons, R. Laurie, and Thomas H. Simmons. *Denver Neighborhood History Project, 1993–94: Five Points Neighborhood.* Denver, CO: Front Range Research Associates, 1995.

Stephens, Ronald J., La Wanna M. Larson, and the Black American West Museum. *Images of America, African Americans of Denver.* Chicago: Arcadia, 2008.

Stewart, Paul W., and Yvonne Ponce Wallace. *Black Cowboys.* Denver, CO: Phillips Publishing, 1986.

Talmadge, Marian, and Iris Gilmore. *Barney Ford, Black Baron.* New York: Dodd, Mead, 1973.

Taylor, Quintard. "They Went West: African-American Pioneers Made Their Way to the Western Frontier Lured by the Promise of Adventure, Opportunity, and Freedom." *American Legacy* (Fall 2001): 41–54.

Taylor, Quintard. *In Search of the Racial Frontier: African Americans in the American West, 1528–1990.* New York: W. W. Norton and Company, 1998.

Wayne, George H. "Negro Migration and Colonization in Colorado, 1870–1920. " *Journal of the West* 15, no. 1 (January 1976): 102–120.

Wilson, Elinor. *James Beckwourth: Black Mountain Man and War Chief of the Crows.* Norman: University of Oklahoma Press, 1972.

CONNECTICUT

Gladys L. Knight

Chronology

1629	The first enslaved Africans arrive in what is now Connecticut.
1633	The Dutch erect a fort, the "House of Hope," near where the city of Hartford now stands. The first English settlers, Puritans from Massachusetts, settle in Windsor.
1636	Thomas Hooker and others establish the Connecticut Colony.
1639	Connecticut ratifies its first constitution.
1643	Connecticut joins the New England Confederation.
1650	The colony of Connecticut legalizes slavery.
1660	Connecticut enacts a law prohibiting blacks from serving in the colonial militia.
1662	John Winthrop obtains an English charter, and the New Haven Colony merges with the Connecticut Colony.
1678	The slave population of the colony numbers fewer than 30 people.
1686	Killing a slave is declared a capital offense in Connecticut.
1690	Blacks and Native Americans in Connecticut are prohibited from traveling beyond town borders without permission.
1703	Black slaves are prohibited from drinking in taverns and inns without permission from their masters.
1717	The colony declares that former slave owners are financially responsible for slaves they free.
1717	A Connecticut law prohibits blacks from owning property.
1717	Black slaves in Connecticut are regarded as "property" for the purposes of taxation and voting, but as "persons" in court, with the right to make contracts, to bring suit, and to trial by jury.
1723	A curfew of 9:00 p.m. is established for black and Native American slaves. Violation of the curfew is punishable by a whipping for the servant and a fine for the master.
1730	A law stipulates whippings for slaves convicted of slander. Slaves are allowed to defend themselves.
1740s	Connecticut experiences a religious revival known as the "Great Awakening."
1749	A colonial survey estimates a population of 1,000 blacks in Connecticut.
1750	A comprehensive act reinforces laws governing enslaved and free blacks and Native Americans that severely restricts their freedoms.
1756	The black population of Connecticut, both slave and free, numbers 3,019 people, less than 3 percent of the total population of the colony.

1762	The black population of Connecticut is 4,590.
1774	The importation of Native American and black slaves is banned. The black population of Connecticut is 5,085.
1775	General George Washington reverses an earlier decision to prevent free and enslaved blacks from serving in the Continental Army; Connecticut supplies the army with one predominantly black unit.
1781	Six blacks volunteer to serve in the Meigs Regiment during the Revolutionary War.
1784	Connecticut enacts a gradual emancipation law that declares that children of enslaved blacks born after March 1, 1784, be granted freedom at age 25.
1788	Connecticut ratifies the U.S. Constitution; the slave trade is outlawed in the state.
1790–1840	The Abolition Movement in Connecticut becomes increasingly active.
1790	The white population in the state is 232,374. The black slave population is 2,759. The free black population is 2,801.
1790	The Connecticut Society for the Promotion of Freedom and the Relief of Persons Unlawfully Held in Bondage, the first abolitionist organization in the state, is formed.
1792	Connecticut prohibits the transportation of slaves to other states for the purpose of selling them.
1797	The Gradual Emancipation Act is modified so that any black child born after August 1, 1797, is granted freedom at the age of 21. The laws enacted in 1750 concerning blacks are abolished; these laws concerned restricted travel, curfew, and harsh punishments for theft.
1800	The white population is 244,721. The black slave population is 951. The free black population is 5,330.
1810	The black slave population of Connecticut is 310.
1818	Connecticut's new constitution denies blacks the right to vote.
1820	Due to Connecticut's gradual emancipation law, the number of black slaves remaining in the state is 97; the free black population is 7,844.
1820	The African Ecclesiastical Society, the first black church in Connecticut, is established.
1828	The Cross Street AME Zion Church is founded in Middletown.
1830–1860	The Underground Railroad is active in Connecticut during this period.
1830	A law legalizes segregated schools in the state.
1833	Prudence Crandall opens her previously all-white girls' school in Canterbury to African Americans, but white opposition eventually forces her to close the school.

1839–1841	After being held in jail in Connecticut, Cinqué and other Africans who had been kidnapped from their homelands are returned to Africa in the aftermath of the *Amistad* trial, adjudicated by the U.S. District Court for the District of Connecticut and then the U.S. Supreme Court. This case was a major victory for the Abolition Movement.
1840	The black slave population of Connecticut is 17. The free black population is 8,105.
1848	The black slave population in the state is only 12 when slavery is abolished.
1850	The free black population of Connecticut is 7,693.
1852	*Uncle Tom's Cabin*, written by Harriet Beecher Stowe, a Connecticut native, is published.
1859	John Brown, an abolitionist and a Connecticut native, leads the infamous antislavery revolt at Harper's Ferry in Virginia.
1860	Abraham Lincoln, the Republican presidential candidate in 1860, visits several cities in the state.
1861–1865	55,000 men from Connecticut serve in the Union Army during the Civil War, including the 16th and 29th Connecticut Volunteers, two all-black regiments. Black Connecticut residents also join the famous 54th Massachusetts Regiment.
1865	(*May 4*) Connecticut ratifies the Thirteenth Amendment to the U.S. Constitution abolishing slavery.
1866	(*June 25*) Connecticut becomes the first state to ratify the Fourteenth Amendment to the U.S. Constitution guaranteeing equal protection to blacks.
1869	(*May 19*) Connecticut ratifies the Fifteenth Amendment to the U.S. Constitution extending the right to vote to blacks.
1869	The first of several all-black companies, the Wilkins Guard, is established.
1874	Edward Alexander Bouchet is the first African American to graduate from Yale University.
1876	(*May*) Edward Alexander Bouchet earns a Ph.D. from Yale University, becoming the first African American to receive a Ph.D. from an American university; he is also believed to be the first African American to be elected to Phi Beta Kappa.
1896	The U.S. Supreme Court rules that racial segregation is constitutional in *Plessy v. Ferguson*.
1900–1940	Whites comprise 98 percent of the state's population. The black population is 2 percent.
1905	The State General Assembly adopts an act ordering full and equal service in all places of public accommodation.
1915–1930	The black population of the state is greatly increased by migrations from the South.

1943	The State General Assembly establishes an Inter-Racial Commission, the nation's first statutory civil rights agency.
1947	The Fair Employment Practices Act prohibits job discrimination.
1948	President Harry S. Truman issues Executive Order 9981, which desegregates the U.S. military.
1949	The Connecticut State Guard is desegregated.
1950	Blacks comprise 3 percent of the state's population.
1954	In *Brown v. Board of Education*, the U.S. Supreme Court rules that segregation in U.S. schools is unconstitutional.
1955	John Clark becomes the first black member of the Hartford City Council.
1960	Blacks comprise 4 percent of the state's population.
1962	Constitution Plaza in Hartford displaces black and Italian sections of the city.
1963	*(March 20)* Connecticut ratifies the Twenty-fourth Amendment to the U.S. Constitution abolishing the poll tax.
1964	The federal Civil Rights Act of 1964 eliminates segregation in public accommodations, public facilities, and employment.
1965	The Voting Rights Act of 1965 eliminates discriminatory practices that restrict black suffrage.
1966	266 African American students are transported to predominately white schools in Hartford.
1967–1969	Race riots erupt in Bridgeport, Hartford, Middletown, New Britain, New Haven, New London, Norwalk, Stamford, and Waterbury.
1968–1969	Demonstrations and racial violence erupt at the University of Connecticut, Trinity College, Wesleyan University, and Yale University.
1970	Blacks comprise 6 percent of Connecticut's population.
1976	A monument commemorating African Americans who served in the Meigs Regiment is erected.
1980	Blacks comprise 7 percent of the state's population.
1981	Thirman Milner becomes the first African American mayor of Hartford.
1981	The Manchester Interracial Council is established.
1989–1996	The *Sheff v. O'Neill* lawsuit challenges segregated conditions in Hartford public schools. The Connecticut Supreme Court rules that racially segregated schools in Hartford violate the state's constitution.

1990   Blacks comprise 8.3 percent of Connecticut's population. The cities with the largest black populations are Hartford (54,338), Bridgeport (37,684), and New Haven (47,157). The cities with the smallest black populations are West Hartford (1,310), Bristol (1,263), and Greenwich (1,245).

1990   Gary Franks becomes the first African American elected to the U.S. House of Representatives from Connecticut and the first black Republican in the House in 50 years.

1991   Civil rights activist Jesse Jackson stages the "Connecticut March to Rebuild America."

1997   The African-American Affairs Commission (AAAC) of Connecticut, a semiautonomous state agency, is established to promote the economic, political, and educational well-being of the state's African American community.

1998   Gary Franks makes an unsuccessful bid for election to the U.S. Senate from Connecticut.

2000   According to the U.S. Census, blacks comprise 9 percent of the total population of Connecticut.

2008   A Comprehensive Management Plan to help integrate public schools in Hartford is established.

2008   Democrat Barack Obama, the first African American nominee for president of a major party, carries Connecticut with 61 percent of the vote.

Historical Overview

Colonial Period to the Start of the Twentieth Century

The life and times of African Americans in Connecticut is well documented in fiction, scholarly works, and Web sites. Numerous monuments and historical buildings stand as lasting reminders of the interconnected history of the state's African and European descendents. Indeed, though the black population has historically been (and continues to be) small compared to other states, Connecticut harbors a wealth of local black history.

Blacks appeared in Connecticut as early as the first half of the seventeenth century. More than likely, slaves were employed by Dutch and English settlers after their arrival in Connecticut in 1633. It was not until 1662 (following the development and merger of three separate English colonies—Saybrook, Connecticut, and New Haven) that Connecticut took its first steps as a colony incorporated by the English. Records show that six years later, there were fewer than 30 blacks in the region. By the eve of the American Revolution, the black population had increased to 5,085. In that same year, 1774, the importation of black slaves was banned. Although slaves were prohibited from owning and carrying weapons, numerous black slaves took up arms during the American Revolution. The call for black men to fight in the war was initiated by John Murray, royal governor of Virginia, who offered slaves their freedom in exchange for joining the royal forces. Shortly thereafter, the Connecticut colonists made the same offer to blacks. Black soldiers throughout the colony enlisted. The names of many of the men who served with distinction in the war are etched on memorials. The lives of black soldiers are explored in books such as *Connecticut's Black Soldiers 1775–1783* (1973).

After the American Revolution, the slave population in the state decreased markedly. In addition to the fact that slaves who fought in the war were granted freedom, the passage of several pivotal pieces of legislation was a major contributing factor to the reduced slave population. Between 1774 and 1788, legislation banned slave importation, prevented the recapture of runaway slaves, and supported gradual emancipation. Although such legislation helped to gather momentum towards its abolition, slavery was still lawful in the state.

Compared with most American states, the slave population in Connecticut was small. In 1790, only two states had slave populations under 1,000: New Hampshire with 157 slaves, and Rhode Island with 958. Although Connecticut's slave population exceeded those figures with a total of 2,759 slaves, the slave populations in Delaware (8,887 slaves), New Jersey (11,423 slaves), and New York (21,193 slaves) put this figure into perspective. By comparison, southern states such as North Carolina, South Carolina, and Virginia had each enslaved over 100,000 blacks by that time, demonstrating that the South was much more dependent on the slave system than the North.

Slavery did not take deep root in Connecticut for various reasons. Connecticut's rocky soil was not conducive to producing commercial crops. Thus the agricultural sector was not extensive enough to sustain a large-scale system requiring a slave-labor force. However, Connecticut did profit from slavery in other ways, by forming ivory-finishing businesses, selling food to support slaves in the West Indies, and selling slaves to other states, where the demand for slaves was much higher. Over time, Connecticut's inclination for industrialization increasingly made the slave system unpopular and unnecessary.

However, slavery in Connecticut was no less turbulent because the slave population was lower than in most states. Any black person could be indiscriminately sold to anyone within or outside of the state, whether or not that meant being separated from family members. Black slaves were subject to numerous laws that controlled their lives. Slave laws, among other things, imposed curfews, restricted travel beyond the periphery of the slaveholder's property and banned alcohol consumption (unless the slaveholder granted written permission), and established punishments such as whipping for myriad offenses. Generally, slaves were not allowed to own property or carry arms.

Slave life was well documented in Connecticut. Former slaves Venture Smith and James Mars both wrote memoirs. Venture Smith, who was born in 1729 in Guinea, West Africa, was the son of an African chief. He was one of three African youths stolen from his homeland in the mid-eighteenth century and sold to Connecticut slaveholders. His book, ambitiously titled *A Narrative of the Life and Adventures of Venture, a Native of Africa, but Resident above Sixty Years in the United States of America, Related by Himself*, was first published in 1798.

Mars never saw his ancestral homeland. He was born (in 1790) into slavery in Canaan, Connecticut. His book, *The Life of James Mars*, was published in 1864. After having obtained his freedom in 1815, he became a prominent member in black communities in Connecticut and Massachusetts, where he actively supported black suffrage and other causes. The slave narratives of Smith, Mars, and many others chronicle the details of black life in slavery and in freedom. They offer poignant accounts of otherwise untold tales and are a significant contribution to American literature. These narratives underscore the inhumanity of slavery and the ever-stalwart opposition to it. Slave narratives were frequently promoted by abolitionists during the antebellum years.

The abolition movement in Connecticut did not pick up steam until the end of the century (previous efforts, waged in particular by Quakers between 1730 and 1750, were much smaller in scale). In 1790, the Connecticut Society for the Promotion of Freedom and the Relief of Persons Unlawfully Held in Bondage became the first abolitionist organization to be established in the state. The formation of this organization launched bigger and stronger efforts toward abolishing slavery. Fiery, outspoken abolitionists whittled away, bit by bit, at the slave system, primarily by speechmaking and lobbying. However, contrary to popular belief, the state was not unanimous in its support of the abolishment of slavery. Indeed, abolitionists risked intimidation and violence for their brazen opposition. Free blacks in Connecticut also supported the abolition movement. Some blacks joined predominately white organizations; many more opted to form separate institutions.

During the early part of the nineteenth century, free African Americans in Connecticut exerted more—albeit still limited—autonomy in their lives. In 1800, the free black population was 5,330, greatly surpassing the slave population, which was 951. Whether compelled by the desire for racial solidarity or forced by social conventions and racism, free blacks in Connecticut tended to live in racially segregated communities. Though they were denied many privileges (for example, they were limited to elementary education and low-status, subservient jobs), within their own communities, black life thrived. Blacks founded their own churches, schools, and businesses. The African Ecclesiastical Society, established in 1820 in New Haven, was the first of numerous black churches to crop up during the first half of the century. One of the most flourishing black communities was in Stamford. Stamford's black population was less than 200, but it included many entrepreneurs. African Americans owned and managed such businesses as a restaurant, dressmaking shop, and coal yard. But it was still a frustrating period, with many setbacks,

as the lives of free blacks in Connecticut were marred not only by discriminatory laws and practices in their own state, but by the pernicious growth of slavery elsewhere in the nation.

As the slave population decreased in Connecticut and other northern states, the influx of slaves in the South rapidly climbed. The continuation and escalation of slavery confounded blacks and white abolitionists, who sought new, creative means to undermine the unjust but deeply entrenched system. Between 1830 and 1860, whites and blacks organized the Underground Railroad. The Underground Railroad was a clandestine operation that facilitated the escape of black slaves, particularly from the South, to the North. Myriad routes ran through Connecticut, leading to free black settlements within the state and further north to Canada. Many well-known abolitionists and lesser-known locals participated in the Underground Railroad in a number of ways: sheltering runaways, funding operations, providing food and clothes, and helping navigate slaves along their journey to freedom. In their own communities, blacks welcomed those fugitive slaves who opted to stay in Connecticut, helping them with the transition toward their new lives.

One of the milestones in the history of abolitionism was the *Amistad* trial, which took place in Connecticut. The *Amistad* was a Spanish vessel, en route to the New World with a cargo of kidnapped West Africans in 1839. Sengbe Pieh (later known as Joseph Cinqué, or, simply, Cinqué) was a man from the Mende society who led a shipboard rebellion. Slaves and crew members were counted among those murdered in the aftermath of Cinqué's revolt and subsequent takeover of the vessel. The surviving crew navigated the vessel to New York, rather than to Africa, where the slaves had wanted to return.

The *Amistad* trial was brought to the attention of abolitionists, who responded with vigor. Abolitionists formed the Amistad Committee, which garnered publicity, support, and money to

Death of Capt. Ferrer, the Captain of the Amistad, July, 1839.

Don Jose Ruiz and Don Pedro Montez, of the Island of Cuba, having purchased fifty-three slaves at Havana, recently imported from Africa, put them on board the Amistad, Capt. Ferrer, in order to transport them to Principe, another port on the Island of Cuba. After being out from Havana about four days, the African captives on board, in order to obtain their freedom, and return to Africa, armed themselves with cane knives, and rose upon the Captain and crew of the vessel. Capt. Ferrer and the cook of the vessel were killed; two of the crew escaped; Ruiz and Montez were made prisoners.

Africans aboard the *Amistad* kill Captain Ferrer. The captives that survived the revolt won their case in the U.S. Supreme Court and returned as free men to Africa. (John W. Barber, *A History of the Amistad Captives*, 1840)

fund the slaves' defense. In 1841, the U.S. District Court of Connecticut ruled in favor of the slaves. For the abolitionists, this was an enormous triumph for their cause and an unprecedented win for justice for the slaves aboard the *Amistad*, who were returned to Africa. The trial has been commemorated by a statue of Cinqué, erected near the City Hall building in New Haven, Connecticut, several exhibits, and a blockbuster film, *Amistad* (1997).

In the wake of this high-profile event, Connecticut experienced further progress in terms of the slave issue. By 1848, only 12 black slaves remained in the state. In that same year, Connecticut abolished slavery. In 1852, Harriet Beecher Stowe, who was born in Litchfield, Connecticut, added fuel to the blazing fire of the national abolition movement with the publication of her seminal book, *Uncle Tom's Cabin*. This fictional work, which was based on the story of a black slave, underscored the immorality of slavery and promoted the abolitionist doctrine. The book enjoyed widespread popularity and increased antislavery support amid escalating tensions between the North and the South. In the South, the dominant white society vigorously defended its slave-based way of life. With no reconciliation

in sight, the North and South went to war in 1861.

African Americans were counted among the soldiers on both the Union and Confederate sides of the war. African Americans in Connecticut joined several Union troops. All-black regiments, such as the 16th and 29th Connecticut Volunteers, were headed by whites. Black Connecticuters also joined the 54th Massachusetts Volunteer Regiment. The heroism of black soldiers changed the perception that many whites had of blacks. The valor of the 54th Regiment in particular spawned numerous memorials, including Saint-Gauden's famous monument, a lithograph entitled "The Storming of Ft. Wagner," and the gripping film *Glory* (1989). *Glory* cast headlining actors such as Matthew Broderick, Denzel Washington, and Morgan Freeman. Washington won an Academy Award for his supporting role as Private Silas Trip.

In the aftermath of the Union victory, the federal government launched monumental human rights legislation. The Thirteenth Amendment abolished slavery throughout the nation. The Fourteenth Amendment guaranteed equal protection to blacks, and the Fifteenth Amendment provided voting rights to blacks.

In the post-war era, African American Connecticuters experienced seemingly colossal progress. Veterans of the war joined the first ever—albeit short-lived—all-black military companies. In 1868, a law integrated public schools in the state. In 1874, Edward Bouchet became the first African American to graduate from Yale. And, in 1905, the General Assembly adopted a public accommodations act ordering full and equal service in all places of public accommodation. However, this act was not always enforced, and blacks in general were frequently subjected to contemptuous treatment.

Amid the still-extant racial tensions and social oppression, black life proliferated. With greater access to education and other opportunities, some blacks in the state enjoyed middle-class status. They owned more businesses, attended black churches, and joined all-black social organizations. New London, Connecticut, offered at least a dozen social organizations, such as the Ambassadors Club, the Colored Men's Democratic Club, the Colored Women's Cultural Club, and the New London Sextet. These organizations demonstrated the commitment of African Americans to their individual and collective advancement, cultural heritage, and civic participation.

A small segment of the black population in the state, particularly those whose ancestry could be traced to long-standing descendants of free blacks, constituted the black bourgeoisie. With social standing (among black circles), position, economic mobility, and access to more modern amenities, the burgeoning black bourgeoisie contrasted sharply with lower-class blacks. Lower-class blacks lived largely in rural settings and retained more African traditions than their wealthier counterparts. With the inevitable urbanization of Connecticut, impoverished blacks would increasingly populate ghettoes in the cities, where they competed with immigrants for housing and employment.

World War I and World War II

Major migrations of African Americans into Connecticut occurred during World War I and World War II, as the wartime economies increased the demand for workers in the manufacturing industries in the North, which lured blacks from the South. This period also saw the flowering of black culture and life in urban areas within the state.

In northern states like Connecticut, the absence of abrasive laws and wanton racial violence made it easy for industrial companies seeking black workers. The Urban League, an organization established in 1910 in New York City by an interracial group of leaders, helped draw numerous blacks to Connecticut for employment. Some black workers stayed; others, such as college students, worked only during the summer months. Hartford was one of several cities that grew considerably as a result of black migration. At the start of the nineteenth century, the black population in Hartford was 1,887. By 1930, the population had grown to 6,510.

The first half of the twentieth century saw an outgrowth of densely populated cities with large black communities, thus changing the cultural climate of previously white-dominated community centers. The cultural climate was greatly influenced by southern culture and national developments in urban African American popular culture. The aroma of southern delicacies wafted through black residential areas. Some restaurants offered foods that catered to the newly transplanted residents. Racially segregated social clubs offered popular black music, such as jazz and blues, and churches with all-black congregations grew. Folklore, fashion trends, hair styles, and vernacular reflected Connecticut's own cultural renaissance. (Harlem, New York, was the home of the most well-known black renaissance, known as the Harlem Renaissance, which spanned the 1920s and 1930s.)

A small jazz ensemble plays at Billy Gardner's restaurant in Milford, Connecticut. (Library of Congress)

With the exception of a few towns, the African American experience in Connecticut was still far from troublefree. Rapidly growing black urban environments were hard hit by mounting social problems such as poverty, overcrowded tenements, unemployment, crime, and racial tensions and conflicts with whites and immigrants. Blacks faced discrimination in housing and employment. Many cities and towns in the state turned a blind eye to unlawful discriminatory practices in public facilities and accommodations. Blacks who lived in predominately white neighborhoods also contended with many trials. For example, black students in mostly white schools were frequently ostracized socially. Black residents in mostly white cities and towns were often excluded from civic involvement and social organizations.

The multifaceted experiences of blacks in the state during this period provided a fertile ground for the close examination and documentation of black life and the issues blacks faced. The Urban League and the Connecticut WPA Federal Writers' Project sponsored surveys in cities such as Waterbury, Bridgeport, New Haven, and elsewhere. Nonfiction books as well as works of fiction, such as Ann Petry's *The Narrows* (1953), shed further light on the black experience in Connecticut.

Civil Rights Movement to the Present

Connecticut was already on the road to addressing many of its racial disparities when, in the 1950s and 1960s, demonstrators in the South made civil rights headline news. Connecticuters, blacks and whites, were numbered among the wave of young adults who went South to take part in sit-ins, marches, and other demonstrations during the Civil Rights Movement. Their bravery in the face of vitriolic resistance and mob violence produced stark images, which captured the attention of both national and world media and played an enormous part in the eventual dismantling of Jim Crowism.

Connecticut's road to civil rights and socioeconomic progress began without the sensation that the Civil Rights Movement generated in the 1960s. In 1943, the Connecticut Interracial Commission was formed to help address and alleviate racial conflict and tension in local communities. The Fair Employment Practices Act, passed in 1947 by the Connecticut General Assembly, was a colossal step forward. For many years, blacks had had no legal protection against employers who discriminated against them. With this act, black Connecticuters now had a legal buttress to pursue jobs to support themselves and their families. Hartford benefited by the election of John Clark, the first black member of the Hartford City Council, in 1955. This was no small victory. African Americans in Connecticut were generally excluded from civic leadership; thus their issues, concerns, and needs were often overlooked or discounted. In the absence of relief and intervention, social problems in black communities persisted and worsened. Hartford's growing black population and the extreme conditions blacks faced in that city necessitated, at the very least, civic representation.

Housing and the public school system were two issues that were addressed to some extent in Connecticut during the mid-1960s. Although the black population in the state was only 4 percent in 1960, Connecticut could ill-afford to ignore escalating racial problems. In Hartford, city leaders made attempts to better race relations by integrating neighborhoods. But black communities remained largely isolated and beset by social crises. In Farnam Courts, a development near New Haven, new housing projects did not include necessities such as safety barriers and play areas for children (not to mention that black neighborhoods were frequently situated in areas where local stores carried low-quality items at exorbitant prices).

In New Haven, Fred Harris emerged as an African American leader by waging a protest movement in his community. Harris, with the support of the Hill Parents' Association, a group consisting of concerned black parents that later merged with the Hill Neighborhood Union, frequently collaborated with the American Independent Movement. Harris and the Hill Parents' Association took action in response to conditions at the Prince Street School, a predominately black school. At Prince Street, students were only provided rough paper for toilet paper and were required to share textbooks. The school principal was negligent in his duties and often incapacitated because of his alcohol abuse. In the wake of a two-day march in front of the school, conditions improved for black students and an African American principal was hired to replace the former principal. After more demonstrations, the city allotted funds to establish a program called Operation Breakthrough, which provided a summer camp for youth, adult education, and other programs.

But African American communities in other Connecticut cities continued to plummet deeper into disrepair. The reports on several cities were alarming. In 1960, unemployment rates showed that 13.6 percent of black women were unemployed compared to 7.6 percent of white women; 10.1 percent of black men were unemployed compared to 5.2 percent white men. Unemployment was not the only problem. Broken families, crime, high dropout rates, and other socioeconomic programs defined many cities in Connecticut as well as in other states across the nation. One writer likened African American ghettoes to an "underdeveloped nation" (Stone, 238). Exacerbating the situation were rampant racism and sweltering racial tension.

Stamford came up with what it thought was a solution to its urban crisis, one that involved urban renewal. The city developed four goals: "(1) Intensifying the core of the city and obviating incompatible land use, (2) Replacing dilapidated housing, (3) Bringing people back downtown by constructing a six lane traffic loop around the central business district, and, (4) Obtaining federal funding and grants that encourage private capital investment" (Stone, 238). This ambitious and heavily funded project resulted in the gentrification or restoration of Stamford, but this was achieved at the cost of displacing African Americans, who remained largely neglected.

Frustrations smoldered within urban black communities in the late 1960s despite substantial gains. The Civil Rights Act of 1964 demolished segregation laws across the nation. In 1965, the Voting Rights Act brought forth stronger support for black suffrage. Specifically, it prohibited the practice of obstructing black suffrage, an issue that was endemic in the South. In 1966, Hartford undertook greater efforts at integrating predominately white schools. But, for urban blacks, problems had reached the breaking point.

Race riots erupted in several cities outside of the South. Many race riots broke out in Connecticut. Between 1967 and 1969, race riots in the state occurred in Bridgeport, Hartford, Middletown, New Britain, New Haven, New London, Norwalk, Stamford, and Waterbury. In response, federal and local governments established programs to directly address impoverished black communities.

The 1970s and 1980s opened greater opportunities for the steadily growing population of African Americans in the state. By 1970, blacks comprised 6 percent of the population in Connecticut. By 1980, 7 percent of the population was black. Critical to the betterment of Connecticut's black population were organizations such as the Greater Hartford Process and the Manchester Interracial Council, which were committed to improving race relations and the quality of life for blacks. The aims of the Greater Hartford Process included the promotion of better housing and educational opportunities and the creation of more opportunities for blacks to participate in the decision-making processes of the city. The council was formed in 1981. It aspired not only to help allay racial hostility in the community, but to diversify the workforce, especially in key leadership positions. Nationally, more doors were opening to blacks than ever before. As a result, more African Americans than ever gained admission to colleges and universities, including predominately white institutions. Employers sought out African Americans for positions and occupations in underrepresented fields.

Myriad efforts to combat poverty and racial disparity brought forth positive developments in Connecticut, including a burgeoning black middle class and black leadership. Black leaders increasingly flourished in the 1980s and 1990s. John Daniels was elected mayor of New Haven, and Carrie Saxon Perry was elected mayor of Hartford. Lloyd Richards was hired as the artistic director of the Yale Repertory Theatre, which featured black players among its ensemble. The number of African American faculty members slowly increased in Connecticut colleges, universities, and schools. Black employment in law enforcement was also a slow going process. Conflict between police officers and black youth has long been a prevalent problem throughout the nation. Manchester hired its first black police officer in 1986. In 1990, the city employed only two African American police officers.

The *Sheff v. Wade* lawsuit, begun in 1989, was named for the fourth-grader Milo Sheff, one of 17 plaintiffs (all Hartford students) who challenged the city's de jure segregated public school system, in which the predominately white schools tended to provide greater opportunities,

Milo Sheff speaks to the media at a news conference at Milner School in Hartford, Connecticut, July 9, 1996. Sheff, 17, was the lead plaintiff in the *Sheff v. Wade* school segregation case, which was filed when he was 10 years old. (AP/Wide World Photos)

resources, and privileges to their students. In 1996, the case finally ended when the Supreme Court ruled that racially segregated schools in Hartford violated the state constitution. In 1991, Jesse Jackson, a prominent civil rights activist, led a "Connecticut March to Rebuild America" to draw attention to the inner city and its unrelenting problems. In the new millennium, Hartford continues to struggle with the problem of diversifying its school system.

In the new millennium, the African American population in the state is still polarized by economic class. While middle- and upper-class blacks access greater levels of material wealth and status and have integrated with more ease into predominantly white neighborhoods and environments, low-income blacks grapple with racial exclusion and a perpetual cycle of poverty. The gap between the haves and have-nots is punctuated by population growth. In 2000, African Americans in Connecticut totaled 9 percent of the population, augmented largely by the immigration of West Indians.

Notable African Americans

Lawson, Ida Napier (1877–1965)

Connecticut's early history is filled with examples of generous African Americans like Ida Napier Lawson, who felt compelled to make great contributions to the well-being, health, and advancement of the African American community. Lawson, a native of Tennessee, became a member of Connecticut's black elite. A graduate of Fisk University in Nashville, Tennessee, Lawson had performed with the famed Fisk Jubilee Singers. A longtime resident of Hartford, she rose to prominence as president of the Women's League of Hartford, where she led middle-class black women in community-building and a variety of lively social activities. Lawson maintained an active schedule outside of the Women's League, sitting on various boards, such as the local YWCA, the Greater Hartford Tuberculosis and Health Education Society, and the National Association for the Advancement of Colored People (NAACP).

Peters, James S. (1917–2008)

James S. Peters, born in Arkansas and raised in Louisiana, resided in Connecticut for over 50 years. Peters was one of many newly transplanted African Americans from the South who would make Connecticut their home during the migrations of the 1940s. Peters, a Navy veteran, received his doctorate at Purdue University in 1954 and taught at several universities. Among his achievements, he was director of the State of Connecticut's vocational rehabilitation program, commissioner of the Hartford Housing Authority, and actively involved in the Greater Hartford Urban League and fraternities. A prolific writer, Peters' third memoir, *Filling in the Gaps*, was published in 2008. A psychologist and educator, Peters spent most of his long years challenging the racism he experienced in the North and sharing his rich life experiences, knowledge, and insight in numerous books, such as *The Saga of Black Navy Veterans of World War II* (1996), *The Spirit of David Walker: The Obscure Hero* (2002), and *Getting Over While Living Black* (2003).

Ruggles, David (1810–1849)

David Ruggles, an entrepreneur and abolitionist, was born free on March 15, 1810, in Norwich, Connecticut. Although he did not attain the high-profile status of some white abolitionist leaders or famous African American leaders like Frederick Douglass and Harriet Tubman, his life was one of significant accomplishments. Norwich was populated by over 3,000 whites, 152 free blacks, and 12 slaves. Although Ruggles' immediate family had eluded slavery, their opportunities and freedoms were limited. Ruggles, however, moved to New York, where he challenged the status quo by becoming an entrepreneur and launching a career in abolitionism. Ruggles, who owned and managed a grocery store and a bookstore, committed his life to abolition work, such as selling abolitionist newspaper subscriptions, actively participating in the Underground Railroad, and confronting whites who had unlawfully abducted slaves. Ruggles aided the return of many Africans. He also lectured, protesting slavery, racial inequalities, and the movement to return African Americans to Africa. African Americans had become distanced from their ancestral homeland over the generations. For better or worse, America was the only home known to them, and many, like Ruggles, would struggle to make it better for all.

Thomas, Rebecca Primus (1836–1932)

In the aftermath of the Civil War, blacks and whites traveled to the South to lend help and support to former black slaves. Societal conventions generally designated women's work as being at home, rearing children and keeping house. Rebecca Primus Thomas was one of many women, black and white, who defied tradition by becoming teachers, leaving home, and providing help to newly freed slaves in desperate need. A Hartford native, Rebecca Primus Thomas traveled to Royal Oak, Maryland, in 1865, where she started a school for children and adults in a church. Soon after, she built a school. The school was named Primus Institute in her honor.

Yearwood, John (dates unknown)

John Yearwood is an accomplished journalist. Born in Trinidad, Yearwood settled in Connecticut with his family in his youth. He attended Weaver High School in Connecticut and graduated with a B.A. in political science from the University of Connecticut in 1986. Since then, Yearwood has achieved many extraordinary accomplishments, interviewing high-profile political leaders in America and around the globe and reporting on world news. He has worked for the *Dallas Morning News* and the *Associated Press* in Connecticut and Oklahoma. He has also worked as a national correspondent for *Focus* magazine and was the news/public affairs director for WHUS Radio in Connecticut. He founded, published, and edited the *IBIS* magazine and was elected president of the San Juan Business Owners Association. He has served on the board of the National Association for Black Journalists and UNITY: Journalists of Color. He is currently the world editor of the *Miami Herald*.

Cultural Contributions

African American museums, historical societies, and historical markers play an important role in making sure the local history and contributions of African Americans remain at the forefront of everyday life. Renowned storyteller Tammy Denease Richardson makes numerous appearances throughout the year, retelling African folktales and performing impressions of great historical African American women, such as aviator Bessie Coleman and slave Elizabeth Keckly.

Among the black elite, organizations play an important role in maintaining identity and expressing racial pride. Exclusive black institutions include Jack and Jill (for high-achieving black youths), sororities, and fraternities. These organizations blend middle-class ideals of economic and social mobility with African American culture. Black fraternities promote black uplift through social networking and long-held African American traditions such as stepping or stomping (a percussive, foot-stomping and hand-clapping dance form) and scarification. Scarification, which originated in Africa, is a form of body modification that is sometimes considered an alternative to tattooing.

Other strong influences in the black communities of Connecticut, rich or poor, are hip-hop music and West Indian culture. Milo Sheff, of the *Sheff v. O'Neill* case, is currently a rising hip-hop star. West Indians have made a definitive mark in Connecticut through their ethnic cuisine, vernacular, language, music, and fashion. West Indian communities have retained much of their traditional culture through the establishment of organizations and by living in tight-knit and secluded neighborhoods. Although African Americans in the state, in 2008, constituted only 10 percent of the national population, Connecticut's small black population belies the strong sense of cultural heritage among African Americans and their influence in the state.

Bibliography

African American Population. *Black Demographics*. (March 2010). http://blackdemographics.com/.

Amistad Trials. *Famous American Trials*. March 2010. www.law.umkc.edu/faculty/projects/ftrials/amistad/Amistd.htm.

Bontemps, Arna. *Five Black Lives: The Autobiographies of Venture Smith, James Mars, William Grimes, The Rev. G.'W. Offley, James L. Smith*. Middletown, CT: Wesleyan University Press, 1971.

Citizen's All: African Americans in Connecticut 1700–1850. February 2010. www.yale.edu/glc/citizens/index.html.

Connecticut Freedom Trail March 2010. www.ctfreedomtrail.ct.gov/site/tour_index.html.

"Connecticut: Population by Race." *CensusScope*, March 2010. www.censusscope.org/us/s9/chart_race.html.

Cruson, Daniel. *The Slaves of Central Fairfield County, Connecticut*. Charleston, SC: History Press, 2007.

Donahue, Barbara. *Speaking for Ourselves: African American Life in Farmington, Connecticut*. Farmington, CT: Farmington Historical Society, 1998.

Gibson, Campbell, and Kay Jung. "Connecticut—Race and Hispanic Origin: 1790 to 1990." *Historical Census Statistics on Population Totals By Race, 1790 to 1990, and By Hispanic Origin, 1790 to 1990, For the United States, Regions, Divisions, and States* March 2010. www.census.gov/population.

Historical Firsts with Tammy Denease Richardson. March 2010. www.historicalfirsts.org.

Lee, Frank F. *Negro and White in Connecticut Towns*. New Haven, CT: Yale University Press, 1961.

Mead, Jeffrey B. *Chains Unbound: Slave Emancipations in the Town of Greenwich, Connecticut*. Baltimore: Gateway Press, 1995.

"New England: Connecticut: Freedom Trail." *Visit New England* February 2010. www.visitconnecticut.com/freedom.html.

Rose, James M., and Barbara Brown. *Tapestry: A Living History of the Black Family in Southeastern Connecticut*. New London, CT: New London County Historical Society, 1979.

Roth, David A. *Connecticut: A History*. New York: W. W. Norton, 1979.

Stone, Frank Andrews. *African American Connecticut: The Black Scene in a New England State; Eighteenth to Twenty-First Century*. Bloomington, IN: Trafford Publishing, 2008.

Strother, Horatio T. *The Underground Railroad in Connecticut*. Middletown, CT: Wesleyan University Press, 1962.

Warner, Robert Austin. *New Haven Negroes: A Social History*. Reprint ed. New York: Arno Press, 1969 [1940].

White, David O. *Connecticut's Black Soldiers 1775–1783*. Chester, CT: Pequot Press, 1973.

DELAWARE

Linda Williamson Nelson

Chronology

1639	"Black Anthony," the first black person to arrive in Delaware, is brought from the Caribbean to Fort Christiana aboard a vessel named the *Grip*.
1721	About 500 black slaves reside in Delaware.
1773	The General Assembly places restrictions on the numbers of blacks brought into the lower counties.
1775	Delaware Quakers begin to free their slaves.
1776	Three lower counties of Pennsylvania break away and adopt a constitution, becoming the state of Delaware.
1778	The Delaware Society for the Gradual Abolition of Slavery is established, largely by Quakers.
1787	New U.S. Constitution is ratified in Dover, making Delaware the first state to join the new Union.
1788–1789	Abolition societies are established in Dover and Wilmington.
1801	The Society of Friends (Quakers) establishes the earliest effort to educate blacks and people of color in the state.
1805	Establishment of Ezion Methodist Episcopal Church in Wilmington.
1813	Blacks reject white control of their worship services at Ezion Church in Wilmington and leave in large numbers to form the Union African Methodist Episcopal Church under the leadership of Reverend Peter Spencer and William Anderson; this is the first denomination in the nation controlled entirely by African Americans.
1814	The Big Quarterly or the August Quarterly, the first black religious festival, is started by the Reverend Peter Spenser; the festival continues in Delaware to this day.
1816	The African School Society opens a school for blacks in Delaware.
1831	A slave insurrection in Virginia led by Nat Turner results in stricter surveillance of free and enslaved blacks in most slave-holding states, including Delaware.
1847	An act to abolish slavery in Delaware is defeated in the state Senate by one vote.
1861	Delaware remains in the Union when most southern slave states secede.
1861–1865	During the Civil War, approximately 12,000 Delaware citizens fight for the Union, while a few hundred fight for the Confederacy.
1863	*(January 1)* President Abraham Lincoln's Emancipation Proclamation frees slaves in the Confederate states, but slaves in slave states that remained in the Union, such as Delaware, remain in bondage until the ratification of the Thirteenth Amendment in 1865.

1865	*(February 8)* The Delaware legislature rejects ratification of the Thirteenth Amendment to the U.S. Constitution abolishing slavery.
1866	The Delaware Association for the Moral Improvement and Education of Colored People establishes schools throughout the state; taxes on the black citizenry for support of their education are levied in 1875.
1867	*(February 7)* Delaware refuses to ratify the Fourteenth Amendment to the U.S. Constitution, which guarantees equal protection of all persons under the law.
1867	Howard High School for blacks is established in Wilmington.
1869	*(March 18)* Delaware refuses to ratify the Fifteenth Amendment to the U.S. Constitution giving blacks the vote.
1875	In response to the passage by Congress of the Civil Rights Act, Delaware legislators pass a "Jim Crow" law, relegating Delawareans to second-class citizenship; the law is not repealed until 1963.
1876	Edwina B. Kruse, who studied at the Hampton Institute, becomes the first black principal of Howard High School.
1880	A Supreme Court decision stating that blacks are not allowed to sit on the jury results in the acquittal of William Neal on rape and murder charges.
1890	Delaware State College for Colored Students is established by an act of Congress.
1892	Delaware State College officially opens with Wesley Webb, a white man, as president, along with two instructors.
1895	W. C. Jason becomes the first black president of Delaware State College
1900	William W. Coage, the son of a Delaware stage line operator, is appointed clerk in the U.S. Census Bureau with the assistance of Senator Henry A. DuPont; Coage is the first African American from Delaware to receive such a federal position.
1901	*(February 12)* The Delaware legislature ratifies the Thirteenth Amendment abolishing slavery, 35 years after the amendment took effect; the Fourteenth Amendment granting citizenship to African Americans, over 30 years after it took effect; and the Fifteenth Amendment ensuring blacks the right to vote, 30 years after it took effect.
1901	Thomas E. Postles is the first black to be seated on the Wilmington City Council.
1903	George White, a black man accused of rape and murder, is lynched by a white mob in Wilmington that was incited to violence by a sermon preached by a racist minister; the minister is later forced to leave town after being denounced in the local press.
1915	A chapter of the National Association for the Advancement of Colored People (NAACP) is established in Wilmington.

1917–1919	An estimated 1,400 black citizens of Delaware serve in the armed forces during World War I.
1919	A white mob in Wilmington tries to lynch two black men accused of killing a police officer; when the mob is fired upon, it invades black neighborhoods and begins vandalizing homes and other property.
1928	Howard High School for blacks in Wilmington receives a grant from Pierre DuPont.
1929	Louis L. Redding becomes the first African American lawyer in the state.
1930	William Coage is appointed recorder of deeds in Washington, D.C.
1941	The Carver Vocational High School for Negro Trainees is rebuilt.
1942	The first basketball game between teams from white and black Delaware high schools occurs when Wilmington Friends School plays Howard High School.
1942–1945	Over 4,000 black citizens of Delaware serve in the armed forces during World War II.
1945	The Delaware State College is granted accreditation offering degrees in the arts, sciences, education, home economics, and industrial arts; there are 175 students in the college and another 145 in a high-school department.
1945	William J. Winchester, a Republican, becomes the first African American elected to the Delaware legislature.
1946	The Carver Vocational High School for Negro Trainees in Wilmington becomes part of Howard High School.
1948	The University of Delaware admits black students.
1950	Louis Redding files a suit on behalf of black children in Claymont and Hockessin for admission to white schools on the grounds that black schools were inferior; Chancellor Collins J. Seitz orders desegregation. Appeals to U.S. Supreme Court result in Delaware being one of the defendants in the famous *Brown v. Board of Education* case.
1952	Paul Livingstone becomes the second African American elected to the Delaware legislature.
1954	The Supreme Court, in its *Brown v. Board of Education* decision, orders desegregation of schools.
1963	(*May 1*) Delaware ratifies the Twenty-fourth Amendment to the U.S. Constitution abolishing the poll tax.
1968	The assassination of Dr. Martin Luther King Jr. and general dissatisfaction with racism results in riots in Wilmington; the National Guard maintains a 10-month occupation in the city.

1970	According to Census figures, African Americans comprise 40 percent of the population of Wilmington, a significant increase over 1960.
1975	William "Judy" Johnson, a former Negro League baseball player, becomes the state's first player elected to the National Baseball Hall of Fame.
1993	James Sills is elected the first black mayor of Wilmington.
1999	Jacqueline Jones, a native of Christiana, wins the MacArthur Genius Award; she is the author of many works, notably her 1986 study, *Labor of Love, Labor of Sorrow: Black Women, Work and Family from Slavery to the Present.*
2008	Census estimates put African Americans at almost 21 percent of the population of Delaware.
2008	Democrat Barack Obama, the first African American candidate for president of a major political party, carries Delaware with 62 percent of the vote; his running mate is Delaware Senator Joseph Biden.

Historical Overview

The Early Years to the Civil War

Writing in 1996, William H. Williams noted that his attempt to write a short history of Delaware 10 years earlier yielded few published materials. Moreover, as he embarked upon his recent study, *Slavery and Freedom in Delaware, 1639–1865,* the resources had not increased appreciably. His text, therefore, is intended to act as a corrective, as it chronicles the period from the first arrival of Africans in this country to the end of legal enslavement in 1865. Indeed, the greater success that recent writers have had in attempting a historical overview of African Americans in that border state is due in large measure to the work of scholars such as Williams, a great many from among the faculty of the University of Delaware in Newark, who have in recent years expended considerable effort to fill a void. Williams' study provides us with a comprehensive overview of the passage of the antebellum years in this small territory "on the periphery of the old south."[1]

Although the repercussions of slavery are still felt in race relations and in the status of African Americans throughout this country, the aftermath of slavery has a peculiar form and substance in those states identified as the southern slave-holding states. This notwithstanding, the specific strength of the leaders, the unique forms of adaptation to dire circumstances, and the spirit of independence within black communities across the country have directed the course of history in this border state and have left their positive identifying marks. Hence we begin to shape our understanding of blacks in Delaware by outlining a historical trajectory beginning with the arrival of the first African. Historians concur that the first African brought to Delaware was a man known as "Black Anthony," who arrived on a Swedish ship, the *Vogel Grip,* in 1639. After his purchase in the West Indies, we are told that he was brought to Fort Christiana, where he served as an assistant to Governor Printz. The earliest settlers were the Swedes, followed by the Dutch, who were subsequently forced out by the English, who were the primary colonists and slaveholders in the area from 1664 onward. In fact by the time the English took control, slavery was firmly rooted in Delaware soil. Nonetheless, mostly due to its size, Delaware did not have a large population of enslaved Africans. In his study of the period of enslavement in Delaware, Williams notes that even at the height of the importation, the population of Africans only reached 20 to 25 percent of the total population of the state. Although most of the enslaved as well as the free blacks worked the soil or served their masters as house servants, a shortage of white indentured servants from Europe resulted in the training of some blacks for more skilled jobs such as tanners, shoemakers, carpenters, and tailors. One Quaker slave owner, seeking to rent farming property, included in the posting that the renter might have the use of Africans, who had been trained as noted above, provided the prospective renter could agree to treat these blacks humanely.

Yet blacks in Delaware did not receive more humane treatment than blacks in other slave states. In 1700, an act called For the Trial of Negroes more precisely codified the legal discrimination of blacks by solidifying their disfranchisement with regard to civil rights. Over the next 150 years, further discriminatory legislation was enacted in Delaware. Blacks were prohibited from carrying arms and from assembling in large groups and were subject to stiffer penalties for certain crimes and to special court procedures. Eventually, blacks in the state were banned from voting, holding office, testifying in court against whites, and marrying whites.

By 1775, 136 years after the first black man set foot on Delaware soil, there were an estimated 2,000 blacks in the state. Among the whites, who feared the possibility of a slave uprising if the numbers of blacks increased, the presence of 2,000 slaves caused sufficient concern to prompt a governmental mandate. At that time, the General Assembly raised the duty to 20 pounds for bringing "an individual slave into the lower counties with the explanation that numerous plots and insurrections in mainland America had resulted in the murders of several inhabitants."[2] In addition, the General Assembly attempted to pass into legislation a prohibition on the import

and export of slaves. While that legislation failed, the Constitution of 1776 said, "No person hereafter imported into this state from Africa ought to be held in slavery under any pretense whatever and no Negro, Indian or Mulatto slave ought to be brought into this state for sale from any part of the world."[3]

The war for independence against England further complicated the issue of slavery for what would seem to be obvious reasons. The influence of the Revolutionary War and the country's subsequent independence actually challenged the very premises of slavery. When the colonists became more and more determined to protect their natural rights against the sovereignty of the British, the question of their enslavement of Africans was underscored in bold relief. The natural rights philosophy argued that the self-governance upon which the colonists insisted was a God-given right, which no person could withhold from them. This laid the groundwork, at least in part, for the abolitionist initiatives on the part of the Quakers and others.

The work of Quakers who were moved by religious and ethical concerns to free their slaves in 1775 contributed significantly to the overall limitations on the growth of slavery in the first state of the Union. By 1787, when the U.S Constitution was completed, Delaware was the first state to ratify it. Official statehood also raised many issues related to slavery. Even the status of free blacks, as opposed to those enslaved, was tenuous at best, as the former still lived in risk of getting kidnapped and sold into slavery. Fighting against what must have been considerable resistance from other inhabitants of the state, groups of Quakers continuously struggled to lessen the vulnerability of blacks at that time; indeed, the Quakers were the leaders in forming the Delaware Society for Promoting Abolition of Slavery in 1788 and the Delaware Society for the Gradual Abolition of Slavery, both growing forces in the move toward cleansing

Delaware of human servitude. Quakers believed that every person was guided by the "Inner Light," a means of direct communication with God. Participation in the buying and selling of other humans would sever one's connection to God's grace and therefore preclude that individual's salvation. Believing thus, Quakers encouraged the manumission of their slaves and went so far as to disassociate from those Quakers who refused to act accordingly.

Moreover, changes in the economy related to the Revolutionary War contributed to the increasing difficulty slaveholders faced in their attempt to maintain slaves. Whitman notes that the war interfered with Delaware's export economy of corn, wheat, and timber, resulting in a shift whereby holding slaves became a liability. Many slaveholders freed slaves informally. In addition, a law passed in 1787 removed the need for the posting of a bond to free a slave between 18 and 35 years old. At the same time, Delaware ended the sale of slaves to the West Indies, the Carolinas, or Georgia, where they would have "little or no chance of freedom."[4] Clearly the collective sentiments within the state at that time were increasingly concerned with the reduction of slave activity. This law restricting the sale of slaves was soon extended to forbid the sale of slaves to Maryland or Virginia.

Both white and black abolitionists, such as Abraham Shadd, a black teacher in Wilmington, and Thomas Garrett, a white businessman and a Quaker, risked their own livelihood and safety to assist runaways. Between 1796 and 1820, the numbers of the enslaved decreased from about 9,000 to 1,798. Economic factors continued to encourage the reduction of slaves during this time. Since Delaware did not produce significant crops of cotton or tobacco, it had less need of slave labor, and Delaware farmers found hiring free black laborers to be more cost effective than keeping slaves. Also, because state law prohibited the sale of slaves outside Delaware, the state

could not profit from the breeding and export of slaves to the Deep South as did Virginia. Nonetheless, those determined to maintain their stakes in the slave economy continued to stealthily remove the slaves from Delaware to Maryland, a practice that kept Quakers and other abolitionists vigilant in their fight to end slavery in Delaware.

As both black and white abolitionists kept up their efforts, Delaware was slowly transforming from a slave state to a locale where slavery was clearly eroding. In 1860, slavery was no longer present in Wilmington, and it was continuously decreasing in lower New Castle County, while free blacks were achieving some measure of stability and an increasing presence. Wilmington seems to have been the focus of forward movement of free blacks. Moreover, in Wilmington, as opposed to other cities, free blacks were employed in occupations outside of domestic service or farming, and some were becoming property owners as well.

By the early to mid-nineteenth century, the flourish of black churches was a substantial force in the uplifting of free blacks and the fight to put an end to slavery overall. To a large extent, progress in the black community was due to the active support of the black churches in the form of education as well as spiritual sustenance. In the foreword to B. Ben Pearce's stunning collection of essays and photos documenting the history of the black church in Wilmington, Reverend Dr. Lawrence M. Livingston remarks that "these congregations radically changed the landscape of Wilmington's population and culture. Without the congregations represented here," he continues, "the City of Wilmington, the mid-Atlantic region, including Maryland's Eastern Shore, and perhaps the nation would be quite different today."[5] For so many, as soon as they gained their freedom, they were drawn in large numbers to worship communities, wherein they found spiritual as well as intellectual sustenance that would assist them in garnering and maintaining the strength that was needed to build their lives as free men and women and to fight the ongoing battle against racial subjugation. Historian Peter T. Dalleo explains that the church was perhaps the "most visible and viable social institution of the Wilmington African American community."[6] Methodism, more than other denominations, seemed to attract large numbers of blacks. In the eighteenth and nineteenth centuries, these churches were more receptive to blacks even though blacks had no presence at the pulpit, nor could they hope to be ordained. While the church provided a consistently nurturing foundation for free blacks, particularly in Wilmington, there were a number of other institutions that sustained black families as well. Among the social and civic organizations were Masonic lodges and other African American lodges, such as the Unity 711 and the Star of Bethlehem 897. Their relevance to the community through uplift and fellowship could be added to the work of the churches. Even the barbershops served as meeting places for social as well as political business.

Wilmington was distinctive for its preponderance of two-parent homes as opposed to the greater number of female-headed households elsewhere in the state. What emerges at this time is a picture of Wilmington's free black society, with the numbers of freed men and women having increased from 444 in 1800 to 3,187 in 1857. Wilmington was clearly as a nascent, but thriving, free African American community, steadily gaining stability from considerable self-help organizations, both secular and religious.

The growth of the African American church in Delaware is marked by its own history of struggle against white domination. The first church mentioned in Reverend Livingston's foreword to B. Ben Pearce's *Historical Vignettes of African American Churches in Wilmington, Delaware* (1998) is Ezion-Mt. Carmel, which he traces back to 1771 and the establishment of a Methodist church led by Francis Asbury and Harry Hoosier,

also known as Black Harry. This early experiment with an integrated congregation failed as Mr. Hoosier's status was apparently undermined. The resulting schism led to the establishment of " 'the first African Society of any kind' in the state of Delaware," namely the African American Methodist congregation of Ezion-Mt. Carmel, which was the daring experiment of Peter Spenser. It is Spenser who must be credited with the eventual development of two African American denominations, Union Church of African Members and the Union American Methodist Episcopal Church. Both were known as "Spenser churches," even though the latter was established after Peter Spenser's death. The Union Methodist Episcopal Church (UAME) burgeoned under the leadership of Reverend Spenser, eventually reaching a membership of 1,200 scattered over several states.

With the aid of free blacks, bolstered by church and community affiliations and white abolitionists, Delaware approached the Civil War with a total of 1,798 slaves, compared to 19,829 free blacks, with at least some of the latter, as noted earlier, employed in sustaining work outside of domestic labor and farming. The white population at the time numbered 90,589. Blacks, therefore, represented more than 25 percent of the population and by all appearances seemed to be moving steadily toward greater enfranchisement.

Any mention of the numbers of free blacks at this time would be egregiously lacking without specific discussion of the work of the most famous Underground Railroad conductor, Harriet Tubman, who was born into slavery in 1821 in Maryland. By 1849, she escaped and made it to Delaware, where she was aided by free blacks and Quakers. One of her closest friends and assistants among the conductors was a name that appears over and again in the history of Delaware. That is the Quaker, iron merchant, and Underground Railroad conductor, Thomas Garrett from Wilmington. In total, Tubman made 19 trips back to the slaveholding areas and brought 100 people to freedom. Masterfully, she carved out a number of routes leading through a locus of cities and towns such as Dover, Blackbird, Middleton, New Castle, Laurel, Smyrna, Delaware City, Wilmington, and others.

Moving Forward after the Civil War

In 1861, Delaware, like other border slave states such as Kentucky, Missouri, and Maryland, did not secede from the Union as did the slave states of the Deep South. Although several hundred Delaware citizens fought for the southern Confederacy, more than 12,000 fought for the Union. Slavery did not end in Delaware until the Thirteenth Amendment, which abolished slavery, was ratified in December 1865. Once the Civil War was over, Delaware, like all the former slaveholding states, faced the task of educating the newly freed black men and women. The Association of Moral Improvement and Education of the Colored People, formed in 1866, gained a presence throughout Delaware in schools established for the education of black children. Nonetheless, only the most naively hopeful would believe at this point that blacks were on a clear path to full citizenry. Shortly after issuance of the Emancipation Proclamation in 1862, white Delawareans expressed their resistance to full black citizenship by writing into law the practice of Jim Crow. A Delaware legislator was able to codify the subordinate status of blacks in the state by asserting at his inaugural address in 1863 that "the true position of the Negro was as a subordinate race, excluded from all political and social privilege."[7]

In the 10 years following emancipation, Delaware Republicans faced formidable odds in their efforts to protect the freed men and women from rampant *de facto* subjugation. The Jim Crow law of 1875 was not repealed until 1963. However, with the aid of the Freedmen's Bureau and the Delaware Association for the Moral Improvement

and Education of Colored People, the availability of basic education gradually took hold. It was not until 1891, however, that serious attention to higher education came to fruition with the establishment of Delaware State College, now Delaware State University. In spite of widespread general education and the growth of the new black college, 70 percent of blacks remained in menial jobs. The overwhelming majority of blacks were effectively barred from white-collar jobs and subject to "arbitrary limitations placed on Negro employment."[8] In her *The Negro of Delaware: Past and Present* (1947), Pauline Young pointed out that "[a]fter V-J Day, the removal of Negroes from the war industries was faster and more complete in Delaware than in any of the other states."[9] Therefore, the figures from the earlier census were relied on. The black and white population figures and comparative employment figures in the 1940 Census clearly reflect the great disparity in the number of employment opportunities available to blacks as opposed to those available to whites. In proportion to their numbers, many more black men and women who were available for employment were unable to secure jobs. Two-thirds of the white women did not need employment, compared to half of the black women. Despite the country's shift at the time toward a war economy, 14.3 percent of available black men were unemployed compared to 6.5 percent of white men. Similarly, the percentage of black women seeking work was 11.7 percent, as opposed to 6.3 percent of white women. There were a paltry number of blacks in professional or semiprofessional jobs as opposed to whites. Most disheartening was the reality that there was a wide range of jobs that blacks could not even approach. Among those were office workers, telephone solicitors, surveyors, street and rail car operators, and department store clerks. These jobs and many others were almost all those jobs for which blacks could have been trained or apprenticed for, if given the opportunity.

Pauline Young's invaluable study is clinical in its detailed discussion of the public service and governmental agencies with doors shut to the black men and women of the era in which she writes. Her discussion, however, like that of most historians of the era, returns to the broad range of civic and religious agencies that have sustained the black community since antebellum days and continues until today. Many, but not all of these, are strictly black organizations: The Young Men's and Young Woman's Christian Association, the National Association for the Advancement of Colored People (NAACP), Democratic and Republican organizations, and some of the historical black fraternities and sororities, notably Alpha Phi Alpha fraternity and Phi Delta Kappa sorority. Many of these had wide participation; the Wilmington branch of the NAACP counted 2,500 members in the 1940s. Among the more mainstream organizations that sought to protect blacks and improve their status, the Wilmington Federation of Teachers exhibited "courageous opposition to racial segregation in its ranks."[10]

Even in the face of overwhelming obstacles, there emerged a group of blacks who were identified both within and outside of their communities as the black middle class. In her study of the famous Redding family, Annette Woolard-Provine reconstructs the complex development of this community through the experiences of one family, which brought forth more than its share of high achievers and leaders. It would be nearly impossible to provide even a brief historical overview of black Delaware without devoting a portion of that report, however small, to the Redding family. In her introduction to this study, Woolard-Provine situates this family in a historical context that is prefigured by the most widely cited work of the famous sociologist/literary artist/historian, W. E. B. Du Bois. It was he who coined the term, "The Talented Tenth," in his incisive study of blacks in America, *Souls of Black Folk* (1903). The Talented Tenth were the upper

10 percent of African Americans who would use their considerable privilege, training, and talents (in comparison to the masses) to lead the masses through the delivery of various services, through education and through the supply to their communities of sorely needed teachers, doctors, lawyers, and other university-trained people, who had the resources and the preparation to wage the strongest battle against racial segregation and assault. The author appropriately reminds us that in large measure these elite had more than the material and intellectual accoutrements of the privileged. Among them were generally lighter-skinned blacks whose color added considerably to their public currency: the closer to white, the more favorably judged by whites. However, in comparison to the white middle class, these families were generally not as well to do, but they were able to live comfortably, to educate their children in more exclusive settings, and to enjoy some of the luxuries, such as vacations and well-appointed homes, which eluded the less fortunate majority of blacks. Willard-Provine's study, *Integrating Delaware: The Reddings of Wilmington* (2003), provides a richly textured portrait of this family, with special attention to the unusual number of high achievers—among them teachers, a famous writer, a lawyer—and the extraordinary service they brought to the black community overall. This discussion offers only a cursory mention of the Reddings, who left an indelible impression and occupy a central position in the history of Wilmington and the state of Delaware. Lewis Redding, identified by Woolard-Provine as "The Patriarch," was one of the first postal workers in Wilmington. Because of his determination to live well and to provide a college education for his children, he worked tirelessly as a postal worker, with a number of side jobs. In this way, he was able to purchase a home in a quiet community where the Reddings were one of the first two families of color. Lest the family's move be read as an escape from their own people, we

should be reminded that the father, Lewis, was ardently loyal to his community, and ever watchful of the white community which he had learned to distrust. Woolard-Provine reports that Redding and his family were members of Bethel AME, a rather staid congregation of other middle-class black professionals, many of whom, like Lewis Redding, took seriously their responsibility to the black community. Redding served as superintendent of the Sunday school for over 40 years. Added to this was Lewis' work with others in founding the Wilmington branch of the NAACP in January 1915. It should come as no surprise that among the children of Lewis and Mary Ann Redding were the famous writer and college professor, Saunders Redding, and the great civil rights attorney Louis Redding, who was the second black person to earn a degree from Harvard Law School and the first black to practice law in Delaware. Both of these Redding children, as well as a daughter, spent all or some part of their undergraduate careers at Brown University in Providence, Rhode Island.

Notwithstanding a visibly active black middle class, Delaware continued to be a border state in terms of geography and race relations. Indeed, the two are certainly not mutually exclusive, as Delaware had the uncertain distinction of being the northernmost slaveholding state. During the 1950s and 1960s, Wilmington blacks, like most blacks across the country in metropolitan areas, continued to fight segregation and were still mostly relegated to service jobs. Louis Redding, the young attorney, was in constant demand as black parents fought to get their children in white schools. A report, *Delaware: Conflict in a Border State*, produced by the Smithsonian's National Museum of American History (the Behring Center), tells how Ethel Louis Belton traveled two hours to the black high school, Howard High, from her home in Claymont. Her mother boldly fought this segregation. Ultimately, Louis Redding represented the black children of

Claymont and Hockessin, arguing against the separate but equal policy that resulted from the *Plessy v. Ferguson* case. The black schools were anything but equal. While Chancellor Collins J. Seitz decided for the plaintiffs, the local school boards took the case to the Supreme Court, where these original two families were joined by seven other families, who were all among the plaintiffs in the *Brown v. Board of Education* case. Louis Redding of Wilmington had a hand in this landmark case, which turned the tide on school segregation.

By the 1960s, Wilmington was clearly transforming into a black city. Wilmington, like so many other urban areas, erupted in violent protest when Martin Luther King Jr. was assassinated, resulting in a National Guard presence for months afterwards. Since the 1970s, the progress of blacks in Delaware has been moderate. The 1993 election of James Sills as Wilmington's first black mayor is a significant symbol of hope and a reminder of the wide-reaching contributions of blacks to the state of Delaware.

The metropolitan Wilmington Urban League reported in 2002 on the "state of people of color in Delaware," offering a comprehensive overview of current labor statistics. In addition to income statistics for a variety of occupations, the report measured the degree of integration or segregation in an area. There was also a study done by the University of Delaware, using 1990 Census data and a more recent study completed by the *News Journal*, whose researchers used the results of the year 2000 Census report. In the first study of census tracts in New Castle County, Delaware, the results are clearly mixed. While New Castle County showed gradual improvement from 1970 to 1990, 21 out of the 100 census tracts that were measured for dissimilarity or degree of integration/segregation revealed that they had become more segregated over that two-decade period. Some positive findings could be seen in the city of Wilmington. When Wilmington was compared to the rest of New Castle County, there was evidence of increased integration in suburban areas of New Castle. The results of the more recent *News Journal*'s report, however, demonstrate progress as well as stagnation. The findings indicate that according to the latest census, 65 percent of Delawareans live in areas that are considered integrated by dissimilarity measures. However, some areas, like Wilmington, are becoming more segregated, with an increase in the African American population from 37,446 in 1990 to 41,646 in 2000. The white population in the city declined from 30,134 to 25,811 during the same time period. This segment of the study concludes with the explanation of the consequences of segregation at this moment in history.

When segregation was enforced, the segregated black communities at least had the benefit of the cohesion that accompanies an arrangement where black people from the range of professions and social classes live, eat, and worship together. In these settings there was inherent stability that came with the juxtaposition of those who could lend support to those who needed support. On the other hand, in today's pattern of segregation, the poor are relegated to areas with lower property values, greater crime statistics, underfunded educational facilities, and greater risk overall to the well-being of the inhabitants. The evidence seems to suggest that where social class intersects with race, opportunities for advancement based upon education and overall living conditions are less in areas where the black citizens are isolated and economically marginalized.

Notable African Americans

Cassells, Cyrus (1957–)

Although a native of Dover, Cassells grew up in Southern California. The title poem in his volume of poetry, *Soul Make a Path through Shouting*, is dedicated to Elizabeth Eckford, a girl who fought against a hostile segregationist group in Little Rock, Arkansas, to integrate a school. Cassells has published four highly acclaimed volumes of poetry, including a selection for the National Poetry Series. Cassells is also a professor and an accomplished actor.

Cornish, Sam (1795–1858)

Sam Cornish was born into freedom in Delaware. He moved to Philadelphia and New York, eventually becoming a Presbyterian minister and the editor of the *Freeman*, which, some claim, was the first black newspaper in the United States.

Holland, Jerome (1916–1985)

Dr. Jerome Holland served as the Head of Delaware State College in the 1940s and later became the president of Hampton Institute. He was a civil rights advocate and a statesman, having served as a representative to the United Nations and as an ambassador to Sweden. In 1985, he was posthumously awarded the Presidential Medal of Freedom.

Jason, William C., Sr. (dates unknown)

The second president of the Delaware State College for Colored Students, Dr. William C. Jason Sr. was a Methodist minister of the Delaware Methodist Episcopal Conference, where he served as president from 1895–1923. Dr. Jason is best remembered for his contribution to the black youth of Delaware, helping them to become aware of the potentials for them in higher education. Without adequate resources, Dr. Jason was expected to build both an academic and an agricultural curriculum at what was to become Delaware State College. While building the institution, he worked to encourage higher education among able black students and recruited extensively from Howard High School. Moreover, he is credited with overseeing the training of highly qualified teachers for most of the black schools in Kent and Sussex counties in Delaware.

Johnson, George Anderson (1889–?)

George Anderson Johnson, the son of a former slave, was born in Shelby County, Kentucky, on April 22, 1889. He moved from Kentucky to Bloomington, Indiana, to live with his father. Like a number of Howard High teachers, he was born outside of Delaware. Yet he has earned his place among Delawareans of note for his dedication to extensive improvements at Howard High. He was hired as principal in 1924 and remained in that position until 1959, during which time he encouraged the endowment of Pierre S. DuPont, whose donation of almost one million dollars resulted in a new building and a great many other improvements, ultimately earning the school Middle States Accreditation in 1930. He has been called "the epitome of the learned scholar who is a leader, teacher and humanitarian."[11] The legacy of Howard High and its role as a center of culture in the black community was due in large measure to this man's contributions.

Jones, Absalom (1746–1818)

Absalom Jones was born into slavery in Sussex County, Delaware. He is best known for his leadership as a clergyman and his founding, along with Richard Allen, of the African Free Society. He was the founder and the pastor of St. Thomas African Episcopal Church. He has been described as the more staid partner in his friendship and collaboration with Richard Allen, the first bishop of the African Methodist Episcopal Church. The two men worked selflessly to assist the victims of a yellow fever epidemic in Philadelphia in 1793 and were praised by whites and blacks alike.

The Reverend Absalom Jones, Rector of St. Thomas African Episcopal Church in Philadelphia. Absalom Jones was the first African American to be ordained to the Episcopal priesthood when he received the ordination of deacon in 1795 and of priest in 1804. He led St. Thomas African Episcopal Church in Philadelphia. (Schomburg Center/Art Resource, NY)

Institute and is credited with developing Howard High into an academically advanced school, with a progressive curriculum. Graduates went to such prestigious schools as Drexel, the University of Pennsylvania, and Lincoln University. She was a teacher and later the principal at Howard High and established schools in the southern or lower two counties of the state.

Kruse, Edwina B. (1848–1930)

Edwina Kruse was born in Puerto Rico; her father was German and her mother Cuban. She was educated in Massachusetts and at Hampton

Lowery, Robert "Boysie" (1914–1996)

Robert Lowery taught jazz for over 50 years. At the time of his death, on September 10, 1996, the *Washington Post* reported that he was

Blues musician Robert Lowery performs on stage at the New Orleans Jazz and Heritage Festival in New Orleans, Louisiana, 1998. (David Redfern/Getty Images)

inspired by his father who was a blacksmith, in addition to being a musician and a band leader. "Boysie" began to teach jazz improvisation in Wilmington in the 1940s. His early students included Clifford Brown, considered one of the best trumpet players of all time. After leaving North Carolina where he was born, he and his brother, Bud, founded the Duces of Rhythm on the Eastern Shore in the 1930s. He settled in Wilmington in the 1940s and began teaching after the Duces disbanded. Even as he continued to teach, he started a new band, the Aces of Rhythm. In 1995, he was honored with the Living Legacy Award.

Nelson, Alice Dunbar (1875–1935)

Alice Dunbar Nelson was born Alice Ruth Moore in 1875 in New Orleans, Louisiana. She graduated from Straight College (now Dillard) and went on to earn a master's degree at Cornell. In addition to being an educator, she was a school administrator, a renowned poet, and a political activist. She was head of the English Department of the Howard High School for African Americans from 1902 to 1920. She served as editor of the *Advocate*, the AME Church Review. Also a well-known figure of the literary period the Harlem Renaissance, she was the author of *Dunbar Speaks*. In addition, she was a social activist who served as secretary of the Peace Committee of the American Friends Service Committee. Her commitment to activism ultimately cost her the teaching position at Howard High that she held for 18 years. She was dismissed due to her absence from her teaching duties to attend Social Justice Day in Ohio in September 1920.

Nutter, Jeanne (dates unknown)

Dr. Jeanne Nutter has a B.A. and M.A. from the University of Cincinnati, and a Ph.D. from Howard University. She was the executive producer of the WHYY documentary, *A Separate Place: Schools That P.S. DuPont Built*. She is the author of the book *Growing Up Black in New Castle County Delaware*, a collection of oral histories of African American individuals who grew up in northern Delaware from the early 1900s through the late 1950s. She has been a college professor and an external affairs manager of the mayor's office in Wilmington. She has also held positions with the Association of Junior Leagues International, the United Nations Institute for Training and Research, and WNBC-TV.

Redding, Louis L. (1901–1999)

A graduate of Brown University in Providence, Rhode Island, Louis L. Redding was one of its commencement speakers in 1923. He was the first African American lawyer in the state and was considered the champion of civil rights in Delaware. Redding filed a suit on behalf of black children in Claymont and Hockessin, Delaware, on

Louis L. Redding, left, and Thurgood Marshall, general counsel for the NAACP, conferring at the Supreme Court during a recess in the court's hearing on racial integration in the public schools, 1955. (Library of Congress)

the grounds that the black schools were inferior. His actions led to Chancellor Collins J. Seitz ordering desegregation of Delaware schools; however, the state legislators blocked the desegregation, resulting in Redding joining the successful team of attorneys who argued the *Brown v. Board of Education* case before the Supreme Court in 1954.

Redding, Saunders (1906–1988)

Another illustrious member of the Redding family of Wilmington, Saunders Redding was the third of seven children. The author of eight books, Redding was a professor of English and a writer who was identified with the Harlem Renaissance period. Saunders Redding went to Howard High and

Brown University, and taught at a number of institutions, including Morehouse College in Atlanta.

Shadd, Mary Ann (1823–1893)

Mary Ann Shadd was the daughter of Abraham D. Shadd, a free black shoemaker in Wilmington who was active in the Underground Railroad. Mary Ann attended a Quaker school in Wilmington and returned to teach black children in Quaker schools after her education in West Chester, Pennsylvania. She was thought to be the first black woman in the country to publish her own newspaper. She wrote a book, *Hints to the Colored People of the North*, in the hopes of helping blacks to lift themselves out of poverty. She distinguished herself by earning a law degree from Howard University at the age of 60, after which she continued to help protect the rights of blacks.

Shadd, Sallie (dates unknown)

Sallie Shadd was the wife of a butcher named Jeremiah Shadd, who reportedly purchased his wife's freedom. He was an independent businessman. His wife joined in the food business and was celebrated among Delaware blacks as the inventor of ice cream. Dolly Madison, the wife of President James Madison, is reported to have made this ice cream a part of her special White House dinners on a regular basis.

Spenser, Peter (1782–1843)

Peter Spenser was born in Maryland, but became a leader in the Delaware black community. Known as "Father Spenser," he was a mechanic, an educator, a businessman, and a founder of the first independent black denomination, the African Union Methodist Protestant Church. Known as the Patriarch, he opposed the efforts of the American Colonization Society to return blacks to Africa. Before his death in 1843, he had founded 31 churches.

Waters, Eldridge (dates unknown)

Eldridge Waters was the first African American man to assume the position of principal of a school in Wilmington in the 1940s. He was also the first basileus of the Upsilon Chapter of Omega Psi Phi fraternity. In 1941, Waters established a committee that renamed a local school Benjamin Banneker Elementary School in honor of the distinguished African American scientist and mathematician.

Young, Pauline A. (d. 1991)

Pauline A. Young was the niece of Alice Dunbar Nelson and followed her illustrious aunt as an educator of black youth at Howard High in Wilmington, which she entered as a teacher and then took the post of librarian. Although born in Medford, Massachusetts, she moved to Delaware to live with her aunt after the death of her mother. After graduating from Howard High, she attended the University of Pennsylvania and then worked at Tuskegee Institute before returning to Wilmington to teach. She traveled to Berlin, the Soviet Union, and Egypt and was present with Martin Luther King Jr. at the Selma-to-Montgomery march. She was an ardent archivist of works on black history and added her own contribution, "The Negro of Delaware: Past and Present" (1947). Her home became a meeting place for scholars and Howard alumni.

Cultural Contributions

The contributions of African American Delaware natives could be easily overlooked, situated as the state is between New York City, Philadelphia, and Washington, D.C. However, from at least the eighteenth century, African Americans of Delaware have made significant and ongoing contributions to the arts and letters. Arguably the most notable repository of art and cultural artifacts in Delaware can be found at the University of Delaware in Newark. The following list identifies some significant exhibits as well as a range of creative artists from Delaware, including Cyrus Cassells, Jacqueline Jones, Edwina B. Kruse, Robert "Boysie" Lowery, Alice Dunbar Nelson, Saunders Redding, Mary Ann Shadd, and Pauline A. Young.

As reported in *Issues in Science and Technology* (2007), the exhibition of the work of Billy Colbert, "The First Taste of the Strange Fruit," was described as "visual folklore." His work is inclusive of multiple genres, including color, imagery, and literature. With a wide-reaching reputation since receiving his M.F.A. in painting in 2000 from the University of Delaware, he has had a number of solo and group exhibitions. His work was featured at the African American Museum in Dallas, as well as the Delaware Center for Contemporary Art in Wilmington. He has taken part in a number of group exhibitions as well, including one entitled "Reasons to Riot," at the Memphis College of Art in Memphis, Tennessee, from February to April 2007. Another, entitled "Jolly Cowboy," was seen at the District of Columbia Art Center in Washington, D.C., from March to April 2007.

In an article entitled "Erasing an Absence," R. Roach reported on the opening of a history-making exhibition of African American Art at the University of Delaware in Newark. One hundred and one African American artists are represented in this collection. When the exhibit was fully assembled, it totaled about 1,000 pieces of art from the collection of Paul R. Jones. This made it one of the largest exhibits of its kind. The University of Delaware is privileged to be the holder of this exclusive exhibit, "A Century of African American Art: The Paul R. Jones Collection." Jones, at 76 years of age, is a treasure himself as the owner of this massive collection of works by a long list of celebrated artists. Among these are works by Romare Bearden, Elizabeth Catlett, James Van Der Zee, Hanry O. Tanner, Leo Twiggs, and Charles White. Although the exhibition has traveled to a number of historically black institutions, Jones chose the University of Delaware, Newark, for its capacity to exhibit the art on the scale of a full museum and to make it available for use in an extensive art curriculum.

Notes

1. William H. Williams, *Slavery and Freedom in Delaware, 1639–1865* (Wilmington, DE: Scholarly Resources, Inc., 1996), xii.

2. James E. Newton, "Black Americans in Delaware: An Overview," in Carole C. Marks, ed., *A History of African Americans of Delaware and Maryland's Eastern Shore* (Wilmington: Delaware Heritage Press, 1997), 12.

3. Ibid., 12–13.

4. T. Stephen Whitman, *Challenging Slavery in the Chesapeake: Black and White Resistance to Human Bondage, 1775–1865* (Baltimore: Maryland Historical Society, 2007), 52.

5. Newton, "Black Americans," xi.

6. Ibid., 169.

7. Ibid., 18.

8. Pauline A. Young, "The Negro of Delaware: Past and Present," in Henry Clay Reed, ed., *Delaware: A History of the First State*, 3 vols. (New York: Lewis Historical Publishing Company, 1947), 544.

9. Ibid., 594.

10. Ibid., 601.

11. Judith Y. Gibson, "Mighty Oaks: Five Black Educators," in Carole C. Marks, ed., *A History of African Americans of Delaware and Maryland's Eastern Shore* (Wilmington: Delaware Heritage Press, 1997), 139.

Bibliography

Bennett, Lerone, Jr. *Before the Mayflower: A History of Black America*. Reprint ed. Chicago: Johnson Publishing Co., 2007.

Center for Material Culture Studies, University of Delaware. *People Were Close. They Looked after One Another*. Newark: University of Delaware and Raven Press, 2005.

Dalleo, Peter. "The Growth of Delaware's Antebellum Free African American Community." In Carole C. Marks, ed., *A History of African Americans of Delaware and Maryland's Eastern Shore*. Wilmington: Delaware Heritage Press, 1997.

Fields, B. J. *Slavery and Freedom on the Middle Ground: Maryland during the Nineteenth Century*. New Haven, CT: Yale University Press, 1985.

Gibson, Judith Y. "Mighty Oaks: Five Black Educators." In Carole C. Marks, ed., *A History of African Americans of Delaware and Maryland's*

Eastern Shore. Wilmington: Delaware Heritage Press, 1997.

Hancock, Harold B. "Mary Ann Shadd: Negro Editor, Educator, and Lawyer." *Delaware History* 15, no. 3 (1973): 187–194.

Hoffecker, Carol E. "The Politics of Exclusion: Blacks in Late Nineteenth-Century Wilmington, Delaware." *Delaware History* 16, no. 1 (1974): 60–72.

Hoffecker, Carol, and A. Wollard. "Black Women in Delaware's History." In Carole C. Marks, ed., *A History of African Americans of Delaware and Maryland's Eastern Shore.* Wilmington: Delaware Heritage Press, 1997.

Hull, Gloria (1976) "Alice Dunbar-Nelson: Delaware Writer and Woman of Affairs." *Delaware History* 17, no. 2 (1976): 87–103.

Lewis, Ronald, L., ed. "Reverend T. G. Stewart and 'Mixed' Schools in Delaware, 1882." *Delaware History* 19, no. 1 (1980): 53–58.

Marks, C., ed. *A History of African Americans of Delaware and Maryland's Eastern Shore.* Wilmington: Delaware Heritage Press, 1977.

Metropolitan Wilmington Urban League. *The Pace of Progress: A Report on the State of People of Color in Delaware.* Newark, DE: Farley Printing Co, Inc., 2002.

Newton, James E. "Black Americans in Delaware: An Overview." In Carole C. Marks, ed., *A History of African Americans of Delaware and Maryland's Eastern Shore.* Wilmington: Delaware Heritage Press, 1997.

Nutter, Jeanne D. *Black America Series: Delaware.* Charleston, SC: Arcadia Press, 2000.

Nutter, Jeanne D., comp. *Growing Up Black in New Castle County, Delaware.* Voices of America series. Charleston, SC: Arcadia Press, 2001.

Pacheco, J. F. *The Pearl: A Failed Slave Escape on the Potomac.* Chapel Hill: University of North Carolina Press, 2005.

Pearce, Ben. B. *Historical Vignettes of African American Churches in Wilmington, Delaware.* Wilmington, DE: The Chaconia Press, 1998.

Pippin, K. A. *Families in Transition: A Smyrna History.* Smyrna, DE: Prison Industries, 1995.

Strickland, A. E., and J. R. Reich. *The Black American Experience: From Slavery through Reconstruction.* New York: Harcourt, Brace Jovanovich, Publishers, 1974.

Whitman, T. Stephen. *Challenging Slavery in the Chesapeake: Black and White Resistance to Human Bondage, 1775–1865.* Baltimore: Maryland Historical Society, 2007.

Williams, William H. *Slavery and Freedom in Delaware, 1639–1865.* Wilmington, DE: Scholarly Resources, Inc., 1996.

Woolard-Provine, A. *Integrating Delaware: The Reddings of Wilmington.* Newark: University of Delaware Press, 2003.

Young, Pauline A. "The Negro of Delaware: Past and Present." In Henry Clay Reed, ed., *Delaware: A History of the First State.* 3 vols. New York: Lewis Historical Publishing Company, 1947.

DISTRICT OF COLUMBIA

Komanduri S. Murty and Carl H. Walker

Chronology

1751 The Maryland Assembly appoints a commission to lay out a settlement—later known as Georgetown—on the Potomac River, near Rock Creek, on land purchased from George Gordon and George Beall.

1788 *(June 21)* The U.S. Constitution is ratified by the states, and gives Congress authority "to exercise exclusive legislation in all cases whatsoever, over such District (not exceeding ten miles square) as may by cession of particular States, and the acceptance of Congress, become the seat of the government of the United States. . . ."

1790 *(July 16)* Passage of the Residency Act, which gives the president power to choose a site for the national Capitol somewhere along a 70-mile stretch on the east bank of the Potomac River.

1791 *(January 24)* President George Washington selects a site for the new federal city that includes portions of Maryland and Virginia.

1791 *(February)* Benjamin Banneker, a free black man with knowledge of mathematics and astronomy, assists in the initial survey of the boundaries of the new federal district.

1792 The foundation is laid for the president's mansion, later known as the "White House."

1800 The Census indicates that the population of the new city of Washington comprises 10,066 whites, 793 free blacks, and 3,244 slaves.

1800 *(November)* President John Adams and his wife Abigail move into the unfinished president's mansion in Washington City.

1800 *(December 1)* The Capitol of the United States is transferred from Philadelphia to the city of Washington, in the territory of Columbia; because the new federal district consists of lands ceded by Maryland and Virginia, the laws of those states, including those pertaining to slavery, remain in force within the District.

1802 *(May 3)* Congress grants Washington a municipal charter, which defines voters as white males who pay taxes and have lived in the city for at least a year; the president appoints the mayor of Washington.

1812 *(May 4)* Congress amends Washington's charter to create an eight-member board of aldermen and a 12-member common council, which jointly elect the mayor.

1814 During the War of 1812, British troops capture the city and burn the Capitol, the president's house, and other federal buildings.

1816 Mount Zion Methodist Episcopal Church, the oldest black congregation in the District, is established. Through its history, Mt. Zion not only served as a spiritual institution for its members, but also as an educational outpost (it housed the first black library) and social support organization. Mt. Zion is also later a stop on the Underground Railroad.

1820 Congress permits direct election of the mayor by the city's voters.

1834   Former slave John Francis Cook opens the first secondary school for blacks in Washington.

1846   *(July 9)* Congress returns the Virginia portion of the federal district—the city of Alexandria and Alexandria County—to Virginia.

1848   Congress adopts a new charter for the city of Washington and expands the number of elected offices to include a board of assessors, a surveyor, a collector, and a registrar.

1848   Construction of the Washington Monument begins. Because of sandy soil where L'Enfant had specified a monument, it is not built at the exact intersection of the axes. Work on the monument ceases in 1854 after the antiforeign Know-Nothing Party seizes the monument to protest the contribution of a memorial stone by Pope Pius IX. Rising sectionalism prevents the resumption of work.

1849   Illinois Congressman Abraham Lincoln introduces a bill providing for the gradual emancipation of all slaves in the federal district; the measure is opposed by southern members of Congress and defeated.

1850   *(September 20)* Congress abolishes the slave trade in the federal district of Columbia as part of the legislative package known as the Compromise of 1850.

1857   In *Dred Scott v. Sandford*, the U.S. Supreme Court rules that slaves are not citizens and have no constitutional rights.

1860   The Census of 1860 finds that 11,131 free blacks and 3,185 slaves are resident in the federal district of Columbia.

1860   By 1860, the Slave Code of the federal district, which is liberal by southern standards, contains provisions allowing slaves to hire out their services and live apart from their masters, while free blacks are permitted to live in the city and to operate private schools.

1862   *(April 16)* Congress abolishes slavery in the federal district of Columbia, five months prior to President Abraham Lincoln's issuance of the Emancipation Proclamation; Congress provides for compensation for federal district slaveholders.

1865   *(April 14)* President Abraham Lincoln is assassinated in Ford's Theatre, a Washington, D.C., landmark.

1866   *(April 19)* The African American citizens of Washington hold a parade celebrating the fourth anniversary of the abolition of slavery in the federal district of Columbia; 5,000 people march up Pennsylvania Avenue led by two regiments of black Civil War veterans.

1867   *(January 8)* Congress grants black males the right to vote in local district elections.

1867   Howard University, one of the nation's oldest historically black colleges, is established in Washington.

1871   Congress abolishes the elected mayor and council of Washington City and replaces with a governor and council appointed by the president; in the same act, Congress merges the

1871 (cont.)	governments of Georgetown and the city and county of Washington into a jurisdiction and territorial government now known as the District of Columbia.
1871	Frederick Douglass, the black abolitionist, lecturer, and author, takes up residence in Washington; he serves as marshal of the District of Columbia from 1877 to 1881 and as recorder of deeds for the District from 1881 to 1886.
1874	Father Patrick Healy becomes president of Georgetown University, the first black man to head a major white university; he serves until 1882.
1879	Calvin T. S. Brent, a black architect, designs St. Luke's Episcopal Church in Washington; almost a century later, in 1976, it is added to the National Register of Historic Places.
1883	(April 16) Frederick Douglass speaks in Washington to commemorate the anniversary of the abolition of slavery in the District of Columbia; in his speech, Douglass calls attention to the continuing struggle of black Americans for full civil rights.
1888	The Washington Monument opens to the public.
1896	The U.S. Supreme Court decision in *Plessy v. Ferguson* establishes a "separate but equal" doctrine, which essentially makes segregation of blacks from whites legal in all aspects of society.
1908	Just one generation removed from slavery, nine African American college women form the first black sorority, Alpha Kappa Alpha, at Howard University.
1914	The Lincoln Memorial is completed.
1919	(January) District Commissioner Brownlow establishes the city's first all-black platoon of firefighters, thus ensuring opportunities for promotion for the department's black veterans.
1919	(July) For five days, white mobs rampage through African American neighborhoods in Washington to avenge the alleged harassment of a white woman by two black men; four people are killed and more than 30 are injured.
1939	African American singer Marian Anderson is refused permission to sing at Constitution Hall in Washington, D.C., by the Daughters of the American Revolution (DAR). Upon learning this fact, First Lady Eleanor Roosevelt resigns from the DAR.
1940	LeDroit Park, formerly a whites-only neighborhood, becomes the residence for many prominent African Americans, including, Ralph J. Bunche (first African American to receive the Nobel Peace Prize), Benjamin O. Davis Sr. (first African American general in the U.S. armed forces), Paul Laurence Dunbar (black poet laureate), and jazz legend Duke Ellington.
1954	The U.S. Supreme Court, in *Brown v. Board of Education*, reverses the "separate but equal" doctrine and provides the basis for integration not only in public schools, but in the larger society as well.
1958	(May 17) The Prayer Pilgrimage for Freedom becomes the first large African American civil rights march in Washington.

1961 *(March 29)* Ratification of the Twenty-third Amendment to the U.S. Constitution gives District of Columbia residents the right to vote for president.

1963 *(August 28)* The March on Washington for Jobs and Freedom, one of the largest political rallies in American history, is highlighted by Dr. Martin Luther King Jr.'s "I Have a Dream" speech.

1967 Walter Washington, the great-grandson of a slave, is appointed mayor of Washington by President Lyndon B. Johnson, thus becoming one of three African American mayors of large U.S. cities.

1967 Edward Brooke of Massachusetts becomes the first African American elected by popular vote to the U.S. Senate.

1967 Thurgood Marshall is nominated to the Supreme Court by President Lyndon Johnson and served as the first African American associate justice until his retirement in 1991.

1968 *(April)* The largest and most destructive riot sparked by the assassination of Dr. Martin Luther King Jr. occurs in Washington between April 4 and April 8; 12 people die in the rioting, almost 1,100 are injured, and property damage exceeds $27 million.

1973 *(December 24)* Congress approves the District of Columbia Self-Government and Governmental Reorganization Act, which establishes an elected mayor and a 13-member council.

1974 *(November 5)* Walter Washington becomes the first elected mayor and the first African American mayor of Washington; he and the city's first elected council take office on January 2, 1975.

1978 (August 22) Congress approves the District of Columbia Voting Rights Amendment, which would give district residents voting representation in Congress—the House and the Senate—but the proposed constitutional amendment fails to be ratified within the allotted seven-year time period.

1979 *(January 2)* Marion Barry takes office as the second African American mayor of Washington.

1983 *(August)* Jesse Jackson and other civil rights leaders speak at a 20th-anniversary commemoration of the March on Washington and Martin Luther King's "I Have a Dream" speech.

1991 *(January 2)* Mayor Sharon Pratt Dixon, the first African American woman to serve as mayor of a major U.S. city, takes office as mayor of Washington.

1991 President George H. W. Bush appoints Clarence Thomas as the second African American to serve on the nation's highest court.

1995 *(January 2)* Marion Barry takes office for an unprecedented fourth term as mayor of Washington.

1995 *(October 16)* Black men converge on Washington as part of the Million Man March organized by Nation of Islam leader Louis Farrakhan to promote self-help and self-reliance as the method for easing the social ills plaguing the African American community.

2001   Appointed by President George W. Bush, Colin Luther Powell becomes the first African American to serve as U.S. Secretary of State.

2003   Congress approves the plan for the Smithsonian National Museum of African American History and Culture. At an estimated cost of $500 million, the museum will feature a variety of exhibits and educational programs on topics such as slavery, post–Civil War Reconstruction, the Harlem Renaissance, and the Civil Rights Movement.

2005   (*October 15*) The Millions More March commemorates the 10th anniversary of the Million Man March.

2005   Condoleezza Rice is appointed by President George W. Bush as the first African American woman to serve as U.S. Secretary of State.

2008   Sojourner Truth becomes the first black woman honored with a bust in the U.S. Capitol.

2008   The Census estimates that African Americans comprise almost 55 percent of the population of the District of Columbia.

2008   Democrat Barack Obama, the first African American presidential candidate of a major political party, carries the District of Columbia with 93 percent of the vote.

Historical Overview

Establishment of the National Capital

The establishment of a capital did not prove to be an easy task for the United States. The efforts to determine the permanent seat of the national government created continuous debate for seven years after the treaty of peace was signed with the British, ending the American Revolution in 1783. The Constitution adopted by the United States in 1789 authorized Congress to govern whatever site, not exceeding 10 square miles, which it might select. From its inception, the nation was faced with two issues that continuously threatened its unity; these were paramount in the many congressional debates on where to locate the capital. The first issue was slavery. Slaveowning southerners opposed keeping Philadelphia as the capital city because the Quakers there favored the abolition of slavery. Northerners were just as determined that the location would not be in a slaveholding area because it would be an indication to the rest of the world that the United States approved of slavery. The second issue was a continuous battle for regional superiority between the agrarian states of the South and the mercantile/commercial interests of the North. The deep feelings concerning both issues were essentially the same ones that had dominated the initial days of the Continental Congress and they did not end with the ratification of the new U.S. Constitution.

The location of the federal capital was such a contested matter that it encouraged both local areas and states as a whole to make offers to Congress during the early summer of 1783. Advocates for the agricultural-based economy of the South clamored to have the national capital within the sphere of their agrarian, low-tariff universe to better influence national representatives and policies. They wanted an environment free of the commercial and manufacturing bias of the northeastern cities. Likewise, the North wished to have the capital in their region of control because of slavery. A compromise was reached and the government decided to use land obtained from the border states of Maryland and Virginia.

Alexander Hamilton exercised a key role in creating an arrangement where southern money would be contributed to funding the national debt. In exchange for that money, the northern states would allow the capital to be located within a day's horseback ride from Mount Vernon, Virginia, the home of George Washington. This compromise allowed the current site of Washington to be selected. The area initially selected was 100 square miles of land from Maryland and Virginia, but the Virginia portion of land south of the Potomac River was given back to that state in 1846.

Pierre L'Enfant was originally appointed designer of the capital city, but his overly grandiose plan could not be carried out. In 1791, Benjamin Banneker, a free black man, was recruited to work on the surveying and mapping of the new Federal City. His inclusion in the project clashed with many congressmen's prejudicial views that blacks were racially inferior and mentally inept. However, Banneker, a talented surveyor, mathematician, and astronomer, successfully surveyed the land designated to build the capital city in accordance with L'Enfant's plan. In 1792, construction of the president's mansion, later known as the White House, began, but the capital city of Washington, D.C., would not become the official seat of government until November 1, 1800, when President John Adams moved into the White House. Banneker's work came to be a source of enormous pride for future generations of African Americans, as evidenced by the fact that several schools, museums, and streets are named in his honor. These include a high school in Atlanta, Georgia; a museum in Annapolis, Maryland; and a circle near L'Enfant Plaza in Washington, D.C.

The Nineteenth Century

It is difficult to identify the first black occupants of the geographical area that became the capital city. In the 1780s, the area selected for the national capital consisted largely of wilderness. When the survey lines of Washington, D.C., were drawn, only a small population of blacks lived there. Nonetheless, African American influence has been in the city since its inception. The Census of 1800 showed the new capital had a population of just over 10,000 whites, 793 free Negroes, and 3,244 slaves. By affirming that the laws of Virginia and Maryland, both slave states, should govern the commerce and liberties of African Americans in the District of Columbia, Congress opted to ignore the dilemma of slavery in the capital. Even after the constitutional provision prohibiting the importation of Africans into the United States from 1808 took effect, Washington, D.C., remained one of the principal slave markets in the nation. It was not until 1862 that black Americans in Washington were officially free, nine months before President Abraham Lincoln's Emancipation Proclamation.

The Civil War of 1861–1865 is arguably the most defining moment in American history. While the South fought, in part, for the right of the states to maintain black slavery, the North fought first to preserve the Union and then to abolish slavery throughout the country. One of the differences between this American war and those preceding it was the significant number of black soldiers who fought. Although African Americans fought in all American wars, including the Revolutionary War, the number of blacks enlisted to fight in the Civil War for their freedom and the abolition of slavery was very important to the outcome. Over 180,000 African Americans served in the Union army alone, not counting the many thousands in the Union navy. There were many accolades given them in recognition of their valor and dedication. It was reported that a Union general said he had never seen such fighting as was done by a "Negro regiment" and he further indicated that the question whether blacks would fight was settled because they were better solders in every respect than any troops he ever had under his command.

The lifeblood and vortex of the Civil War conflict was in Washington, D.C. The decision to engage the Confederate states, the policy establishing the inseparability of the states, the Emancipation Proclamation, and the terms by which the conflict would end were all either formulated or defined in Washington. Because of continuing racial discrimination in the South, Washington experienced a major influx of African Americans into the city from the end of the Civil War to 1900, causing the black population of Washington, D.C., to increase eightfold. With more newly freed blacks in the city, the Freedmen's Bureau decided it was time to make education a priority for the mostly illiterate black population. Howard University (named in honor of General Oliver Otis Howard, head of the Freedman's Bureau) was created from an elementary school and social center for the teaching of reading, writing, and religion. Howard University was established in Washington, D.C., in 1866 and became one of the nation's oldest black universities. The institution was the capstone of black American higher education and encouraged an environment of education and achievement throughout the surrounding area.

The history and activities of Washington, D.C., at some points are synonymous with those of the United States itself. The Reconstruction era (1865–1877) is an excellent case in point. The federal government did not follow the emancipation of the slaves with a workable program of racial adjustment. The return of the seceded states to the Union turned the Reconstruction period into a time of bitterness and hatred. Yet many positive achievements emerged from Washington during Reconstruction, such as passage of the Thirteenth Amendment abolishing slavery (1865), of the Fourteenth Amendment guaranteeing due process to all Americans (1868), and of the Fifteenth Amendment extending the vote to African Americans (1870). The

Reconstruction period also saw the passage of the Civil Rights Acts of 1866 and 1875; the creation of the Freedman's Bureau by Congress; the emergence of black political leaders, like Frederick Douglass; and the election, between 1869 and 1875, of 16 blacks from seven southern states to the U.S. Congress, including six from South Carolina, three from Alabama, three from Mississippi, and one each from Florida, Georgia, Louisiana, and North Carolina. By the end of 1876, the Reconstruction governments in the southern states had all but passed away. Not long after his inauguration in 1877, President Rutherford B. Hayes ordered the removal of federal troops from public buildings in the South. The president's decision began the closing of the door of freedom in all aspects of blacks' lives in the South, a situation that would continue to some degree

Editor, orator, and abolitionist Frederick Douglass was the foremost African American leader of the nineteenth century in the United States. He was also an advocate for women's suffrage. (National Archives)

until the end of the twentieth century. To make matters worse for black people, after 1877, the federal government declared itself powerless against lawlessness in an individual state.

The Twentieth Century

At one point between 1880 and 1910, Washington, D.C., was reported to have the highest urban black population in the nation. White violence directed at blacks and the rise of white racist terror organizations were developments that reached their zenith during the post-Reconstruction era of 1877–1920. Blacks throughout the nation began to develop resistance to the violence. Washington, D.C., experienced its share of the turmoil. Even though the city did not adopt a segregation ordinance like other American cities in the early 1900s, white property owners made most areas available for white residence only. Washington blacks found it increasingly difficult to find suitable places to live. They often lived in small clusters near white neighborhoods, making them vulnerable to hateful attacks. It remained for the black citizens in the capital of the nation to show the real potential of black resistance to racial violence in the post-Reconstruction era. The only thing black Washingtonians could do that their counterparts in Richmond, Atlanta, or Birmingham could not was ride in the front of city buses within the city limits. The 1930s brought on an unforeseen political shift in Washington, D.C., with the "New Deal" programs of President Franklin D. Roosevelt. Although meant to combat the Great Depression that gripped the nation after 1929, the New Deal did make some headway with civil rights with the appointment of a black leader like Mary Bethune to a higher governmental position, thereby achieving a new visibility for African Americans on Capitol Hill.

Three of the most repressive governmental political decisions foisted upon the black residents of Washington during the twentieth century were the following:

1. A denial of the right to vote.
2. Congressional governance of the District of Columbia.
3. Urban renewal programs that displaced thousands of poor and low-income black citizens.

An act of Congress on May 15, 1820, allowed Washington City to popularly elect its mayor, its eight-member board of aldermen, and its 12-member board of common council. Neither blacks nor women were allowed to vote. In February 1871, Congress repealed the city's 69-year-old charter. Georgetown, Washington City, and Washington County were merged. Alexandria had been given back to Virginia in 1846. The loss of the charter also discontinued voting rights for D.C. citizens. It was not until November 3, 1964, that the residents of Washington, D.C., were allowed to vote for the president of the United States; the district's three presidential electors cast their votes for Lyndon Baines Johnson.

Perhaps the most significant thought in the minds of D.C. residents in the 1950s and 1960s was a desire to be able to elect their own local government. This was referred to as "home rule." There was also an active movement known as the D.C. Statehood Party. For much of the twentieth century, Washington, D.C., has been governed by a congressional committee. Congressional committees have served as the primary instrument by which Congress managed its business for most of the past two centuries. When considering the issues of determining local rules and legal requirements for a major city like Washington, this was a unique and puzzling anomaly in a democracy. Both houses of Congress had committees for the District of Columbia, but the House committee was more repressive, apparently because it had control of the budget for the District. The Legislative Reorganization Act of 1946 created an arrangement that lasted for over 50 years and vested a great deal of power in committee chairmen, collectively known as "cardinals." The House committee also appeared to justify its repression because the population was black and the congressmen involved were mostly southern white men who behaved in the most racist manner possible. Many local blacks attributed their racist behavior to a psychological desire to "run a plantation." The flexibility and arbitrary power of committee members derived largely from the realization that they were free to set their own model, since neither the Constitution, federal law, nor congressional rules established the "committee system" uniformly.

In 1967, the Lyndon Johnson administration sought to move the home rule process along by consolidating the old three-man commission government into a single appointive mayor-commissioner and council-type government. Many residents saw this attempt as being cosmetic only. In November 1968, elections were held for the new 11-member board of education, which was the first time in 92 years that the citizens of the District of Columbia voted for local officials. In December 1973, President Richard Nixon signed the District of Columbia Self-Government and Reorganization Act, also known as the "Home Rule Act." This law gave Washington the right to an elected mayor and a 13-member city council. The law also eliminated the three presidentially appointed positions created by Congress in 1874. The new act was limited, since D.C. residents did not get a voting representative in Congress. In addition, Congress kept control over the District's court system and budget, as well as the right to override legislation passed by the D.C. city council. By 1977, the U.S. Senate had eliminated its District of Columbia Committee. During the middle 1990s, the House of Representatives dismantled the Committee on the District of Columbia and made it a subcommittee of the Committee on Government Reform and Oversight. Later, at the beginning of the 109th Congress in 2005, the House eliminated its District of Columbia subcommittee.

In 1948, the U.S. Supreme Court ruled that racially restricting covenants were illegal. This enabled middle-class blacks and black professionals to purchase and own homes in several neighborhoods in Washington, such as Brookland, Sheppard Park, and Brightwood. However, the tragedy of Washington's racism in housing for poor and disadvantaged blacks was illustrated by the sweeping plan of the District of Columbia Redevelopment Land Agency for urban renewal in Southwest Washington. Nearly 23,500 persons (most of whom were blacks with a family income less than $2,500 per year) were moved out between 1954 and 1958. This move occurred despite the strong negative reaction of the black community's religious and community leaders to the planned programs. The fate of these families caused by inadequate planning for their resettlement was quite obvious to the leaders. The evolution of such negative D.C. governmental actions against its black citizens was somewhat ironic since the removal measures were designed by the grandson of one of the most progressive leaders of the Reconstruction era—President Ulysses S. Grant. In the 1870s, President Grant's administration had promoted some of the racial policies advocated by Washington resident Frederick Douglass, including the betterment of living conditions for blacks in the District of Columbia. Ulysses S. Grant III, as head of the National Capital Park Planning Commission, was the architect of a master plan of racial segregation. He was empowered to design a Washington free of slums. In 1947, General Grant III unveiled a proposal calling for the massive removal of the city's black population away from Foggy Bottom, the southwest area, and Georgetown to the farthest regions of Anacostia. By 1960, most of the old southwest area disappeared.

Although many African Americans had fought for the United States during World War II and had come to expect that racial conditions in the country after the war would improve because of their service, racism still reigned supreme in the Deep South. However, the 1950s witnessed the start of a strong Civil Rights Movement in the South. Beginning with Rosa Parks' refusing to give up her seat on a Montgomery, Alabama, bus in 1955, and followed by sit-ins in diners in North Carolina and elsewhere in 1960, racial tension was mounting. Politicians and national leaders were forced to pay attention to African American demands for equality. In 1961, "freedom rides" from the North, including Washington, D.C., were initiated into the southern states to show the solidarity among those, black and white, fighting for the cause of racial justice. The freedom rides were journeys by activists on interstate buses into the segregated southern United States to test the U.S. Supreme Court decision in the case *Boynton v. Virginia* (1960), which ended segregation in bus and train terminals for passengers traveling between states. The freedom ride movement culminated in 1963.

From 1966 to 2009, Washington, D.C., saw a quick progression of "firsts," as African American leaders took their position in government. These firsts included Robert Weaver as secretary of the Department of Housing and Urban Development under Lyndon Johnson; Patricia Harris as the first black female cabinet member as secretary of the Department of Housing and Urban Development under Jimmy Carter in 1977; General Colin Powell as secretary of state from 2001 to 2004 and Condoleezza Rice as the first black female secretary of state from 2005 to 2009 under President George W. Bush. Senator Barack Obama of Illinois defeated Senator John McCain of Arizona in the 2008 presidential campaign and was inaugurated as the 44th president of the United States and the first African American president in January 2009. As the seat of the national government, Washington, D.C., remains central for the establishment of equality for all Americans.

Notable African Americans

Adams, Numa Pompilius Garfield (1885–1940)

In 1929, Numa Adams became the first black dean of Howard University Medical School. He established the first residencies, including the surgical residency program in 1936, for doctors wishing to pursue specialties in medicine.

Augusta, Alexander Thomas (1825–1890)

Alexander Thomas Augusta was in charge of Freedmen's Hospital in the District of Columbia from 1863 to 1864. He was the first black person to head a hospital in the United States. He also taught anatomy at Howard University.

Bailey, Pearl (1918–1990)

Pearl Bailey was a Washington resident who attained worldwide fame as a jazz singer and actress. Although born in Virginia, it was early in her career that she gained fame performing at two famous nightclubs on Washington, D.C.'s historic U Street.

Banneker, Benjamin (1731–1806)

Benjamin Banneker was chosen to help survey the boundaries for what is now the District of Columbia. He also published an almanac using his own astronomical calculations.

Barry, Marion Shepilov (1936–)

Marion Barry was mayor of Washington, D.C., from 1979 to 1991 and from 1995 to 1999. Between and following his terms as mayor, he served three terms on the D.C. City Council. Barry came to politics from the Civil Rights

Benjamin Banneker was one of the country's first and greatest intellectuals, and as an African American helped to dispel the notion that intelligence varies according to skin color. Banneker's accomplishments ranged from self-taught astronomy and mathematics to writing influential essays and improving irrigation techniques. (National Archives)

Movement of the 1960s, where he served as the first president of SNCC. Barry remained a controversial figure throughout a large portion of his career, including an arrest for possession of crack cocaine in 1990.

Bell, George (c. 1761–1843)

George Bell helped found the Bell School in 1807, which was the first district schoolhouse for black children. He dedicated his life to educating blacks in Washington, D.C.

Cardozo, Francis Louis (1837–1903)

Francis Louis Cardozo helped organize and shape Preparatory (later M Street) High School into the country's top educational institution for blacks. He taught Latin at Howard University from 1871 to 1872.

Cardozo, William Warrick (1905–1962)

William Cardozo practiced medicine in Washington and was a pioneer in the research of sickle cell anemia. He was a grandson of Francis L. Cardozo and was an instructor at Howard University College of Medicine.

Davis, Benjamin O., Sr. (1877–1970)

In 1940, Benjamin O. Davis became the first African American to be promoted to the rank of General in the U.S. military. He was a native of Washington, D.C.

Davis, Benjamin Oliver "Chappie," Jr. (1912–2002)

"Chappie" Davis was the second African American to become a U.S. military general and the first black in the U.S. Air Force to become a lieutenant general. He became a four-star general in 1998. Chappie Davis was also a native of Washington, D.C.

Drew, Charles Richard (1904–1950)

Charles Drew is known for his groundbreaking research in blood plasma. During World War II, he modified the technology for producing blood plasma so that it could be mass-produced for shipment. Drew was a professor of surgery and later became the head of the Howard University Medical School Department of Surgery.

Eckstine, William Clarence "Billy" (1914–1993)

Billy Eckstine was known as the greatest black crooner during the 1930s and 1940s. He attended Armstrong High School and began his professional singing career in Washington, D.C.

Civil rights leaders, including Dr. Martin Luther King Jr., during the March on Washington in Washington, D.C., on August 28, 1963. (Library of Congress)

Ellington, Edward Kennedy "Duke" (1899–1974)

Duke Ellington has been called the single most important figure in jazz history. He composed five film scores and ballet music for leading ballet dancers, and also recorded over 160 compositions between 1928 and 1931. He received 16 honorary doctorates, honors from two U.S. presidents, and many other awards. Duke Ellington was a native of Washington and a graduate of Armstrong High School.

Fauntroy, Walter (1933–)

Walter Fauntroy was the first elected nonvoting delegate to represent Washington, D.C., in the U.S. Congress. A graduate of Yale University Divinity School, he was a civil rights activist. As a member of the staff of S.C.L.C., he helped coordinate the March on Washington in 1963. He was D.C.'s delegate to Congress from 1971 to 1990, and afterwards made an unsuccessful run for mayor of Washington.

Frazier, E. (Edward) Franklin (1894–1962)

E. Franklin Frazier left a legacy of research and publications on race relations, family life, black youth, and the black middle class that has served scholars for generations. In 1942, he was appointed a Library of Congress Resident Fellow and he founded the District of Columbia Sociological Society. He was also a professor and chairman of Howard University's Sociology Department.

Houston, Charles Hamilton (1895–1950)

Charles Hamilton Houston was the first African American to win a case before the U.S. Supreme Court. He helped to found the Washington Bar Association and was a Howard University Law School professor.

Johnson, Mordecai Wyatt (1890–1976)

Mordecai Johnson was the 11th president of Howard University and the first president of African descent. He served as president from 1926 to 1960, when he retired.

Just, Ernest Everett (1883–1941)

Ernest Just was a pioneer in experimental embryology, fertilization, and cellular physiology. His research opportunities were limited by his race, and after being denied admittance by white research institutions, he sought to concentrate on his research in Europe. In 1911, he and three others established Omega Psi Phi, the first fraternity to be founded at a historically black college or university. Dr. Just was an instructor of physiology and director of the Department of Zoology at Howard University from 1912 until 1941.

Locke, Alain Leroy (1886–1954)

Alain Locke was a major proponent of the New Negro Movement, or the Harlem Renaissance. He was an editor and mentor to many young writers, artists, and scholars of the time. He was an early advocate of an African studies program, and from 1912 until 1925 he taught English and philosophy at Howard University.

Manuel, Charles (a.k.a. Daddy Grace) (1881–1960)

Bishop Daddy Grace founded the United House of Prayer for All People in 1926. The church became famous for providing food for the hungry, particularly in the black community. The church was said to have more than three million members in more than 60 cities. In the 1920s, the national headquarters for the church was established in the nation's capital.

An aerial view of the Million Man March at the Capitol in Washington, D.C., on October 16, 1995. Hundreds of thousands of African American men, the largest assemblage of African Americans since the 1963 March on Washington, took part in the rally. (AP/Wide World Photos)

Michaux, Elder Lightfoot Solomon (1885–1968)

Elder Michaux founded the Church of God Movement and established the Church of God in 1928 in Washington. He staged massive baptisms in Griffith Stadium and the Potomac River and held other events, including community marches, around the city.

Norton, Eleanor Holmes (1937–)

Eleanor Holmes Norton is a non-voting delegate to the U.S. Congress. A graduate of Yale University Law School, she was active in the Civil Rights Movement of the 1960s, serving as an organizer for SNCC. She also participated in the Mississippi protests, known as the Mississippi Freedom Summer of 1960. She was first elected to Congress in 1990.

Washington, Walter (1915–2003)

Walter Washington was the first elected mayor of Washington, D.C. A native of Dawson, Georgia, he had served as chair of the New York City Housing Authority before becoming mayor of Washington. In 1968, he helped calm the city after rioting broke out in Washington following the assassination of Martin Luther King Jr. Criticized by many for his low-key approach to governing, Washington finished third in the 1978 Democratic mayoral primary and left office in January 1979.

Williams, Daniel Hale (1856–1931)

Dr. Daniel Hale Williams was one of the first physicians to perform open-heart surgery in the country. He became the surgeon-in-charge of Freedmen's Hospital in Washington in 1894. At Freedmen's,

Martin Luther King Jr. waves to the crowd as he delivers his famous "I Have a Dream" speech during the March on Washington in Washington, D.C., on August 28, 1963. King was awarded the Nobel Peace Prize in 1964 for his work in the area of human rights. (AP/Wide World Photos)

he organized the first program for interns, and established the Training School for Nurses.

Woodson, Carter Godwin (1875–1950)

Carter G. Woodson is best known for his founding of the Association for the Study of Negro (now African American), the founding of the *Journal of Negro* (now *African American*) *History*, and the creation of Negro History Week in 1926. He spent a lifetime dedicated to research in black history and consequently became known as the "father of black history." The headquarters of his association was in Washington and he was a longtime resident of the city. He was a professor of history and dean of liberal arts at Howard University.

Cultural Contributions

African American culture has had a pervasive, transformative impact on many elements of mainstream American culture, and Washington, D.C., remains an exemplar of this veracity. The African American culture is a multifaceted social phenomenon that became distinct because of slavery, segregation, and racial discrimination. The core of the culture is survival in a hostile land. The mechanisms for survival created a different language, a reliance upon various art forms for genuine expression and specific mannerisms in personal interactions. Those characteristics usually evolved to the point that they were visibly different than the European-based culture in the United States. Other aspects of the African American culture like religion, a standard of beauty for African Americans, and family life concepts were not so easily visible for white Americans until the twentieth century. Washington has been a center of cultural development for black Americans, especially after the Civil War. African Americans found out after

Reconstruction that they would have to rely on their own value and social systems. The newly freed slaves placed a high value on education and this was reflected throughout the nation and was especially true for Washington. In time, Howard University was thriving and producing notable scholars like Thurgood Marshall and Carter Woodson, among many others. African Americans have repeatedly met the challenges of racism by outstanding achievements in many fields such as medicine, law, the performing arts, religious leadership, and civic and political participation. Despite the oppressive Jim Crow laws, Washington blacks were among the many around the nation to pave the way to a bright future for African American culture.

Washington, D.C., continues to serve as a major depository of historical contributions of African American culture in the United States. The following 10 institutions and points of interest suggest the width and depth of those cultural contributions while simultaneously recognizing both individual and collective accomplishments. This list of course does not enumerate all of the cultural resources and locations available in the capital city.

1. *The Anacostia Museum.* This museum celebrates African American culture and history through the use of several media. The museum is located in what was once known as Uniontown, a community settled in the wake of the Civil War by freed slaves. It contains a black cultural gallery, and there are demonstrations of black music, art, and dance.

2. *The Bethune Museum and Archives.* This Victorian townhouse served as headquarters for the National Council of Negro Women. It is now a center for black women's history and a national historic site.

3. *The Carter G. Woodson Home.* Dr. Woodson was a Washington historian who effectively promoted recognition of black American contributions to this country. His home at 1538 Ninth Street, NW, is a national historic landmark.

4. *The Frederick Douglass National Historic Site* (also known as Cedar Hill). This was the suburban home of Frederick Douglass, who lived there from 1877 until his death in 1895. This home has been restored by the National Park Service and is now a National Historic Site and museum.

5. *Howard University.* Howard University is one of the outstanding cultural and educational institutions, not only for Washington D.C., but for the United States as well. The Founders Library on the south side of the quadrangle contains black history exhibitions, and the Moorland-Spingarn Research Center contains the nation's largest collection of black literature.

6. *Lincoln Park.* Two of the city's finest and most moving statues are located in this park. The sculpture of educator Mary McCleod Bethune portrays her passing her legacy to her children. The other is a life-size statue of Abraham Lincoln holding the Emancipation Proclamation.

7. *The Martin Luther King Jr. Library.* The main branch of the D.C. public library system focuses on more than books. It sponsors a citywide arts program and houses a permanent collection of paintings, sculptures, photographs, and probably the largest collection of D.C.-related information in the world.

8. *Metropolitan AME Church.* Members of the congregation once hid slaves escaping on the Underground Railroad behind the facade of the national church of African Methodism. Funeral services for Frederick Douglass were held here.

9. *The National Museum of African Art.* The contents of this museum are rare in the United States since the museum is dedicated to the traditional arts of sub-Saharan Africa. The

collection demonstrates how the 900 distinct cultures of Africa weave art into daily life. They express religious beliefs and practices in masks and figures created for ceremonial purposes and also objects of everyday existence. The art works give an incomparable view of the cultures that shaped the African American, which, in time, transformed this country.

10. *The Sumner School Museum and Archives.* This historic red brick schoolhouse built in 1872 was the first school for black children in D.C. after the Civil War.

During the period 1862 to 1900, the U Street Corridor, also known as "Washington's Black Broadway," was developed. This was a collection of shops, restaurants, nightclubs, galleries, and residences located along a nine-block stretch of U Street in northwest D.C. The dawn of the twentieth century proved to be a golden age for blacks in Washington, D.C., especially in entertainment. With the influence of the Harlem Renaissance, artists like Pearl Bailey and Louis Brown realized their talents with performances in the District and subsequently became known throughout the nation. African Americans throughout the nation consider restaurants and nightclubs with talented musicians and singers as being essential to the culture. Washington would be included in the top tier of cities having some of the best food, drink, and talent.

The intersection of culture and race was never more vivid than the several experiences of black Americans exercising their right to the use of public-owned land like Lincoln Memorial on the Mall in Washington for expression of both their culture and political power. The world beyond the District line did not often take notice of the city's difficult race relations, but in 1939, it did so briefly. Many citizens made efforts to enjoy a concert in the District of Columbia by one of the greatest singers in the world, who happened to be black. The Daughters of the American

Marian Anderson singing from the steps of the Lincoln Memorial at memorial service for Harold L. Ickes, 1952. (Library of Congress)

Revolution refused to allow the opera singer Marian Anderson to sing in their auditorium, Constitution Hall. The country and the world took notice of this situation. The Interior Department of the U.S. government suggested that the concert take place outdoors on the steps of the Lincoln Memorial. On Easter Sunday 1939, people gathered along the Reflecting Pool and down the Mall to the Washington Monument. Marian Anderson performed before 75,000 citizens, black and white. This image was included in schoolbooks used across the nation for black children for many years.

Bibliography

Bailey, Thomas. *The American Pageant: A History of the Republic.* Lexington, MA: D. C. Heath and Company, 1975.

Borchert, James. *Alley Life in Washington: Family, Community, Religion, and Folklife in the City,*

1850–1970. Urbana: University of Illinois Press, 1980.

Brawley, Benjamin. *A Social History of the American Negro.* Mineola, NY: Dover Publications, Inc., 2001.

Brinkley, David. *Washington Goes to War.* New York: Alfred A. Knopf, 1988.

Geschwender, James A. *The Black Revolt.* Englewood Cliffs, NJ: Prentice-Hall, Inc., 1971.

Glaab, Charles N., and Theodore A. Brown. *A History of Urban America.* New York: Macmillan Publishing Company, 1976.

Graham, Katharine. *Katharine Graham's Washington.* New York: Alfred A. Knopf, 2002.

Hosmer, John, and Joseph Fineman. "Black Congressmen in Reconstruction Historiography." *Phylon: The Atlanta University Review of Race and Culture* 39, no. 2 (1978): 97–107.

Lewis, David L. *District of Columbia: A Bicentennial History.* New York: W. W. Norton, 1976.

Perret, Geoffrey. *Lincoln's War.* New York: Random House, 2004.

President Abraham Lincoln's letter to Horace Greeley, Editor, *New York Tribune,* August 22, 1862. http://showcase.netins.net/web/creative/lincoln/speeches/greeley.htm.

Smithsonian Anacostia Museum and Center for African American History and Culture. *The Black Washingtonians.* Hoboken, NJ: John Wiley & Sons, 2005.

Thum, Marcella. *Hippocrene USA Guide to Black America.* New York: Hippocrene Books, 1991.

Untermayer, Louis. *Library of Great American Writing Volume 1.* Chicago: Britannica Press, 1960.

U.S. Census Bureau: State and County Quick Facts. May 5, 2009. http://quickfacts.census.gov/qfd/states/11000.html.

Whitney, David C., and Robin V. Whitney. *The American Presidents.* 8th ed. Pleasantville, NY: Reader's Digest Association, Inc., 1996.

FLORIDA

Seth A. Weitz

Chronology

1513	First known African, Juan Garrido, sets foot in Florida.
1565	Blacks help the Spanish found St. Augustine.
1738	Fort Mose is constructed by Spanish as accommodations for blacks in Florida.
1763	Black rights are stripped away when Great Britain assumes control of Florida.
1790	Spain officially suspends the practice of giving refuge in Florida to runaway slaves from the United States.
1816	American troops destroy Fort Negro and kill most of the "Black Seminoles" inside the fort.
1821	Florida becomes a U.S. territory and African American rights are once again stripped away.
1834	Seminole Indians sign the Treaty of Payne's Landing and agree to hand over African Americans to "white" authorities.
1835–1842	African Americans fight alongside the Seminoles in the Second Seminole War.
1840	According to the 1840 Census, the population of Florida is almost 55,000 people, with nearly half being African American slaves.
1845	(*March 3*) Florida enters the Union as a slave state.
1861	(*January 10*) Florida secedes from the Union.
1862	U.S. General David Hunter issues General Order 11, which emancipates slaves in Florida, Georgia, and South Carolina; the order is soon rescinded by President Abraham Lincoln.
1864	Colored regiments take part in the Battle of Olustee. After the battle, reports surface of atrocities committed by Confederate troops against African American soldiers.
1865	The Emancipation Proclamation is read in Tallahassee more than a month after General Robert E. Lee surrendered in Virginia.
1865	(*December 28*) Florida ratifies the Thirteenth Amendment to the U.S. Constitution abolishing slavery several weeks after the amendment had taken effect.
1868	(*June 9*) Florida ratifies the Fourteenth Amendment to the U.S. Constitution guaranteeing full civil rights to African Americans.
1868	Florida is readmitted to the Union; its new state constitution guarantees civil rights and gives African Americans the right to vote.
1868	Jonathan C. Gibbs is appointed as Florida's secretary of state.

1869	Josiah Walls is elected to the Florida legislature.
1869	(*June 14*) Florida ratifies the Fifteenth Amendment to the U.S. Constitution guaranteeing the right to vote to blacks.
1869–1871	The Jackson County War claims the lives of close to 100 people, including many African Americans.
1871	Josiah Walls is elected to the U.S. House of Representatives.
1885	Florida's new constitution mandates a separation of the races in all public facilities, including schools.
1887	The State Normal College for Colored Students (today Florida A&M University) begins classes.
1897	James Weldon Johnson becomes the first African American admitted to the Florida Bar.
1909	The State Normal College for Colored Students changes its name to Florida Agricultural and Mechanical College for Negroes.
1920	Whites destroy black homes and churches and kill at least eight black residents of Ocoee in Orange County; later termed the "Ocoee Massacre" by the National Association for the Advancement of Colored People (NAACP), the violence may have begun when several blacks attempted to vote.
1923	(*January*) Whites attack and largely destroy the African American community of Rosewood, Florida, killing many of the town's residents after a local white woman accuses a black man of assaulting her.
1923	Mary McLeod Bethune helps found Bethune-Cookman Institute.
1951	Civil rights activist Harry T. Moore and his wife are murdered when a bomb explodes at their house.
1953	The Florida Agricultural and Mechanical College for Negroes changes its name to Florida Agricultural and Mechanical University (FAMU).
1956–1957	Tallahassee Bus Boycott leads to the integration of the city's buses.
1963	(*April 18*) Florida ratifies the Twenty-fourth amendment to the U.S. Constitution abolishing the poll tax.
1964	Dr. Martin Luther King Jr. leads successful protests in St. Augustine.
1970	Gwendolyn Cherry becomes the first African American woman elected to the state legislature.

1973	Racial tensions erupt at a northwest Florida high school when the school's sports teams use Confederate imagery as their mascot.
1975	Five African American fishermen from the Pensacola area disappear under suspicious circumstances; while local authorities declare their deaths accidental drowning, many area blacks believe they were murdered by whites.
1975	Joseph W. Hatchett becomes the first African American to serve on the Florida Supreme Court.
1975	(*December 22*) When a white sheriff's deputy in Escambia County shoots and kills Wendel Blackwell, a black motorist, local African American leaders hold demonstrations and rallies demanding a federal investigation of the incident.
1976	(*February 24*) A riot erupts in Pensacola when police use force to break up a demonstration protesting the recent killing by a police officer of black motorist Wendel Blackwell.
1978	Jesse J. McCrary Jr. is appointed Florida secretary of state, becoming the second African American to hold the office.
1980	(*May 17*) Miami is rocked by three days of rioting in the African American communities of Liberty City, Overton, and Coconut Grove, where black rioters rise up after white police officers are acquitted of the beating death of a black man; 17 people died in the riots and property damage was put at more than $100 million.
1982	A riot erupts in Miami after a Hispanic police officer shoots and kills a young black man.
1989	Riots erupt again in Miami after another Hispanic officers shoots and kills an African American; the officer is eventually convicted and sent to prison.
1990	Leander Shaw is selected to be the chief justice of the Florida Supreme Court.
1992	After serving 17 years in the Florida legislature, Carrie Meek becomes the first African American woman elected to Congress from Florida as well as the first African American sent to Washington by the state since Reconstruction.
2002	Kendrick Meek is elected to Congress, succeeding his mother as representative of Florida's 17th District.
2008	(*November 4*) Democrat Barack Obama, the first African American nominee for president of a major political party, carries Florida with about 51 percent of the vote.
2010	Kendrick Meek is defeated in his bid to become the first African American U.S. senator from Florida.

Historical Overview

Early History to 1800

While Native Americans have been in Florida for more than 10,000 years, the first known African American in Florida was Juan Garrido, a conquistador who arrived in 1513 as part of Juan Ponce de Leon's expedition. While there were other black conquistadors, one of the first blacks to permanently inhabit Florida was Estevanico, a slave from Morocco who was owned by one of the earliest Spanish explorers. Later in the sixteenth century, blacks, both slave and free, helped Pedro Menendez de Aviles found the city of St. Augustine in 1565 (the oldest settled city in what is today the United States). Aside from these events, and Estevanico's time in Florida, African Americans were not a sizeable presence until the late seventeenth century, numbering only 27 out of a nonnative population of 491 in 1600. Despite their small numbers, blacks were still a vital cog in Spanish Florida's economy as they were counted on to replace native labor as the natives died off, mostly due to contracting European diseases they had no immunity to combat. Most of the slaves initially came directly from Spain, but later most came to Florida from Cuba, where they were already acclimated to the tropical climate.

Even though the labor system was rigid and set in place by the late sixteenth century, many slaves enjoyed higher levels of freedom and dignity (which they were not afforded later under English and American rule). Spain set up a system of laws and traditions centered on what they deemed morality and guided by the Catholic Church, which gave slaves more freedoms and a sense of identity. Unlike other institutions of slavery in the Americas, slaves in Florida could own and transfer property legally as well as use the judicial system when a crime was committed against them. Many slaves were also able to obtain their freedom through various methods, including purchasing it or through the generosity of their owners.

Runaway slaves began to arrive in North Florida from the Carolinas in the 1680s, escaping their English colonial masters by seeking refuge in Spanish Florida. To accommodate the runaways, the Spanish constructed Fort Mose in 1738 outside of St. Augustine, and this soon became the first settlement of free blacks anywhere in North America. Fort Mose was also known as Gracia Real de Santa Teresa de Mose. The free blacks not only lived in the settlement and worked on the land in the surrounding area, but also helped the Spanish defend St. Augustine and Florida from several British attacks. Over time the community expanded and free blacks worked and lived within the city of St. Augustine as well as within the walls of the fort. They performed numerous jobs such as working as blacksmiths, tailors, and carpenters along with more traditional agricultural duties.

At the conclusion of the French and Indian War in 1763, Florida was transferred from Spain to Great Britain and it was during this time that the African American population of Florida grew dramatically. One of the largest increases in population came during the Revolutionary War when English loyalists moved south from Georgia and the Carolinas as their plantations came under attack from patriot forces. It was also a time when Florida's slaves lost the freedoms they had enjoyed under Spanish rule. English planters tried to recreate the plantations they had already established in other colonies in the Americas where the slaves worked under harsh conditions cultivating tobacco, cotton, indigo, and rice. The British in Florida copied the South Carolina Slave Code verbatim, which called for harsh punishments for the slave population. In spite of the fact that many of the slaves left with their masters when Florida once again became a Spanish possession after the American Revolution, Florida's black population, both slave and free, was on the rise and this trend would continue through the

American Civil War. From the time when Florida was transferred back to Spain, through the end of Spanish rule, the black population, both slave and free, increased from 27 percent to 54 percent of Florida's total population.

As the Spanish resumed control, they once again loosened the reins on the black population, and many slaves took advantage of this, and also of the confusion and chaos during the transfer, to run away from their masters and hide out in the Florida wilderness. Some did not even have to run away to gain their freedom as 251 slaves were freed, due to their claim that they were fleeing Anglican religious persecution. Under Spanish law, they were granted their freedom once they accepted Catholicism. One other avenue to freedom was service with the Spanish army, including the "black militia," which had helped the Spanish repulse several British attacks against St. Augustine.

Over the course of the seventeenth and eighteenth centuries, African Americans had lived alongside the Spanish in Florida, but as the United States won its independence from Great Britain in 1783, and began to expand in the early part of the nineteenth century, the status of the small free black population there was threatened. In the early years of the American republic, planters in neighboring Georgia began to vociferously protest the fact that slaves from their state were being given asylum in Spanish Florida. Feeling threatened by the United States, Spain, in 1790, agreed on paper to stop granting freedom and protection to runaway slaves, though they maintained that they would protect the freedom of those blacks who had already escaped to Florida. In fact, in spite of Spain's compliance with American complaints, Florida remained a haven for runaways and also remained a thorn in the side of the United States.

Early Nineteenth Century

After the conclusion of the War of 1812 and the defeat of the Creek Indians in the Creek War in Alabama and Georgia, the United States looked south to Florida. The Spanish Empire was crumbling in the "New World" and Americans saw an opportunity to stake claim to a piece of this land. When the British left Florida, they maintained a presence in the region by funneling ammunition, money, and other supplies to the natives as well as blacks living in the area. They also left the natives and their black allies a well-armed fort, known to white Americans as Fort Negro or Negro Fort, located in present-day Franklin County on the Apalachicola River, not far from the Gulf of Mexico. While most of the natives left the area, some 300 blacks, mostly runaway slaves, stayed behind and set up a refugee camp at the fort, which was open to anyone seeking refuge from what they perceived to be white encroachment. Not only did the fort dominate the river, it alarmed white planters and settlers as far north as Georgia and Alabama. To deal with this problem, General Andrew Jackson offered the natives money if they would attack the fort, and when they refused he pressured the Spanish, who also refused. Finally, the Americans decided to attack the fort themselves in July 1816. Troops under the command of Colonel Duncan L. Clinch fired at the fort from the mouth of the river until a lucky shot hit the ammunition supply in the fort, causing an enormous explosion that killed 270 of the 344 defenders and also wounded all but three. Soon, seeing no point in trying to halt American expansion, Spain decided to cede Florida to the United States.

When the United States took possession of Florida following the Adams-Onis Treaty, blacks saw their quality of life steadily decline. As the "Old South" was created in Florida, African Americans were seen as inferior, even those who were not slaves. In 1821, when Florida became a U.S. territory, the land held fewer than 8,000 people, including slaves. This soon changed as settlers flocked to Florida, seeking a new and better life. Florida was the nation's and the South's newest frontier and despite over 300 years of Spanish and British rule, Florida was largely a virgin land to whites in the 1820s. It was considered part of the "old Southwest," which can account for why many felt Florida was a land of opportunity where white settlers could begin new lives. Most of the settlers came from the established plantation systems of Virginia, the Carolinas, and Georgia.

When white Floridians called a convention to draw up a territorial constitution, the document produced was proslavery in every aspect. The new legislature was not allowed to ban the importation of slaves into the territory, it could not emancipate slaves for any reason, and it also banned blacks from entering Florida while maintaining that all free blacks present in Florida would have a grace period of 30 days to leave the territory or face enslavement. This was important because it affected the lives of close to half of Florida's population by 1830.

Not all free blacks left Florida, and many remained, living with the Seminole Indians in Central Florida. Some of the African Americans, or Black Seminoles as they were often called, were technically the property of the natives, but they not did suffer the same horrible fate of most slaves owned by white masters. In most cases they were slaves in name only, and lived comfortably within or on the peripheries of the Seminole settlements. When President Andrew Jackson decided that it was in the best interest of the United States to remove Native American tribes to land west of the Mississippi River, the Seminoles were one of the tribes that were targeted. When asked about their population, the Seminoles noted that they had 4,883 natives living on their land, but refused to make a distinction between pure-blooded natives and blacks. When the Seminoles signed a treaty with the U.S. government, it also called for the natives to hand over their slaves and free blacks living within their communities to white American authorities.

In almost every case, the Seminoles did not abide by these stipulations and the blacks retreated further into the swamps away from the reach of white society.

When they felt they could no longer peacefully resist the whites, the Seminoles took up arms. When the Second Seminole War broke out in 1835, blacks, both slave and free, aided the Seminole warriors who attacked Major Francis L. Dade and his 110 U.S. soldiers as they left Fort Brooke and marched towards Fort King in what is referred to as the Dade Massacre. The fact that the Seminoles killed over 100 American troops only heightened the resentment that whites felt towards free blacks, as well as runaway slaves, and in many cases provided slave owners with excuses to impose harsher punishments and restrictions on their slaves.

Slavery soon became the most important economic institution in much of Florida, especially the area known as Middle Florida, in which the new capital of Tallahassee resided. Florida's population when it entered the Union as a state in 1845 was estimated at 66,500, of which at least 27,181 were slaves. In 1845, slaves made up 48.7 percent of Florida's population. Also, 47 percent of the population resided in Middle Florida, which was known as Florida's "Black Belt" due to the soil as well as the large number of slaves. The counties in this region all had slaves make up more than 50 percent of their populations. By 1850, Florida had surpassed South Carolina and Georgia in the production of black seeded, long staple cotton, further proof of the importance of slavery.

Slavery in Florida varied depending on the region of the state. In East and South Florida, planters normally employed the task system, which was favored by the slaves and in which the slaves were assigned different tasks or jobs. These slaves were often finished with their work by midday. In Middle Florida, which was home to the state's larger plantations, the gang system was used. This system in which large numbers of slaves worked in groups for most of the day was despised by the slaves and most forms of resistance were aimed at this system. While there were no major slave revolts in Florida during the antebellum period, most slaves practiced day-to-day resistance such as feigning illnesses or breaking tools to sabotage work. Since Florida was sparsely populated, running away was an option, and more successful for slaves than in other Deep South states. From 1821 to 1860, 742 slaves were classified as runaways.

Civil War and Reconstruction

When the Civil War broke out in 1861, Union troops occupied many of the forts along Florida's coast as well as occupying several coastal cities such as Key West and Jacksonville. Jacksonville was occupied on four separate occasions and every occupation offered the opportunity for slaves to run away to what they felt was the safety of the Union lines. Even though Union troops did not stay in Jacksonville for long periods of time, naval gunboats remained on the St. Johns River and encouraged slaves to leave their masters. In early 1862, Union troops returned some of the runaways to their masters, but many went against the wishes of President Abraham Lincoln and refused, referring to the former slaves as contraband of war. In May 1862, General David Hunter, who was in charge of the Union troops in Florida, Georgia, and South Carolina, issued an order abolishing slavery. Lincoln overturned the edict, but by July 1862, Lincoln had changed his tune, and slaves were no longer returned to their masters in Florida. In response, many slave owners moved their slaves inland or sold their slaves to Georgia or other states that were not directly threatened by Union troops.

Many of the adult male runaway slaves eventually entered into service in the Union army, composing large portions of the 1st, 2nd, and 3rd South Carolina Volunteers, who were later consolidated into the 21st, 33rd, and 34th U.S. Colored Infantry. By 1865, more than 1,000 slaves and free blacks from the Jacksonville area alone served in these regiments. In November 1862, Company A of the South Carolina Volunteers was sent to Florida to engage in actions against the Confederate positions on the coast. The black troops were involved in several small raids and skirmishes in 1862 and 1863; but black troops did not play a major role in the Civil War in Florida until 1864, when 5,500 Union troops left Jacksonville and marched toward Tallahassee. On February 20, they met a force of about 5,000 Confederate troops at Ocean Pond, near present-day Lake City. The ensuing Battle of Olustee was the bloodiest and most important battle fought in Florida during the war. It was also important to African Americans since they made up a large percentage of the Union troops. The 54th Massachusetts Infantry, made famous by the movie *Glory*, participated in the battle along with the 35th U.S. Colored Infantry. While the battle was a victory for the Confederates, the black troops performed admirably under fire and also provided valuable cover for Union troops retreating toward Jacksonville. One controversy that emerged from the battle, and was directly linked to the high casualty rate, was the fact that many Union troops and newspapers claimed that Confederate troops refused to take black prisoners, killing many of those who tried to surrender or who were injured and left on the battlefield.

While many slaves gained their freedom in Florida earlier than in other states because of the continual presence of Union troops in various parts of the state, the Emancipation Proclamation was not read in Tallahassee until May 1865, a month after General Robert E. Lee had surrendered in Virginia. Because Tallahassee was the only Confederate capital east of the Mississippi River never to fall into Union hands during the war, many slaves in Middle Florida were not aware of their freedom or even the end of the war until after the conclusion of hostilities. Even though blacks had now gained their freedom, many whites in Florida did not want them to be able to act on this freedom during the period of Reconstruction and the decades which followed.

Following the end of the Civil War, federal troops occupied the South, including Florida. Many of the troops who occupied Florida were African Americans, some who had fought in Florida, and many who had once been slaves in the state. Most white Floridians resented any Northern army occupying their state, but were appalled at the fact that their former slaves made up a large portion of the force. At the outset of Reconstruction, numerous prominent white Floridians, who had either moved to the state from the North, or had been Union sympathizers during the war, organized Republican Party "Clubs," which attracted many African Americans. In fact, in 1867, more African Americans were registered to vote than whites and 18 blacks were selected to represent various districts at the state's constitutional convention in 1868. In the state's first election after being readmitted to the Union, 18 African Americans were elected to the legislature and Governor Harrison Reed named Jonathan C. Gibbs, an African American, as Florida's secretary of state.

Encouraged by President Andrew Johnson's seeming lack of interest in protecting the rights of African Americans in the South, southern states, including Florida, soon devised ways to bypass the "rights" afforded to the former slaves. These states passed what came to be known as the Black Codes, whose single purpose was to reduce blacks to a legal form of slavery or servitude by regulating every aspect of their lives. The laws in Florida resembled those of other southern states but in many cases were more severe. They stipulated that no African American was allowed to have any weapon of any kind without a license, could not join white religious congregations, could not use the same public facilities as whites, and could only do labor dictated by the law, which in most cases were the same jobs they performed as slaves. Punishment for not adhering to these laws was often whipping. While these codes were harsh, in many locations it was left to local officials to enforce them, and in some areas they were strictly enforced, while in other areas, African Americans were not subject to harsh punishments. In fact, Governor Reed deemed the section of the codes that made it illegal for blacks to own or possess firearms to be unconstitutional, and therefore this stipulation was largely ignored by officials, even though on a local level, groups such as the Ku Klux Klan confiscated firearms from African Americans.

At the end of the decade, many whites turned to violence to oust Republicans from power, as well as to intimidate African Americans and keep them from voting. A major outbreak of violence occurred in 1869 in what is now known as the Jackson County War. Jackson County, west of Tallahassee, saw a rise in violence aimed first at Republicans, but later, mostly at African Americans. Groups such as the Ku Klux Klan and other white supremacist organizations were responsible for a lot of the terror, which killed an estimated 168 civilians, both black and white, from 1869 to 1871.

After federal troops left Florida, Reconstruction came to an end and the state was redeemed by "Bourbon" Democrats—they drafted a new constitution in 1885 that included provisions for poll taxes as a prerequisite for voter registration and voting, thus virtually eliminating black voters. As if this were not enough, literacy tests were issued along with property taxes. When these methods did not stop black voting, intimidation by white supremacist groups was commonplace. By 1890, African Americans accounted for 47 percent of Florida's population of 269,000, but they had been virtually disfranchised, and would remain that way until the middle of the twentieth century.

Late Nineteenth and Early Twentieth Centuries

One aspect of African American life that prospered during the late nineteenth century was education. State-supported education for blacks began in 1883 when the legislature apportioned $4,000 annually for schools for both races, with the first schools opened for African Americans in Gainesville and Tallahassee in 1884. What is today Florida A&M University was founded in 1887 as the State Normal School for Negroes with 1,500 students and was the only black public university in the state at the time. Waters College was founded in 1883 and run by the African Methodist Episcopal Church and Florida Memorial four years earlier in 1879 by the Southern Black Baptist Church. These advances in education also came with consequences as whites often resented gains made by African Americans, especially those in the field of education, and in many cases these advances were met with violent resistance.

The 1920s also saw the growth of racial violence in Florida, largely traced back to the rebirth of the Ku Klux Klan in 1915. Two of the most horrific incidents in Florida's history occurred at Ocoee in 1920 and Rosewood in 1923. At Ocoee, 250 members of the Ku Klux Klan attacked the black section of the town in an effort to prevent African Americans from voting, and over 50 African Americans were killed in the incident. Three years later, Rosewood, a self-sufficient black community located in Levy County, was also attacked. The "Massacre at Rosewood" began when a black man was falsely accused of raping a white woman. Whites from the neighboring town of Sumter retaliated by attacking, burning, and razing the entire town to the ground. The exact number of dead remains undetermined, estimates range from as few as 6 to as many as 40. African

Americans not killed in the massacre fled to the swamps, where most escaped with the help of a local white citizen. None of the survivors returned to the town, and Rosewood, along with the incident, remained largely unknown until the 1980s.

Many African Americans felt their lives would improve with the outbreak of World War II, but many white Floridians did not feel they could trust the loyalty of the African American community. Governor Spessard Holland was concerned that African Americans were ripe for subversive activity, and in an effort to combat any "subversive" activity, Holland pushed for the creation of the Negro Defense Council led by Florida A&M President John Robert Edward Lee. African Americans were highly active in the Negro Defense Council as well as serving in the armed forces once the war broke out. Despite seemingly being able to prove critics wrong, African Americans remained after the war "outsiders" in Florida as well as throughout the South.

Civil Rights Era and Beyond

Following the end of the Second World War, African Americans around Florida as well as the nation strove to tear down Jim Crow society, which legally kept them as second-class citizens. In Florida, Harry T. Moore led the charge for equality in education as well as registering African Americans to vote. Moore paid for his activism with his life when a bomb exploded in his house on Christmas Day 1951, killing Moore and his wife.

On May 17, 1954, the U.S. Supreme Court struck down school segregation in the famous *Brown v. Board of Education* decision, but in Florida, and many places throughout the South, the fight was just beginning. Most high schools in Florida did not integrate until the late 1960s and early 1970s. The University of Miami became the first major white university in the state to admit African Americans, doing so in 1961. In

Florida A&M University student Ruby Powell thumbs a ride during the pro-integration Tallahassee Bus Boycott, June 1, 1956. It was the fifth day of the boycott. (AP/Wide World Photos)

May 1956 in Tallahassee, two female FAMU students directly challenged the city's segregated bus laws, leading to the Tallahassee Bus Boycott, which was led by the Reverend C. K. Steele and the Inter Civic Council. As a result, Tallahassee's buses were integrated in 1957.

Activism continued to rise, and in 1960, Tallahassee was the scene of numerous sit-ins and other protests that helped to integrate public facilities, but the biggest civil rights battle in Florida took place in St. Augustine, where college students tried to integrate the city's beaches and swimming pools through wade-ins. After local African American activists were attacked by the Ku Klux Klan, Martin Luther King Jr. temporarily moved his operations to the city in 1964 and was arrested and jailed in May. Throughout the summer of 1964, black and white protesters absorbed physical and verbal abuse from the Ku Klux Klan, until President Lyndon Johnson signed the Civil Rights Act of 1964. African American protesters in St. Augustine played an important role in highlighting the violence and discrimination that blacks faced throughout the nation.

In spite of gains made by African Americans in Florida, in early 1980 Miami exploded with a series of riots in African American neighborhoods after four white police officers were acquitted by an all-white jury of killing a black insurance salesman during a traffic stop. Three people were killed and 23 wounded during the first day of the riots. In the end, 15 people died and close to 200 were wounded. Another series of riots broke out in 1982 when two Hispanic cops were acquitted in the shooting death of an African American in a bar, and a final riot broke out in Miami in 1989 after another shooting death of an African American by a Hispanic police officer. This time the officer was found guilty and sentenced to seven years in prison.

In spite of the violence, by the end of the twentieth century, African Americans made up close to 16 percent of the state's population and three African Americans represented Florida in the U.S. House of Representatives, while many more held positions in local and state politics. African Americans traveled an often tumultuous road throughout Florida's history, but have persevered in spite of more than 500 years of oppression, and today play a vital role in every aspect of the state.

Notable African Americans

Armwood, Blanche (1890–1939)

Blanche Armwood was an educator as well as civil rights activist who grew up in Tampa. From 1922 to 1930, she was the supervisor of Negro schools for Hillsborough County and during her tenure worked to try and gain equality in education for African Americans. She was successful in helping to establish the first black high school in the county. She was also executive secretary of the Tampa Urban League and later graduated from Howard Law School. She also worked as a civil rights activist alongside Mary McLeod Bethune and others during the 1920s and 1930s.

Bethune, Mary McLeod (1875–1955)

Mary McLeod Bethune was an educator credited with helping bring higher education to African American females. Bethune won a scholarship to the Moody Bible Institute in Chicago, where she was the only African American student. After working with the poor in Chicago, Georgia, and South Carolina, she moved to Florida after marrying fellow teacher Albertus Bethune. After working as a teacher in Palatka, she opened the Daytona Normal and Industrial Institute for Negro Girls in 1904. In 1923, she merged her school with a boys' school in the area to form Bethune-Cookman Institute, today Bethune-Cookman University. She served as president of the college from 1923 to 1942 and again from 1946 to 1947.

Mary McLeod Bethune fought fiercely to achieve social, economic, and educational opportunities for African Americans, and particularly for African American women. (Library of Congress)

In 1917, she was named president of the Florida chapter of the National Association of Colored Women, a title she held until 1925. In 1932, after working to help elect Franklin D. Roosevelt to the presidency, she became a member of his Federal Council of Negro Affairs or "Black Cabinet," an unofficial group of advisors. In 1935, she founded the National Council of Negro Women, and in 1938 was named director of Negro Affairs for the National Youth Administration, one of Roosevelt's New Deal agencies. Bethune was also a close friend of First Lady Eleanor Roosevelt, and she helped to educate Roosevelt on lynchings and pushed to get an antilynching bill passed by Congress.

Charles, Ray (1930–2004)

Ray Charles was a world-renowned singer and songwriter who was born in Albany, Georgia, but grew up poor in Greenville, Florida. Charles showed a love for music from an early age, but by the time he was seven was completely blind. In spite of this disability, as a teenager, Charles made money playing the piano in bars and clubs in various cities across Florida before moving to Seattle, at age 14.

Cherry, Gwendolyn Sawyer (1923–1979)

Gwendolyn Cherry was born in Miami, attended Florida A&M University (FAMU) and later New York University before returning home to Miami, where she taught public school for 18 years before she became the first African American to attend the University of Miami Law School. She eventually graduated from FAMU's law school, where she taught before running for the state legislature in 1970. Her victory made her the first African American woman elected to the state legislature.

Fortune, T. Thomas (1856–1928)

T. Thomas Fortune was born a slave in Marianna in 1856. After the Civil War, he learned how to read and write at a school set up by former Union soldiers and eventually landed jobs writing for the *Marianna Courier* and the *Jacksonville Daily-Times Union*. He moved to Washington, D.C., to study law and eventually moved to New York, where he became the editor and owner of several newspapers including the *New York Age*. He also published a book, *Black and White: Land, Labor, and Politics in the South*, in 1884 and six years later helped to establish a civil rights organization, the National Afro-American League. He was instrumental in helping W. E. B. Du Bois found the Niagara Movement and later the NAACP and was one the earliest proponents of using the term "Afro-American." Throughout his career he worked to combat lynching and, later in his life, became an editor of *Negro World*, the periodical published by Marcus Garvey's Universal Negro Improvement Association.

Gibbs, Jonathan C. (1827–1874)

Jonathan C. Gibbs was born in Pennsylvania and earned a degree from Dartmouth College. Following the conclusion of the Civil War, he moved to North Carolina, where he opened a school for former slaves, before moving to Florida to work with freedmen in that state. In 1868, he served as a delegate to the state's constitutional convention before Governor Harrison Reed appointed Gibbs as his secretary of state, a position he held until 1872. Gibbs was next made state superintendent of public instruction by Governor Ossian Hart. Gibbs was instrumental in improving education for African Americans as well as whites and helping to significantly raise the literacy rate in the state. He died suddenly in 1874, leading some to believe that he was poisoned since he had accumulated numerous death threats from white supremacists.

Hastings, Alcee (1936–)

Alcee Hastings represents Florida's 23rd district in the U.S. Congress. A native of Altamonte Springs, Florida, he was educated at Fisk and

Howard Universities and received a law degree from Florida A&M University. Before being elected to Congress in 1993, he was appointed a U.S. District Court judge by then President Jimmy Carter in 1979. Ten years later, he was impeached, convicted, and removed from office on charges of corruption.

Hatchett, Joseph W. (1932–)

Joseph W. Hatchett was the first African American to serve as a justice on the Florida Supreme Court as well being the first African American to sit on a Supreme Court in any Southern state. Before becoming a justice, Hatchett was a civil rights attorney, Assistant U.S. Attorney in Jacksonville, and U.S. Magistrate for the Middle District of Florida. He was appointed to the Florida State Supreme Court in 1975 by Governor Reubin Askew. Under Florida law, justices had to seek reelection and Hatchett was successful, making him the first African American elected to a statewide office since Reconstruction. In 1979, President Jimmy Carter named him as a federal circuit judge on the Fifth U.S. Circuit Court of Appeals.

Hawkins, Virgil (1906–1988)

Virgil Hawkins became the focal point in the fight for African American equality in education when he tried to enter the University of Florida's School of Law in 1949. Even though he met the entrance requirements, Hawkins was denied admission because he was black. Hawkins filed suit with the Florida Supreme Court and the state offered to pay for Hawkins' tuition if he agreed to attend school outside of Florida, but Hawkins refused. The state tried a new tactic by agreeing to open a law school for African Americans in Tallahassee. Before the school was completed, the state agreed that Hawkins could take classes at Florida, but the Gainesville school now denied him admission based on merit. He again

went to court in 1952, but the state Supreme Court dismissed his case.

In 1956, the U.S. Supreme Court ordered the University of Florida to admit Hawkins, but the school still refused, claiming there would be outbreaks of violence on their campus. In 1958, a federal district court judge ordered all Florida graduate schools open to all races, but Hawkins was again denied admission based on his credentials. Hawkins eventually attended an unaccredited law school in Boston but was not able to take Florida's Bar exam since the school he had attended was not accredited. In 1975, at the age of 69, Hawkins asked to be allowed to take the state bar exam; a year later, he was allowed to become a lawyer without taking the exam and opened an office in Leesburg, Florida.

Hayes, Robert Lee (1942–2002)

Bob Hayes was a world-class sprinter and professional football player who was nicknamed the "World's Fastest Human" in 1963 after shattering the world record in the 100-yard dash. Hayes played football and ran track at Florida A&M in the early 1960s and in 1964 signed with the Dallas Cowboys. In 1964, Hayes also competed at the Tokyo Olympics, where he won two gold medals.

Hurston, Zora Neale (1891–1960)

Zora Neale Hurston grew up in Eatonville, Florida, a town that was completely governed and inhabited by African Americans. Hurston earned a scholarship to Barnard College, where she was the only African American student, graduating in 1927. Despite holding a degree in anthropology, she made a name for herself as a writer. She began writing plays and poems in the 1920s during the Harlem Renaissance before moving on to books in the 1930s. Her most

Portrait of James Weldon Johnson, author and civil rights activist during the Harlem Renaissance. (National Archives)

Zora Neale Hurston was an American novelist, folklorist, anthropologist, and prominent member of the circle of writers associated with the Harlem Renaissance of the 1920s. (Library of Congress)

famous book, *Their Eyes Were Watching God*, was written in 1937, and was met with criticism from whites and blacks alike at the time, but has since been recognized by *Time* as one of the best 100 novels written between 1923 and 2005.

Johnson, James Weldon (1871–1938)

James Weldon Johnson was born in Jacksonville during Reconstruction and would eventually become an author, composer, poet, scholar, civil rights activist, and even diplomat serving the United States in Venezuela and Nicaragua. He attended Atlanta University, and after graduation, became the principal of Stanton School in Jacksonville. In 1897, he became the first African

American admitted to the Florida Bar since Reconstruction. Johnson is most known for his role in the arts, especially music. In 1900, he wrote the words to "Lift Every Voice and Sing," which has become recognized as the "Black National Anthem" after it was adopted in that capacity by the NAACP. Johnson was also a civil rights activist and helped to organize the NAACP in the 1910s, becoming the first black secretary of the organization in 1920. He used this position to try and secure the passage of a federal antilynching bill.

Lloyd, John Henry "Pop" (1884–1964)

John Henry Lloyd was born in Palatka and made a name for himself as both a baseball player and manager in the Negro League. Lloyd was a shortstop and is considered to be one of the best to ever play that position regardless of race. He played for seven teams beginning in 1906. He went on to help found the Columbus Buckeyes and later managed several other teams. In 1977, he was posthumously inducted into the Baseball Hall of Fame.

Meacham, Robert (1835–1902)

Robert Meacham, who was born to a slave mother and a white father, became one of the leaders of Florida's African American community during Reconstruction. He was also a minister who helped establish the African Methodist Episcopal Church in Tallahassee in 1865 before moving to nearby Monticello where he worked in a church as well as a school educating former slaves. After Florida was readmitted to the Union, he helped frame the state's 1868 Constitution and was later elected to the state Senate and also superintendent of schools in Monticello. He survived an assassination attempt in 1876 and later served as postmaster in Punta Gorda before retiring from public life.

Meek, Carrie (1926–)

Carrie Meek was elected to the U.S. House of Representatives in 1992, along with two other African Americans, Alcee Hastings and Corrine Brown, making them the first African Americans elected to Congress from Florida since Reconstruction. After graduate school, Meek worked at Miami-Dade Community College, where she became the assistant to the president. After Gwendolyn Cherry's untimely death, Meek decided to run for her seat and she defeated 13 other candidates to win the seat. She then ran for a seat in the state Senate, which she won in 1982, making her the first African American woman to hold that distinction. Meek won election to the U.S. Congress in a landslide in 1992 and retired when her term expired in 2003.

Meek, Kendrick (1966–)

Kendrick Meek, the son of Carrie Meek, succeeded his mother in Congress. Meek first became interested in politics while he was a member of the Florida Highway Patrol, where he was assigned to Lieutenant Governor Buddy McKay's security detail. In 1995, he was elected to the Florida House of Representatives, and to the Florida Senate in 1998. In 2002, he was elected to the U.S. House of Representatives with 100 percent of the vote and subsequently reelected unopposed in 2004, 2006, and 2008. He was defeated in a Senate run in 2010.

Moore, Harry T. (1905–1951)

Harry T. Moore was a civil rights leader who was known as the first NAACP activist to be murdered. Moore became a teacher in Brevard County in the 1920s and then became the principal of Titusville Colored School. In 1934, along with his wife Harriette, Moore founded the Brevard County Chapter of the NAACP. In 1937, he filed a lawsuit intended to equalize the salaries of black teachers, and in 1944, he took control of the Progressive Voters League, an organization that sought to end all-white primaries in the Deep South as well as register African Americans to vote.

Because of their activism, the Moores were blacklisted from Florida's public schools in 1946 and Moore began to work full time for the NAACP, becoming the executive director of the Florida chapter. On Christmas night 1951, the Moores' house in Mims, Florida, was bombed by white supremacists. Moore died on the way to the hospital and his wife died nine days later. No one was charged with the crime in the 1950s but the case was reopened in 2005, and a year later Florida concluded that they were victims of a conspiracy by four members of the Ku Klux Klan, three whom had died within a year of the attack, and one in 1978.

Randolph, Asa Philip (1889–1979)

Asa Philip Randolph was a civil rights activist as well as a union organizer. He moved from Florida to New York when he was 22 and soon became known for his activism. In 1917, Randolph founded *The Messenger*, a magazine that campaigned against lynching, opposed U.S. participation in World War I, and urged African Americans to oppose the draft since the armed forces were segregated. In 1925 he organized the Brotherhood of Sleeping Car Porters, an attempt to earn rights for African Americans working as porters for the Pullman Company. In 1937, after more than a decade-long fight, the company awarded the porters more than $2 million in pay increases as well as other concessions.

During World War II Randolph again urged African Americans to not answer the call when drafted and pressured President Roosevelt by creating the March on Washington Movement, which called for an end to segregation in the armed forces as well as defense industries. While the defense industries were integrated, the armed forces remained segregated until Randolph pressured President Harry S. Truman to issue an executive order in 1948. Randolph was also influential in helping Dr. Martin Luther King Jr. organize the March on Washington for Jobs and Freedom in 1963.

Shaw, Leander (1930–)

Leander Shaw became the first African American chief justice of the Florida Supreme Court in 1990. Shaw taught at Florida A&M University in the 1960s before practicing as a lawyer, representing African Americans in civil rights cases. In 1983, he was appointed to the state Supreme Court. He was reelected in 1984 and voted to become chief justice by his fellow justices in 1990.

Steele, Charles Kenzie (1914–1980)

Reverend C. K. Steele was an influential civil rights leader in Florida and close associate of Dr. Martin Luther King Jr. Steele moved to Tallahassee in 1951 and became minister of the Bethel Baptist Church. In 1956, he helped lead the Tallahassee Bus Boycott after two female African American students from Florida A&M University were arrested after refusing to give up their seats to white passengers. Steele helped to form and lead the Inter-Civic Council to protest the city's segregation policies. Steele was arrested on several occasions and in spite of violent threats from the Ku Klux Klan, Tallahassee integrated its buses. Steele's famous quote from the boycott was, "We would rather walk in dignity than ride in humiliation." Steele was also vice president and a charter member of the Southern Christian Leadership Conference, which was led by Dr. King.

Walls, Josiah (1842–1905)

Josiah Walls, originally from Virginia, was forced into service for the Confederacy before being captured by the Union and joining their ranks in 1863, eventually serving in Florida. After the war, Walls settled in Alachua County where he became a teacher and eventually a delegate to the state Republican Convention in 1867. In 1869, he was elected to the state legislature, and in 1871, he was elected to serve as Florida's only representative in the U.S. Congress. In 1874, he won reelection, but his victory was challenged and he was unseated in 1876, ending his political career. In 1873, he bought a newspaper in Gainesville, making Walls the first African American to own a paper in Florida.

Cultural Contributions

African Americans have played a key role in shaping Florida's history and heritage and have made numerous cultural contributions to the Sunshine State, beginning during Spanish colonial rule, and moving through the antebellum period, when most of the state's African Americans were slaves, to the present day.

Besides the contributions made to the fields of music and literature by such native Floridians as Ray Charles and Zora Neale Hurston, African Americans have contributed to the culture of Florida in other ways and many are evidenced in neighborhoods across the state. One such neighborhood is the Smoky Hollow Historic District in Tallahassee. This black neighborhood was home to Wallace Amos, the founder of "Famous Amos" cookies. Another historically black neighborhood, whose history and culture add to Florida's heritage, is the Lincolnville area of St. Augustine, which has been nicknamed "Africa," and was where Ray Charles attended a school for the deaf and blind in order to learn how to read music. In South Florida, the neighborhood of Coconut Grove, inside Miami's city limits, is home to a large Bahamian population, and these immigrants have added flair to Miami by holding an annual festival, the Goombay Festival, which just celebrated its 33rd year. What began as a small street festival in 1976 has grown to be one of the largest black heritage festivals in the United States. From their early days aiding Spanish conquistadors, through their time as slaves, until the present day, African Americans have helped to shape the culture and heritage of the Sunshine State.

Among the other cultural contributions of blacks in Florida are the world-famous Florida A&M University Rattlers Marching Band, which has performed at major sports events, presidential inaugurations, and other national celebrations. Floridians also celebrate Black History Month, sometimes under state sponsorship. Among notable historical sites and museums are the African Heritage Project at the University of South Florida, which seeks to rediscover records of African American history; the African American Museum of the Arts in Fort Lauderdale; the African Americans in Florida Oral History Project at the University of South Florida in Tampa; the African American Research Library and Cultural Center in Bradenton; the Pinellas County African American History Museum in Clearwater; the African American Museum at Florida A&M University; and American Beach, formerly a luxurious oceanfront resort for African Americans on the south end of Amelia Island.

Bibliography

Colburn, David. *Racial Crisis and Community Conflict: St. Augustine, Florida, 1877–1980.* Gainesville: University Press of Florida, 1992.

Colburn, David R., and Jane L. Landers. *The African American Heritage of Florida.* Gainesville: University Press of Florida, 1995.

D'Orso, Michael. *Like Judgment Day: The Ruin and Redemption of a Town Called Rosewood.* New York: G. P. Putman's Sons, 1996.

Dunn, Marvin. *Black Miami in the Twentieth Century.* Tallahassee: University Press of Florida, 1997.

Dunn, Marvin, and Bruce Porter. *The Miami Riots of Nineteen Eighty: Crossing the Bounds.* New York: Simon & Schuster, 1984.

Gannon, Michael. *Florida, a Short History.* Gainesville: University Press of Florida, 1993.

Jones, Maxine D., and Kevin M. McCarthy. *African-Americans in Florida.* Sarasota, FL: Pineapple Press, 1993.

Newton, Michael. *The Invisible Empire: The Ku Klux Klan in Florida.* Gainesville: University Press of Florida, 2001.

Porter, Bruce, and Marvin Dunn. *The Miami Riot of 1980: Crossing the Bounds.* Lanham, MD: Lexington Books, 1984.

Stewart, Martina. "Meek Announces Senate Run." (Online, January 2009). CNN Web site. http://politicalticker.blogs.cnn.com /2009/01/13.

Tebeau, Carlton W. *A History of Florida.* Coral Gables, FL: University of Miami Press, 1971.

GEORGIA

Alton Hornsby, Jr.

Chronology

1730	*(July)* James Oglethorpe and his associates petition for a royal charter to establish a new colony south of Carolina.
1732	*(April)* George II signs the Georgia charter for Oglethorpe and his associates.
1733	Leading a group of English colonists, James Oglethorpe founds the town of Savannah.
1735	Slavery and rum are prohibited in the Georgia colony.
1749	*(May 19)* Georgia's trustees ask the king to allow the repeal of the colony's ban on slavery.
1749	*(October 26)* The king approves the trustees' petition asking for the repeal of Georgia's slavery prohibition.
1751	*(January 1)* African slavery is officially authorized in Georgia.
1758	To encourage the settlement of skilled white laborers in the colony, the Georgia Assembly bans African slaves from working in various trades, including carpentry, masonry, and bricklaying.
1773	First African Baptist, Georgia's oldest African American church, is established
1788	*(January 2)* Georgia ratifies the U.S. Constitution, becoming the fourth state to enter the Union.
1793	*(February 12)* Congress passes the Fugitive Slave Act.
1793	*(June 20)* Eli Whitney applies for a patent for his cotton gin, which he developed at the Georgia plantation of Revolutionary War General Nathaniel Greene.
1798	Georgia prohibits the further importation of slaves.
1847	Atlanta, formerly Marthasville, is incorporated.
1850	As part of the Compromise of 1850, Congress passes a new, stronger fugitive slave act, substituting federal for state jurisdiction over fugitive slaves.
1859	Georgia again prohibits the postmortem manumission of slaves by last will and testament and permits free blacks to be enslaved if they have been indicted for vagrancy.
1861	*(January 19)* Georgia votes to secede from the Union.
1861	*(February 8)* Georgia is admitted to the Confederate States of America.
1864	After the Battle of Atlanta, the city is occupied by Union forces; Union forces take Savannah.
1865	*(January 16)* General William T. Sherman issues Special Field Orders No. 15, which grants abandoned coastal lands in Georgia, southern South Carolina, and northern Florida to "negroes now made free by the acts of war."

1865	*(December 6)* Georgia ratifies the Thirteenth Amendment to the U.S. Constitution abolishing slavery; Georgia's ratification gives the amendment the 27 state approvals it needs to take effect.
1865	Atlanta University is founded.
1865	With the end of the Civil War, Georgia is placed under U.S. military control.
1866	*(November 9)* Georgia rejects the Fourteenth Amendment to the U.S. Constitution guaranteeing full civil rights to African Americans.
1868	Blacks are elected to, then expelled from, the Georgia legislature.
1868	*(July 21)* Georgia ratifies the Fourteenth Amendment, almost two weeks after the amendment took effect.
1868	*(July 21)* Georgia is readmitted to the Union.
1869	Georgia is denied representation in Congress, and the U.S. Army reoccupies the state.
1870	*(February 2)* To have its representatives recognized by Congress, Georgia ratifies the Fifteenth Amendment to the U.S. Constitution granting blacks voting rights.
1870	African American representatives restored to seats in the Georgia legislature.
1870	*(July 15)* Georgia is again readmitted to the Union.
1871	African American Jefferson Long of Macon is elected to the U.S. House of Representatives.
1871	U.S. military forces leave Georgia.
1877	Georgia institutes cumulative poll taxes for voting.
1882–1930	458 blacks are lynched in Georgia, more for the period than in any other state except Mississippi.
1883	The U.S. Supreme Court declares the Civil Rights Act of 1875, which opened public accommodations to blacks, unconstitutional.
1891	Various segregation laws are passed by the Georgia legislature.
1895	Booker T. Washington addresses the Cotton States and International Exposition in Atlanta, where he expresses a willingness to accept segregation in return for white help in advancing educational and economic opportunities for blacks, an idea later known as the "Atlanta Compromise."
1896	The U.S. Supreme Court, in *Plessy v. Ferguson*, upholds the concept of separate but equal.
1900	Georgia Democrats institute all-white primaries.

1906	A serious race riot erupts in Atlanta, leaving an estimated 25–40 blacks and two whites dead.
1908	Georgia institutes literacy tests for voting.
1910	Three blacks in Uvalda are killed in rioting following Jack Johnson's defeat of James Jeffries, the so-called "great white hope."
1912	White residents of Forsyth County drive African Americans out of the county.
1915	A new Ku Klux Klan is organized on Stone Mountain.
1917	The first Georgia chapter of the National Association for the Advancement of Colored People (NAACP) is founded.
1933	Blacks and whites in Georgia are to be educated in separate schools.
1935	A Georgia state law requires segregation on all public transportation.
1935	Separate mental health hospitals are required for blacks.
1936	Margaret Mitchell's *Gone with the Wind*, a novel about Civil War Georgia, is published.
1945	(*April*) U.S. President Franklin D. Roosevelt dies of a cerebral hemorrhage at his retreat in Warm Springs.
1945	A new Georgia constitution calls for separate schools for whites and blacks.
1946	Two black sharecroppers, one man and one woman, are lynched by a mob at Moore's Ford Bridge, in one of the last mass lynchings in the United States.
1947	John Roosevelt (Jackie) Robinson, a native of Cairo, becomes the first African American Major League Baseball player.
1949	WERD, the first black-owned radio station in the country, goes on the air in Atlanta; its founder is Atlanta businessman Jesse B. Blayton.
1955	Georgia repeals its poll tax.
1957	Georgia declares that no public funds are to be allocated for integrated schools.
1960	Martin Luther King Jr. returns to Atlanta, where he was born, to be copastor with his father at Ebenezer Baptist Church.
1961	The University of Georgia and the Atlanta public schools are desegregated.
1961	Martin Luther King launches his first direct action campaign to end segregation and discrimination in Albany, Georgia, but the "Albany Movement" has little success due to divisions in the city's black community.

1966	Citing his opposition to the Vietnam War, the Georgia legislature denies Julian Bond his seat in the legislature by a vote of 184–12. Later in the year, the U.S. Supreme Court orders Bond seated.
1968	After her husband's assassination, Coretta Scott King founds the Martin Luther King Jr. Center for Nonviolent Social Change in Atlanta.
1972	Vernon Jordan, an Atlanta native and former president of the United Negro College Fund, is named president of the National Urban League.
1972	Andrew Young becomes the first black congressman from Georgia since Reconstruction, by winning election from a district with a white majority.
1973	Maynard Jackson is elected as the first black mayor of Atlanta.
1973	The Atlanta NAACP, headed by Lonnie King, agrees to a compromise plan whereby the Atlanta chapter ends its demands for busing to achieve school desegregation in return for black control of the Atlanta public schools administration. The national NAACP suspends King, a former leader of the Atlanta sit-in movement.
1974	(*April*) Henry (Hank) Aaron, a native of Alabama and a member of the Atlanta Braves, hits his 715th home run, breaking the record long held by legendary white player Babe Ruth.
1981	Ed McIntyre is elected as the first black mayor of Augusta.
1984	Ed McIntyre resigns as mayor of Augusta after being convicted on federal extortion charges.
1986	John Lewis, a Democrat, becomes the second African American elected to Congress from Georgia in the twentieth century.
1992	Cynthia McKinney becomes the first black woman elected to Congress from Georgia.
1993	William "Bill" Campbell is elected mayor of Atlanta.
1996	Atlanta hosts the Centennial Olympic Games, which former Atlanta mayors Andrew Young and Maynard Jackson were influential in bringing to the state.
2001	Shirley Clarke Franklin is elected mayor of Atlanta, becoming the first black woman to be mayor of a large southern city.
2002	(*July 27*) Savannah dedicates a bronze statue to Africans brought into Georgia as slaves through the port of Savannah.
2004	Denise Majette wins the Democratic nomination for a U.S. Senate seat, becoming the first woman to win a Senate nomination in Georgia; Majette loses the general election to Republican Johnny Isakson.

2006	Former Atlanta mayor Bill Campbell is sentenced to 30 months in prison and fined $6,000 after being convicted of tax evasion. The jury had previously acquitted him of bribery charges.
2008	Barack Obama, an African American senator from Illinois, defeats Hillary Clinton in the Georgia Democratic primary, winning about 66 percent of the vote; Obama loses Georgia to John McCain in the general election, winning about 47 percent of the vote.
2008	The 25th anniversary of the mayor's Masked Ball is held in Atlanta. The ball, which raises money for the United Negro College Fund, was initiated by Billye Aaron, wife of baseball star Hank Aaron and former regional director of the UNCF.
2009	Kasim Reed, a former Georgia state senator, is elected mayor of Atlanta. The 59th mayor of the city, Reed continues a string of more than 35 years of consecutive black mayors; however, he defeated his white opponent, Mary Norwood, by fewer than 900 votes.

Historical Overview

When the colony of Georgia was established in 1733, the intention of the charter was to provide a place for poor persons who were unable to support themselves in England and to establish a frontier for Carolina, which because of its small number of white inhabitants was very much exposed to hostile Native Americans and Spaniards. It was felt that it was unlikely that the poor people who would be sent from England as well as any poor person who would later enter the colony voluntarily to escape religious persecution or for other reasons would be able to purchase slaves or to maintain them if they were made available free of cost. At the time the average cost of a bondsperson was $150. The trustees' desire to prohibit slavery in Georgia soon, however, came under strong attack. Faced with mounting expenses for military protection against the Spaniards and a decline in private contributions for the aid of the colony, the Georgians were, by 1738, short on military supplies and even food. On December 9, 1738, a group of 121 white males met at Savannah and drew up a petition to the trustees concerning the economic crisis. In the petition, they said that their poor conditions could partially be alleviated by the use of slaves

"with limitations." The trustees, however, refused to allow slavery in the colony at this time.

Some prominent voices continued to be raised, however, in support of black servile labor in the colony. Among these was evangelist George Whitefield. Whitefield had become convinced that the lack of slaves was one of the principal causes of the poor condition of the colony. Nevertheless, the trustees remained firm in their stand against slavery. In the face of the trustees' opposition, some Georgians felt they had no other recourse other than to evade the law and move forward with their plans for black slaves.

When news of these evasions and laxity of enforcement of the law reached the trustees, they told the local authorities to end the illegal activities. But the proslavery steamroller could not be stopped. In January 1749, a new petition was sent to the trustees asking for immediate authorization to use black slaves in Georgia. The trustees could resist no longer. They asked the king for approval of a repeal of the act prohibiting slavery. In 1751, African slavery was authorized in Georgia.

In authorizing the bondage of Africans in Georgia, the trustees added certain provisions. Enslavers were encouraged to permit their bondspersons to attend church on Sundays and no work was to be required on that day. Penalties

The First African Baptist Church, in Franklin Square, Georgia, ca. 1940. (Library of Congress)

were ordered for any interracial sexual cohabitation, and interracial marriage was forbidden. Finally, the trustees declared that enslavers should not exercise unlimited powers over their slaves and that each slavetrader and slaveholder be required to pay a tax for each person held in bondage.

When the first General Assembly of Georgia was held in 1775, a new slave code was adopted. It prescribed that all persons who were slaves at the time of the first colonial General Assembly in 1775 should be assigned to bondage forever. The statute prohibited cruel and unusual treatment of slaves but did not require murderers of slaves to face the full penalty for murder until a second offense. Slaves could not, without a permit, sell food products, own a horse or cattle, or any boat or canoe. They could not sell or purchase liquor. Bondspersons were to receive severe penalties for any crimes they committed: arson, malicious mischief, certain thefts, and homicide

against a white person were all punishable by death.

In the beginning, Georgia's bondspersons raised rice and worked as domestic servants. Later as cotton became king in the area, most worked in the cotton fields. Aside from religious services, often in the company of whites and other times autonomous, the slaves' social activities were limited to occasional recreation with the enslaver and their own late night, weekend, or holiday entertainment in the slave quarters.

Georgia Blacks in the American Revolution

At the outbreak of the American Revolution, it was general and official policy in most American colonies to exclude blacks from the colonial militias, but military necessities often made these rules invalid. By 1775, blacks were serving in the militias of several colonies. At the national level, General George Washington and the Continental Congress vacillated on the use of blacks as soldiers first approving, then disapproving, then approving again, but only free blacks.

By 1778, manpower shortages and the worsening military situation on the American side suggested the recruitment of soldiers wherever they could be found. Several New England colonies and New York authorized the use of slaves. Most of these colonies promised the slaves their freedom after the war if they served faithfully. In the summer of 1780, Maryland took the lead among southern colonies in authorizing the use of slaves as soldiers. Georgia law prohibited slaves from carrying firearms for any purpose.

At the national level, the Continental Congress had, since 1779, been recommending the employment of slaves as soldiers. After the British had occupied Savannah and opened a second campaign to subdue the South, the Congress sent a specific request to Georgia and South

Carolina to enlist slaves. These were to be formed in separate battalions with white officers. Owners of the slaves were to be paid $1,000 for each able-bodied man under 35 years of age. They were not to receive any salary, but those who served "well and faithfully" to the end of the war were to be freed and given the sum of $59. Despite the perils and despite the pleas and offers of the Congress, both South Carolina and Georgia refused to employ slaves as soldiers.

Although Georgia never authorized the use of slaves as soldiers, the colony at a very early stage in the war used blacks in noncombat roles. In November 1775, the authorities ordered that 100 blacks be pressed into service to help General Charles Lee enclose the military storehouse at Savannah. In June 1776, blacks were hired to build entrenchments at Sunbury. And in June 1778, blacks were hired to repair the roads between the Ogechee and the Altamaha Rivers. The Georgia officials ordered the use of blacks, even though in many cases their enslavers were opposed.

The British, also like the Americans, employed a number of blacks as laborers, guides, scouts, and spies. In the fall of 1779, for example, the British commander General Augustine Prevost was trying to decide whether or not he should surrender to the Americans and their allies. During the 24-hour period in which he had to make up his mind, he was reenforced by a detachment under the command of Colonel John Maitland. Success in reaching Savannah for Prevost was attributed to his black guides. At the Dawfuskie River en route from Beaufort, South Carolina, Maitland was blocked by French forces. Some blacks in the area volunteered to lead him to the enemy. The British force used obscure, winding waterways, swamps, and marshes and the covering of a dense fog to reach Savannah undetected. The route had never been used before except by "bears, wolves, and runaway Negroes."

Georgia did not exhibit the same attitude toward free blacks as soldiers as it did toward slaves. Free blacks were probably fighting in Georgia as early as 1775. But because of the very small number of free blacks, only about 300, living in the state during the Revolutionary War, this class was destined to be an almost negligible factor as combatants. The most notable black arms bearer for the patriots in Georgia was an artilleryman, Austin Dabney. Dabney's enslaver, Richard Aycock, brought him to Wilkes County, Georgia, from North Carolina shortly after the beginning of the Revolutionary War. After Aycock was called to serve in the Georgia militia, he used the rule of substitution, where persons who could furnish able-bodied substitutes could be exempt from military service, to ask that young Dabney be permitted to take his place: Aycock swore that the young boy, allegedly the son of a Virginia white woman and a black father, was indeed a free person of color, since the law forbade slaves from bearing arms for any reason.

As a soldier, Dabney was probably the only black person to participate in the fierce battle of Kettle Creek in 1779. Two years later, he was wounded in the thigh at Augusta. The wound crippled him for life and ended a brief, but distinguished military adventure.

Free Blacks in Antebellum Georgia

The free blacks in antebellum Georgia never comprised more than 1 percent of the total population of the colony and state. Yet despite their small number, the white community sought to control them through social restrictions and legal enactments. The fear was that the existence of even this small number of persons had a disturbing influence on the larger system of slavery. The free black clearly demonstrated to the slave that there was an alternative condition for black people in Georgia. To keep the free black class small, the Georgia legislature in 1859 forbade the freeing of slaves by will and testament.

The free blacks found almost all of their social associations within their own group, as they were almost totally cut off from the slave community and interacted with the white community only under specified arrangements. Much of this interracial interaction was on the same basis as that of slaves and white persons as servants and laborers of one kind or another for whites. Nevertheless, in Georgia a number of free blacks, despite the caste system, achieved notable successes. The Revolutionary War hero Dabney, in later years, became a rather prosperous landowner and sportsman in Pike County, Georgia. Other affluent blacks in the pre–Civil War era included Andrew Marshall, a free black drayman of Savannah who was worth $5,000 in 1850, James Oliver of Savannah, and Jeffrey Moore of Augusta. All of these blacks owned either gigs and/or carriages.

In the Revolutionary period, two blacks, George Leslie and Andrew Bryan, organized the First African Church at Savannah, Georgia, probably the first stable black Baptist Church in the American colonies. In 1773, the church, founded by the ex-slaves, opened its doors to a small congregation. Both men had only a modest amount of education and had begun preaching at very young ages.

In addition to Austin Dabney, the Reverends Bryan and Leile, Marshall, Oliver, and Moore, the best known of Georgia's free blacks were Anthony Odingsells and Solomon Humphries. Odingsells, who was perhaps the son of his enslaver, was freed in 1809. He soon came into possession of several items of property, including land and slaves. Even in 1860, he retained much of his valuable holdings. In an unusual circumstance as a black person, he owned property in the city and was a successful merchant and cotton broker.

Civil War

By 1860, the conflict between the North and the South over whether slavery should be allowed to exist or be banned in the western territories had reached the boiling point. With the election of Abraham Lincoln, whom the South viewed as a radical abolitionist Republican, as president that year, the die was cast. South Carolina seceded and attacked the federal Fort Sumter. President Lincoln responded by calling for 75,000 volunteers to defend the Union. The Civil War had begun.

The Georgia Secession Convention of 1861 met in Milledgeville from January 16 to March 23, 1861, and not only voted to secede the state from the Union but also created Georgia's first new constitution since 1798. The vote for secession was 208 to 89. After the vote, celebrations were held all over the state.

Emancipation and Reconstruction

On September 22, 1862, five days after the Union victory at Antietam, President Abraham Lincoln issued a proclamation, which in effect declared that all slaves held in bondage in states still in rebellion against the United States as of January 1, 1863, would be free. Since the Union controlled only a small portion of southern territory on that date, real emancipation would come with military victory and the Thirteenth Amendment to the Constitution.

Abraham Lincoln—and after his assassination in 1865, his successor Andrew Johnson of Tennessee—had wanted to get the South back in the Union as soon as possible. Hence they favored lenient terms of reconstruction. They were ambivalent about the terms of African American citizenship. Another group in Congress were Republicans who wanted to punish the South and possibly achieve political dominance there by making blacks citizens and enfranchising them. In 1866, this group began to override Johnson's intentions, instituted military or radical reconstruction of the South, made blacks citizens of the United States and of the states wherein they resided, and gave them civil and voting rights.

The Reconstruction Acts of 1867 called for new constitutions to be drawn up in the rebel states, new legislatures to be elected, and the Thirteenth Amendment ratified, among other things. When military reconstruction began in Georgia in 1867, there were 465,000 blacks and 591,000 whites residing in the state. After the registration of voters was completed it was found that 95,000 blacks and whites were eligible to cast ballots. In the ensuing elections to the constitutional convention, 33 blacks and 137 whites were elected. Clearly the blacks had not exercised a proportionate degree of their newly won political influence in the election of members of their own race to office. The explanation for the failure of black voters to vote black or not to vote at all lies in several areas. First, despite the presence of federal troops, antiblack violence continued. Much of this violence was directed at would-be voters. Second, since so many blacks were dependent upon southern whites for their livelihood, economic intimidation was always a real possibility.

In the constitutional convention that met in Atlanta in 1867–1868, only 19 percent of the delegates were black. But some of them made their voices heard by introducing measures to enhance the economic, educational, and judicial status of the state. In the 1868 elections, four blacks were elected to the state Senate and 29 to the House of Representatives. Here, again, the black representatives introduced measures for education and to strengthen the executive branch. Meanwhile, many white Democrats devised a plot to unseat the black legislators. They contended that the new constitution of 1868 did not permit people of color to hold office. Finally in the late summer of 1868, by lopsided votes in the Senate and the House, all of the black legislators were removed.

The ouster of the black legislators caused consternation among African Americans and some white Republican leaders in the state as well as Republicans in Congress. National attention was first attracted by a memorable oration delivered by black Senator Henry McNeal Turner

immediately following the dismissals in which he chastised the white lawmakers, and by inference the white race, for making war on defenseless blacks. In 1870, the blacks were ordered reinstated by the U.S. Supreme Court.

With the return of the black legislators, conservative white Georgians had suffered a setback, but not a defeat. Violence and intimidation still kept many black voters from the polls, and following the elections of 1870 and the new withdrawal of military rule, whites again reigned supreme. Only two blacks were elected to the Georgia Senate until Leroy Johnson accomplished the feat in 1964. The last black to serve in either house of the legislature prior to the election of Johnson was W. H. Rogers of McIntosh County, who left in 1907.

Jim Crow Georgia

Booker T. Washington, a founder of the Tuskegee Institute in Alabama in 1881, had become by the mid-1890s the preeminent African American leader in the United States. Thus he was asked to represent his people as a principal speaker at the Cotton States International Exposition in Atlanta in 1895. There he outlined what he hoped would be a formula for racial peace and African American advancement. He discouraged the seeking of political office on the part of blacks, discounted the importance of social equality, and asked that whites support blacks in their quest for economic opportunity. This speech, denounced by his critics as the Atlanta Compromise, won wide acceptance by whites, North and South, and many blacks. The next year, the U.S. Supreme Court, in the case of *Plessy v. Ferguson*, ruled that separate public facilities could be provided for blacks and whites as long as they were equal.

After 1900, Georgia, like most southern states, passed a series of laws that separated the races in schools and in public accommodations.

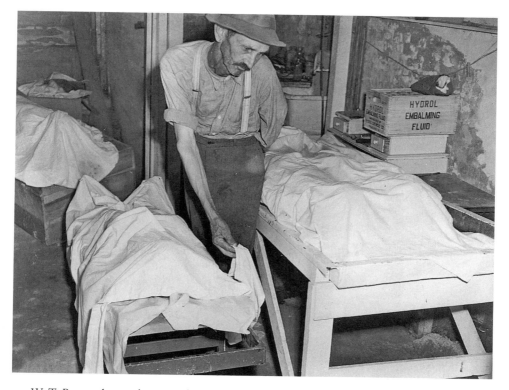

Coroner W. T. Brown places a sheet over the body of one of four African American mob victims in a funeral home at Monroe, Georgia. The four people, two men and two women, were seen while riding with a white farmer and were taken into the woods and shot. (Library of Congress)

Yet the facilities and the opportunities provided for blacks were not equal, and they were subjected to discrimination in every walk of life. At the same time acts were enacted that severely restricted black political participation through such extralegal devices as literacy and understanding tests, poll taxes, and whites-only primary elections. With these measures, added to violence and intimidation, blacks were destined to remain for nearly half a century a negligible factor in the political life of the state.

Under the doctrine of white supremacy, some individuals and groups sought to aid and abet the government in "keeping blacks in their place." In many instances they resorted to violence. Foremost among these was the Ku Klux Klan, which was revived in Georgia in the early 1900s. Also

there were disastrous race riots and lynchings, which further terrorized blacks. One of a series of riots that occurred in various parts of the nation during the 1900s was one at Atlanta in 1906. Spurred by inflamed newspaper reports of black men attacking white women, mobs of whites roamed through Atlanta and its suburbs killing and injuring blacks. The final toll left at least three dozen blacks and a handful of whites dead and scores, mostly black, injured.

Also between 1882 and 1930, there were 450 lynchings in Georgia, a total only exceeded by Mississippi's 538. From 1890 to 1900, Georgia lynchers killed more than one black person per month. The lynchings declined in the first decade of the twentieth century, but by 1911 rose again when 19 black Georgians were murdered.

After 1919, there was another decrease, and between 1927 and the New Deal, there were few official reports of lynchings. However, in 1946, in what may have been the last mass lynching in the country, two young black sharecroppers, a man and a woman, were taken by a mob to the Moore's Ford Bridge, on the Apalachee River at the border of Walton and Oconee counties, beaten, and shot several times. The lynching was reported in the national media and sparked mass protests in several places, including New York City and in Washington, D.C. Georgia governor Ellis Arnall, one of the first moderates to occupy the governor's office in modern times, requested the Georgia Bureau of Investigation to seek out members of the lynch mob. The NAACP also asked President Harry S. Truman to investigate. Later, the FBI did investigate but no one was ever indicted in the murders. But the Moore's Ford lynching did motivate civil rights groups to press anew for federal antilynching legislation in Congress, and helped stir Truman to create the President's Committee on Civil Rights.

In 1999, the Moore's Ford Memorial Committee and the Georgia Historical Society erected a historical marker commemorating the 1946 lynching. It is the only known official marker for a lynching in Georgia.

Following the Atlanta race riot of 1906, some African American leaders, especially in Atlanta, sought racial peace mainly through the type of accommodationism proposed by Booker T. Washington. Others, however, continued in the historic tradition of protest that preceded the riot and that was manifested by the blacks who resisted the white mobs. For example, in the 1890s, there had been boycotts of segregated street cars in Macon, Savannah, and Atlanta. But these efforts failed when leaders of the movement became divided over strategy. Other actions involved challenging segregation in Pullman railroad sleeping cars. W. E. B. Du Bois,

J. W. E. Bowen, Reverend H. H. Proctor, and Henry McNeal Turner filed actions, including an unsuccessful complaint to the Interstate Commerce Commission.

During the disfranchisement debate of the early 1900s, several black leaders, including Du Bois and college president John Hope, signed a petition opposing the measure. And in 1912 there was a brief boycott of segregated cruise ships in Savannah. African American leaders were also, at least initially, very active in the defense of Angelo Herndon, a young African American communist who was convicted of insurrection for trying to organize black and white workers during the Great Depression. The conviction was subsequently overturned by the U.S. Supreme Court.

Yet even in the throes of Jim Crow, African Americans in Georgia continued to live their lives through parallel institutions. The key to African American success in these years was the black church, which not only gave the race emotional solace, but became its principal social and often economic and political institution. At the close of the Civil War, African American churches were established throughout Georgia, in both rural and urban areas. Some of the oldest included the First African Baptist Church in Savannah, the Springfield Baptist Church and Walker's Tabernacle Church in Augusta, and the Friendship Baptist Church and the Bethel AME Church in Atlanta. The early pastors of these churches also became some of the earliest African American political and civil rights leaders in the state—men such as Charles Walker of Walker Tabernacle in Augusta, E. K. Love of Savannah, Edward R. Carter of Friendship, and Wesley John Gaines and Henry McNeal Turner at Bethel in Atlanta.

In addition to the major denominational churches, there were many storefront churches, some adhering to the traditional denominations, others calling themselves evangelical or healing or free will and other such names. More recently, megachurches preaching an economically based gospel as well as black Muslim mosques and black Christian nationalist churches have also sprung up, especially in the major cities.

Although there were clandestine black schools during the era of bondage, real systems of black education did not emerge until after the Civil War. Most of these were sponsored by the federal Freedmen's Bureau and northern missionary societies. These first institutions were elementary schools, often housed in black churches. But many rapidly evolved into colleges and universities. Most of the latter were in Atlanta, starting with what became Atlanta University in 1865 and ending with Morris Brown College, the only one founded solely by African Americans, and Spelman College in 1881. By this time Atlanta had become the largest educational center for blacks in the world. Later another private school, Paine College, was founded at Augusta, and three state schools, Savannah State, Albany State, and Fort Valley State, the latter in a rural area, were also established.

While a few free blacks owned land and acquired a degree of wealth in the slave era, the growth in black property owning and black entrepreneurship coincided with freedom and the attainment of education, particularly higher education. Since Atlanta had the largest number of black colleges, it also became a capital of black business, including insurance companies, banks, cemetery associations, hotels, and restaurants. Yet to a smaller extent, such enterprises also existed in Augusta, Columbus, Macon, Albany, and other places.

Politically, although African Americans, especially in Atlanta, had been having sporadic influence on some local general and special elections since the early 1900s, the real breakthrough in electoral participation and office holding did not occur until after 1946. Two years earlier the

U.S. Supreme Court had removed a major hurdle to African Americans' exercise of the franchise by declaring, in *Smith v. Allwright*, the Democratic white primary (which had really been the only important election) unconstitutional. Following this decision, the Court sustained its opinion in a case brought from Columbus, Georgia—*Chapman v. King*. Atlanta's black leaders, who had been protesting for full voting rights and urging their fellow blacks to register to vote, launched new voter registration initiatives. Within a few short months, they added thousands of new black voters to the polls. By 1949, they had become the balance of power in local elections. This had a profound impact on race relations in the city, as major white officeholders had to respect the black political influence. In 1953, a coalition of black voters and upper-income white voters elected Rufus Clement, the president of Atlanta University, to the Atlanta Board of Education—the first African American to occupy a political office in Georgia since the early 1900s.

An Era of Civil Rights

The decision of the U.S. Supreme Court in *Brown v. Board of Education* in 1954 ushered in the era of civil rights. This decision and several which followed it, together with the Civil Rights Act of 1964 and the Voting Rights Act of 1965, were supplemented by direct action campaigns beginning with bus boycotts in Montgomery, Alabama, and elsewhere in the 1950s and sit-ins, freedom rides, and other public demonstrations in the 1960s and 1970s. In this new Civil Rights Movement, an Atlanta native, Martin Luther King Jr., emerged as the principal leader.

School desegregation in Georgia began in 1961 with the desegregation of the University of Georgia and the Atlanta public schools. The former occurred after days of rioting; the latter occurred peacefully and won national commendation from President John F. Kennedy and the international media. The occurrences in Atlanta broke a cycle of violence that had accompanied much of school desegregation in the South since the Supreme Court's 1954 decision. While the desegregation in Atlanta was comparatively peaceful, it was also token. Within a few years, the schools were mostly resegregated. Acknowledging the massive opposition to school desegregation, especially through busing across neighborhoods and jurisdictional lines, the Atlanta NAACP agreed to a compromise that involved the cessation of the pressures for busing in return for black administrative control of the predominantly black school system. Elsewhere, in the Atlanta suburbs and in smaller cities and in rural areas, over time, much more school desegregation was accomplished.

Following the beginning of the sit-in movement in Greensboro, North Carolina, in February 1960, the first major sit-ins in Georgia occurred the next month in Atlanta. They were followed by protests in Savannah, Albany, Augusta, Columbus, and other places. The Atlanta sit-ins, however, faced a major roadblock as Atlanta merchants refused to relent. A major breakthrough occurred in the fall of 1960 when Martin Luther King Jr. joined local college students in a sit-in, was arrested, and then sent to the state's maximum-security prison for violating probation on a previous traffic charge in another county. This arrest caused the Atlanta mayor Bill Hartsfield to urge a truce in the sit-ins until he could try to get white merchants to seriously negotiate. Then when the campaign of presidential candidate John F. Kennedy expressed concern for King and was reportedly instrumental in obtaining his release on bail, the Atlanta sit-ins gained international attention. Some scholars contend that the switch of many black votes in the nation to Kennedy over Vice President Richard Nixon provided the margin of victory for the Massachusetts senator. Nevertheless, the Atlanta sit-

in stalemate persisted and public accommodations were not desegregated until the fall of 1961 following school desegregation.

Another major battleground of the Civil Rights Movement in Georgia was in Albany and it too involved a stalemate and the participation of Martin Luther King Jr. The Congress on Racial Equality (CORE) provided the first initiative for the Freedom Rides. In Georgia, the riders used Atlanta as a staging area as they moved throughout the region. Within the state, they also stopped at Savannah, Thomasville, and at Albany. The visits to Albany were to set the stage for one of the most famous mass movements of the era.

In an attempt to avoid negative publicity that might aversely affect economic prosperity, the town fathers in Albany adopted a policy of "killing them [the demonstrators] with kindness." The local strategy, combined with some miscommunication and division among Albany's blacks, many scholars now contend, perplexed Martin Luther King Jr., and gave him one of his first major setbacks.

Elsewhere in the state, from Savannah on the southeast coast to Rome in north Georgia, there were protests. Some, as in Savannah, were almost immediately successful; others were more protracted; some turned violent. Blacks in Augusta and Columbus, for example, often faced setbacks similar to those in Albany, but the police were more hostile, there was violent opposition from white racists, and sometimes editorial opposition from the white press. The achievement of desegregation, other than in schools, came much later and more grudgingly to Georgia's smaller cities and towns.

Nevertheless, the Student Nonviolent Coordinating Committee (SNCC) led by Charles Sherrod, a Virginian, did confront entrenched and violent white racism in the Georgia Black Belt, taking on such places as "Terrible" Terrell and "Bad" Baker counties in southwest Georgia. The young SNCC volunteers lived in the area for several months attempting to convince local blacks to register and vote. Several were arrested, some were beaten and even shot. In 1963, some were charged with insurrection, a capital crime, by authorities in Americus. They were subsequently released, but such tactics made their work among local blacks much more difficult. Yet undeterred, some of them, like Sherrod, became residents of the area.

Although civil rights protesters in Georgia, as in the rest of the South, most often followed the nonviolent principles and practices of Martin Luther King Jr., there were several instances of violence across racial lines during the civil rights era. In 1966 and 1967, riots in Atlanta, blamed on SNCC leaders but provoked by police shootings of blacks, were small and contained. But a larger riot occurred in Augusta in 1970, sparked by the torture and murder of a black teenager in a city jail. As late as 1987 civil rights leaders led a march in Forsyth County—a county that warned black visitors not to "let the sun go down on your head." In 1972, the police chief in Darien, a small town on the Georgia coast, shot and seriously wounded a black garbage worker for allegedly disturbing the peace by drinking and arguing with his girlfriend. The incident so angered local blacks that they began the first Civil Rights Movement in McIntosh County.

Among the major gains of the civil rights era was the election of African Americans to high political offices in the South. Although some blacks, especially in Atlanta, had been elected to local offices since the 1950s, the greater number took office during the time of the Civil Rights Movement. The biggest prize came in 1973 with the election of Maynard H. Jackson Jr., in Atlanta as the first African American mayor of a major southern city. In this period, African American mayors were also elected in Augusta, Macon, and Savannah, as well as in smaller towns

like Keysville and Washington. The era also saw the election of many county commissioners, county sheriffs, state legislators, state department heads, and many other lesser offices.

The civil rights era also witnessed new economic opportunities for Georgia blacks. Although wealthy blacks had existed in Atlanta and other Georgia cities since the early 1900s and there were substantial middle-income communities of professional and businesspeople, the removal of Jim Crow discriminations in the 1960s and 1970s expanded the African American middle class. Now blacks attained middle-management positions in manufacturing, commerce, and finance as well as in education, fast-food franchises, and technology. Many blacks became owners of auto dealerships and of computer and other technology facilities.

Yet there were great disparities between urban areas and rural areas and even within urban Georgia. While the wealth of some blacks expanded into the Atlanta suburbs, African American poverty in the central city remained among the highest in the nation.

The Post–Civil Rights Era

Even in the antebellum period, free blacks in Savannah and elsewhere had formed churches and other social organizations among themselves. After the Civil War, even exclusive social clubs were formed in Atlanta and elsewhere. Still, the African American middle and upper classes spent considerable energies taking care of the less fortunate members of the race. As in much of the nation, in addition to the churches, this work was done by fraternal groups, like the Prince Hall Masons, the Eastern Stars, the Odd Fellows, and college fraternities and sororities. Major self-help was also provided by orphanages, the YMCA, the YWCA, the Neighborhood Union, the Concerned Black Clergy, the 100 Black Men, the NAACP, and the Urban League—both of the latter had local offices in the major cities of the state and regional offices in Atlanta. The Concerned Black Clergy and the 100 Black Men, both founded in the 1980s, were unique organizations—the former bringing together representatives of more than 125 Atlanta-area churches to address not only social issues but civil rights matters as well, and the latter raising money through balls and an annual football classic to fund college scholarships for deserving black youth and to mentor disadvantaged youth.

This social formation continued throughout the post–civil rights era, even as African Americans found increasing opportunities for biracial social activities and community service. In 2010, it was estimated that the African American population in Georgia, 30 percent of the total of 9,830,000, was the third largest in the nation after Mississippi and Louisiana. The major cities of the state, Atlanta, Augusta, Columbus, Savannah, and Macon, contained most of that population. By 2010, metropolitan Atlanta had added more African American residents than any other city in the nation and had the second-largest black population in the country. It also had one of the two richest African American communities in the nation.

Notable African Americans

Abernathy, Ralph David (1926–1999)

Ralph David Abernathy, born in Alabama, was a minister and civil/human rights leader who spent much of his life in Atlanta as a chief associate of Martin Luther King Jr., and succeeded King as president of the Southern Christian Leadership Conference (SCLC) after his assassination in 1968.

Abbott, Robert Sengstacke (1870–1940)

Robert S. Abbott was the founder and publisher of the *Chicago Defender*. He was born on St. Simons Island and moved to Chicago in the early 1900s.

Barber, Jesse Max (1878–1919)

Jesse Max Barber was a journalist and civil/human rights activist. He published the *Voice of the Negro*, a militant periodical. He was highly critical of white and black leaders in the aftermath of the Atlanta Riot of 1906 and was ordered to leave the city by influential whites.

Bolden, Dorothy (1923–2005)

Dorothy Bolden was a labor and womanist leader and community activist. She founded the Domestic Workers Union and served on the Georgia Commission for Women.

Borders, William Holmes (1905–1993)

William Holmes Borders was a minister, civil/human rights leader, and politician. He guided Atlanta's Wheat Street Baptist Church into a position as one of the leading black churches in the United States in his 50 years as pastor there. He was the principal leader of a group of ministers who demonstrated against bus segregation in Atlanta in 1957 and became the chairman of an adult committee that advised students during the Atlanta sit-ins of the 1960s. He was one of the top leaders in the Atlanta black power structure, but failed on two occasions to be elected to public office.

Bowen, John Wesley Edward (J. W. E.) (1855–1933)

J. W. E. Bowen was a Methodist minister who rose to be a bishop and college president He was born in New Orleans and moved to Atlanta in 1893. He was president of Gammon Theological

Seminary when he was detained and assaulted by police during the Atlanta Riot of 1906.

Butler, Selena Sloan (c. 1872–1964)

Selena Sloan Butler was an educator and community activist. She was the founder of the Georgia Colored Parent-Teacher Association in 1920 and the National Congress of Colored Parents and Teachers in 1926.

Carter, Edward R. (E. R.) (1858–1944)

E. R. Carter was a minister and civil rights leader. As pastor of the Friendship Baptist Church in Atlanta, he was instrumental in the founding of Spelman College in 1881. He wrote the first comprehensive history of black Atlanta, *The Black Side*, in 1894.

Clayton, Xernona (1930–)

Xernona Clayton was born in Oklahoma and moved to Atlanta in 1965 to work with Dr. Martin Luther King Jr. at the headquarters of the SCLC. She was one of the first African American women to host a television show in the Deep South. Later she became a vice president at Turner Broadcasting and established the Trumpet Awards, presented annually to African American achievers in various fields.

Crogman, William Henry (W. H.) (1841–1931)

W. H. Crogman was an educator and community leader. He was born in the British West Indies and arrived in Atlanta in 1883 to attend Atlanta University. He became the first African American president of Clark University (later Clark Atlanta University) in 1903 and served for seven years before returning to teaching. He walked to most places in Atlanta rather than ride segregated street cars.

Cummings, Mary Moss Young (1944–2010)

Mary Moss Young Cummings was a civil rights leader and politician. She began her civil rights activism as a teenager in Fitzgerald, Georgia, and continued in college and in the city of Albany. She was also a state representative from the Albany area in the Georgia House. She was the first female to be elected president of the Georgia Association of Black Elected Officials (GABEO).

Dobbs, John Wesley (1882–1961)

John Wesley Dobbs was the grand-master of the Prince Hall Masons of Georgia from 1932 until 1961. He was also a leader in efforts to attain voting rights for blacks in Georgia and to have blacks register and vote intelligently. He was also a national vice president of the NAACP.

Finch, William (1832–1911)

William Finch was a minister and the first black elected to the Atlanta City Council in 1870. He was a staunch advocate for public schools for African Americans.

Flipper, Henry Ossian (1856–1940)

Henry Ossian Flipper, born in bondage, was West Point's first African American graduate in 1878. In 1881, he was dismissed from the military for allegedly embezzling funds. Flipper vehemently denied the charges. He and others suggested that racism may have been involved. He was exonerated posthumously by the military in 1976.

Franklin, Shirley Clarke (1945–)

Shirley Clarke Franklin was the first female mayor of Atlanta and the first African American woman to be elected mayor of a major southern city.

Hamilton, Grace Towns (1907–1992)

Grace Hamilton was the first African American woman elected to the Georgia legislature. She served in the state Senate from 1965 to 1984. Working as a moderate, she was able to have much influence with both the legislative and executive branches during her tenure. Prior to entering politics, she had been the first female executive director of the Atlanta Urban League from 1943 to 1961.

Harper, Charles Lincoln (C. L.) (1877–1955)

C.L. Harper was an educator and civil rights leader. He was the first principal of the Booker T. Washington High School in Atlanta, which was opened in 1924. He was also a founder and president of the Atlanta NAACP.

Hayes, Roland (1887–1977)

Roland Hayes was a world-renowned classical singer. He first performed in Europe in the 1920s, after facing little appreciation in America for an African American employing that style of music. When he returned to the United States in 1923, he won wide acceptance as one of the best classical musicians in the world. In 1924, he was awarded the NAACP's highest honor, the Spingarn Medal.

Herndon, Alonzo Franklin (1858–1927)

Alonzo Franklin Herndon was born in bondage, but became one of the wealthiest African Americans of his time after founding the Atlanta Life Insurance Company in 1905.

Herndon, Norris Bumstead (1897–1977)

Norris Bumstead Herndon succeeded his father, Alonzo F. Herndon, as president of the Atlanta Life Insurance Company in 1928. He was also a philanthropist who supported churches, colleges, social service organizations, and the NAACP through a family foundation. *Ebony* magazine listed him as the richest African American in the United States in 1962.

Hill, Jesse (1926–)

Jesse Hill, born in St. Louis, became a business and civil rights leader in Atlanta. As president of Atlanta Life Insurance Co., he helped found the *Atlanta Inquirer*, a leading organ of the civil rights movement in Atlanta in the 1960s. He was also the first African American president of the Atlanta Chamber of Commerce. A street in Atlanta is named for him.

Holley, Joseph Winthrop (1874–1958)

Joseph Winthrop Holley was born in South Carolina and moved to Georgia in 1902 where he planned to establish a school for black children. The school eventually evolved into Albany State College in 1943. Holley served as president of the institution from the time it started as an elementary school in 1903 until it became a four-year college in 1943. Holley was also a founder of the Georgia Teachers and Educators Association, the first professional organization of black educators in the state, in 1933.

Hollowell, Donald Lee (1917–2004)

Donald Lee Hollowell was an attorney and civil rights leader. A native of Kansas, he moved to Atlanta in the 1940s. He was the principal attorney in most of the major civil rights cases in Georgia in the 1960s, including the desegregation of state universities and the Atlanta public schools. A street in Atlanta is named for him.

Holsey, Lucius Henry (1842–1920)

Lucius Henry Holsey was a clergyman and educator. In 1903, he became the senior bishop of the

Colored Methodist Episcopal (CME) Church. He was a founder of two schools, Paine College in Augusta and Holsey Institute in Cordele.

Hope, John (1868–1936)

John Hope was an educator and civil rights leader. In 1906, he became the first African American president of what became Morehouse College. He was also the first African American president of Atlanta University, which he led from 1929 to 1936. He early disagreed with Booker T. Washington's educational and racial philosophies and was the only African American college president to attend the Niagara Conference called by W. E. B. Du Bois, William Monroe Trotter, and others in 1906.

Hope, Lugenia Burns (1871–1947)

Lugenia Burns Hope was born in St. Louis and lived in Chicago and Nashville before moving to Atlanta with her husband John Hope in 1898. When John Hope became president of Morehouse College, Lugenia Burns Hope not only served as first lady for the students, she became a community activist, holding office in the local NAACP, leading voter registration drives, and founding the Neighborhood Union, a social service agency.

Howard, David T. (1849–1934)

David T. Howard was a businessman who achieved substantial wealth as an undertaker in Atlanta. He extended his business enterprises into real estate. He is believed to have smuggled weapons into Atlanta for blacks during the 1906 riot.

Hubert, Benjamin Franklin (d. c. 1947)

Benjamin Franklin Hubert was an educator. He was president of Georgia State Industrial College (now Savannah State College) from 1926 to 1947. During his tenure as president he doubled the number of buildings on campus and recruited some of the most talented faculty in the country. He subscribed to the agricultural-industrial mode of black education promoted by Booker T. Washington. Hubert was also a founder of the Association for the Advancement of Negro Country Life and the Log Cabin Center in Hancock County in the 1930s.

Jackson, Maynard Holbrook, Jr. (1938–2003)

Maynard Jackson, a native of Texas, moved to Atlanta with his family at an early age. He was elected vice mayor of the city of Atlanta in 1969 and in 1973 was elected mayor—the first African American ever to hold the office and the first African American to be elected mayor of a major southern city.

Johnson, Georgia Douglas Camp (1886–1966)

Georgia Johnson was one of the nation's most successful literary figures. She was born in Atlanta and moved to Washington, D.C., in 1909. Her repertoire included poetry, drama, and short stories: Her better known works include *The Heart of a Woman and Other Poems* (1918), "Blue Blood" (1927), and *Share My World* (1962).

Johnson, Leroy (1928–)

Leroy Johnson was the first black person elected to the Georgia legislature since 1907. In the state Senate he rose to be one of the most influential members of that body. He made an unsuccessful run for mayor of Atlanta in 1973.

King, Chevrone Bowers (C. B) (1924–1988)

C. B. King was an attorney, civil rights leader, and politician in Albany. He represented Martin Luther

King Jr., Ralph David Abernathy, and other civil rights demonstrators in 1962. In 1969, he ran unsuccessfully for a congressional seat, and the next year was an unsuccessful candidate for governor.

King, Coretta Scott (1927–2006)

Coretta Scott King, a native of Alabama, was a civil rights leader and organization executive. Following the assassination of her husband, Martin Luther King Jr., in 1968, she founded the Martin Luther King Jr. Center for Nonviolent Social Change in Atlanta and began a successful lobbying campaign to make his birthday a national holiday. A school for girls in Atlanta is named in her honor.

King, Martin Luther, Jr. (1929–1968)

Martin Luther King Jr. was the principal leader of the American Civil Rights Movement from the late 1950s until his assassination in 1968. In 1964, he was awarded the Nobel Peace Prize.

King, Martin Luther, Sr. (1899–1984)

Martin Luther King Sr. was a minister, investor, and civil/human rights leader. Born in poverty in rural Georgia, he married the daughter of the pastor of Ebenezer Baptist Church and civil rights leader A. D. Williams and upon his death succeeded him as pastor of the Atlanta church. As early as the 1930s, King led a voting rights march in Atlanta and participated in demonstrations for black policemen in the city. He invested in Atlanta's black banks and other businesses and became one of the city's wealthiest African Americans.

Laney, Lucy Craft (1854–1933)

Lucy Craft Laney was an educator. She was the founder of one of the first schools for African Americans in Augusta. Laney named the school in honor of Francine Haines, corresponding secretary of the Women's Executive Committee of Home Missions of the Presbyterian Church who had helped raise money for the school at a crucial time in the late 1880s. By the beginning of the First World War, the Haines Normal and Industrial Institute enrolled nearly 1,000 students and had a faculty of 30. Economic hardships forced the school to close in 1949. It was succeeded by the Lucy C. Laney High School. A portrait of Ms. Laney now hangs in the Georgia state capitol.

Law, Westley Wallace (W. W.) (1923–2002)

W. W. Law was a civil/human rights leader who spent his life in Savannah, but earned the title "Mr. Civil Rights of Georgia." He led both the Savannah and the state NAACP and was active in all of the actions to attain improved civil rights, human rights, and living conditions in Savannah and Georgia for more than half a century. A community center and library in Savannah are named for him.

Lewis, John R. (1940–)

John Lewis, born in Alabama, is a civil rights leader and activist. He achieved a certain amount of immortality after being severely beaten by police during a voting rights march in Selma, Alabama, in 1965. He is Georgia's longest-serving African American congressman.

Long, Jefferson Franklin (1836–1900)

Jefferson Franklin Long was Georgia's first African American congressman. He served in the U.S. House of Representatives for about 15 months. Yet he was the first African American representative to speak on the floor of Congress. He made a speech arguing against a proposal to remove the laws restricting office holding by former Confederates.

John Lewis was one of the most courageous leaders of the Civil Rights Movement and has served as Democratic U.S. representative for Georgia's Fifth Congressional District since 1986. (U.S. House of Representatives)

Lowery, Joseph Echols (1921–)

Joseph Echols Lowery is a minister and civil rights leader. He was a close aide to Martin Luther King Jr. and has been president of the SCLC. In 2009, Lowery was asked to give the benediction at the inauguration of President Barack Obama. The president awarded him the Medal of Freedom in August 2009. A street in Atlanta is named for him.

Mays, Benjamin E. (1894–1984)

Benjamin E. Mays was a native of South Carolina, but spent most of his life in Atlanta. He was an educator and civil rights spokesman. In 1940, he became president of Morehouse College and helped enhance the school's national reputation for academic excellence. After he retired

from Morehouse in 1967, he became president of the Atlanta Board of Education. He was a counseler to Martin Luther King Jr. while he was a student at Morehouse College and after he became the nation's foremost civil rights leader.

McCown, John L. (1934–1976)

John L. McCown was born in South Carolina and moved to New York City. In the 1960s, he was in Georgia working with the Equal Opportunity Authority in Savannah. In 1966, he was accused of stirring up rioting blacks in Atlanta. During that same year, he went to Hancock County to work for an antipoverty agency. The next year, he became the executive director of the Georgia Council on Human Relations. He also established the East Central Committee for Economic Opportunity in Hancock County. A controversial figure, he became known as the "political boss" of Hancock County. He was under investigation for corruption when he died in a plane crash in 1976.

McKinney, Cynthia (1935–)

Cynthia McKinney was the first African American female elected to Congress from Georgia. She served six terms between 1992 and 2006. In and out of the Congress she was a controversial figure as she vocally supported radical causes, including antiwar protests. In 2008, she was the Green Party's candidate for president.

Paschal, James (1920–2008)

James Paschal was a leading African American entrepreneur in Atlanta. He and his brother Robert opened Paschal's restaurant in Atlanta in 1959. They later opened a nightclub and a hotel. In the 1970s, they began operating restaurants and lounges at the Atlanta airport. The Paschal's hotel and restaurant was a favorite meeting place for Martin Luther King Jr. and other leaders as they planned Civil Rights Movement strategies.

Proctor, Henry Hugh (H. H.) (1868–1933)

H. H. Proctor was a clergyman who was born in Tennessee and moved to Atlanta in 1894 to become the pastor of a small congregational church. Proctor solicited the goodwill of leading whites after the Atlanta riot of 1906 to help keep the peace and to help him build his church. First Congregational Church was able to make substantial improvements to its structure. Proctor also made it one of the first institutional churches—serving the spiritual as well as physical and social needs of the community—in the nation. Yet it acquired and continued to maintain a reputation as "a silk stocking church."

Rucker, Henry A. (1852–1924)

Henry A. Rucker was a politician and businessman who was born in bondage. When he reached adulthood he used his earnings from various jobs to buy a barber shop, which he leased out. The shop, which catered to whites, became prosperous and so did Rucker. A lifelong Republican, he attended several Republican National Conventions. He was a Republican appointee as a clerk in the Internal Revenue Service district office in Atlanta before being named head of that office by President William McKinley in 1897. At about the same time, Rucker began to expand his business enterprises into real estate. In 1904, he built the first professional office building for blacks in Atlanta. He died as one of the wealthiest blacks in the nation.

Russell, Herman, Sr. (1930–)

Herman Russell Sr. is an Atlanta entrepreneur, civic leader, and philanthropist. He began his career as owner of an Atlanta construction company and branched out into other enterprises including hotels, restaurants, and the media in other parts of the country. He is one of the country's wealthiest African Americans.

Scott, Cornelius Adolphus (C.A.) (1908–2000)

C. A. Scott was a publisher, editor, and voting rights activist. He used the pages of the *Atlanta Daily World*, the longest continuously running black daily newspaper in the country, to campaign for black voting rights and to encourage black voter registration. He opposed direct action protests to end segregation, but vociferously opposed police brutality and waged a long, successful fight for African American policemen in Atlanta.

Sherrod, Charles (1937–)

Charles Sherrod was a key civil rights leader in the SNCC and its efforts in Albany and southwest Georgia during the Civil Rights Movement. He was first field secretary and SNCC director of southwest Georgia. He also began an agricultural cooperative called New Communities Inc. In 1976, Sherrod was elected to the Albany City Council, serving until 1990. In 1996, he ran unsuccessfully for the Georgia State Senate.

Turner, Henry McNeal (1834–1915)

Henry McNeal Turner, clergyman, politician, human rights leader, and Pan Africanist, was born in South Carolina and moved to Georgia in 1865 as an agent of the Freedmen's Bureau. Within a year he left this position to solicit for the AME church. In 1867, he was also assigned as an organizer among blacks for the Republican Party. His work with the church and the party led to his election to the Georgia Constitutional Convention of 1867 and to the House of Representatives in 1868 and 1870. After having been dismissed from his legislative seat in 1870, he became increasingly bitter, denouncing the American flag as "a dirty rag" and advocating emigration to Africa.

Walden, Austin Thomas (A. T.) (1885–1965)

A. T. Walden was an attorney and civil rights leader. He defended Georgia blacks in hostile courtrooms and was lead or cooperating attorney on all of the major civil rights cases in Atlanta from the 1940s until the time of his death. He was president of the Atlanta NAACP and vice president of the national NAACP. As a cofounder of the Atlanta Negro Voters League, he became a principal broker with Atlanta's white leaders for improved living condition for blacks and improved race relations. He has been called the most influential member of Atlanta's "black power structure" from the 1940s to the 1960s.

White, Walter Francis (1893–1955)

Walter White, a writer and civil rights leader, was born in Atlanta and moved to New York in 1918. He witnessed, as a boy, the Atlanta Race Riot of 1906 and, although blonde of hair and blue of eyes, then decided to cast his lot with the African race. In Atlanta he was a member of the organizing committee for the local NAACP and a member of the black leadership group which was pressing for a black high school. In New York, he rose from an assistant secretary to acting secretary and to executive secretary of the national NAACP between 1918 and 1955. During the Harlem Renaissance of the 1920s, he authored such works as *Flight* and *Rope and Faggot*.

Williams, Adam Daniel (A. D.) (1863–1931)

A. D. Williams was a clergyman and civil rights leader. He helped build the Ebenezer Baptist Church in Atlanta to one of the South's largest black churches. He was an early president of the Atlanta NAACP, a leader in the campaigns

Walter White served the cause of African Americans as assistant and executive secretary of the National Association for the Advancement of Colored People from the 1920s until the 1950s. He came to be the most devoted fighter in the effort to stamp out lynching in the United States after World War I. (Library of Congress)

for black voting rights and for a black high school.

Williams, Hosea Lorenzo (1926–2000)

Hosea Lorenzo Williams was a civil/human rights leader. He became known as the ramrod of the Civil Rights Movement for his aggressive, although nonviolent, tactics in confronting white racism. He became a leader in the SCLC and directed its Operation Breadbasket in Georgia. He held elective office in the city of Atlanta and DeKalb County. He gained national attention when he began an annual "Feed the Hungry and Homeless" dinners at Thanksgiving and Christmas in 1970. Starting in a church in Atlanta, the dinners moved to larger quarters in gymnasiums and stadiums and drew thousands of people from all walks of life.

First as a civil rights activist, then as a congressmember, diplomat, and mayor, Andrew Young has devoted his life to improving the quality of life for African Americans and poor people both in the United States and around the world. (Library of Congress)

Williams, Samuel Woodrow (1912–1970)

Samuel Woodrow Williams, a native of Arkansas, was a minister, an educator and one of Atlanta's most vocal and active civil rights leaders in the 1960s. He was a principal advisor, as head of the Atlanta NAACP, to student sit-ins in Atlanta as well as to students who desegregated Georgia's schools. He was one of the two plaintiffs in the suit that desegregated Atlanta buses in 1959.

Wright, Richard Robert, Sr. (1855–1947)

Richard Robert Wright Sr. was an educator, businessman, and journalist. In 1880, he helped

with developing Ware High School for blacks in Augusta, while editing a newspaper, the *Augusta Weekly Sentinel*. In 1890, he was named the first president of the Georgia Industrial College for Colored Youth (later Savannah State College). He retained this position for 30 years and became known as one of the most prominent African American educators in the nation. In the controversy among the black leadership of the time over educational and political goals, Wright straddled the fence between the Booker T. Washington and W. E. B. Du Bois camps, and considered both men his friends.

Young, Andrew Jackson (1932–)

Andrew Young was born in New Orleans and moved to Atlanta to work with Martin Luther King Jr. and the SCLC. After King's assassination in 1968, Young entered politics. He was elected to Congress from the Atlanta area—becoming the first African American from Georgia to serve in the U.S. House of Representatives since Jefferson Long left in 1872. After being ambassador to the United Nations in the administration of President Jimmy Carter, he was elected mayor of Atlanta in 1981.

Cultural Contributions

Black Georgians have made outstanding cultural contributions to the nation and to the world. The state has been home to internationally acclaimed classical musicians like Mattiwilda Dobbs, Roland Hayes, and Jessye Norman; rhythm-and-blues and soul singers James Brown, Ray Charles (whose rendition of "Georgia on My Mind" has become a modern-day classic), Little Richard, Otis Redding, and Gladys Knight; rappers Ludacris and Outkast; artist Benny Andrews; writers and playwrights Tina Ansa, Pearl Cleage, Jean Toomer, James McPherson, Alice Walker, and Frank Yerby; dramatist and producer Kenny Leon; actress Jasmine Guy; and actor and producer Tyler Perry.

The state's African American colleges and universities have had a long history of outstanding choruses and orchestras such as the Morehouse College Glee Club, the Clark Atlanta University Philharmonic Orchestra, and the Morris Brown College Band. The Atlanta-Morehouse-Spelman Chorus has presented a series of Christmas carol concerts dating back to the 1920s, which attract biracial audiences from throughout the state. The Atlanta-Morehouse-Spelman Players have a long history of presenting outstanding dramatic performances.

There are major festivals, some of them with international reputations, such as the National Black Arts Festival, which is held annually in Atlanta. Several areas of the state have annual jazz festivals and annual African and African American film festivals. Many black Georgians celebrate the Juneteenth holiday and the alternative Christmas observance known as Kwanzaa.

Among the major African American art galleries and museums in the state are the Atlanta University Art Gallery, the Spelman College Art Gallery, the APEX Museum, and the Herndon House (the mansion once occupied the family of Alonzo Herndon, the founder of the Atlanta Life Insurance Company), all in Atlanta; the Harriett Tubman Museum in Macon; and the Lucy Craft Laney Museum in Augusta.

The Martin Luther King Jr. birthplace and the Martin Luther King Jr. Center for Nonviolent Social Change are in the Martin Luther King Jr. Historic District in Atlanta. African American sites on the National Historic Register also include the "Sweet Auburn" Business District (site of an early major hub of black enterprise); Stone Hall at Morris Brown College, also in Atlanta; the Morton Building and Theatre in Athens; the Albany Civil Rights Institute; The Nicholsonville Baptist Church in Chatham County; the Lucy Laney Museum in Macon; The Zach Community Center

Historic District in Hancock County; the Georgia Music Hall of Fame and the Georgia Sports Hall of Fame in Macon; and the First African Baptist Church and Laurel Grove South Cemetery, both in Savannah.

The Laurel Grove Cemetery, like the Oakland Cemetery in Atlanta, has separate burial areas for blacks and whites. Both are resting places for Confederate veterans as well as distinguished African Americans. However, in the case of Laurel Grove, the separate section for blacks was designated Laurel Grove South. There are many other historic African American cemeteries in Georgia, including some in churchyards, especially in rural areas. Two of the oldest established by African American cemetery associations are the Southview and Lincoln cemeteries in Atlanta. Martin Luther King Jr. was first interred at Southview, and his parents are interred there now. The crypts of King and his wife Coretta are now at the Martin Luther King Jr. Center on Auburn Avenue.

Places providing important resources for the study of African American culture and history include the Robert W. Woodruff Library of the Atlanta University Center, the Auburn Avenue Research Library on African Americans, the Atlanta History Center, and the Robert W. Woodruff Library of Emory University, all in Atlanta; the Albany Civil Rights Institute; and the National Park Service Research Study of the Gullah/Geeche culture on Georgia's southeastern coast.

Bibliography

Bartley, Numan V. *The Creation of Modern Georgia.* Athens: University of Georgia Press, 1990.

Bayor, Ronald H. *Race and the Shaping of Twentieth-Century Atlanta.* Chapel Hill: University of North Carolina Press, 1996.

Cobb, James C. *Georgia Odyssey.* Athens: University of Georgia Press, 1997.

Dittmer, John. *Black Georgia in the Progressive Era, 1900–1920.* Urbana: University of Illinois Press, 1980

Georgia Encyclopedia. www.georgiaencyclopedia.org.

Grant, Donald L. *The Way It Was in the South: The Black Experience in Georgia.* Secaucus, NJ: Carol Publishing Group, 1993.

Hornsby, Alton, Jr. *A Biographical History of African Americans.* Montgomery, AL: E-Book Time Publishers, 2005.

Hornsby, Alton, Jr. *Black Power in Dixie: A Political History of African Americans in Atlanta.* Gainesville: University Press of Florida, 2009.

Hornsby, Alton, Jr. *The Negro in Revolutionary Georgia.* Atlanta: Georgia Commission for the Bicentennial Celebration, 1977.

Hornsby, Alton, Jr. *A Short History of Black Atlanta, 1847–1990.* Richland, TX: Ivy Halls Publishers, 2005.

Hornsby, Alton, Jr. *Southerners Too? Essays on the Black South, 1733–1990.* Lanham, MD: University Press of America, 2004.

Hunter, Tera. *To Joy My Freedom: Southern Black Women's Lives and Labors after the Civil War.* Cambridge, MA: Harvard University Press, 1997.

Inscoe, John. C., ed. *Georgia in Black and White: Explorations in Race Relations, 1865–1950.* Athens: University of Georgia Press, 1994.

Pomerantz, Gary M. *Where Peachtree Meets Sweet Auburn: The Saga of Two Families and the Making of Atlanta.* New York: Scribner, 1996.

Thompson, C. Mildred. *Reconstruction in Georgia: Economic, Social, Political, 1865–1872.* New York: Columbia University Press, 1915.

Tuck, Stephen G. N. *Beyond Atlanta: The Struggle for Racial Equality in Georgia, 1940–1980.* Athens: University of Georgia Press, 2001.

HAWAII

Miles Jackson

Chronology

1778	The English explorer James Cook lands in Hawaii.
1798	Ebenezer Townsend, sailing in Hawaii waters on the *Neptune*, writes in his diary that he saw two Portuguese African men with three white men building a boat on Kauai.
1811	Anthony Allen, a former slave and the first fully documented African American in the islands, arrives in Hawaii.
1823	Betsy Stockton, a former slave and the first documented African American female in the islands, arrives in Hawaii.
1898	T. McCants Stewart, the first African American attorney and civil rights attorney in New York City, moves to Hawaii with his family.
1898	The United States annexes Hawaii, which becomes a U.S. territory.
1900	The federal Census records 233 blacks in Hawaii.
1901	The first group of African American contract laborers from Alabama, Tennessee, Mississippi, and Louisiana are recruited for work on sugar plantations on Maui and the island of Hawaii.
1901	William Lineas Maples, a physician and Howard University graduate, becomes the first African American medical doctor to practice in Hawaii.
1910	The U.S. Census records 695 blacks in Hawaii, a tripling of African American residents over the last decade.
1913	The all–African American 25th Infantry Regiment with 2,000 men is assigned to Schofield Barracks on Oahu. The U.S. Department of the Army moves the regiment in 1918 to Nogales and Yuma, Arizona.
1914	William F. Crockett, an African American attorney, is elected to the Hawaii territorial legislature.
1915	Alice Ball, an African American chemist at the University of Hawaii, begins research on a cure for leprosy.
1915	Nolle Smith, an African American engineer from Wyoming, establishes a construction firm in Hawaii.
1928	Nolle Smith is elected to the Hawaii territorial legislature and becomes an influential political leader in Hawaii.
1941	(*December 7*) The Japanese attack the U.S. naval base at Pearl Harbor on Oahu. The attack leads next day to a U.S. declaration of war on Japan.
1941–1945	An estimated 30,000 African American military personnel and civilian war workers are stationed and living in Hawaii at various times during the war.

1944	Walter White, executive secretary of the National Association for the Advancement of Colored People (NAACP), visits military installations in Hawaii because of complaints by military personnel and civilians about discrimination on Oahu.
1945	A chapter of the NAACP is established in Hawaii.
1950	The U.S. Census counts 2,651 African Americans living in Hawaii, indicating that many of the blacks who went to Hawaii during the war did not stay once it was over.
1950	Wendell F. Crockett, an African American attorney, is elected to the Hawaii territorial legislature.
1959	*(August 21)* Hawaii enters the Union as the 50th state.
1968	African American educator Charles Campbell is elected to the Hawaii state legislature.
c. 1970	A chapter of Links, Inc., a national organization of African American women, is established in Hawaii.
1980	Sandra Simms becomes the first African American appointed to be judge of the first circuit court of Hawaii.
1985	The African American Heritage Foundation of Maui is founded to foster and preserve African American culture in Hawaii.
1991	The Hawaii legislature enacts a law making Martin Luther King Jr. Day a state holiday.
1991	Sandra Simms becomes the first African American woman appointed as judge of the state district court.
1995	The Dr. Martin Luther King Coalition of Hawaii is founded to promote the Martin Luther King holiday as a day of community service in the state.
1997	The African American Diversity Cultural Center of Hawaii is founded to document, archive, preserve, and maintain the documents and artifacts of African American history in the state.
2000	African American real estate broker Helene Hale is elected to the Hawaii legislature.
2000	The African American population reaches 44,000, including military personnel and their dependents, revealing that the population growth for African Americans in Hawaii is moderate in comparison to other groups.
2008	*(November 4)* Barack Obama, born and raised in Hawaii, is elected as the first African American president of the United States; Obama carries Hawaii with about 72 percent of the vote.

Historical Overview

The Hawaiian Islands, or Sandwich Islands as they were known in the eighteenth and early nineteenth centuries, are located in the middle of the Pacific. When the Englishman Captain James Cook arrived in 1778, he met Polynesians who had inhabited the islands for at least eight centuries. After Cook's visit, word soon spread to Europe and America about the opportunities that were waiting for the adventurous in the tropical islands of the Pacific. King Kamehameha I welcomed into the kingdom foreigners from all over the world and from all walks of life. Hawaii had become a major rest stop because of its central location in the Pacific. It was a convenient stop for whaling fleets and ships trading with countries in Asia. The ships stopped in Hawaii because of the natural harbor on Oahu, for fresh water, and replenishment of supplies.

Among the crew members of many of the ships were men of African ancestry. Some were from Portugal's African colonies, including the Cape Verde Islands and colonies on the African continent. Also among ship crews were freedmen or former slaves and runaway slaves from the United States and the Caribbean islands. Samuel Kamakau, a nineteenth-century Hawaiian writer, stated that "many races—the red, the black, and the white—came in the early days to Hawaii." Kamehameha and other chiefs recruited from these newly arrived foreigners were men with many skills, including navigators, armorers, blacksmiths, sailmakers, and even musicians. Among the men who remained ashore, most found the Polynesian people hospitable and many found a niche that allowed them to earn a living. Anthony D. Allen, a former slave from Schenectady, New York, left his ship in 1811 and worked for a short while as steward to Kamehameha when he sailed to neighboring islands in the kingdom. Allen was awarded six acres of land by the high priest of Oahu, Hevaheva. By the time the first missionaries arrived in 1820, Allen had an established farm with cattle, goats, and fresh vegetables; a boarding house; a saloon; and a small hospital that specialized in caring for sailors that had become ill while at sea. He married a Hawaiian woman and had three children, Peggy, Anthony Jr., and George. One missionary wrote that "Among the residents of this island is a Black man . . . named Allen. He has been our constant friend, has daily furnished us with milk and once or twice a week fresh vegetables."[1] Allen had an enclosure that consisted of 8–10 houses that served as sleeping, eating, storage, and cooking facilities. In 1835, he died, leaving a family that eventually became assimilated into Hawaii's growing multiracial population.

In 1823, Betsey Stockton, a former slave from Princeton, New Jersey, arrived in Honolulu with the Second Company of Missionaries. Stockton was assigned to Maui as a teacher, where she established the first school for Hawaiian commoners. Unfortunately, after two years she had to accompany one member of her missionary group who became ill back to New Jersey.

In 1834, the crew members who came ashore could very well have been entertained by a musical group consisting of black men. David Shattuck and David Curtis were hired by Kamehameha III to organize a band. The king agreed to provide his musicians living quarters and free clothing for themselves and their wives. By 1845, a larger band was organized with George Wyatt as leader and Charles Johnson as captain. The remaining members were from other ethnic groups. The musicians were expected to entertain at special events. Several blacks became successful in the barbering business in Honolulu. Fredrick Bins not only cut hair, but gave shampoos in the "Chinese Fashion," according to an advertisement in the local newspaper. There were enough blacks in Honolulu at various times to organize the "African Relief Society." According to the journal of Stephen Reynolds, a missionary, the main work of the organization was to provide assistance to destitute African seamen and provide burial services to those who died while in Honolulu.

Hawaii and Slavery

The Kingdom of Hawaii never experienced black slavery as practiced in the American colonies and states. However, Hawaii's experience with slavery was largely through the sympathies of American missionaries who arrived in Hawaii as early as 1820. They came under the auspices of the American Board of Commissioners for Foreign Missions, which had many of its members active in the antislavery, abolitionist movement. In fact, an antislavery society was formed in the kingdom in 1841 among the American missionaries, but they spoke out against slavery several years earlier. Thomas Lafon, a missionary in the Hawaii group, resigned from his post in 1841 when he learned that the Board of Commissioners for Foreign Missions had accepted money from southern slave owners.

Blacks and the Plantation Experience

By the early 1870s, Hawaii's ports no longer bustled with business brought by whaling ships that had, until recently, so frequently anchored in Hawaii's harbors. The discovery of oil in Pennsylvania had rendered the use of whale oil obsolete in the United States. Although the declining whaling industry no longer provided Hawaii with the revenue it once did, a new sugar-based economy seemed promising to investors. In 1850, the Hawaiian government had passed laws allowing foreigners to buy land in fee simple, and consequently, huge tracts of land had been purchased by investors and set aside for the cultivation of sugar. Growing the sugarcane was one thing, harvesting it was yet another. The success of the sugar industry required increasingly large numbers of laborers, many more than the dwindling native Hawaiian population could provide, and so contract laborers came to Hawaii to work on the sugar plantations.

The first laborers to arrive were Chinese, and by the time the Hawaiian Kingdom had restricted Chinese immigration with regulations passed in 1884 and 1885, the population of Chinese in Hawaii had reached 18,000. These workers were followed by 148 Japanese laborers in 1868, but in 1870, further immigration of Japanese workers was also stopped, but for different reasons. The Hawaiian government had restricted Chinese immigration, but it was the Japanese government that refused to allow any more workers to settle in Hawaii. Because of negative reports about working conditions on Hawaii's plantations, the Meiji government halted any further recruitment of Japanese workers. Emigration of Japanese laborers would not resume until 1885, when an agreement was signed between officials of both Hawaii and Japan; by 1900, over 60,000 Japanese laborers had arrived to work on Hawaiian sugar plantations. Plantation laborers had also been recruited from Italy, Germany, Norway, Spain, Russia, and Portugal.

The Portuguese workers adapted very quickly and comfortably to island life, and by 1884, nearly 10,000 were in residence. Men of African ancestry from Cabo Verde, a group of islands off the coast of West Africa settled by the Portuguese, were already in residence in Hawaii as the sugar industry gained importance in Hawaii's economy. These men had arrived earlier to the islands as whalers and when contract laborers for the plantations were needed, other Caboverdeanos, Africans, or Portuguese Africans continued to sail to Hawaii as contract laborers. Although some laborers also arrived from the South Pacific, including approximately 400 Melanesians from the New Hebrides, most South Sea Islanders did not stay but returned home at the end of their contracts; the Melanesians had also been recruited to work on Australia's expanding sugar plantations in Queensland.

As early as 1870, Walter Murray Gibson, an American adventurer, legislator, and confidant of King Kalakaua, investigated the possibility that southern blacks might work Hawaii's plantations. While visiting the United States, Gibson proposed recruiting blacks with plantation experience, but nothing resulted from his initial investigations. In 1872, a few leaders of the Hawaii Sugar Planters Association (HSPA) reiterated Gibson's notion that African Americans from the American South represented an experienced labor force comfortable with plantation life, but, once again, the suggestion of recruiting blacks as plantation workers was not well received by many planters, missionaries, and some Hawaiians. In 1879, further discussions were held by the Bureau of Immigration on this earlier HSPA proposal. The Bureau wrote for advice to Samuel Chapman Armstrong, the son of a prominent missionary family who had arrived in Hawaii with the Fifth Missionary Company. As a young man with family in Hawaii and also with important contacts in the American South, the bureau hoped that Armstrong might be able to give them both insight and real information.

As a young man, Armstrong had traveled to study at Williams College, and when the Civil War erupted, he had volunteered for the Union Army and was given command of the 5th Infantry Regiment, an African American unit. He rose quickly through the ranks and by the war's end had been promoted to brevet general. After the war, Armstrong worked with the Freedman's Bureau and noted a great need for education and training programs for African American youth. Dedicated to the notion of resolving that need and supported by Northern philanthropy, he founded in 1868 the Hampton Institute in Virginia to educate African American youth in industrial trades. Unfortunately, although the dialogue of the HSPA with Armstrong may have been important, it was, ultimately, inconsequential. John E. Bush, a part-Hawaiian and head of the Bureau, wrote Armstrong that:

> the last legislature was decidedly adverse to Negro immigrants, even to opposing New Hebrides people. There was a resolution passed opposing the immigration of blacks, and we do not deem it advisable to ignore the House and would therefore ask you to discontinue further investigation of that class of immigrants.[2]

Like the Chinese before them, blacks, it appeared, would be kept from entering Hawaiian society as workers. Without the support of the legislature, plantation owners would find it difficult to encourage black workers from the Southern United States to immigrate to Hawaii. Nonetheless, in 1882, following the discussion between the sugar planters and Armstrong, James E. Blaine, U.S. secretary of state, did propose another plan to recruit African Americans for work on Hawaii's plantations, but this plan also received little support.

Although it may be difficult to determine precisely why and how divisive racial attitudes prosper in any society and why the Hawaii legislature in particular would choose to exclude immigrants because of race alone, evidence of racial prejudice and discrimination in nineteenth-century Hawaii civilian society is abundant. For example, the Reverend Sereno E. Bishop, editor of *The Friend*, had frequently expressed in print that any admixture of African would be disastrous for the people of Hawaii, writing derogatory editorials that referred to both those of African ancestry and other nonwhites as "low in mental culture." Such attitudes expressed by influential community members might have easily influenced legislative decisions. After annexation and gaining territorial status, the new government with an American-appointed governor felt subtle pressure from the U.S. Department of Labor to consider recruiting African American contract laborers from the American South.

The prospect of bringing African American families to Hawaii was beginning to seem reasonable to many plantation owners, and, as prosperous businessmen, their opinions were heard by legislators. An influx of black workers might provide field hands with much-needed plantation experience, and the women who accompanied them might also offer personal and household assistance for wives of plantation owners. An article printed in the magazine *Paradise of the Pacific* quotes one plantation manager as saying that his plantation would accept 25 families "and, furthermore, two Negroes can do the work of three Japanese.... The women will work as well as the men at about two-thirds the wages. Interest has also been awakened among housewives as to the desirability of Negroes as cooks, nurses, etc. and many think they may supplant the Japanese in household duties."[3] James B. Castle of Alexander and Baldwin, sugar plantation owners, established recruiting agencies in Nashville, Tennessee, and Montgomery, Alabama. Agents for the HSPA began recruitment in the surrounding black communities during the fall of 1900. Flyers, newspapers, and pastors of Nashville and Montgomery churches announced opportunities in Hawaii for African Americans, emphasizing both the astounding beauty of these faraway islands in the middle of the Pacific and the ample salaries of $26 per month plus free housing, healthcare, and firewood. Black workers, however, did not need the lure of gentle tradewinds to convince them to leave Southern plantations. By the end of 1901, approximately 400 blacks were recruited to work and live on Maui and on Hawaii's plantations.

Trouble at Wailuku

Life on Hawaii's plantations was not as idyllic as those early transplanted workers might have hoped. After working for a month, the Nashville laborers were told that their pay would be only 60 cents per day, considerably less than the salary recruiters had indicated they would be receiving. Many workers were handed only $3 for a month's labor along with an explanation that deductions had been made for items provided by the plantation store, including bedding, food, utensils, and other necessary household items. Four single men, led by Will Aliston, protested and went on strike, stating that they had been misled and overcharged for household goods.

Aliston tried to convince fellow workers to join the strike, but with little success. Plantation manager Wells ordered the four protesters off the plantation immediately; they were not allowed to return to their cabins to retrieve personal belongings. This brutal method of labor control was not a new practice; in past years, strikers and their families had been frequently evicted from plantation homes, often with the help of local police. Penniless and with only the clothes on their backs, Aliston and other protesters made their way to Kahului, hoping to find employment. Unfortunately, the manager of the Wailuku plantation had already informed potential employers in Kahului that Aliston and his group were troublemakers. Forced to acknowledge the impossibility of finding work on Maui, the group of strikers raised money for passage to Honolulu by singing and dancing for street crowds. The four men found employment in Honolulu. By December 1903, as contracts expired, many workers imported from the South found means and ways to leave the plantations and Hawaii. The African Americans who had imagined that Hawaii held possibility for a new life were bitterly disappointed, and many left the islands in search of places that would allow their dreams for freedom to be translated to reality.

Between 1898 and 1915, Hawaii was seen as a new frontier by a small group of professional blacks from the continental United States. They

Admiral Chester W. Nimitz pins the Navy Cross on Dorie Miller at a ceremony onboard a U.S. Navy warship in Pearl Harbor, Hawaii, 1942. (Library of Congress)

sought their fortunes in the islands as many others did from around the world. The black population, according to the U.S. Census, had increased to 695 by 1910. Perhaps more would have come after annexation, but the great distance of the islands from the mainland and the high cost of travel did not encourage very many blacks to migrate to Hawaii. Among the professionals represented in those early years who arrived in the islands were several lawyers, a physician, an engineer, several teachers, and others with technical skills who established themselves in the islands before 1915.

Black Military Presence

The need for security for the United States' new territory suggested a need to have permanent naval and army bases on Oahu to protect American investments and citizens. In 1913, the 25th Infantry Regiment was assigned to Schofield Barracks located in central Oahu. This all-black unit had already made a name for itself in battles during the Spanish American War in 1898. The presence of 2,000 black soldiers made an impression on the local community because of their outstanding athletes and talented musicians. The local press covered the unit's baseball games on a regular basis as they played local baseball teams and the unit's band gave concerts in various communities. Many of Oahu's rural residents had never had contact with such a variety of black males, but it did not take long for friendships to form. A few of the men whose enlistment ended in Hawaii chose to remain in the islands. In 1918, the unit was transferred to Yuma and Nogales, Arizona.

When the Japanese attacked Pearl Harbor on December 7, 1941, Dorie Miller, a U.S. Navy mess attendant assigned to the USS *West Virginia* at Pearl Harbor, helped moved his mortally wounded commander to shelter and then manned a .50-caliber machine gun. With no previous combat or training on this particular weapon, Miller shot down four Japanese planes. On May 27, 1942, Miller was awarded the Navy Cross for his extraordinary heroism, the first African American to be recognized with this honor. It is estimated that approximately 30,000 black military and civilian war personnel were assigned to Hawaii between 1942 and 1945. They came from various parts of the country and most found Hawaii's Polynesians and Asians to be welcoming. However, there was racial tension that existed between blacks and whites, military and civilian. Most of the interracial problems stemmed from mainland racial attitudes that were brought to Hawaii by many of the white southerners. The black civilian workers brought to Hawaii to work in the war effort were assigned segregated housing on military bases; all military units were segregated in Hawaii as they were throughout the nation.

The racial problems were serious enough that an interracial committee was requested by the NAACP to investigate the patterns of discrimination on military installations and in the community. Walter White, executive secretary of the NAACP, visited Hawaii in 1944. His report was critical of federal and local racial practices and recommended that a chapter of the NAACP be established in Honolulu. The first year of the charter in 1946, there were 150 new members. Rumors spread in 1948 that at least 30 members of the Honolulu branch were members of the Communist Party. The national board of directors was fearful that communists and communist sympathizers were about to take over the Honolulu branch. White, who became NAACP executive secretary in 1955, recommended to the board that the branch's charter be revoked. The board agreed at its November 1949 meeting. It was not until May 1960 that a new NAACP charter was granted. Today, there is an active branch of the organization on Oahu. Although Hawaii is free of most of the problems faced by blacks on the mainland, there still remains a need to have a civil rights organization such as the NAACP available in Hawaii.

Establishing Community

Following World War II, most of the blacks connected with the war effort in Hawaii returned to the mainland. Nevertheless between 1950 and 1960, the black population nearly doubled from 2,651 to 4,943. By 2000, the U.S. Census estimated 33,000 blacks, including military, their dependents, and civilians, were residing in Hawaii. The 2007 U.S. Census update for Hawaii estimated that the total African American population was 44,000, with 60–65 percent connected to the military. Most blacks who migrated to Hawaii have always entered the existing social

structure, especially in employment, according to their educational background, skills, and experience. Those who migrate are either professionals or skilled technicians, and some are retired from the military. The blacks who chose to move to Hawaii had undoubtedly been successful in their fields on the mainland. Martha Hansen, a sociologist, feels that because there is no separate spatial black community in Hawaii, there has evolved a socio/psychological community based on historical and common American experiences. Despite not having a spatial community, blacks in Hawaii have found each other. There are several predominantly black churches that worship in the traditional ways of the black church on the mainland. They have formed fraternal, social, and cultural organizations that allow them to come together for regular meetings. During the war years, the Bachelor's Club was organized by single black civilians employed at Pearl Harbor Naval Base. Later, the Wai Wai Nui Club, a black women's social and service group, was organized and was active in a variety of community activities that included service to hospitals and the mentoring of teenage girls.

In 1979, Alpha Kappa Alpha (AKA) sorority, first established at Howard University in Washington, D.C., in 1908, became the first all-black chapter of a "Greek letter" sorority to be established in Hawaii. Soon after other predominantly black "Greek letter" chapters were established and include Alpha Phi Alpha fraternity, Delta Sigma Theta sorority, Zeta Phi Beta sorority, Phi Beta Sigma fraternity, and Omega Psi Phi fraternity. Some of the members in these societies are active-duty military officers who joined the organizations when they were undergraduate college students. In Honolulu, graduate chapters perform a variety of community services designed to strengthen community. AKA sorority, as an example, awards an average of $20,000 annually from its scholarship program for Hawaii high-school graduates.

The Prince Hall Grand Lodge of Free and Accepted Masons of Hawaii has been chartered in Hawaii since 2001. Prince Hall Masonry in Hawaii supports all principles necessary to build character, to render service to others, and to improve Hawaii's social, cultural, and economic conditions. The Hawaii chapter of Links, Inc., was established in Honolulu in the 1980s and today sponsors African American educational and cultural programs on Oahu. In cooperation with the Honolulu Academy of Arts, the Honolulu chapter of Links, Inc., sponsors an annual program celebrating African American art, music, dance, and storytelling. This annual cultural program attracts many people from the community of various ethnic backgrounds, and provides an understanding of African American culture and the black presence in Hawaii.

Education

Betsey Stockton was with the first group of missionary teachers who moved quickly to Maui in 1823 to assemble students and establish the first missionary schools. She was liked by the Hawaiians, mainly because she immediately began learning the Hawaiian language and was able to establish rapport with the parents of the students she taught.

Carlotta Stewart arrived in Honolulu as a young woman in 1898. She was the oldest daughter of T. McCant Stewart, an attorney who moved his family to Honolulu. She completed the teacher-training program at Oahu College and started her teaching career at Sacred Hearts Convent. By the time she was 28, she was the principal of Koolau Elementary School earning $1,200 annually, a comfortable middle-class salary then. She spent 40 years on Kauai as a teacher and principal. In 1916, she married Yun Tim Lai, a Chinese businessman of Anahola, Kauai. He was killed in 1935 in an accident while visiting Hong Kong. Lai never had children and did not remarry.

Annie V. Crockett arrived on Maui in 1901 and was formerly a teacher in the public schools of Montgomery, Alabama, and Washington, D.C., before beginning her teaching career on Maui. Her daughter Grace also retired from the Maui school system. In 1980, the Hawaii Department of Education was criticized by the federal government and minority leaders in the state for the lack of adequate representation of some of Hawaii's minorities. Much of the impetus for correcting the imbalance in minority representation on the teaching staff in the department was Dr. Donnis Thompson, an African American professor of education at the University of Hawaii. Dr. Thompson was appointed Hawaii's superintendent of education in 1981. She was the first woman to head Hawaii's public schools. During her three years in office she led the way in bringing more black, Filipino, Hawaiian, and Samoan teachers into the school system.

There are four universities in Hawaii: The state-operated University of Hawaii has 10 campuses, including the community college system; Chaminade University; Brigham Young University–Hawaii; and Hawaii Pacific University. Black students are enrolled in all of the institutions of higher education in the state. The biggest challenge in attempts to diversify students, faculty, and staff at these institutions has been to increase the number of blacks attending and employed at these institutions. Approximately 2 percent of the students enrolled in the University of Hawaii system are black and fewer than 1 percent of the faculty is black.

The Church

The first group of blacks who were recruited from the South arrived in 1901, and accompanying them were two preachers from Montgomery,

Alabama, the Reverends James A. Henderson and Augustus Hutchinson. The *Maui News* noted that both men were leading their flocks of workers who "are as a class moral men and women and will prove to be a reliable class of labor."[4] Henderson was a graduate of Tuskegee Institute in Alabama and had served as pastor of the well-respected Mount Zion Church in Montgomery. Reverend Henderson and Mrs. M. E. Henderson were leaders in organizing the "Christian Endeavor Club" among workers at Alabama Camp, which had as its primary mission to encourage a Christian life among the several hundred workers and their families. The Sunday school was well supported and popular among the children and parents of the camp. The *Evening Bulletin* reported that the Alabama laborers were popular in Wailuku because of the Negro spirituals they sang in the evenings. The Hawaiians on the plantation were always delighted to hear their southern neighbors sing. Unfortunately, Reverend Henderson died of a stroke when he was 49 years old. His obituary that appeared in the local Maui newspaper said that he was "honest and upright in character as well as a sincere and zealous Christian. He rounded out a beautiful life, rich in love and esteem for all who knew him." Reverend J. Nua of the Native Church officiated at his funeral service and his remains were interred in Wailuku. Reverend Hutchinson left the Pu'unene Plantation in mid-1902 and opened a barber shop in the lobby of the Maui Hotel in Wailuku. Hutchinson died in late 1902 and his burial was handled by the local lodge of the Odd Fellows at the Wailuku cemetery.

It was not until 1943 that another black church was established in Hawaii. The New Era Baptist Church was established at Pearl Harbor Naval Base. Today, there are several churches with predominantly black congregations on Oahu. The two largest are Trinity Baptist Church and City of Refuge Christian Church. The other churches are smaller and have congregations with fewer than 100 members. They meet in storefronts, homes, and public buildings (mostly schools), and even tents. The stated mission of all the churches is to meet the religious needs of local people and a few do have congregants from other ethnic groups. However, most of these churches minister primarily to the black congregations. The gospel choirs of Trinity Baptist Church and City of Refuge Christian Church are very popular and their concerts are well attended by people of all faiths in the community. Many blacks worship at churches with multiracial congregations.

Hawaii's Multiracial Mix

The blacks who settled in Hawaii during the nineteenth century selected Hawaiian wives. Broussard stated that "today most of the descendants of (Anthony D.) Allen and his fellow harbingers are unaware of the role their ancestors played in the Hawaiian Kingdom. In fact, many do not even know they are of African ancestry." Dr. Romanzo Adams, professor emeritus of the University of Hawaii, more than 70 years ago predicted that Hawaii would probably be one big race in a couple of hundred years. No doubt Adams was thinking what is commonly referred to as "Hawaii's Melting Pot." According to the most recent U.S. Census, Hawaii's interracial-marriage rate is one of the highest in the nation. In 1920, interracial marriages were about 10 percent of all Hawaii's marriages. By 1950, interracial marriages had increased to 30 percent. In 2000, 65 percent of blacks marrying in Hawaii married outside of their own ethnic group. Similar patterns of interracial marriage exist among Hawaii's other racial groups. Today, the racial issue by and large is not a sensitive one in Hawaii because so many people are of multiracial mix. Quite often they will identify with the predominant cultural practices they experience in the home and in growing up. There is evidence that

Chemist Alice Ball. Ball was the first African American woman to graduate from the University of Hawaii and was renowned for her work on Hansen's disease. (Library of Congress)

as the rate of interracial marriages continue, distinct racial categories could blur even more and perhaps in the distant future disappear as Romanzo Adams predicted.

In summary, it is likely the black population in Hawaii will continue to have only modest growth. Some observers view Hawaii's black population and its assimilation into the multiracial mix in the islands as a possible model of what could happen as blacks are dispersed in urban areas to non-black communities throughout the nation.

Notable African Americans

Allen, Anthony D. (1774–1835)

Anthony D. Allen was born on the German Flats of New York and was a slave in Schenectady. He arrived in Hawaii as a seaman in 1811. Allen became a friend of the early missionaries and of Hawaii's royalty. He became a successful entrepreneur in several enterprises, which included a boarding house, a tavern, the first bowling alley in Hawaii, and selling food supplies to ships stopping in Honolulu.

Ball, Alice (1892–1916)

Alice Ball was the first African American woman to graduate from the University of Hawaii with a master's degree in chemistry. As a young pharmaceutical chemist she was engaged in groundbreaking research on a cure for Hansen's disease (leprosy). At the age of 24 she became seriously ill and died after a short illness. Her injectable ethyl ester of chaulmoogra oil to Hansen's disease patients was recognized years later as a remarkable cure for this dreaded disease.

Crockett, William F. (1861–1943)

William F. Crockett arrived on Maui in 1901 with his wife, Annie V. Rider of Washington, D.C., and his two children, Wendell Francis and Grace. He first worked as a representative for the first black laborers to come to Maui from the South. A year or so after arrival, he established a successful law practice in Wailuku and became active in Republican politics, was elected to the Hawaii legislature, and was appointed to a judiciary post on Maui.

Hale, Helene (1916–)

Helene Hale moved to Hawaii in 1947 where she taught school before entering politics. She is the first woman mayor of the island of Hawaii. Elected in 1962, she was instrumental in introducing the county system to Hawaii. In 2000, she was elected to the Hawaii legislature and served for two terms as a state representative.

Lai, Carlotta Stewart (1881–1952)

Carlotta Stewart Lai arrived in Hawaii in 1898. She was a teacher and administrator in the

Hawaii public school system for 40 years and was the oldest daughter of T. McCants Stewart. She married Yun Tim Lai, a Chinese businessman of Anahola, Kauai, in 1916. He died while on a business trip to Hong Kong.

Smith, Nolle (1888–1982)

Nolle Smith was a popular political leader in Hawaiian local and state politics. He was an engineer and graduate of the University of Montana. He arrived in Honolulu in 1915 and was employed by local government as an engineer; eventually he established his own construction company. He became active in Republican politics and was elected to the territorial legislature in 1928. Smith is known as the key person who introduced a statewide civil service system in Hawaii.

Stewart, T. McCants (1854–1923)

T. McCants Stewart was a well-respected attorney in New York before he moved to Honolulu in 1898. He established a law practice in Honolulu and became an active member in the local Republican Party. He practiced before the Hawaii Supreme Court and was successful in handling immigration cases for Chinese aliens. Stewart enjoyed popularity among the Hawaiians and settled land case disputes for Hawaiian families. He sensed an increase in racial animosity in Honolulu and decided to leave for the mainland and later Liberia. Carlotta, his daughter, remained in Hawaii.

Stockton, Betsey (1798–1865)

Betsey Stockton was a missionary teacher in Hawaii. She was born in Princeton, New Jersey, as a slave, but was manumitted in 1817 by her owner. In 1823, she was accepted as a member of the Second Missionary Company by the American Board of Commissioners for Foreign

Missionaries to go to the Hawaiian Islands. On her way to Maui, she was a guest in the Anthony Allen home in Honolulu. She was assigned to establish the first school for children of Maui from nonroyal families. Her stay was cut short because she had to leave Hawaii due to the illness of her sponsor.

Cultural Contributions

African Americans' cultural contributions in Hawaii have been mainly in the arts. On December 11, 1889, a troupe from the 49th Regiment staged an extravaganza at the Orpheum Theater in downtown Honolulu. In port for only a short time, the black soldiers from the troopship *Sherman*, bound for the Philippines, presented an exhilarating performance. Since that date, blacks have continued to make substantial contributions to the arts in Hawaii. With their talents they have enriched the lives of Hawaii's people.

Jazz first arrived in the islands in 1920, when Hawaii's musicians began to play new and unfamiliar music. Local musicians left the islands to play, study, and travel to the major cities on both coasts of the U.S. mainland. Many of the local musicians listened to and played with black jazz musicians. Hawaii's musicians who could not leave the islands could listen to black jazz musicians and singers who stopped briefly in Honolulu on their way to and from major cities in Asia and the Pacific. During World War II, some of the top jazz performers entertained troops, but also local audiences. Later, top entertainers such as Billy Eckstein, Sarah Vaughn, Nat King Cole, and bands of Count Basie, Cab Callaway, and Duke Ellington played dates in Honolulu and these extraordinary musicians helped win the hearts of new local jazz enthusiasts. A few black musicians who settled in Hawaii, such as the late Trummy Young (trombonist), Azure McCall (vocalist), Chuck James (drummer), and M. Merrill Jackson (bassist), made an impact on the jazz scene in Hawaii.

African Americans have played a role in introducing local theater audiences to black theater. The African American Theater, led by Gregg Harris, and the African American Repertory Theater, founded by Leonard Piggee, have been active in offering acting classes to the community, and several of August Wilson's plays have been produced and played to Hawaii's enthusiastic multiracial audiences.

The poet Frank Marshall Davis moved his family to Hawaii in 1948. Before coming to the islands to live, he had published several volumes of poetry and had many anthologized during the Harlem Renaissance literary era. Davis died in 1987, the last of the black poets of the twilight years of the Depression. In contemporary Hawaii, the tradition of poetry continues. Kathryn Waddell Takara is a prolific poet with three volumes of poetry published since 2000. Takara's work is recognized because it represents the blending of the African American and Hawaiian experiences. Ayin Adams, who resides on Maui, is a prolific writer and has had her poetry selected for national awards. Despite the small number of blacks in Hawaii, a thriving community exists and contributes decisively to the multicultural and multiethnic environment of the islands.

Notes

1. Sylbil Bingham, *Journal*, June 20, 1820, Hawaii Mission Children's Society, Honolulu.

2. Charles T. Gulick, *Report to the President of the Bureau of Immigration to the Legislative Assembly of 1886* (Honolulu: Kingdom of Hawaii, 1886), 143.

3. *Paradise of the Pacific*, September 1897, 10: 132.

4. *Maui News*, February 16, 1901, 3.

Bibliography

Adams, Romanzo Colfax. "Census Notes on Negroes in Hawaii Prior to the War." *Social Process in Hawaii* 9–10 (1945): 25–27.

Broussard, Albert C. "Carlotta Stewart Lai, a Black Teacher in the Territory of Hawaii." *Hawaiian Journal of History* 29 (1990): 129–154.

Broussard, Albert C. "There Is One Black Man, Anthony Allen." In Miles M. Jackson, ed., *They Followed the Trade Winds: African Americans in Hawaii*. Honolulu: University of Hawaii Press, 2005, 24–55.

Home, Gerald. *The White Pacific: U.S. Imperialism and Black Slavery in the South Seas after the Civil War*. Honolulu: University of Hawaii Press, 2007.

Jackson, Miles M. *And They Came: A Brief History of Blacks in Hawaii*. Durham, NC: Four G. Publishers, 2001.

Jackson, Miles M., ed. *They Followed the Trade Winds: African Americans in Hawaii*. Honolulu: University of Hawaii Press, 2004.

Kamakau, Samuel M. *Ruling Chiefs of Hawaii*. Honolulu, HI: Kamehameha Schools Press, 1961.

Lee, Lloyd. "A Brief Analysis of the Role of the Negro in the Hawaiian Community." *American Sociological Review* 13 (1948): 419–437.

IDAHO

Margaret Blair Young

Chronology

1804	Meriwether Lewis and William Clark are dispatched by President Thomas Jefferson to explore uncharted territory, including what is now Idaho. With them is Clark's slave, York, who is the first black man the Native Americans of the area have ever seen.
1832	Biracial trapper Jim Beckwourth attends a rendezvous with other trappers and Native Americans in Idaho (then called Oregon Country).
1860s–1870s	Miners of all ethnicities come to Idaho.
1863	President Abraham Lincoln signs an act creating Idaho Territory, combining parts of Washington Territory and Dakota Territory.
1866	Territorial law bans nonwhite students from attending public school until 1873.
1867	Elvina Moulton, a former slave, settles in Boise.
1879	Miner George Washington Blackman settles in Hailey; Blackman Peak in the White Cloud Mountains is named after him.
1880s	African American Mormons, who had been living in Utah, begin homesteading in the Idaho Falls/Milo area. Other African American homesteaders, trappers such as Dan Brockman (for whom Brockman's Creek was named), and businessmen such as Francis Grice also come to Idaho during these years.
1886	Gobo Fango, an African who had come from England with Mormon pioneers, is murdered in Oakley; his murderer, who is known, is ultimately acquitted.
1890	Idaho enters the Union as the 43rd state; few African Americans live in the new state.
1892	African American soldiers from the 24th Infantry are sent to Coeur d'Alene to quell a mining dispute.
1896	*Plessy v. Ferguson* establishes "separate but equal," validating the nation's segregation. Idaho has had de facto segregation, but, with blacks being such a minority, has integrated its schools.
1899	The 24th Infantry, now stationed at Fort Douglas, Utah, returns to Coeur d'Alene when mining disputes reignite. Shortly thereafter, many of these soldiers fight in the Philippines.
1899	Jennie Hughes becomes the first black student to graduate from the University of Idaho.
1903	Green Flake, vanguard Mormon pioneer, dies in Gray's Lake.
1903	The African American League and the Women's Athenian Club, both working for equal rights, are founded in Boise.

1909	St. Paul Baptist Church (African American) is established in Boise. It will later become the first home of Idaho's Black History Museum.
1910	African American soldiers help fight fires in northern Idaho.
1919	The Treasure Valley (Idaho) Branch of the National Association for the Advancement of Colored People (NAACP) is organized.
1920	Ku Klux Klan activity begins in Idaho.
1924	Boise's mayor demands that Klan members remove their masks before parading. A black policeman known as "Yellowstone Jack" prepares to defend the AME Church in Pocatello, but it is not attacked.
1930	Black cowboy Tracy Thompson (grandfather of the first black mayor of Pocatello, Thomas "Les" Purse) dies in a rodeo competition; the circumstances of his death are suspicious.
1933	Gene Harris, a jazz musician who will eventually establish Idaho roots, is born in Michigan.
1940	The famous singer Marian Anderson comes to sing in Boise. She is not permitted to stay at the Hotel Boise, but is permitted to stay in the Owyhee Hotel, provided she uses the back entrance.
1945	Vernon Baker fights heroically in a segregated unit during World War II, but is not recognized for his valor for another 50 years.
1948	President Harry S. Truman ends segregation in the military by executive order.
1968	Reverend Dr. Martin Luther King Jr. is assassinated. Idaho Governor Don Samuelson does not order the statehouse flag to be flown at half-mast. Boise's African Americans and other civil rights supporters protest. In Governor Samuelson's absence, Lt. Governor Jack Murphy orders the flag lowered to half-mast.
1969	Idaho passes a civil rights bill. The Idaho Human Rights Commission is formed.
1970	White supremacists set up headquarters in Hayden Lake at a compound owned by Richard Butler, and eventually hold an annual World Congress of Aryan Nations there.
1972	Dr. Mamie Oliver becomes the first African American professor at Boise State University.
1973	Thomas "Les" Purce is the first African American elected to the city council in Pocatello; he goes on to become the state's first black mayor.
1980s	There is a rise of some "survivalist" political groups in Idaho, including neo-Nazis. These groups are generally found in Idaho's panhandle, and particularly around Coeur d'Alene (near Hayden Lake).

1982	Mamie Oliver, Idaho's first African American professor and a prominent historian, founds the Treasure Valley Council for Church and Social Action.
1985	The University of Idaho at Moscow names its jazz festival for musician Lionel Hampton, who had worked with the school since 1980 developing its jazz music program.
1990	Idaho enacts a law making the third Monday of January Martin Luther King Jr./Idaho Human Rights Day.
1995	The Black History Museum is founded in Boise—the only African American museum in the Pacific Northwest.
1997	Idaho resident Vernon Baker accepts the Medal of Honor for previously unacknowledged valor shown during World War II.
1998	Musician Gene Harris founds a jazz festival at Boise State University.
2000	The Aryan Nations organization loses a $6.3 million lawsuit and is bankrupted. Its compound in Hayden Lake is confiscated. Government officials and other supporters of human rights soon commission a human rights memorial in a park with quotations about human rights—in Boise.
2001	The Idaho State Senate passes Resolution 4RC101, making Idaho the fifth state to recognize Juneteenth Day as a state holiday.
2003	African American Joe McNeal is elected mayor of Mountain Home.
2004	Richard Butler, who had headed the Hayden Lake Aryan Nations compound, dies. The compound is turned into a park dedicated to peace.
2006	The Lionel Hampton Center in Moscow is opened. It includes an archive of jazz materials starting with jazz donations from Hampton himself.
2007	Dr. Mamie Oliver is awarded the Idaho Bridge Award from the Idaho Black History Museum for her contributions in documenting African American history in Idaho.
2008	*(February 5)* Barack Obama, an African American senator from Illinois, wins the Idaho Democratic caucuses, winning almost 80 percent of the vote to defeat Senator Hillary Clinton of New York. Obama fails to carry Idaho in the November general election.

Historical Overview

Early Years

The area we now call Idaho was for years part of an expanse referred to simply as the Northwest and later as Oregon Country. In 1803, President Thomas Jefferson purchased the Oregon Country from Napoleon Bonaparte, paying 3 3/5 cents per acre. Shortly thereafter, Jefferson dispatched Meriwether Lewis and William Clark to explore and map the new purchases of the United States, including Oregon Country.

With William Clark came his slave, York—the first African American whom Native Americans of the area (mostly Shoshone [sometimes called Snake] Indians) had ever seen. Lewis' journal notes that the Indians were fascinated by York's color and attempted to rub the blackness from his skin. For years after York's appearance in Idaho, there was little African American presence there, other than a few mountain men and trappers, most notably James Beckwourth. Although Beckwourth's presence in Idaho was fleeting, given the transient lifestyle of fur trappers and mountain men, he symbolizes the presence of other lesser-known African American mountain men who frequented the area.

There was no permanent African American presence in Idaho until after the Civil War. In 1867, Elvina Moulton ("Aunt Viney"), a former slave from Kentucky, became the first African American woman to live in Boise. A few African American homesteaders ventured to Idaho after Elvina Moulton, but 20 years passed before there were any significant African American pockets in the territory. Francis and Mary Grice were among the settlers who joined the black community in Boise in the late 1880s. They had been living in Utah, but false accusations of poisoning a white man's livestock prodded them to leave their restaurant business and home in Salt Lake City and move to Idaho.

Grice's Utah restaurant had been the scene of some tragic events in Utah in 1883, when a black man, a former soldier named Sam Joe Harvey, shot a white marshal and was subsequently lynched. The false accusations against the Grice family began soon after the lynching. The Grice home in Utah remained vacant for decades after their departure to Idaho, and was eventually torn down.

Homesteaders

Starting around 1880, the first African Americans from the Mormon migration began relocating from Utah to Idaho, usually as homesteaders. Latter-day Saint converts from the South had often brought slaves with them to Utah. Of those emancipated blacks who remained in the Rocky Mountain area, several chose to settle around Idaho Falls. Other former slaves who had become Mormons during their enslavement came to Utah when they were free to do so after the Civil War ended.

Prominent among this group was Green Flake. In 1838, Flake, age 10, had been given as a wedding gift to James Madison and Agnes Love Flake. He was 15 years old at the time he and the other Flake family members were baptized into the Church of Jesus Christ of Latter-day Saints. By then, he already weighed nearly 200 pounds. Oscar Crosby and Hark Lay, two half brothers, were also slaves of Mormon converts. These three men were hand-selected to be a part of the first company of Mormon pioneers. Their duties included building bridges across the Platte River, clearing trails, and repairing wagons. As was York, Green Flake was the first black man many Native Americans (Pawnee) had seen.

In later years, when Green Flake was honored as a vanguard pioneer at a celebration near Gray's Lake, Idaho, he described slavery in the following words:

Slavery has been around a long time, and the colored folks got sold like they were a horse, a cow, or some other animal. They become the owner's property, and they are to work long and hard for the master. Most everyone don't want to be a slave and be in bondage to another, because you cannot have even your own thoughts and dreams. You cannot plan for the future when all decisions get made by someone else.[1]

After the 1885 death of his wife Martha (also a former slave who shared the same mother as Hark Lay and Oscar Crosby), Green moved to Idaho to be with his children, Lucinda and Abraham, who had settled in the Idaho Falls area. He died in Gray's Lake in 1903. His body was then transported to the Union Cemetery in Salt Lake City, to be buried beside his wife. Green had already chosen his epitaph and reportedly helped carve it: "In my Father's House are Many Mansions."

Around the time the Flake children moved to Idaho, Edward (Ned) and Susan Leggroan joined them. Once liberated from slavery, the Leggroans had come west with Ned's sister, Amanda, and her husband Samuel Chambers, who had been baptized a Mormon at age 12 while still enslaved. Both Ned Leggroan and Samuel Chambers had lost their first wives, who had been sold off during slave times. The wives they brought west with them were considerably younger than either man.

Lucinda Flake, daughter of Green and Martha Flake, and her part-Mexican husband George Stevens had 13 children, most of whom lived to maturity. Likewise, Ned and Susan Leggroan had a large posterity, most of their 10 children reaching maturity. Because the African American population was so small in Utah and Idaho, several marriages were formed between these two families, as well as between some Utah blacks—the children and grandchildren of black Mormon pioneers Jane Manning and Isaac James in addition to the posterity of former slaves, whose surnames included Perkins, Bankhead, Williams, Thomas, and Hooper. The families were so involved with each other that when Nettie James Leggroan died in her 20s, Martha Stevens Perkins (granddaughter of Green and Martha Flake) raised Nettie's two daughters until their father remarried.

Ned Leggroan's 1926 obituary is significant given the year, since the Ku Klux Klan had become prominent throughout the nation—including in Idaho. White supremacist activity had surfaced there six years previously, with the Klan appearing in Twin Falls, Nampa, and Payette. As the following excerpt indicates, Ned Leggroan's obituary provides a picture of the life of a homesteader in untamed Idaho and acknowledges his tenacity:

Out there alone and completely surrounded by desert and sage brush, he had a hard struggle for the first few years, particularly against jack rabbits which was [sic] so thick that they used to eat the settlers out of house and home....

He has lived to see the U.S. engaged in three big wars. There are few who have passed through as many historical stages as had Ned Leggroan. Born and reared in bondage he lived to become not only a highly respected citizen, but a voter and land owner as well. It took character, industry, and brains to accomplish what Ned Leggroan has accomplished during his life.[2]

Soldiers

Though often mistreated and segregated from white soldiers, black troops have served in all wars the United States has fought. They have also been part of the peacekeeping military efforts within the nation and were so used in Idaho.

African American soldiers in the old West were often referred to as buffalo soldiers, reportedly because some Native Americans compared their hair to a buffalo's. Buffalo soldiers were sometimes assigned to fight Native Americans and were used in whatever internal or external conflicts in which the United States was engaged.

As the century neared its end, black soldiers from the 24th Infantry were assigned as peacekeepers to Coeur d'Alene, Idaho, where mining conflicts had broken out. Though the soldiers were a temporary presence, they did impact the state, staying for four months during 1892. In 1899, when the 24th Infantry was stationed at Fort Douglas, Utah, some troops returned to Coeur d'Alene to quell a resurgence of the mining disputes. At this time, there were conflicts between the newly organized Western Federation of Miners and the Mine Owners' Association. The miners and their union leaders were demanding higher pay, and their protests became literally explosive—with 200 pounds of dynamite blowing up the smelter building. Anticipating an escalation in violence, Idaho Governor Frank Steunenberg requested that President McKinley send more troops. As the soldiers of the 24th arrived (some having recently fought in Cuba during the Spanish-American War), martial law was declared in Coeur d'Alene.

Peace was eventually established, and the soldiers of the 24th returned to Fort Douglas. Shortly thereafter, some of these troops were sent to fight in the Philippines (part of the land won from Spain in the Spanish-American War), where President McKinley had determined that islanders were not ready for independence. There (as in Cuba) many of the soldiers contracted malaria, some succumbing to it. African American soldiers were segregated from their white counterparts until after World War II and were often unrecognized for their bravery. Idaho resident Vernon Baker, who was awarded the Medal of Honor in 1997, was in one of the last segregated military units of the Second World War. On July 26, 1948, President Harry S. Truman officially ended segregation in the U.S. military through an executive order.

Cowboys

After the Civil War, a large number of former slaves became cowboys, many in the West. The most famous, Nat Love, may have ventured into Idaho but did not stay long. Cowboys served as ranch hands and sometimes as rodeo performers. Idaho's best-known cowboy was Tracy Thompson, who was a homesteader and railroad worker in the winter and a rodeo performer in the summer. He was killed in Bozeman, Montana, in 1930. His saddle strap was cut just before a horse-bucking competition, resulting in his fall from the horse and subsequent death.

White Supremacists

African Americans populated the larger cities of Idaho sparsely in the years after homesteading and have remained a slim minority. Eventually, Idaho sustained a reputation for being a haven for white supremacists. This was largely due to the work of Richard Butler.

Butler's Aryan Nation compound in Hayden Lake, Idaho, was regarded by many white supremacists as their international headquarters. Butler hosted summer festivals where attendees of all ages were indoctrinated in the white supremacist ideology. Youth conferences attracted skinheads to celebrate Hitler's birthday. Though those attending Butler's festivals were relatively few (200 at most), the very presence of the group and the compound tainted the outside perception of Idaho.

Butler and his organization lost a lawsuit in 2001, brought by Native Americans Victoria Keenan and her son Jason. Security guards Jesse Warfield and John Yeager were already serving prison terms for attacking the Keenans in 1998. The Keenans had been chased by these guards, shot at, forced into a ditch, and then beaten with rifle butts. The Keenans' lawsuit argued that Butler's group had been negligent in training its security guards. Famous civil rights attorney Morris Dees of the Southern Poverty Law Center (which focuses on eradicating hate groups) represented the Keenans, with the trial held in Coeur d'Alene. A month after the jury announced its $6.3 million judgment against Butler's organization and compound, he filed for bankruptcy. The compound was ultimately auctioned off, with the Keenans as the only bidders. They got not only the compound but its intellectual property, including the titles "Aryan Nations" and "Church of Jesus Christ Christian."

Richard Butler died in 2004. His white supremacist compound was turned into a park devoted to peace. Pockets of Aryan societies are still present in Idaho, but they are fragmented.

Modern-Day Idaho

African Americans remain a slim minority in Idaho, but their presence has unquestionably impacted the state, from the Lewis and Clark expedition through the years of segregation, until more recent times, when Idaho has had two African American mayors: Thomas "Les" Purce in Pocatello and Joe J. McNeal in Mountain Home. Though born elsewhere, Gene Harris and Lionel Hampton established important centers for jazz in Idaho. Indeed, more and more blacks claim Idaho as their home and serve in important positions at universities, businesses, and government. The NAACP is well organized throughout the state and has strong branches supported by all ethnicities. Every major city in Idaho has some predominantly African American religious congregations, including the African Methodist Episcopal Church and Church of God in Christ. Though Idaho still contends with a reputation for hosting white supremacist groups, it has responded to that reputation by establishing monuments to peace and civil rights. Most significant is the monument to Anne Frank erected in Boise in 2000, which includes the following words:

> May this memorial stand as a tribute to her memory, as a warning to any who would dare trespass upon the freedom of others, and as an inspiration to all whose lives are devoted to love, respect, understanding, peace, and good will among the totality and diversity of the human family. May this memorial inspire each of us to contemplate the moral implications of our civic responsibilities.[3]

Notable African Americans

Baker, Vernon (1919–)

A resident of northern Idaho, Vernon Baker has been the subject of a documentary and the author of a successful memoir about his military service in World War II. In April 1945, as a soldier in Viareggo, Italy, Baker single-handedly killed nine enemy soldiers and destroyed three machine gun positions as well as an observation deck. For these and other actions, President Bill Clinton belatedly awarded Baker the Medal of Honor in 1997. Baker's memoir, *Lasting Valor*, which describes his experiences as a black officer, was published in 1997.

Beckwourth, James (1798–1866)

James Beckwourth was the son of Englishman Sir Jennings Beckwourth and one of his slaves. Though his father acknowledged him, Beckwourth was nonetheless enslaved. After moving to Missouri and apprenticing with a blacksmith in St. Louis, Beckwourth left home, eventually working for the American Fur Trading Company. He lived for eight years with the Crow tribe and in his autobiography claimed that he was named the head chief of the Crow Nation. Beckwourth was reputed to stretch his tales, so we cannot know if this claim was strictly true, but it is clear that he at least observed the most significant events of western development in the early nineteenth century. For example, he was present at one of the largest rendezvous with Native Americans and other traders, held in 1832 in what is now Idaho. The annual rendezvous included trading, dancing, drinking, and various competitions.

Buckner-Webb, Cherie (dates unknown)

Cherie Buckner-Webb, a native of Idaho, is a motivational speaker and a vocalist in blues, gospel, and jazz. She is the founder and principal of Sojourner Coaching and is a featured inspirational keynote speaker, trainer, coach, and consultant for public and private business, groups, and organizations.

Fango, Gobo (1854–1886)

Gobo Fango was from a Bantu tribe in Africa. After some intertribal wars, he was adopted at age three as a servant to the Talbot family, British converts to the Mormon religion. He settled in the Oakley area of Idaho around 1880 with the Talbots, who were part of a group of Mormon pioneers. Gobo Fango was three years old at the time of that journey. When threatened with discovery in pre–Civil War America, he had been hidden under the skirts of one of the pioneer women.

As a young man in the West, Gobo stayed with the William and Mary Ann Hunter family as a sheepherder, but was not considered an equal to the Caucasians. He slept outside even in the dead of winter, which resulted in his feet being frozen and left him with a permanent limp.

In 1886, conflicts over grazing rights between cattlemen and sheepherders were common in Idaho. In February 1886, Gobo, although not involved in any of the conflicts, was accosted and shot in the stomach by a man named Frank Bedke. Mortally wounded, he nonetheless managed to walk and crawl four miles to a ranch, covering his wound with his hands and some sagebrush. Three days later, he died. Although the assailant was known, he was never convicted. Bedke's first trial ended in a mistrial; his second in acquittal. The jury found that Gobo's murderer had shot and killed him in "self-defense," although Gobo had been unarmed. The Gobo Fango case was thus the first case in Idaho where race clearly played a part in the jury's verdict.

Folklore circulated that Gobo wrote his will in his own blood, deeding all his money to the Hunter family and the Grantsville LDS Relief Society. In fact, he did not write his will in his own blood (he signed the will with an X), but did ask that some of his money be donated to the building of the Salt Lake Temple.

Flake, Green (1828–1903)

Green Flake was born enslaved in Anson County, North Carolina, and given as a wedding gift to James and Agnes Love Flake, who moved to Mississippi shortly after their marriage. Green Flake was a baptized Mormon and became one of three "colored servants" (slaves) in the vanguard company of Mormon pioneers, which brought him some fame. Emancipated around 1849, he spent the last years of his life in the Gray's Lake area of Idaho and died there, although he was buried in Utah. His two children both settled in the Idaho Falls area.

Harris, Gene (1933–2000)

Gene Harris was a renowned jazz pianist. He was born in Benton Harbor, Maryland, and retired to Boise in 1977, but even after retirement joined the Ray Brown Trio and led his own groups as well. Prior to his death from kidney failure, he organized the Gene Harris Jazz Festival in Idaho, which continues to bring jazz aficionados into Idaho annually. He is perhaps best known for his "Ode to Billy Joe."

Leggroan, Edward (c. 1840–1926)

One of the early homesteaders in Idaho, Edward "Ned" Leggroan was honored for his tenacity in taming Idaho's difficult terrain. He and his wife Susan had come west after the Civil War and were the parents of many children who, as they married other African Americans in the Idaho and Utah areas, formed the nucleus of the black community in these states. Although most of the Leggroan descendants eventually moved from Idaho, a few still remain.

McNeal, Joe J. (1936–)

Joe J. McNeal became president of the Boise/Ada/Elmore Branch of the NAACP in 1990. He also was a strong proponent of Idaho's successful efforts to recognize Juneteenth Day as a state holiday. He became the first African American mayor of Mountain Home.

Thomas "Les" Purce, right, answers questions during a news conference as part of the Higher Education Day, 2007. On the left is V. Lane Rawlins, president of Washington State University. (AP/Wide World Photos)

Moulton, Elvina (1837–1917)

Elvina Moulton (Aunt Viney) was born enslaved in Kentucky. After the Civil War, she made her way west, settling in 1867 in Boise, where she worked as a laundress. She became a charter member of Boise's First Presbyterian Church.

Oliver, Mamie (dates unknown)

Mamie Oliver became the first African American professor (Boise State University) in Idaho when she accepted a faculty position at Boise State University in 1972. She and her students conducted foundational research on the history of African Americans in Idaho and she is a principal creator of the museum exhibit titled "The Invisible Idahoan: 200 Years of Blacks in Idaho." Dr. Oliver accepted a position of professor of social work at Northwest Nazarene University in 2001. She

has been widely recognized for her contributions to public service and to the study of Idaho African American history. In 2005, she and her late husband, Dr. H. Lincoln Oliver, were both inducted in the Hall of Fame of the Treasure Valley chapter of the NAACP. In 2007, she received a Congressional Award for community service from Idaho Senator Mike Crapo.

Purce, Thomas "Les" (dates unknown)

Thomas "Les" Purce was the first black mayor in Idaho (serving in Pocatello). Dr. Purce is currently president of Evergreen College in Washington state, a position he has held since July 2000. Before that he held various governmental positions in Idaho and also served as vice president of Extended University Affairs and dean of Extended Education Programs at Washington State University.

Kimberly Moore, the new director for the Idaho Black History Museum, stands in the center of the museum, 2006, in Boise, Idaho. The museum is set in a tiny former black Baptist church, a space that Moore hopes to quadruple in size. (AP/Wide World Photos)

Thompson, Tracy (c. 1880–1930)

Tracy Thompson, the most famous cowboy of Idaho, was a champion rodeo rider. He worked as a homesteader at Arimo, but moved to Pocatello in 1919. He worked on Idaho's railroads in the winter months and spent summers on the rodeo circuit. He died after a suspicious rodeo accident in Bozeman, Montana, in 1930.

York (1770–1832)

York, a slave of William Clark of the Lewis and Clark expedition, was the first African American to set foot in what is now Idaho. Although he risked his life to save Clark in a flash flood and was a part of the exploration team in every way, he was returned to slavery after the expedition concluded.

Cultural Contributions

Black History Museum

Though few African Americans have settled in Idaho, Boise sponsors a Black History Museum on Julia Davis Avenue, which chronicles the contributions of the African Americans in Idaho, ranging from York (William Clark's enslaved companion on the Lewis and Clark expedition), to the buffalo soldiers, and up to current times.

Jazz

Through the formidable contributions of Gene Harris and Lionel Hampton, Idaho attracted jazz musicians, who can study jazz at the well-endowed facilities in the University of Idaho at Moscow and can attend the annual Gene Harris Festival in Boise.

Anne Frank Human Rights Memorial

This educational park, located in Boise, contains over 60 quotes about human rights. Opened in 2002, the memorial is toured by thousands of schoolchildren each year. A world-class educational park, the memorial has been profiled in several national publications, including the book *Etched in Stone: Enduring Words from Our Nation's Monuments* by National Geographic.

Notes

1. John Fretwell, "Miscellaneous Family Papers." The quote is from the undated Millcreek, Idaho, Pioneer Appreciation Day, transcribed by Rachel Simmons.
2. The *Times Register* (later called the *Post Register*), February 2, 1926, from Idaho Falls, ID.
3. Idaho Anne Frank Human Rights Memorial (online, July 2007), www.idaho-humanrights.org/Memorial.

Bibliography

Baker, Vernon, and Ken Olsen. *Lasting Valor.* New York: Bantam/Dell, 1999.

Burley, Idaho, Recorder's Office. Letter of Kenneth Larson, September 15, 1951. (Reports events related to the life and death of Gobo Fango.)

Burley, Idaho, Recorder's Office. Letter of J. Newell Dayley. December 16, 1948. (Details the events of Gobo Fango's murder from firsthand accounts.)

Carter, Kate. *Negro Pioneer.* Salt Lake City: Daughters of Utah Pioneers, 1964.

Clark, Michael J. "Improbable Ambassadors: Black Soldiers at Fort Douglas, 1896–99." *Utah Historical Quarterly* 46 (1978): 282–301.

Coleman, Ronald. "A History of Blacks in Utah, 1825–1910." Ph.D. dissertation, University of Utah, 1980.

Fretwell, John. "Miscellaneous Family Papers on Green Flake." Unpublished.

Katz, William Loren. *The Black West.* Seattle, WA: Open Hand Publishing, 1987.

Taylor, Quintard. *In Search of the Racial Frontier: African Americans in the American West, 1528–1990.* New York: W. W. Norton, 1998.

Web Sites

Idaho Black History Museum. Online, July 2007. www.ibhm.org.

Idaho Human Rights Education Center. Online, July 2007. www.idaho-humanrights.org.

Idaho Public Television. Mountain Man Rendezvous—Yesterday and Today. Online, July 2007. http://idahoptv.org/outdoors/shows/buckskinbrigade/rendezvous.cfm.

PBS. "Stories of Valor: Vernon Baker." Online, July 2007. www.pbs.org/weta/americanvalor/stories/baker.html.

University of Idaho. "Lionel Hampton: His Life and Legacy." Online, July 2007. www.uidaho.edu/hampton/bio.html.

ILLINOIS

Tiffany K. Wayne

Chronology

1720   The first African slaves are brought by the French to the Illinois country to work in mines.

1724   The French government issues "Black Codes," or the *Code Noir*, to regulate slavery in French colonies.

1779   Haitian-born trader Jean Baptiste Pointe du Sable establishes a permanent settlement on the western shores of Lake Michigan that becomes Chicago.

1787   Under the Northwest Ordinance, the U.S. Congress prohibits slavery in the new western territories, including Illinois.

1800   The Indiana Territory, including Illinois, is established, and William Henry Harrison, a slaveholder, is appointed governor.

1809   Illinois becomes a separate territory, retaining the territorial law that requires blacks to be registered as long-term indentured servants and prohibiting free blacks from entering Illinois.

1818   *(December 3)* Illinois is admitted to the Union as the 21st state; its state constitution contains a provision that protects the rights of current slaveholders but prohibits slavery from this point forward.

1836   "Free" Frank McWorter, a former slaver from Kentucky, founds the town of New Philadelphia, Illinois.

1837   The Illinois legislature condemns abolitionist societies and activities, and supports the rights of slaveholders in southern states.

1837   Abolitionist newspaperman Elijah Lovejoy is killed by a proslavery mob in Alton.

1848   The Illinois state constitution ends slavery in the state, but includes an article requiring legislation to "prohibit free persons of color from immigrating to and settling in this state; and to effectually prevent the owners of slaves from bringing them into this state for the purpose of setting them free."

1848   Baptist minister Samuel S. Ball of Springfield travels to Liberia to report on conditions for Illinois African Americans interested in relocating to the region.

1857   In *Dred Scott v. Sandford*, the U.S. Supreme Court denies the claim to freedom made by Scott, a slave from Missouri, who based his claim on his residency in the Wisconsin Territory and in the free state of Illinois.

1863   Slaves in Illinois are not freed by Lincoln's Emancipation Proclamation, which applies only to slaves in the rebel states.

1864   The 29th U.S. Colored Infantry is organized at Quincy, Illinois, and suffers severe losses in the Civil War.

1865   *(February 1)* Illinois becomes the first state to ratify the Thirteenth Amendment to the U.S. Constitution, abolishing slavery in the United States.

1867	(*January 15*) Illinois ratifies the Fourteenth Amendment to the U.S. Constitution guaranteeing full citizenship to blacks.
1869	(*March 5*) Illinois becomes the third state to ratify the Fifteenth Amendment to the U.S. Constitution extending voting rights to African Americans.
1874	Illinois outlaws segregation in public schools.
1876	John W. E. Thomas of Chicago is the first African American elected as a representative to the Illinois state legislature.
1878	The *Chicago Conservator* newspaper is founded by Ferdinand L. Barnett; he later sells the paper to his wife, antilynching activist Ida B. Wells-Barnett.
1885	The Illinois Civil Rights Act forbids racial discrimination in public facilities.
1886	Augustus Tolton is ordained as the first black Catholic priest in the United States; his first assignment is as pastor of St. Joseph's Church in Quincy.
1893	National black leaders such as Ida B. Wells and Frederick Douglass protest the exclusion of African Americans from exhibits at the World's Columbian Exposition held in Chicago.
1905	The *Chicago Defender*, the largest black newspaper in Illinois, is founded by Robert S. Abbott.
1908	(*August*) Race riots in Springfield leave seven people dead and much black property destroyed.
1909	In part as a response to the race riots in Springfield, the National Association for the Advancement of Colored People (NAACP) is founded.
1917	(*July*) Race riots break out in East St. Louis over job and housing tensions; dozens are killed and thousands of African Americans flee the city.
1919	(*July and August*) Several days of race riots in Chicago leave dozens dead. The riots begin as a dispute over separate black and white areas of the beach and the drowning death of a black boy.
1919	Chicago journalist and businessman Claude Barnett founds the Associated Negro Press, a service that eventually distributes stories to more than 200 black newspapers around the country.
1920	Violette N. Anderson becomes the first black woman lawyer in Illinois and later becomes the first black woman admitted to argue before the U.S. Supreme Court.
1924	Adelbert H. Roberts of Chicago is the first African American to serve in the Illinois State Senate.
1928	Oscar Stanton DePriest of Chicago is elected to the U.S. House of Representatives, the first African American elected since the Reconstruction era and the first black congressman from a northern state.
1933	The Illinois legislature outlaws racial discrimination in government contracts and employment.
1940	In *Hansberry v. Lee*, the U.S. Supreme Court strikes a blow against restrictive covenants in home sales, the practice of preventing African Americans from living in white neighborhoods.

1940 (cont.)	The subject matter of the case, which referred to restrictions in a Chicago neighborhood, was later incorporated by the plaintiff's daughter Lorraine Hansberry into her 1959 play, *A Raisin in the Sun*, in which the family moves into a white neighborhood.
1934	Arthur W. Mitchell is elected to the U.S. House of Representatives from Illinois, becoming the first black Democrat elected to Congress from any state.
1941	The Illinois legislature forbids racial discrimination in state defense contracts and employment.
1942	William L. Dawson, a black attorney from Chicago, is elected to the U.S. House of Representatives from Illinois.
1943	Governor Dwight H. Green establishes the Illinois Interracial Commission, the first publicly funded state committee on race, to address problems of racial tension and discrimination in areas such as housing and education.
1950	Poet Gwendolyn Brooks of Chicago becomes the first black woman to win a Pulitzer Prize.
1955	The body of 14-year-old Emmett Till, murdered in Mississippi, is viewed in Chicago.
1961	A Fair Employment Practices Commission is created in Illinois to investigate cases of employment discrimination.
1962	*(November 14)* Illinois becomes the first state to ratify the Twenty-fourth Amendment to the U.S. Constitution abolishing the poll tax.
1966	Dr. Martin Luther King Jr. leads marches through all-white neighborhoods in Chicago to protest housing discrimination.
1967	*(July)* Three days of race riots and protests occur in Cairo after the suspicious death of a young black man who is found hanged in the town jail.
1968	*(April)* Riots erupt in Chicago and other cities across the nation after the assassination of Martin Luther King Jr. in Memphis, Tennessee. In Chicago, at least 11 African Americans are killed and hundreds of others are injured or arrested.
1969	George W. Collins, an African American attorney who had worked as a deputy sheriff of Cook County, is elected to the U.S. House of Representatives in a special election held to fill the unexpired term of the late white Congressman Daniel J. Ronan; Collins is elected to a full term in 1970.
1969	*(December)* A police raid on the Chicago headquarters of the Black Panther Party results in the death of two members, Mark Clark and Fred Hampton.
1971	James E. Williams Sr. becomes the first black mayor of East St. Louis.
1971	Chicago civil rights activist Jesse Jackson founds the interracial organization Operation PUSH: People United to Serve Humanity.
1973	Cardiss Collins is elected to the U.S. House of Representatives from Illinois, filling the seat left vacant by the death of her husband George W. Collins.

1979	African American attorney Roland Burris is elected as comptroller of Illinois.
1980	Chicago attorney and politician Harold Washington is elected to the U.S. House of Representatives from Illinois.
1983	Harold Washington is elected the first black mayor of Chicago.
1983	Chicago civil rights activist Charles A. Hayes is elected to the U.S. House of Representatives in a special election to fill the seat vacated by Harold Washington upon his election as mayor of Chicago.
1991	Roland Burris is elected as Illinois attorney general.
1992	Carol Moseley-Braun of Chicago is elected the first black woman to the U.S. Senate.
1996	Civil rights activist and Chicago alderman Danny K. Davis is elected to the U.S. House of Representatives from Illinois.
2004	Barack Obama, a Chicago community activist, becomes the first African American man elected to the U.S. Senate from Illinois.
2008	Barack Obama, U.S. senator from Illinois, is elected as the first African American president of the United States; Obama carries Illinois in the election with about 62 percent of the vote.
2009	Roland Burris is sworn in to fill out Barack Obama's unexpired term in the U.S. Senate.

Historical Overview

With more than 12 million residents in 2000, Illinois is one of the most populous and diverse midwestern states. The capital of Illinois is Springfield, but Chicago and its surrounding suburbs is the state's largest metropolis. Chicago, especially, has attracted large numbers of African Americans since the Great Migration of the early twentieth century. In 2000, African Americans made up 15 percent of the population of the state of Illinois, while the population of Chicago was more than 37 percent black.

Since its admission as the 21st state in 1818, Illinois has been at the center of national politics and has often been considered a microcosm for issues affecting the entire nation. African Americans have been central to the history and political development of Illinois, from the slavery debates of the nineteenth century, to the civil rights movement of the mid-twentieth century, to the election of Barack Obama as the first African American president.

Africans in Early Illinois

What is now the state of Illinois was part of the larger Mississippi River Valley region explored by French trappers and traders beginning in the 1670s. The first Africans were brought into the region in 1720 to work in the mines. By 1732, a French census listed some 300 Africans in the Illinois settlement, a population that would have been subject to the French *Code Noir* (or Black Code) regulating the colonial slave workforce. The Code Noir allowed some rights for slaves and slave families, but also protected the rights of slaveholders to punish their slaves as they saw fit. The Code Noir also set a precedent in the Americas for severely limiting the rights of free blacks, a population that would be regulated, excluded, and discriminated against in Illinois through the nineteenth century.

One of the first documented Africans in Illinois was Jean Baptiste Pointe du Sable, born in Haiti to a black slave mother and a French father.

Du Sable was educated in France and then returned to North America as a trader and explorer. He traveled to New Orleans, Louisiana, and then up the Mississippi River and into Michigan, where he married a Native American woman and was known as a "Black Chief." Later deemed "the father of Chicago," sometime before or around 1779, du Sable reached the western shores of Lake Michigan, where he established a permanent settlement and a centrally located trading post for fur and agricultural goods.

The slave population slowly increased as more French settlers acquired agricultural and household laborers. The British gained control of Illinois in 1763, at the end of the Seven Years' War; and after the American Revolution, the region was part of the Northwest Territory to be organized and regulated by the new United States. The Northwest Ordinance of 1787 prohibited slavery in the territory, but the territorial government allowed for settlers in the region to retain slaves and servants already owned before the United States had claimed the region. The Northwest Territory was eventually divided into separate regions; in 1800, Illinois became part of the Indiana Territory, and in 1809, the Illinois Territory was established. European Americans began settling in the region in greater numbers. Most were farmers coming to Illinois from northeastern states in search of opportunity. These were not wealthy settlers, and although there were still very few slaves in the Indiana Territory in the early decades of the nineteenth century, some had been brought by slave owners from nearby Kentucky or Missouri, or brought in from other regions to work on new industrial and mining projects. As slavery was officially prohibited in the territory, the territorial government enacted legislation to allow lengthy, even indefinite, terms of "indentured servitude," making it possible to meet frontier labor needs while preventing African American workers from gaining their freedom.

Slavery and Statehood

This conflicted history of slavery in the Illinois Territory, and the combination of slave and free populations, was still not resolved when Illinois sought admission as a state. As it was in the economic interest of the region to lure wealthier slaveholding whites from nearby Missouri, some politicians advocated for admitting Illinois as a slave state. After much debate, Illinois was added to the Union as a free state in 1818, although the new state constitution still allowed for existing slaves to remain slaves. In the coming years, the Illinois legislature enacted laws severely limiting the freedoms of free blacks and preventing the migration of free blacks into the state from other regions.

In 1819, future Illinois Governor Edward Coles migrated from Virginia, specifically searching for a place to free his own inherited slaves. He ultimately freed 10 slaves and gave each family 160 acres of land when they reached Illinois. Coles was elected governor in 1822 and challenged the state's slave laws; he was subsequently sued (unsuccessfully) for violating those laws himself by bringing his slaves to Illinois with the intention of freeing them. In 1829, a group of fugitive and former slaves from St. Louis, Missouri, fled across the Mississippi River, establishing an all-black community that thrived for years in Brooklyn, Illinois.

Even after admission as an officially "free" state, the issue of slavery continued to dominate Illinois politics. Throughout the early 1820s, proposals were made to change the state constitution and allow slavery. The proslavery proposals were narrowly defeated, and not due to abolitionist sentiment but due to fear of the slaveholding class of whites gaining political control and fear of blacks themselves; in other words, while some wanted to lure wealthy slaveholding whites to the region, others feared the black slave population they would bring with them. The Illinois legislature eventually completely outlawed black migration into the state, forbade intermarriage between blacks and whites, and enacted some of the harshest laws regarding free blacks already living in the state. Free blacks were denied any political or legal rights, and Illinois developed as a heavily segregated society. In 1837, the legislature went so far as to officially condemn the existence and activities of those who opposed slavery as abolitionists. That same year, Elijah Lovejoy, publisher of an abolitionist newspaper and founder of the Illinois Anti-Slavery Society, was killed by a proslavery mob in Alton, Illinois.

Because of a rising abolitionist network and because of the proximity to several slave states, Illinois became an important route along the Underground Railroad for slaves fleeing the South and heading to freedom in Canada. These factors also set the stage for the most famous freedom suit of the 1850s, that of Dred Scott, a Missouri slave who argued for his freedom because he had lived with his owner in the "free" areas of the Wisconsin Territory and Illinois. In *Dred Scott v. Sandford* (1857), the U.S. Supreme Court not only denied Scott's appeal for his freedom, but claimed that African Americans, slave or free, were not U.S. citizens and therefore could not even file such a lawsuit.

Civil War and Beyond

The debate about slavery in Illinois was taken to the national stage when two Illinois politicians ended up on the presidential ticket in 1860. Two years earlier, Abraham Lincoln and Stephen Douglas had engaged in a series of debates about slavery held across Illinois as part of their campaign for a U.S. Senate seat. Douglas won, and served as senator from Illinois before securing the Democratic nomination for president in 1860. Douglas, who had played a prominent role in the Kansas-Nebraska territorial slavery debates of 1854, united the interests of his southern and northern constituents by refusing to take a

position on the moral question of slavery and running instead on a platform of popular sovereignty and free territorial elections to decide the question of slavery.

Abraham Lincoln returned as Douglas' opposition as the Republican presidential candidate in 1860 on the platform of free soil, free labor. The Republican party of Lincoln did not initially embrace or attract many Illinois abolitionists. Lincoln looked back to the original intent of the Northwest Ordinance prohibition on slavery to determine that the goal was not ending slavery as it already existed in the South, but merely preventing its further spread westward into free territories.

With Lincoln's election to the presidency in 1860, and the outbreak of Civil War just a few months later, Illinois was again at risk of being split over the question of slavery. Although some residents of southern Illinois considered joining the Confederacy, Illinois remained with the Union and more than 1,800 African Americans from Illinois ultimately joined the Union army. Although Lincoln's Emancipation Proclamation of January 1863 freed slaves only in the rebel Confederate states, it angered northern Democrats and their white working-class constituency when the Union army began bringing freed slaves into Illinois from the South.

After the war, whites in Illinois were still not eager to embrace an expanded free black population. Even Republicans who advocated for black civil rights focused their energies on "reconstructing" the South and providing opportunities for blacks there, not expecting or encouraging black migration to the North. Still, in February 1865, Illinois became the first state to ratify the Thirteenth Amendment to the U.S. Constitution, ending slavery throughout the nation. Although Illinois had a smaller black population and therefore fewer blacks in political office than many other northern and midwestern states, the post–Civil War Illinois legislature went on to enact civil rights and antisegregation legislation in the 1870s and 1880s.

Black Migrations

While the Jim Crow South has its own history of discrimination and horrors, the northern states were not exempt from the problems of segregation, racial tension, and violence of the late nineteenth and early twentieth centuries. Despite these problems, however, the early decades of the twentieth century saw a "Great Migration" of African Americans fleeing poverty and discrimination in the South in search of education and employment opportunities in the North.

Beginning in the last decades of the nineteenth century, the black population of Illinois, and of the city of Chicago in particular, increased multiple times over. While many black men enlisted and served in both World War I and World War II, at home the wars brought increased demand for factory workers in cities such as Chicago. At the same time that military needs created demand for production, there were also fewer white workers available due to not only male military service, but a decrease in new European immigration during the wars. For every better-paying factory or railroad job, however, there were many more blacks who came to Chicago and other northern cities only to be segregated into low-paying service jobs.

Between 1910 and 1940, the black population in Chicago alone increased from 40,000 to more than 270,000. This population found itself segregated into poor neighborhoods on the South Side, where urban poverty, segregated public schools, and housing discrimination would become the focus of a new Civil Right Movement. On the positive side, that movement would be sustained by this concentrated community and its networks of black churches and social and political organizations, newspapers, and cultural institutions.

The increase in the urban black population, and the increased politicization of that population, led to new forms of white resentment and, again, the North was not immune to some of the worst racial violence of the century. In 1908, rioting broke out and two black men were lynched in the capital city of Springfield. Several whites were also killed, others were injured, and many black homes and businesses were destroyed. The Springfield riots were so disruptive and shocking that white and black activists together were moved to create a national civil rights organization, and the NAACP was founded the following year. The violence did not end, however. Ida B. Wells-Barnett, wife of Chicago newspaperman Ferdinand L. Barnett, was the leading voice of the antilynching campaign. Race riots continued, including one of the worst in the history of Illinois and of the nation in Chicago in 1919. That summer, a week of protests, fires, and looting left several dead and hundreds more injured.

Depression and World War

The 1930s and 1940s brought the beginning of dismantling the history of discrimination and segregation. Jobs were scarce for everyone during the Great Depression, and black workers protested and boycotted businesses that served their community but would not hire black workers. Black newspapers in Chicago and other cities advertised and encouraged the boycotts, putting pressure on white business owners that was then backed up by state and federal legislation against employment discrimination in the public and government sectors. Housing was another area in which the black community began to fight back. In the early twentieth century, restrictive covenants were used to prevent blacks from living in certain neighborhoods. These were legally binding contracts that allowed white homeowners to refuse to sell or rent to African Americans. In

1940, a Chicago case went all the way to the U.S. Supreme Court. In *Hansberry v. Lee*, the Court did not declare restrictive covenants unconstitutional, but it did set a precedent for questioning their legality and brought attention to this form of discrimination.

Illinois blacks had answered the call to service in the Civil War, the Spanish-American War, and World War I, but an even greater number took on a variety of roles during World War II. Ellsworth Dansby of Decatur, Illinois, was part of the famous Tuskegee Airmen trained as the first black fighter pilots. Illinois was also the training ground for the first African American officers to serve in the U.S. Navy, known as the "Golden Thirteen." Besides combat roles, African Americans worked behind the scenes for the war effort. Chemist Ralph Gardner-Chavis of Chicago was one of a small number of African American scientists involved in the U.S. government's secret Manhattan Project to develop the atomic bomb. Not all avenues were open to blacks or to women, however. Janet Bragg of Rockford and later Chicago purchased her own plane and started her own flying club in order to become a pilot in the 1930s. During World War II, she was one of a number of black women whose applications to fly for the Women's Auxiliary Service Pilots (WASPs) were denied.

Civil Rights Movement and Beyond

The war ended with the desegregation of the military and the beginning of intense civil rights campaigns to desegregate schools and public facilities. Such efforts again provoked a violent response from whites threatened by black attempts at social equality. One of the defining events of the new Civil Rights Movement of the 1950s involved a young boy from Chicago but took place in Mississippi, where 14-year-old Emmett Till was visiting relatives in the summer of 1955 and was murdered after being accused

of speaking to a white woman. Till's family had his body put on display in Chicago in order to inspire outrage about the event and about race relations in the United States.

In the 1960s, Chicago became a hotbed of civil rights activity, perhaps the most active northern city during the Civil Rights Movement. In 1966, Dr. Martin Luther King Jr. joined with local activists to form the Chicago Freedom Movement, leading marches through all-white neighborhoods to protest housing discrimination and segregation. The crowd threw stones at King and the other marchers and, in a television interview, King said that he had experienced more racial hostility in Chicago than in many southern cities. The following years saw major race riots and protests in Cairo, Illinois, and again in Chicago following the news of King's assassination in April 1968. King had inspired a new generation of Chicago and national civil rights leaders, including the Reverend Jesse Jackson.

Millions of African Americans continued to migrate north through the 1960s. By 1970, blacks made up one-third of the Chicago population, and by the year 2000, Chicago had the second-greatest urban population of African Americans, behind New York City. In Chicago, this meant the growth of the inner city, the poor and working population concentrated on the south and west sides of Chicago, but also the continued growth of a small black middle class. These factors have led to Illinois (and Chicago in particular) becoming an important proving ground for black politicians who began to take control of their South Side neighborhoods or wards beginning in the early 1900s and had moved into city, state, and national politics by the mid-twentieth century. Harold Washington was elected the first black mayor of Chicago in 1983, and in 1992, Illinois sent the first African American woman, Carol Moseley-Braun, to the U.S. Senate. By 2010, there had been only six African American senators, but three of those were from the state

Dr. Martin Luther King Jr. in front of City Hall with hundreds of supporters and members of the Chicago Freedom Movement during a protest calling for the firing of School Superintendent Benjamin Willis by Mayor Daley over the former's delays in integrating area schools, Chicago, Illinois, 1965. (Getty Images)

of Illinois (Moseley-Braun, Barack Obama, and Roland Burris, who in 1991 had been Illinois' first black attorney general). In 2007, Barack Obama, U.S. senator and former Chicago community organizer, announced his bid for the presidency and in November 2008 was elected the first African American president of the United States. At the beginning of the twenty-first century, however, Illinois' African American citizens continue to struggle with problems of discrimination and segregation, particularly in the battles over school desegregation and employment and housing discrimination.

Notable African Americans

Brooks, Gwendolyn (1917–2000)

Poet Gwendolyn Elizabeth Brooks was the first African American to receive a Pulitzer Prize. Born in Topeka, Kansas, Brooks and her family

moved to Chicago when she was just an infant. She published her first poem at the age of 13 and began submitting poetry to the black newspaper, the *Chicago Defender*, at age 17. Most of her poems deal with black urban life. Her first book, *A Street in Bronzeville* (1945), was critically acclaimed, but it was *Annie Allen* (1949) which earned her the Pulitzer Prize in poetry. Brooks was named poet laureate for the state of Illinois in 1968, and in 1985 was appointed U.S. poet laureate. She received numerous other awards and honors, including the National Medal of Arts in 1995.

Burnett, Chester Arthur "Howlin' Wolf" (1910–1976)

Chester Arthur "Howlin' Wolf" Burnett was a singer, guitarist, harmonica player, and composer who exemplified the new urban Chicago-style blues of the mid-twentieth century. Born and raised in rural Mississippi, Burnett sang in local nightclubs before moving to Chicago after recording his first hit album, *Moanin' at Midnight*, in 1951. Along with Muddy Waters and other Chicago blues artists, Burnett had a significant influence on the development of rock and roll in the 1960s and 1970s, and he recorded with artists such as the Rolling Stones and Eric Clapton. His 1956 recording, "Smokestack Lightning," and other songs were later acknowledged by both the Grammy Hall of Fame and the Rock and Roll Hall of Fame as an important early influences in rock music.

Davis, Miles (1926–1991)

Miles Dewey Davis III was a trumpet player and composer and one of the most celebrated jazz musicians of the twentieth century. Responsible for many new musical fusions, he helped spread the popularity of cool jazz and bebop, as well as playing with and launching the careers of many other musicians. Davis was born in Alton, Illinois, to a middle-class family who then moved to East St. Louis. He began trumpet lessons at age 13 and by age 17 had joined a blues band. He moved to New York in 1944 to study at Juilliard and to play with his idol, Charlie Parker. Davis first recorded as leader of the Miles Davis Sextet in 1946 and his most significant album, *Kind of Blue*, was recorded in 1959.

Dunham, Katherine (1910–2006)

Katherine Dunham was a choreographer and dancer known for bringing African and Caribbean influences into modern American dance. Born in Chicago and raised in Glen Ellyn and Joliet, Illinois, Dunham studied anthropology at the University of Chicago. Her research on the culture of the African diaspora influenced her choreography and her formation of an all-black dance school and touring troupe; it also influenced her later political work on behalf of Haitian refugees. She opened the Dunham School of Dance in New York, where she taught both folk and classical dance; and in 1968, she founded the Dunham Center for the Performing Arts (now the Katherine Dunham Centers for Arts and Humanities) at Southern Illinois University.

Gregory, Dick (1932–)

Richard Claxton Gregory is a comedian and activist well known for his books and comedy routines on racism and the struggles of African Americans. Born in St. Louis, Missouri, Gregory studied at Southern Illinois University before joining the army during World War II. After the war, he moved to Chicago where he performed at nightclubs and was soon discovered by television executives. He gained national exposure on the *Tonight Show* in the early 1960s but used his celebrity to turn attention to the civil rights and antiwar movements. He launched a political career at the same time that he published several books of racial and political humor and criticism based on his experiences.

Comedian and activist Dick Gregory being interviewed on the telephone, 1964. (Library of Congress)

Jackson, Jesse (1941–)

Jesse Jackson is a minister, civil rights activist, and politician, and one of the most prominent African American activists and leaders of his time. Born Jesse Louis Burns in South Carolina, Jackson attended the University of Illinois and later the Chicago Theological Seminary. He worked with Dr. Martin Luther King Jr.'s Southern Christian Leadership conference (SCLC) in Chicago beginning in 1965 and was in Memphis, Tennessee, when King was assassinated in 1968. In 1971, Jackson founded Operation PUSH (People United to Serve Humanity), which later merged with his Rainbow Coalition. Jackson ran for president of the United States in 1984 and 1988. He failed to capture the Democratic nomination either time, although he won 29 percent of the popular vote in the 1988 primary.

Jackson, Mahalia (1911–1972)

Mahalia Jackson was the most successful gospel singer of the twentieth century, recording more than 30 albums and selling more than 8 million copies of her 1946 recording of "Move On Up a Little Higher." Born in New Orleans, Jackson moved to Chicago as a teenager, where she sang at church services, was invited to join a touring gospel choir, and began a lifelong collaboration with composer Thomas A. Dorsey. Jackson became an international star and sang at Carnegie Hall, the 1963 March on Washington, and the 1968 funeral of Martin Luther King Jr. When Jackson died in 1972, thousands came to Chicago to pay tribute. Mahalia Jackson was inducted into the Grammy Hall of Fame and the Rock and Roll Hall of Fame as an important early influence on rock music.

Metcalfe, Ralph (1910–1978)

Ralph Harold Metcalfe was an Olympic sprinter once known as the "World's Fastest Human."

Born in Atlanta, Metcalfe was raised in Chicago and entered his first Olympic games while still a student at Marquette University. He earned a silver medal in the 100-meter dash and a bronze in the 200-meter at the Olympics held in Los Angeles in 1932. At the controversial 1936 games held in Berlin, he won his only gold medal, in the 4×100-meter relay, and a silver in the 100-meter. After graduating from college, Metcalfe was a university track and field coach and then joined the army during World War II. After the war he began a career in politics, serving on the Chicago City Council and representing Illinois in the U.S. Congress during the 1970s.

Motley, Archibald (1891–1981)

Archibald Motley was an artist associated with the Harlem Renaissance black cultural movement, although he was trained and lived in Chicago. Motley is best known for his scenes of urban black night life, inspired by the "jazz culture" of Chicago in the 1920s and 1930s. Born in New Orleans, he was raised in Chicago and graduated from the School of the Art Institute in 1918. Raised in an all-white neighborhood, and later married to a German-American woman, Motley became known for destabilizing ideas about race and color through his depictions of African Americans of various skin tones. His celebratory scenes of city life were also in stark contrast to southern stereotypes of poor rural blacks.

Muddy Waters (McKinley Morganfield) (1915–1983)

Born McKinley Morganfield in Mississippi, Muddy Waters became known as one of the founders of the Chicago blues style in the 1950s. Waters played with Big Bill Broonzy, Howlin' Wolf Burnett, Willie Dixon, and others in the Chicago blues movement. Recording at the famous Chess Record Studio in the late 1940s, Waters added a more amplified urban sound to the

Barack Obama is sworn in as the 44th president of the United States by Chief Justice John Roberts in Washington, D.C., January 20, 2009. Obama's wife Michelle holds the Bible on which President Abraham Lincoln took his oath of office. (U.S. Department of Defense)

traditional folk blues with his use of the electric guitar, inspiring both American and British rock and roll artists of the 1960s and beyond. His 1950 song "Rollin' Stone" inspired the Rolling Stones in their name, and his songs were recorded by or identified as the influence behind songs by Led Zeppelin ("Whole Lotta Love"), Foghat ("I Just Want to Make Love to You"), and AC/DC ("You Shook Me All Night Long").

Obama, Barack (1961–)

Barack Hussein Obama II was elected the 44th president of the United States in 2008. He was born in Hawaii to a father who was an economist in Kenya and a mother who was a native of Kansas. He lived in Indonesia as a child before returning to live with his white grandparents in Honolulu, Hawaii. He attended Columbia University in New York and graduated from Harvard Law School, where he became the first black to serve as president of the *Harvard Law Review* before moving to Chicago, where he worked as a community organizer on the South Side, and as a civil rights attorney and professor of constitutional law at the University of Chicago before serving in the Illinois Senate. In 2004, he was elected to the U.S. Senate and gave the keynote address at the Democratic National Convention. In 2008, he was named the Democratic nominee for president and was elected to office as the first black president in November 2008. He was awarded the Nobel Peace Prize in 2009. Obama authored two best-selling autobiographical books, *The Audacity of Hope* and *Dreams from My Father* (2008).

Pryor, Richard (1940–2005)

Richard Franklin Lennox Thomas Pryor III was a stand-up comedian and film actor known for his outrageous and controversial humor. Pryor translated his difficult childhood of poverty, abuse, and racism into comedy and entertainment, paving the way for many other black comedians who would later credit his influence. Born in Peoria, Illinois, Pryor dropped out of school and served in the U.S. Army for two years before returning home to perform in comedy clubs. He moved to New York in 1963, eventually taking his comedy routine on the road and gaining national exposure that led to television (*Saturday Night Live*, *The Richard Pryor Show*) and film deals (*Jo Jo Dancer, Your Life Is Calling, Superman III, Silver Streak,* and others).

Wells-Barnett, Ida B. (1862–1931)

Ida Bell Wells-Barnett was a journalist and activist who led the antilynching campaign at the turn of the twentieth century. Wells traveled throughout the United States and Europe and published several newspaper articles and pamphlets to expose the false accusations and lynchings of African Americans. Born in Mississippi during the Civil War, Wells later moved to Memphis, Tennessee, where she taught school and brought a lawsuit against a railroad company for segregated seating. She began speaking out on and recording incidents of lynching after three of her friends were murdered in Memphis. She encouraged blacks to leave the South and, under personal threat from the white community, she moved to Chicago in the 1890s, where she met and married newspaper editor Ferdinand L. Barnett and continued her civil rights campaigns.

Wright, Richard (1908–1960)

Richard Nathaniel Wright was a writer whose works dealt with race relations and racism in

Ida B. Wells was a civil rights activist, journalist, and crusader against lynching. During World War I, she campaigned for racial equality in the military. (Library of Congress)

twentieth-century America. His most famous novel, *Native Son* (1940), tells the story of a young black man growing up in the ghetto of Chicago's South Side. Wright was born in Mississippi and raised in the South before moving to Chicago in 1927. He was associated with the Communist Party in the 1930s, but was disillusioned by racism within the party. His first novel, *Cesspool*, was published in 1935, but his second book, *Native Son*, became a bestseller and was produced on Broadway. It was followed in 1945 by the semi-autobiographical novel, *Black Boy*. Wright later moved to New York and then, hoping to escape American racism, to France.

Cultural Contributions

Illinois' large, diverse, and politically active African American community has left an important legacy in music, entertainment, sports, and literature that has impacted Illinois and the nation at large. Beginning with the Great Migration of African Americans in the early twentieth century, southern blacks developed new musical forms and traditions in their new home in the North, particularly with the blues and jazz music. The "Chicago blues" style developed when musicians from the Mississippi Delta, and from New Orleans, St. Louis, and other vibrant arts communities, came north to Chicago, where their music developed a more urban upbeat rhythm and white and black musicians began to influence and promote one another.

Chicago was a thriving metropolis of black and white music during the jazz age of the 1920s and beyond. In the 1940s and 1950s, Muddy Waters, Willie Dixon, Meade Lux Lewis, Big Bill Broonzy, Howlin' Wolf Burnett, and other Chicago musicians achieved mainstream success and had a direct influence on the emergence of rock and roll, soul, and rhythm-and-blues music. Besides the blues, Illinois nurtured some of the greatest black gospel voices of the century, such as Mahalia Jackson and Etta Moten Barnett, a Broadway singer who once sang for President Franklin Delano Roosevelt. After the 1960s, the next generation continued to develop the black urban sound with rap and hip-hop. Kanye West, raised in Chicago, is one of the most innovative of this generation. West has been a Grammy Award–winning artist as well as a producer of other major acts.

The African American traditions and community in Illinois nurtured numerous black writers, artists, and entertainers as well. With midcentury writers such as Richard Wright, Margaret Walker, Lorraine Hansberry, Willard Motley, Archibald Motley, Frank Marshall Davis, and Gwendolyn Brooks, Chicago had its own literary and artistic renaissance to rival that of Harlem in New York in the early twentieth century. These writers and artists often focused on the

celebrations and struggles of black urban life, providing an alternative tradition to chronicles of slavery and the southern experience.

Other Illinois writers and entertainers went on to careers in film and television. William Attaway was born in Mississippi in 1911, but was raised and educated in Chicago. Attaway wrote novels and plays and was one of the first black writers for television and film. A true Renaissance figure, he also wrote more than 500 songs for artists such as Harry Belafonte. Oscar Brown Jr. was another early playwright, songwriter, and television personality. He was Chicago's (and perhaps the nation's) first African American newscaster, and he later recorded his own jazz albums, performed with Miles Davis, and wrote songs for popular artists such as Mahalia Jackson and Lena Horne. Brown is also credited with discovering the Jackson Five musical group in Indiana.

Illinois has also produced its share of national and international sports stars, from Olympic athletes to major league players. In the early years of baseball, Andrew "Rube" Foster was responsible for founding the Negro National League and for managing the Chicago American Giants, founded in 1920. After integration, Ernie Banks was the first black player for the Chicago Cubs in the early 1950s.

Black athletes from Illinois also achieved notoriety in basketball. The all-black Chicago basketball team, the Savoy Big Five, was owned and coached by a white coach, Abe Saperstein, who renamed them the Globetrotters. They played their first Globetrotters game in 1927 in Hinckley, Illinois, and the following year they changed their name to the Harlem Globetrotters, to identify with the mystique and culture of the more well-known African American community in New York. Soon touring all over the nation and then internationally, the Globetrotters are an incredibly long-lived team of athletes and performers.

Perhaps Chicago is best known for basketball because it is the home team of one of the most popular players of all-time. Michael Jordan became one of the biggest sports celebrities of the 1980s and 1990s, playing with the Chicago Bulls, winning Most Valuable Player status multiple times, and taking the Bulls to six championships. Born in New York, Jordan grew up in North Carolina and played basketball in college before being drafted by the Bulls in 1984, retiring from the team in 1999.

Olympic athletes from Illinois have included Jacqueline "Jackie" Joyner-Kersee, a world-record holder and Olympic medalist in the women's heptathlon (a combined seven events) and long jump, considered one of the best female athletes of the twentieth century. She was born in East St. Louis, Illinois, and set a state record for the long jump while still in high school. She went on to compete in four Summer Olympic games (1984–1996), earning three gold medals, a silver, and two bronze medals overall. In the Winter Olympic games, Chicago-born Shani Davis is a world champion speed skater, winning both gold and silver Olympic medals in 2006 and again a gold and silver in 2010.

Bibliography

Armfield, Felix L. *Black Life in West Central Illinois*. Chicago: Arcadia Publishing, 2001.

Carrier, Lois. *Illinois: Crossroads of a Continent*. Urbana: University of Illinois Press, 1993.

Generations of Pride, African Americans in Illinois, Abraham Lincoln Presidential Library and Museum. www.alplm.org/events/aa_history/AA_History_Timeline.

Gove, Samuel Kimball. *Illinois Politics and Government: The Expanding Metropolitan Frontier*. Lincoln: University of Nebraska Press, 1996.

Grossman, James. *Land of Hope. Chicago, Black Southerners and the Great Migration*. Chicago: University of Chicago Press, 1989.

Hendricks, Wanda A. *Gender, Race, and Politics in the Midwest: Black Club Women in Illinois*. Bloomington: Indiana University Press, 1998.

Jensen, Richard J. *Illinois: A Bicentennial History*. New York: Norton, 1978.

Leonard, Gerald. *The Invention of Party Politics: Federalism, Popular Sovereignty, and Constitutional Development in Jacksonian Illinois*. Chapel Hill: University of North Carolina Press, 2002.

Meyer, Douglas K. *Making the Heartland Quilt: A Geographical History of Settlement and Migration in Early-Nineteenth-Century Illinois*. Carbondale: Southern Illinois University Press, 2000.

Muirhead, John W. *A History of African-Americans in McLean County, Illinois, 1835–1975*. Bloomington, IL: Bloomington-Normal Black History Project, McLean County Historical Society, 1998.

Petterchak, Janice A., ed. *Illinois History: An Annotated Bibliography*. Westport, CT: Greenwood, 1995.

Pratt, Mildred. *We the People Tell Our Story: Bloomington-Normal Black History Project*. Normal, IL: Bloomington-Normal Black History Project, 1987.

Sanders, Walter R. "The Negro in Montgomery County, Illinois." *Illinois State Genealogical Society Quarterly* 10, no. 1 (Spring 1978).

Simeone, James. *Democracy and Slavery in Frontier Illinois: The Bottomland Republic*. DeKalb: Northern Illinois University Press, 2000.

Williams, Erma Brooks. *Political Empowerment of Illinois' African-American State Lawmakers, from 1877–2005*. Lanham, MD: University Press of America, 2008.

INDIANA

Alton Hornsby, Jr.

Chronology

1787　Congress enacts the Northwest Ordinance, which bans slavery in the northwestern territories, an area that includes the present-day state of Indiana.

1800　*(May 7)* Congress organizes the Indiana Territory.

1816　*(December 11)* Indiana enters the Union as the 19th state.

1836　The Bethel AME Church is established in Indianapolis.

1850　As part of the Compromise of 1850, which seeks to resolve the question of the expansion of slavery in the western territories, Congress passes a new Fugitive Slave law.

1851　The new Indiana state constitution prohibits blacks from entering the state.

1851　*(November 9)* Marshals from Kentucky abduct abolitionist minister Calvin Fairbank from Jeffersonville and carry him to Kentucky to be tried for helping a slave escape.

1864　*(March 31)* The 28th Indiana Colored Infantry Regiment, the only black regiment formed in the state during the Civil War, is mustered in at Camp Fremont; the regiment sees action in Virginia, losing over 200 men.

1865　*(February 13)* Indiana ratifies the Thirteenth Amendment to the U.S. Constitution abolishing slavery.

1867　*(January 23)* Indiana ratifies the Fourteenth Amendment to the U.S. Constitution guaranteeing full civil rights to African Americans.

1869　*(May 14)* Indiana ratifies the Fifteenth Amendment to the U.S. Constitution guaranteeing voting rights to African American men.

1874　The Sisters of Charity, an African American self-help organization, is founded in Indiana.

1879　The *Indianapolis Leader*, Indiana's first black newspaper, is founded.

1898　Flanner House, a social service agency, opens in Indianapolis.

1912　A chapter of the National Association for the Advancement of Colored People (NAACP) is organized in Indiana.

1920s　The Ku Klux Klan, at its height, claims over 250,000 members in Indiana, amounting to over 30 percent of the state's white male population.

1922　The Indiana legislature passes a bill creating Klan Day at the Indiana State Fairgrounds, though the bill is vetoed by the governor.

1926　Investigations reveal that over half the members of the Indiana General Assembly are also members of the Ku Klux Klan.

1927　Black entrepreneur Madame C. J. Walker opens a theater in Indianapolis.

1930　Two blacks are lynched by a white mob in Marion.

| 1958 | (*August 29*) Michael Jackson, pop singer and entertainer, is born in Gary, the seventh of nine children. |

1958   (*August 29*) Michael Jackson, pop singer and entertainer, is born in Gary, the seventh of nine children.

1958   (*December 12*) Dr. Martin Luther King Jr. delivers a speech in Indianapolis calling for racial harmony.

1961   (*November 24*) Death threats are made against Martin Luther King Jr. when he returns to Indianapolis to speak at a Southern Christian Leadership Conference (SCLC) fundraiser.

1963   (*February 19*) Indiana ratifies the Twenty-fourth Amendment to the U.S. Constitution abolishing the poll tax.

1967   Richard Hatcher is elected as the first black mayor of Gary.

1968   Bobby Kennedy speaks to a black audience in Indianapolis just after hearing of the assassination of Martin Luther King. His speech registers the enormity of the event and begins the work of healing. Riots over the next few days hit 76 American cities, but Indianapolis remains quiet.

1969   (*June 5–6*) A riot erupts along Indiana Avenue in the heart of Indianapolis' black district after police break up a fight; members of the local Black Panther Party seek to calm the crowds.

1969   (*July 27*) A three-day race riot begins in Gary. Policemen aim at snipers after the third night of racial unrest. Sixty-four people are taken into custody.

1971   (*June 19*) Debut of the Indiana Black Expo, a celebration of the cultural and educational contributors of blacks to Indiana history.

1980   In Fort Wayne, an attempt is made to assassinate Vernon Jordan Jr., the president of the National Urban League.

1982   A jury in South Bend acquits self-avowed racist Joseph Paul Franklin for the 1980 attempted assassination of Vernon Jordan Jr.

1991   (*September 9*) An Indiana grand jury indicts boxer Mike Tyson on three counts, including one for the rape of Desiree Washington, a Miss Black America contestant. Tyson is convicted on February 10, 1992, and is imprisoned.

1996   Acquitted sniper Joseph Paul Franklin tells a newspaper that he did shoot and wound Vernon Jordan outside an Indiana hotel in 1980.

1997   Julia Carson is elected to the U.S. House of Representatives from Indiana.

2008   (*November 4*) Andre Carson is elected to the U.S. House of Representatives from Indiana.

2008   (*November 4*) Barack Obama, the first African American presidential nominee of a major party narrowly carries Indiana with about 50 percent of the vote; Obama's victory marks the first time a Democrat has won Indiana since 1964.

Historical Overview

In the pre–Civil War era, hundreds of free blacks migrated to Indiana, mainly from North Carolina, as well as a number of escaped slaves. But these early black settlers experienced blatant racial discrimination, and they and their abolitionist supporters often faced violence, sometimes leading to deaths. They were denied political rights, could not testify in courts against whites, and could not serve on juries. Early on they were not afforded education in the public schools. Under an 1831 law, they had to post a $500 bond "as security for their good behavior." Those who failed to post such bonds could be sold to the highest bidder for six months of work.

The first African American residents first arrived in Indiana in the 1820s. They were brought in to the area by white men to work in domestic service. Among the earliest blacks in the state were John G. Britton and his wife Cheney Lively. Britton was a former bondsman from Ohio who became active in the national Negro Convention movement in the 1830s. Cheney Lively was the only black female head of household listed in the 1830 Census. Other early African American residents were Ephraim Ensaw and David Mallory, who was the first barber in Indianapolis. African Americans made up less than 10 percent of the state's population in the antebellum period. Nevertheless, as of 1836, in Indianapolis and in rural areas, they were beginning to establish their own settlements. And on the eve of the Civil War, there were more than 60 such settlements carrying names such as "Colored Town," "Colored Freedom," "Lyles Station," "Roberts settlement," and "Lost Creek." After the Civil War, most of the settlements gradually ceased to exist as blacks moved into their own neighborhoods in large central cities.

As a result of the Fugitive Slave Law of 1850, some of the bondspersons left southern Indiana where they had originally stopped and headed for other parts of the state. At the time, there were approximately 2,500 African Americans in Indiana. A large number of these were employed in skilled trades, menial labor, and domestic service. They were generally poorly housed and poorly clothed.

In 1851, a new Indiana constitution prohibited blacks from entering the state. A provision of the law also called for fines to be levied on anyone who hired blacks who entered Indiana in violation of the act. Indiana voters approved the new proscriptions, disregarding the opposition of blacks and some white abolitionists, clergymen, and legislators.

The antiblack provisions of the 1851 constitution seemed to accelerate the emigration of African Americans from Indiana. John G. Britton and other black leaders urged blacks to emigrate to Jamaica. Some urged a "Back to Africa" movement. But, despite the heavy burden of racial discrimination in Indiana, most of the state's blacks were opposed to large-scale colonization or emigration outside of the country. They did, however, show a preference for urban life. The 1850 Census showed that there were 2,500 African Americans in the major cities of Indiana. The majority of these were laborers, but there were also a sizeable number of professional people, including barbers, physicians, and dentists.

Although at first Indiana, like other northern states, thought that the enlistment of black soldiers in the Civil War would be a dangerous thing, as the war continued and manpower shortages increased, the state government changed its position. Some Indiana blacks had already shown their loyalty and their courage by going to Massachusetts to join the famous 54th Massachusetts all-black regiment (the outfit that was the subject of the popular movie *Glory*). In 1863, the 28th U.S. Colored Regiment of Indiana was formed. The regiment was first deployed to Virginia in 1864, where they performed admirably in combat, but suffered heavy casualties because of poor leadership from white officers.

During and immediately after the Civil War, the major institutions in black communities were the church and the school. While there were some blacks who worshipped in white churches, the overwhelming majority attended all-black churches. Like African Americans elsewhere they tended to be Baptists and Methodists, including African Methodists (AME). Unlike in other communities, particularly in the Deep South, it was the AME Church which became predominant in the state. The first AME Church in Indianapolis, Bethel church, dated from the 1830s. The Indiana Conference of the AME Church was approved in 1940. The AME Church also was a pioneer in supporting black schools throughout the state. One of the most important AME ministers in the post-emancipation era was the Reverend John Henry Clay. This Georgia-born, ex-slave preacher served as minister of churches in west central Indiana from 1878 to 1881. After 1881, he pastored in Bloomington, New Albany, and Terre Haute before landing in Indianapolis, where he was minister to the largest black AME congregation in the state. He was a pivotal figure in building the AME Church in rural Indiana and in aiding the black migration from the South to the area in the late 1870s and early 1880s.

While most of Indiana's houses of worship have always been segregated, the state has always had a few racially mixed churches. One such structure was the Christ Temple Apostolic Church. The church, which dates from the early 1900s, began with fewer than 100 members. But by 1924, it had built a new building seating 1,500 members, which was called the finest edifice for black worship in Indianapolis. The church has had as many as 40 percent white worshippers. But not all whites have been receptive to its racially diverse membership. As early as 1908, a brick shattered the windows in the church.

In post–Civil War Indiana, black education, except that supported by churches, was disorganized.

In some places, because of the small black population, blacks were permitted to attend school with whites. In 1869, the state of Indiana authorized the admission of blacks into the state public school system. But most local systems interpreted the law to mean that blacks should be educated in separate elementary schools. As elsewhere, but certainly in the South, the prevailing educational philosophy was that blacks were incapable of learning beyond the elementary grades. But in 1877, the legislature stipulated that if there were no local schools for blacks in an area, they could attend white schools. Slowly, as in Gary, some black students began to receive secondary education, although sometimes in a racially discriminatory manner. For example in 1920, three Gary high schools—two of them technical schools—admitted blacks, but segregated them in the classroom and in extracurricular activities. In 1927, most whites boycotted Emerson High School, from which Oscar winner Karl Malden graduated. Then, in 1945, there was a boycott at the Froebel school, which lasted for several months. That boycott drew national attention as celebrities, including Edna Ferber, Carl Sandburg, and Frank Sinatra, went to Gary and denounced the racially inspired protests. As a result of the actions taken at the time, an additional 116 African American students were enrolled in all-white schools.

A first major step toward changing Indianapolis' segregated system came in 1949, when the state passed a desegregation law. The Indianapolis public schools then announced a plan of compliance and abolished separate elementary schools for blacks and whites. Yet where desegregation or partial desegregation existed, there was often strong opposition, not only from the growing Ku Klux Klan, but from white citizens across all social and economic lines and genders. In Indianapolis a virulent prosegregation group, the White Supremacy League, was largely composed of women. The segregationists were particularly concerned about racial mixing at the high-school level and mounted letter-writing campaigns and appeared at forums, often proclaiming white supremacy. Early on, blacks organized a massive counteroffensive against the segregationists. But soon divisions arose between those who demanded desegregation and those who would accept separate but equal schools. Thus in December, the local school board approved a separate high school for blacks. The school eventually became known as Crispus Attucks High School. The Indianapolis example was soon replicated in most of the urban areas of the state.

In 1998, an agreement brought an end to the federal court busing order that began with a lawsuit in the 1960s. The agreement did not end busing immediately; instead it called for a phaseout over an 18-year period. Meanwhile, officials were to work on additional efforts to desegregate the schools in the area. As a result of the turmoil over desegregation, enrollment in the Indianapolis public schools dropped from 108,000 in 1971 to 47,000 by the early 1990s. Much of this was apparently the result of efforts of the Ku Klux Klan and other manifestations of white supremacy as demonstrated in the city's anti-immigrant, antiblack, anti-Catholic, antiforeigner attitudes at the time. While Indianapolis escaped the extreme violence that accompanied desegregation in other cities such as Boston, the city experienced a white flight to suburbs and an exodus from urban public schools.

Antiblack violence continued in Indiana after the Civil War. In 1930, at least 10,000 whites stormed into the Grant County jail in Marion seeking three African American teenagers who had been charged with robbing and murdering a white man and raping his girlfriend. Two of the blacks were lynched. The incident has been called one of the last such lynchings ever to occur north of the Mason-Dixon line. Much of the racial violence was initiated by the Ku Klux Klan. In 1933, for example, the Klan demonstrated on the statehouse steps; then fighting broke out and several people were injured. Some 35 Klansmen showed up for the rally. They were countered by more than a thousand opponents.

The Klan had been a factor in Indiana political life since its first Indiana chapter was founded in Evansville in 1920. It soon established chapters in every county. D. D. Stephenson, a salesman, arrived in Evansville from Oklahoma and eventually was named grand dragon of Indiana and 22 other states. Membership in the Klan increased dramatically to about 250,000 statewide. In Indianapolis, as many as 40 percent of all native-born white men in the city paid their $10 fee and joined the hate group. The Klan became the largest social organization in Indianapolis and a dominant force in the city from 1921 to 1928. At some of the Klan rallies, as many as 50,000 people were in attendance.

As elsewhere, the primary targets of the Klan's vitriolic hate were blacks, Catholics, and Jews. But it was Catholics who drew the most attention. At the time there were about 32,000 Catholics in the city. The Klan charged that they were un-American as they owed their loyalties to Rome and not to American governments. Some believed that Catholics would one day revolt and claim the country for the Church of Rome. As to the Klan's direct role in Indiana politics, this can be seen in the primary election of 1924. The Klan-backed candidates were elected. To celebrate, an estimated 25,000 Klansmen, women, and children gathered at the Indiana State Fairgrounds. Later, some 6,500 Klansmen and their supporters paraded through downtown while a crowd of 75,000 to 100,000 lined the streets. A Klan newspaper was jubilant at the organization's success, proclaiming; "Protestant Ticket Sweeps State" and "National Papal Machine Smashed." Shortly thereafter, however, Stephenson was arrested and convicted of second-degree murder charges in the death of Madge Oberholtzer. She was a statehouse worker whom Stephenson had been dating in 1925. He was sentenced to a long prison term. The Klan's involvement in bribery and corruption of government officials began to come out. Political scandals led to the ouster of Indianapolis' mayor

Bodies of Tom Shipp and Abe Smith, two victims of lynching in Indiana, 1930. (AP/Wide World Photos)

and the governor at the time, and interest in the Klan declined sharply.

Black-initiated racial violence was rare in Indiana until recent times. Although Indianapolis and Gary African Americans were commended for remaining relatively calm following the assassination of Martin Luther King Jr. and Senator Bobby Kennedy's fervent appeal to them to remain so, racial tensions did lead to rioting in Indianapolis in the summer of 1969. For two nights, bottles were thrown, windows were smashed, and there were fires, shootings, and looting. The Indianapolis riot was sparked by rage at police handling of a fight between black men at a local apartment complex. When the violence was brought under control, there had been thousands of dollars in property damages, at least 20 arrests, and several injuries, but apparently no fatalities. Amid the violence, it was reported by local media

that a black youth and members of the local chapter of the Black Panther Party actively sought to ease the tensions and the disorder.

Meanwhile, African Americans continued to go about their daily tasks, finding refuge in their own community activities. Black social life in Indiana, as elsewhere in black America, was often focused on church-related activities, but there were plenty of nonchurch activities to attract both saint and sinner. In Indianapolis, for example, there was the Walker Theatre. Founded by the daughter of wealthy black hair products manufacturer Madame C. J. Walker in 1927, the theater remained open until the late 1970s. In the words of its founder, it was built to serve as a cultural and social center for Indianapolis. In addition to the theater, the building housed a beauty shop, a coffee shop, and a drugstore, all owned by the Walkers, and a casino.

The Walker Theatre featured major films mainly by white producers and featuring white actors and actresses. Later "blacksploitation" films were added, but by the time the theater closed in the late 1970s, African American public opinion had turned against such movies. In the major cities of the state, branches of the YMCA and YWCA were organized. Other activities designed to promote such social welfare and self-help included the Sisters of Charity, which was founded in 1874 to provide healthcare for the poor. This group and others did establish a few small hospitals for blacks in the periods when black access to healthcare was severely restricted, but they were short-lived. More lasting were the efforts of fraternal groups and women's clubs. These latter groups, which could be traced back to the early nineteenth century, sought to tend to the morals, education, and social welfare of young women, including sponsoring lectures by womanist leaders and black intellectuals, both female and male. They also established reading clubs and fairs: notably African American women in Indianapolis founded the Alpha House for the Aged in Indiana as early as 1883.

Another of the major self-help organizations was Flanner House. The current building at 2424 Dr. Martin Luther King Jr. Street is not the original structure. The House is supported by a women's group known as the Flanner House Guild, a 99-year-old social service group. Opened in 1898, Flanner House, the home, has been called "an open door, a passageway for people searching for better lives." The home served African American migrants from the post–Civil War South.

The first building was donated by Frank Flanner, a local mortician. As a social service agency, the Flanner House was, in many ways, ahead of its time. African American domestic workers left their children there while they went to serve affluent white families.

In recent times, the home has been supported by the United Way. The child-care center now serves about 150 families; a kindergarten is also on site; in-home services are offered for the elderly and disabled; and a prosecutor's office offers child support assistance. In a new program with the Indianapolis Museum of Art, African artifacts are displayed in large cases in the lobby.

A chapter of the NAACP was organized in Indianapolis three years after the founding of the national organization in 1909. Although there had been civil rights laws in Indiana as early as 1885, which, among other things, prohibited discrimination in public accommodations, the laws were rarely enforced. Suits were brought by the NAACP over these issues as well as school segregation, which ultimately brought relief in the 1940s.

Educated black women played a major role in the struggle for civil rights in Indiana. For example, during the First World War, the Indiana Federation of Colored Women's Clubs adopted resolutions protesting lynchings and the treatment of blacks in the South and for the end of racial discrimination in Indiana.

As in most states, gains in civil rights also led to new and greater progress in political rights and political opportunities. These gains were particularly significant for African American women. In 1964, Daisy Riley Lloyd became the first black woman elected for the Indiana legislature. In the 1970s, Julia Carson was elected first to the Indiana House and then, in 1976, as the first black woman to the state Senate. In 1997 she was elected to the U.S. Congress.

Prior to Carson's election to Congress, the major political achievement for African Americans in Indiana was the election of Richard Hatcher as mayor of Gary in 1967. Following the Civil Rights Acts of 1964 and 1965, blacks began to be elected mayors in predominately black cities of the North. Hatcher was one of the first of those elected.

Gary had become a magnet city for African American migrants from the South during World War I. They were drawn there by the hope of a promised land free from racial oppression and offering economic opportunities. Though the city possessed all of the racial animosity of other places in Indiana at the time, labor shortages forced employers to extend a welcome hand to blacks. But the welcome was only intended for relatively cheap labor with little chance to advance into higher positions. And segregation in schools, places of recreation, and places of public accommodations persisted.

In 1910, there had been only about 400 African American residents in Gary. Ten years later, they were 10 percent of the city's population. In 1990, Gary was 85 percent black. Also by this time, although blacks had firm political control of the city, the economy declined as steel mills closed and the Sun Belt South became more industrialized. The beautiful city on Lake Michigan, as it was called, experienced white flight to the suburbs and inner-city decay, both structurally and socially.

A major force in the quest for African American civil and political rights in Indiana has been the black press. The first black newspaper in Indiana was the *Indianapolis Leader*, founded in 1879. Three years later, the *Colored World* (which later became the *Indianapolis World*) was launched. These pioneer organs were followed by the *Freeman* (1884), which had a national audience, and the *Indianapolis Recorder* (1885), the longest-lasting black newspaper. The *Recorder* is also the third-oldest African American newspaper with continuous publication in the country. Two other black newspapers began publishing in the twentieth century, the *Indiana Herald* in 1959 and the Muncie *Times* in 1990. Newspapers such as the *Evansville Argus* and the Indianapolis *Freeman* have highlighted grievances and agitated for equal opportunity in education, employment, healthcare, housing, and public facilities. As these newspapers declined and often folded in the civil rights and post–civil rights eras, the African American communities lost an important voice of advocacy as well as an important economic enterprise.

Notable African Americans

Carson, Julia May (1938–2007)

U.S. Congresswoman Julia May Carson was born in Louisville, Kentucky, but the family moved to Indianapolis when Julia was a child. Carson received her higher education from Martin University in Indianapolis and Indiana University in Bloomington. Before going to Congress, Carson served in the state House of Representatives (1973–1977) and the state Senate (1977–1990). Seven years later, she was sent to the U.S. House from a predominantly white district in Indianapolis. She was returned to her position in four subsequent elections. Carson, who had a history of serious health problems, died of cancer in 2007. She was succeeded by her grandson, André Carson.

Edmonds, Kenneth Brian "Babyface" (1958–)

Born in Indianapolis, "Babyface" Edmonds is a rhythm-and-blues producer, singer, songwriter, and musician. A portion of Interstate 65 in Indiana has been named for him.

Fisher, Aaron Richard (dates unknown)

Aaron Fisher was an African American in the all-black 366th Infantry during World War I. He is generally regarded as the most distinguished black soldier from the state of Indiana to serve in that war. This distinction was based upon his brave and courageous actions against German forces in France on September 3, 1918.

Fox, Lillian Thomas (1866–1917)

Lillian Fox was a journalist and community leader in Indianapolis. Born in Chicago, she came to Indiana in the early 1880s from Wisconsin. She became a writer for the *Freeman*, a prominent black newspaper in Indiana, and became active in the black women's club movement. She also chided white newspapers for not covering black community activities.

Hall, Katie Beatrice (1938–)

U.S. Congresswoman Katie Beatrice Hall was born in Mound Bayou, Mississippi. She was educated at Mississippi Valley State University and Indiana University at Bloomington. Before being elected to the U.S. Congress from Indiana in 1982, Hall served terms in the Indiana state House of Representatives and the state Senate (1974–1976; 1976–1982). After only one term in the U.S. House, Hall was defeated in the Democratic primary in 1984.

Hatcher, Richard G. (1933–)

Richard G. Hatcher was the first African American mayor of Gary and a civil rights leader. He hosted black political and economic leadership summits in his city during his tenure as mayor between 1968 and 1987. He was also chairman of the Jesse Jackson for President Campaign in 1984.

Hayward, Garfield T. (d. 1931)

Garfield T. Hayward was an African American minister. Known as a great orator, he once held office as presiding bishop of his denomination. A portion of a street in Indianapolis is named in his honor.

Jackson, Michael (1958–2009)

Michael Jackson was an internationally acclaimed singer, actor, writer, record producer, and philanthropist. In 1964 he joined with four of his brothers to form the rhythm-and-blues group the Jackson Five. A controversial figure because of his dress, his facial changes, and friendship with children, he died suddenly in 2009 and was celebrated as "the king of Pop."

Lewis, Henry Jackson (c. 1837–1891)

Henry Jackson Lewis was born in bondage in Mississippi. In freedom the family lived in Arkansas. Lewis moved to Indianapolis in 1889, where he joined the staff of the *Freeman* newspaper.

Montgomery, Wes (1923–1968)

Wes Montgomery was a jazz guitarist, called one of the best of the modern era and a successor to Charlie Christian.

Plato, Samuel M. (d. 1957)

Samuel M. Plato was an architect. Born in Alabama, he studied in North Carolina and at Tuskegee Institute in his native state. He later moved to Marion, Indiana, in 1902. Among his more notable designs are schools, apartments, and houses that are listed on the national Register of Historic Places. He also designed the First Baptist Church of Marion.

Scott, William Edouard (1884–1964)

William Edouard Scott was a painter who studied at the Chicago Art Institute. He also studied in France, where he came under the tutelage of the famed black artist Henry O. Tanner at the Julian Academy. While there he had three of his works accepted at the prestigious Salon des Beaux Arts at Toquet. Among his more noted paintings, accepted by such galleries as the Salon at La Loque in France and the Royal Academy in London, is *La Pauvre Voisine*.

Pop artist Michael Jackson performs at opening night of his Victory Tour at Dodger Stadium in Los Angeles, California, December 1, 1984. (AP/Wide World Photos)

Sisslie, Noble (1889–1975)

Noble Sisslie was a jazz composer, bandleader, singer, and playwright. He also was a filmmaker. He is perhaps best known for his collaboration with songwriter Eubie Blake. Among the duo's best known productions are "Shuffle Along" and "The Chocolate Dandies."

Stewart, George P. (dates unknown)

George P. Stewart was the founder of the *Indianapolis Recorder* newspaper in 1885. He was also a champion of civil rights, speaking out forcefully for desegregation of public accommodations and against those merchants who profited from black trade but who would not advertise in African American newspapers.

Walker, Madame C. J. (1867–1919)

Although born in Louisiana, Madam C. J. Walker established several of her economic enterprises, including a theater, in Indiana.

Cultural Contributions

In addition to painter William Edouard Scott, architect Samuel M. Plato, actor Guinea "Blue" Fainsworth, and musicians "Babyface" Edmonds, Michael Jackson, and Noble Sissle, Indiana's African American communities have produced Deotis Hardeman, a classical pianist. Indiana is also the home of the McArthur Conservatory, where musicians have been trained since the 1940s. McArthur, founded by an Indianapolis music teacher, Ruth McArthur, has a notable faculty including Jerry Daniels of the Ink Spots as well as members of the Indianapolis Symphony Orchestra. The McArthur Marching Band, the McArthur Orchestra, and its vocal group the Choraliers have performed jazz and classical numbers, and Haitian and African American dance music at nightclubs as well as at the state fairgrounds.

The Freetown Village is a community of artists who reenact life in post–Civil War Indiana. Founded in the 1980s by a former schoolteacher, Ophelia Umar Wellington, the story is told in acting, song, dance, and exhibits. It is presently housed in the Indiana State Museum.

In the 1990s, Indiana's black historians began developing a listing of African American historic sites. As of 1995, they had identified several places in Indianapolis, including the Crispus Attucks Middle School and several historic black churches.

In the early part of this century, Indiana residents began the development of a "trail of freedom," mapping out the state's role in the Underground Railroad. "Indiana Freedom Trails" will show the routes of the many "stations" of the railroad—the network of abolitionist homes and other places where escaping slaves were housed en route to the North and to Canada. It is estimated that there were at least 300 such sites, mainly in southeastern Indiana.

Culturally, Indiana is perhaps best known for Black Expo. The festival was begun in 1971 and held at the Indiana State Fairgrounds. Its goal was to highlight, through culture, education, and entertainment, the contributions of black Indiana. During the first exposition in 1971, an estimated 5,000 people, including civil rights leaders Ralph David Abernathy and Jesse Jackson and athletes John Mackey and Bill Russell, were in attendance. Abernathy's and Jackson's appearances reflected the cosponsorship by the SCLC's Operation Breadbasket of the event.

Since 1971, the event has attracted more than 20,000 people annually from all over the country and has featured exhibit booths, artists, markets, song, and dance.

More than 50,000 people attended the two-day event in June 1971, which featured 75 exhibitor booths, a concert, and an ABA versus NBA basketball game. The success of the event depended on getting sponsors and exhibitors. White business leaders initially resisted invitations to participate, but changed their minds when Eugene S. Pulliam, publisher of the *Indianapolis Star* and the *News*, offered his support.

By the late 1970s, Black Expo was in financial trouble again with a debt that had grown to over $100,000. One of those who tried to help was entertainer Sammy Davis Jr., who donated $10,000. In 1988, an *Indianapolis Star* investigation discovered management problems and little financial accountability.

By the time Black Expo celebrated its 20th anniversary in 1990, it was out of debt and the celebration was expanded to a full week. That year, the first Founder's Award was given to singer, songwriter, and producer Kenneth "Babyface" Edmonds. The Expo also began presenting a Freedom Award. That award has gone to individuals like boxing promoter Don King and entertainer Stevie Wonder.

More recently, the Expo has added conferences for businesspeople and jobs fairs, a children's program, music festivals, a health fair, and a National Youth Summit. The event was hosting more than 800 exhibit booths.

But the event has also had its share of troubles, including crime in a nearby neighborhood and a fatal shooting of men at the 1994 and 1998 Soulfests. This led to the canceling of the 1999 Soulfest. When the celebration resumed in 2000, it was relocated and renamed the Family Fun Fest. But new problems arose in 2002 when there were several complaints of racist behavior by the Indianapolis police.

On the more positive side, a rejuvenated celebration was honored with a visit by President

Jesse Jackson speaks into a microphone, surrounded by marchers at a demonstration in Indianapolis, Indiana, 1975. (Library of Congress)

George Bush in 2005. Bush spoke at the business luncheon and was presented with a Lifetime Achievement Award.

Another growing cultural enterprise in Indiana is Indianapolis' Asante Children's Theatre. The group presents plays depicting phases of African American history. One of the popular presentations is "The Step and Stand Tall Blues" which uses the blues to interpret black history.

A growing cultural site for tourists is the six-square-block neighborhood in Indianapolis called Ransom Place, which was once the center of black life and culture in Indianapolis. In the early 1900s on Indiana Avenue, there were many thriving local businesses, including Madam C. J. Walker's beauty supply plant and the theater named for her. This main artery just west of downtown was also home to many churches, barber shops, funeral parlors, and local jazz clubs.

The Ransom Place Historic District was named for Freeman B. Ransom (1882–1947), an attorney and general manager of the Walker business enterprises. He lived on the 800 block of California Street. In the 1920s, this block of fashionable black homes was called the "Negro Meridian Street." Today, Ransom Place remains the most intact neighborhood associated with Indianapolis' early black history.

The area is also home to the Heritage Learning Center Museum, an 1830 Queen Anne cottage that houses the history and artifacts of early Ransom Place residents.

Another attraction is the "Museum Without Walls," an open-air museum documenting the lives and homes of early Ransom Place residents. Signs along the streets in the neighborhood tell the addresses, family names, and occupations of the neighborhood's earliest residents. For example, one sign marks the site where Senator Robert Lee Brokenburr lived. He was a two-term Indiana senator who also wrote the articles of incorporation for the Madame C. J. Walker Company. Ransom Place was entered on the National Register of Historic Sites in 1992.

Freetown Village seeks to replicate black life in Indiana in the 1870s. It accomplishes this through living-history performances. The activities include an annual "Evening Dinner with Freetown Village." The organization also collects and preserves artifacts and prepares exhibits for other programs. It is sponsored in part by the Arts Council of Indianapolis and produced in cooperation with the Tourism Division of the Indiana Department of Commerce.

Bibliography

Baker, Ronald L., ed. *Homeless, Friendless and Penniless: The WPA Interviews with Former Slaves Living in Indiana.* Bloomington: Indiana University Press, 2000.

Bigham, Darrel E. *We Ask Only a Fair Trial: A History of the Black Community of Evansville, Indiana.* Bloomington: Indiana University Press, 1987.

Black Soldiers in Civil War Indiana. http: civilwarindiana.com/black_soldiers.html.

Bodenhamer, David J., and Robert G. Barrow, eds. *The Encyclopedia of Indianapolis.* Bloomington: Indiana University Press, 1994.

Carmony, Donald F. *Indiana, 1816–1850: The Pioneer Era.* Indianapolis: Indiana Historical Bureau and Indiana Historical Society, 1998.

Cayton, Andrew R. L. *Frontier Indiana.* Bloomington: Indiana University Press, 1996.

Frantz, Edward. "A March of Triumph? Benjamin Harrison's Southern Tour and the Limits of Racial and Regional Reconciliation." *Indiana Magazine of History* 100, no. 4 (December 2004): 293–320.

Gibbs, Wilma L., ed. *Indiana's African American History: Essays from Black History News and Notes.* Indianapolis: Indiana Historical Society, 1993.

Hamm, Thomas D, April Beckman, Marissa Florio, Kirsti Giles, and Marie Hopper. " 'A Great and Good People': Midwestern Quakers and the Struggle Against Slavery." *Indiana Magazine of History* 100, no. 1 (March 2004): 3–25.

Hendrick, George, Willene Hendrick, Levi Coffin, and William Still. *Fleeing for Freedom: Stories of the Underground Railroad.* Chicago: Ivan R. Dee, 2004.

Indiana's African-American History. www2. indystar.com/library/factfiles/history/black_ history.

Kotlowski, Dean J. " 'The Jordan Is a Hard Road to Travel': Hoosier Responses to Fugitive Slave Cases, 1850–1860." *International Social Science Review* 78, no. 3/4 (2003): 71–89.

Lutholtz, M. William. *Grand Dragon: D.C. Stephenson and the Ku Klux Klan in Indiana.* West Lafayette, IN: Purdue University Press, 1991.

Madison, James H. *Indiana through Tradition and Change: A History of the Hoosier State and Its People, 1920–1945.* Indianapolis: Indiana Historical Society, 1982.

Madison, James H. *The Indiana Way: A State History.* Bloomington: Indiana University Press, 1986.

Nation, Richard F. "Violence and the Rights of African Americans in the Civil War Era." *Indiana Magazine of History* 100, no. 3 (September 2004): 215–230.

Nelson, Jacquelyn S. *Indiana Quakers Confront the Civil War.* Indianapolis: Indiana Historical Society, 1991.

Onuf, Peter S. *Statehood and Union: A History of the Northwest Ordinance.* Bloomington: Indiana University Press, 1987.

Taylor, Robert M., Jr., and Connie A. McBirney, eds. *Peopling Indiana: The Ethnic Experience.* Indianapolis: Indiana Historical Society, 1996.

Thornbrough, Emma Lou, and Lana Ruegamer. *Indiana Blacks in the Twentieth Century.* Bloomington: Indiana University Press, 2000.

Thornbrough, Emma Lou. *The Negro in Indiana before 1900: A Study of a Minority.* Bloomington: Indiana University Press, 1993.

Tucker, Todd. *Notre Dame vs. the Klan: How the Fighting Irish Defeated the Ku Klux Klan.* Chicago: Loyola Press, 2004.

Vincent, Stephen A. *Southern Seed, Northern Soil: African-American Farm Communities in the Midwest, 1765–1900.* Bloomington: Indiana University Press, 1999.

IOWA

Lisa N. Nealy

Chronology

1673	Louis Jolliet and Father Jacques Marquette are first Europeans to set foot on Iowa soil.
1803	Iowa becomes a U.S. possession as part of the Louisiana Purchase, a vast tract of territory purchased from France by President Thomas Jefferson.
1804	Accompanied by a black slave named York, Meriwether Lewis and William Clark enter Iowa as they ascend the Missouri River during their exploration of the newly acquired Louisiana Territory.
1812	Congress organizes the Missouri Territory, which includes present-day Iowa.
1820	Passage of the Missouri Compromise, which proclaims all territory north of the southern border of Missouri to be free, ensures that Iowa will be a free state.
1832	The Black Hawk War ends with Indians ceding to the United States a strip of land west of the Missouri known as the Black Hawk Purchase; permanent white settlement of Iowa begins, and Fort Des Moines is eventually established at the confluence of the Mississippi and Des Moines Rivers.
1834	Congress creates the Michigan Territory, which includes present-day Iowa.
1836	With Michigan statehood, Iowa is transferred to the Wisconsin Territory.
1838	*(July 4)* Congress establishes the Iowa Territory, the northern boundaries of which extend into present-day Minnesota and the Dakotas.
1839	The territorial legislature enacts a series of black codes to discourage black settlement in Iowa. This series of measures requires blacks to produce a certificate of freedom and post a $500 bond to enter the territory, and prohibits them from voting, joining the militia, serving in the legislature, testifying against whites in court, and attending public schools.
1840	The Iowa territorial legislature bans interracial marriages.
1840	The United States counts 188 African Americans living in Iowa.
1845	The slavery issue delays Iowa statehood when a debate erupts over the future state's northern boundary. Iowa leaders propose a border that extends to modern Minneapolis, but northern leaders in Congress want a smaller Iowa to leave land for more future free states. The issue is settled by a compromise.
1846	*(December 28)* Iowa enters the Union as the 29th state.
1846	Mormons migrate across southern Iowa.
1847	The University of Iowa in Iowa City is chartered.

1850s	Iowa abolitionists such as Josiah Grinnell, James Jordan, and the Reverend John Todd serve as conductors on Iowa's Underground Railroad, helping runaway slaves to freedom in Canada and the North.
1853	Alexander Clark, the African American owner of a barber shop in Muscatine, attends the National Colored Convention in Rochester, New York.
1857	Thirty-three African American delegates attend a convention in Muscatine that demands full citizenship for Iowa's black residents.
1857	Iowa voters reject a proposal for black suffrage.
1858	The General Assembly requires all Iowa school boards to maintain separate schools for black students.
1859	Iowa abolitionist Josiah Grinnell provides shelter for John Brown, who is on the run after his acts of violence against proslavery settlers in Kansas.
1861–1865	Iowa sends 80,000 men to the Union army during the war.
1863	1,153 Iowa blacks are recruited into the 1st Iowa Volunteers of African Descent, a unit later designated as the 60th Regiment Infantry, U.S. Colored Troops.
1866	*(January 15)* Iowa ratifies the Thirteenth Amendment to the U.S. Constitution, which abolishes slavery in the United States; Iowa's ratification comes several weeks after the amendment itself gained sufficient state approvals to take effect.
1868	*(February)* The Iowa State Colored Convention meets in Des Moines to discuss ways to work for full civil rights for African Americans in the state.
1868	*(March 16)* Iowa ratifies the Fourteenth Amendment to the U.S. Constitution guaranteeing African American citizenship.
1868	In *Clark v. Board of Directors*, the Iowa Supreme Court declares that requiring black children to attend separate schools violates the 1857 state constitution.
1868	Iowa becomes the first state outside New England to grant African American men the right to vote.
1870	*(February 3)* Iowa ratifies the Fifteenth Amendment to the U.S. Constitution, which secures the African American right to vote; Iowa's ratification gives the amendment sufficient state approvals to take effect.
1871	Bethel African Methodist Episcopal (AME) Church is founded in Cedar Rapids.
1874	Thanks to the 1868 *Clark v. Board of Directors* decision of the Iowa Supreme Court, all public schools in the state are now open to children of all races and religions.
1880s	More than 300 African American families own and run farms in Iowa.

1880	The Iowa state constitution is amended to remove the words "free white" from the qualifications for serving in the state legislature.
1884	The state legislature passes a civil rights law guaranteeing full and equal access to public accommodations for anyone regardless or race, religion, or ethnic group.
1890	*(August 16)* President Benjamin Harrison appoints Iowa civil rights activist G. Alexander Clark as U.S. minister to Liberia.
1915	The first Iowa branch of the National Association for the Advancement of Colored People (NAACP) is founded in Des Moines.
1917	Fort Des Moines becomes the site of the Colored Officers Training Camp; by bringing black military families to the city, the camp spurs an increase in Des Moines' African American population.
1941	Lulu Johnson, a native of Gravity, Iowa, becomes the first African American woman to receive a Ph.D. from the University of Iowa and the first African American woman in the United States to receive a Ph.D. in history.
1946	The dormitories at the University of Iowa are integrated.
1948	*(July 7)* Accompanied by her daughter and two friends, Edna Griffin—who will later be known as the "Rosa Parks of Iowa"—stages a sit-in at Katz Drug Store in Des Moines when she is refused service at the lunch counter because she is black.
1949	The Iowa Supreme Count upholds the conviction of the Katz Drug Store manager under Iowa's 1884 civil rights law in the landmark civil rights case *State of Iowa v. Katz.*
1949	*(December 2)* Civil rights attorneys for the local NAACP chapter negotiate an end to the discriminatory practices of Katz Drug Store in Des Moines.
1954	President Dwight Eisenhower appoints Archie Alexander, the first African American to play football for the University of Iowa, and owner of a successful Des Moines construction company, governor of the U.S. Virgin Islands.
1963	*(April 24)* Iowa ratifies the Twenty-fourth Amendment to the U.S. Constitution abolishing the poll tax.
1964	James H. Jackson of Waterloo and Willie Stevenson Glanton of Des Moines are elected as the first male and female African American state legislators in Iowa history.
1965	A new Iowa Civil Rights Act is passed; it creates the Iowa Civil Rights Commission to work for the ending of racial discrimination in the state.
1984	Only 54 African American families own and run farms in Iowa, down from an estimated 170 families in 1970.
1987	The Iowa legislature passes the state's first hate crimes legislation.

1988	The Iowa Commission on the Status of African Americans is established to report on the status of African Americans in Iowa and to make recommendations as to programs, legislation, policies, and services that will improve the quality of life for African Americans in the state.
1989	Iowa begins celebrating Martin Luther King Jr. Day on the third Monday in January.
1992	Virginia Harper, one of the women who integrated the dormitories at the University of Iowa in 1946, is elected to the Iowa Women's Hall of Fame.
1993	Massive flooding of the Mississippi and Missouri Rivers and their tributaries causes many deaths and widespread loss of homes in Iowa.
1998	(May 15) The mayor of Des Moines declares this day "Edna Griffin Day" in honor of the Iowa civil rights activist who helped end the discriminatory practices of Des Moines businesses in the late 1940s.
2000	The U.S. Census records 61,852 African Americans in Iowa, comprising 2.1 percent of the state's population.
2003	(September 19) The African American Museum of Iowa opens in Cedar Rapids.
2006	African American Museum of Iowa chapters are opened in eight communities across the state.
2008	(November 4) Democrat Barack Obama, the first African American nominee for president of a major party, carries Iowa in the presidential election with 54 percent of the vote.

Historical Overview

Because the Missouri Compromise of 1820 prohibited slavery north of the southern border of Missouri, Iowa was always a free territory and in 1846 became a free state. Slavery never existed there. In 1839, the African American presence in Iowa first became visible. Iowa's territorial Supreme Court heard the case of an African American named Ralph, a slave from Missouri who had been sent by his master to work in the lead mines at Dubuque. After Ralph lived in Iowa for two years, Ralph's master came from Missouri to take him home. But Ralph alleged that he was no longer a slave, since for the past two years he had been living on free soil. The court ruled in Ralph's favor. Under Iowa law, he was a free man.

From its founding, Iowa had never permitted slavery within its borders. During the 1840s and 1850s, Iowans were gradually swept up in the nation's passionate debate over the slave issue. Missouri, Iowa's neighbor to the south, had entered the Union as a slave state. Frequently, runaway slaves from Missouri fled into Iowa. Many headed north to Canada on the Underground Railroad, a secret network of safe houses or "stations," where fugitives could find food and shelter. "Conductors" on the railroad transported runaway slaves from one station to another, often hiding them in wagons beneath bales of wheat or rows of corn. To aid an escaping slave violated federal law. The conductors and their families risked imprisonment in order to live by their belief that slavery was morally wrong. One fugitive who made use of the Underground Railroad was not a runaway slave but an ardent white abolitionist: John Brown. Brown fled to Tabor, Iowa, and hid in the home of conductor John Todd because his antislavery activities in Kansas got him into trouble with the law.

Brown dreamed of sparking an uprising among southern blacks that would end slavery forever. He and his followers stayed in Springdale, a Quaker settlement, for several months, making secret plans. They then marched into Missouri, killed a slaveholder, and brought 11 slaves to Iowa. With "still wanted" notices offering a reward for his capture, Brown finally left the Hawkeye State. Brown was hanged for treason along with several of his men, including Edwin and Barclay Coppoc, two brothers who were Quakers from Springdale. The Coppoc brothers joined Brown in seizing the arsenal at Harpers Ferry, Virginia, in October 1859.

Indeed, the question of slavery had divided the nation, and in 1844, Iowa asked to be admitted to the Union as a state. Southern congressmen protested that if Iowa became a state, it would tip the balance in the U.S. Congress between slave and free states. In the final compromise, Iowa, the first free state west of the Mississippi River, entered the Union hand in hand with Florida, the last slave state east of the Mississippi. Slave and free states remained equally represented in Washington, D.C. On December 28, 1846, President James K. Polk signed the bill that made Iowa the 29th state to join the Union.

Iowa became a leading state in passing civil rights legislation. Alexander Clark, an African American barber, was one of the Iowans at the forefront of activism in the state. He protested the state's discriminatory laws, campaigned for black suffrage, and fought for the right for his daughter to attend an all-white school. The efforts of Clark and other Iowans did not go in vain. In 1868, an amendment to the state constitution extended the vote to African

American men. Another constitutional amendment, passed in 1880, permitted African Americans to serve in the Iowa General Assembly. Several court decisions eliminated segregation in public schools. Mississippi steamboats had to be integrated as they passed though Iowa waters. President Ulysses S. Grant once called Iowa "the nation's one bright radical star."[1]

Between the late nineteenth century and the early twentieth century, Iowa saw the emergence of an increasingly economically and socially mobile black population. African Americans worked on steamboats and railroads and in factories (though they often received less pay than their white counterparts). Many blacks also went into business for themselves. One of the thriving towns of the state was Buxton. Although many African Americans were drawn to the mining industry in Buxton, not everyone worked in the mines. Minnie B. London, who lived in Buxton, recalled that blacks were well represented in assorted professions, such as "doctors, lawyers, teachers, druggists, pharmacists, undertakers, postmaster, Justice of the Peace, constables, clerks, [and] members of the school board."[2] Indeed, African Americans in Buxton were among the most successful blacks in the state in that time.

African Americans in Buxton also fared better than many blacks in the nation in terms of racial experiences. Racial hostility and conflict was virtually nonexistent in the town. Blacks enjoyed unprecedented levels of racial equality. African Americans in cities such as Keokuk and Des Moines also experienced less racism and discrimination than other cities in the United States. Elsewhere in the state, however, discrimination in restaurants, housing, and employment was prevalent.

In ensuing years, black Iowans became more involved in mainstream society. Some "600 men earned commissions as captains and lieutenants at the World War I Black Officer Training Camp at Ft. Des Moines."[3] Black women were

Members of the Women's Army Auxiliary Corps standing in front of their commander, Captain Frank Stillman, at Fort Des Moines, Iowa, 1942. (Library of Congress)

employed in the Women's Army Auxiliary Corps. African Americans also participated in World War II and, during the postwar years, integrated more state institutions, such as the military and universities. Black Iowans experienced still more gains in the wake of the Civil Rights Movement of the 1950s and 1960s. Blacks attained a number of firsts as judges, legislators, and other high-level positions. In the 1970s and 1980s, the number of blacks who achieved economic and social success continued to grow, resulting in a thriving black middle class. By the 1990s, racial discrimination decreased further.

The luminous success stories of black Iowans and racial progress notwithstanding, blacks in the state faced challenges into the twenty-first century. White supremacist organizations have staged rallies in the state. These organizations and their messages of hate and intolerance pose challenges to growing populations of African Americans and immigrants. As many blacks prospered, many more have been inundated with social problems and disparities. A report noted that "the median income of black families in 2008 was $27,000, compared with $61,663 for all Iowans"; the unemployment rate was 8.9 percent for blacks and 3.9 percent for all others, and more African Americans were imprisoned in the state than any other race.[4] As blacks in the state grapple with challenges and celebrate successes in the new millennium, the world around them changes, becoming increasingly diverse.

Ethnic Communities

Large numbers of blacks seeking job opportunities and refuge from crime have migrated to Iowa in recent years, bringing the percentage of blacks in the state up to 2.7 percent. This percentage is still far less than the national average of 12.4. Regardless, African Americans form one of the state's largest minority groups. Almost 93 percent of the state population is described as non-Hispanic Caucasians. The majority of Iowans are white and most have ancestors who came to

America many generations ago. Approximately 35 percent of Iowans are descended from Germans, the largest of Iowa's nineteenth-century immigrant groups. German-speaking communities exist today in what are known as the Amana colonies and among the state's Amish villages in Washington and Johnsan counties. Some 98 percent of modern Iowans were born in the United States. A small but growing number of Asians live in the state. A small number of Native Americans, most of them belonging to the Mesquakie tribe, live near the Iowa River in Tama County.

Nearly 90 percent of Iowa's population identify with one of the Christian denominations. Roman Catholics, however, make up the largest single religious group in the state. Catholics are concentrated in the Mississippi River cities. Many religious denominations, such as Baptists, Presbyterians, Lutherans, and Methodists, are represented in Iowa. Iowa's Jewish population tends to be clustered in larger cities. A large Muslim community lives in Cedar Rapids. Amish and Mennonite people live in the farming areas.

Population

Iowa ranks fourth in the nation in percentage of people over the age of 65. The state's population declined during the 1980s because the number of deaths caught up with the number of births. Many senior citizens left Iowa for a warmer climate. In a phenomenon known as the "brain drain," thousands of well-educated women and men in their 20s sought new jobs out of state.

Although Iowa is one of the nation's most productive farm states, the majority, 59 percent of the people, live in cities and towns. Until 1960, however, more than half of all Iowans lived in rural areas. The largest concentration of people in the Hawkeye State lives within the "Golden Triangle." Five of the state's six largest cities are located in the Golden Triangle region. Iowa has about 30 cities with populations greater than 10,000. In terms of population, the six largest

cities are Des Moines, Cedar Rapids, Davenport, Sioux City, Waterloo, and Dubuque.

Politics

The Republican Party has been the driving force in Iowa politics since the Civil War. But Iowa Republicanism swerves from the norm. While Republicans from other states often favor a strong national defense and a tough foreign policy, Iowa Republicans, reflecting the will of their people, tend to be "doves" (a political term for one who favors negotiation over war). Voters in the state were decidedly against America's involvement in the Vietnam War. The state's most influential newspaper, the *Des Moines Register*, regularly advocates policies that would lead to the reduction of world armaments.

The Iowa caucus or primary is the nation's first step in electing the president. During the caucus, voters gather in schools, public buildings, and even private homes to express their choice for a national leader. The Iowa caucus carries little weight in the actual nominating process, but it is the first test of a candidate's popularity. During the 1988 caucus, Iowa's white voters gave a surprising 9 percent of their votes to the Reverend Jesse Jackson.

Notable African Americans

Alexander, Archie (1888–1958)

Archie Alexander became University of Iowa's first African American football player after his family moved to Des Moines. Alexander refused to let racial barriers prevent him from becoming a successful engineer and presidential appointee.

Alexander was born in Ottumwa, the son of a coachman. He was 12 years of age when his family moved to Iowa. He earned an engineering degree in 1912 and then worked for a bridge-building firm in Des Moines before launching his own business in 1914 with a friend, George Higbie, who was white. Their company built freeways, apartments, airfields, sewage systems, and power plants. In 1944, he and his wife, Audra, broke the color barrier with the purchase of a home in the Chautaugoa Park neighborhood. In 1947, the University of Iowa named Alexander one of 100 outstanding alumni among 30,000 graduates.

Alexander gained an international reputation when President Dwight Eisenhower appointed him governor of the Virgin Islands. He served from April 1954 until August 1955, resigning when islanders thwarted his plans to help empower impoverished communities. He continued his construction projects, with offices in Des Moines and Washington, D.C. Alexander was a trustee for Howard University, where he also lectured. Alexander died of a heart attack but left almost $200,000 in scholarship money to help others.

Clark, G. Alexander (1826–1891)

G. Alexander Clark was an African American civil rights leader who became the first black to graduate from the University of Iowa. Clark was one of the most influential men of his time, who was tireless in his efforts to improve the lives of African Americans. He arguably did more for civil rights than anyone else in nineteenth-century Iowa.

Clark is best remembered for refusing to accept segregated schools. In 1867, when the Muscatine School District prohibited Clark's daughter, Susan, 12 years old, from attending the same public school that white students attended, he sued. The Iowa Supreme Court ruled in his favor in 1868, declaring that all children could attend a common school. The decision was an important one, preceding the landmark 1954 ruling in a Topeka, Kansas, case. The U.S. Supreme Court, in *Brown v. Board of Education*, reversed the "separate but equal" education policy. Clark's lawsuit made Iowa one of the first states to integrate its public school system.

Clark was born on February 25, 1826, in Washington County, Pennsylvania, to John Clark, a former slave, and Rebecca Darnes Clark, of African descent. Clark's main occupation was as a barber, where he began his career until 1868. On October 9, 1848, Clark married Catherine Griffin of Iowa, who had been freed from slavery in Virginia at age three. The Clarks had five children, two of whom died in infancy. During the Civil War, Clark organized the 1st Iowa volunteers of African Descent, later redesignated the 60th Regiment Infantry, U.S. Colored Troops, a Union regiment of 1,100 black soldiers from Iowa and Missouri. Clark himself enlisted in 1863 and was appointed a sergeant major. A disability forced him to focus his energies on soldier recruitment.

In 1869, a state convention appointed him a delegate to the Colored National Convention in Washington, D.C., where he had the opportunity to meet with President Grant. In 1873, Grant offered Clark an appointment as ambassador to Haiti. However, Clark turned down the position, because he felt the salary was too small. Active in both the Masonic Lodge and the Republican Party, Clark traveled extensively for both, and his speaking skills earned him the title "Colored Orator of the West." Clark's final achievement came when President Benjamin Harrison appointed him U.S. minister to Liberia on August 16, 1890. Clark died in Monrovia, Liberia, on June 3, 1891. He was buried with honors at Muscatine's Greenwood Cemetery on February 16, 1892.

Estes, Simon (1938–)

Simon Estes is an African American opera singer born on March 2, 1938, in Centerville. He was one of five children of Ruth Jeter Estes and Simon Estes. Estes' father was a slave who worked a variety of jobs after toiling in coal mines. Estes first performed in church and school choirs.

Opera singer Simon Estes at his home, 2000. (AP/Wide World Photos)

At age 13, his clear soprano voice won him first place when Bill Riley brought his "Talent Search" to town. Estes attended the University of Iowa from 1957 to 1963. He first majored in pre-med, then changed to theology and later social psychology. He finally settled on vocal music with encouragement from his teacher Charles Kellis. After Estes studied at Julliard School of Music for one year, he left for Germany, making his professional stage debut in 1965 in Berlin as Ramfis in "Aida." He made his Metropolitan Opera debut in 1982. In his long career, Estes has performed throughout the world. He sponsors a youth choir in South Africa but returns to his home state frequently.

Farmer, Arthur Stewart (1928–1999)

Arthur Stewart Farmer was a famous African American jazz musician born on August 21, 1928,

in Council Bluffs. His family moved away from Iowa four years later. As children, Farmer and his twin brother, Addison, took music lessons. Farmer began piano lessons at six. Later, he received instruction on the violin. When he wanted to participate in a school marching band, Farmer took up the bass tuba because that was the only instrument available. In the 1940s, Farmer joined a dance band and was introduced to the world of jazz. When big bands and swing bands came to town, the Farmer brothers often invited musicians to their home for jam sessions. From the moment Farmer heard a professional jazz band perform, his goal was to pursue a career in jazz music. He decided to learn how to play the trumpet.

In 1952, Farmer toured Europe with Lionel Hampton. In the following year, he made New York City his home base, playing with Hampton alongside trumpeters Quincy Jones and Clifford Brown and saxophonist Gigi Gryce. In 1959,

Farmer and saxophonist Benny Gholson formed their hard-bop Jazztet, continuing the group until 1962. With musical tastes turned upside down in the 1960s and a turbulent political scene, Farmer decided to move to Europe, where jazz still had a strong following. He joined the Austrian Radio Orchestra in 1968, settling down in Vienna with his family. As a freelancer, Farmer traveled extensively to clubs and jazz festivals in London, Paris, Italy, Scandinavia, and Switzerland.

After 1977, Farmer spent equal time in Vienna and New York. He enjoyed music and often practiced from five to seven hours a day. An inventive musician, Farmer believed in the "less is more" theory, conveying much in a few notes, eventually choosing the flugelhorn over the trumpet. He preferred a softer, more intimate lyrical sound.

Farmer received recognition for his illustrious career. In 1994, Farmer was awarded the Austrian Gold Medal of Merit. In the same year, Lincoln Center held a concert to honor Farmer. Following his death in New York City on October 4, 1999, musical performances and jazz festivals were organized to celebrate his life and achievements. In 2001, Farmer was inducted into the Jazz Hall of Fame.

Griffin, Edna (1909–2000)

Edna Griffin was a local civil rights leader. Born in Kentucky in 1909, Griffin grew up in New Hampshire as the daughter of a dairy-farm supervisor. Griffin graduated from Fisk University in 1933, married a doctor, Stacey Griffin, and became a schoolteacher. The couple moved to Des Moines in 1947.

In 1948, Griffin sat down at a Des Moines lunch counter and ordered an ice cream soda and was refused service because of her skin color. Griffin led sit-ins and picketed the drugstore and sued owner Maurice Katz. The Iowa Supreme Court supported Griffin's charge. Katz was found in violation of an 1884 Iowa statute making it a crime to discriminate in public accommodations. In a civil case, an all-white jury awarded Griffin a decisive ruling.

Griffin founded the Iowa chapter of the Congress for Racial Equality (CORE), and in 1963, she organized Iowans to attend Dr. Martin Luther King Jr.'s March on Washington. At age 75, Griffin sat in the middle of a Nebraska highway in an attempt to prevent nuclear warheads from being shipped into the local SAC Army base. Griffin was inducted to the Iowa Women's Hall of Fame and the Iowa African American Hall of Fame. Des Moines Mayor Preston Daniels declared May 15 as Edna Griffin Day in 1998. In that same year, the Flynn building, where the Katz Drug Store was once located, was renamed to honor Griffin.

Redd, Ernest "Speck" (1914–1974)

Ernest "Speck" Redd was the top African American jazz pianist in Des Moines, Iowa. He acquired his nickname because of his many freckles. Redd, one of seven children of a Baptist minister and his wife, was born in Huntsville and moved to Des Moines, Iowa, in 1941. Redd became known with appearances on KRNT radio and television. His latest engagement was at the Best Western Inn in Ankeny. After Redd died, friends and fans gathered for a special party to exchange recordings and tapes of his music.

Winston, Ivory (1911–1996)

Ivory Winston was named "Iowa's First Lady of Song" and "Iowa's Popular Concert Artist." Winston was born in Ottumwa on August 11, 1911, the only child of E. P. Green, minister of the Second Baptist Church, and his wife Effie. The church provided the child's foundation in music, and in her later career, she loved to share Negro spirituals with her audiences. As a child of 12, when she began studying piano, she dreamed of becoming a concert pianist like her idol, Inane Paderewski. Friends encouraged her to develop her talent. Winston began studying privately, working eight hours a week for her lessons. She earned enough money by ironing on Tuesdays and cleaning houses on Fridays to pay for two voice lessons per week.

Winston later studied at Ottumwa Heights College, Parsons College, and Drake University. Acclaimed concert singer Marion Anderson was her role model. Winston made her recital debut at Ottumwa Heights College in May 1946. In 1948, Winston sang for President Harry Truman on his birthday when he made a campaign swing through the Midwest.

In June 1950, Winston won a top ranking at the *Des Moines Register and Tribune* Cavalcade of Music festival. The event was held at the Drake University stadium, with 3,000 contestants entered from seven states. When Wilson was invited to sing at the state Republican Convention at Des Moines' theater in July 1950, she wrote a special song for the occasion and performed before Republicans from every county, as well as Governor William Beardsley. She began her singing career at a time when few opportunities existed on the concert stage for African Americans. The coloratura soprano was in demand at colleges, high schools, community celebrations, conventions, clubs, churches, and civic groups.

Cultural Contributions

African Americans in Iowa have made a wide variety of cultural contributions. Black Iowans, like Simon Estes, an opera singer, and Ivory Winston, a concert artist, have exhibited extraordinary talent in classical music forms that were historically dominated by whites. African Americans in Iowa were strongly influenced by the jazz and big band era of the 1940s and 1950s. Jazz, which was created by African Americans, was brilliantly performed by celebrated Iowans such as Ernest Redd and Arthur Farmer. Margaret Walter, born in Alabama, and Alice Walker,

from Georgia, attended the University of Iowa Writers' Workshop and went on to achieve literary success. Margaret Walker is well known for her poem "For My People," which celebrates black life, culture, and triumph in spite of oppression. One of Alice Walker's most seminal novels was *The Color Purple* (1982), which was adapted into a film directed by Steven Spielberg and a musical produced by Quincy Jones, Oprah Winfrey, and others. *The Color Purple* features songs, dance, religious traditions, and vernacular from the black experience in the 1930s. Since the 1990s, Iowan Tionne Tenese Watkins, otherwise known as T-Boz, has produced R&B and hip-hop music as a member of the massively popular group TLC. The prolific careers and talents of African Americans in Iowa have enriched the state and the world over.

Notes

1. Robert R. Dykstra, *Bright Radical Star: Black Freedom and White Supremacy on the Hawkeye Frontier* (Cambridge, MA: Harvard University Press, 1993), 227, 268.

2. Dorothy Schwieder, Thomas Morain, and Lynn Nielsen, *Iowa Past to Present: The People and the Prairie* (Ames: Iowa State University Press, 1991), 126.

3. "African-Americans in Iowa, 1838–2005," www.iptv.org/iowapathways.

4. William Petroski, "New Report: Blacks Make Big Gains in Iowa Population," www.desmoinesregister.com/article/20100403.

Bibliography

"African-Americans in Iowa, 1838–2005." (April 2010). www.iptv.org/iowapathways.

Alex, Lynn M. *Iowa's Archeological Past*. Iowa City: University of Iowa Press, 2002.

Carpenter, Allan, and Randy Lyon. *Between Two Rivers: Iowa Year by Year, 1846–1996*. Ames: Iowa State University Press, 1997.

Dykstra, Robert R. *Bright Radical Star: Black Freedom and White Supremacy on the Hawkeye Frontier.* Cambridge, MA: Harvard University Press, 1993.

Fradin, Dennis B. *From Sea to Shining Sea: Iowa.* Connecticut: Grolier Publishing. 1993.

Holmberg, James J. *Exploring with Lewis and Clark: The 1804 Journal of Charles Floyd.* Norman: University of Oklahoma Press, 2004.

Kent, Deborah. *America the Beautiful: Iowa.* Chicago: Children Press, 1991.

Landau, Diana. *Iowa: Art of the State.* New York: Harry N. Abrams, Inc., 1998.

Longden, Tom. "DesMoines Registry." www.FamousIowans.com. May 30, 2007.

Martin, Michael. E. *World Almanac Library of the States: Iowa.* Milwaukee, WI: World Almanac Library. 2002.

Petroski, William. "New Report: Blacks Make Big Gains in Iowa Population." *Des Moines Register,* April 2010. www.desmoinesregister.com/article/20100403.

Riley, Glenda, ed. *Prairie Voices: Iowa's Pioneering Women.* Ames: Iowa State University Press, 1996.

Sage, Leland L. *A History of Iowa.* Ames: Iowa State University Press, 1974.

Schwieder, Dorothy. *Iowa: The Middle Land.* Ames: Iowa State University Press, 1996.

Schwieder, Dorothy, Thomas Morain, and Lynn Nielsen. *Iowa Past to Present: The People and the Prairie.* Ames: Iowa State University Press, 1991.

Wall, Joseph Frazier. *Iowa: A Bicentennial History.* New York: W. W. Norton & Company, 1978.

KANSAS

William Gibbons and Gordon E. Thompson

Chronology

1803	The United States acquires the Louisiana Territory from the French; the new territory, including Kansas, nearly doubles the size of the United States.
1804	Lewis and Clark explore Kansas on their way to the Pacific Coast. Accompanying the expedition is an African American, York, who plays a prominent role in the expedition.
1820	The first African Americans whose arrival can be documented come to Kansas. Some were free and others purchased their freedom, but most were enslaved and in the fur trade.
1852	Clement Shattio, a white farmer, and his free black wife, Ann Davis Shattio, are some of the first residents of Topeka in the Kansas Territory.
1854	(May 30) The Kansas-Nebraska Act is passed by Congress opening the territory to settlement and giving Kansas territorial status. The act repeals the Missouri Compromise of 1820 and permits the admission of Kansas and Nebraska territories to the Union after their populations decide on slavery.
1854	"Bleeding Kansas" is an outgrowth of the controversy over the Kansas-Nebraska Act. Between 1854 and 1858, armed groups of pro- and antislavery factions, often funded and sponsored by organizations in the North and South, compete for control of Kansas Territory, initiating waves of violence that kill 55 people. Bleeding Kansas becomes a preview of the Civil War.
1854	The Republican Party is formed in the summer in opposition to the extension of slavery into the western territories.
1855	Abolitionist John Brown arrives in Oswatomie to fight proslavery factions.
1855	(July 2) The first territorial legislature meets at Pawnee, and later at Shawnee it legalizes slavery in Kansas.
1856	(May 21) The Lawrence Massacre results in the deaths of 150 abolitionists when proslavery groups attack the antislavery town of Lawrence.
1856	(May 23) Abolitionist John Brown leads a group of abolitionist settlers in the so-called "Pottawatomie Massacre," which results in the deaths of five proslavery settlers living near Pottawatomie Creek.
1858	(December 25) On Christmas night, John Brown leads a group of abolitionists into Missouri to rescue 11 enslaved Missourians. Before and after this Christmas Night Raid, fugitive black slaves make their way to freedom in Kansas Territory.
1860	Kansas adopts a constitution prohibiting slavery. African Americans in neighboring slave states immediately flee to Kansas to work as free people; the African American free population of Kansas increases to 625 from 192 in 1855.

1861	(*April 12*) The Civil War begins with the Confederate bombardment of Fort Sumter in the harbor of Charleston, South Carolina.
1861	Kansas enters the Union as the 34th state.
1862	(*February*) The Kansas Emancipation League is founded by black and white abolitionists meeting at the First Colored Baptist Church in Leavenworth.
1862	(*June*) Congress abolishes slavery in the territories of the United States.
1862	(*October 17*) The 1st Kansas Colored Infantry is organized near Fort Lincoln in Bourbon County.
1863	(*July 17*) The 1st Kansas Colored Infantry arrives at Fort Scott, becoming the first African American unit to see action in the Civil War.
1863	(*October*) Twenty-three delegates representing approximately 7,000 black Kansans gather in Leavenworth for the first Kansas State Colored Convention demanding political equality and an end to racial discrimination.
1864	The Ladies' Refugee Aid Society is established in Lawrence.
1865	The Thirteenth Amendment to the U.S. Constitution outlaws slavery throughout the United States.
1865	Kansas' African American population increases to 12,527; many African Americans find work as farm laborers, domestic servants, and soldiers.
1866	Congress authorizes the formation of two all-black cavalry regiments, the 9th and 10th, and two infantry, the 24th and 25th; the 10th Cavalry was stationed at Fort Leavenworth.
1867	(*January 10*) Congress passes the Territorial Suffrage Act, which allows African Americans in the western territories to vote. The act immediately enfranchises about 800 black male voters in those territories.
1867	(*November*) White male voters in Kansas overwhelmingly reject efforts by both African American males and all women to obtain the ballot. In a vote on both propositions, African American suffrage fails by 19,421 to 10,438, while women's suffrage is defeated by 19,857 to 10,070.
1868	(*July 21*) The Fourteenth Amendment to the U.S. Constitution is ratified, granting citizenship to any person born or naturalized in the United States.
1869	(*February 26*) Congress sends the Fifteenth Amendment to the U.S. Constitution to the states for approval. The amendment guarantees African American males the right to vote.

1870	Exodusters begin migrating from the South to the Midwest; between 1875 and 1881, an estimated 60,000 African Americans from the southern states head for Kansas with dreams of owning land on the western frontier.
1877	(July 30) African American settlers from Kentucky arrive to establish the town of Nicodemus, which is the first of hundreds of all or mostly black western towns; Nicodemus reaches its peak in 1910 when the federal Census reports 595 colored residents.
1878	Edwin McCabe arrives in Nicodemus advertising himself as an attorney and land agent. In April 1880, Kansas Governor John P. St. John appoints McCabe the first clerk of newly organized Graham County. In November 1881, McCabe is elected to a full term as county clerk.
1878	William L. Eagleson founds the *Colored Citizen*, the first black newspaper in Topeka.
1878	Benjamin "Pap" Singleton leads his first group of Tennessee emigrants to Kansas. The party of 200 settlers establishes the Dunlap Colony on the east bank of the Neosho River in Morris County.
1879	African American parents in Topeka begin a campaign to desegregate the local schools. They receive a setback in 1890 when the Kansas Supreme Court in *Reynolds v. Board of Education of Topeka* decides the state's school segregation law is constitutional. Their multi-generational efforts at desegregation continue until *Brown v. Board of Education* strikes down school segregation in 1954.
1879–1880	Approximately 6,000 African Americans leave Louisiana and Mississippi counties along the Mississippi River for Kansas in what will be known as the Exodus. In response to the Exodus, Kansas Governor John P. St. John creates the Kansas Freedmen's Relief Association (KFRA) to provide assistance for the mostly destitute refugees. The association receives nationwide support, including donations from pre–Civil War abolitionist William Lloyd Garrison, who leads fund-raising efforts in Boston, and from Philip D. Armour, the Chicago meatpacker.
1880	The African American population of Kansas exceeds 48,000.
1881	Western University is founded to provide professional training and services in Kansas City.
1882	Edwin McCabe of Nicodemus is elected the state auditor of Kansas at the age of 32. He is the first African American elected to a statewide office outside the South.
1885	Blanche K. Bruce becomes the first African American to graduate from the University of Kansas.
1886	(*May 13*) The *Western Cyclone* newspaper is established by A. G. Tallman in the township of Nicodemus.
1886	Young George Washington Carver homesteads 160 acres in Ness County, Kansas, for two years before leaving the area to continue his education at Iowa State University.

1887	(August 17) The *Enterprise* newspaper is established by H. K. Lightfoot in Nicodemus.
1889	Edwin McCabe creates the Oklahoma Immigrant Association, headquartered in Topeka, to encourage African American migration from the South to the new territory. McCabe and his wife Sarah arrive in Oklahoma in April 1890 and help found Langston City, which they name after Virginia Congressman John Mercer Langston.
1895	The Kansas Industrial and Education Institute is founded in Topeka as a kindergarten, sewing school, and reading room by Elizabeth Reddick and Edward Stephens, two African American elementary school teachers in Topeka. The institute will eventually become, after the endorsement of Booker T. Washington and a substantial donation from Andrew Carnegie, a major facility for the teaching of industrial arts and scientific agriculture to black Kansans. In 1919, the state of Kansas assumes control of the facility and renames it the Kansas Vocational Institute.
1895	Hattie McDaniel is born in Wichita; she is best known for her role as Mammy in *Gone with the Wind*, for which she won an Oscar. She was the first black to win an Oscar and the first black star to attend these ceremonies.
1897	The Kansas legislature gives cities with populations above 10,000 the authority to establish racially separate grade schools; Leavenworth and Topeka do so.
1899	Alfred Fairfax, a Republican from Chautauqua County, is the first African American state legislator.
1899	Nick Chiles founds and edits the *Plain Dealer*, a newspaper in Topeka that published until 1958.
1899	Aaron Douglas, an African American painter and major figure in the Harlem Renaissance, is born in Topeka.
1919	Lorenzo Fuller Jr. is born in Stockton; he is considered by some to be the first African American to host a national television show—a 15-minute show airing on NBC in 1947.
1925	Kansas City (Missouri and Kansas) becomes the center of a black jazz network that stretches throughout the West and eventually includes Shanghai, Hong Kong, and Manila.
1940	The African American population of Kansas reaches 65,138.
1940	(*February 29*) Hattie McDaniel receives an Oscar for best supporting actress for her role in *Gone with the Wind*.
1941	(*June 25*) Executive Order 8802 desegregates war production plants throughout the West and creates the Fair Employment Practices Committee (FEPC).
1948	(*July 26*) President Harry S. Truman issues Executive Order 9981 directing the desegregation of the armed forces.

1950	Four percent of African Americans earned their living in professional jobs.
1951	*(February 28)* Thirteen African American families in Topeka, Kansas, file a lawsuit against the local school board for its policies that permit racially segregated schools. The case will eventually be known as *Brown v. Board of Education.*
1954	*(May 17)* The U.S. Supreme Court in *Brown v. Board of Education* declares segregation in all public schools in the United States unconstitutional, nullifying the earlier judicial doctrine of "separate but equal."
1955	Wilt Chamberlain attends the University of Kansas to play basketball.
1958	*(July 19)* Ronald Walters, a Wichita State College freshman and president of the Wichita National Association for the Advancement of Colored People (NAACP) Youth Council, leads the city's first sit-in demonstration. The group protests Dockum Drugstore's ban on black customers using the lunch counter. The protest ends a few days later when drugstore officials promise to end the discriminatory policy.
1958	James P. Davis, a Democrat from Wyandotte County, is elected to the Kansas House of Representatives.
1966	Billy Q. McCray, a Democrat from Sedgwick County, is elected to the Kansas House of Representatives.
1970	The University of Kansas' Department of African American Studies is established.
1970	Nine percent of African Americans earn their living in professional jobs.
1974	The First National Black Historical Society is formed in Wichita to save the Old Calvary Baptist Church, which is placed on the National Register of Historic Places in 1993.
1975	*(March)* The Kansas Black Legislative Caucus is formed by seven African American members of the Kansas legislature.
1976	*(January 7)* The Nicodemus Historic District, commemorating Nicodemus, the first black settlement in Kansas in 1877, is designated a National Historic Landmark.
1990	Sixteen percent of African Americans earn their living in professional jobs.
1997	The Kansas legislature creates the Kansas African American Affairs commission (KAAAC) to serve as a conduit of information for groups and organizations addressing the affairs of the state's African American community.
1999	The First National Black Historical society in Wichita becomes the Kansas African American Museum.
2000	Valdenia Winn, a professor at Kansas City Community College, is elected to the Kansas House of Representatives.
2000	African Americans comprise 0.5 percent of Kansas' population, about 154,198 people.

2004	The *Brown v. Board of Education* National Historic Site and Museum opens in the Monroe Elementary building, a formerly segregated school in Topeka.
2004	Melody McCray-Miller, a Wichita city commissioner, is elected to the Kansas House of Representatives.
2006	The U.S. Census documents 153,560 African Americans in the state of Kansas.

Historical Overview

The history of Kansas contains some of the most extraordinary African American events and personalities in the United States. The list of famous blacks to emerge from Kansas is impressive, and includes the historic Reconstructionist U.S. Senator Blanche Kelso Bruce, Bishop John A. Gregg, Oscar winner Hattie McDaniel of *Gone with the Wind* fame, the dynamic tenor sax player Coleman Hawkins, muralist extraordinaire Aaron Douglas of the Harlem Renaissance, and the Pulitzer Prize–winning poet Gwendolyn Brooks. Other notables include those who either moved to Kansas or made significant achievements there such as the landmark black scientist George Washington Carver, the black poet laureate James Langston Hughes, and the great Wilt Chamberlain of the Globetrotters and the Los Angeles Lakers.

African American entry into Kansas differed from the emigration patterns of their white brethren, as was true in the western states overall. Unlike their white counterparts who arrived by wagon train, many blacks initially walked from Missouri and the border states of Kentucky and Tennessee, or traveled by railroad or steamboat from Virginia and the Deep South states such as Mississippi and Louisiana. Among the more dramatic events of this time was the flight from Mississippi of Henry Clay Bruce, the brother of Senator Blanche K. Bruce. Henry escaped with his fiancée from Missouri in 1863 with a pair of Colt 45s, and made the run, as he describes it in his autobiography, by crossing the Missouri River.

Early on, African Americans were drawn by knowledge of Kansas' famous abolitionist tradition, associated with John Brown, but also James H. Lane, James Montgomery, and Charles Jennison. In fact, with the entry into the state of religious groups such as the Quakers, Presbyterians, and Congregationalists who proclaimed their devotion to the freedom and uplift of African Americans, African Americans got the impression that Kansas was a haven for freedom and fair play. Indeed, these are the very abolitionists who established the Kansan wing of the Underground Railroad.

Bleeding Kansas

The state was known as "Bleeding Kansas" for its many internal wars over the Kansas-Nebraska Act of 1854 that left the decision to the people living in each territory to determine whether or not their territory would enter the Union as a slave state. Yet, since such battles were not waged in the Deep South, they indicated that powerful forces in Kansas stood in opposition to slavery. As such, many blacks saw this battle-torn state as a refuge, the city of Lawrence in particular.

Kansas, moreover, would become one of the first states to ratify the Thirteenth Amendment. Abolitionists, known as Free Staters, descended on Kansas to influence the decision and to counteract slaveholders from the South who were beginning to settle in the region. Black Laws were passed making it illegal on pain of death to aid a fugitive slave or spread antislavery opinions. Upon repeal of the Black Laws, the Free Staters succeeded in creating Kansas as a free state.

Kansas' bloody warriors are exemplified by men like John Brown. A champion for the abolition of slavery, Brown was neither a native-born Kansan nor a black man. He came to Kansas in 1855 from Ohio, fought and killed for his cause, and died after having led a quixotic but spectacular raid on the U.S. Army arsenal at Harpers Ferry in 1859. Among his men was an ancestor of Langston Hughes. Brown was perhaps only the most colorful and violent of a large host of folks, slave and free, white and black, who, as actors on the Underground Railroad, led slaves from Missouri through Lawrence and Topeka on the way to Canada.

Statehood and a Growing Black Population

When it declared in its constitution that it would be a free state, Kansas saw blacks make their way there in droves. The black population was about 192 in 1855, jumped to 655 in 1860, and by 1865 had increased to over 12,500. This large increase was the consequence, of course, of the Civil War, during and immediately after which blacks found their way to Kansas in skiffs, by swimming, or even walking across the ice floes of the Missouri River. Blacks, like their white counterparts, were also inspired to come to Kansas by what has been called "Kansas Exodus Fever," a movement spurred by the advertising campaign of the railroads and other land speculators who hailed Kansas as a little Eden. The second great wave of blacks arrived in 1877, augmenting the size of the black population to more than 48,000 by 1880.

The number of blacks in Kansas exploded with the Exodusters, black slaves who amazed their contemporaries as they fled in masses from Missouri and the Deep South to Kansas, Nebraska, and Colorado. From 1875 to 1881, 60,000 blacks headed for Kansas, led by Benjamin Singleton, called "Pap," who was an important figure of the Exoduster movement. Credited with bringing thousands of blacks from border and Deep South states, he organized colonies of black farmers in the settlements of Dunlap, Singleton, and Nicodemus. Having spearheaded the migrant Exodusters, Singleton also established the colony named after him and founded an emigration agency called the Edgefield Real Estate and Homestead Association.

If these first blacks arrived as individuals or as isolated families, many later entered Kansas with the assistance of the Edgefield Real Estate and Homestead Association or similar emigration agencies. Putting aside racism, blacks felt encouraged to make this transition by the expectation of higher wages and the hope of becoming homesteaders. After all, the federal government, in the Homestead Acts of 1862, made cheap land on reasonable loan rates available to every man or woman, black or white, that agreed to live on the land for at least six months.

Towns

Based on its proximity to Missouri, the eastern corner of Kansas developed more rapidly than the western portion of the state. It is no surprise, then, that the towns and cities with the heaviest population of blacks—propelled by the mass migration during the Exoduster phenomenon—were located in the east. Yet, while some of the Exodusters were also the founders of the first all-black settlement of Nicodemus, it resides, interestingly enough, in an isolated, western portion of the state, way out in western Kansas in that great expanse of prairie linking Kansas with Colorado.

Founded by W. H. Smith, Nicodemus was named after a slave who was said to have been an African prince who predicted the coming of the Civil War and purchased his freedom. So far west is Nicodemus, this early black frontier settlement, from the other major settlements in Kansas that blacks attempting to homestead there seemed to have made every effort to flee slavery

View of Washington Street in Nicodemus, Kansas, circa 1885. Nicodemus was an African American town settled by former slaves. (Library of Congress)

along with all forms of white oppression. From 30 colonists in 1877 to more than 480 in 1880, African Americans represented 11 percent of Graham County in which Nicodemus lies. Despite its typical high-plains topography and weather, settlers managed to grow wheat and corn on this flat terrain. The settlement developed from structures that were little more than dugouts to encompass a livery stable, a blacksmith shop, the St. Francis Hotel, newspapers, a two-story stone building erected in 1879, a general store, pharmacy, and a schoolhouse. Three churches—Baptist, Free Methodist, and African Methodist Episcopal—thrived for a while.

Despite Nicodemus' national reputation as a symbol of black successful self-management, it quickly went into decline as a reflection of the poor weather and unsuccessful dealings with the railroad companies that bypassed their township. But during its heyday, Nicodemus caught the attention of many migrants like George Washington Carver and one, Edwin P. McCabe, hailing from as far away as Troy, New York, who eventually was elected the auditor of the state. To this day, Nicodemus remains an unincorporated black town in Graham County, far from the railroad or any major highways.

While blacks still reside in Nicodemus, Lawrence and Leavenworth are towns where blacks experienced their greatest successes and most promising early years. Later, the majority of blacks would eventually settle in Kansas City and Topeka.

With the advent of the Civil War and in its wake, the population of black Kansans increased significantly. The towns of Leavenworth and Lawrence were among the most popular, with more than 72 percent of the black population of Kansas residing there alongside a larger population of white settlers. One great inducement for free blacks and slaves alike during the Civil War was the offer of work for freedom, in which slaves grew and harvested the wheat and other crops in place of white males who had enlisted in the army. In 1863, blacks distinguished themselves by producing one of Kansas' best harvests of all time.

Leavenworth had a large black community of about 2,455 in 1865, representing about 16 percent of its population. As the population increased, their destitution was such that the town fathers, white men, immediately set about to ameliorate the situation. For this purpose, the Kansas Emancipation League was founded with the combined efforts of men such as William Mathew, one of the first blacks to become an officer in the Union army; the town's preacher, Reverend Robert Caldwell; the educator, Lewis Overton; and the druggist Dr. R. C. Anderson, who worked hand in hand with famous white citizens such as Susan B. Anthony's brother, Colonel Daniel R. Anthony, and Richard J. Hinton, a well-known abolitionist.

Prominent church leaders such as Jesse Mills and Moses White founded the African Methodist Episcopal Church in Leavenworth. Not only did the church operate to help end slavery, but it also worked to assist fugitive slaves entering the state. The Kansas Emancipation League was initiated at a meeting of the First Colored Baptist Church in 1862, and together with the Ladies Refugee Aid Society, it supported blacks fleeing Missouri and other slave states. Other self-help groups such as the Kansas Federation of Colored Women's Clubs, previously known as the Ladies Refugee Society, collected food and clothing and raised funds for the weary black migrants. For those who were gainfully employed, the choice of work consisted of porters and waiters, cooks, maids, and manual laborers such as teamsters.

Leavenworth was also the site in 1863 for the first Kansas State Colored Convention, which met to agitate for equal rights; for black male suffrage; for the right to serve on juries; to end discrimination, particularly in regard to public transportation; to gain wider access to public education; and to demand federal pay for soldiers, specifically the 1st Kansas Colored Regiment. They also argued in opposition to black American colonization efforts in Africa, urging more blacks to become homesteaders and farmers.

Once Kansas became a state in 1861, blacks entered in large numbers. Lawrence was particularly popular as an antislavery town, and by 1862, a significant number of blacks had arrived in the town by way of the Underground Railroad. The "railroad" ran from western Missouri into Lawrence toward Topeka and from there into Nebraska Territory, Iowa, Chicago, and finally into Canada.

In urban areas such as Lawrence, half of black workers were unskilled and lived in virtual poverty. Still, they attended public schools during the day and night, and in 1862, they founded the first black house of worship in Lawrence called Freedmen's Church. By 1865, the black population of Lawrence had increased to 1,000. While blacks were self-supporting, most hovered very near the poverty line. Of the 1,000, only 369 were listed in the census as employed. The largest numbers were soldiers, followed by day laborers. Women were mostly domestics—washerwomen, housekeepers, servants, and cooks—decreasing in number respectively. Among the remaining unskilled laborers, approximately half were teamsters, blacksmiths, and barbers.

The formal education of blacks was strongly encouraged by the white citizens who volunteered to teach the black children during the day and the adults at night. The preacher from the Freedmen's Church together with the town's tradesmen, such as the printer, the shoemaker, the carpenter, and even a saloonkeeper, strengthened the civic infrastructure of the black community of Lawrence.

Topeka was the site of the drafting of the state constitution that would have outlawed both slavery and black immigration into Kansas. It took a lot of work to eliminate such clauses from the early drafts of the constitution. As a stop on the Underground Railroad, Topeka also saw an early influx of blacks. Despite the rush in Topeka to form a state free of blacks, Topeka may have been the first racially integrated residential area in the United States. Yet its residents, though freestaters, disliked blacks almost as much as they disliked slavery. Neither the white population nor, strangely, the previously established black community welcomed the new arrivals. As a consequence, a color line was established in Topeka that lasted for over a century. Segregation was maintained in the churches; and the destitute Exodusters were sent to facilities at the edge of town, which became permanent black enclaves and, eventually, strong cohesive communities, with many Exodusters finding work as mechanics, teamsters, maids, and laborers.

In addition, Topeka, with a population of over 10,000, was one of the cities that the Kansas legislature would allow to segregate its schools, which it did in 1879. Still, blacks were allowed to enroll in the state's public colleges and universities. Yet they did not always receive equal treatment in the internal administration of these campuses: in some instances the cafeterias, swimming pools, various cultural events, and classrooms were segregated. Even though school segregation was authorized in 1879, many high schools in Kansas were mixed until 1905. In fact, blacks received a relatively good education in Kansas, raising the stakes all the more in face of another half century of educational inequality. Nevertheless, the Kansas Industrial and Educational Institute was established in homage to Booker T. Washington's Tuskegee Institute.

The recalcitrance in a state with a moderately inclusive sentiment toward blacks is what led, in part, to the *Brown v. Board of Education* lawsuit of 1954. Kansas and particularly Topeka were prime locations for the arguments presented in *Brown v. Board of Education*. Having established branches of the NAACP, Kansas would find its education system used as a test case by the U.S. Supreme Court in 1954.

Wichita was the site of the first sit-in in response to the high court's decision in *Brown v. Board of Education*. Several black high-school and college students refused to leave the lunch counter of the local drugstore when they were spat upon and verbally abused upon requesting service. After eight days, the owners of the lunch counter gave in, ending for all intents and purposes segregation in that city. This was a landmark event, of course, and its influence would spread throughout the South and across the country.

The Army

Black Kansans, emboldened by Kansas' joyous embrace of the Emancipation Proclamation, became the first to enlist as soldiers in the Union army, preceding many other blacks residing in this western region. A determined abolitionist, Senator James H. Lane, was crucial to the settlement of blacks in Kansas, but as a military man and a senator, he was mainly interested in fending off the Missouri secessionists. For this purpose he raised a 1,200-man fighting force and invaded southwest Missouri. Apparently a champion of black interests, Lane invited fugitive slaves into his command as early as August 1861 and provided safe passage for the women and children into Kansas. The blacks that sought out his camp joined him and became the first African American bluecoats in the Union army.

In 1862, Brigadier General James G. Blunt—an ally of John Brown and a powerful abolitionist and friend to African Americans—authorized the

War Department of Kansas to enlist African Americans. Later that year, Senator Lane announced that he would enlist any fit black who wanted to join the 1st Kansas Colored Infantry Regiment. In response, the state created two regiments of black soldiers who were eager to abolish slavery, to help free relatives and friends, and to establish themselves as Americans. These enlistees came to represent about one of every six African Americans in Kansas. The commanders of the western army, who had no problem leading black soldiers, further abetted their successful enlistment. The 1st Kansas Colored would, in fact, become the first black group to engage the Confederate army.

Yet the creation of the regiment was callously done. Lane's mustering of black men into the 1st was apparently overly harsh, with Lane declaring that he would draft them if they did not volunteer. In fact, it is said that Lane did indeed use unsavory practices to draft or dragoon blacks into his regiment. But by 1865, one-sixth of the African American population, over 2,000 men, had joined Kansas' black regiments. These men would go on to fight Confederate guerrillas in the Battle of Honey Springs, the largest engagement in Indian Territory. Later, in the fall of 1864, while they again fought valorously at Honey Springs, they suffered a devastating defeat. As early as 1863, thousands of black Kansans staged the first Kansas State Colored Convention to celebrate these valiant men. Then, in 1883, the 1st Kansas Colored joined the U.S. Army of the Frontier, which consisted, remarkably, of Native Americans, whites, and blacks.

Twentieth Century

Overall, while between 1885 and 1940, the black population moderated, it subsequently rose dramatically, reaching 65,000 by 1940. From then on, blacks would enter Kansas in increasingly large numbers, in anticipation of employment spurred by the increased activity of the defense industry. After the *Brown v. Board of Education* ruling in 1954, another court decision called *Baker v. Carr* ordered legislative reapportionment in the state. The positive outcome of this order led to another surge in the black population in major Kansas cities. By 1990, the black population jumped in the state to 143,076, and by 2000, African Americans comprised 0.5 percent of the population, over 154,000 people.

One black sat in the Kansas legislature in 1956 and, six would serve in it by 1976. Towns and cities such as Leavenworth, Coffeyville, and Abilene would elect black mayors for the first time in the 1980s. It is also significant that in 1994, the federal government officially recognized the African and African-American Studies Department at the University of Kansas as a national resource center.

Notable African Americans

Brooks, Gwendolyn Elizabeth (1917–2000)

Pulitzer Prize–winning poet Gwendolyn Elizabeth Brooks was born in Topeka, Kansas, in 1917. She began writing poetry when she was seven and had her first work published at the age of 13. David and Keziah Brooks on her mother's side were fugitive slaves who fought for Kansas in the Civil War. Brooks grew up, for the most part, in Chicago. In 1945, her first book of poetry, *A Street in Bronzeville*, was an instant sensation. In 1949, her second book of poetry, *Annie Allen*, won the Pulitzer Prize for poetry, the first given to an African American. She went on to publish dozens of books of poetry, anthologies, and essays before her death on December 3, 2000, from complications due to cancer. In 1968 she was named poet laureate of Illinois, succeeding the late Carl Sandburg. President Bill Clinton awarded Brooks the National Medal of Art.

Poet Gwendolyn Brooks, holding a copy of her book, *A Street in Bronzeville*, published in 1945, was the first African American woman to win a Pulitzer Prize. (Library of Congress)

Bruce, Blanche Kelso (1841–1898)

Educator and politician Blanche K. Bruce was the second African American U.S. senator from Mississippi. He was born into slavery in Virginia in 1841. He moved with his master to Missouri before the Civil War. By 1861, Bruce had escaped from slavery and made his way to Lawrence, Kansas, where he survived Quantrill's raid. Blanche Bruce was credited with organizing the first school in the country for Negroes. Moving on to Mississippi by 1868, Bruce became the first black U.S. senator elected to a full term, 1875–1881 (Hiram R. Revels, the first from the state, served only from February 1870 to March 1871).

Carver, George Washington (c. 1861–1943)

Pioneer chemist and agriculturalist, George Washington Carver was born into slavery in Diamond Grove, Missouri, in the mid-1860s. An orphan, he moved to Fort Scott in 1878 to attend school. After finishing high school, Carver farmed for two years near Beeler in Ness County. He went on to Iowa State University, where he received his master's degree in 1896 in the area of agricultural science. Carver soon joined the faculty of Tuskegee Institute in Alabama, where he invented new uses for various crops, including making soybeans into plastic, sweet potatoes into cereal, and peanuts into more than 300 by-products such as milk, coffee, and shaving cream. Impressed with his work, Thomas Edison offered him $100,000 a year to come and work for him, but he thought he could do more good at Tuskegee. Although George Washington Carver received many awards for his work, he refused to accept any royalties from the sale of his products.

Chamberlain, Wilton Norman (1936–1999)

Basketball legend Wilt Chamberlain was born in Philadelphia, Pennsylvania, in 1936. When he entered Philadelphia's Overbrook High School, he was already 6' 11", and when he left Overbrook in 1955, the basketball team's record stood at 56–3. After this amazing high-school career, over 200 universities attempted to recruit him. Chamberlain decided to play college basketball at the University of Kansas. His astonishing success landed him on the pages of *Time, Life, Look,* and *Newsweek* magazines before he was 21 or had turned professional. In 1958, during a lull in this meteoric rise, he was offered $50,000 to join the Harlem Globetrotters. The amount was astounding for the times.

The next year, he finally entered the professional ranks with the Philadelphia Warriors. He was league Most Valuable Player (MVP) in 1960. When the team developed financial problems, Chamberlain was traded in 1965 to the Philadelphia 76ers. He was awarded a second MVP in 1966 when the 76ers posted a 55–25 record for the 1965–1966 NBA season. He was again league MVP in 1967 and 1968. In 1968, he was traded to the Los Angeles Lakers. Chamberlain latter coached the Conquistadors, sponsored a professional volleyball and a track-and-field team, went into business, entertainment, real estate, reopened the popular club Small's Paradise in Harlem, and made money in advertising. He wrote and published several books before his death.

Douglas, Aaron (1899–1979)

Aaron Douglas, painter and muralist extraordinaire, was born in 1899 in Topeka, Kansas. He graduated from Topeka High School in 1917 and received his B.A. degrees from the University of Nebraska–Lincoln in 1922 and the University of Kansas in 1923. In 1925, Douglas moved to Harlem, New York City, resigning his two-year post as teacher at Lincoln High School in Kansas City, Missouri. In Harlem, Douglas would develop into a great American painter and muralist of the Harlem Renaissance and earn a master's in fine arts from Teacher's College at Columbia University in New York in 1944. After founding the Art Department at Fisk University, Douglas taught there until his death on February 3, 1979. Art historian David Driskell dubbed Douglas the "father of Black American art," an honor based greatly on Douglas' mural series "Aspects of Negro Life," completed in 1934 for the 135th Street branch of the New York Public Library. The titles of the four murals are: "The Negro in an African Setting," "An Idyll of the Deep South," "From Slavery through Reconstruction," and "Song of the Towers."

McDaniel, Hattie (1895–1952)

Actress Hattie McDaniel of *Gone with the Wind* fame was born on June 10, 1895, in Wichita, Kansas, to former slaves and Civil War soldier Henry McDaniel and Susan Holbert. For best supporting actress as Mammy in *Gone with the Wind* (1939), she was the first black actress to win an Academy Award. Over the course of her career, McDaniel appeared in more than 300 films, receiving screen credits for about 80. In 1975, she was inducted into the Black Filmmakers Hall of Fame, and in 2006 became the first black Oscar winner honored with a U.S. postage stamp.

Parks, Gordon (1912–2006)

Photographer, film director, and novelist Gordon Parks was born on a small farm outside Fort Scott, Kansas, in 1912. He is known for his historic photographs, and his powerful essays and films. Born the youngest of 15 children, Parks' success as photographer at *Life* magazine, where he spent 20 years, led to his autobiography, *The Learning Tree* (1963), about his youth in Kansas. Subsequently turned into a screenplay, *The Learning Tree* (1969) led in 1971 to a highly acclaimed motion picture, *Shaft*.

Thompson, Linda Brown (1943–)

In 1951, Linda Brown Thompson was a third grade student at the all-black Monroe Elementary School in Topeka, when her father, Oliver L. Brown, brought a suit on her behalf to desegregate the city's public schools. The eventual U.S. Supreme Court decision, which desegregated the nation's schools in 1954, took the name of *Brown v. Board of Education of Topeka, Kansas*. In 1992, Monroe Elementary School was designated a national historic site.

Cultural Contributions

Fort Leavenworth

After the Civil War, northerner antipathy for blacks was so deep and raw that despite their heroism during the war, blacks found that whites greatly resisted integrating them into the regular army. In great part this led to the construction of Fort Leavenworth, the oldest military base west of the Mississippi. Housed here were the 9th and 10th Calvary regiments, consigned to protect white settlers from Native Americans in the western territories. As such, these regiments fought battles from Kansas to Arizona, including parts of Texas and New Mexico. It is still an active military base, having attained additional fame when its men served alongside Teddy Roosevelt and his Rough Riders in Cuba during the Spanish-American War. They also engaged in the historic pursuit of Pancho Villa in 1916.

John Brown Memorial State Park

John Brown Memorial State Park is where John Brown had executed five proslavery men in retaliation, it is said, for a raid on Lawrence, a town in support of Kansas becoming a free state. In return the proslavery forces attempted to burn down the nearby town of Osawatomie. One may find here a statue of Brown, a memorial to his men killed in the attack on Osawatomie, and a log cabin in which Brown lived and, it is believed, sheltered fugitive slaves. Whatever John Brown's criminal actions may have been, ignoring his raid on Harper's Ferry, an arsenal of the federal government, and the subsequent execution of him and his men, Osawatomie's citizens, toward the end of June, regularly celebrate his memory with a John Brown Jamboree.

Carver Homestead

Beeler is proud to be the "homestead of a genius"—George Washington Carver—who

After John Brown attended his first abolitionist meeting in 1837, he dedicated his life to the abolition of slavery. Over the next 20 years, Brown grew increasingly violent as he fought for this cause, and after a failed attack on the town of Harper's Ferry, Virginia (in present-day West Virginia), he was hanged by the U.S. government for murder, treason, and insurrection. (Library of Congress)

arrived in the state, like so many of his brethren, seeking to homestead in a region with far less racism than that found in Missouri where he was born. Carver, who predicted the location of oil in western Kansas, sold his 160-acre homestead long before oil was actually found. He raised corn and vegetables, and then left for college in Iowa, ensuring his illustrious career in education at Booker T. Washington's Tuskegee Institute in Alabama.

Fort Scott National Historic Site

The 1st Kansas Colored Infantry was housed at Fort Scott. Built in 1843, it was slated to close in 1853, but remained open and later housed the

Buffalo soldiers (late-nineteenth-century African American cavalry) in camp. Illustration by Frederic Remington. (Library of Congress)

Kansas Colored Volunteers and the 1st Kansas Colored Infantry.

Other African American historical sites in Kansas include the Richard Allen Cultural Center of Bethel AME Church, which commemorates contributions of African Americans to every phase of American life; the Buffalo Soldier Monument, which was begun at the behest of former Secretary of State Colin Powell at Fort Leavenworth; the Nicodemus Historic Site, reconstructing five historic structures in the all-black town of Nicodemus, including an AME and a Baptist church, a school, the Fletcher Hotel, and Township Hall; and the Kansas African American Museum in Wichita, housed in the Old Calvary Baptist Church (1917), presenting and preserving African American culture in visual arts, documents, exhibits, and special programs.

Bibliography

Athearn, Robert G. "Black Exodus: The Migration of 1879." *The Prairie Scout* 3 (1975): 86–97.

Athearn, Robert G. *In Search of Canaan: Black Migration to Kansas, 1879–1880.* Lawrence: University Press of Kansas, 1978.

Baigell, Matthew. "The Relevancy of Curry's Paintings to Black Freedom." *Kansas Quarterly* 2 (Fall 1970): 19–24.

Berwanger, Eugene H. *The Frontier against Slavery: Western Anti-Negro Prejudice and the Slavery Extension Controversy.* Urbana: University of Illinois Press, 1967.

Berwanger, Eugene H. "Hardin and Langston: Western Black Spokesmen of the Reconstruction Era." *Journal of Negro History* 64 (Spring 1979): 101–115.

Berwanger, Eugene H. *The West and Reconstruction.* Urbana: University of Illinois Press, 1981.

Boyer, James B. "A Voice from the Heart: Gospel Music in the African American Tradition." *Kansas Heritage* 1 (Spring 1993): 11–13.

Burton, Art A. *Black, Buckskin, and Blue: African American Scouts and Soldiers on the Western Frontier.* Austin, TX: Eakin Press, 1999.

Carper, James C. "The Popular Ideology of Segregated Schooling: Attitudes toward the Education of Blacks in Kansas, 1854–1900." *Kansas History* 1 (Winter 1978): 254.

Carroll, John M., ed. *The Black Military Experience in the American West.* New York: Liveright, 1971.

Chafe, William. "The Negro and Populism: A Kansas Case Study." *Journal of Southern History* 34 (August 1968): 404–419.

Chaudhuri, Nupur. " 'We All Seem Like Brothers and Sisters': The African American Community in Manhattan, Kansas, 1865–1940." *Kansas History* 14 (Winter 1991–1992): 270–288.

Cooper, Arnold. " 'Protection to All, Discrimination to None': The Parsons Weekly Blade, 1892–1900." *Kansas History* 9 (Summer 1986): 58–71.

Cornish, Dudley Taylor. "Kansas Negro Regiments in the Civil War." *Kansas Historical Quarterly* 20 (May 1953): 417.

Cox, Thomas C. *Blacks in Topeka, Kansas, 1865–1915: A Social History.* Baton Rouge: Louisiana State University Press, 1982.

Crockett, Norman I. *The Black Towns.* Lawrence: Regents Press of Kansas, 1979.

Dandridge, Deborah L., and William M. Tuttle. "Kansas." *Encyclopedia of African-American Culture and History.* Vol. 3. New York: Simon & Schuster, 1966, 1519–1522.

Dunham, Philip, and Everett L. Jones. *The Negro Cowboys.* Reprint ed. Lincoln: University of Nebraska Press, 1965.

Durham, Philip. "The Negro Cowboy." *American Quarterly* 7 (Fall 1955): 291–301.

Fisher, Mike. "The First Kansas Colored Massacre at Poison Springs." *Kansas History* 2 (Summer 1979): 121–128.

Fleming, Walter L. " 'Pap' Singleton, The Moses of the Colored Exodus." *American Journal of Sociology* 15 (July 1909): 61–68.

Fowler, Arlen L. *The Black Infantry in the West, 1869–1891.* Westport, CT: Greenwood, 1971.

Frehill-Rowe, Lisa M. "Postbellum Race Relations and Rural Land Tenure: Migration of Blacks and Whites to Kansas and Nebraska, 1870–1890." *Social Forces* 72 (September 1993): 77–92.

Garvin, Roy. "Benjamin, or 'Pap,' Singleton and His Followers." *Journal of Negro History* 33 (January 1948): 7–23.

Gatewood, Willard B., Jr. "Kansas Negroes and the Spanish-American War." *Kansas Historical Quarterly* 37 (Autumn 1971): 300.

Gordon, Jacob U. *Narratives of African Americans in Kansas, 1870–1992: Beyond the Exodust Movement.* Lewiston, NY: Edwin Mellen Press, 1993.

Greenbaum, Susan D., et al. *The Afro-American Community in Kansas City Kansas: A History.* Kansas City: City of Kansas City, Kansas, 1982.

Grenz, Suzanna M. "The Exodusters of 1879: St. Louis and Kansas City Responses." *Missouri Historical Review* 73 (October 1978): 54–70.

Hamilton, Kenneth Marvin. *Black Towns and Profit: Promotion and Development in the Trans-Appalachian West, 1877–1915.* Urbana: University of Illinois Press, 1991.

Hamilton, Kenneth Marvin. "The Origins and Early Promotion of Nicodemus: A Pre-Exodus, All-Black Town." *Kansas History* 5 (Winter 1982): 220.

Haywood, C. Robert. "The Hodgeman County Colony." *Kansas History* 12 (Winter 1989–1990): 210–221.

Haywood, C. Robert. "'No Less a Man': Blacks in Cow Town Dodge City, 1876–1886." *Western Historical Quarterly* 19 (May 1988): 161–182.

Hickey, Joseph V. "'Pap' Singleton's Dunlap Colony: Relief Agencies and the Failure of a Black Settlement in Eastern Kansas." *Great Plains Quarterly* 11 (Winter 1991): 23–36.

Higgins, Billy D. "Negro Thought and the Exodus of 1879." *Phylon* 32 (Spring 1971): 39–52.

Hulston, Nancy J. "'Our Schools Must Be Open to All Classes of Citizens': The Desegregation of the University of Kansas School of Medicine, 1938." *Kansas History* 19 (Summer 1996): 88–97.

Kansas State Historical Society, Historic Sites Survey. *Historic Preservation in Kansas. Black Historic Sites, A Beginning Point*. Topeka: Kansas State Historical Society, 1977.

Katz, Milton S., and Susan B. Tucker. "A Pioneer in Civil Rights: Esther Brown and the South Park Desegregation Case of 1948." *Kansas History* 18 (Winter 1995–1996): 234–247.

Katz, William Loren. *Black Pioneers: An Untold Story*. New York: Athenaeum Books, 1999.

Klassen, Teresa C., and Owen V. Johnson. "Sharpening the Blade: Black Consciousness in Kansas, 1892–1897." *Journalism Quarterly* 63 (Summer 1986): 298–304.

Kluger, Richard. *Simple Justice: The History of Brown v. Board of Education and Black America's Struggle for Equality*. New York: Alfred A. Knopf, 1976.

Leckie, William H. *The Buffalo Soldier: A Narrative of the Negro Cavalry in the West*. Norman: University of Oklahoma Press, 1967.

Lewallen, Kenneth A. "'Chief' Alfred C. Sam: Black Nationalism on the Great Plains, 1913–1914." *Journal of the West* 16 (January 1977): 49–56.

Marshall, Marguerite Mitchell. *An Account of Afro-Americans in Southeast Kansas, 1884–1984*. Manhattan, KS: Sunflower University Press, Wheatland Books, 1986.

McCoy, Sondra Van Meter. "Black Resistance to Segregation in the Wichita Public Schools, 1870–1912." *Midwest Quarterly* 20 (Autumn 1978): 64–77.

McCusker, Kristine M. "'The Forgotten Years' of America's Civil Rights Movement: Wartime Protests at the University of Kansas, 1939–1945." *Kansas History* 17 (Spring 1994): 26–37.

McKenzie, Sandra Craig. "Paul Wilson: Kansas Lawyer." *University of Kansas Law Review* 37 (Fall 1988): 1–59.

Meltzer, Milton. *Langston Hughes, a Biography*. New York: Thomas Y. Crowell Company, 1969.

Miller, Timothy. "Charles M. Sheldon and the Uplift of Tennesseetown." *Kansas History* 9 (Autumn 1986): 125–137.

Moore, Deedee. "Is There Anything Gordon Parks Can't Do?" *Smithsonian* 20 (April 1989): 147–164.

O'Connor, Patrick J. "The Black Experience and the Blues in 1950s Wichita." *Mid-America Folklore* 21 (Spring 1993): 1–17.

Painter, Nell Irvin. *Exodusters: Black Migration to Kansas after Reconstruction*. New York: Alfred A. Knopf, 1977.

Pantle, Alberta, ed. "The Story of a Kansas Freedman." *Kansas Historical Quarterly* 11 (November 1942): 341–369.

Parks, Gordon. *A Choice of Weapons*. Reprint ed. St. Paul: Minnesota Historical Society, 1986.

Parks, Gordon. *Gordon Parks: A Poet and His Camera*. New York: Viking Press, 1968.

Parks, Gordon. "A Look Back." *Kansas Quarterly* 7 (Summer 1975): 25–29.

Parks, Gordon. *Voices in the Mirror, an Autobiography.* New York: Doubleday, 1990.

Peoples, Morgan D. "Kansas Fever in North Louisiana." *Louisiana History* 11 (Spring 1970): 121–135.

Porter, Kenneth Wiggins. *The Negro on the American Frontier.* New York: Arno Press and the New York Times, 1971.

Quarles, Benjamin, ed. "John Brown Writes to Blacks." *Kansas Historical Quarterly* 41 (Winter 1975): 454.

Ravage, John W. *Black Pioneers: Images of the Black Experience on the North American Frontier.* Salt Lake City: University of Utah Press, 1997.

Reese, Linda Williams. " 'Working in the Vineyard': African-American Women In All-Black Communities." *Kansas Quarterly* 25, no. 2 (1994): 7–16.

Savage, W. Sherman. *Blacks in the West.* Westport, CT: Greenwood Press, 1976.

Schultz, Elizabeth. "Dreams Deferred: The Personal Narratives of Four Black Kansans." *American Studies* 34 (Fall 1993): 25–51.

Schwendemann, Glen. "The 'Exodusters' on the Missouri." *Kansas Historical Quarterly* 29 (Spring 1963): 25–40.

Schwendemann, Glen. "Nicodemus: Negro Haven on the Solomon." *Kansas Historical Quarterly* 34 (Spring 1968): 10.

Schwendemann, Glen. "St. Louis and the 'Exodusters' of 1879." *Journal of Negro History* 46 (January 1961): 32–46.

Schwendemann, Glen. "Wyandotte and the First 'Exodusters' of 1879." *Kansas Historical Quarterly* 26 (Autumn 1960): 233–249.

Scott, Mark. "Langston Hughes of Kansas." *Kansas History* 3 (Spring 1980): 2–25.

Sheridan, Richard B. "From Slavery in Missouri to Freedom in Kansas: The Influx of Black Fugitives and Contrabands into Kansas, 1854–1865." *Kansas History* 12 (Spring 1989): 28–47.

Strickland, Arvarh E. "Toward the Promised Land: The Exodus to Kansas and Afterward." *Missouri Historical Review* 69 (July 1975): 376–412.

Suggs, Henry Lewis, ed. *The Black Press in the Middle West, 1865–1985.* Westport, CT: Greenwood Press, 1996.

Taylor, Quintard. *In Search of the Racial Frontier: African Americans in the West.* New York W. W. Norton & Company, 1999.

Tidwell, John Edgar. "Frank Marshall Davis, ' Ad Astra, Per 'Aspera'." *Kansas History* 18 (Winter 1995–1996): 270–283.

Tillery, Tyrone. *Claude McKay: A Black Poets Struggle for Identity.* Amherst: University of Massachusetts Press, 1992.

Tuttle, William M., Jr., and Surenda Bhana. "Black Newspapers in Kansas." *American Studies* 13 (Fall 1972): 119–124.

Van Deusen, John G. "The Exodusters of 1879." *Journal of Negro History* 21 (April 1936): 111–129.

Williams, Nudie E. "Black Newspapers and the Exodusters of 1879." *Kansas History* 8 (Winter 1985–1986): 217.

Wilson, Paul E. *A Time to Lose: Representing Kansas in* Brown v. Board of Education. Lawrence: University Press of Kansas, 1995.

Wintz, Cary D. "Langston Hughes: A Kansas Poet in the Harlem Renaissance." *Kansas Quarterly* 8 (Spring 1976): 58–71.

Woods, Randall B. "After the Exodus: John Lewis Waller and the Black Elite, 1878–1900." *Kansas Historical Quarterly* 43 (Summer 1977): 172.

Woods, Randall B. *A Black Odyssey: John Lewis Waller and the Promise of American Life,*

1878–1900. Lawrence: Regents Press of Kansas, 1981.

Woods, Randall B. "Integration, Exclusion, or Segregation? The Color Line in Kansas, 1878–1900." *Western Historical Quarterly* 14 (April 1983): 181–198.

Woods, Randall B., and David A. Sloan. "Kansas Quakers and the 'Great Exodus': Conflicting Perceptions of Responsibility within a Nineteenth Century Reform Community." *Historian* 48 (November 1985): 24–40.

KENTUCKY

Dwayne Mack

Chronology

1770s	First American settlers in Kentucky bring slaves with them.
1792	*(June 1)* Kentucky joins the Union as the 15th state; the first state constitution legalizes slavery.
1808	Carter Tarrant and David Barrow, both Baptist ministers, found the Kentucky Abolition Society.
1815	The Kentucky legislature enacts a law limiting the importation of black slaves into the state.
1820	Slaves comprise almost 26 percent of the population of Kentucky.
1822	The Kentucky Abolition Society begins publishing one of the first antislavery periodicals produced in the United States.
1833	Kentucky legislators implement the Non-Importation Act, outlawing the importation of slaves into the Commonwealth through sale.
1842	Henry Bibb, a slave on a plantation in Oldham County, escapes to Detroit; Bibb later becomes a noted abolitionist and author of a famous autobiography, *Narrative of the Life and Adventures of Henry Bibb, An American Slave, Written by Himself.*
1845	Cassius Marcellus Clay begins publishing an antislavery newspaper, the *True American*, in Lexington, but death threats and mob violence force him to move the paper to Cincinnati within a few months.
1847	The antislavery *Louisville Examiner* begins publication; the newspaper remains in business until 1849.
1848	*(August)* In the largest coordinated slave escape attempted in the United States, some 50–70 armed slaves from various Kentucky counties flee their masters, though most are soon caught by the state militia.
1849	The passage of Kentucky's new proslavery constitution repeals the ban on the importation of slaves into the state.
1850s	With more that half of its white residents owning slaves, Louisville is a center of the slave trade, selling 3,000–4,000 blacks a year into slavery in the Deep South.
1855	Abolitionist John G. Fee opens Berea College to educate both blacks and whites.
1859	The racial backlash from John Brown's raid on Harper's Ferry, Virginia, forces abolitionist John Fee to close Berea College and flee Kentucky.
1860	Slaves comprise less than 8 percent of the population of Kentucky, a sharp decrease since 1820. The decrease is due to the declining need for slave labor on Kentucky's small farms, the movement of Kentucky slaveholders to Tennessee and Missouri, and the importation of Kentucky slaves to the Deep South.

1861	(May 20) Kentucky officially declares its neutrality in the war between the states.
1861	(September) Kentucky's neutrality breaks down and military forces from both sides operate in the state. The elected government of the state is Unionist, but pro-Confederate groups meet and enact an ordinance of secession in December; however, this act has little effect and Kentucky officially remains within the Union.
1861–1865	An estimated 75 percent of Kentucky's slaves are freed or escape to Union forces during the Civil War.
1863	(January 1) President Abraham Lincoln issues the Emancipation Proclamation, but his home state of Kentucky is excluded because the decree frees slaves only in those states that have seceded from the Union.
1864	Camp Nelson becomes an important Union recruiting post and training camp for African American soldiers; thousands of fugitive slaves seek refuge at the camp.
1865	(February 24) Kentucky refuses to ratify the Thirteenth Amendment to the U.S. Constitution abolishing slavery in the United States.
1866	John G. Fee reopens Berea College to black and white students.
1867	(January 8) Kentucky rejects the Fourteenth Amendment to the U.S. Constitution, which guarantees due process to all Americans.
1869	(March 12) Kentucky refuses to ratify the Fifteenth Amendment to the U.S. Constitution, which extends voting rights to African Americans.
1870	The congregation of Quinn Chapel AME Church in Louisville organizes the first protests against racial discrimination in the state by opposing segregation on city streetcars.
1892	The Kentucky General Assembly passes the Separate Coach Law, mandating separate interstate railroad cars for blacks and whites.
1896	U.S. Supreme Court Justice John Marshall Harlan, a native of Boyle County, dissents in Plessy v. Ferguson, which rules that "separate but equal" treatment for blacks and whites is constitutional. Jim Crow laws are now legalized by the Supreme Court.
1904	The Day Law, aimed specifically at Berea College, segregates public and private schools in Kentucky.
1908	The U.S. Supreme Court refuses to overturn the Day Law.
1912	Lincoln Institute near Louisville opens as a primary and secondary school for blacks.
1914	In response to lynching and white mob violence against blacks, African Americans in Louisville establish a branch of the National Association for the Advancement of Colored People (NAACP); the chapter also challenges the new Louisville Residential Segregation Ordinance, a restrictive housing ordinance that prohibits blacks from moving into homes previously owned by whites.

1917	In *Buchanan v. Warley*, the U.S. Supreme Court rules that the 1914 Louisville Residential Segregation Ordinance is unconstitutional.
1935	Charles W. Anderson, a Louisville attorney, becomes the first black elected to the Kentucky House of Representatives since Reconstruction; he sponsors bills to pay out-of-state tuition for African American students refused admittance to Kentucky colleges and universities.
1941	Charles Eubanks sues the University of Kentucky to attend its College of Engineering.
1948	Lyman T. Johnson is a plaintiff in a lawsuit to admit African Americans to the University of Kentucky's graduate school.
1949	The University of Kentucky allows blacks to attend its graduate and professional schools.
1950	The Day Law is amended to allow colleges and universities to admit black students.
1954	The U.S. Supreme Court, in *Brown v. Board of Education*, outlaws segregation in public schools. The University of Kentucky begins admitting black undergraduates.
1956	Louisville public schools begin the process of peaceful integration. Eight black students attempt to attend Sturgis High School, but a white mob stops them from entering the school.
1959	After the management of Louisville's Brown Theater refuses to admit blacks into showings of the movie *Porgy and Bess*, the NAACP Youth Council demonstrates in front of the theater.
1960	A chapter of the Congress of Racial Equality (CORE) is established in Louisville. The organization initiates nonviolent protests at downtown businesses that discriminate against blacks.
1960	The general assembly launches the Kentucky Commission on Human Rights, which is responsible for monitoring and prohibiting discrimination in employment.
1961	Civil rights activists boycott downtown Louisville clothing stores. The activists urge the community to purchase "nothing new for Easter" from stores that practiced discrimination. The campaign influences similar peaceful protests throughout the Commonwealth.
1961	Whitney Young Jr., a Kentucky native, is named executive director of the National Urban League.
1962	The Kentucky General Assembly directs cities to form their own commissions on human rights to prohibit discrimination in public accommodations and the hiring of teachers.
1963	(*June 27*) Kentucky ratifies the Twenty-fourth Amendment to the U.S. Constitution abolishing the poll tax.

1964	The federal government passes a Civil Right Act. In an effort to lobby Kentucky legislators to pass a strong statewide public accommodations bill, Dr. Martin Luther King Jr. addresses over 10,000 activists during the March on Frankfort.
1966	Kentucky becomes the first southern state to pass a Civil Rights Act. The law bans discrimination in employment, housing, and public accommodations.
1967	Mae Street Kidd, an African American, is elected to the Kentucky House of Representatives.
1968	*(May 27)* A riot erupts in Louisville's Parkland neighborhood when civil rights demonstrations are upset by rumors that a scheduled speech by Stokely Carmichael has been delayed by officials.
1968	Georgia Powers, an African American, is elected to the Kentucky State Senate.
1969	The Kentucky Commission on Human Rights establishes centers in Louisville and Lexington to assist African Americans in moving into white neighborhoods.
1969	African American students take control of an administration building at the University of Louisville to request that the campus add black studies courses.
1975	Court-enforced, cross-district busing to equalize the number of black and white public school students in Louisville causes two years of sporadic violent protests by whites.
1976	*(March 18)* Mae Street Kidd successfully lobbies the Kentucky General Assembly to ratify the Thirteenth, Fourteenth, and Fifteenth amendments to the U.S. Constitution.
2000	Denise Clayton is the first black woman appointed to a circuit judgeship in Kentucky.
2000	According to the 2000 Census, African Americans comprise about 300,000 of Kentucky's 3.6 million residents.
2001	Anthany Beatty becomes Lexington police chief.
2003	Robert C. White becomes Louisville chief of police.
2004	Elaine Farris becomes the first black superintendent of Shelby County Schools.
2004	Protests erupt after a white Louisville police officer shoots and kills Michael Newby, an African American teenager and the third black male to die at the hands of Louisville police in little more than a year.
2006	William E. McAnulty becomes the first African American justice of the Kentucky Supreme Court.
2007	The U.S. Supreme Court reverses itself and strikes down court-enforced school integration in Seattle and Louisville with a 5–4 vote.

2008   Conservative Kentucky voters support Hillary Clinton nearly 2 to 1 over African American Senator Barack Obama in Kentucky's Democratic presidential primary; during the general election, Obama does not campaign in Kentucky, which he loses to John McCain by winning only about 41 percent of the vote.

Historical Overview

Eighteenth Century to the Civil War

Decades before Kentucky joined the Union in 1792, the black experience there began in slavery. In the 1750s, blacks came to this untamed, wild, Appalachian region of the United States, as servants and/or slaves of their white masters. They were brought there to clear dense forests, plant and harvest crops, construct forts, and build the plantation infrastructure. During Kentucky's frontier years, whites also used their bondsmen to repel Indians who were trying to reclaim their land. In 1778, pioneer Daniel Boone relied on his slaves to protect his new settlement of Boonesborough from Indian attacks. When the Commonwealth of Kentucky was established, the fate of blacks was sealed that same year, as the state legalized slavery in Article IX of its constitution. According to historian George C. Wright in an article in the *Oral History Review* (1982, 76), slavery would become "the pillar of Kentucky's antebellum society and economy."

As early as the 1780s, thousands of slaves began to arrive in the commonwealth with white settlers. During the early republic years, the first federal government census of Kentucky was carried out in 1790, recording 11,830 slaves, 16 percent of the state population. Ten years later, over 40,000 slaves lived in the state, by then making up 18 percent of the population. By 1830, that slave population had jumped to some 165,000, 24 percent of Kentucky's population. Based on demographic profiles, the practice of slavery in Kentucky differed greatly from the way it was practiced in other Southern states. Unlike the large gang labor–driven plantations of the Lower South, most Kentucky slaves worked on farms in small groups of about five where they often labored in close proximity to the master.

At the peak of slavery, only 20 percent of bondsmen worked on big farms that had more than 20 slaves. On average, roughly 12 percent of slave owners had more than 20 bondsmen. In all, not more than 70 masters in the state at any one time held more than 50 slaves. Although Kentucky's slave population only ranked ninth out of the 15 slave states in 1860, the commonwealth had the third-highest total of slaveholders. Despite the small black population, slavery was well entrenched in Kentucky, however. And free black labor was relied on in every single county. By 1860, the then sizable urban city of Louisville contained close to 5,000 slaves, the largest population of slaves in the state. Slaves also lived in counties that touched the banks of the Ohio River, including Oldham and Henderson, the tobacco-rich counties of Trigg and Todd in the south-central part of the Commonwealth. In the mountainous eastern and southeastern sections, a much smaller number of slaves lived on small farms.

Kentucky had the most diverse agricultural economy and labor pool in the South. The climate and soil was not conducive to growing cotton as it was in Alabama and Mississippi, or sugarcane as in Louisiana or rice as in the Low Country of South Carolina. When it came to labor, most slaves worked more than 14 hours a day under brutal and dangerous conditions. The fields of Kentucky yielded bountiful crops; and male and female slaves of all ages cultivated corn, tobacco, and hemp.

By the mid-1800s, for example, hemp was the largest and most lucrative crop in Kentucky. Slaves were involved in every aspect of the production of that herb, from tilling the soil, plowing the fields, and dispersing seeds. Once the plant was harvested, slaves worked in factories that processed hemp into manufactured goods like cordage, bale rope, durable bags to hold cotton, and canvas ship sails. The state eventually produced close to 18,000 tons of hemp; half of the total amount produced in the country. The number of hemp-producing plantations by the early 1850s totaled over 3,500. This profitable crop contributed to Fayette County having one of the largest slave populations and becoming the biggest hemp producer in Kentucky. Slaveholders maintained a sizable workforce in that county, an area where whites barely outnumbered blacks.

In addition to the profitable hemp industry, Kentucky slaves also cultivated corn. In the 1840s, Kentucky was the second-largest corn producer in the country. In the 1850s, the large plantations of Robert Wilmot Scott of Franklin County and Merit Williams of Scott County produced thousands of bushels of corn. The plantation system used children as young as eight to work in the labor-intensive corn and hemp fields.

Though slaveholders ran efficient, economically prosperous operations, they barely provided for their slaves. Blacks survived in squalid conditions. Two to three families often shared small, dark, poorly ventilated, windowless, dirt floor cabins. They slept on homemade mattresses of straw or corn shuck. Under such conditions, illness and disease often spread throughout the slave cabin and the entire slave quarters. When it came to apparel, most masters only purchased clothing or cloth once a year; slaves made their own clothes. As a result of the heavy wear-and-tear on slave clothes from working in the fields, bondsmen wore tattered clothing, and the majority went without shoes. Their nutritiously (vitamins and calories) deficient diets consisted of only small weekly rations of fatty meat (typically pork fat: heads and feet), cornmeal, and molasses. Rarely did masters give slaves the independence

to hunt animals or to grow nutritional vegetables near their cabins to supplement their meager diets. In addition to experiencing backbreaking field labor and poor living conditions, thousands of slaves worked in the large urban cities of Louisville and Lexington as carriage and wagon drivers, tailors, and washerwomen. Highly skilled slaves labored as cooks, carpenters, brick masons, shoemakers, coopers, and blacksmiths. By the time of the Civil War, approximately a quarter of the slaves in Louisville were hired workers. This system of hiring out their surplus of bondsmen for money allowed masters to earn more revenue during the harvesting off-season. Slaveholders earned over $200 by contracting out their skilled slaves. It also forced slaves to labor hard year-round without breaks between jobs. While some slaves worked in skilled trades, others worked as waiters, house servants, factory workers, stevedores, and on bridge and road construction crews. Even in this environment, children labored long, hard hours to fulfill production quotas in bagging, brick, nail, and leather tanning factories. In rural areas like Greenup County, slaves and free blacks worked alongside each other in the profitable distillery industry. In Madison County, the same group labored in a meatpacking plant that earned $216,000 annually.

Slave labor also played a major role in producing and manufacturing raw materials for national consumption. In the eastern part of the state, slaves worked in the dangerous, but profitable, extractive industries at salt and iron works, coal mines, and in the lumber industry. For example, in Clay, Floyd, Greenup, Lewis, and Pulaski counties, slaves satisfied the statewide and national markets by mining and manufacturing hundreds of thousands of barrels of salt each year.

In the early 1800s, Kentucky plantation owners found it profitable to export livestock, corn, and slaves to meet the demands of other southern markets and plantations. Historically, one of the most horrific aspects of slave trading was the permanent breakup of the black family. The agents of slave trading firms regularly scoured the countryside in search of slaves to purchase by circulating handbills and posters and/or by placing ads in newspapers like the Lexington *Observer and Reporter* or Frankfort's *Commonwealth*. Both regularly announced slave market auctions in Lexington, Louisville, Winchester, and other cities. Advertised as "Bucks" and "Wenches," slave fathers, mothers, husbands, wives, and even children were auctioned off by the thousands. As part of the interstate trade process, slave coffles, jails, and holding pens, which contained heavily chained bondsmen, were a common sight throughout the Bluegrass State. Prices for individual slaves in Kentucky ranged from as low as $10 to as high as several thousand dollars. For example, women beyond the childbearing age were sold for only a couple of hundred dollars; whereas fertile "fancy girls" (beautiful, young mulatto women) were sometimes purchased for over $2,000 for the future as concubines or prostitutes.

Moreover, Kentucky masters, like most other slave masters in other southern states, sexually assaulted black women. The sexual abuse often yielded progeny. These biracial offspring helped fulfill the master's desire to increase the slave population for either trading or labor. For the purpose of breeding slaves, masters also often maintained more women than men on a plantation.

With a firm grip on the interstate slave trade, Kentuckians between 1830 and 1860 exported some 77,000 blacks to other southern plantations. During that period, the state passed the Non-Importation Act of 1833, which prohibited bondsmen from entering Kentucky by purchase or to trade to other southern markets. The law slowed the rapid growth of slaves in Kentucky. Although the law was repealed in 1849 by proslavery legislators, on the eve of the Civil War, the slave population had only gradually increased to 225,483, or approximately 19 percent of the total population of the state.

Although no major slave revolts occurred in Kentucky, state legislators were fixated on preventing rebellion. Despite such a small slave population, commonwealth officials adopted stringent Slave Codes in 1792 in an effort to deny blacks an opportunity to gain their freedom. The codes were then intensified over time. Since slaves were not considered citizens, the repressive laws prohibited them from marrying, testifying in court against whites, traveling without a pass, challenging whites either verbally or physically, owning weapons, stealing, conspiring to revolt, violating curfew, and numerous other offenses. Those slaves accused of breaking these laws received swift and brutal punishment from the slaveholder, overseer, or trusted black driver. Masters used various inhumane methods to discipline slaves. Whipping a bondsman in public at a post in the town square or on a plantation was the most common way to punish blacks and deter other blacks from rebelling. For more serious offenses like running away or fighting with a white, slaves of both sexes experienced mutilation, including cropped ears and even a chopped-off foot or finger(s). The use of the hot iron to brand the face, buttock, breast, palm, leg, and/or arm of a slave was another cruel method that masters used to terrorize slaves.

Similar to the repressive nature of slavery in the Deep South, Kentucky masters treated their slaves just as inhumanely. As a result, Kentucky slaves longed for their freedom and used various forms of resistance to register their discontent with what some scholars call the "peculiar institution." To stop production, some feigned sickness, broke tools, or burned fields or barns. One of the most extreme forms of rebellion was poisoning a slaveholder or entire slaveholding family with arsenic. The most dramatic form of resistance was running away to free states or even to Canada.

The free northern states of Ohio, Indiana, and Illinois that bordered Kentucky were popular escape destinations for fugitive slaves traveling

John Rankin House, Ripley, Ohio, home of the famed abolitionist and conductor, whose involvement in the Underground Railroad was truly a family affair. (Tom Calarco)

the Underground Railroad. Runaways followed the North Star and stopped at stations or checkpoints along the Ohio River where their white and/or black conductors would lead them to freedom. At the home and Underground Railroad stop of one white abolitionist, John Rankin, in Ripley, Ohio, slaves enjoyed temporary refuge once they crossed over the river before they continued northward on their quest for freedom. Some of the more successful runaway slaves included Lewis Clarke, Josiah Henson, and Henry Bibb. Once they gained their freedom, they all became ardent abolitionists.

Despite the heavy shadow of slavery, a small free black population was able to coexist with bondsmen. For example, in 1860, 10,600 blacks lived outside of bondage in Kentucky in close proximity to slaves. However, even this free black population endured repressive laws. Paying an annual fee, free blacks were required to register and carry their documentation at all times to prove their social status. If charged or even accused of a crime, such as assaulting whites, carrying an unconcealed weapon, selling alcohol, conspiring with slaves, hiding fugitive slaves, free blacks were punished by whipping, incarceration, enslavement, or death. The efforts of some whites opposed to slavery began as early as the 1790s. Although he never manumitted his slaves, David Rice, a Presbyterian preacher, in 1792 published

Overlooking the Ohio River Valley from the John Rankin House in Ripley. (Tom Calarco)

the state's first antislavery pamphlet, titled *Slavery Inconsistent with Justice and Good Policy*. During sermons in Woodford County, Carter Tarrant, a Baptist minister, spoke out against slavery. His unpopular position caused his excommunication from the Baptist Church in 1806. He continued his advocacy, however, and the following year he founded an antislavery organization, the Baptized Licking-Locust Association, Friends of Humanity.

Other antislavery organizations in the early 1800s, such as the Kentucky Abolition Society (KAS) and the Kentucky Colonization Society, intensified the call for an end to slavery. The KAS, for example, spread its antislavery message through its periodical, the *Abolition Intelligencer and Missionary Magazine*. As the states moved closer to war, individuals such as white Kentuckian lawyer James Speed passionately opposed

slavery. He worked to convince state officials that slavery was a sin. By 1864, he had become pessimistic about the commonwealth becoming an instrument to abolish slavery and instead called on the federal government to emancipate slaves.

Civil War and Reconstruction

Although the Civil War brought a glimmer of hope, Kentucky slaves continued to face more challenges. In the early years of the war, Union soldiers returned slaves who had fled to their military camps to their masters by the thousands. In some cases soldiers even turned them away to starve and die. As the war progressed, Kentucky's slaveholders remained committed to the Union and expected President Abraham Lincoln to preserve slavery in that state. On January 1, 1863, Lincoln signed the Emancipation Proclamation, freeing slaves in those states at war with the Union (not including the commonwealth), thus keeping the institution intact in Kentucky. However, after the proclamation, Union soldiers at Camp Nelson in Kentucky and elsewhere ended the policy of returning fugitive slaves. Despite their mistreatment in the military, approximately 25,000 black Kentuckians fought to preserve the Union. Of the slave states, Kentucky ranked second highest in terms of the number of black soldiers serving the North.

White Kentuckians after the Union victory in 1865 were slow to free their bondsmen. In early 1865, they voted against the Thirteenth Amendment, which freed slaves and made them citizens and equal to whites. The ratification of that amendment by other states in December finally emancipated all Kentucky blacks. Whites in Kentucky then challenged the legality of the Fourteenth and Fifteenth Amendments. Despite white opposition to black freedom, however, the former slaves made social, political, and economic progress during Reconstruction (1865–1877). The Freedmen's Bureau, black churches, African American politicians, and northern philanthropists collaborated to establish and operate public schools, hospitals, orphanages, and nursing homes for former slaves.

With the end of Reconstruction in 1877, black Kentuckians began to experience major setbacks. Despite the passage of the Civil Rights Act of 1875, which outlawed discrimination in public accommodations, the federal government failed to stem violence against blacks or declare illegal state-implemented, repressive black codes. By the late nineteenth century, white racist attitudes appeared as Jim Crow laws. Such de jure segregation in Kentucky foreshadowed and paralleled ongoing segregation legislation. Four years before the groundbreaking *Plessy v. Ferguson* decision in 1896 in which the U.S. Supreme Court supported "separate but equal," the Kentucky General Assembly passed the separate coach law,

mandating separate interstate railroad cars for black and white passengers. Despite strong opposition from the mostly black members of the Anti-Separate Coach Movement, the U.S. Supreme Court upheld the law in 1900.

Early Twentieth Century

At the beginning of the twentieth century, the black population of Kentucky totaled 285,000 out of 1.86 million whites. Blacks migrated during the new century in large numbers to northern states like Indiana, Illinois, Ohio, and Michigan to earn better wages. Louisville and Lexington contained the largest black populations. These urban areas also received the largest number of blacks migrating from racially repressive rural areas.

During the first half of the twentieth century, most African Americans worked in labor-intensive positions. In rural Kentucky, some African Americans remained on former plantations, existing as sharecroppers. A small number of blacks became prosperous farmers. In urban Louisville, black men found positions as janitors, waiters, bartenders, store clerks, restaurant kitchen helpers, chauffeurs, bellhops, and busboys. Black women found corresponding types of work as cooks, hairdressers, manicurists, housekeepers, and waitresses. Most black women worked in private households as domestics.

Some blacks became entrepreneurs during this time. They owned and operated their own restaurants, taverns, grocery stores, construction companies, junkyards, cab companies, drugstores, physician offices, beauty solons, and barbershops. In the small city of Henderson, the African American barbers, tailors, and shoemakers served both white and black clienteles. In the larger cities, as in most urban areas, some black-owned financial-service-oriented companies did emerge. For example, by the early twentieth century, the Louisville-based companies, Mammoth Life and

Accident Insurance Company and the Domestic Insurance Company, sold insurance policies to blacks throughout the state, becoming one of the nation's largest black-owned businesses. Before the collapse of most banks during the Great Depression, two black-owned Louisville banks, American Mutual Savings Bank and the First Standard Bank, also thrived.

Besides the various occupations blacks worked in, the black church served as the foundation of the community. During periods of economic hardship—unemployment or bereavement— these churches became unofficial welfare agencies for African Americans who needed financial assistance. Kentucky churches maintained emergency funds to help with delinquent debt and served not only as meeting places for spiritual and social comfort, but also as schools.

Black churches also contributed to the educational attainment of the black community. Some churches founded black colleges. In Louisville, Reverends Charles H. Parrish and William J. Simmons and other African American leaders solicited money from white philanthropists to open Eckstein Norton Institute in Cane Springs in 1890 (the school closed in 1911).

Unfortunately, Kentucky still lagged far behind other southern states in providing blacks with primary, secondary, and postsecondary education. By 1916, only nine black public high schools existed in the commonwealth. Other than the Kentucky Normal and Industrial Institute for Colored Persons (the school was renamed Kentucky State University in 1972), some of the only colleges and universities opened to African Americans from 1904 to 1948 were Simmons College, West Kentucky Industrial College for Colored Persons, and Louisville Municipal College for Negroes.

In conjunction with some progress in educational attainment, black Kentuckians still faced similar racial discrimination to their counterparts in the lower South. In 1882, the federal circuit court ordered in the case of *Commonwealth of Kentucky v. Jesse Ellis* that Kentucky legislators provide equal funding to black and white schools, but then Kentucky officials breached the decision by withholding adequate funds to black schools. As director of the Kentucky Commission on Interracial Cooperation, James Bond in 1924 conducted a survey of the public school system and reported that the state's inadequate support of black schools cheated African American educational institutions. To increase funding for these schools, Bond traveled statewide, where he was successful in encouraging citizens to pass bond proposals to build black schools and lobbying school boards to raise the pay of black teachers. State officials also enforced segregation on the college level. In 1904, the general assembly passed the Day Law, aimed specifically at Berea College, a private, integrated college that since Reconstruction had enrolled an equal number of black and white students. The law prohibited integrated education in Kentucky and in 1908, the U.S. Supreme Court in *Berea College v. Kentucky* refused to overturn the state's decision. Berea officials quickly responded by using part of its endowment to establish Lincoln Institute in 1912, a private primary and secondary school for blacks in Lincoln Ridge near Louisville.

Kentucky's government officials also utilized other legislative measures to limit black progress. Jim Crow laws outlawed interracial marriage and prohibited blacks from entering public accommodations, including hotels, restaurants, hospitals, libraries, public and private schools, and public parks. In housing, blacks were confined to impoverished neighborhoods.

In the early twentieth century, African American Kentuckians reenergized their struggle for equality through new civil rights organizations. A few years after the founding of the NAACP in New York in 1909, concerned blacks in Kentucky created local chapters. For example, the Louisville NAACP branch vigorously worked with the national legal redress team to

Students at Berea College, including both white and African American, 1899. (Library of Congress)

end housing discrimination in that city. In 1917, the U.S. Supreme Court in *Buchanan v. Warley* reversed the Louisville residential segregation ordinance.

Black Kentuckians also experienced lynching. In accordance with the general racist sentiment of the time, state legislators refused to outlaw lynching. Between 1885 and 1940, white lynch mobs murdered over 250 blacks in Kentucky alone. The "Red Summer" of 1919 produced 25 race riots in American cities, and racist mobs in Corbin, Kentucky, terrorized blacks, getting them to flee that small rural town. During the next decade, white mobs in Bell, Estill, and Mercer Counties would also try to physically force blacks from their lands.

Despite such wholesale white violence, African Americans continued to persevere. During the Great Depression, African Americans still sought racial equality and financial relief. President

Franklin Delano Roosevelt signed into law in 1933 an economic stimulus program known as the New Deal that established government agencies and projects that created jobs and strengthened the economy. Most New Deal programs eluded black Kentuckians. However, some African Americans gained from Roosevelt's initiatives. During the 1930s and early 1940s, three segregated African American Civilian Conservation Corps (CCC) camps were established—Fort Knox in Hardin County, Russellville in Logan County, and Mammoth Cave in Edmonson—to attend to Kentucky's neglected woodlands.

At Mammoth Cave, black enrollees from Camp 510 fought fires, dug firebreaks, completed reforestation and soil erosion projects, constructed parks and recreational areas, strung telephone and electrical wires, laid roads, placed sewers and waterlines, and erected lookout towers. Camp 510 eventually transformed the area's infrastructure into a popular national park by building cottages and cabins and paving a parking lot for visitors. The hard work of these African American enrollees enriched the quality of life for visitors to the longest cave system in the world.

By World War II, African American Kentuckians were mounting major challenges to Jim Crow laws. Lyman T. Johnson, president of the Louisville Association of Teachers in Colored Schools from 1939 to 1941, succeeded in pressuring the state to end salary inequality for Louisville black teachers. Johnson's activism intensified during the burgeoning Civil Rights Movement. He served as a member of the Kentucky Civil Liberties Union and as president of the Louisville NAACP branch, where in 1948 he became a plaintiff in an important civil lawsuit that in 1949 gave black students the opportunity to attend law, pharmacy, engineering, and graduate schools at the University of Kentucky in Lexington.

Civil Rights Era and Beyond

In 1950, still some four years before the monumental *Brown v. Board of Education* case, Berea College reintegrated with the repeal of the Day Law. College officials slowly readmitted African Americans; approximately 10 black students attended Berea from 1950 to 1954. In 1954, Jessie Reasor Zander became the first African American student to earn a degree after Kentucky desegregation when she graduated from Berea with a degree in elementary education.

After the *Brown* decision in 1954, the Kentucky public school system was slow to support the ruling, however. In 1955, only 200 black students integrated into white schools. In the western part of the state, whites were even more resistant to desegregation. In Sturgis, Kentucky, known as a Ku Klux Klan haven, 500 segregationists brandished pitchforks and shovels while screaming "go home nigger" as they blocked black students from entering Sturgis High School in 1956. The

protests that year forced black students to abandon their integration efforts, but the following academic year they were admitted to the high school. In that same decade, whites also protested school desegregation in Hopkins County and Henderson County. Fortunately, not all efforts to desegregate were met with virulent white opposition. Louisville became one of the first urban southern cities to desegregate its public school with slight white opposition.

By 1960, Kentucky's black population had increased to 216,000 compared to 2.82 million white residents. Despite this small African American population, the Civil Rights Movement gained momentum. Frank Stanley Jr., an African American community activist, led a series of demonstrations with African American youth. Some of the children were junior members of the CORE and the NAACP. Inspired by college students in the Deep South, Raoul Cunningham, an African American teenager and Louisville NAACP youth leader, mobilized his peers to participate in these nonviolent demonstrations under Stanley's direction outside of Louisville's segregated department stores. The activists, singing freedom songs, carried signs that urged people "Don't buy here" and "nothing new for Easter" from stores that practiced discrimination. The campaign influenced similar direct-action protests throughout the commonwealth.

After the federal government passed the Civil Rights Act in 1964, segregation in the commonwealth still managed to continue. In 1964, African American activist Frank Stanley Jr. founded the Allied Organization for Civil Rights (AOCR) in Kentucky to lobby the state to pass a progressive public accommodations and fair employment law to reinforce the federal law. On March 5, Dr. Martin Luther King Jr. marched with 10,000 activists at an AOCR co-organized protest in Frankfort. The marchers included hundreds of students from Kentucky State University, Berea College, the University of Kentucky, and the University of Louisville. On the steps of the state capitol, King, along with James Farmer, Wyatt T. Walker, Jackie Robinson, and other civil rights supporters, lobbied for strong civil rights legislation.

A year later, both black and white Kentuckians displayed strong support for the Civil Rights Movement in the Deep South. On March 25, 1965, hundreds of Kentuckians marched with King, this time in Montgomery, Alabama, during the last leg of the Selma-to-Montgomery march. The participation of Kentucky students and other activists from around the world contributed to the passage of the 1965 Voting Rights Act. This federal legislation would increase the number of black voters not only in the Black Belt states of the Deep South, but also in Kentucky. Later in the decade, the new voting bloc enabled more Bluegrass blacks to win political positions.

Back in Kentucky, after two years of continued pressure, the state passed the Civil Rights Act on July 27, 1966. Blacks now had access to public accommodations, and the law empowered the Kentucky Commission on Human Rights (KCHR) to promote the law. In 1966, the KCHR was an 11-member board that included Frank L. Stanley Sr., the African American editor of the *Louisville Defender*, a black newspaper, and a staff of eight field investigators that included black young college graduates. They all had experience advocating social change as participants in the Civil Rights Movement. That first year, the KCHR investigated and mediated dozens of discrimination cases.

In the late 1960s, black churches continued to contribute to civil rights. Even after passage of the Civil Rights Act, most African American Kentuckians still experienced housing discrimination. In 1966, African American churches in Louisville, including Plymouth Congregational and Broadway Temple African Methodist Episcopal Zion, mobilized behind the brother of Dr. Martin Luther King Jr., A. D. King, through open housing marches to challenge that form of racism. A combination of

marches, newly elected state Senator Georgia Davis Powers urging colleagues in the Senate to support a fair housing bill, and black representatives Mae Street Kidd and Hughes McGill lobbying the House convinced the Kentucky General Assembly to pass the Fair Housing Law of 1968. It was a monumental law in the South.

Following the assassination of Martin Luther King Jr., many American cities, including some in Kentucky, erupted in racial violence. Blacks in urban areas like Louisville and Lexington and rural areas like Owensboro experienced their greatest race-related disturbances in years. In 1968, the Commission on Human Rights reported that the state had experienced seven racially motivated bombings. Black churches, an African American community center, and a black-owned pharmacy were destroyed.

In late May 1968 in Louisville's West End, two black teenagers were slain; 472 African Americans were arrested during violent protests. Over 1,400 National Guard troops restored order. Racial violence was not limited to urban areas. In September, a group of black Bereans challenged members of the National States' Rights Party, a white supremacy group. At a public rally, the racist supremacy group provoked members of the small black community with inflammatory comments. When the African Americans confronted them, a gun battle ensued, leaving Elza Rucker, a white, and Lenoa Bogg, a black Madison County resident, both dead. With the passage of the Kentucky Civil Rights Act, the decade of the '60s concluded on a high note. Armed with solid legal authority, the KCHR reported that by the last year of the decade, private businesses and government agencies had hired hundred of blacks; hundreds of African Americans had graduated from colleges; white-owned restaurants were serving blacks; and hundreds of homes in white neighborhoods and thousands of apartments in white complexes had became available to blacks.

In no area did African Americans in the Bluegrass State achieve more success than in politics in the 1960s. By the close of the decade, African Americans filled city council and mayoral seats in both large and small cities. Jerry D. Sanders of Nicholasville and Joseph K. Hobbs of Versailles became council members in their respective cities. In Glasgow, Luska J. Tyman was elected mayor. Some 24 African Americans served as state, county, city, and school officials in cities such as Danville, Paducah, Russellville, Shelbyville, and Munfordville.

As blacks gained politically, the Civil Rights Movement intensified further. Some African American Kentuckians joined the Black Power Movement. When colleges and universities in the commonwealth denied blacks adequate educational opportunities, they responded as their counterparts did at other schools such as Howard University and San Francisco State College. At the University of Louisville on May 1, 1969, members of the Black Student Union (BSU) seized control of the office of the Dean of Arts and Sciences and successfully convinced the university to adopt a black studies program.

In the next decade, the concerns of activists young and old shifted. In 1970, members of the University of Louisville's BSU focused its energies on removing crime and drugs in the black community by founding Stop Dope Now. In the political arena, in the late 1970s, Lyman T. Johnson became a member of the Jefferson County Board of Education. During her Senate tenure, Dorothy Powers chaired two important committees. Kentucky finally, in 1976, ratified the Thirteenth Amendment. In the 1980s, black Kentuckians also influenced national politics. In 1984 and again in 1988, Powers served as the state chairperson for Jesse Jackson's presidential bids.

In 2000, there were 300,000 African Americans in Kentucky compared to 3.64 million whites, and blacks continued to face new and familiar economic, political, and social challenges. Compared to whites, a disproportionate number of African Americans have been stricken with HIV/AIDS. Poverty, high unemployment, inadequate education, drug and alcohol addiction, and crime continue to plague black communities in the commonwealth. In recent years, police brutality in urban areas, such as Louisville, has gained national attention. For example, in 2004, the city's west end area experienced more racial controversy when during an arrest, a white officer, McKenzie Mattingly, fired three shots into the back of handcuffed suspect Michael Newby, an African American teenager, killing him. Newby's death sparked emotional protests and marked the third time in 13 months that Louisville police had killed a black male.

Despite these problems, some blacks in the Bluegrass State have experienced success. In the new millennium, the two largest urban cities in Kentucky selected African Americans to head their police forces. In 2001, Lexington hired Anthany Beatty as police chief, and two years later, Louisville hired Robert C. White as chief. In education, in 2004, Elaine Farris became the first black superintendent of Shelby County Schools. In 2000, Denise Clayton became the first black woman appointed to a circuit judgeship in Kentucky, and in 2006, William E. McAnulty became the first African American state Supreme Court justice.

Kentucky blacks originally arrived in the commonwealth as slaves, and upon their emancipation, they faced invasive discrimination. After some reasonable social progress during Reconstruction, blacks again experienced intense racism in the form of Jim Crow laws that defined their subordinate status as less than that of full citizenship. Still, African Americans pushed forward, establishing their own churches, schools, and social and political organizations. These organizations served as major social and spiritual outlets to strengthen many blacks and sustain them well into the twentieth century. By the 1960s, African American Kentuckians were indeed well prepared to challenge racial discrimination in their state. They relied on the judicial process and direct action campaigns to gain their civil rights. The activism of the 1960s opened increased political, social, and economic opportunities for African Americans. Nonetheless, black Kentuckians continue today to encounter old and new challenges, and it is obvious their historical resiliency will continue to sustain them in the years ahead.

Notable African Americans

Ali, Muhammad
(Cassius Marcellus Clay, Jr.) (1942–)

Muhammad Ali was born Cassius Marcellus Clay in Louisville in 1942. Under the guidance of Fred Stoner, an African American boxing coach in Louisville, Clay took up boxing and won six Kentucky Golden Gloves titles before winning a gold medal in boxing at the 1960 Olympics. In February 1964, Clay defeated Sonny Liston for the heavyweight title, even though the fight was almost cancelled when the promoter discovered that Clay had been seen with controversial Nation of Islam leader Malcolm X. After the fight, Clay announced his conversion to Islam and the change of his name to Muhammad Ali. During the 1960s and 1970s, Ali evolved into an athlete activist during the height of the civil rights movement and the anti–Vietnam War movement. During the war, boxing officials stripped Ali of his heavyweight title for his refusal to serve in the military. When the boxing commission reinstated his license, Ali won his title back two more times, becoming the first boxer to win the heavyweight title three times. Today, although Ali suffers from Parkinson's disease, the former champion has become a humanitarian and ambassador of good will.

Muhammad Ali wearing the 24-carat gold-plated championship belt, 1964. (Library of Congress)

Bibb, Henry (1815–1854)

Henry Bibb, a fugitive slave, was born in Shelby County, Kentucky, on May 10, 1815. His father was the white state Senator James Bibb, and his mother was Mildred Jackson, a slave. As a child, Bibb witnessed his siblings sold to different slave owners. After several failed escape attempts, he successfully escaped in 1837. Bibb later returned to Kentucky to free his family but was captured. He eventually permanently escaped. In 1842 Bibb, along with other well-known black abolitionists Frederick Douglass and William Wells Brown, began a lecturing tour against slavery. Bibb also joined the antislavery Liberty Party. In 1849, in recognition of his activism, the Anti-Slavery Society published his autobiography, *Narrative of the Life and Adventures of Henry Bibb, An American Slave*. In 1851, in an effort to persuade runaways and free blacks to live in Canada, Bibb and fellow fugitive slave, Josiah Henson, founded the Refugees' Home Colony in Canada. He also founded Canada's first black newspaper, *Voice of the Fugitive.*

Hudson, J. Blaine (1949–)

J. Blaine Hudson, African American civil rights leader and educator, is a native of Louisville, Kentucky. Hudson serves as a history professor and chairman of the Pan-African Studies Department and associate dean for retention and diversity in the College of Arts and Sciences at the University of Louisville. He also serves as chairman of the Kentucky African American Heritage Commission. Hudson first experienced racial discrimination as a youngster in the late 1950s when he was denied entrance into a Louisville movie theater. While a student at the University of Louisville, he participated in a Black Student Union (BSU) demonstration at the dean's office in Arts and Sciences, where he and other students demanded improvements in course offerings for African American students. The protesters were arrested and charged under the Kentucky Anti-Riot Act, but the state eventually dropped the charges. The protest resulted in the university deciding to hire more black faculty and introduce black studies courses into the curriculum.

Kidd, Mae Street (1909–1999)

Mae Street Kidd was an African American civil rights leader and politician. She served in the Kentucky House of Representatives from 1968 to 1984, representing Louisville's 41st legislative district. She cosponsored legislation to make Dr. Martin Luther King Jr.'s birthday a state holiday and also the 1968 Fair Housing Act, which provided accessible, low-income housing to all Kentucky residents. In the 1970s, Kidd continued her housing advocacy efforts, and following a two-year battle on the House floor, she introduced House Bill No. 27 to the House, and it

became law in 1972. The law established the Kentucky Housing Corporation, which promoted and financed low-income housing. In 1948, Kidd founded the Louisville Urban League Guild, and at one time served as president of the Lincoln Foundation. The NAACP honored Kidd with the Unsung Heroine Award, and she also earned the Louisville Mayor's Citation for Outstanding Community Service. In 1976, after years of campaigning in the General Assembly to have Kentucky ratify the U.S. Constitution's Thirteenth, Fourteenth, and Fifteenth Amendments, that legislative body voted unanimously to ratify all three.

Powers, Georgia D. (1923–)

Georgia D. Powers, civil rights leader and politician and also a native of Kentucky, was the first African American and first woman elected to the state Senate in 1967. In the early 1960s, Powers joined the Allied Organization for Civil Rights to advocate for a statewide public accommodations and fair employment law. That same year, she co-organized the March on Frankfort in which keynote speaker Dr. Martin Luther King Jr. urged Kentucky officials to support public accommodations legislation. As a result, the Kentucky legislature passed the 1966 Public Accommodations Act. During her five terms in the Senate, Powers introduced and witnessed passage of bills prohibiting housing, employment, age, and sex discrimination. She also successfully lobbied for improvements in education for the mentally and physically challenged. In the Senate, she chaired two legislative committees—Health and Welfare (in 1970 and again in 1976) and Labor and Industry (1978–1988). During her long, successful political career, Powers became a political force in the state by managing mayoral, gubernatorial, congressional, and presidential campaigns for other Democrats. In 1968, she addressed the Democratic National Convention in Chicago.

On the local scene, Powers became the first African American woman to serve on the Jefferson County Democratic Executive Committee. In 1989, she retired from political office.

Cultural Contributions

Despite the various social, economic, and political struggles Kentucky blacks faced, they had managed to create a community structure. African Americans continued to form economic, social, cultural, and religious institutions similar to those in other parts of the country and forged alliances between residents to endure and combat racism. Several black churches, mostly Baptist, addressed the spiritual and social needs of African Americans and became the core of many Kentucky communities. The churches sponsored picnics, plays, fairs, athletic teams, and literary clubs—social outlets that sustained the African American community. Churches also created the social and political agenda for the black working class. In the 1890s, African American congregations from Louisville, Lexington, and Owensboro challenged the Separate Coach Law in their own cities.

Around the turn of the century, secular black political clubs, fraternal organizations, cultural associations, social clubs, and literary societies evolved from the Kentucky black churches. These included the Prince Hall Masons, the Odd Fellows, and the Knights of Pythias. Often, those who did not belong to the same religious congregation became members of the same club or fraternal order or socialized together at barbecues, dances, and sporting events. Next to churches, black fraternal orders had the most diverse membership in the commonwealth. These strictly bourgeois organizations represented all social, economic, and religious categories. For example, in the early twentieth century, African Americans launched dozens of black Masonic lodges in Kentucky. The Louisville, Paducah, Rand Lexington Masons, and other Kentucky orders offered financial assistance to blacks enduring economic hardship.

During the Great Depression, welfare agencies in Kentucky denied help to destitute black families. In response, black churches collaborated with African American fraternal organizations to help. The women's auxiliary of the Masons, the Cecelia Dunlap Grand Chapter Order of the Eastern Star, was an organization of black women that adhered to a strict code of ethics, including a strong belief in God, honesty, and charity. In cities like Berea and Richmond, the Eastern Star was mostly a charitable agency that provided college scholarships, donated money to worthy causes, and distributed fruit baskets during the Christmas holiday. In Kentucky, and also nationally, the Eastern Star was one of the earliest supporters of the national civil rights struggle.

Black women continued to be instrumental in improving social conditions in Kentucky. Women's clubs contributed to the growth of Winchester, Bowling Green, Paducah, Owensboro, and other Kentucky communities. Many groups contained people who wanted to pursue recreational, cultural, political, and social interests with others of the same race. In 1904, the African-American Married Ladies Industrial Club of Owensboro was formed to fund the building of a nursing home, sturdy homes, and to educate children in the black community. African American women from four different church congregations in Berea's black hamlets of Bobtown, Middletown, Farristown, and Peytontown socialized monthly as members of the Merry Workers' Club.

Besides religion and organizations serving as spiritual, social, and political outlets for blacks, some African Americans thrived in sports. In a state known for producing thoroughbred horses, African Americans in Kentucky excelled as horse trainers and jockeys. Abe Perry and Edward Brown both trained Kentucky Derby winners in the late 1800s. As jockeys, 15 blacks won the Kentucky Derby in the early years of the event's existence. Oliver Lewis, William Walker, Isaac B. Murphy, Erskin Henderson, Babe Hurd, and Isaac Lewis all rode winners in the prestigious horse race. Perhaps the best-known sports figure from Kentucky is Muhammad Ali, who gained wide respect for his civil rights activism and his refusal to be inducted into the military for service in Vietnam.

Bibliography

Baskin, Andrew. "Berea College and the Founding of Lincoln Institute." *The Griot: The Journal of African American Studies* 13 (1994): 9–13.

Cole, Jennifer. "For the Sake of the Songs of the Men Made Free: James Speed and the Emancipationists' Dilemma in Nineteenth-century Kentucky." *Ohio Valley History* 4 (2004): 27–48.

Coleman, Winston J. *Slavery Times in Kentucky.* Chapel Hill: University of North Carolina Press, 1940.

Dunaway, Wilma A. *The African-American Family in Slavery and Emancipation.* New York: Cambridge University Press, 2003.

Dunaway, Wilma A. *Slavery in the American Mountain South.* New York: Cambridge University Press, 2003.

Hardin, John A. *Fifty Years of Segregation: Black Higher Education in Kentucky, 1904–1954.* Lexington: University Press of Kentucky, 1997.

Howard, Victor B. *Black Liberation in Kentucky: Emancipation and Freedom, 1862–1884.* Lexington: University Press of Kentucky, 1983.

Jones, Reinette F. *Library Service to African Americans in Kentucky, from the Reconstruction Era to the 1960s.* Jefferson, NC: McFarland and Company, 2002.

Kentucky Commission on Human Rights. "The 1966 Kentucky Civil Rights Bill Becomes Law: Equal Opportunity in Employment and Accommodations." Fifth Annual Report (1965–1966).

Kentucky Commission on Human Rights. "The First Year of Kentucky's Fair Housing Act." Eighth Annual Report (1968–1969).

Kentucky Educational Television (KET): "A Kentucky Civil Rights Timeline." www.ket.org/civilrights/timeline.

Kentucky Educational Television. *An Online Reference Guide to Kentucky African American History.* www.ket.org/civilrights.

K'Meyer, Tracy E. "The Gateway to the South: Regional Identity and the Louisville Civil Rights Movement" *Ohio Valley History* 4 (Spring 2004): 43–60.

Kurian, Thomas George, ed. *Datapedia of the United States: American History in Numbers.* 3rd ed. Lanham, MD: Bernan Press, 2004.

Lucas, Marion B. *A History of Blacks in Kentucky: From Slavery to Segregation, 1760–1891.* Frankfort: Kentucky Historical Society, 1992.

Lucas, Marion B. "Slave Life in Kentucky." In James C. Klotter, ed., *Our Kentucky: A Study of the Bluegrass State.* 2nd ed. Lexington: University Press of Kentucky, 2000, 106–119.

Mack, Dwayne A. "Ain't Gonna Let Nobody Turn Me Around: Berea College's Participation in the Selma to Montgomery March." *Ohio Valley History* 5 (2005): 43–62.

Schmitzer, Jeanne Canella. "CCC Camp 510: Black Participation in the Creation of Mammoth Cave National Park." *Register of the Kentucky Historical Society* 93 (1995): 446–464.

Wolfford, David L. "Resistance on the Border: School Desegregation in Western Kentucky 1954–1964." *Ohio Valley History* 4 (2004): 41–62.

Wright, George C. *A History of Blacks in Kentucky: In Pursuit of Equality, 1890–1989.* Vol. 2. Frankfort: Kentucky Historical Society, 1992.

Wright, George C. *Life Behind a Veil: Blacks in Louisville, Kentucky, 1865–1930.* Baton Rouge: Louisiana State University Press, 1985.

Wright, George C. "Oral History and the Search for the Black Past in Kentucky." *Oral History Review* 10 (1982): 73–91.

Wright, George C. "Race Relations after 1865." In James C. Klotter, ed., *Our Kentucky: A Study of the Bluegrass State.* 2nd ed. Lexington: University Press of Kentucky, 2000, 122–135.

Wright, George C. *Racial Violence in Kentucky, 1865–1940.* Baton Rouge: Louisiana State University Press, 1990.

LOUISIANA

Howard J. Jones

Chronology

1662	Robert Cavalier Sieur de LaSalle claims Louisiana for France.
1716–1719	Importation of slaves into Louisiana from the West Indies begins.
1718	Official date for the founding of New Orleans.
1724	The French Edict in the Code Noir for Louisiana prohibits interracial marriage between blacks and whites.
1751	Sugarcane is introduced into Louisiana by Jesuits.
1795	A slave uprising occurs in Pointe Coupee Parish.
1800	James Dernham of New Orleans is recognized as the city's first black physician.
1801	Louisiana is ceded to France by Spain in the secret treaty of San Ildefonso.
1802	The Spanish governor of Louisiana, Sebastián Nicolás de Bari Calvo de la Puerta, Marqués de Casa Calvo, issues a lengthy regulation governing black militiamen in Louisiana.
1803	The United States purchases the Louisiana Territory from France; the present-day state of Louisiana is only a small portion of the territory.
1804	The Louisiana Purchase is divided into two parts—the southern Territory of Orleans and the northern District of Louisiana.
1806	Inventor Norbert Rillieux, the son of a white father and free black mother, is born in New Orleans; Rillieux is best known as the inventor or an energy-efficient evaporator that helped the growth of the Louisiana sugar industry.
1811	*(January 8–10)* Charles Deslondes, a Louisiana slave, leads the German Coast Uprising, one of the largest slave rebellions in American history; the uprising involves several hundred slaves from St. John the Baptist and St. Charles parishes along the Mississippi River and results in the deaths of several plantation owners and 40–50 slaves, including Deslondes.
1812	*(April 30)* Louisiana enters the Union as the 18th state.
1814	Andrew Jackson issues a proclamation in New Orleans urging blacks to fight for the Americans against the British.
1815	*(January 8)* Several hundred free Negroes participate in the Battle of New Orleans.
1816	New Orleans adopts an ordinance officially segregating theaters and public exhibition areas.
1827	Louisiana passes an act stipulating that anyone who wants to emancipate a slave must provide the parish judge with a reason for doing so.

1830	Suspicious fires, which are blamed on slaves, sweep New Orleans.
1861	(*January 26*) Louisiana secedes from the Union.
1861	(*February 4*) The Confederate States of America is formed.
1861	(*February 8*) Louisiana is admitted to the Confederate States of America.
1861	(*April 12*) The Civil War begins with the Confederate firing on Fort Sumter, in the harbor of Charleston, South Carolina.
1862	(*May 1*) New Orleans is officially occupied by U.S. forces under General Benjamin Butler.
1862	(*May*) Federal troops occupy the Louisiana state capital at Baton Rouge.
1863	(*January 1*) New Orleans and 13 neighboring parishes under federal control are excluded from President Abraham Lincoln's Emancipation Proclamation.
1863	(*June 7*) Black Louisiana troops help repulse white Texas Confederate troops at the Battle of Milliken's Bend.
1863	The Grand Lodge of Prince Hall Masons in Louisiana is organized.
1863	Black troops from Louisiana participate in the Port Hudson campaign.
1863	Major Andre Cailloux distinguishes himself when the African American 3rd Louisiana Native Guards make two unsuccessful attempts to capture Port Hudson.
1864	Union General N. P. Banks issues an order that establishes the second public school system for blacks in the United States in New Orleans.
1864	The Louisiana Constitutional Convention meets and abolishes slavery.
1864	Equal pay for black and white soldiers is authorized by Congress.
1864	The first issue of *L'Union and La Tribune* appears in New Orleans.
1864	The *New Orleans Tribune* begins publication, becoming the first daily black American newspaper.
1865	(*February 17*) Louisiana ratifies the Thirteenth Amendment to the U.S. Constitution abolishing slavery.
1865	The Confederacy sanctions the policy of arming slaves.
1865	The Newman Normal School is established in New Orleans.
1865	The Bureau of Refugees, Freedmen and Abandoned Lands (Freedmen's Bureau) is created by Congress.
1865	The Black Codes of Louisiana are approved by Governor J. M. Wells.

1866	Congress overrides the veto of President Andrew Johnson and extends the life of the Freedmen's Bureau.
1866	A serious race riot erupts in New Orleans.
1867	*(February 6)* Louisiana rejects the proposed Fourteenth Amendment to the U.S. Constitution, which would guarantee full civil rights to African Americans.
1867	The Louisiana Constitutional Convention is convened.
1867	William Nichols tries to precipitate a test case by boarding a segregated streetcar in New Orleans.
1867	Blacks in New Orleans stage a streetcar ride-in to protest segregation in the city.
1867	New Orleans streetcars are unofficially desegregated.
1868	Louisiana adopts a new state constitution.
1868	A black man, Oscar J. Dunn, is elected lieutenant governor of Louisiana.
1868	An ordinance is passed that requires integrated schools in Louisiana.
1868	Antoine Dubuclet is elected Louisiana state treasurer.
1868	A racially mixed state legislature is convened in New Orleans.
1868	*(July 9)* Louisiana becomes the fifth state of the former Confederacy to be readmitted to the Union.
1868	*(July 9)* Louisiana ratifies the Fourteenth Amendment to the U.S. Constitution.
1868	A race riot erupts in New Orleans.
1868	A massacre of blacks occurs at Brownlee in Bossier Parish.
1868	Race massacre occurs at Opelousas where, reportedly, two or three hundred blacks are killed.
1868	John Willis Menard becomes the first African American elected to Congress when he wins a special election in Louisiana's 2nd District. When his opponent disputes the outcome, Menard becomes the first black to address the U.S. House of Representatives. When Congress decides for his opponent, Menard loses his seat.
1869	The governor of Louisiana signs a public accommodation bill barring discrimination.
1869	*(March 5)* Louisiana ratifies the Fifteenth Amendment to U.S. Constitution guaranteeing black men the right to vote.
1870	Leland University is incorporated.

1872–1873	*(December 9, 1872–January 13, 1873)* P. B. S. Pinchback becomes the first black man to serve as governor of a state when, as lieutenant governor, he succeeds his impeached predecessor for a period of 35 days.
1874	Charles E. Nash, a black Republican, wins election to the U.S. House of Representatives from Louisiana's 6th District.
1881	Southern University is chartered in Baton Rouge.
1892	Homer Plessy boards a train for Covington and is arrested for sitting in the white section of a railroad car in Louisiana; the incident leads to the 1896 U.S. Supreme Court case, *Plessy v. Ferguson*, which upheld the practice of racial discrimination.
1897	Homer Plessy is finally fined $25 in local court for his 1892 violation of the segregation laws.
1898	Louisiana enacts its first grandfather clause for voting purposes. It ties the rights of Louisiana blacks to vote to the rights enjoyed by their grandfathers, thus stripping many African Americans of the vote.
1900	*(July)* A race riot erupts in New Orleans after Robert Charles, a black laborer, shoots a white police officer, thus initiating a manhunt that results in the deaths of almost 30 people, including Charles and several New Orleans police officers.
1915	Xavier University is opened in New Orleans.
1916	The Zulu Social Aid and Pleasure Club is incorporated in New Orleans.
1920	The first issue of *The Shreveport Sun* is published by founder M. L. Collins Sr.
1930	New Orleans University and Straight College merge to form Dillard University.
1938	W. C. Williams is lynched near Ruston; this is supposedly the last daytime lynching witnessed by nonlynchers in Louisiana.
1946	The Louisiana Negro Normal and Industrial Institute officially becomes Grambling College.
1946	War veteran John Jones is lynched at Minden.
1953	Reverend T. J. Jemison leads a bus boycott over racial discrimination in Baton Rouge.
1954	The U.S. Supreme Court's decision in *Brown v. Board of Education* declares an end to legal racial segregation.
1954	Shreveport employs its first black policemen in modern times—William Hines and Joseph Johnson.
1955	Archbishop Rummel orders New Orleans parochial schools to desegregate at the upcoming term.

1955	The modern Civil Rights Movement begins with Rosa Parks refusing to give up her bus seat to a white passenger in Montgomery, Alabama.
1956	Federal Judge Skelly Wright orders the Orleans Parish schools to desegregate with all deliberate speed.
1956	Louisiana's attorney general begins a campaign to suppress the National Association for the Advancement of Colored People (NAACP) in Louisiana.
1957	Judge Skelly Wright rules that all New Orleans bus segregation laws are unconstitutional.
1957	Attempts at bus desegregation begin in Shreveport.
1957	A Freedom March from Bogalusa to Baton Rouge ends on the state capitol steps.
1958	New Orleans bus and trolley cars are desegregated.
1958	Louisiana Governor Earl Long approves closing public schools threatened with integration.
1960	In Shreveport, Dr. C. O. Simpkins and five students from Grambling College and Southern University are arrested for trying to use library facilities.
1960	Members of the NAACP Youth Council are arrested for talking with a department store manager about the possibility of desegregating the store's lunch counter.
1960	Ruby Bridges enters previously all-white William Frantz School in New-Orleans.
1963	The City of New Orleans agrees to remove racial signs from all public buildings.
1964	(*January 23*) The Twenty-fourth Amendment to the U.S. Constitution abolishing the poll tax is ratified; Louisiana has not ratified the amendment as of 2010.
1965	Black pro football players boycott the AFL All-Star football game played in New Orleans.
1967	H. Rap Brown of Baton Rouge becomes the new chairman of the Student Nonviolent Coordinating Committee (SNCC).
1969	The U.S. Supreme Court directs the Fifth Circuit Court of Appeals to order the immediate termination of dual schools in Louisiana.
1970	Governor John McKeithen urges Louisianians to defy court-ordered busing to achieve school desegregation.
1971	Dorothy Maede Lavallade Taylor becomes the first black woman elected to the Louisiana state legislature.
1972	Alphonse Jackson from Shreveport becomes the first black person since Reconstruction to become a state legislator from North Louisiana.

1974	Shreveport desegregates its fire department.
1974	Grambling College becomes Grambling State University.
1977	Ernest N. Morial is elected as the first African American mayor of New Orleans with 95 percent of the black vote and about 20 percent of the white vote.
1983	The Louisiana State Senate joins the Louisiana House of Representatives in repealing the Louisiana Racial Classification Law.
1985	Coach Eddie Robinson of Grambling becomes the winningest collegiate football coach with 324 victories.
1990	William J. Jefferson, a black Democrat, is elected to the U.S. House of Representatives from Louisiana's 2nd District.
1992	Marc Morial, a black Democrat and son of the former mayor of New Orleans, is elected to the Louisiana State Senate.
1992	Cleo Fields is elected to the U.S. House of Representatives from Louisiana's 4th District.
1994	Marc Morial, the son of former mayor Ernest Morial, is elected mayor of New Orleans.
1995	Congressman Cleo Fields runs unsuccessfully for the Democratic nomination for governor of Louisiana.
2001	The New Orleans City Council approves a measure to rename the New Orleans International Airport in honor of Louis Armstrong.
2002	Ray Nagin is elected mayor of New Orleans.
2005	(*August*) Hurricane Katrina descends on New Orleans, devastating many black areas of the city.
2006	The "Jena 6," a group of six black high-school students from Jena, Louisiana, are convicted of beating a white student after a series of racial incidents and confrontations at the school.
2007	Shelton J. Fabre, a Louisiana native, becomes the first black auxiliary bishop of the Archdiocese of New Orleans.
2008	(*February 9*) Barack Obama, an African American senator from Illinois, defeats Senator Hillary Clinton of New York in the Louisiana Democratic presidential primary by winning about 57 percent of the vote; Obama loses Louisiana to Republican John McCain in the November general election.
2008	Official designation by the state of the Louisiana African-American Heritage Trail.
2009	Five defendants plead "no contest" in the Jena 6 case, bringing the case to a close.

Historical Overview

Pre–Civil War

From 1718 to 1750, thousands of Africans were transported to Louisiana from West Africa. Both free and enslaved populations increased rapidly during the years of Spanish rule, as new settlers and Creoles imported large numbers of slaves to work on plantations. Although some American settlers brought slaves with them who were native to Virginia or North Carolina, most slaves brought by traders came directly from Africa. In 1763, there were 3,654 free persons and 4,598 slaves. By the 1800 Census, which included West Florida, there were 19,852 free persons and 24,264 slaves in Lower Louisiana.

Rice, indigo, and sugarcane made the French realize the importance of having the Africans in their midst. However, soon after their arrival, the French began setting them apart from the rest of the population. In 1724, the Code Noir for Louisiana was adopted. Among the initial prohibitions was interracial marriage.

Being brought to Louisiana and being forced to serve others did not always set well with the people from Africa. A major slave revolt occurred in Pointe Coupee Parish in 1795. Almost simultaneously, people of African descent were proving that they could make lasting progress in spite of racial restrictions. In 1800, James Derham, in New Orleans, became recognized as the first black medical doctor in America.

At the beginning of the nineteenth century, as a result of his troubles in Haiti, the French Emperor Napoleon I decided to sell France's American territories. In 1803, the United States purchased the Louisiana Territory from France. The United States then split the newly acquired region into two territories, with the southern Territory of Orleans becoming the state of Louisiana in 1812. The northern District of Louisiana became the basis for a series of later states, including all or parts of Arkansas, Missouri, Iowa, Minnesota, Oklahoma, Kansas, Nebraska, North and South Dakota, Colorado, Wyoming, and Montana. In 1810, President James Madison issued a proclamation annexing what were to become the Florida Parishes of eastern Louisiana from the short-lived West Florida Republic.

The Haitian Revolution of 1804 also caused a major emigration of refugees into Louisiana, particularly New Orleans. These Haitian immigrants included many free people of color, as well as whites and enslaved Africans. These immigrants enlarged Louisiana's French-speaking community, and the free people of color who immigrated from Haiti substantially increased the number of Creoles of color in New Orleans.

Periodically, Africans continued to show their disdain for their enslavement. In 1811, the German Coast Uprising, considered by some scholars the largest slave revolt in American history, erupted in Louisiana. Led by a slave named Charles Deslondes, a buggy driver from Haiti who worked in a plantation just above New Orleans, as many as 500 slaves from the plantations of the German Coast, about 40 miles from New Orleans, marched to within 20 miles of the city. The revolt, which took place on January 8 and 9, was bloodily suppressed by the Louisiana militia, who executed Deslondes without trial. Deslondes' execution was brutal. First, his hands were cut off, then he was shot in each leg, shattering his bones. As he lay dying, he was wrapped in straw and set on fire. These harsh acts were meant as a warning to other bondspersons of the dire consequences of defying the slave system.

Statehood to Reconstruction

Louisiana became a U.S. state on April 30, 1812. Nevertheless, African Americans could be counted on to serve the state and nation in time of war or other emergencies. During the War of 1812, at least 600 African American men, both free and enslaved, fought with Andrew Jackson in the Battle of New Orleans. Joseph Savary became one of the men of color who distinguished himself. He rose to the rank of second major. After the war, Jackson, at the behest of white New Orleanians, ordered Savary and all blacks who still possessed arms out of New Orleans. Savary ended up in Texas.

By this time the Port of New Orleans had become a major port for the export of cotton and sugar. The city's population grew and the region became quite wealthy. More than the rest of the Deep South, it attracted immigrants for the many jobs in the city. By 1840, New Orleans had the largest slave market in the United States, and it had also become one of the largest and wealthiest cities in the nation. Also by this time, the federal ban on the importation of slaves had increased demand in the internal market. It is estimated that in the antebellum period, more than one million enslaved African Americans were sent from the Upper South to the Deep South, two-thirds of them in the internal slave trade.

Following the Louisiana Purchase, as more white southerners inhabited the state, racial lines grew tighter. In 1835, New Orleans cemeteries were segregated. The next year, black prisoners were given different duties than white ones—most of the menial work. Another setback to Louisianans of color came on June 8, 1816, when an ordinance was adopted that segregated theaters and public exhibitions. Twelve years later, New Orleans' Mardi Gras balls were segregated. And in 1856, card playing in taverns was segregated.

Again, in spite of restrictions, people of color continued to contribute to human progress. In 1846, Norbert Rillieux, a Louisiana-born Creole, invented a multiple-effect evaporator that revolutionized the sugar industry by enabling sugar to be produced more efficiently than the cumbersome system known as the Jamaica Train. Rillieux's invention, which made sugar whiter and grainier, also was used in making soap and glue. Rillieux

himself, however, faced discrimination in Louisiana and eventually left the state for France. While Rillieux and other Creoles were educated in France, others were educated in New Orleans—something that was not available to other African Americans. In 1847, for example, Madame Bernard Couvert provided for a Creole school in New Orleans. Also, on the eve of the Civil War, although Rillieux and others had left the state, there were still more than 18,000 free African Americans—one of the largest free black populations in the country. Many of these persons were of mixed racial heritage and were middle class, well educated, and property owners. At the same time, however, more than 300,000 African Americans remained enslaved, almost half of the state's total population.

The question of whether the United States would remain half slave and half free was not solved, as many had hoped the Compromise of 1850, which sought to maintain that delicate balance, would do. Within a short time, the issue of the expansion or restriction of slavery in the western territories had increased tensions between the North and the South to the boiling point. The election of Abraham Lincoln, viewed by the South as a radical abolitionist Republican, as president of the United States in 1860 led to the secession of South Carolina and an attack on the U.S. arsenal at Fort Sumter, South Carolina. When the war came, Louisiana became a major player. In 1861, Louisiana seceded from the United States and became a state in the Confederate States of America (CSA).

In 1862, Union General Benjamin Butler formed the black Native Guards. In 1863, Major Andre Cailloux, a Creole, distinguished himself in the Battle of Port Hudson. Louisiana black troops also fought in the Battle of Miliken's Bend. Also during this same period in New Orleans, General Banks ordered down all physical signs pointing to blacks as slaves. So when the Louisiana Constitutional Convention met in 1864, it abolished slavery. Education had become even more significant in the black community. Thus, in 1864, General Banks issued an order establishing a new public school system for African Americans. At the same time there were 5,200 freedmen enrolled in 49 schools in New Orleans. Greater literacy led to a push in the African American community for universal suffrage. Among the men leading this effort were Oscar J. Dunn, P. B. S. Pinchback, and P. B. Randolph.

Louisiana was quickly defeated in the Civil War. The state's defeat was a part of the Union's strategy to cut the Confederacy in two by seizing the Mississippi River. On April 9, 1865, the Civil War came to a close. A few months earlier, in desperation, the CSA had authorized the use of black troops. But few blacks served their cause before the end of the war. Then in December 1865, the Thirteenth Amendment to the U.S. Constitution abolished slavery. Not until several years later did African American men become important players in the politics of Louisiana. Education and the ballot became exceedingly significant in the black world.

Reconstruction to World War II

In early 1865, Newman Normal School was established in Louisiana. A year earlier, freedmen groups had 90 men and women teaching over 5,000 black students in over 40 schools in Louisiana. There followed Union Normal School, Thompson University, Leland University, Southern University, and others. Blacks also began a renewed attack on segregation with much of the activity aimed at streetcars in New Orleans. This led to an "unofficial" desegregation of the streetcars in 1867. Black students tried unsuccessfully to desegregate at least two schools in New Orleans.

Several terrorist organizations sprang up in Louisiana during the Reconstruction era. They primarily aimed to intimidate Republican voters and officeholders of both races, obstruct implementation of Radical Republican policies, and restore Louisiana to rule by native whites. The main instruments of white terror in Louisiana were the Knights of the White Camellia, formed in 1868, and their successor group, the White League, which had spread across the state by 1874.

On the political front, during Reconstruction when blacks came to play a major role because of casting votes, Louisiana became a state with a different political climate. Starting with the 1868 Constitutional Convention, blacks were granted citizenship. Some historians have indicated that as many as half the delegates might have been black, and so were the members of the 1868 legislature. But it is certain that blacks never came to dominate Reconstruction in Louisiana. Blacks were more significant in the executive and legislative branches of government than in the judiciary. Three African American Creoles who served as lieutenant governor were Oscar J. Dunn, P. B. S. Pinchback, and C. C. Antoine. Robert H. Isabelle, who served as temporary chairman of the Louisiana House, introduced a bill abolishing all discrimination. Pinchback, after the impeachment of the sitting governor, Henry Clay Warmouth, served as governor of the state for 43 days. Three others held statewide offices—Antoine Dubuclet (1868–1878), state treasurer; W. G. Brown (1872–1876), state superintendent of public education; and P. G. Deslondes (1872–1876), secretary of state. In 1868, about half the members of both Houses of the 1868 state legislature were men of color. At the same time, J. W. Menard was elected to Congress from Louisiana's second district.

The Constitution of 1868, the first in Louisiana history to include a bill of rights, disfranchised former confederates. It also guaranteed full civil rights, including voting rights, to African Americans, created a free, integrated school system, and provided equal access for all citizens to public accommodations. At the time, Louisiana's state constitution was one of the most progressive in the country. The Black Codes of 1865 were abolished, as were all property qualifications for holding office. However, the new constitution had little effect on racial discrimination. Despite black legal challenges, antidiscrimination laws were rarely enforced, and most African Americans in Louisiana could not afford to eat in restaurants, attend cultural events, or ride trains and steamboats. During Reconstruction, African American leaders in the state differed from the masses of former slaves they sought to lead. They tended to be literate and prosperous professional men who had been free before the Civil War. A few had even held slaves.

Meanwhile, some whites, mainly Democrats, sought to use legal and extralegal means, including violence, to regain political power. On September 14, 1874, for example, the metropolitan police in New Orleans clashed with Democratic militants calling themselves the Crescent City White League, in a conflict known as the Battle of Liberty Place. The metropolitan police, numbering about 600, assisted by an additional 3,000 black militia, lost to the White Leaguers, who numbered about 8,400. Eleven policemen were killed and 60 wounded. The White Leaguers suffered 16 killed and 45 wounded. President Ulysses S. Grant called in federal troops from Mississippi to restore the Republican governor to office. He maintained his position until the end of Reconstruction.

National political developments eventually determined the course of reconstruction in Louisiana and the rest of the South. The two major political parties disagreed over which presidential candidate, Democrat Samuel J. Tilden or Republican Rutherford B. Hayes, had truly won the election of 1876. A compromise worked out in February 1877 gave the disputed votes to Hayes, and Hayes agreed to let southern Democrats, also known as redeemers, take over governments in the three remaining militarily occupied states—Florida, South Carolina, and Louisiana.

Once the federal government agreed to pull its troops out of Louisiana, a mostly Democratic convention wrote a new constitution that voters ratified in 1879. White redeemist Democrats were now firmly back in control of the state government.

During the Reconstruction era, one man of color, Charles E. Nash, served the state in the Congress. Another, P. B. S. Pinchback, was elected but was refused his seat as a U.S. senator. The issue was whether or not the legislature that elected him was legitimate; in 1876, the Senate said no. Amid these political successes, ugly racial violence raised its head. In 1868, there was a race riot in New Orleans and racial massacres at Opelousas and Brownlee. In 1873 and 1874, there was racial violence in Colfax and Coushatta, while white mobs continued to force African Americans out of white schools. Yet progress continued as can be seen by a public accommodations act barring discrimination in 1869, the chartering of New Orleans University in 1873, and the attempted desegregation of an all-white, all-girls school in New Orleans in 1874.

After losing the right to hold political office with the end of Reconstruction, Louisiana's blacks had to fight just to retain any civil rights at all. With Jim Crowism, the Mississippi Plan, and grandfather clauses, blacks had a real fight on their hands. The first Mississippi Plan of 1870 involved bands of armed whites intimidating prospective black voters. The second Mississippi Plan of 1890 required every citizen 21 to 60 years of age to display a poll tax receipt, and read and interpret the Constitution. This allowed all-white registration officials to deny the vote to black illiterates, while allowing whites, even though illiterate, to register to vote. Having no representation in the legislative or executive branches of government, blacks were segregated and discriminated in almost all areas of public life. Generally, their schools and other institutions and the public services provided for them were inadequate. They mostly worked in menial occupations such as unskilled labor and domestic service.

After the election of 1876, following the victory of Francis T. Nicholls and the Democrats, and the withdrawal of Union troops the next year, the federal government seemed to have abandoned blacks. The 1879 state constitution reversed most of the equalities black people had fought for and gained, including the right to vote. Ironically, at about the same time, the state capitol was moved from New Orleans with its large African American population to Baton Rouge. Some black Louisiana residents became so disillusioned that they joined the Exodus Movement to Kansas and other places in the Southwest. In 1896, this oppression culminated in the case of *Plessy v. Ferguson*.

The case was brought by Homer Plessy, a Louisiana Creole, who was seeking equal accommodations and equal treatment on railway cars. The Supreme Court rejected his plea and sanctioned the doctrine of "separate but equal." But separate was not equal in Louisiana and the rest of the South before *Plessy* and was not equal after *Plessy*. In this period, the most favorable thing that blacks got from segregation was the establishment of Southern University at Baton Rouge in 1881. A few years later, a land purchase was made that eventually led to Grambling State University. In spite of these educational venues, the pattern of segregation continued to grow, as the Louisiana legislature required segregation in public accommodations in 1890.

1900 to Present

There seemed to be some light ahead in the political situation when, in 1915, in the case of *Guinn v. United States*, the Supreme Court ruled the grandfather clause unconstitutional. Although the case arose from Oklahoma, it could be applied to all of the southern states, including Louisiana, which had the disfranchising clause. Not to be outdone, Louisiana legislators, like their southern counterparts elsewhere, came up with new devices, including a literacy and understanding test, to keep blacks away from the polls and out of political offices. Since many blacks were semiliterate or illiterate, there was little chance that they could read and understand the passages that were handed to them. In any case, all-white registration officials would make the determination. Still, in tandem with much of the rest of the South, Louisiana erected a seemingly impregnable barrier to black voting by declaring that the Democratic Party was really a private club for whites only. The so-called white primary, once the Republican Party became negligible, was the only election that really counted.

Under these conditions and with economic distress continuing or worsening, thousands of Louisiana blacks left the state for the North and Midwest in the Great Migration. Some even went west, as far as California, seeking relief from Jim Crow and seeking better jobs in industry. For those African Americans who remained in the state, the Great Depression furthered their financial woes, while New Deal measures for relief did not reach far enough. Louisiana's governor at this time was the flamboyant Huey Long. Calling himself a populist, he appealed to and favored poorer whites. To further the political involvement of this group, Long removed the poll tax. Blacks, too, ostensibly would benefit from the end of the poll tax. But the white primary remained in effect.

After the Supreme Court, in *Smith v. Allwright*, ruled the white primary unconstitutional in 1944, Louisiana erected new barriers to black voting. Meanwhile, African American voting strength plummeted in the state, going to less than 10 percent in the 1950s. But it was also during this time that the state prescribed only a citizenship test to register to vote. This encouraged black leaders in the NAACP and other organizations to launch voter registration drives. The campaign was successful in raising black voter registration to

20 percent. By 1934, 32 percent of eligible black citizens were voters—a significant increase in the decade, but still far short of the total number of eligible voters. It would take the Civil Rights Act of 1965 to clear the way for unfettered black voting and to give many blacks the confidence to actually register and vote. The fruits of this effort included the election of a series of black mayors in New Orleans, including Ernest "Dutch" Morial in 1972 and Ray Nagin in 2002. Black mayors were also elected in Baton Rouge, Shreveport, and Monroe.

Civil Rights Movement and Beyond

Meanwhile, African Americans were growing bolder in their quest for equality. In 1953, a year before *Brown v. Board of Education* and two years before the Montgomery Bus Boycott, a Baton Rouge minister, the Reverend T. J. Jemison, led a bus boycott in that city. Over the next several years from every corner of the state, north and south, there were freedom demonstrations by black Louisianians. There was also a bus desegregation demonstration in Shreveport in 1957, and New Orleans desegregated its buses and trolleys in 1958. But in 1960, baseball star Jackie Robinson was denied service at the cafeteria at the Shreveport airport. Also in Shreveport, members of the NAACP Youth Council were arrested just for talking with the manager of a department store about the possibility of desegregating his lunch counter, and black teenagers were arrested in Winnfield, Louisiana, for disturbing the peace after they tried to borrow books from the public library there. These incidents, however, were overshadowed by the tumultuous events in New Orleans that year. The city was under federal court order to begin school desegregation.

In 1954, the U.S. Supreme Court struck down segregation in its *Brown v. Board of Education* decision. In 1956, Federal District Court Judge

J. Skelly Wright ordered the Orleans Parish School Board to devise plans to effectively desegregate public schools in New Orleans. Local opposition to the ruling was immediate and fierce, as parents and other whites sought state legislation to overturn the judge's decision. The school board delayed complying with Wright's order for four years, but in 1960, it finally implemented an integration plan for two schools in the impoverished Ninth Ward. Starting with the first grade, the plan called for one grade to be integrated per year. On November 14, 1960, armed U.S. Marshals protected Leona Tate, Tessie Prevost, and Gaile Etienne as they integrated McDonough 19 and Ruby Bridges as she entered William Frantz School. As a result of this action, riots led by segregationists erupted throughout the city and enrollments at McDonough 19 and William Frantz declined significantly, as many parents enrolled their children in local private schools. Integration in New Orleans drew national attention, with many outside the state condemning Louisiana's segregationists for their hostile reaction. The disorders in New Orleans even prompted famed American painter Norman Rockwell to paint "The Problem We All Live With," which depicted federal marshals escorting six-year-old Ruby Bridges to school.

Over the years, much of the social, political, and economic life of black Louisiana was tied to the black press. Louisiana had the first African American newspaper in the South, *L'Union*, and with the *New Orleans Tribune*, the first African American daily newspaper in the nation. *L'Union* was founded in 1862 by Dr. Charles Roudanez, a wealthy financier, published bimonthly, then biweekly. Roudanez and his editor were also civil rights leaders. The newspaper mainly advocated for Louisiana's free people of color. The newspaper folded in July 1864. The *New Orleans Tribune* was the successor to *L'Union*, with Paul Trenigne serving as editor. Unlike *L'Union*, the *Tribune* was published

U.S. Navy air crewmen survey damage to a residential area from Hurricane Katrina as they fly over Mississippi on September 1, 2005, en route from Florida to provide relief to victims of the hurricane. The Navy's assistance in relief operations was directed by the Federal Emergency Management Agency. (U.S. Department of Defense)

partially in French and partially in English and advocated for both free people of color and the recently freed blacks. This paper was published weekly, but was rather short-lived.

But in 2005, it was not only the black media, but media from around the world which published and broadcast news that during a huge hurricane, the levees protecting the city were breached and flood waters engulfed much of the city and surrounding areas. Warnings of the hurricane had prompted the evacuation of New Orleans and other areas, but thousands of people, mostly African Americans, were left behind and stranded by the flood waters. Cut off in many cases from food, medicine, or water, or packed into public places like the Superdome and Convention Center, they were pictured by international television as refugees, as if from a Third World country. At least 1,500 people in

New Orleans died, as government at all levels failed to prepare for the emergency or to react quickly and adequately to it. When President George W. Bush and his administration as well as state and local authorities belatedly responded to the crisis, reconstruction in the mainly black areas of town remained painfully slow.

Two years after Katrina, Louisiana again was thrust into the national spotlight over a racial matter. The previous year, six black youths were charged as adults for allegedly beating a white high-school classmate. This incident followed several instances of white students hanging nooses from a tree at Jena High School. To protest what many believed were harsh charges and sentencing against the black youths, more than 20,000 persons, mostly black, held a one-day demonstration in the small town of 3,000 people

A crowd marches through Jena, Louisiana, in support of six black teenagers initially charged with attempted murder in the beating of Justin Barker, a white classmate, 2007. (AP/Wide World Photos)

on September 20, 2006. Most of the charges were later reduced and the black youths pled guilty to the lesser offenses.

Notable African Americans

Armstrong, Louis (1900–1971)

Louis Armstrong was born in New Orleans and moved to Chicago in 1922. He was an entertainer who revolutionized jazz with his improvisations on the trumpet and with his orchestra. The U.S. State Department sponsored several of his European and African tours and he became known as an unofficial goodwill ambassador.

Augustine, Israel Meyer, Jr. (1924–1994)

Israel Meyer Augustine was the first African American district court judge in Louisiana. In 1971, he presided over the trial of a group of Black Panthers, a case that drew national attention.

Clark, Joseph Samuel (1871–1944)

Joseph Samuel Clark was an educator who served as one of the first presidents of Southern University—his tenure was from 1913 to 1938.

Louis Armstrong is one of the towering figures in the history of jazz. (Library of Congress)

Davis, Abraham Lincoln (1914–1978)

Abraham Lincoln Davis was a minister and one of the founders of the Southern Christian Leadership Conference (SCLC) in 1957.

Delile, Henriette (1813–1862)

Henriette Delile was an educator, feminist, and social worker. She founded the Sisters of the Holy Family.

Dent, Thomas Covington (1932–1998)

Thomas Covington Dent was a dramatist and civil rights activist. In 1965, he was a cofounder of the Free Southern Theater, a collective of artists, intellectuals, and civil rights activists who used art to combat racism.

Gaines, Ernest James (1933–)

Ernest James Gaines is a writer best known for his novels *A Lesson before Dying*, *A Gathering of*

Old Men, and *The Autobiography of Miss Jane Pittman*. He has been the recipient of the National Book Critics Award, the American Academy of Arts and Letters Award, and a National Humanities Medal.

Glapion, Roy E., Jr. (1935–1999)

Roy E. Glapion Jr. was an educator and politician who was active in the Zulu Social Aid and Pleasure Club and became its president in 1976. In 1994, he was elected a member of the New Orleans City Council.

Haley, Oretha Castle (1939–1987)

Oretha Castle Haley was born in Tennessee and moved to New Orleans in 1947. She was a civil rights activist who became head of the New Orleans chapter of the Congress of Racial Equality (CORE). She was also a deputy administrator of New Orleans' Charity Hospital—the city's large health facility for indigent patients.

Lafon, Thorny (1810–1893)

Thorny Lafon was a businessman and philanthropist. He made substantial contributions to the Underground Railroad and to orphanages, homes for the elderly, universities, and Charity Hospital.

Landry, Lord Beaconsfield (1878–1934)

Lord Beaconsfield Landry was a physician, soloist, and civic leader. He sang in the famed Fisk Jubilee Singers, directed the Osceola Five, and became the first black mayor of Donaldsonville, Louisiana.

Morial, Ernest Nathan "Dutch" (1929–1989)

Ernest "Dutch" Morial was a lawyer, judge, state legislator, and the first African American mayor of New Orleans.

Morial, Marc Haydel Morial (1958–)

Marc Morial, the son of Ernest "Dutch" Morial, succeeded his father as mayor of New Orleans and head of the National Urban League.

Nagin, Ray (1956–)

Ray Nagin was mayor of New Orleans from 2002 to 2010. He received mixed reactions for his handling of the floods in his city following Hurricane Katrina. When he left office after serving a two-term limit, he was succeeded by Mitchell "Mitch" Landrieu, the first white mayor in more than two decades.

Pinchback, P. B. S. (1837–1921)

P. B. S. Pinchback was elected as a delegate to the 1867 Louisiana Constitutional Convention. After this, he was elected as a state senator. Upon the death of the elected lieutenant governor of Louisiana, Oscar J. Dunn, Pinchback was chosen to become the new lieutenant governor on December 6, 1871. On December 9, 1872, Louisiana Governor Henry Clay Warmoth was impeached for "high crimes and misdemeanors." Pinchback then served as acting governor for 35 days (December 9, 1872, to January 13, 1873). In the elections of 1874 and 1876, Pinchback was in "contested elections" chosen as a U.S. congressman from Louisiana and in the latter year, chosen as a U.S. senator from Louisiana, He lost both elections to Democrats who now controlled the state. While in Louisiana, he helped found Southern University, and earned a law degree at Straight University. He then moved to Washington, D.C.

Plessy, Homer (1863–1925)

Homer Plessy was the plaintiff in the case of *Plessy v. Ferguson* (1896), in which the Supreme Court pronounced its separate but equal doctrine for race relations.

Robinson, Edward Gay (Eddie) (1919–2007)

Eddie Robinson was a legendary football coach who spent his career at Grambling State University of Louisiana. Edward Gay Robinson began work at Grambling in 1941 and retired in 1997 with a record of 408 wins for Grambling. He also led the school to 17 SWAC (Southwestern Athletic Conference) titles. Under his leadership, Grambling won nine black football national championships. In his honor, the Football Writers Association has named the award presented to the best football coach in Division I the Eddie Robinson Award.

Spears, Mack Justin (d. 1988)

Mack Spears was an educator who became the first African American to become president of the Louisiana Schools Board Association. He was also the first black to serve on the Orleans Parish School Board, where he was elected seven times during a period of 18 years.

Taylor, Dorothy Mae Delavallade (1928–2000)

Dorothy Taylor was the first African American woman elected to the Louisiana House of Representatives in 1971, and in 1984, she became the first African American woman to be appointed to head a state department—the Department of Urban and Community Affairs.

Thierry, Camille (1814–1875)

Camille Thierry was a prolific Francophone poet. He came from a wealthy New Orleans family and spent many years in France. His romantic poetry included "To the One I Love" and "The Corsair's Sweet Heat."

Walker, Madam C. J. (Sarah Breedlove) (1867–1919)

Madam C. J. Walker was born in Louisiana and moved to St. Louis where she developed and revolutionized hair care products for black women. She became one of the wealthiest African American women in the country.

Cultural Contributions

In addition to world-renowned jazz musician Louis Armstrong and gospel singer Mahalia Jackson, Louisiana has had many other musicians who have contributed much to American culture. They include Afro-Creole jazzman Jelly Roll Morton, Kid Ory's Original Creole Jazz Band, and the King Oliver Band. There have also been literary giants like Arna Bontemps, Camille Thierry, Ernest Gaines, and Thomas Dent, a founder of the Free Southern Theater (FTS). The FTS, founded in the 1960s, has used art and drama to depict the oppressive nature of racism, discrimination, and segregation and efforts to overcome them.

Highlights of African culture in Louisiana are the Mardi Gras celebrations and the unique krewes of people of color. Although celebrations are held throughout the state, the larger ones are centered in New Orleans and Baton Rouge. The Original Illinois Club is one of the oldest black krewes. It was formed by Creole-of-Color community leaders in 1894. It sponsors a dance called "The Chicago Glide." Although it has only about 50 members, their ball draws over 700 guests. The Zula Aid and Pleasure krewe held its first parade in 1914. It has about 400 members and is the only krewe where the king gets to choose his own queen. Louis Armstrong was the king in 1949. During the Mardi Gras festivities, any

friend of a member can pay a fee and ride in the parade.

Louisiana has perhaps more African American theater companies than any other American state. They include the Vestage Theater Company in Baton Rouge and the Anthony Bean Community Theater, Arts for Life, Chakula Chua Jua Theater, Creative Artists, Striving Together, Curtain Call Theater, Dashik Theater, Ethiysian Theater, Junebug Productions, and Winfield Productions, all in New Orleans.

Prominent African American museums include the Ama Bontemps African American Museum in the birth home of author Bontemps in Alexandria; the River Road African American Museum, which sponsors an annual Juneteenth Festival in Donaldsonville; and the Tangipoor African American Heritage Museum and Black Veterans Archives in Hammond. In New Orleans, there are many museums, several of which are along Louisiana's African American heritage trail.

The heritage trail begins at the famed French Market, designed by Joseph Abeilard, a free man of color in the early 1700s. The next stop is in the historic neighborhood of Tremé, just north of the French Quarter. From the early 1800s, this neighborhood was home to a large community of prosperous free people of color. Tremé is in the area once known as Congo Square, which is now a part of Louis Armstrong Square. Beginning in the era of bondage, enslaved blacks would gather on Sundays and conduct traditional African rituals, engage in conversations, and dance and sing. As the trail moves further up Governor Nicholls Street, one finds the African American Museum of Art, which features rotating exhibits and a collection of African arts and crafts. In the same area, one will find the St. Louis Cemeteries, which contain the gravesites of prominent Creoles, including Homer Plessy of the *Plessy v. Ferguson* case and Ernest "Dutch" Morial, New Orleans' first African American mayor. Nearby is the Providence Park

Cemetery, where the remains of legendary gospel singer Mahalia Jackson are interred. Louisiana, especially the New Orleans area, is famous for its jazz festivals each spring and summer. Other cities, such as Shreveport, sponsor black theater festivals and Juneteenth festivals.

Bibliography

African American Heritage Museum, Louisiana. www.africanamericanheritagemuseum.com.

Bell, Caryn Cossé. *Revolution, Romanticism, and the Afro-Creole Protest Tradition in Louisiana, 1718–1868*. Baton Rouge: Louisiana State University Press, 1997.

Davis, Edwin Adams. *Louisiana: A Narrative History*. Baton Rouge, LA: Claitor's Books, 1965.

Fairclough, Adam. *Race and Democracy: The Civil Rights Struggle in Louisiana, 1915–1972*. Athens: University of Georgia Press, 1995.

Gentry, Judith F., and Janet Allured, eds. *Louisiana Women: Their Lives and Times*. Athens: University of Georgia Press, 2009.

Hornsby, Alton, Jr. *A Biographical History of African Americans*. Montgomery, AL: E-Book Time, 2005.

Jackson, Joy. *New Orleans in the Gilded Age: Politics and Urban Progress, 1880–96*. Baton Rouge: Louisiana State University Press, 1969.

Schafer, Judith Kelleher. *Slavery, the Civil Law, and the Supreme Court of Louisiana*. Baton Rouge: Louisiana State University Press, 1994.

Shugg, Roger W. *Origins of Class Struggle in Louisiana: A Social History of White Farmers and Laborers During Slavery and After, 1840–75*. Reprint ed. Baton Rouge: Louisiana State University Press, 1968.

Taylor, Joe G. *Louisiana: A Bicentennial History*. New York: Norton, 1976.

Taylor, Joe G. *Louisiana Reconstructed, 1863–77*. Baton Rouge: Louisiana State University Press, 1974.

Taylor, Joe G. *Negro Slavery in Louisiana*. Westport, CT: Greenwood Press, 1977.

Tregle, Joseph George. *Louisiana in the Age of Jackson: A Clash of Cultures and Personalities*. Baton Rouge: Louisiana State University Press, 1999.

Vincent, Charles. *The African American Experience in Louisiana: From Jim Crow to Civil Rights*. Baton Rouge: Louisiana State University Press, 2002.

Wall, Bennett. *Louisiana: A History*. Baton Rouge: Louisiana State University Press, 2002.

Winters, John D. *The Civil War in Louisiana*. Baton Rouge: Louisiana State University Press, 1979.

MAINE

Demetrius Lamar

Chronology

1600s	Africans assist in the settlement of the island of St. Croix, Maine, as servants to French colonist Pierre Du Gua Sieur de Monts.
1633	Oliver Weeks is possibly a servant of George Cleves on Richmond Island and in Falmouth (now Portland). A sailor, Weeks is a witness to a land-possession case in 1640.
1641	Massachusetts, which at this time includes Maine, legalizes slavery.
1671–1673	Antonius Lamy of York County is the first African American medical doctor in Maine.
1775–1783	The American Revolution is fought.
1775	Richard Earle of Machias participates in the first naval battle of the American Revolution, June 11, 1775, and is considered Maine's first recorded black patriot and hero. Earle is one of many African Americans who served in the American Revolution in exchange for their freedom.
1783	Slavery is abolished in Massachusetts, which then included Maine. Due in part to the petitioning efforts of Captain Paul Cuffee, a black shipmaster and ship owner, voting rights for male blacks and Indians are granted in Massachusetts.
1820	*(March 15)* Maine enters the Union as the 23rd state.
1823	Christopher Christian Manuel (1781–1845) of Portland becomes a barber, band co-ordinator, business owner, and human rights leader.
1826	John Brown Russwurm (1799–1851) is the first black graduate from Bowdoin College in Brunswick.
1844	Macon Bolling Allen (1816–1894) is accepted as a member of the Maine Bar.
1851	Harriet Beecher Stowe begins writing *Uncle Tom's Cabin*, the great antislavery novel of the antebellum period, in Brunswick.
1860	Dr. Thomas G. Brown (1805–1887) is listed as Bangor's first black physician.
1865	*(February 7)* Maine ratifies the Thirteenth Amendment to the U.S. Constitution abolishing slavery.
1867	*(January 19)* Maine ratifies the Fourteenth Amendment to the U.S. Constitution guaranteeing full civil rights to African Americans.
1869	*(March 11)* Maine ratifies the Fifteenth Amendment to the U.S. Constitution guaranteeing African Americans the right to vote.
1875	James Augustine Healy (1830–1900) becomes the first black Roman Catholic priest and later the first black bishop of the Roman Catholic Diocese of Maine and New Hampshire.

1881	Maine repeals a state law against interracial marriage.
1909	Louis George Gregory (1874–1951) becomes a member of the Baha'i Faith and a champion of racial unity.
1920	A National Association for the Advancement of Colored People (NAACP) branch is established in Bangor.
1937	Ted "Tiger" Lowry (1920–) begins his boxing career and fights the champion boxers of his day.
1940s	James A. Johnson (1901–1979), an inventor, educator, and author, helps to establish the vocational and technical schools in Augusta and South Portland.
1964	(January 16) Maine ratifies the Twenty-fourth Amendment to the U.S. Constitution abolishing the poll tax.
1964	Martin Luther King Jr. speaks in Maine; the National Civil Rights Act is passed.
1972	Gerald E. Talbot (1932–) becomes the first black elected to the Maine legislature.
1975	Dr. Stanley J. Evans starts the Alcohol Institute at Eastern Maine Medical Center, Bangor.
1977	Legislation to remove racially offensive place names in Maine is passed.
1978	Barbara Ware Nichols (1937–), originally of Portland, is elected president of the National American Nurses Association.
1988	William D. Burney Jr. (1951–) becomes the first black elected mayor of Augusta.
1990	Census figures show that African Americans comprise less than 0.5 percent of Maine's population.
1996	Sallie Chandler becomes the first black woman to be elected to public office in Maine when she is elected as town clerk in Lebanon.
2000	Rick Lawrence becomes the first black judge in Maine.
2004	Jill Doson is elected the first black mayor of Portland.
2008	(November 4) Democrat Barack Obama, the first African American nominee for president of a major party, carries Maine with about 58 percent of the vote.

Historical Overview

Although today black Mainers constitute less than 1 percent of the state's population, they have been an integral part of Maine even before its conception. Perhaps as early as the sixteenth century, the first wave of Africans came to what is now Maine as baiters for Portuguese fisherman, as servants for English settlers, and as co-explorers and discoverers as well as language translators for French and French Canadian colonists and explorers. Existing records show that the first Africans came to this part of North America in small numbers as bonded and freemen to contribute to the growing number of cultural and commercial enterprises that dominated the period, ranging from fishing and whale hunting to sugar refining and molasses production.

Due to their limited number, black Mainers were found in only a few parts of Maine and obtained transient servitude status near the seaports. These African pioneers, however few, were occasionally connected with the South, but there are few existing family records of this. It appears that those black Mainers who had extended family beyond the shores of Maine seldom found their way back to the South or Canada, but the majority seem to have stayed in New England as contracted or indentured servants.

By the late sixteenth and early seventeenth centuries, British North America, being part of the British Empire's continued epic push for geographical expansion and material conquest, would take on a life of its own, as African indentured servitude gradually eroded into institutionalized slavery. Slavery became America's bedrock, giving it a headstart toward technical development by facilitating the birth of a much-needed leisure class whose restless energy would be used to create culture and to perpetuate unending innovation. During this period, there were also free Africans who continued to arrive in Maine and elsewhere, but in small numbers, for the vast majority of the newly arriving Africans were being shipped to the United States to partake in an enterprise of free labor.

The New England slave traffic was led by Massachusetts (including Maine), particularly Boston, with Rhode Island and Connecticut close behind. Still part of Massachusetts and feeling the pressures of industrialization initiated by Old England, Maine became a major shipbuilding state and played no insignificant part in American black slavery. Despite the importance of ushering in a market economy and later the machine age, the social condition of this period was one of profound morbidity in which New England would

copy the Spaniards, who, up to the eighteenth century, often enslaved not only African but also Native American or Indian and white people.

The New England merchants primarily sold Africans to the West Indies and to the southern colonies. The purpose of the slaves was to work the plantation fields of cotton, sugar, tobacco and rice—highly desired items by the leisure class. Thus, the slave trade in New England was comparatively limited and is said to have lacked the inhumane cruelty practiced in the antebellum South. It is estimated that fewer than 1,000 slaves existed in all of colonial New England in 1700. By 1790, this figure would reach 16,822 out of over one million inhabitants. The early history of Maine regarding blacks is well documented and is chronicled in the first permanent newspaper published in North America, the *Boston News Letter*.

The colonial era—owing in part to one country's exploitation of another country's people and resources for its own benefit—produced some of the first measurable African migration into Maine. In untold ways this second stream of new arrivals, whose history was once veiled in near total obscurity, would greatly help Maine's economy. Prior to the American Revolution, slavery was the capstone to economic stability and was justified spiritually as well as legally. The profits resulting from New England slave-trading stimulated American cultural development and philanthropy, but slave trading triggered a slow and catastrophic cultural decline on the African continent.

In 1780, three years before the close of the American Revolution, Massachusetts emancipated its American slaves. The end of American slavery took many forms in New England and elsewhere. Slaves would achieve the status of freedmen by either purchasing their liberty or by being born legally free. For example, children of mixed racial parentage were born free. Some conscientious slave owners, convinced that slavery was wrong, set their slaves free. Others were liberated by earning their freedom as participants in the revolutionary armies. Some slaves, eager for their independence, "stole themselves" by running away.

After the Revolution, former slaves in Maine who once held a broad array of employment now found work unavailable. Many African slaves held skilled positions in Maine's flourishing maritime period, working in such vital areas as iron forgers, house carpenters, coopers, blacksmiths, shipbuilders, and distillers, but these trades became limited after the colonial slave era. Before the Revolutionary War, 25 percent of mariners were black. Now these jobs were available only to American whites, sometimes even to former white indentured servants. In some respects this trend has continued to this day.

Thus the inauguration of the post-Revolution period in Maine was a time of enormous difficulty both for the former slaves and their immediate descendants. Despite such obstacles, some of the ancestors of African slaves would start on the difficult road of avoiding bondage, making a living, establishing families and careers, and social integration. This process would take place in port towns, particularly Portland.

From the middle of the eighteenth century forward, Portland merchants were engaged in coastal, regional, transatlantic, and global commerce and trade. Since Portland was a major New England port city, most blacks who found work there were employed as seamen. Some worked as career seamen and others as stewards and waiters. Even today, Portland has the largest overall population and the largest black population.

In spite of these limitations and occupational handicaps, the nineteenth and twentieth centuries became an age of movement, growth, and assimilation for many Maine freedmen. The process of assimilation in a budding new nation-state that sought to imitate Old England by showing an appetite for industrialization (expansion and perpetual innovation), social hierarchy (class distinctions), and material acquisition (property accumulation) led many freedmen and women to bend to these pressures and pursue an economic society with a zeal equal to their white counterparts.

When the maritime era came to a close, the railway industries were introduced. Blacks sought to take full advantage of these new jobs, working as coachmen, bootblacks, engineers, cooks, and porters, as well as trackmen and matrons on the railroad system. Essentially the railway in Maine, particularly in Portland, was dependent on black labor. In Maine, blacks played a key role throughout the railway age, all the way through World War II. Other occupations became rungs on the ladder of vertical mobility in which blacks made stellar cultural contributions to Maine.

Some black Mainers bought property and became small business entrepreneurs, for property acquisition was a stepping-stone to wealth, stability, and independence. Others would inherit property from their progressive masters, allowing former slaves for the first time to own a home and to raise a family. Early black entrepreneurs also selected barbering, carpentry, clothes manufacturing, public accommodations, and farming as their means for making a living. Still others would seek new lives by immigrating to the British Empire, migrating to Canada, or marching west to pursue the open frontiers.

In the early twentieth century class distinctions and race inequality in Maine played an important role in determining who got what. Those blacks with white ancestry had more opportunities, responsibilities, and freedoms than darker-skinned blacks because it was believed that darker-skinned blacks were pure-blooded Africans and therefore less culturally able than the mixed American black or mulatto. Nevertheless, the sprawling nature of this early American racial caste system would have a direct effect on how influence and opportunity would be distributed in every nook and cranny of Maine's society.

For a time the few blacks living in Maine were forced to confine themselves to servicing the black community. Maine's aristocracy, once the primary class who owned slaves, now seldom hired them as wage laborers. This shift of status—from working with Maine's white merchants, planters, and financiers to working within an isolated human-made social framework—would produce a group of American blacks who had high expectations for black progress. Borne out of a confluence of factors, this spirit of black uplift reached its high-point during Reconstruction, when society at large, but most particularly in the South, was facing immense social maladjustment. Some American blacks sought to adopt the cultural way of life of those with whom they worked, including high interactions with American whites. Others felt the pain of open oppression and discrimination and found refuge by matriculating into higher education and finding work in the professions. A third division recognized that true equality would not be achieved without civic action and sought political office.

In the subsequent years of gradual erasure of legal bondage, Maine had the second-largest number of free blacks in New England (Massachusetts had the largest). The general footprint of this early post-colonial period can be seen from east to west, for today the posterity of early black Mainers now plays a crucial role in every aspect of the state, as inventors, civic leaders, barbers, prize-fighters, spiritual councilors, nurses, lawyers, physicians, legislators, and mayors.

Notable African Americans

Allen, Macon Bolling (1816–1894)

A native of Indiana, Macon Bolling Allen obtained a license to practice law in Maine in 1844, but never actually practiced in the state. According to the U.S. Census of the time, he was a mulatto or mixed heritage, being of Scottish, Native American, and African descent. He migrated to the Commonwealth of Massachusetts and then to Portland, Maine, where he changed his name from A. Macon Bolling to Macon Bolling Allen.

Allen actually began his practice in Massachusetts. Although Maine was a state that strongly supported the antislavery cause, the black population was still very small and business was scarce for black litigators. Seeking to find a better life, Allen moved from Maine back to Massachusetts, becoming, in 1845, the first African American to be admitted to the Massachusetts Bar as well. After practicing for more than two decades there, he later became a justice of the peace in the Massachusetts commonwealth.

Burney, William D., Jr. (1951–)

William Burney Jr. was born in Augusta and became the first black elected mayor in Maine, when he became mayor of Augusta in 1988. Burney comes from a rich line of dynamic and accomplished African Americans. His mother, Helen Nicholas Burney, and father, William D. Burney Sr., were from Poughkeepsie, New York, and Macon, Georgia, respectively. For more than half a century, both parents contributed to the papermaking industries and church missions, and Helen as an airplane rivet inspector during World War II. The Burneys were also charter members of the NAACP, with Burney Sr. consequently becoming one of the first presidents of the Central Maine chapter of the NAACP.

Burney graduated from Cony High School in Augusta, where he played sports and earned membership in the National Honor Society. He earned a B.S. in public communications from Boston University in 1973 and a law degree from the University of Maine School of Law in 1977.

Before becoming Maine's first elected African American mayor, Burney served in a variety of civil and legal capacities, among them eight years on Augusta's City Council and four years as chairman of Augusta's Board of Education. He has spent nearly 20 years as a development officer and planner at the Maine State Housing Authority. Between 1988 and 1996, Burney was elected to four consecutive two-year terms as mayor of Augusta; his election was considered unusual because blacks made up only 1 percent of the population. He now works for the U.S. Department of Housing and Urban Development.

Geary, Roscoe, Sr. (1885–1964)

A native of Pennsylvania, Roscoe Geary was the first known black to practice law in Maine. On the 50th anniversary of his practice, he was honored by the Maine Bar Association.

Healy, James Augustine (1830–1900)

James A. Healy became the first black Roman Catholic priest and later the first black bishop of the Roman Catholic Diocese of Maine and New Hampshire. Bishop Healy was born in Georgia of mixed ancestry. His mother, Mary Eliza, was a former slave of African origins, but most probably mixed. His father was an Irish American plantation owner, from Roscommon, Ireland.

Bishop Healy graduated first in his class from Holy Cross College, Worcester, Massachusetts, in 1849, the year the college was established. He along with two of his siblings went to seminary school abroad. Ordained as a priest at the Cathedral of Notre Dame, in Paris, France, in 1854, Bishop Healy worked for over two decades as secretary to Bishop James Bernard Fitzpatrick of Boston, Massachusetts, before leaving for Maine in 1875 to become bishop, a post he held until his death in 1900.

During his lifetime Bishop Healy accomplished much. Working tirelessly, he not only brought enumerable religious orders to Maine, but he also increased the number of parishes and convents and was responsible for more than a dozen new schools in the diocese. Traveling throughout Maine, sometimes in a canoe, Bishop Healy would meet and confirm children, especially orphans. He anointed more than 4,000 children during his administration, giving him the namesake "Children's Bishop."

Beyond having a zeal for organization, Bishop Healy had a talent for the French language, which would also improve his Catholic following. Being well versed in the French language was a requirement of his priests, for Maine had a large population of French Canadians. But Bishop Healy's road to success was not an easy battle. He faced discrimination because of his skin color and, at the beginning of his tenure, a church was set afire in disapproval of his presence in Maine. There was also a history of medical neglect due to his African ancestry—nursing sisters found him too different to be tended to. Yet there is little to no documented history of Bishop Healy publicly condemning racism. Two months before he died, Bishop Healy was made an assistant to the papal throne and was honored for his nearly 50 years of service. He is interned at Calvary Cemetery in South Portland, as he requested.

Johnson, James A. (1901–1979)

James A. Johnson, an inventor, educator, and author, helped to establish the vocational and technical schools in Augusta and South Portland, Maine. Johnson was born in Cape Elizabeth, Maine, but grew up in Portland. He went to the Franklin Institute in Boston, Massachusetts, and later earned his B.S. from the University of Southern Maine (1976).

Johnson was best known for being one of the founders of the Maine Vocational and Technical Institute (MVTI)—now called Southern Maine Community College. The institution came about when Johnson saw a need for World War II military veterans to learn a trade to gain employment.

Thus, he decided to train veterans in automotive repair. This idea blossomed and Johnson was soon teaching thousands of students at MVTI.

Johnson is also known for his inventions. In 1959, he invented the Trig Stato-DiNamic Wheel Balance for cars. In 1972, he authored a textbook, *Automotive Tune-up and Diagnosis*. He also invented the truck Trig Balancer in 1976. In 1968, after 20 long years, he fulfilled one of his personal dreams, to build his own automobile.

Lowry, Ted "Tiger" (1920–)

Ted "Tiger" Lowry is a boxer whose claim to fame is going the 10-round distance twice with the legendary power puncher Rocky Marciano, a boxing feat never before achieved. Lowry's life started in austere circumstances. Although born in New Haven, Connecticut, he was raised by his mother Grace in Portland. Lowry attended Portland High School and participated in sports. Immediately following high school, he entered the ring to become a prize fighter. At 18, in his debut match, he knocked out three opponents in one night. Lowry received his boxing credentials in New Bedford, Massachusetts. There he would be trained to become a professional pugilist.

Lowry's 16-year boxing career was put on hold because of World War II. He distinguished himself as a member of an all-black 555th parachute battalion called the Triple Nickels. This crew put out forest fires created by Japanese-launched incendiary balloons in Washington and the Pacific Northwest.

Although not a true heavyweight, at age 23 Lowry volunteered to put on a three-round exhibition fight with the heavyweight Champion Joe "the Brown Bomber" Louis. After the match, Louis informed Lowry that he had a future in the sport of boxing. These comments coming from, in the minds of some, the greatest American professional boxer of all time made Lowry pursue his career unstintingly. Lowry would soon

fight all over the country, often for very little financial reward.

Lowry left the ring with a 64–65–9 record with 41 knockouts. Among his opponents were Sonny Liston, Archie Moore, Joey Maxim, and Rusty Payne. He was knocked out only three times in his entire career. Lowry authored a book, *God's in My Corner* (2007). On November 28, 2008, he at age 87 was inducted into the Connecticut Boxing Hall of Fame.

Manuel, Christopher Christian (1781–1845)

Christopher C. Manuel of Portland became a barber, band coordinator, business owner, and human rights leader. A native of Cape Verde, Manuel is thought to have immigrated to the United States as a mariner. In 1820, he married Nancy Pier, a daughter of perhaps one of the leading black families in Portland, that of Peter and Elizabeth Pierre. Following his first wife's death, Manuel married Sophia Ruby. Sophia Ruby was the sister of Reuben Ruby, an influential antislavery activist and Underground Railroad leader.

As a barber, a highly regarded occupation at the time, Manuel was an important person in the black community, as many would congregate at his place of business for haircuts, humor, and serious dialogue. He was also a flutist who organized the first reported brass band in Maine. Manuel, along with several other contributors, would go on to help create the Abyssinian Religious Society and the Abyssinian Congregational Church, which still stands. On June 1, 1842, the Abyssinian Congregational Church would become the site for the founding of the Portland Union Anti-slavery Society, and Manuel would subsequently become its first elected president.

His wife, Sophia, survived him by 30 years, and today their bodies rest at the Eastern Cemetery, recently discovered to be a popular grave site of Maine's African American abolitionists.

Nichols, Barbara Ware (1937–)

Born in Gardiner, Barbara Ware Nichols became the first minority person to be elected president of the American Nurses Association in 1978. Born to Mildred Ware Rogers, Nichols was an only child. She attended Portland High School, where she was one of two blacks in her class (1956). Three years later, she earned her nursing credentials from Massachusetts Memorial Hospital School of Nursing in Boston. She went on to earn her B.S. from Case Western Reserve University in 1966 and an M.A. from the University of Wisconsin–Madison in 1973.

Nichols has also been a consultant to ministries of health and nurses' associations. She has written many articles and given over a thousand speeches. The rewards and citations she has received are endless, including four honorary degrees.

Russwurm, John Brown (1799–1851)

John Brown Russwurm was the first black graduate from Bowdoin College, Brunswick, Maine. Born in Port Antonio, Jamaica, on October 1, 1799, Russwurm grew up in a wealthy family. Of German extraction, his father owned a sugar plantation and is said to have owned more than 50 slaves. Russwurm's maternal heritage is not entirely clear, but records show that his mother was a West Indian woman, perhaps even a slave mistress.

After Russwurm's mother's death, his father moved his family to Back Cove, Maine (now Portland), and remarried. Russwurm's stepmother, Susan Blanchard, was a widow who already had children of her own. After Russwurm's father's death in 1815, his stepmother married William Hawes, who co-owned a paper mill.

With this upper-class background, Russwurm was known to attend leading schools of his time, starting with a boarding school in Quebec,

Canada. He later went to Hebron Academy, a college preparatory school, owing to his stepparents' desire to see him succeed. Later, while teaching in Boston, Massachusetts, Russwurm encountered racism and thereafter devoted his life fighting against racism and for the civil rights of black people.

He returned to Maine in the 1820s and matriculated at Bowdoin College. There he studied, among other things, anatomy, medicine, and chemistry, but was also rather fond of politics and history. In 1826, he would become Bowdoin College's first black graduate and only the third American black to graduate from college. Highly regarded by his classmates, he gave the commencement oration on "The Conditions and Prospects of Hayti," a document that remains insightful and worthy of being read to this day (Price and Talbot, 227).

Within the year, Russwurm moved to New York, where many thousands of free blacks lived, and became junior editor of *Freedom's Journal*, the country's first black newspaper. This short-lived publication not only disclosed the tragedies faced by blacks in America but it helped stimulate ideas of social progress and was the initial impetus to Russwurm's relationship with the early "back to Africa" movement. *Freedom's Journal* folded in 1829 (Meier and Rudwick, 107).

Russwurm later emigrated to Liberia, West Africa, taking a position as editor of the *Liberia Herald*. He also became the governor of the Maryland colony of Liberia. As governor he played a critical role in uplifting the standard of living in Liberia, including encouraging agriculture, establishing a legal system, outlawing peonage, and instituting currency exchange.

He died in Cape Palmas, Liberia, and his tombstone reads: "John Brown Russwurm: Able, Learned, Faithful, An Honor to His Race." Today there are several buildings, a national journalism award, and a school honoring the work of John Brown Russwurm.

Talbot, Gerald E. (1932–)

Gerald E. Talbot is the first black elected to the Maine legislature. Deeply involved in the Civil Rights Movement throughout New England, Talbot is a member of a family with a long history on the eastern ridge of North America. The Talbots have lived in Maine for more than eight generations. It is likely that Gerald E. Talbot's ancestors either came to settle in Maine via Nova Scotia or New Brunswick, Canada, or from the South following the Revolutionary War.

Gerald Talbot was born in 1932 in Bangor, Maine. Talbot graduated from Bangor High School where he was nicknamed "Timber" and later played on the Carver Club, a semipro basketball team. He joined the army in 1953 and served three years before marrying Anita Cummings.

Talbot grew up in a time when racism, although often subtle. Still the Talbot family withstood those tough times, as did so many other black families. According to Talbot, by the 1940s, nearly 75 percent owned their own homes (Price and Talbot, 173).

During Talbot's time, the Bangor black community was closely connected and everyone knew intimately what everyone else was doing. In his now popular book, *Maine's Visible Black History*, Talbot recounts the history of the Bangor black community, name by name, street by street, and brick by brick. For example, he documents how one of his high-school classmates went on to join the U.S. Army, earning a Purple Heart in the European theater. He also documents how another member of the community became a professional boxer; another a Boston Latin High School teacher for more than 40 years; another a major in the U.S. Army; another a cook; another a house keeper; and another a long-distance runner.

Talbot himself directly faced racism in the housing rental market in Portland, Maine. Talbot, who has light-colored skin, tells of a horrific story of having secured housing due to his light skin hue, but once the landlord discovered his friends (and he) were black, "a light went off in his head and racism took over" (Price and Talbot, 293). Talbot and his family had to move out before they moved in. They later found a home in the Munjoy Hill area, once the cradle of Portland's black community.

Talbot's service to Maine and its black heritage is very impressive. In the 1960s, he was the president of the Portland NAACP branch, a position he would hold two more times before the end of the 1980s. In a joint effort with some engaged white activists and NAACP members, as branch president he played a critical role in establishing the Fair Housing bill into law, initiating public accommodations legislature, contesting Portland's all-white police department's hiring practices, providing clothes and improved textbooks to libraries and public schools, addressing unemployment challenges, as well as shelter for the homeless.

In 1980, he formed BEACH: Black Education And Cultural History. This program was conceived to help reach out to the children of Maine who were seeking to further their educational prospects. Since then BEACH has created educational scholarships, sponsored conferences on racism, interracial marriage and adoption, and held tribute to the 10 outstanding black women throughout Maine.

In 1972, Talbot became the first black to become a Maine state legislator, and during his tenure, he displayed black history in the legislative halls of the statehouse. He also introduced the first legislation to establish a state holiday in honor of Dr. Martin Luther King Jr., in 1973. The bill finally passed in 1986. Also in this capacity, he fought for and passed a bill to eliminate derogatory black place names in the state of Maine. In 1984, he became the first black to chair the Maine State Board of Education. He also served as a trustee to the Maine Vocational Technical Institute. In 1995, Mr. Talbot donated a world-class black history collection to the University of Southern Maine. He and his wife, Anita, have lived and worked in Portland for more than half a century.

Cultural Contributions

Black Mainers' cultural contributions cover the full gamut of life, and are only now beginning to be recognized. Although Maine has the third smallest black population among the states, black Mainers have contributed more than their small size might suggest.

By the twentieth century, an automotive engineer, James A. Johnson, Sr., was recognized for his contributions in education, literature, and technology. He cofounded the Maine Vocational and Technical Institute, which is perhaps his greatest legacy.

Bob Greene of South Portland, Maine, has given us a litany of informative articles, ranging from an interview with President Harry S. Truman to covering Dr. Martin Luther King Jr.'s funeral, while working as a journalist for the Associated Press for 45 years.

Bibliography

Foley, Albert S. *Bishop Healy: Beloved Outcaste*. New York: Farrar, Straus and Young, 1954.

Greene, Lorenzo. *The Negro in Colonial New England*. New York: Columbia University, 1942.

Meier, August, and Elliott Rudwick. *From Plantation to Ghetto*. Rev. ed. New York: Farrar Straus Giroux, 1970.

Mladinich, Robert. "Tiger Ted Lowry by the Tale." (Online January 2006.) The Sweet Science Web Site. www.thesweetscience.com.

National Bahai Archives. *Louis G. Gregory: Champion of Racial Harmony*. (Pamphlet.) Wilmette, IL, 1995.

Price, H. H., and Gerald E. Talbot. *Maine's Visible Black History: The First Chronicle of Its People*. Gardiner, ME: Tilbury House Publishers, 2006.

Roman Catholic Diocese of Portland. Online, 2006. www.portlanddiocese.net.

Sammons, Mark J., and Valerie Cunningham. *Black Portsmouth: Three Centuries of African American Heritage*. Durham: University of New Hampshire Press, 2004.

Smith, Jessie Carney, ed. *Blacks First: 2,000 Years of Extraordinary Achievement*. Detroit: Gale Research Inc., 1994.

Smith, J. Clay, Jr. *Emancipation: The Making of the Black Lawyer, 1844–1944*. Philadelphia: University of Pennsylvania, 1993.

The Louis G. Gregory Bahai Museum. (Online 2003.) www.louisgregorymuseum.org.

MARYLAND

John A. Wagner

Chronology

1634   Although it has a Protestant majority from the beginning, the settlement of St. Mary's City is founded by Cecil Calvert, Lord of Baltimore, a Catholic who intends his new colony to be a haven for his co-religionists. Supposedly named for Charles I's wife, Queen Henrietta Maria, the colony is really named for the Virgin Mary.

1634   A black man named Matthias De Sousa arrives in Maryland aboard the *Ark* as an indentured servant. He will be freed after seven years of servitude.

1634   Slavery is introduced into Maryland.

1642   As a member of the Maryland General Assembly, Matthias De Sousa becomes the first African American to sit and vote in an American colonial legislature.

1663   Maryland enacts a law enslaving all African Americans brought into the colony.

1664   Maryland considers drafting a law declaring that the baptism does not confer freedom on a child born to slaves.

1664   Maryland enacts a law declaring that any white woman who marries an African slave should serve her husband's master for life.

1681   Maryland declares children born to white mothers and African American fathers and children born to free black mothers to be free.

1692   Maryland sentences white men who marry or have children with black women to seven years of servitude and also prohibits African American men from having sexual relations with white women.

1700   The number of slaves in British North America is about 28,000, with most living in the South.

1725   The number of slaves in the British colonies reaches 75,000.

1731   (*November 9*) Benjamin Banneker is born to free parents in Ellicott, Maryland.

1754   Benjamin Banneker constructs the first clock made entirely in America.

1760   There are over 325,000 slaves in the American colonies, with most residing in the South.

1767   Kunta Kinte, the ancestor of Alex Haley who was immortalized in Haley's book *Roots* in the twentieth century, arrives in Annapolis as part of a cargo of slaves.

1784   The Methodist Church orders its members to free their slaves within a year, but the directive faces so much opposition in the South, including Maryland, that it has to be suspended.

1784   Blacks in Baltimore withdraw from the Methodist Church and form Bethel African Methodist Episcopal Church.

1787   The U.S. Constitution provides for a male slave to count as three-fifths of a human being in determining representation in Congress.

1787	One of Baltimore's first African American congregations, the Sharp Street United Methodist Church, is established.
1788	(*April 28*) Maryland enters the Union as the seventh state.
1789	Josiah Henson, who is believed by some to have been the inspiration for "Uncle Tom" in Harriet Beecher Stowe's 1852 novel *Uncle Tom's Cabin*, is born in Charles County, Maryland.
1789	The Maryland Society for Promoting the Abolition of Slavery and the Relief of Poor Negroes and Others Unlawfully Held in Bondage is established in Baltimore.
1791	Benjamin Banneker publishes the first edition of his almanac and works on the survey laying out the District of Columbia for the nation's new capital.
1793	Refugees from the Haitian slave uprising arrive in Baltimore.
1793	Congress passes the first fugitive slave law.
1796	Maryland forbids the importation of black slaves for sale and allows the voluntary emancipation of slaves.
1798	Joshua Johnston of Baltimore becomes the first African American portrait painter to receive widespread recognition for his work.
1800	According to the U.S. Census, more than one million black slaves reside in the United States, comprising almost 19 percent of the population.
1805	Maryland forbids free blacks from selling corn, wheat, or tobacco without a license.
1807	Congress bans the importation of slaves into the United States.
1809	James W. C. Pennington is born into slavery in Maryland; he will later become the only black member of the Hartford Central Association of Congressional Ministers.
1810	Maryland denies the vote to free blacks.
1815	Clergyman and abolitionist Henry Highland Garnet is born in Maryland.
1816	Daniel Payne Coker, pastor at Bethel AME Church in Baltimore, becomes the first African American Methodist Episcopal bishop.
1817	Black abolitionist and author Frederick Douglass is born into slavery in Tuckahoe, Maryland.
1825	Frances Ellen Watkins Harper, a black novelist and poet, is born in Baltimore to free parents.
1825	Free blacks in Maryland cannot sell tobacco without a license from a justice of the peace witnessed by at least two white citizens.
1825	Josiah Henson leads a group of runaway slaves from Maryland to freedom.
1827	The Maryland Colonization Society is founded in Baltimore.
1829	The first boarding school for black girls, St. Frances Academy, opens in Baltimore.

1832	Maryland reacts to Nat Turner's Rebellion in Virginia by enacting laws restricting free blacks in the state.
1836	Congress passes the "gag rule" to prohibit any antislavery bill or petition from being introduced, read, or discussed.
1838	Frederick Douglass escapes from slavery in Baltimore.
1842	A slaveholders' convention meets in Annapolis.
1843	A native Marylander, James W. C. Pennington, represents Connecticut at the World Anti-Slavery Convention in London.
1845	Frederick Douglass publishes *The Narrative of the Life of Frederick Douglass: An American Slave.*
1847	Frederick Douglass publishes the first issue of his newspaper, *The North Star.*
1849	Harriet Tubman escapes from slavery in Dorchester County, Maryland, to freedom in Pennsylvania.
1849	Escaped slave James W. C. Pennington publishes his autobiography, *The Fugitive Blacksmith.*
1849	Josiah Henson, who escaped from slavery in Charles County, Maryland, publishes his autobiography.
1852	Frederick Douglass delivers perhaps his most famous speech, "The Meaning of the Fourth of July to the Negro," at the Independence Day celebrations in Rochester, New York.
1852	A convention of free blacks from across the state of Maryland meets in Baltimore.
1852	Reverend Harvey Johnson founds the Union Baptist Church in Baltimore; the church will become a center of the Civil Rights Movement in Baltimore in the twentieth century.
1857	In its decision in the Dred Scott case, the U.S. Supreme Court denies slaves citizenship and denies Congress the power to restrict slavery in federal territory.
1860	A bill calling for the enslavement of free blacks in Maryland is defeated by the General Assembly.
1861	*(May)* Federal troops occupy Baltimore, where secessionist mobs have caused disorder and attacked Union troops passing through the city.
1861	*(September)* Secessionist members of the Maryland General Assembly are placed under arrest.
1862	The enlistment of slaves and free blacks into the Union army is authorized by Congress.
1862	The Confiscation Act, which frees the slaves of any slave owner who helps the Confederacy, is passed by Congress.
1863	*(January 1)* President Abraham Lincoln's Emancipation Proclamation ends slavery in areas in rebellion against the United States, but does not touch the institution in loyal states and areas, such as Maryland.

1864	Slavery is abolished in Maryland via the state's new constitution.
1864	For his bravery at Fort Gilmore, near Richmond, Virginia, Sergeant Major Christian A. Fleetwood of Maryland is awarded the Congressional Medal of Honor.
1865	(*February 3*) Maryland ratifies the Thirteenth Amendment to the U.S. Constitution abolishing slavery.
1865	Frederick Douglass dedicates the Douglass Institute in Baltimore.
1866	The Chesapeake Marine and Dry-dock Company, owned by the future founder of the Black Labor Union, Isaac Myers, opens in Baltimore.
1869	(*July*) Isaac Myers and black caulkers in Baltimore found the National Black Labor Union.
1870	(*February 26*) Maryland rejects the Fifteenth Amendment to the U.S. Constitution guaranteeing voting rights to African Americans.
1874	Frederick Douglass becomes president of the Freedman's Savings and Trust Company.
1877	Frederick Douglass becomes a U.S. Marshal.
1880	Frederick Douglass is appointed recorder of deeds for Washington, D.C.
1882	Colored High School is opened in Baltimore.
1885	African American leaders in Baltimore establish the Mutual Brotherhood of Liberty.
1889	Frederick Douglass becomes American consul-general to Haiti.
1890	Harry S. Cummings is elected to the Baltimore City Council, becoming the first black to win a major elective office in the state.
1892	The Baltimore *Afro-American* newspaper is founded by John H. Murphy, Sr.
1904	Maryland passes a Jim Crow public accommodations statue.
1905	The proposed Poe amendment to the Maryland constitution, which would have disfranchised blacks, is defeated.
1909	The proposed Straus amendment to the Maryland constitution, which would have limited voting by blacks, is defeated by voters.
1909	Maryland native Matthew Henson becomes the first person to reach the North Pole.
1911	The proposed Digges amendment to the Maryland state constitution, which would have used property qualifications to effectively disfranchise many black voters, is defeated.
1912	The Arch Social Club, Baltimore's oldest African American social club, is founded.
1913	The Baltimore chapter of the NAACP is formed.
1922	Ku Klux Klan rallies are held in Baltimore and Frederick.

1922   The Douglas Theater, one of the first theaters in the United States owned and operated by blacks, opens in Baltimore.

1926   Baltimore equalizes pay for the city's black and white teachers.

1931   A white mob lynches a black man in Salisbury, Maryland.

1933   A white mob lynches a black prisoner at Princess Anne, Maryland.

1935   The University of Maryland Law School is opened to blacks after Thurgood Marshall, a lawyer for the NAACP, brings suit; Donald Gaines Murray becomes the first African American to enter the law school.

1938   A state court orders that equal pay be provided for black and white teachers throughout Maryland.

1942   African Americans in Baltimore protest police brutality and demand black representation on the local school board.

1946   The Maryland Congress against Discrimination meets in Baltimore.

1948   The Baltimore County Medical Society becomes the first American Medical Association affiliate in a southern state to open its membership to African Americans.

1948   (*July 11*) At Druid Hill Park in Baltimore, 24 black tennis players leave the Negro courts to play on the park's whites-only courts and are arrested.

1950   The University of Maryland School of Nursing is opened to African Americans via a successful lawsuit.

1950   Juanita Jackson Mitchell becomes the first African American graduate of the University of Maryland Law School.

1951   The Maryland Commission on Interracial Problems and Relations is established.

1951   Baltimore city golf courses are opened to African Americans.

1952   Polytechnic High School in Baltimore is integrated.

1953   Maryland state parks are opened to African Americans.

1953   Nine black actors and actresses in Baltimore form the Arena Playhouse, Inc., which is now the oldest continuously operated black community theater in the United States.

1954   The University of Maryland is integrated, becoming the first major southern university to do so.

1955   The desegregation of Maryland public schools begins.

1955   Maryland National Guard units are integrated.

1956   Baltimore enacts an equal employment ordinance.

1958   Irma Dixon and Verda Freeman Welcome become the first African American women elected to the Maryland House of Delegates.

1959   Maryland ratifies the Fourteenth Amendment to the U.S. Constitution guaranteeing full civil rights to African Americans; the amendment took effect in 1868.

1962   Verda Freeman Welcome becomes the first African American woman elected to the Maryland State Senate.

1963   (*February 6*) Maryland ratifies the Twenty-fourth Amendment to the U.S. Constitution abolishing the poll tax.

1963   (*June 14*) Severe race riots erupt in Cambridge; the disorders resulted in the negotiation of a non-binding agreement known as the "Treaty of Cambridge," which listed a series of actions to be undertaken by the Cambridge City Council to improve conditions for the city's black residents.

1963   (*July*) Clergymen of both races force the integration of Gwynn Oak Amusement Park just outside Baltimore.

1966   The Maryland legislature enacts a fair employment law.

1967   Frederick Douglass of Maryland becomes the first civil rights leader to be honored on a postage stamp.

1968   (*April*) Riots erupt in Baltimore following the assassination of Martin Luther King Jr.

1969   The Maryland Commission on Negro History and Culture is authorized.

1970   Parren James Mitchell is elected to the U.S. House of Representatives from Maryland, becoming the first African American elected to Congress from Maryland and the first elected from the South in the twentieth century.

1970   Milton B. Allen becomes the first African American elected state's attorney for the city of Baltimore.

1971   Roland Nathaniel Patterson is the first African American appointed superintendent of schools in Baltimore.

1973   (*May 7*) Maryland ratifies the Fifteenth Amendment, 103 years after the amendment took effect.

1976   Oprah Winfrey becomes coanchor and reporter for WJZ-TV in Baltimore, becoming the first African American woman in the country to hold such a position.

1977   Aris T. Allen becomes the first African American chairperson of the Maryland Republican Party.

1978   Harriet Tubman becomes the first African American woman honored on a postage stamp.

1978   Black Classic Press is founded in Baltimore to publish significant works by and about African Americans.

1978   Aris T. Allen becomes the first African American to run for state office.

1984   Bishop Robinson becomes the first African American police commissioner of Baltimore.

1986   Kweisi Mfume of Baltimore is elected to the U.S. House of Representatives from Maryland, replacing the retiring Parren James Mitchell.

1986   The NAACP moves its national headquarters to Baltimore.

1987   Kurt Lidell Schmoke is elected the first African American mayor of Baltimore.

1991   Vera Hall becomes the first African American woman chairperson of the Democratic Party of Maryland.

1992   Albert R. Wynn, an African American member of the Maryland State Senate, is elected to the U.S. House of Representatives from Maryland's Fourth District.

1995   Elijah E. Cummings is elected as the first black speaker pro tem of the Maryland House of Delegates.

1996   Kweisi Mfume resigns from the U.S. Congress to become president of the NAACP.

1996   Elijah E. Cummings, an African American member of the Maryland House of Delegates, is elected to the U.S. House of Representatives from Maryland to replace Kweisi Mfume after his resignation.

2008   Donna Edwards becomes the first African American woman elected to the U.S. Congress from Maryland.

2008   (*November 4*) Democrat Barack Obama, the first African American nominee for president of a major party, carries Maryland with about 62 percent of the vote.

2009   Maryland Congresswoman Donna Edwards is arrested outside the Sudanese embassy in Washington, D.C., while protesting the genocide in Darfur.

Historical Overview

Seventeenth and Eighteenth Centuries

The Italian navigator Giovanni da Verrazano is thought to have explored the Chesapeake region in about 1524, but the first certain European exploration of the area was made by Pedro Menéndez Marqués, governor of Spanish Florida, in 1574. The first English explorers in the region were Bartholomew Gilbert, who visited in 1603, several years before the founding of Jamestown, and Captain John Smith, who explored the Chesapeake from Jamestown in 1608. Colonization of the area comprising present-day Maryland began in the 1630s. In 1632, Charles I granted George Calvert, Lord Baltimore, a former secretary of state and privy councilor, feudal rights to the land between the Potomac River and 40°N latitude, a boundary description that was vague enough to cause a series of border disputes between Maryland and the colony/state of Virginia down to 1930. A Catholic who was long interested in colonization, both for profit and as a refuge for his coreligionists, Baltimore died before the grant was finalized, but his son Cecilius Calvert, second Lord Baltimore, then undertook the foundation of the colony. Although named Maryland ostensibly in honor of Queen Henrietta Maria, the French Catholic wife of Charles I, the colony in fact was named for the Virgin Mary.

The first settlers arrived in 1634 aboard the ships *Ark* and *Dove*. Although Protestants comprised the majority of the population of St. Mary's City, the first settlement, most of the colony's officers under the first governor, Leonard Calvert, Lord Baltimore's brother, were Catholics, a unique circumstance within the British colonial empire. Among the 1634 settlers was Matthias De Sousa, a black indentured servant. Freed after seven years of servitude, De Sousa by 1642 was a member of the Maryland General Assembly, thus becoming the first black man to sit in an American colonial legislature. De Sousa's example illustrates the fluid nature of race relations in early Maryland. Although slavery existed in the colony almost from the beginning, many blacks, like many whites, came as indentured servants and were freed when their term of service ended. Black and white laborers lived and worked together and even many black slaves were able to gain their freedom—slavery before the 1660s was not necessarily a lifelong status. Many of Maryland's later free black families originated in this period from marriages or relationships between free, indentured, or enslaved African men and free or indentured white women.

As in the other English colonies, the late seventeenth century saw a hardening of racial lines within the colony. The development of tobacco agriculture, particularly in southern Maryland, increased demand for agricultural labor and led to the codification of the institution of slavery into Maryland law. In 1663, the General Assembly passed an act enslaving all Africans brought into the colony. Thus, black servants and their children were henceforth enslaved for life and considered the property of their masters, who could buy and sell them as they wished. In 1664, the Maryland General Assembly debated a bill declaring that Christian baptism did not

confer freedom on the children of black slaves. Maryland also moved to discourage interracial marriages by enacting a law that forced all white women who married black slaves to serve their husband's master for life. In 1692, laws were passed prohibiting any sexual relations between black men and white women and sentencing to seven years servitude any white men who married or had children with black women. Nevertheless, in 1681, children born to white mothers of black fathers or born to free black women were declared to be free.

In the eighteenth century, slavery was an increasingly important component of the Maryland economy, especially in such southern counties as St. George's, where slaves comprised almost 60 percent of the population by 1800. Many newly enslaved Africans came into the colonies through the ports of Annapolis and Baltimore, which developed into important commercial centers in the American colonies in the eighteenth century. Kunta Kinte, who was made famous in the twentieth century by his descendent Alex Haley, was brought into America in a cargo of slaves that landed in Annapolis in 1767. However, by the end of the century, during the decades following the Revolutionary War, profits from tobacco declined, causing an accompanying decline in the demand for black fieldhands. In 1783, the state of Maryland outlawed the further importation of slaves, and the state's policy over the next decade shifted from acquiring more slaves to grow tobacco to seeking means to limit or reduce the state's black population, both slave and free.

Antislavery sentiment also developed in Maryland in the late eighteenth century. In 1784, the Methodist Church ordered its slaveholding members to free their slaves within a year, although resistance to the edict caused it to be suspended. In 1789, one year after Maryland entered the Union as the seventh state, the Maryland Society for Promoting the Abolition of Slavery and the Relief of Poor Negroes and Others Unlawfully Held in

Bondage was established in Baltimore. In 1793, a wave of black refugees from the Haitian slave rebellion arrived in Baltimore, enlarging that city's black community. In 1796, the state allowed the voluntary manumission by owners of their slaves.

Nineteenth Century to the Civil War

In the antebellum period, Maryland, like Virginia, became a source of new slaves for the cotton-growing states of the Deep South. As Maryland itself became less agricultural, many of the state's slave owners sought to make profits from selling slaves or supported efforts to recolonize slaves in Africa. The Maryland chapter of the American Colonization Society was founded in 1827 and largely supported by slave owners who found slavery to be no longer economically viable, but who feared to free their slaves and have the state overrun by free blacks. In 1831, the Maryland General Assembly appropriated $10,000 to be made available to transport slaves and free blacks to Africa. The colony of Maryland in Africa was established in 1834, its population composed mainly of ex-slaves and free blacks from Maryland. In 1857, the Maryland colony was annexed by Liberia.

To encourage free blacks to leave the state, Maryland in 1832 placed severe restrictions upon them. They were officially denied the vote, the right to hold office, or the ability to serve on juries. Free blacks had to carry proof of their free status or they risked being sold into slavery. In Prince George's County, freed blacks had to prove that they were employed and had to obtain a license to sell any goods or commodities they produced upon pain of imprisonment or reenslavement. Any free blacks who visited from other states or areas had to leave within 10 days, and any free black who left the state without license for more than 30 days was not allowed to return. Any children born to a free black who married a slave were born slaves, and any child born to free parents had to be apprenticed to a trade as soon as practical or their apprenticeship would by arranged by the state Orphan's Court. Driven in part by fears arising from the violence of Nat Turner's rebellion in Virginia in 1831, these Maryland measures were designed to encourage free blacks to emigrate and so limit their numbers within the state.

Despite these measures, more than 25,000 free blacks, as well as 2,200 slaves, lived in Baltimore in 1860. According to the 1860 Census, the number of slaves in Maryland as a whole exceeded 87,000. Also in 1860, the Maryland legislature considered but did not enact a bill calling for the enslavement of all free blacks in the state. This bill was part of a trend seen throughout the South in the last years before the Civil War in which slave states tried to control or eliminate free blacks within their borders.

Although a slave state, Maryland was an important conduit through which runaway slaves were funneled into the Underground Railroad. Many Maryland-born slaves, such as Frederick Douglass, Josiah Henson, and Harriet Tubman, escaped to freedom in the North, where they became leaders of the abolitionist movement or helped other slaves to escape the South or settle successfully in the North. Baltimore, with its large community of free blacks, was the center of a network of stations run by both black and white conductors. These conductors, the most famous of whom was the ex-slave Harriet Tubman, strove to get runaways across the Mason-Dixon line into free Pennsylvania, where more formal networks often run by northern abolitionists helped slaves into freedom in New England or Canada. But it was people like Tubman, or free black vendors on the streets of Baltimore or Washington, who actually aided runaways in escaping successfully from slave territory. Many escape routes emanated from Maryland, and particularly from Baltimore. Harriet Tubman often led runaways up Maryland's Eastern Shore into Delaware, where a number of Underground Railroad stations were concentrated around Wilmington. From there, the runaways made their way to Philadelphia, before setting out for places of settlement further north. Many other slaves boarded boats in Baltimore or elsewhere along the Chesapeake and then sailed north, aided by black ship pilots and black crewmen, both slave and free.

The coming of the Civil War split the state. There was much sympathy for the southern cause, but most of the state's commercial and business community opposed secession and there were fears that fighting would be centered in the state should it leave the Union. And once Virginia seceded in April 1861, the Lincoln administration was determined that Maryland should not secede as well and thus surround Washington by Confederate territory. On April 19, 1861, federal troops marching though Baltimore on their way to Washington were attacked by a secessionist mob. In the ensuing battle, 42 men of the 6th Massachusetts Regiment were killed or wounded, while a dozen of the attackers were slain and scores injured. A month later, federal troops were sent to occupy Baltimore. The incident inspired Baltimore native James Ryder Randall to write a poem that was soon set to music as "Maryland, My Maryland," which became the unofficial anthem of Maryland secessionists, many of whom fought for the Confederacy. Maryland did not, however, leave the Union, and in 1864 its new constitution abolished slavery within the state.

Late Nineteenth and Early Twentieth Centuries

Maryland ratified the Thirteenth Amendment abolishing slavery in February 1865 and the Fifteenth Amendment guaranteeing the voting rights of black men in February 1870. However, the state took no action on the Fourteenth Amendment guaranteeing black citizenship, which it did not ratify until 1959, which was 91 years after the amendment took effect. In the postwar years, Maryland, like other border states, fully supported a policy of racial segregation. In 1870, the state declared that taxes paid by African Americans be set aside to support separate African American schools. In 1872, state schools for blacks were formally mandated, although no distract had to establish such a school unless the size of the local African American population warranted it. In 1884, the legislature passed an antimiscegenation statute that prohibited all marriages between whites and blacks or anyone of black descent within three generations. Violators faced up to 10 years in prison and ministers performing such marriages were fined $100.

In 1904, Maryland railway and steamboat companies were required to provide separate cars or areas for white and black passengers, and public accommodations within the state were segregated. Any company refusing to comply risked fines of up to $1,000, and any passenger refusing to comply could face fines of up to $50, 30 days in jail, or both. In 1908, segregation was extended to streetcars, which now had to designate separate seats for white and black riders. In 1924, miscegenation was declared a felony and racially segregated schools were required throughout the state. Although laws requiring segregation in public accommodations were repealed in 1951, the antimiscegenation laws were strengthened in the 1950s. In 1955, any white woman who gave birth to a child fathered by a black or mulatto man was liable to up to five years' imprisonment, and in 1957, it became a crime for a white woman to conceive a child with a black man, although the law was struck down as unconstitutional within the year. However, the state's antimiscegenation laws were not fully repealed until 1967.

Several attempts were also made to limit black voting. In 1905 and 1909, two proposed amendments to the Maryland constitution designed to disfranchise African Americans were defeated by voters. A third attempt, the Digges Amendment,

THE FIFTEENTH AMENDMENT.
CELEBRATED MAY 19ᵗ 1870.

This commemorative montage depicts the May 19, 1870, parade in Baltimore celebrating the passage of the Fifteenth Amendment. One of three Reconstruction amendments enacted in the years immediately following the Civil War, the Fifteenth Amendment was adopted by the U.S. Congress on February 26, 1869, to protect the voting rights of African American men. (Library of Congress)

sought to use property qualifications for voting to achieve the same purpose, but it was also defeated in 1911.

Meanwhile, this same period saw the rise of vibrant African American communities in and around Baltimore. African American leaders opened a black high school in the city in 1882 and established the Mutual Brotherhood of Liberty in 1885. John H. Murphy founded the *Baltimore Afro-American* newspaper in 1892, and the Baltimore chapter of the NAACP was formed in 1913. Many black-owned or directed businesses or organizations also appeared in the state in this period. Isaac Myers founded the national Black Labor Union in Baltimore in 1869, and the Arch Social Club, the oldest black social club

in Baltimore, was established in 1912. The Douglas Theater, one of the first black-owned theaters in the United States, opened in Baltimore in 1922. Nonetheless, racism became more overt in the state in the early twentieth century. In 1919, serious riots erupted in Baltimore as whites, unhappy that blacks were moving into previously all-white neighborhoods, harassed blacks with taunts and jeers. In one instance, blacks, who were frustrated by the failure of the police to respond to their complaints, confronted a mob of white youths and were then attacked with rocks, bottles, and bricks. In the 1920s, Ku Klux Klan rallies were held in Baltimore and other Maryland cities and the lynching of black citizens by white mobs occurred in the state as late as 1933.

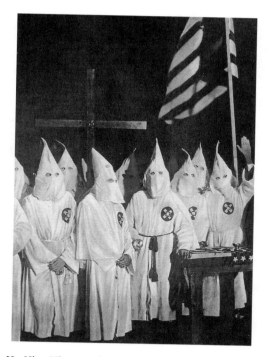

Ku Klux Klan members attend an initiation ceremony in Baltimore, Maryland, in 1923. The Klan was founded in the South after the Civil War for the purpose of intimidating the newly freed slaves and preventing them from taking advantage of their new rights. Klan members dressed in white robes and hoods to conceal their true identities. (The Illustrated London News Picture Library)

Civil Rights Era and Beyond

In 1934, African Americans launched a "Don't Buy Where You Can't Work" campaign along Baltimore's Pennsylvania Avenue, which concluded with the hiring by local merchants of several black employees. In 1935, a lawsuit by Thurgood Marshall, who had earlier been denied admittance to the school, opened the University of Maryland Law School to African Americans. In 1938, a state court ordered that equal pay be provided to Maryland's black and white teachers. In 1942, African American civil rights activists staged the "March to Annapolis" to protest white

police brutality against blacks. An interracial tennis match held at Druid Hill Park in Baltimore in 1948 led to the arrest of 34 people when police arrived to stop the match. When in the same year a court ruled that Baltimore's municipal golf courses had to be opened to blacks, the parks board evaded the ruling by designating certain days on which the courses were open to blacks only.

The Maryland Teachers Association was integrated in 1951 and blacks were hired for the first time by the Baltimore Fire Department in 1953. Although 500 white students refused to attend classes to protest school integration in the wake of the 1954 U.S. Supreme Court *Brown v. Board of Education* decision, Catholic and Quaker schools in Baltimore announced that they would integrate. The University of Maryland also integrated in 1954, and the desegregation of Maryland public schools began in earnest in 1955. In 1963, Gwynn Oak Amusement Park outside Baltimore was integrated after hundreds of antisegregation demonstrators were arrested at the park and then insulted by white patrons as they were led away.

In June 1963, riots erupted in Cambridge with shootings by both blacks and whites, brick throwing, and numerous fires started by Molotov cocktails. The governor sent the National Guard to Cambridge to restore order, but on July 11, further violence erupted when two carloads of armed whites drove down Pine Street, the main black thoroughfare, firing guns in all directions. To end the disorder, local civil rights activist Gloria Richardson, a leader of the Cambridge Nonviolent Action Committee, met with city and Justice Department officials to negotiate the so-called Treaty of Cambridge, which listed a series of nonbinding initiatives the City Council could undertake to improve conditions for black residents. In April 1968, the assassination of Martin Luther King Jr. sparked riots in Baltimore that resulted in more than 5,000 arrests, 1,000 arson fires, and over 700 persons injured. The governor called in federal troops and the National Guard to restore order after three days of rioting. The year 1968 also saw the founding of the Baltimore branch of the Black Panther Party, which opened its "People's Free Clothing Program" in the city.

Since the 1950s, African Americans have made significant political gains in the state. In 1954, three African Americans were elected to the Maryland General Assembly—Emory Cole and Truly Hatchett to the House of Delegates and Henry Cole to the state Senate. In 1958, Verda Freeman Welcome and Irma Dixon became the first African American women elected to the Maryland House of Delegates, and in 1962 Welcome won election to the state Senate. In 1970, Maryland sent its first African American representative to the U.S. Congress in the person of Parren James Mitchell; he was the first African American elected to Congress from a southern state in the twentieth century. Mitchell retired in 1986 and was replaced in Congress by Kweisi Mfume, who served until his resignation in 1996 to become president of the NAACP. Kurt Schmoke became the first black mayor of Baltimore in 1987, and Albert R. Wynn, a member of the Maryland State Senate, was elected to Congress in 1992. Elijah E. Cummings, the first African American speaker pro tem of the Maryland House of Delegates, was elected to replace Mfume in Congress in 1996. Donna Edwards became the first black woman elected to Congress from Maryland in 2008, the same year Maryland gave over 60 percent of its popular vote for president to Barack Obama, the black Democratic senator from Illinois.

Notable African Americans

Banneker, Benjamin (1731–1806)

Benjamin Banneker was born free near Ellicott City. His father was an escaped slave and his mother was freeborn, the daughter of a white woman, Molly Welsh, and her former slave, Banneka, whom Molly freed and married. Taught to read by his grandmother and by Peter Heinrichs, a Quaker farmer who established a school in the neighborhood, Banneker taught himself astronomy as an adult, using books and equipment lent to him by George Ellicott, a Quaker neighbor. In 1791, Banneker was hired by Ellicott to assist the survey team laying out the boundaries of the new federal district. Between 1792 and 1797, Banneker published a series of almanacs containing many astronomical calculations. He also kept a series of journals and a diary. In 1791, he sent a letter to Thomas Jefferson, criticizing Jefferson's treatment of his slaves and calling for justice and equality for blacks.

Blake, James Hubert "Eubie" (1887–1983)

Born in Baltimore to former slaves, Eubie Blake was one of the greatest American composers and performers of ragtime and jazz of the twentieth century. He started playing the organ at age 5, and by his early teens was performing on the piano at nightclubs, saloons, and brothels in Baltimore. In 1921, Blake and his long-time collaborator Noble Sissle wrote *Shuffle Along*, one of the first Broadway musicals to be written and directed by African Americans. Among Blake's other well-known compositions are "Bandana Days," "Charleston Rag," "Love Will Find A Way," "Memories of You," and "I'm Just Wild About Harry." In 1978, a musical entitled *Eubie*, which featured Blake's music, opened on Broadway. Blake received the Presidential Medal of Freedom from President Ronald Reagan in 1981, two years before his death.

Calloway, Cabell "Cab" III (1907–1994)

Born in Rochester, New York, but raised in Baltimore, Cab Calloway was a band leader, jazz singer, and master of scat, a style of singing that uses random syllables or no words at all to make the voice sound as if it were performing an instrument solo. Calloway briefly attended law school before achieving national fame as leader of one of the most popular African American big bands in the 1930s and 1940s. In 1931, Calloway's band, which included such jazz greats as Dizzy Gillespie and Doc Cheatham, performed at the famous Cotton Club in Harlem, replacing Duke Ellington's band while it was on tour. So popular was Calloway's band that it began touring nationwide, appearing on Walter Winchell's radio program and with Bing Crosby in New York. Through these performances, Calloway, along with Ellington, helped break the color barrier for black performers at major broadcast networks. Calloway's most famous song was "Minnie the Moocher," recorded in 1931. Calloway continued to perform up to his death in 1994.

Douglass, Frederick (1818–1895)

Douglass was born into slavery in Tuckahoe in Talbot Country; his mother, Harriet Bailey, was a slave who died when Douglass was seven, and his father is obscure but may have been Harriet's master. Taught the alphabet by the wife of his master, Douglass then secretly taught himself to read and write. Escaping from slavery in 1838, he settled in Massachusetts, where his great ability as a speaker and writer made him a leader of the abolitionist movement. In 1845, he published his influential autobiography *Life and Times of Frederick Douglass*. During the Civil War, he was an advisor to President Abraham Lincoln, and after the war, he worked for equal rights for African Americans. He was the first African American to hold high rank in the federal government, serving as U.S. minister and consul-general to Haiti. In 1888 at the Republican National Convention, he became the first black man to receive a vote for president.

Gaddy, Beatrice (1933–2001)

Born in North Carolina, Beatrice Gaddy moved to Baltimore in 1964. In 1981, unemployed and on food stamps, she used $290 from a winning lottery ticket to feed herself and 39 neighbors at Thanksgiving, starting an annual Thanksgiving event that eventually fed thousands. Soliciting donations from grocers and other suppliers, Gaddy opened a food kitchen run by those in need. Her work led to the creation of the Bea Gaddy Foundation and caused her to become widely known throughout the city as the "Mother Teresa of Baltimore" and "Saint Bea." She also directed a food pantry, a furniture bank, clothing drives, shelters for women and children, and a program to refurbish abandoned row houses. She was mentioned by President George H. W. Bush as one of his "thousand points of light." The anniversary of her death, October 3, is known as Bea Gaddy Day in Baltimore.

Harper, Frances E. W. (1825–1911)

Born free in Baltimore, Frances Harper was a poet, writer, and abolitionist leader. She published her first book of poetry, *Forest Leaves*, in 1845. She became a traveling lecturer for the American Anti-Slavery Society in 1853 and involved herself through speaking and writing in most of the important political and social issues of the nineteenth century, including abolition, anti-lynching campaigns, and women's rights. In 1859, she published *The Two Others*, which is considered the first short story published by an African American in the United States Featuring a female protagonist, her most famous work is her novel *Iola Leroy*, which was published in 1892 when she was 67. In 1897, she was elected president of the National Association of Colored Women.

Henson, Josiah (1789–1883)

Born a slave in Charles County, Henson escaped from bondage in 1830 and settled in Canada, where he founded a school and a community known as Dawn Settlement for other ex-slaves. In 1849, he published his autobiography *The Life*

Josiah Henson, 1876. Henson is believed by some to have been the inspiration for "Uncle Tom" in Harriet Beecher Stowe's 1852 novel, *Uncle Tom's Cabin*. (Library of Congress)

of Josiah Henson, Formerly a Slave, Now an Inhabitant of Canada, as Narrated by Himself, which was later used by Harriet Beecher Stowe in writing her novel *Uncle Tom's Cabin*. Because of this, it is believed that Stowe's character of Uncle Tom is based upon Henson. He also became a Methodist preacher and an abolitionist lecturer. In 1876, continuing interest in his life generated by his connection with Stowe's novel led him to publish an updated version of his autobiography entitled *Uncle Tom's Story of His Life: An Autobiography of the Rev. Josiah Henson*. He died at Dawn Settlement in 1883.

Henson, Matthew (1866–1955)

Born on a form near Nanjemoy in Charles County, Henson went to sea as a cabin boy after his parents died when he was only 13. He educated himself and became a skilled navigator while sailing around the world as a merchant seaman. In 1887, he met the explorer Robert Peary, who, impressed by Henson's navigational skills, recruited him for various voyages of exploration, including expeditions to Nicaragua and the Arctic. During the 1909 Arctic expedition, Henson appears to have been the first member of Peary's team to reach the North Pole, where Henson planted the American flag. Although Peary was widely honored for the achievement, Henson was largely ignored, and Henson's 1912 book, *A Negro Explorer at the North Pole*, angered Peary, who saw it as an attempt to encroach on his fame. In 1944, Congress awarded Henson a duplicate of the silver medal given to Peary.

Holiday, Billie (1915–1959)

Born in Philadelphia with the name Eleanora Fagan, but raised in Baltimore largely by relatives and friends of her mother, who was a Baltimore native, Eleanora took the stage name Billie Holiday in about 1929 when she started singing in clubs, bars, and brothels in Harlem, where she had moved with her mother in 1928. She made her recording debut with Benny Goodman in 1933, after record producer John Hammond heard her singing at a local club. Holiday transformed the art of jazz singing with her distinct and deeply personal vocal style, which illustrated novel methods of manipulating phrasing and tempo. Holiday, who later performed at Carnegie Hall and starred opposite Louis Armstrong in the 1947 film *New Orleans*, also cowrote a number of well-known jazz songs, including "God Bless the Child," "Don't Explain," "Fine and Mellow," and "Lady Sings the Blues." Widely known by her nickname, "Lady Day," Holiday was also famous for several of the jazz standards she performed, including "Easy Living" and "Strange Fruit," which condemned the lynching of African Americans and which, in Holiday's version, was inducted into the Grammy Hall of Fame in 1978.

Leonard, Ray Charles "Sugar Ray" (1956–)

Born in North Carolina, Ray Leonard moved to Palmer Park in Prince George's County when he was 11. Leonard stated boxing at the recreation center in Palmer Park in 1969. Named for his mother's favorite singer, he got his nickname when a boxing coaching told his trainer that as a boxer Leonard was "sweet as sugar." He won the national Golden Gloves lightweight championship in 1973 and won the gold medal as a light welterweight at the 1976 Olympics. He made his professional debut in 1977 and, before retiring in 1998, became the first boxer to win over $100 million in purses and championships in five weight divisions, defeating most of the top boxers of his era. Considered one of the best boxers of all time, he was named "Boxer of the Decade" for the 1980s. He has worked as a boxing analyst for various networks since his retirement.

Lewis, Reginald F. (1942–1993)

Born in Baltimore, Reginald Lewis earned a degree in economics from Virginia State College in 1965 and a law degree from Harvard Law School in 1968. In the early 1980s, he bought McCall Pattern Company, which he brought to great profitability and sold for $90 million. In 1987, he bought Beatrice International Foods, a snack foods, beverage, and grocery conglomerate that he renamed TLC Beatrice International. The company became the first African American–owned enterprise to achieve more than $1 billion in profits. In 1992, *Forbes* Magazine named Lewis one of the 400 richest Americans with a net worth of about $400 million.

Marshall, Thurgood (1908–1993)

Born in Baltimore, the great-grandson of slaves, Marshall graduated from Baltimore's Frederick Douglass High School in 1925 and from Lincoln University in Pennsylvania in 1930. Denied entrance to the University of Maryland because of his race, he earned a law degree from Howard University and in 1935 successfully sued the University of Maryland in *Pearson v. Murray*, thereby ending segregation at the university's law school. In 1940, he became chief counsel for the NAACP and thus became lead attorney for the landmark 1954 case *Brown v. Board of Education*, which overturned the "separate but equal" doctrine and opened the door to integration of public education. In 1967, President Lyndon Johnson nominated Marshall as the first African American justice on the U.S. Supreme Court. He died in 1993 and is buried at Arlington National Cemetery.

Mitchell, Clarence M., Jr. (1911–1984)

Born and raised in Baltimore, Clarence Mitchell was educated at Old Douglass High School and then at Lincoln University in Pennsylvania. He saw the aftermath of a lynching in Cambridge while working for the *Baltimore Afro-American* newspaper, which spurred him to become active in the fight for civil rights. For almost 30 years, he was chief lobbyist for the NAACP, where his advocacy for a series of civil rights measures, including the 1964 Civil Rights Act, the 1965 Voting Rights Act, and the 1968 Fair Housing Act, won him the Spingarn Medal in 1969 and earned him the nickname of "the 101st U.S. Senator." In 1980, he received the Presidential Medal of Freedom from President Jimmy Carter. After his retirement, he wrote a Sunday editorial column on civil rights for the *Baltimore Sun*. After his death, Baltimore renamed its courthouse after him.

Pennington, James W. C. (1807–1870)

Born a slave in Washington County, James Pennington escaped to Pennsylvania and in 1828 moved to New York. Settling in New Haven,

Connecticut, where he plied his trade as a black-smith, Pennington attended classes at Yale Divinity School, becoming the first African American student at Yale. He was later ordained a minister and in 1849 received an honorary doctorate of divinity from the University of Heidelberg. In 1841, he published *The Origin and History of the Colored People*, considered the first history of African Americans, and in 1850, he published his famous autobiography, *The Fugitive Blacksmith*. Self-taught, Pennington, through his speeches and writings, became a leader of the antebellum antislavery movement.

Richardson, Gloria (1922–)

Born in Baltimore, the granddaughter of a city councilman, Gloria Richardson grew up in Cambridge, where she became a founder of the Cambridge Nonviolent Action Committee (CNAC) and a leader of the Cambridge Movement, a campaign to win civil rights for the city's black community. In June 1963, serious race riots erupted in Cambridge, leaving the city under martial law. Richardson was part of the negotiations conducted by a Department of Justice team that included Robert Kennedy and that led to the signing of the so-called Treaty of Cambridge, which listed various actions the Cambridge City Council could undertake to improve conditions for the city's blacks. When a city charter amendment calling for desegregation of public accommodations was put up for a vote, Richardson broke with Martin Luther King Jr. and other civil rights leaders and called on blacks to stay away from the polls because a group's basic civil rights should not be put up for vote. Richardson left Cambridge in 1964 and today works for New York City's Department for the Aging.

Tindley, Charles Albert (1851–1933)

Born in Berlin, the son of a free mother and a slave father, Charles Tindley was himself considered free, although he grew up with slaves. Tindley moved to Philadelphia after the Civil War and taught himself Greek and Hebrew. He put himself through school while working as a church janitor, eventually earning a doctorate and achieving ordination as a Methodist minister. He founded one of the largest African American Methodist congregations in the country in Philadelphia. Tindley also made a name for himself as a composer of gospel hymns, and is often called the "Father of Gospel Music." He composed almost 50 hymns and published a collection of hymns entitled *New Songs of Paradise* in 1916. Tindley's two best-known compositions are "I'll Overcome Some Day," which is believed to be the basis for the later civil rights anthem "We Shall Overcome," and "Stand by Me," which was later remade by Ben E. King.

Tubman, Harriet (1820–1913)

Born a slave in Dorchester County, Harriet Tubman escaped from bondage in 1849 and immediately returned to Maryland to help members of her family to freedom. Over the next decade, she is believed to have made 19 trips into slave territory and to have helped over 300 slaves escape to freedom via the Underground Railroad. Known as "Moses," she famously told an audience after the Civil War that she "never lost a single passenger" as a conductor on the railroad. During the war, Tubman worked for the Union army as a cook, nurse, and then as an armed scout and spy. She led a military raid into South Carolina in 1863, which resulted in the liberation of almost 700 slaves. After the war, Tubman was active in the women's rights movement.

Cultural Contributions

There are numerous institutions and organizations that celebrate the African American history of Maryland. The Reginald F. Lewis Museum of

Portrait of Harriet Tubman, a leader of the Underground Railroad. (Library of Congress)

Maryland African American History and Culture opened in Baltimore in 2005. Dedicated to preserving Maryland's black heritage, the museum is the second-largest African American museum in the world. The Sports Legends Museum at Camden Yards, the home of the Baltimore Orioles baseball team, also opened in 2005. It contains many artifacts relating to the Negro Baseball Leagues and specifically to Baltimore's two African American teams, the Baltimore Elite Giants and the Baltimore Black Sox. Elmer and Joanne Martin founded the Great Blacks in Wax Museum in Baltimore in 1983. Today the museum contains over 100 wax figures of prominent African Americans, including Malcolm X, Langston Hughes, Sojourner Truth, and a full-scale replica of a slave trading ship. In January, the museum offers a special exhibit commemorating the life of Martin Luther King Jr. The Eubie Blake National Jazz Institute and Cultural Center in Baltimore contains permanent collections illustrating the lives of such Baltimore jazz legends as Eubie Blake, Cab Calloway, and Chick Webb. The center also sponsors jazz concerts, cultural events, and performing arts classes.

Maryland also offers a number of African American cultural festivals and programs. In February, the Black Heritage Art Show is held at the Baltimore Convention Center. The annual event brings together the works of African American artists from across the country, and also features workshops, seminars, and poetry readings. The African American Renaissance Grand Tour is held the last Friday of February; it features actors in period costumes reenacting important episodes from Baltimore's African American history and black heritage sites throughout the city. During the summer, Baltimore offers the weekly Showcase of Nations Ethnic Festivals, which showcase African American and other ethnic foods, crafts, music, dance, and other entertainments. Jazzy Summer Nights is a free concert series featuring the best of local jazz bands and performers. The African American Heritage Festival is held in June at Camden Yards ballpark in Baltimore. The festival offers crafts, music, and artwork by local and national artists. Baltimore's three-day Juneteenth Festival, commemorating the arrival of news of emancipation in Texas and the Southwest, offers jazz, blues, and gospel music; food and cooking contests; a celebrity basketball game; arts and crafts exhibitions; historical lectures; and storytelling.

Baltimore also has a number of African American cultural and historical sites. The Frederick Douglass "Path of Freedom" walking tour covers numerous sites associated with Douglass' life in Baltimore and Maryland. These sites include several eighteenth-century buildings associated with Douglass during his youth as a slave in Maryland, as well as houses where he lived, churches where he worshipped, and places where he was educated.

Also on the tour are the five historic townhouses that he built in Baltimore after the Civil War. Baltimore's Civil War walking tour also covers many important African American sites in the city, including some associated with slavery days and others with the black communities that developed around the city after the war. The Thurgood Marshall walking tour covers 12 sites in and around Baltimore associated with the country's first black Supreme Court justice. Finally, the "Finding a Way to Freedom" tour covers sites in and around Cambridge that are associated with Harriet Tubman and the Underground Railroad, including a Harriet Tubman museum and a country general store where she is said to have prevented the capture of a runaway slave.

Bibliography

Argersinger, Jo Ann E. *Toward a New Deal in Baltimore: People and Government in the Great Depression.* Chapel Hill: University of North Carolina Press, 1988.

Bode, Carl. *Maryland: A Bicentennial History.* New York: Norton, 1978.

Brackett, Jeffrey R. *The Negro in Maryland: A Study of the Institution of Slavery.* Reprint ed. Lenox, MA: HardPress, 2008.

Browne, Gary Lawson. *Baltimore in the Nation, 1789–1861.* Chapel Hill: University of North Carolina Press, 1980.

Brugger, Robert J. *Maryland, A Middle Temperament: 1634–1980.* Baltimore: Johns Hopkins University Press, 1996.

Callum, Agnes Kane. *Colored Volunteers of Maryland, Civil War, 7th Regiment, United States Colored Troops, 1863–1866.* Baltimore: Mullac Publishers, 1990.

Callum, Agnes Kane. *9th Regiment United States Colored Troops, Volunteers of Maryland, Civil War, 1863–1866.* Baltimore: Mullac Publishers, 1999.

Chapelle, Suzanne Ellery, and Glenn O. Phillips. *African American Leaders of Maryland: A Portrait Gallery.* Baltimore: Maryland Historical Society, 2003.

Diggs, Louis S. *From the Meadows to the Point: The Histories of the African American Community of Turner Station and What Was the African American Community in Sparrows Point.* Baltimore: By the Author, 2003.

Diggs, Louis S. *Holding On to Their Heritage.* Baltimore: Uptown Press, 1996.

Diggs, Louis S. *In Our Voices: A Folk History in Legacy (African American Community of Baltimore, Maryland).* Baltimore: Uptown Press, 1998.

Diggs, Louis S. *It All Started on Winters Lane: A History of the Black Community in Catonsville, Maryland.* Baltimore: By the Author, 1995.

Diggs, Louis S. *Since the Beginning: African American Communities in Towson.* Baltimore: Uptown Press, 2000.

Diggs, Louis S. *Surviving in America: Histories of Seven Black Communities in Baltimore County, Maryland.* Baltimore: Uptown Press, 2002.

Dozer, Donald. *Portrait of the Free State: A History of Maryland.* Cambridge, MD: Tidewater, 1976.

Durr, Kenneth D. *Behind the Backlash: White Working-Class Politics in Baltimore, 1940–1980.* Chapel Hill: University of North Carolina Press, 2003.

Farrar, Hayward. *The Baltimore Afro-American: 1892–1950.* Westport, CT: Greenwood Press, 1998.

Fields, Barbara J. *Slavery and Freedom on the Middle Ground: Maryland during the Nineteenth Century.* New Haven, CT: Yale University Press, 1985.

Fuke, Richard Paul. *Imperfect Equality: African Americans and the Confines of White Racial Attitudes in Post-Emancipation Maryland.* New York: Fordham University Press, 1999.

Heinegg, Paul. *Free African Americans of Maryland and Delaware from the Colonial Period to 1810.* Baltimore: Clearfield Company, 2000.

Hoffman, Ronald. *A Spirit of Dissension: Economics, Politics, and the Revolution in Maryland.* Baltimore: Johns Hopkins University Press, 1973.

Kulikoff, Allan. *Tobacco and Slaves: The Development of Southern Cultures in the Chesapeake, 1680–1800.* Chapel Hill: University of North Carolina Press, 1988.

McCormac, Eugene Irving. *White Servitude in Maryland, 1634–1820.* Westminster, MD: Willow Bend Books, 2002.

Middleton, Arthur Pierce. *Tobacco Coast: A Maritime History of Chesapeake Bay in the Colonial Era.* Baltimore: Johns Hopkins University Press, 1984.

Papenfuse, Edward C., et al. *Maryland: A New Guide to the Old Line State.* Baltimore: Johns Hopkins University Press, 1976.

Phillips, Christopher. *The African American Community of Baltimore, 1790–1860.* Urbana: University of Illinois Press, 1997.

Poe, William A. *African Americans of Calvert County.* Mt. Pleasant, SC: Arcadia Publishing, 2008.

Risjord, Norman K. *Chesapeake Politics, 1781–1800.* New York: Columbia University Press, 1978.

Switala, William J. *Underground Railroad in Delaware, Maryland, and West Virginia.* Mechanicsburg, PA: Stackpole Books, 2004.

Walsh, Richard, and William Lloyd Fox, eds. *Maryland: A History.* Baltimore: Maryland Hall of Records, 1983.

Wennersten, John R. *Maryland's Eastern Shore: A Journey in Time and Place.* Atglen, PA: Schiffer Publishing, 1992.

MASSACHUSETTS

Fred Lindsey

Chronology

1630	Massachusetts passes the first law protecting any slaves who flee brutal treatment by their masters.
1635	First African slaves in Massachusetts arrive in Salem in exchange for Native Americans sent in bondage to the West Indies.
1641	Massachusetts is the first colony to legalize slavery for African Americans, Native Americans, and mulattos, but their natural rights include use of the legal system.
1652	Massachusetts enacts a law requiring all African American and Native American servants to undergo military training to enable them to help defend the colony.
1656	Fearing the potential for a slave uprising, the Massachusetts colonial legislature reverses the 1652 statute and prohibits African Americans from arming or training as militia.
1670	The Massachusetts legislature passes a law that enables its citizens to sell the children of enslaved Africans into bondage, thus separating them from their families.
1673	The Massachusetts legislature passes a law that forbids European Americans from engaging in any trade or commerce with African Americans.
1693	The Society of Negroes, a self-help organization, is founded in Boston.
1700	Massachusetts Chief Justice Samuel Sewall publishes *The Selling of Joseph*, a book that advances both economic and moral reasons for the abolition of the African slave trade.
1746	Lucy Terry (1724–1821) composes "Bars Fight," the first known poem by an African American. A description of an Indian raid on Terry's hometown, the poem is passed down orally and published in 1850.
1754	A Massachusetts Census counts the total population of enslaved blacks in the colony; 647 male slaves and 342 female slaves are counted in Boston.
1764	African Americans are granted the right to vote in Boston.
1770	(*March 5*) Crispus Attacks, a runaway slave, is killed in the Boston Massacre.
1770	(*April 19*) Free blacks fight alongside white Minutemen in the initial skirmishes of the Revolutionary War at Lexington and Concord.
1773	Phillis Wheatley, a slave of the Wheatley family of Boston, authors the first book of poetry by an African American; it is published in London.
1773–1778	Prince Hall, spiritual leader, and other free blacks petition the Massachusetts legislature for the same rights and privileges as their white peers.
1774	(*March 8*) The Massachusetts General Assembly passes the first act forbidding the importation of black slaves. It was suspended by the royal governor the following day.

1775	*(June 17)* Two African Americans, Peter Salem and Salem Poor, are commended for their service on the American side at the Battle of Bunker Hill.
1778	Phillis Wheatley is legally freed upon the death of her master.
1780–1783	The Massachusetts state constitution provides a Declaration of Rights, which includes equality for all men. Under the constitution, the first test cases of Quock Walker and Mumbet (Elizabeth) Freedom lead to the declaration that slavery is unconstitutional.
1783	Paul Cuffee and his brother John are leaders of a lawsuit that gives African Americans civil equality in the state by allowing them to vote.
1784	The first African Lodge of Free Masons in Massachusetts is formed with Prince Hall as master.
1787	Prince Hall petitions the Boston School Committee for a separate school for "colored" children.
1788	*(February 6)* Massachusetts enters the Union as the sixth state.
1788	After three Boston free black men are kidnapped and taken to the West Indies, Prince Hall and 21 associates petition to the legislature, and the kidnapped men are returned to Boston.
1796	Boston's African Society is established.
1798–1800	A private school for "Africans" is established in the house of Prince Hall.
1808	*(January 1)* By an act of Congress, the transportation of enslaved Africans into the United States is outlawed.
1815	Abiel Smith, a wealthy white businessman, dies and leaves money to establish an African school in Boston.
1816	The American Colonization Society is formed to encourage the emigration of free blacks from the United States to West Africa. Paul Cuffee, a ship captain and wealthy Westport African American, leads an expedition to Sierra Leone in West Africa for settlement.
1822	After decades of absence, African Americans are linked to the whaling industry, as Abaslon Boston commands an historic voyage on the ship *Industry*, with an all-black crew.
1825	Under the leadership of David Walker, the Massachusetts General Colored Association is founded to abolish slavery and improve conditions for blacks.
1829	Jacob Perry is the first and only African American teacher in the African school in Nantucket.
1829	David Walker (1785–1830) publishes the *Appeal to the Colored Citizens of the World* (David Walker's *Appeal*). The *Appeal* called for violence against slaveholders. Walker

1829 (*cont.*)	is murdered in 1830, at his business on Beacon Hill. He was wanted "dead or alive" for $1,000.
1832	(*February 22*) A group of "females of color" in Salem form the first black women's anti-slavery society in the United States. The abolitionist press documents the existence of a variety of women's antislavery societies during this period. Freed black women actively participate in the racially mixed societies.
1841	John Quincy Adams of Massachusetts, a former president of the United States, successfully defends black mutineers in the *Amistad* case before the U.S. Supreme Court.
1844	Richard Theodore Greener becomes the first African American to graduate from Harvard.
1845	The Massachusetts legislature passes a law that requires integrated schools.
1845	(*May 3*) Macon B. Allen (1816–1894) of Worcester becomes the first black formally admitted to the bar in any state. He had been allowed to practice in Maine two years earlier.
1847	Frederick Douglass begins editing *The North Star* newspaper.
1849	In *Roberts v. Boston*, a lawsuit seeking to end racial discrimination in Boston public schools, the Massachusetts Supreme Judicial Court rules in favor of Boston, finding no constitutional cases for the suit.
1850	(*June 27*) Robert Morris becomes the first African American lawyer to pass the bar in Boston.
1850	John V. DeGrasse is the first black doctor admitted to the Massachusetts Medical Society. He graduated from Bowdoin Medical School (Maine) in 1849.
1851	Black abolitions rescue a fugitive slave from a Boston courtroom.
1853	Sarah Parker Remond is ejected from a Boston theater for refusing to sit in the section reserved for blacks. Injured during her ejection, she sues and recovers damages. The theater is later desegregated.
1855	A law is passed calling for the integration of all public schools in the Commonwealth of Massachusetts.
1859	Former slave and community activist Lewis Hayden becomes the first black political appointee in Boston, when he is made messenger to the Massachusetts secretary of state.
1860	The Census reports 2,260 African Americans (1.3 percent of the African American population of Massachusetts) live in Boston.
1863	The all-black Massachusetts 54th Infantry Regiment is formed in Boston. Eight hundred African Americans become part of the 54th Regiment, but more than 4,000 African Americans take up arms for the North in the Civil War.

1865–1869	The Freedmen's Bureau sponsors a program that relocates African Americans from the Tidewater region of Virginia to Boston; during the program, more than a thousand African Americans move to Boston and Cambridge.
1865	(*February 7*) Massachusetts ratifies the Thirteenth Amendment to the U.S. Constitution abolishing slavery.
1866	Charles Lewis Mitchell (1829–1912) and Edward Garrison Walker (1831–1910), the son of David Walker, are elected to the Massachusetts legislature, becoming the first African Americans elected to a state legislature. Mitchell also serves as the first African American inspector of customs in Boston, and Walker becomes a prominent Boston lawyer and a Democrat, a surprising switch of party for the time.
1867	(*March 20*) Massachusetts ratifies the Fourteenth Amendment to the U.S. Constitution guaranteeing full citizenship rights to African Americans.
1868	(*February 23*) William Edward Burghardt Du Bois, one of the twentieth century's greatest intellectuals and a founder of the National Association for the Advancement of Colored People (NAACP), is born in Great Barrington.
1869	(*March 12*) Massachusetts ratifies the Fifteenth Amendment to the U.S. Constitution guaranteeing blacks the right to vote.
1870	The official number of African Americans living in Boston reaches 3,445.
1890	The black population of Boston reaches 8,000.
1890	(*June 25*) W. E. B. Du Bois graduates, cum laude, from Harvard University, the first African American to receive a Ph.D. from Harvard.
1899	In Cambridge, Maria Baldwin becomes the North's first African American headmaster of a predominantly white school.
1915	When Massachusetts blacks object to the racist film *Birth of a Nation*, Governor Edward Walsh bans the film in Massachusetts outside Boston.
1938	Malcolm Little (later Malcolm X) moves to Boston to attend the eighth grade. He stays in the Boston area for the next eight years.
1951	(*September*) Martin Luther King Jr. arrives at Boston University to study for his Ph.D. While in Boston, King meets his future wife Coretta Scott, another southerner attending the Boston school.
1962	Edward Brooke is elected attorney general of Massachusetts, becoming the first African American to serve as an elected attorney general of a state.
1963	(*March 28*) Massachusetts ratifies the Twenty-fourth Amendment to the U.S. Constitution abolishing the poll tax.
1963	(*June 18*) 3,000 blacks boycott Boston's segregated public schools.

1966	Edward Brooke is elected to the U.S. Senate from Massachusetts, becoming the first black elected to the Senate by popular vote.
1973	Roxbury Community College is founded after Boston's African American community pressures the state.
1974	The federal court orders the integration of Boston public schools.
1974	The Boston offices of the NAACP are firebombed to protest the busing of children to integrate public schools.
1985	Black Bostonians vote on a referendum to secede from Boston and form their own city with Roxbury and Dorchester. The new city, which was to be called Mandela, is voted down.
1992	Ralph Martin becomes the first African American elected as Suffolk County's (Boston) District Attorney.
2004	Andrea J. Cabral, an African American, is elected the first female sheriff in the history of Suffolk County (Boston).
2006	Deval L. Patrick of Milton wins a landslide victory to become the first African American elected governor of Massachusetts.
2008	Democrat Barack Obama, the first African American nominee for president of a major party, carries Massachusetts with about 62 percent of the vote.
2009	(*July*) Henry Louis Gates, a prominent African American professor at Harvard, is arrested after a confrontation with a white police officer at his home. The officer had been called by a neighbor who thought Gates and his driver, who were working on a stuck door, were trying to break into the house. The resulting controversy involved President Obama, who invited both Gates and the officer to the White House to discuss the incident.

Historical Overview

The Colonial Period to the Civil War

The first African Americans came to Massachusetts and were taken to Noodles Island, in Boston Harbor, as slaves in 1638. They came to a Puritan colony that was already attempting to deal with the problem of how to relate to another group of people who were different from themselves, the Native Americans. In 1641, the Bay Colony's leaders produced the document called the "Massachusetts Body of Liberties," which,

among other things, paved the way for the possible future enslavement not only of Native Americans, but African Americans, as well, because it gave them the right to enslave "lawful captives taken in just wars," meaning the Native Americans, in particular, but was broadened to include African Americans.

In 1646, the Puritan leadership took a strong stand against the concept of "man stealing." Although this did not prevent Massachusetts merchants from becoming actively involved in the slave trade, it kept the number of African

Americans in the colony very small. The rocky soil was not conducive to large-scale agriculture, and there was sufficient free or indentured white labor for most farming and artisanal tasks. Those African Americans who were brought in became either house servants or farm laborers, who lived with their masters. Massachusetts was similar to other colonies that passed laws to regulate the conduct of slaves. In 1656, the Bay Colony followed Virginia and Maryland's lead, taking away from all blacks the right to bear arms. This was followed in 1705 by a strict law prohibiting racial intermarriage, but contrary to other states, African Americans could own property, serve as witnesses, and sue in court, which was a right of importance in the bringing of freedom suits. While African Americans never became more than 2 percent of the population, by 1720, there were 2,000 African Americans in the colony, most of whom were slaves. By 1776, the number of African Americans had increased to 5,250 based on a total Massachusetts population of 349,094.

As sentiment in Massachusetts against slavery and the slave trade grew, the campaign by Samuel Sewall for an import duty on slaves, with the hope of ending the trade, was largely ineffective. When the rebellion against the English escalated, white Americans attacking British tyranny began to take action against slavery. James Otis was one of many who argued that there was no law permitting slavery in Massachusetts. A bill was passed banning the slave trade in 1771, but Royal Governor Thomas Hutchinson vetoed it. At the same time, Massachusetts African Americans, led by Prince Hall, began to petition for the end of slavery in the colony. These petitions were ignored by legislators, who wished to maintain white unity against the British. Many Massachusetts African Americans actively supported the revolutionary cause, including Crispus Attucks, who was killed in the Boston Massacre of March 5, 1770. Soldiers Salem Poor and Peter

Salem and others distinguished themselves at the Battle of Bunker Hill on June 17, 1775.

In 1780, Massachusetts adopted a new state constitution, which included the declaration of natural rights. The next year, Quock Walker of Worcester County sued successfully for his freedom. When his former owner prosecuted him as a runaway in 1783, Massachusetts Chief Justice William Cushing ruled that Walker, and therefore every other African American in the Commonwealth of Massachusetts, was free. This initial decision went largely unnoticed and slaves continued to be sold. However, public opinion had formed solidly against slavery in Massachusetts and as blacks and white sympathizers began to press freedom suits based on Cushing's precedent, owners began to manumit their slaves rather than lose them in legal challenges. And as a consequence, slavery came to an end in the state. The 1790 Massachusetts Census reported 5,369 free blacks and no slaves in the state.

After African Americans were freed, they continued to face discrimination in Massachusetts and they were denied voting rights. In 1786, the law banning intermarriage was strengthened. In 1821, the state legislature appointed a committee to investigate methods of restricting free African Americans from entering Massachusetts. Education, where it existed for African Americans, remained segregated. Paul Cuffee, a wealthy black merchant and ship owner from the southeastern part of the state, vowed not to pay his taxes until granted voting rights. Eventually, he gave up hope of equal treatment and became involved in black colonization schemes in Sierra Leone.

In 1825, African Americans led by William G. Nell established the Massachusetts General Colored Association, an abolitionist group which also defended the rights of free Massachusetts blacks. The organization was soon joined by David Walker, whose appeal to the colored citizens of the world, published in 1829, denounced slavery and urged slaves to resist the institution by any means possible. Walker questioned the exclusion of blacks from Massachusetts juries and government and attacked the law against intermarriage as a caste system. By 1830, Boston had become the center of America's fledgling abolitionist movement. In 1833, black abolitionists such as Robert Purvis, James McCrummell, John B. Vashon, and Peter Williams worked with whites led by William Lloyd Garrison and Arthur Tappan to form the interracial American Anti-Slavery Society, based in Boston. It was crucial in the organizing of abolitionist newspapers and meetings. In 1841, Frederick Douglass started his career as an activist when he was hired as an agent by the Massachusetts Anti-Slavery Society.

During the antislavery period, Massachusetts had a very active African American community. Black opponents of slavery were supported by white abolitionists such as William Lloyd Garrison, in the years before the Civil War. The agitation centered on Boston, where nearly 25 percent of Massachusetts blacks lived, and where African Americans faced their harshest bigotry from white merchants, who had southern connections, and Irish immigrants, who were in competition with blacks for jobs. However, as a result of black and white pressure, racial intermarriage was legalized in 1843, and in the same year, state railroads stopped running Jim Crow cars. In 1885, following a 15-year struggle led by the militant integrationist William Cooper Nell, the state legislature passed a bill banning Boston's Jim Crow schools, the state's only segregated schools at the time. Still, in 1857, there were times when Boston blacks were refused permission to serve in the state militia despite repeated petitions, and after they had purchased their own uniforms and arms.

Civil War to Twentieth Century

When the Civil War began, Massachusetts' African Americans raised money for the Union's cause. In 1863, blacks were recruited as soldiers for the Union army. Blacks from across the state volunteered, although many of Boston's black residents, who were bitter from the militia struggles and angry at being forced to serve in segregated units, refused to commit to service. The 54th Massachusetts Regiment was one of the first black units formed, and the 54th distinguished itself by a courageous charge at Fort Wagner, Morris Island, South Carolina, in November, 1863. There is a memorial to the 54th on Beacon and Park Streets at the Boston Common. It is considered a landmark of civic black pride.

In 1865, a year before the first federal Civil Rights Act, Massachusetts passed a comprehensive civil rights bill. African Americans were guaranteed the right to vote and to be admitted to all "licensed" public establishments. Unlicensed establishments were added in 1874 and other facilities in 1895. These laws were laxly enforced, and even Civil War hero Roberts Smalls had difficulty obtaining a hotel room when he visited Boston in 1880.

The first blacks were elected to the Massachusetts legislature in 1866. One of them, Edwin Garrison Walker of Charleston (the son of David Walker), continued serving until the turn of the century. During this period, African Americans voted the Republican Party ticket, but when Governor Benjamin Butler broke with the party in 1883, African Americans voted for him in large numbers, and he rewarded his supporters by appointing a black municipal judge in Charlestown. African Americans also served as customs collectors and held other political patronage positions.

By the turn of the century, Massachusetts had largely abandoned its commitment to black equality, but even so, the state was one of the least difficult places to live for an African American. White sympathizers, including abolitionists and their descendants, fought along with blacks for civil rights. When the Spanish-American War broke out in 1898, Massachusetts blacks formed a militia company to support it. When southern whites protested the inclusion of black troops, white Massachusetts supported the African American units. The soldiers went to Cuba and were the only black volunteer troops to see action in the conflict.

In the decades following the Civil War, Massachusetts' black population merged into two distinct and sometimes antagonistic groups. One was the small "colored elite," led by such figures as Archibald Grimke, William Monroe Trotter, Maria Louise Baldwin, William H. Lewis, and W. E. B. Du Bois. Du Bois, born in Great Barrington, was closely associated with the group during his years at Harvard University. The "colored elite," as they loved to call themselves, were composed of native-born Massachusetts residents, most of whom were brought up in largely white towns and suburbs. They were Massachusetts college graduates (Harvard being their favored institution). Some white southerners refused to attend classes with them. And they usually worked in prestigious professions such as the law or higher education. They felt strongly the need to uplift African Americans and they defended blacks' civil rights against white attacks. The elite spoke collectively in Monroe Trotter's Boston newspaper, the *Guardian*, and they helped organize political groups, notably the Niagara Movement of 1906, to effect change.

The other group of blacks in Massachusetts was composed of the masses who migrated north in the latter part of the nineteenth century and who settled mostly in Boston. These African Americans had been slaves or were children of slaves, and they were fleeing the hardships of the South. Most were poor, and very few of them had much education. Even in the North, they faced hardship and discrimination. Outnumbered by the large number of immigrants from Ireland and later from other places, they were excluded from unions, denied jobs in factories, victimized by de facto segregation and crowded into

dilapidated, unhealthy housing and poor schools. As the state's economy declined, at the turn of the century, black political and economic powers were further reduced.

Although there were class tensions among Massachusetts' African Americans, the two groups did unite for common objectives. One notable success they scored was the 1915 boycott of the racist film *Birth of a Nation*. While then–Boston Mayor Michael Curley only mildly objected to the movie, Governor Edward Walsh ordered the film banned in Massachusetts outside of Boston.

A third group of African Americans in nineteenth- and twentieth-century Massachusetts was the community of immigrants—the only large group of voluntary African travelers to the New World—from the Cape Verde Islands, a group of Portuguese-owned islands off the coast of Africa, and their descendants. They may have come to Massachusetts as early as the 1780s to work on the whaling ships that sailed the Atlantic Ocean, as well as working in the maritime trades. Later, many Cape Verdeans migrated to Massachusetts as seasonal laborers, working in the cranberry bogs. Most settled in the old whaling towns such as New Bedford and Fall River. The Cape Verdeans were mainly Roman Catholic and spoke Creole (Kriolu), a mixture of Portuguese and African languages. They fit oddly into American racial patterns, since their dark skin caused them to suffer discrimination, yet their culture and history differed from that of black Americans.

Many Cape Verdeans, who saw the stigma placed on blackness in the United States, tended to call themselves "Portuguese" rather than "black." The experience of Cape Verdeans has been close to that of other immigrants. They had worked at heavy labor for low pay, socialized predominantly within their own communities, and struggled to educate their children and enable them to enter the middle class. In the wake of the Civil Rights Movement, the majority of Cape

Verdeans have since taken a new pride in their blackness.

In the years since World War II, Massachusetts' black population has increased several times, but blacks still represent a small percentage of the state's population. Most African Americans still live in Boston and are trapped in poverty. Other African Americans have settled in Springfield, Worcester, and Williamstown, all of which were sites of racial conflict during the 1960s. At times, there appears to be a major contradiction in the state. While Boston carries the perception of being one of the most liberal cities in the United States, it has harbored many racial animosities. Still, in 1966, Massachusetts Republican Edward Brooke became the first African American U.S. senator since Reconstruction. He won reelection in 1972, both times relying heavily on white votes. In 1980, African American leader Mel King came in a strong second in Boston's mayoral election. The race forced a runoff with Raymond Flynn. Flynn was a moderate on many racial issues, which has helped set a statewide pattern that was slow to change.

Nevertheless, there were still serious racial problems in Massachusetts. In the 1960s and the 1970s, the African American community's demand for quality education led to court-ordered school integration and forced the busing of schoolchildren. This resulted in white riots and violence, which inflamed racial tensions. It was the media coverage of this calamity that exposed a national audience to the racial problems of Massachusetts, much as the Charles Stuart affair, in which a community of African Americans were falsely suspected of murdering a white woman and were harassed by police, would do in the 1980s. Welfare and the greatly discussed debate over workfare in the early 1990s brought attention to the problems of African Americans finding suitable employment, even in a state as relatively wealthy as Massachusetts, but with the election in Suffolk (Boston) County of African American

Massachusetts Governor-Elect Deval Patrick speaks during an Associated Press interview, December 19, 2006, in Boston. Patrick was inaugurated into office on January 4, 2007. (AP/Wide World Photos)

Ralph Martin as district attorney, the election of an African American woman Andrea J. Cabral as the first female sheriff, and Deval L. Patrick as the first African American governor in the history of the state, things may be changing.

The 2000 resident census population for Massachusetts was 6,349,097, with 5,367,286 whites (76%); 428,729 Hispanic/Latinos (6.8%); 343,454 African Americans (5.4%); 238,234 Asians (3.8%); 15,015 American Indians (0.2%); and 382,729 other combined races (6.0%). The five largest cities are Boston, its capital (589,141), Worcester (172,648), Springfield (152,082), New Bedford (93,768), and Fall River (91,983). The eastern half of this relatively small state is mostly urban and suburban. The west is primarily rural. Massachusetts is the most populous of the

Crispus Attucks, an African American victim of the Boston Massacre, became a symbol of the American struggle for independence. (Library of Congress)

six New England states and ranks third in overall population density among the 50 states. Plymouth, Massachusetts, was the second permanent English settlement in North America.

Notable African Americans

Attucks, Crispus (1723–1770)

Crispus Attucks, a runaway slave, was shot and killed in the Boston Massacre of 1770. Crispus Attucks Day was begun by African Americans in 1958 and is still celebrated.

Brooke, Edward William (1919–)

In 1962, Brooke became the first African American in the United States to be elected as a state attorney general. In 1966, he was elected to the U.S. Senate. He was the first African American senator since 1881 and was the only person of African descent in the U.S. Senate until 1993. After leaving the Senate, he returned to his law practice and led the National Low-Income Housing Coalition.

Carney, William H. (1840–1908)

William H. Carney was the first African American soldier to earn the Medal of Honor. He was a member of the 54th Massachusetts Infantry Regiment, an all-black unit—with the exception of senior officers and a few senior noncommissioned sergeants—that proved by its Civil War service that black men could be good soldiers.

Born a slave, February 24, 1840, in Norfolk, Virginia, Carney escaped slavery by way of the Underground Railroad and settled in New Bedford, Massachusetts, in the 1850s. In 1863, he became a member of the 54th Massachusetts Regiment and had the opportunity to prove his mettle on July 18, 1863, at the Battle of Fort Wagner, outside of Charleston, South Carolina. His bravery earned him a promotion to sergeant and the U.S. military's most prestigious award, the Medal of Honor.

Cuffee, Paul (1759–1817)

Paul Cuffee was born a free child, on Cuttyhunk Island near New Bedford of a Native American mother and a father from the Ashanti tribe of West Africa, who was captured and brought to America at the age of 10. Cuffee learned to be a carpenter. He and his brother, John, built their own boat and began their trading business, which included running British blockades with American supplies. This small business gradually became a large fleet of merchant vessels, including his own shipyard, which helped him to become one of America's wealthiest men. He became a part of the Back to Africa Campaign. Cuffee, eventually, set sail for Sierra Leone, West Africa, with a group of free blacks, with the intent to end slavery in the colony by building a free and prosperous, industrial Africa. He became ill and died before his dream was realized.

Douglass, Frederick (1818–1895)

After Frederick August Washington Bailey, a runaway slave from Maryland, and Anna Murray, a free black woman, were married in 1838, the year Bailey escaped from slavery, they moved to New Bedford, where he adopted the name Frederick Douglass. It was in New Bedford that this prominent American abolitionist lecturer and author wrote *The Narrative of the Life of Frederick Douglass: An American Slave* (1845), which became an instant bestseller.

54th Massachusetts Regiment (1863–1865)

The 54th was a Massachusetts infantry unit made up of African Americans that were active during the Civil War. The 54th Regiment was famous for its battlefield fighting prowess and for the great courage of its members. The African American infantry unit was immortalized in the 1989 film *Glory*.

Hall, Prince (1735–1807)

Prince Hall was one of the most prominent free black citizens of Boston during and after the American Revolution. A former slave, Hall was freed by his master, William Hall of Boston, shortly after the Boston Massacre in 1770. Hall worked as a leather dresser and is considered the founder of black freemasonry. He helped establish the African Grand Lodge in Boston in 1791 and served as its grand master until his death. He was also involved in the African Society, another institution for the social, political, and economic improvement for African Americans. In addition, Hall had a defined role in the abolition of slavery,

worked for the legal end to the slave trade in Massachusetts, and sought to improve the education of African Americans.

Nell, William Cooper (1816–1874)

Nell is considered the first African American to publish a significant collection of African American biographies. He is also distinguished as the first black American to hold a federal civilian post. He worked as a U.S. postal clerk from 1861 until his death in 1874.

Wheatley, Phillis (c. 1753–1784)

Born in Senegal, Africa, she was sold into slavery at the age of seven to John and Susannah Wheatley

Published according to Act of Parliament, Sept. 1, 1773 by Arch.d Bell, Bookseller N.o 8 near the Saracens Head Aldgate.

Phillis Wheatley, born in Africa and brought to America as a slave, became an accomplished poet in Boston and traveled to London to publish her work. (Library of Congress)

of Boston on July 11, 1761. Her first name was derived from the ship that carried her to America, *the Phillis*. Wheatley was the author of *Poems on Various Subjects Religious and Moral*, the first book of poetry by an African American, published in London in 1773. At her young age, Wheatley was chosen to be a domestic servant and companion to Mrs. Wheatley. Speaking no English upon her arrival in this country, she proved to be a precocious learner and was tutored by Wheatley's daughter Mary in English, Latin, history, geography, religion, and the Bible. She was treated more as a family member than a servant or slave and her education was that of a young woman in an elite Boston family. Wheatley was the first African woman to earn an income from her writings, as well as the first woman writer encouraged and financed by a group of women.

Cultural Contributions

The Parting Ways Cemetery and the Royal House—both in Medford—are open from May to October. The latter features a pictorial study of African American families who have lived in the area since their arrival 300 years ago. Four African American families formed Parting Ways settlement on the town line between Kingston and Plymouth.

The Museum of Afro-American History, Boston and Nantucket, is dedicated to preserving, conserving, and accurately interpreting the contributions of African Americans. The Museum of the National Center of African American Artists, in Boston, presents contemporary, historical, and expressive art from the global black world. The Boston African American National Historic Site—the largest such site in the United States—comprises two dozen pre–Civil War black-owned structures (homes, businesses, schools, churches) located in Boston in the Beacon Hill neighborhood. The oldest standing African American church in the country is part of the site, which is administered by the National Park Service. The structures are linked by the self-guiding Black Heritage Trail.

The Frederick Douglass Memorial, New Bedford, commemorates the noted orator and abolitionist. After escaping slavery in Maryland, Douglass came to New Bedford via the Underground Railroad. It was in New Bedford where Mr. Douglass changed his name from Frederick Bailey to Douglass to avoid escaped slave catchers. He lived there from 1838 to 1841 and had two children, Rosetta and Lewis, born there. It was in New Bedford that he became a part of the abolitionist movement.

Cambridge's African American Heritage Trail is a collection of markers spread throughout the city at places where prominent African Americans lived or worked. African Americans have lived in Cambridge since 1630, but it was in the 1840s that the population doubled due to arrivals from the South and other areas.

Bibliography

Brown, Richard D., and Jack Tager. *Massachusetts: A Concise History*. Amherst: University of Massachusetts Press, 2000.

Burchard, Peter. *One Gallant Rush: Robert Gould Shaw and His Brave Black Regiment*. New York: St. Martin's Press, 1990.

Duncan, Russell. *Where Death and Glory Meet: Colonel Robert Shaw Gould and the 54th Massachusetts Infantry*. Athens: University of Georgia Press, 1999.

Greene, Lorenzo. *The Negro in Colonial New England*. New York: Columbia University Press, 1942.

Greenwood, Janette Thomas. *First Fruits of Freedom: The Migration of Former Slaves and Their Search for Equality in Worcester, Massachusetts, 1862–1900*. John Hope Franklin Series in

African American History and Culture. Chapel Hill: University of North Carolina Press, 2010.

Grover, Kathryn. *The Fugitive's Gibraltar: Escaping Slaves and Abolitionism in New Bedford, Massachusetts.* Amherst: University of Massachusetts Press, 2001.

Lemire, Elise. *Black Walden: Slavery and Its Aftermath in Concord, Massachusetts.* Philadelphia: University of Pennsylvania Press, 2009.

Logan, Rayford W. *The Negro in American Life and Thought: The Nadir, 1877–1901.* New York: Collier Books, 1965.

Manegold, C. S. *Ten Hills Farm: The Forgotten History of Slavery in the North.* Princeton, NJ: Princeton University Press, 2009.

Minardi, Margot. *Making Slavery History: Abolition and the Politics of Memory in Massachusetts.* New York: Oxford University Press, 2010.

Piersen, William D. *Black Yankees: The Development of an Afro-American Subculture in Eighteenth Century New England,* Amherst: University of Massachusetts Press, 1988.

Titcomb, Caldwell, Thomas Underwood, Randall Kennedy, and Werner Sollors. *Blacks at Harvard: A Documentary History of African-American Experience at Harvard and Ratcliffe.* New York: New York University Press, 1993.

Yacovone, Donald. *We Fight for Freedom: Massachusetts, African Americans, and the Civil War.* Boston: Massachusetts Historical Society, 2001.

MICHIGAN

Julius Thompson

Chronology

1700–1814	Three colonial groups are active in the area that became known as Michigan: the French, between 1700 and 1760; the British from 1760 and 1776; and the Americans from 1814.
1701	Antoine de la Mothe Sieur (a French military officer and explorer) establishes Detroit as a French base in North America.
1736–1865	Slavery exists in Michigan.
1805	Congress creates the Michigan Territory, with William Hull as governor.
1837	Michigan enters the Union as the 26th state.
1839	An early black religious institution, the Second Baptist Church, is established in Detroit, with the Reverend William Monroe serving as its first pastor.
1845	The Colored Methodist Church (Bethel AME) is established in Detroit.
1861–1865	The 102nd Infantry Regiment, U.S. Colored Troops of Michigan, serves in the Civil War and sees duty in Florida, Georgia, and South Carolina; 1,446 officers and men serve in this regiment, and 138 of them die during the war.
1865	*(February 3)* Michigan becomes one of the first states to ratify the Thirteenth Amendment abolishing slavery in the United States.
1867	*(January 16)* Michigan ratifies the Fourteenth Amendment to the U.S. Constitution guaranteeing full civil rights to African Americans.
1868	The Michigan state legislature outlaws school segregation.
1869	*(March 5)* Michigan ratifies the Fifteenth Amendment to the U.S. Constitution guaranteeing voting rights for African Americans.
1900	The city of Detroit has a population of 288,704 people, of which 4,111 are African Americans.
1911	The Detroit branch of the National Association for the Advancement of Colored People (NAACP) is established and becomes one of the major black organizations in the city to seek solutions for problems facing the black community in Michigan and the nation.
1915	*The Freedman's Progress*, a celebration of the black experience in Michigan from 1865 to 1815, is published with state funds.
1918	The Detroit branch of the National Urban League is organized; its community outreach programs have been successful in aiding the advancement of blacks in Detroit.
1920	The Detroit branch of the Universal Negro Improvement Association (UNIA) is formed and soon has over 300 local members. An organization of working-class blacks, the group has a major impact on black pride consciousness in Detroit.

1923	Elijah Poole (Elijah Muhammad) migrates to Detroit as the Great Black Migration to the North continues; he becomes an early associate of Wallace D. Fard, the founder of the Nation of Islam.
1925	A local black dentist, Dr. Ossian H. Sweet, and his family are attacked by whites for seeking to buy a house in a white neighborhood. In the ensuing protests, one white person is killed. The Sweet family and friends are later cleared of the charge of murder; the case, however, does not improve race relations in Detroit.
1926	10,000 black men (out of 110,000 total employees) work for the Ford Motor Company in Michigan.
1930s–1940s	The area in Detroit known as Paradise Valley is noted as the central business and commercial district for African Americans in the city.
1936	The *Michigan Chronicle* is established in Detroit and becomes the leading black newspaper in the state.
1940	"The Brown Bomber," Joe Louis, defeats Max Schmelling and wins the heavyweight championship of the world.
1943	(*June 20–21*) The Detroit Race Riot becomes one of the largest racial disturbances in the United States during World War II. Blacks in the city protested the conditions under which they lived and clashed over jobs and housing with white immigrants from Europe. Thirty-four people are killed, 25 of them African Americans; 85 percent of the people arrested during the riot are black, while property damage totals more than $2 million.
1950	Ralph Bunche, a native of Detroit, becomes the first African American to be awarded the Nobel Peace Prize for his work to make peace between Arabs and Israelis in the Middle East.
1950	Charline White (1920–1959) becomes the first African American woman to win a seat in the Michigan legislature.
1950	Charles C. Diggs Jr. becomes the first African American elected in the Michigan State Senate.
1952	Cora M. Brown (1914–1972) is the first African American woman (and the first woman of any race in the state) to win election to the Michigan State Senate.
1954	Charles C. Diggs Jr. is the first African American elected to the U.S. Congress from Michigan; a Democrat from Detroit, Diggs represents the state's 13th District.
1959	Berry Gordy, founds Motown Records in Detroit.
1960	Fifteen young people attempt to desegregate a chain store in Ann Arbor and are arrested by local authorities.
1960	Otis M. Smith (1922–) is elected auditor general of Michigan, the first black to win such a statewide position since Reconstruction.

1960s–1970s	Detroit is a major center for the production and distribution of African American music in the forms of civil rights songs, soul music, soul jazz, and modern jazz avant garde.
1963	(*February 20*) Michigan ratifies the Twenty-fourth Amendment to the U.S. Constitution abolishing the poll tax.
1964	John Conyers Jr., a future founder of the Congressional Black Caucus (1971), is elected to Congress as a Democrat from Michigan's 14th District.
1965	Viola Liuzzo, an American of Italian descent from Detroit, is assassinated when she travels to Alabama to participate in the Selma-to-Montgomery civil rights march.
1965	Librarian and poet Dudley F. Randall founds Detroit's Broadside Press, a company committed to promoting black poetry and other black literary works in the United States.
1967	(*July*) The Detroit Rebellion is noted by many activists and scholars as the most extensive urban rebellion in the last century of American history; 39 blacks are killed, plus 5 from other ethnic groups, 2,000 people are injured, 7,331 arrests are made, and 5,000 people are left homeless in the city.
1968	The League of Revolutionary Black Workers, an organization intended to fight for improved working conditions, is formed by African American workers at a Dodge factory in Detroit.
1970	Richard H. Austin (1913–) becomes Michigan secretary of state, the first black person to hold the office.
1973	Naomi Long Madgett, educator and poet, creates Lotus Press, in Detroit, to aid the production and distribution of black literature (especially black poetry) in Michigan and other states.
1973	A study by the Office for Civil Rights notes that Michigan is home to 186 black physicians.
1973	Coleman Young is elected the first African American mayor of Detroit; he serves as mayor until 1993.
1978	Carolyn Cheeks Kilpatrick is elected to the Michigan House of Representatives and becomes the first African American woman to serve on the State House Appropriations Committee.
1979	Loren Eugene Monroe becomes the first African American state treasurer of Michigan.
1980	George William Crockett Jr., an attorney who defended civil rights workers during the Mississippi Freedom Summer project in 1964, is elected to succeed Charles Diggs as representative for Michigan's 13th Congressional District.
1981	Barbara-Rose Collins is elected to the Detroit City Council.

1983	Congressman John Conyers Jr. of Michigan introduces into Congress the legislation calling for the creation of a Dr. Martin Luther King national holiday.
1985	According to the Bureau of the Census, blacks in Detroit compose 63.1 percent of the city's total population in the mid-1980s.
1990	Barbara-Rose Collins is elected to Congress from Michigan's 13th District.
1993	Dennis W. Archer, a Democrat, is elected as the second black mayor in the history of Detroit.
1996	After defeating incumbent Barbara-Rose Collins in the Democratic primary, Carolyn Cheeks Kilpatrick wins election to the U.S. Congress from Michigan's 13th District; she is the first African American woman to serve on the Appropriations Committee of the U.S. House of Representatives.
2001	Kwame Kilpatrick, a Democrat, wins election as mayor of Detroit.
2007	Lotus Press publishes *Pilgrim Journey: An Autobiography* by Naomi Long Madgett, a leading black poet and educator.
2008	(*November 4*) Democrat Barack Obama, the first African American nominee for president of a major party, carries Michigan with about 57 percent of the vote.

Historical Overview

The earliest known history of the African American people in the state of Michigan extends from 1701 to 1837, during a period of slavery in this important area, known as the Wolverine State and the Great Lake State. Yet, an antislavery perspective developed early in the history of Michigan, which was greatly influenced by the Northwest Ordinance of 1778 prohibiting the institution of slavery in the territory. On January 26, 1837, Michigan became the 26th state of the United States, with its capital at Lansing, and with Detroit as its largest city. Geographically, Michigan covers 58,527 square miles and contains two large land areas, the Lower and Upper Peninsulas.

In the eighteenth and nineteenth centuries, small numbers of African Americans were attracted to Michigan because of its rich agriculture potential, fur trading, and lumber industries. However, many early black settlers suffered discrimination in Michigan, including a lack of political rights for voting, and economic and social inequalities. Perhaps these issues had a bearing on the growth of the black population in Michigan. Table 1, "The Black Population in Michigan, 1820–1910," notes this historically significant factor. The black population in Michigan increased very slowly in the nineteenth century, from 67 blacks in 1829 to 126 in 1830, from 138 in 1834 to 707 in 1840, and 2,583 in 1850, followed by a somewhat more rapid increase between 1860 and 1910, when 17,115 blacks lived in the state in the latter year. In the twentieth century, and especially

Table 1   The Black Population in Michigan, 1820–1910

Year	Population
1820	67
1830	126
1834	138
1840	707
1850	2,583
1860	6,799
1880	15,100
1910	17,115

during the era of World War I (1914–1919), a "Great Migration" of African Americans brought thousands of them to Michigan, and most settled in the city of Detroit. One important study notes that: "Michigan's African-American population grew from 17,115 (6.1 percent) in 1910 to 208,345 (4 percent) in 1940 and to 1,289,012 in 1990 (13.9 percent)." Table 2, "The Black Population in Detroit, 1840–1960," displays the growth of the black population in this important industrial center for over a century. Certainly the greatest concentration of blacks in Detroit took place between 1920 and 1960. The newer black migrants to Michigan came in search of political, social, and economic freedoms. They discovered some advantages in Michigan, such as factory positions at Ford Motor Company, where by 1920, 1,675 African Americans had secured employment. Yet, overall they suffered in terms of housing, mistreatment at the hands of police, and economic disadvantages. But, they were able to increase their representation in unions, improve their educational opportunities, and forge a way for more political activity in the years ahead.

In the Lower Peninsula, where most blacks lived in Michigan by the twentieth century, they placed an emphasis on developing black social and economic institutions, such as the black church, the black press, private black schools, and small business establishments—including

Table 2   The Black Population in Detroit, 1840–1960

Year	Population
1840	193
1860	1,403
1900	4,111
1910	6,000
1920	40,838
1930	120,000
1950	300,506
1960	382,506

barbershops, restaurants, salons, nightclubs, funeral homes, insurance companies, and Michigan outlets of national civil rights organizations, such as the National Association for Advancement of Colored People, the Southern Christian Leadership Conference, the Universal Negro Improvement Association, the National Urban League, the Congress of Racial Equality, the Student Non-Violent Coordinating Committee, the Black Panther Party, and others, including local groups formed by concerned blacks in such cities as Detroit and Flint.

Black churches have had a long history of service in Detroit. The Second Baptist Church was established in 1836 in Detroit and is recognized by some blacks as the oldest black congregation in the midwestern region of this country. Other churches followed this and include the Bethel African Methodist Episcopal Church (1839) and St. Matthew's Protestant Episcopal Church, created in 1846. Since this early period, hundreds of black churches have been found in Michigan, and many blacks also attend the services at historical white churches. By the 1920s, a new movement had emerged among black churches for spiritual associations. These black church groups were the National Colored Spiritualist Association (1922); Universal Hagar's Spiritual Church (1925); and the Spiritual Israel Church and its Army. In the 1930s, the Nation of Islam emerged in Detroit as a new religious group, headed by Wallace D. Fard, and, later, Elijah Muhammad. A small black professional middle class also served the healthcare, dental, legal, and other needs of the black community in Michigan. As late as 1973, the state contained 186 black physicians with a concentration of these in Detroit.

One of the major challenges facing contemporary blacks has been a growth of racial tension in the state, an increase in white racism, police brutality, the impact of migration between World War I and II, and race riots in Michigan. In fact,

Passengers climb from rear of streetcar stopped by mob during race riots in Detroit, Michigan, 1943. (Library of Congress)

during World War II, on June 20–21, 1943, Detroit experienced a major race riot that resulted in 34 deaths and over 700 injuries—a record for this historical period. Major riots also broke out during the 1960s, with the largest of these in Michigan occurring in Detroit on July 23, 1967, and ending with "forty deaths (thirty-two black), 2,250 injuries, and property losses estimated at $250 million."[1] Poverty, crime, white migration from Detroit, unemployment, and other social ills continued to create hardships for modern blacks in Michigan. These challenges are still before the community today.

The black press in Michigan, consisting of newspaper, magazine, radio, and television, has been active for over 150 years in promoting the media needs of the African American people in the state. The early development of the state's black press occurred in the period 1865–1920, when the Detroit *Plaindealer*, a weekly, served as the major newspaper for blacks. The paper was edited by W. H. Anderson, B. B. Pelham, W. H. Stowers, and R. Pelham Jr. By 1888, the organ contained 20 pages and noted for the world that its outlook was as follows:

> To overcome mistrust; to [promote] the welfare of Afro-Americans; to set an example that there is no field of labor which cannot be successfully explored and cultivated by the Afro-American who is energetic and painstaking; to provide a medium for the encouragement of literacy work, for the creation of a distinctive and favorable Afro-American sentiment, for the dislodgment of prejudice and the encouragement of Patriotism.[2]

Yet the organization of the black press was also important, for this segment of the black press in Michigan began with:

> the establishment in 1911 of the Detroit branch of the National Association for the Advancement of Colored People, under the leadership of the executive secretary Gloster

B. Currnet; and the city's chapter of the National Urban League, created in 1916, and headed by John C. Dancy.

Yet the influence of Booker T. Washington, the dominant national black leader form 1895 to 1915, was greatly felt in the black business and political community of Detroit. The influence of Marcus Garvey's black nationalist perspective was also powerfully expressed in Detroit by 5,000 local black members and their leader Joseph A. Craigne, who served as executive secretary of the Universal Negro Improvement Association's branch in the city, established in 1920.[3]

In the modern period from 1920 to the present, the *Michigan Chronicle*, published in Detroit since 1936, has been the major black newspaper in Michigan for blacks. Louis E. Martin served the organ as its major editor for many years, and by the 1940, he had developed a weekly circulation of 5,000 copies of this paper for the community. By 1952, the *Michigan Chronicle* had a circulation of 21,619. During the decade of the 1950s, four editors helped to guide the paper into the future. They were Russell Cowans, Longworth M. Quinn, William C. Matney Jr., and Charles J. Wartman. These editors took an activist perspective for the paper's coverage of political, economic, and social news and commentary. By 1979, they published an average edition of 30,856 copies of the paper.

On the mass communication front, blacks in Michigan as late as the 1970s promoted seven black-oriented radio stations in the state. Yet, only three of these stations, all in Detroit, were in fact owned by blacks—WCHB-AM, WCHD-FM, and WGPR-FM. Black ownership of television also remained a problem. One study observes that in 1975, "the black International Masons established the first black-owned television station in the United States, WGPR, Channel 62, a UHF station in Detroit."[4]

Blacks in Michigan have been very active in the political history of the state. Their votes have obtained leadership positions for blacks on the local, state, and national levels. Black political leaders from Michigan who have been especially recognized for their political contributions are: Ralph J. Bunche (1904–1971), a United Nations officer who received the 1950 Nobel Peace Prize; representatives in Congress Charles C. Diggs (D), and John Conyers Jr. (D); and Coleman Young (1918–1997), the first black elected major of Detroit in 1974 to 1994.

The historical presence of blacks in Michigan, most notably form the nineteenth century to the present, has produced a rich legacy of political, economic, social and cultural contributions to advance the African American community in the state, and developments on the national scene in the United States. Michigan remains an important state, and although Detroit has suffered much in the last 40 years, it still remains an important symbol of the struggles of black people and others to promote equality, justice, and an open society for all of the people.

Notable African Americans

Archer, Dennis W. (1942–)

Dennis W. Archer was elected as the second black mayor in Detroit in 1993. A lawyer, Archer served on the Michigan Supreme Court for the period 1986–1991.

Boyd, Melba J. (1950–)

Melba J. Boyd is a leading black intellectual, poet, and editor who became a major professor at Wayne State University in the 1990s. She is the author of *Wrestling with the Muse: Dudley Randall and the Broadside Press* (2003), among other books.

Boyer, Jill Witherspoon (1947–)

Jill Witherspoon Boyer is a local Detroit poet who published *Dream Farmer* (1975) and edited

The Broadside Annual (1972, 1973), a series of anthologies of poetry by black poets. She is the daughter of poet Naomi Long Madgett.

Bunche, Ralph Johnson (1904–1971)

Ralph Bunche became the first African American to be awarded the Nobel Peace Prize in 1950, for his efforts in helping to foster peace in the Middle East. He was also an outstanding scholar of political science and a noted author. Bunche wrote several books, including *World View of Race* (1936) and *The Political Status of the Negro in the Age of FDR* (1973).

Carson, Benjamin Solomon, Sr. (1951–)

Dr. Benjamin Carson, who grew up as a poor youth in Detroit, is known around the world as a leading neurosurgeon and heads the Pediatric Neurosurgery unit at Johns Hopkins Medical Center in Baltimore, Maryland. He has worked on very difficult medical cases in the United States and in foreign countries, helping to save the lives of many children in his career. He has written three important books on his life work, including *Gifted Hands* (1992).

Cleage, Albert Buford (1911–2000)

Albert Cleage was the creator of a new black church movement in 1952, which became known as the Shrine of the Black Madonna, the "Mother Church" of the Black Christian Nationalist Movement. Minister Cleage wrote two major books, *The Black Messiah* (1968) and *Black Christian Nationalism* (1972).

Conyers, John, Jr. (1929–)

A Democrat, John Conyers was first elected to Congress to represent Detroit in 1964. He has been the powerful chairman of the Government Operations Committee and serves on other important congressional committees.

John Conyers Jr. has served in the U.S. House of Representatives since 1965. A Democrat and native of Detroit, Conyers represents Michigan's 14th District. (U.S. House of Representatives)

Crockett, George W., Jr. (1909–1997)

George Crockett was a prominent African American jurist who served on the Detroit Recorders Court, as a judge, in 1946–1966, 1972–78, and presiding judge, 1974–1978; he was also an important member of the U.S. House of Representatives from Detroit, in 1980–1990. Historically, he was the first black lawyer in the U.S. Department of Labor. Crockett was also a member of the African Resolution, which sought the release of Nelson Mandela and his then-wife, Winnie Mandela, from prison and banning in South Africa.

Dancy, John Campbell, Jr. (1888–1968)

John C. Dancy served the National Urban League's Detroit branch as director from 1918 to 1959. Under his leadership, the Detroit branch, located at 553 E. Columbia, near St. Antoine, was very effective in developing outreach programs in education, health, employment, and recreational needs (the Green Pastures Camp for children was established in 1931) to meet the needs of the local black community in Detroit. Dancy wrote *Sands Against the Wind: The Memories of John Campbell Dancy, Jr.* (1966).

Diggs, Charles C., Jr. (1922–1998)

A Democrat, Charles Diggs was first elected to Congress to represent Detroit in 1954. While in Congress, he developed a special interest in civil rights and African affairs. Historically, he was the first African American member of Congress from Michigan and the founder and first chairperson of the Congressional Black Caucus. Diggs was a key member on the Committee on the District of Columbia for many years, and he helped to secure partial self-government status for the District, as chair of the committee, in 1972. In 1978, he was convicted on charges of mail fraud and falsifying payroll forms. After the U.S. Supreme Court refused to review the decision, Diggs resigned from Congress in 1980.

Dyson, Michael Eric (1958–)

Michael Dyson is one of the leading black public intellectuals of the last 20 years in the United States. His books have had a profound influence on black thinking in this country and include a work of essays entitled *Between God and Gangsta' Rap* (1994).

Elijah Muhammad (Elijah Poole) (1897–1975)

Elijah Muhammad migrated to Detroit in 1923, and became an associate of Wallace D. Fard, the founder of the Nation of Islam. By 1926, Elijah Muhammad led the new movement.

Promotional poster of Aretha Franklin, 1971. (Library of Congress)

Franklin, Aretha (1942–)

A major rhythm-and-blues singer who also has an interest in gospel music, Aretha Franklin grew up in Detroit and began her career singing in her father's Baptist Church choirs. She is known today as the "Queen of Soul."

Franklin, Clarence Lavaughn (C. L.) (1915–1984)

Clarence Franklin was pastor of Detroit's New Bethel Baptist Church in 1946, when he became a leading religious figure in the city and the state of Michigan. Because of his fame as a preacher, a number of other black ministers tried to imitate his religious style. He was also known for making effective use of radio religious broadcasts to reach his audience. In 1953, his radio broadcast sermons were recorded, and he sold over a million copies of this work. In the 1960s, he was a major supporter of Martin Luther King Jr. and of efforts to uplift the black community in this country. He also helped his daughter, Aretha Franklin, develop into a major musician in the United States.

Gordy, Berry, Jr. (1929–)

Born in Detroit, Berry Gordy became an important record producer in the late 1950s to the present. In 1959, he created Motown Records, which became a leading producer of black music in the 1960s and 1970s. He worked with many important black singers and groups, such as Diana Ross, Smokey Robinson, Marvin Gaye, and Michael Jackson. By 1973, his company was the largest black-owned business in the United States, yet, he sold Motown to whites in 1998.

Berry Gordy Jr. had enormous influence on American music in the 1960s as the founder and owner of the Motown Record Corporation. (AP/Wide World Photos)

Hayden, Robert (1913–1980)

Born in Detroit, Robert Hayden was a leading black poet and teacher who taught for many years at Fisk University and the University of Michigan. In 1976–1978, he served as Consultant in Poetry for the Library of Congress, Washington, D.C. Hayden wrote or edited at least 10 books during his career.

Hood, Nicholas, Sr. (1923–)

Nicholas Hood Sr. was a key senior black minister of Plymouth United Church of Christ in Detroit from the late 1950s. He created an outstanding outreach ministry in the 1960s to help people in the community. In 1965, he was elected to the Detroit City Council.

House, Gloria (Aneb Kgositsile) (dates unknown)

Gloria House is a leading Detroit educator and intellectual, poet, and publisher of Broadside Press since 2002. Her career has included academic posts at such institutions as Wayne State University, Detroit.

Johnson, Earvin "Magic," Jr. (1959–)

A star on the 1979 Michigan State national champion basketball team, "Magic" Johnson became a major star with the Los Angeles Lakers in the 1980s. He helped the Lakers win five National Basketball Association titles. Johnson ended his career in 1991 with an announcement that he was HIV positive. In recent years, he has worked hard to increase AIDS prevention and awareness in American society.

Kilpatrick, Kwame (1970–)

In November 2001, Kwame Kilpatrick, then 31, was elected as the youngest mayor in Detroit's history. He also served in the Michigan legislature as a state representative for the West Side of the City of Detroit. Because of his youth, he has been a very controversial mayor of the Motor City.

Madgett, Naomi Long (1923–)

Naomi Madgett has served as publisher and editor of Lotus Press, Detroit, from 1973 to the present. She was also an outstanding professor at Eastern Michigan University and has published over 10 books in a career of 50 years. In 2001, she was appointed the Poet Laureate of the City of Detroit. Madgett is also the author of an outstanding auto-biography—*Pilgrim Journey* (2006).

Martin, Louis (1912–1997)

As editor of the *Michigan Chronicle* in the 1930s and 1940s, Louis Martin helped to develop the paper's proactive positions on the New Deal policies of President Franklin Roosevelt and union sympathies among black workers, while maintaining its social outlook for black consciousness, pride, and self-help.

Massey, James Early (1929–)

James E. Massey was a leading religious minister and scholar in the Church of God. In the period 1949–51, he served as an associate minister at the Church of God in Detroit; as a senior pastor at the Metro Church of God, 1954–1976; as an educator at Anderson College, School of Theology, 1969–1977 and 1981–1984; as Chapel and University Professor of Religion, Dean, 1984–1989; and as Professor of Preaching and Biblical Studies, dean emeritus and Professor at Large, during his retirement years.

Milner, Ron (1938–2004)

Ron Milner was an outstanding theater writer and aided the development of Concept East Theatre, established in 1962 at Detroit. Milner is considered one of the most important Black Arts Movement writers to come out of Detroit. In 1962–1963, he was awarded a John Hay Whitney Award; followed in 1965, by a Rockefeller Foundation grant. Such aid helped him to develop into a major African American playwright for the period of the 1960s to the turn of the century.

Parks, Rosa (1913–2005)

Rosa Parks was a noted NAACP civil rights activist in Alabama who played a major role in the 1955–1956 Montgomery Bus Boycott movement led by Martin Luther King Jr. She was also a dressmaker, life insurance agent, housekeeper, staff member for Congressman John Conyers of Detroit (1965–1988), and youth worker in Detroit. She helped to create the Rosa and Raymond Parks Institute for Self-Development in 1987. She co-authored, with Jim Haskins, *Rosa Parks, My Story* (1992).

Quinn, Longworth (1907–1989)

Longworth Quinn was an editor at the *Michigan Chronicle* during the period of the 1960s, when he served the paper as general manager, and promoted an editorial policy, during this decade, and in the 1970s, of a progressive and liberal nature for the historical era.

Randall, Dudley F. (1914–2000)

Dudley Randall was a major black poet, who created Detroit's Broadside Press, in 1965, to promote the publication of black poetry and other literacy works among African American writers. In 1981, Mayor Coleman A. Young, appointed Randall as the first Poet Laureate of Detroit. Randall published over 10 books in his career, including *A Litany of Friends, New and Selected Poems* (1981). He is widely known in history as the "Father of the Black Poetry Publishing Movement."

Sweet, Henry Ossian (1895–1960)

The H. O. Sweet case in 1925 represented an attempt by local Detroit whites from preventing the black doctor Henry Sweet and his family from a buying a house in a white neighborhood. One white protester was killed by a gunshot, which local authorities charged came from the black home, and several members of the Sweet family and their friends were alleged to have contributed to the killing. The NAACP took an active interest in the case, and all of the blacks were acquitted. The case is viewed as a setback overall for improved race relations in Michigan.

Truth, Sojourner (Isabella) (c. 1797–1883)

Sojourner Truth was a leading antislavery activist and supporter of women's rights in the United States during the nineteenth century. In 1857, she settled in Battle Creek, Michigan, and became associated with the Michigan Progressive Friends, a Spiritualist Movement of Americans at Harmonia, near Battle Creek.

Vest, Hilda (1933–)

Hilda Vest was an important poet and publisher in Detroit. She was a teacher in the Detroit public schools from 1959 to 1988. On assuming ownership, with Don S. Vest Sr. of Broadside Press in 1985, she became the new publisher and editor of the company. She is the author of *Sorrow's End* (1993).

Wonder, Stevie (Steveland Judkins) (1950–)

A leading black musician of the last 40 years, Stevie Wonder was born in Saginaw, Michigan. He has had a tremendous influence on the field of music, human rights concerns, and securing a national holiday in honor of Dr. Martin Luther King Jr.

Wright, Charles (1919–2002)

Charles Wright established the Museum of African American History in Detroit in 1965. The institution has developed into one of the largest black museums in the United States.

Young, Coleman (1918–1997)

Coleman Young was elected as the first black major in Detroit's history in 1973, and served five terms in office until 1993. He was also a professor of Urban Affairs at Wayne State University, Detroit.

Cultural Contributions

Motown Records

Motown Records was created by record producer Berry Gordy Jr. (1929–), in 1959, in Detroit, Michigan. His early career had centered on writing songs as a young student in high school; he also worked in the automotive industry of Detroit and had a sports interest in boxing. In the 1950s, he wrote a series of popular black musical hits for record star Jackie Wilson, while working out of New York City.

Working from Detroit in 1959, Gordy created the most important black music company in American history. He was able to promote the careers of dozens of new artists, especially in the area of rhythm and blues. Besides Jackie Wilson, his list of outstanding artists included Smokey Robinson, the Four Tops, the Temptations, Marvin Gaye, Stevie Wonder, the Jackson Five, Diana Ross and the Supremes, and many others.

In the 1970s, *Black Enterprise* magazine, recognized Motown Records as the largest black business enterprise in the United States. Gordy was thus a major factor in the lives and work of many black artists. Also in the 1970s, Gordy turned his attention to movie production. His most important production was headlined by star Diana Ross, *Lady Sings the Blues* (1972).

By the early 1980s, Gordy relocated Motown Records to Los Angeles, California, a leading center of the music industry in the nation. Finally, after several decades of success, Gordy sold Motown Records in 1988 to white business interests in California. He continues to live and work in California. The older Motown Company, in Detroit, is now a national museum on "the Motown Sound" in modern American music.

Lotus Press

Next to Broadside Press, Detroit has also been the home base of a second premier publisher of black poetry in the United States, Lotus Press. Poet Naomi Long Madgett, with the aid of local Detroit supporters, established this company in 1972. As the following excerpt indicates, Madgett viewed the work of Lotus Press as an aid in keeping

> the best of black poetry alive by making inexpensive, attractive paperbound volumes available to the bookstores and libraries of the world. To provide a worldwide audience to black poets of excellence, regardless of their ideology, subject matter, or style. Our goal is literary excellence. We are not interested in work that is political without being technically sound; nor are we interested in beginners who have not studied the fundamentals of their craft.[5]

Lotus Press published 18 books between 1972 and 1979, including titles by major black poets such as James A. Emanuel, May Miller, Naomi Long Madgett, Herbert Woodward Martin, Lance Jeffers, and Houston A. Baker. Most Lotus Press books were priced between $3 and $4.

During its early history, Lotus Press also published 20 broadsides of poetry, with 11 of these by male poets, and 9 by women. This body of work represented some of the best poetry written by African American poets, with contributions to the series by such poets as Michael S. Harper, Etheridge Knight, Pinkie Gordon Lane, Robert Hayden, Naomi Long Madgett, Gloria C. Oden, Dudley Randall, and Margaret Walker, among others.

Lotus Press remains active at the turn of the new century in promoting and publishing at least two new books of poetry each year by outstanding black poets in America. Thus, Madgett at Lotus Press, and the staff at Broadside Press, have continued the special efforts required to bring more black poetry before the American public.

Notes

1. Wes Boruki, "Michigan," in Waldo E. Martin Jr. and Patricia Sullivan, eds., *Civil Rights in the United States*, Vol. 2 (New York: McMillan Library Reference USA/an Imprint of the Gale Group, 2000), 4765.

2. I. Garland Penn, *The Afro-American Press and Its Editors* (Springfield, MA: Wiley, 1891; reprint, New York: Arno Press and the New York Times, 1969), 160.

3. Julius E. Thompson, "An Urban Voice of the People: The Black Press in Michigan, 1865–1985," in Henry Lewis Suggs, ed., *The Black Press in the Middle West, 1865–1985* (Westport, CT: Greenwood Press, 1996), 137.

4. Ibid., 160.

5. Donald Franklin Joyce, "Reflecting on the Changing Publishing Objectives of Secular Black Book Publishers, 1900–1986," in Cathy N. Davidson, ed., *Reading in America: Literature and Social History* (Baltimore: Johns Hopkins University Press, 1989), 234–235.

Bibliography

Baer, Hans, and Merrill Singer. *African-American Religion in the Twentieth Century: Varieties of*

Protest and Accommodation. Knoxville: University of Tennessee Press, 1992.

Boykin, Ulysses. *A Handbook on the Detroit Negro.* Detroit, MI: The Minority Study Associates, 1943.

Boyle, Kevin. *Arc of Justice: A Saga of Race, Civil Rights, and Murder in the Jazz Age.* New York: Henry Holt and Co., 2004.

Byrd, Rudolph P., ed. *Generations in Black and White: Photographs by Carl Van Vechten from the James Weldon Johnson Memorial Collection.* Athens: University of Georgia Press, 1993.

Carson, Clayborne, Emma J. Lapsansky-Werner, and Gary B. Nash. *African American Lives: The Struggle for Freedom.* New York: Pearson/Longman, 2005.

Ciment, James. *Atlas of African-American History.* New York: Facts On File, 2001.

Clegg, Claude. *An Original Man: The Life and Times of Elijah Muhammad.* New York: St. Martin's Press, 1997.

Dancy, John C., Jr. *Sands against the Wind: The Memories of John C. Dancy, Jr.* Detroit, MI: Wayne State University Press, 1966.

Detroit Chapter of the Association for the Study of African-American Life and History. *Black Historic Sites in Detroit.* Detroit, MI: Detroit Historical Department, 1989.

Hinds, Patricia M., ed. *50 of the Most Inspiring African-Americans.* New York: Essence Communications Partners and Time, Inc. Home Entertainment, 2005.

Holt, Thomas C., and Elsa Barkley Brown, eds. *Major Problems in Afro-American History, Volume II: From Freedom to "Freedom Now," 1865–1890: Documents and Essays.* Boston: Houghton Mifflin, 2000.

Katzman, David. *Before the Ghetto: Black Detroit in the Nineteenth Century.* Urbana: University of Illinois Press, 1973.

Madgett, Naomi Long. *Pilgrim Journey.* Detroit, MI: Lotus Press, 2007.

Martin, Waldo E., Jr., and Patricia Sullivan, eds. *Civil Rights in the United States.* Vol. 2. New York: McMillan Library Reference USA/An Imprint of the Gale Group, 2000.

McMickle, Marvin A. *An Encyclopedia of African-American Christian Heritage.* Valley Forge, PA: Judson Press, 2002.

Penn, I. Garland. *The Afro-American Press and Its Editors.* Springfield, MA: Wiley, 1891. Reprint, New York: Arno Press and the New York Times, 1969.

Reynolds, Barbara, ed. *And Still We Rise: Interviews with 50 Black Role Models.* Washington, DC: USA Today Books/Gannett Co., 1988.

Schomburg Center for Research in Black Culture and the New York Public Library. *African American Desk Reference.* New York: John Wiley & Sons, 1999.

Sisson, Richard, Christian Zacher, and Andrew Cayton, eds. *The American Midwest: An Interpretive Encyclopedia.* Bloomington: Indiana University Press, 2007.

Smith, Jessie Carney, ed. *Black Firsts: 2000 Years of Extraordinary Achievement.* Canton, MI: Visible Ink Press, 2003.

Smith, Sande, ed. *Who's Who in African-American History.* Greenwich, CT: Brompton Books, 1994.

Suggs, Henry Lewis, ed. *The Black Press in the Middle West, 1865–1885.* Westport, CT: Greenwood Press, 1996.

Thomas, Richard W. *Life for Us Is What We Make It: Building Black Community in Detroit, 1915–1945.* Bloomington: Indiana University Press, 1992.

Thompson, Julius E. *Dudley Randall, Broadside Press, and the Black Arts Movement in Detroit,*

1960–1995. Jefferson, NC: McFarland & Co., Publishers, 1999.

U.S. Department of Health, Education, and Welfare. *Availability Data on Minorities and Women*. Washington, DC: Office for Civil Rights, 1973.

Ward, Jerry W., Jr., ed. *Trouble the Water: 250 Years of African-American Poetry*. New York: Mentor/Penguin Books, 1997.

Writer's Program of the WPA. *Michigan: A Guide to the Wolverine State*. New York: Oxford University Press, 1941.

MINNESOTA

Tiffany K. Wayne

Chronology

1787	The first recorded African slave in what is now Minnesota, Pierre Bonga, is freed.
1787	Eastern Minnesota is designated part of the Northwest Territory of the United States of America regulated by the Northwest Ordinance, which prohibits slavery in the region.
1803	The United States claims western Minnesota as part of the Louisiana Purchase.
1805	Lieutenant Zebulon Pike negotiates an agreement with the Dakota people for 100,000 acres of land in southern Minnesota, including the area that now includes the Twin Cities.
1818	The northern boundary of Minnesota is established at the 49th parallel.
1825	Fort Snelling is completed at the confluence of the Mississippi and Minnesota Rivers.
1836	The Wisconsin Territory (which includes Minnesota) is established.
1836	The slave Dred Scott is brought to Fort Snelling by his owner.
1848	Wisconsin becomes a state, and a separate Minnesota Territory is organized.
1855	The Minnesota Republican Party is formed on a platform of opposition to the western spread of slavery.
1857	In *Dred Scott v. Sandford*, the U.S. Supreme Court rules against Scott, a slave from Missouri who claimed a right to his freedom based on residency in the "free" territory of Minnesota.
1858	*(May 11)* Minnesota is admitted to the Union as the 32nd state and as a free state.
1862	An uprising of the Dakota Indians in Minnesota is suppressed.
1865	*(February 23)* Minnesota ratifies the Thirteenth Amendment to the U.S. Constitution abolishing slavery.
1867	*(January 22)* Minnesota ratifies the Fourteenth Amendment to the U.S. Constitution extending full citizenship rights to African Americans.
1868	The Minnesota legislature grants the vote to black men, as well as to some Native Americans.
1870	*(January 13)* Minnesota ratifies the Fifteenth Amendment to the U.S. Constitution extending the right to vote to black men.
1885	The *Western Appeal* (later the *Appeal*), a black newspaper, is founded in St. Paul.
1885	Frederick McGhee is the first black lawyer admitted to the bar in Minnesota.
1898	J. Frank Wheaton becomes the first African American elected to the Minnesota House of Representatives.
1905	Frederick McGhee is involved in the Niagara Movement, a precursor to the founding of the National Association for the Advancement of Colored People (NAACP).

1920   *(June)* Three black men are lynched in Duluth after being accused of raping a white teenage girl.

1921   Minnesota passes an antilynching law, requiring police offers to protect victims from mobs and making it possible for victims' families to receive damages.

1921   Lena O. Smith becomes the first black woman lawyer admitted to the bar in Minnesota.

1934   The *Minneapolis Spokesman-Recorder* is founded by Cecil E. Newman.

1948   Minneapolis Mayor Hubert H. Humphrey calls for an end to racial discrimination in a speech at the Democratic National Convention in Philadelphia.

1955   St. Paul civil rights leader Roy Wilkins is elected executive director of the NAACP.

1963   *(February 27)* Minnesota ratifies the Twenty-fourth Amendment to the U.S. Constitution abolishing the poll tax.

1993   Alan Page becomes the first African American elected to the Minnesota State Supreme Court.

1994   The Confederation of Somali Community in Minnesota is established to coordinate services to new immigrants.

2006   Keith Ellison is elected as the first African American congressman from Minnesota and first Muslim in the U.S. Congress.

2008   *(November 4)* Democrat Barack Obama, the first African American nominee of a major party, carries Minnesota in the general election, winning about 54 percent of the vote.

Historical Overview

Admitted as the 32nd state in 1858, Minnesota has historically had a very small black population. According to the 2000 U.S. Census, African Americans make up only 4.6 percent of the state's population, while 85 percent of population is white. Most of the white population is of German and Scandinavian descent, as these are the European immigrant groups who began coming to the region in the mid-nineteenth century. There were few African slaves brought to Minnesota, which until the 1840s was the furthest western outpost of Anglo-American settlement.

Minnesota is known for its prairies, forests, and lakes, and the region's economy was historically based on logging, mining, and farming. It was not until the early twentieth century that industrialization and wartime labor needs drew more African Americans from the South to the northern cities in search of employment opportunities. Throughout the twentieth century, most of the state's overall population (60 percent in the year 2000)—and most of the black population—were concentrated in the urban areas of the capital city, St. Paul, and the state's largest city, Minneapolis, which together are referred to as the "Twin Cities" metropolitan area.

Africans in Early Minnesota

French fur traders began exploring the Minnesota territory in the late 1600s and the fur trade remained the primary economic interest in the region well into the 1800s. Minnesota was part of the imperial struggle for control of land and resources and was at various times controlled by the French, Spanish, or British. The British maintained outposts in the area through the time of the American Revolution, and it was a British officer who brought the first recorded African into what is now Minnesota. Pierre Bonga, born into slavery in the West Indies, was brought to Minnesota and subsequently freed around 1787, at about the same time that the new United States gained control of the area. Bonga (sometimes spelled Bungo) lived near Duluth and was an explorer, fur trapper, and trader who married an Ojibwe woman and was a skilled negotiator and translator between the British and native Americans.

Pierre Bonga's two sons, Stephen and George, were also traders, translators, and guides. George Bonga was born sometime around 1802 and was also able to achieve some success as a person of African descent in this sparsely populated outpost where diverse cultures mixed and traded. He became well known in the region and among U.S. officials, and several Minnesota landmarks, including Lake Bonga, are named for the contribution of the Bonga family.

Once the new United States gained control of the region, Minnesota was part of the territory regulated by the Northwest Ordinance of 1787, which prohibited slavery in the territory. After Pierre Bonga was freed that same year, however, there were no other recorded African slaves in the far western and northern reaches of Minnesota until at least the 1820s. The western part of Minnesota was not acquired by the United States until the Louisiana Purchase of 1803; in 1805, Zebulon Pike negotiated the agreement that resulted in the Dakota people ceding some 100,000 acres of southern Minnesota to the United States for military use. Construction on Fort Snelling began at the confluence of the Mississippi and Minnesota Rivers in 1819 and the fort was completed in 1825. A sawmill town at St. Anthony Falls was built a few years later in the area that now includes the cities of St. Paul and Minneapolis.

Slavery in Minnesota

The military fort and mill activities drew greater numbers of government appointees, settlers, and migrants from the South, and some African slaves were brought to Fort Snelling by officers in the 1820s. U.S. Indian agent Lawrence Taliaferro was one of these early slaveholders, having inherited several slaves from his Virginia father. One of Taliaferro's slaves was Harriet Robinson, who later married Dred Scott in a ceremony officiated by Taliaferro himself. Scott (originally from Missouri) later used his residency in the free territory as the foundation of his appeal for his freedom, which was denied by the U.S. Supreme Court in 1857. Two decades before the infamous Scott case, another enslaved person, identified simply as Rachel, had also sued in the Missouri courts for her freedom based on time spent in the Wisconsin and Minnesota territories.

The population of Minnesota expanded greatly after it was organized into a separate territory in 1849 and settlers came for the bountiful farmlands and timber. Throughout the 1850s, an era in which the nation was increasingly divided over the issue of slavery, most territorial migrants came from the Northeast and generally did not bring slaves with them. The Minnesota territorial census of 1850 showed only a small community of free blacks—about 40 persons—living mostly in the town of St. Paul. Among these blacks, most were themselves new migrants to Minnesota, having been born in Virginia, Kentucky, and other southern slave states.

Even before the Dred Scott case, and despite the small number of blacks in Minnesota by the 1850s, the slavery debates throughout the United States raised concerns about attracting fugitive or freed slaves into the territory. An 1849 law prohibited African Americans from voting in local and territorial elections. After the Kansas-Nebraska Act of 1854, white Democrats in the Minnesota Territory supported the idea of popular sovereignty, of white voters deciding whether to allow slavery in the territory. In opposition to this idea, the Minnesota Republican Party was formed in 1855 on a platform of preventing the western spread of slavery, also known as a free soil, free labor platform. The Republican Party gained strength in rural areas among white emigrants coming to settle and farm the vast western lands, while the Democratic numbers were stronger in the lumber mill towns.

Slavery was thus an issue in Minnesota's bid for statehood, including in the selection of delegates for and terms of the constitutional convention. Minnesota Democrats called their political rivals "Black Republicans" because of their support for free labor (if not outright abolition of slavery) and black suffrage. In 1857, the Democratic newspaper in St. Paul argued for "White Supremacy against Negro Equality." After the Dred Scott case denied African Americans claims to citizenship, much less freedom, Minnesota Republicans debating the black suffrage provision decided the issue would too greatly risk the passage of the state constitution, and so they allowed the issue to go to voters, as Democrats had wanted. Reflective of such compromises, Minnesota was granted statehood in May 1858 as a free state with a Democratic governor.

Civil War and Reconstruction

Minnesota was one of the last states admitted to the Union before the outbreak of Civil War. Minnesota had only 259 black residents in 1860, and yet more than 100 of those enlisted to fight. In the midst of the Civil War, Minnesota became involved in another battlefront against Native Americans in the Dakota War (also known as the Sioux Uprising) of 1862. Several "contraband" laborers (former slaves captured from the Confederate enemy) were sent to the Fort Snelling military outpost to assist in the conflict.

With many whites leaving the state to join the Union army, Minnesota offered other opportunities for black migrants looking for work in the 1860s. Some companies even sent representatives to recruit thousands of black workers from St. Louis and other areas. Other African Americans made their way north to Minnesota as workers on steamboats who migrated up the Mississippi River to St. Paul. After the Emancipation Proclamation went into effect in January 1863, the Union army helped facilitate the escape of enslaved people from the South, while others took it upon themselves to leave. In the spring of 1863, Robert Hickman led a group of some 75 African American refugees on a raft up the Mississippi River from Missouri. They were eventually towed by Union troops to St. Paul. Hickman went on to found the Pilgrim Baptist Church in St. Paul, an important beacon in the Minnesota African American community. Other early black churches in Minnesota included an AME church founded in Minneapolis in 1860 and St. Mark's Episcopal Church in 1867.

After the Civil War, Minnesota was one of the earliest states to adopt a suffrage law allowing black men (and Native Americans) the right to vote, two years before the passage of the Fifteenth Amendment to the U.S. Constitution extending that right across the nation. The Minnesota state government also passed its own civil rights legislation, outlawing segregation in the public schools in 1869. If Minnesota seemed to be a more egalitarian place for African Americans in the post–Civil War era, the number of blacks migrating into the state was still relatively small compared to other locations. Minnesota in general was experiencing tremendous population growth in the final decades of the nineteenth century, but the state census showed only 500 additional African American individuals living in the state in 1870 compared to 10 years earlier. By 1900, their numbers had increased significantly to more than 14,000 "colored" people living in Minnesota. Although this seemed like a phenomenal influx of African Americans into the state, they still made up less than 1 percent of the total population of Minnesota.

Racial Tensions and Politics in the Twentieth Century

Although the numbers were small, and although blacks had been actively recruited into the state as laborers and Indian fighters during the Civil War, hostility toward African Americans increased in the new century. Conflicts arose between black and white communities in St. Paul and Minneapolis, and efforts were made by some whites to prevent more blacks from migrating into the state. Even with such tensions, and with the discrimination that left blacks relegated to low-paying service jobs, a steady stream of black migrants coming to the northern cities drew rural Minnesota blacks into urban areas. These migrants sought the promise of educational and employment opportunities, as well as an escape from the Jim Crow conditions of the South. Other European immigrants and migrants also moved to Minnesota in the late nineteenth and early twentieth centuries, and ethnic neighborhoods developed in the cities.

Blacks, like other groups, were drawn to existing communities for support and opportunity, but the black community's growth and movement in St. Paul and Minneapolis were limited by de facto segregation, as they were unwelcome in surrounding German, Swedish, Norwegian, and Irish Catholic neighborhoods. Some blacks, however, moved into new Russian-Jewish neighborhoods in the early 1900s. The Rondo neighborhood, in particular, became a well-known black enclave. In these urban areas, blacks worked in skilled and building trades, in service industries, and for the railroad lines that were headquartered in St. Paul.

African Americans in cities such as St. Paul, Minneapolis, and Duluth created vibrant communities centered around black businesses, churches, newspapers, benevolent organizations, and newspapers. The *Western Appeal* was founded in 1885 at a time when there were fewer than 1,500 black residents in the Twin Cities area, and the *World* newspaper was founded in Duluth in 1895. This period saw the rise of a small black middle class of doctors, lawyers, and ministers as community leaders. Fredrick McGhee received his law degree in Tennessee in 1885 and set up practice in St. Paul and Minneapolis. He was the first black lawyer admitted to the bar in Minnesota and later became an important figure in the Civil Rights Movement. The neighborhood organizations, churches, and newspapers provided institutional support for the black community as well as the foundations of black political life throughout the twentieth century.

In 1889, an Afro-American League was founded with chapters in several Minnesota towns, and Minnesota delegates John Q. Adams (publisher of the *Appeal* newspaper) and lawyer Fredrick McGhee were central players in the national Afro-American League's meeting in St. Paul in 1902. Three years later, in 1905, McGhee was among those national black leaders (along with W. E. B. Du Bois) who met and formed the Niagara Movement, a civil rights organization that opposed the accommodation strategy of Booker T. Washington. The Niagara Movement was short-lived as a group, but led to the formation of the NAACP in 1909.

Nationally, many black men also moved into leadership positions in the Republican Party at the turn of the century. The St. Paul and Minneapolis black population was still relatively small compared to other northern cities, and was made up of primarily working-class and new migrants, so that black political representation and influence were rather limited. Again, Fredrick McGhee emerges as an example of limits for blacks in the Republican Party during this era; frustrated by white Republicans who protested his selection as a presidential elector in 1892 when the party's national convention was held in Minneapolis, McGhee was among the first prominent black leaders to change their affiliation and join the Democratic Party.

Great Migrations

Black migration continued into Minnesota during World War I and World War II as industrial labor needs, coupled with the decrease in new European immigrations, opened up job opportunities. By the 1920s, black neighborhoods had established community institutions to help the poor and new migrants. The Piyllis Wheatley House was one such organization founded in Minneapolis in 1924; the Hallie Q. Brown Community Center was founded in 1929. These and other church and neighborhood centers were not only available for meeting and entertainment space for blacks often barred from white-owned hotels and restaurants, but also offered services such as educational workshops, healthcare, housing assistance, and child care.

By 1920, the majority of blacks living in Minnesota were still new migrants, having been born in other states. Their numbers, and the rate of increase, then, were still small compared to other midwestern cities which swelled during the Great Migration, such as Detroit, Chicago, or Cleveland. The Twin Cities remained segregated from the early decades of the twentieth century, well into the 1960s and 1970s, even after the establishment of government housing programs and efforts to end housing discrimination. Even the proud black enclave of the Rondo neighborhood had been separated along class lines, with middle and working-class residents living on different streets. Resident Evelyn Fairbanks later wrote an autobiographical account of growing up black in St. Paul in the 1930s and 1940s entitled *Days of Rondo* (published in 1990). The neighborhood was divided by a highway in the 1960s, but beginning in the 1980s, the African American community began organizing an annual Rondo Days Festival (held in July) to remember and celebrate this community.

Still, the racial tensions underlying life in Minnesota exploded in one particularly jarring incident, the lynching of three black men in Duluth in the summer of 1920. Several black circus workers had been accused of raping a white teenage girl and, on June 15, 1920, three of the men, Elias Clayton, Elmer Jackson, and Isaac McGhie, were pulled from the jail by a mob, beaten, and hanged. Although thousands had participated in the mob, only a handful were indicted for rioting and 12 individuals were charged with murder. In the end, no one was ever convicted or held accountable for the murders of Clayton, Jackson, and McGhie. Two other men, Max Mason and William Miller, went on trial for the rape and were defended by black lawyers. While Miller was acquitted, Mason was found guilty and ultimately served four years of a prison sentence.

In the aftermath of the lynchings, many African Americans left the city, disillusioned. Others stayed and a Duluth branch of the NAACP was founded in September 1920, with national leader W. E. B. Du Bois brought as a speaker in early 1921. Activists such as Nellie Francis and lawyer William T. Francis (who had represented Max Mason) of St. Paul began pressing for a state antilynching law, which was passed in April 1921.

Depression and World War II

The Great Depression affected the African American community of Minneapolis and St. Paul just as in many other industrial cities. The railroad industry, in particular, was hard hit and by 1939, at the end of the Great Depression, 60 percent of blacks in the Twin Cities remained unemployed, compared to an unemployment rate of 25 percent among whites. As in many cities, the Communist Party appealed to many laboring and unemployed people during the Depression and several Minnesota blacks participated in city and statewide organizations. Other blacks sought to address their grievances through labor unions. The St. Paul chapter of the Brotherhood of Sleeping Car Porters was accepted into the American Federation of Labor (AFL) in 1934. Local activist Nellie Stone Johnson was a union leader who organized black workers and also helped found and became vice president of the Local 665 Hotel and Restaurant Employees Union.

The post–World War II era saw another large influx of blacks into the Twin Cities. Newly arrived residents continued to protest discriminatory practices that kept blacks confined to low-paying service jobs. Black newspapers helped spread the word about employment opportunities and about boycotts of businesses that refused to hire blacks. When the war broke out, many industries were still reluctant to hire black workers, and blacks organized to protest exclusion from government defense work, which was finally outlawed at the federal level by President Roosevelt in June 1941.

Tensions remained, however, and during the war, in the summer of 1943, race riots broke out in several cities across the nation, including Detroit, Los Angeles, and New York. The Minnesota governor was concerned about discrimination and economic inequality and preemptively organized a committee to report on the condition of black communities in Minnesota. The report of the Governor's Interracial Commission—one of the first such state groups of its kind—was later published as *The Negro Worker's Progress in Minnesota*. Still, Minnesota did not pass fair employment legislation until 1955 and housing discrimination continued, supported by state laws that allowed restrictive covenants and discrimination in home loan programs. The postwar housing shortage was made even worse by urban renewal programs that broke up black neighborhoods, disrupting community institutions and fueling white resentment about black movement into other areas of the city.

Civil Rights and Beyond

The next greatest influx of blacks into Minnesota was during the decade of the 1960s, as a new wave of migrants sought to escape the violence of the South during the civil rights struggles. These migrants were a younger and more politicized population and staged civil rights protests in Minnesota in scenes that were repeated around the country. Activists picketed the Woolworth's lunch counter in St. Paul in 1960, and black students took over the admissions office of the University of Minnesota in 1969, leading to the establishment of an Afro-American Studies program and greater recruitment and retention efforts of black students. In the 1970s, the NAACP expanded beyond the Twin Cities with branches in areas such as Duluth and Rochester.

White Minnesotans were also involved in the Civil Rights Movement against segregation and discrimination. Hubert H. Humphrey had been the mayor of Minneapolis during the 1940s and was committed to ending employment discrimination against blacks in his city. Soon to be a U.S. senator, Humphrey addressed the 1948 Democratic National Convention with a speech on the need for the party to commit to human rights and civil rights issues. As senator and then as vice president under Lyndon B. Johnson, Humphrey was involved in the passage of the Civil Rights Act of 1964 and other important social programs of the era.

Through and beyond the 1970s, Minnesota as a whole remained overwhelmingly white, with blacks concentrated in the urban areas of the Twin Cities and Duluth. In the 1980s and 1990s, a new wave of blacks to enter Minnesota

Democratic Representative Keith Ellison, the first Muslim elected to Congress in 2006, looks at his hands before placing them on the Quran once owned by Thomas Jefferson. From left are Speaker of the House Nancy Pelosi, Ellison's wife Kim Ellison, and their daughter Amirah. (AP/Wide World Photos)

came not from the southern states, but from Africa. Minnesota has welcomed political refugees from several war-torn African countries with economic and civil unrest, the greatest number of these (as many as 40,000) from Somalia. According to the 2000 Census, as many as 20 percent of Minnesota's black population are foreign-born. These immigrants have different experiences than African Americans with ties and histories in the American South, as well as different access to educational and employment opportunities. New African immigrants are also more likely to be spread out across Minnesota, as opposed to African Americans who are concentrated in urban areas with long traditions of support through churches, newspapers, and local politics.

In the late twentieth century, more African Americans were elected to political office in Minnesota. In 1994 the city of Minneapolis elected its first female and first black mayor, Sharon Sayles

Belton, and another black woman, Jean Harris, served as mayor of Eden Prairie, Minnesota, during the same years. Only a small number of African Americans have ever lived in rural Minnesota and, at the end of the twentieth century, African Americans in the Twin Cities, in particular, are among the most educated and most affluent black communities in the nation.

Notable African Americans

Ellison, Keith (1963–)

Keith Maurice Ellison was the first African American member of the U.S. Congress from Minnesota, and the nation's first Muslim elected to Congress, representing his Minneapolis district as a Democrat in the House of Representatives. Born and raised in Detroit, Michigan, Ellison attended Wayne State University and then earned a law degree from the University of Minnesota. He served in the Minnesota state legislature and was elected to the U.S. Congress in 2006 and reelected in 2008. Ellison has advocated for the rights of Muslims in the United States, especially in light of the terrorist attacks of September 11, 2001, which led to an increase in anti-Muslim sentiment. In 2007, Ellison took his oath of office using a copy of the Quran once owned by Thomas Jefferson.

Jones, Frederick McKinley (1892–1961)

Frederick McKinley Jones was an inventor who received more than 60 patents, most of these related to refrigeration systems he developed for trucks and railroad cars. Born in Ohio and raised in Kentucky, Jones served in World War I and was self-taught as a mechanic, engineer, and inventor. He moved to Minnesota in 1912 and worked in both the railroad and the emerging motion picture film industries. He invented his automatic cooling system in 1935, which not only allowed fresh produce to be shipped long distances, but also had later applications for the military and medical industry. In 1935, he and partner Joe Numero founded the Thermo-King Corporation in Minneapolis.

Marshall, Bobby (1880–1958)

Robert "Bobby" Wells Marshall was a baseball and football player, one of the earliest and best athletes in Minnesota history. Born in Milwaukee, Wisconsin, he was raised in Minneapolis, Minnesota. He attended the University of Minnesota, leading the college team to championship status in the early 1900s. Marshall earned a law degree in 1907 but played professional baseball for the St. Paul Colored Gophers, the Minneapolis Keystones, and Rube Foster's Chicago Giants. In the 1920s, he was one of the first African Americans to play professional football in the NFL. He played for the Minneapolis Marines (Minnesota's first

NFL team), the Duluth Kelleys, and the Rock Island Independents of Illinois.

McGhee, Fredrick (1861–1912)

Fredrick L. McGhee was a civil rights pioneer and the first black lawyer admitted to the bar in Minnesota. McGhee was born to slave parents in Mississippi in October 1861, just months after the start of the Civil War. He earned his law degree in Tennessee and practiced law in Illinois before moving to St. Paul, Minnesota, where he had many white clients but also became involved in civil rights activism. McGhee was one of the founders of the Niagara Movement, working with W. E. B. Du Bois in an organization that led to the formation of the NAACP.

Newman, Cecil (1903–1976)

Cecil E. Newman was a journalist, civil rights activist, and publisher of the *Minneapolis Spokesman-Recorder*, which he used as a forum for motivating and organizing the black community. Newman was born in Kansas City, Missouri, and worked for the *Kansas City Call* before moving to Minneapolis, Minnesota, around 1922. He worked as a bellhop and a Pullman porter before becoming a partner and reporter for the *Twin Cities Herald*. He began his own paper, the *Spokesman-Recorder*, in 1934, which he published until his death in 1976; the paper continues to be published by his granddaughter.

Page, Alan (1945–)

Alan Cedric Page was a Hall of Fame football player with the Minnesota Vikings before having a distinguished career as a lawyer, activist, and Minnesota Supreme Court justice. Born in Canton, Ohio, Page studied political science in college before joining the Minnesota Vikings from 1967 to 1978, during which time the team made

Minnesota Supreme Court Justice Alan Page. (Minnesota Supreme Court)

Undated photo of the rock star Prince. (AP/Wide World Photos)

it to the Super Bowl four times; he went on to play with the Chicago Bears for three years. In 1978, he earned a law degree from the University of Minnesota. After retiring from football, he was assistant state attorney general and then became an associate justice on the Minnesota State Supreme Court in 1993, the first African American on that court. He was reelected in 1998 and 2004.

Prince (1958–)

Musician and songwriter Prince introduced a new "Minneapolis sound" to pop music. Born Prince Rogers Nelson in Minneapolis to jazz musician parents, Prince started his own band in high school and recorded his first album by age 20. He was one of the most successful recording artists of the 1980s, earning seven Grammy Awards as well as an Academy Award for the title song of his 1984

film, *Purple Rain*. He has nurtured dozens of other acts and written hundreds of hit songs for other pop artists. In the 1990s, he gave up the name Prince and was known only by a copyrighted symbol and as "The Artist Formerly Known as Prince." In 2010, he wrote a song for the Minnesota Vikings football team, "Purple and Gold."

Puckett, Kirby (1960–2006)

Kirby Puckett was a Hall of Fame baseball player who played for the Minnesota Twins (1984–1995) and is considered one of the best athletes in Minnesota sports history. Born in Chicago, Illinois, the youngest of nine children, Puckett won All-American honors in high-school baseball. He played college baseball in Chicago and in a California league before being drafted by the Twins in 1984. During his tenure, the Minnesota Twins won two World Series championships, in 1987 and again in 1991. Puckett developed glaucoma at the age of 35 and was forced to retire in 1995. He moved to Arizona where, in 2006, he suffered a stroke and died at the age of 45.

Smith, Lena O. (1885–1966)

Lena Olive Smith was a pioneer civil rights activist and lawyer, the first black woman admitted to the bar in Minnesota. Smith was born in Kansas and moved to Minneapolis, Minnesota, around 1906. She graduated from Northwestern College of Law and was admitted to the Minnesota bar in 1921. Smith focused her Minneapolis law practice on civil rights and equality issues such as housing discrimination and the right of blacks to join labor unions. She was a founding member of the Minneapolis Urban League, and between 1935 and 1939, she served as the first female president of the Minneapolis chapter of the NAACP.

Wigington, Clarence Wesley "Cap" (1883–1967)

Clarence Wesley "Cap" Wigington was considered the first African American municipal architect, working on public projects and buildings. Born in Kansas, his family moved to Omaha, Nebraska, when he was just an infant. While still a teenager, he won several prizes for drawing at the Trans-Mississippi World's Fair in 1899 and, after his high-school graduation, worked as a clerk for a local architect. Wigington eventually had important commissions in Omaha and in Wyoming before moving to St. Paul, Minnesota in 1913. In a career that spanned three decades, he designed more than 60 buildings and projects in the St. Paul area, including many which remain as Minnesota historical landmarks.

Wilkins, Roy (1901–1981)

Roy Wilkins was one of the most important Minnesota and national civil rights leaders of the mid-twentieth century, serving as executive director of the NAACP from 1955 to 1977. Born in St. Louis, Missouri, Wilkins attended the University of Minnesota and began his career as a newspaper editor. He began working with the NAACP in the 1930s, serving as editor of the organization's paper, *The Crisis*, and in a variety of administrative roles before becoming executive director in 1955. Under his tenure, the NAACP played a key role in every major civil rights victory, including the 1963 March on Washington, the Civil Rights Act of 1964, and Voting Rights Act of 1965.

Wilson, August (1945–2005)

August Wilson was a playwright who received two Pulitzer Prizes. Born Frederick August Kittel Jr. in Pittsburgh, Pennsylvania, as a young adult he began using his mother's name, Wilson. He cofounded the Black Horizon Theater in Pittsburgh in 1968. By 1978, Wilson had moved to St. Paul, Minnesota, and was eventually affiliated with the Penumbra Theatre Company, which produced (and still produces) many of his plays. He is best known for *The Pittsburgh Cycles*, a 10-play series that chronicles the African American experience over the twentieth century. He earned Pulitzer Prizes for two of the plays in the series, *Fences* (1987) and *The Piano Lesson* (1990); he also won a Tony Award in 1985 for *Fences*.

Winfield, David (1951–)

David Mark Winfield is one of Minnesota's top all-time athletes, although he joined the baseball Hall of Fame as a player with the San Diego Padres. Winfield was born in St. Paul and attended the University of Minnesota on a full athletic scholarship. He led the Golden Gophers baseball team to the College World Series in 1973 and was subsequently recruited by teams in three different sports (baseball, basketball, and football), including the Minnesota Vikings, although he had not played college football.

Winfield chose to play baseball with the San Diego Padres (1973–1980) and went on to play with the New York Yankees and several other teams, spending the 1993–1994 season on his hometown team, the Minnesota Twins.

Cultural Contributions

Black athletes have had a prominent role in Minnesota sports history, especially in football and baseball. Bobby Marshall played both baseball and football and was one of the first African Americans to play for a National Football League team. He joined Minnesota's first NFL team, the Minneapolis Marines, in 1908. Several generations later, Alan Page was a Hall of Fame football player with the Minnesota Vikings, leading the team to four Super Bowl competitions in the 1960s and 1970s.

Black baseball in Minnesota began with the St. Paul Colored Gophers, a team that was founded in 1907 and led to the creation of the Negro League. Bobby Marshall played for the Colored Gophers and for the Minneapolis Keystones, another early black team. Walter Ball later played for teams in Chicago and New York, but he had been one of the founding players, a pitcher, for the Colored Gophers and the Keystones in the early twentieth century. In the next generation of integrated baseball, Roy Campanella was, along with Jackie Robinson, one of the first black players with the Brooklyn Dodgers, but he had spent one season (1948) with the St. Paul Saints. Likewise, Willie Mays became a major league Hall of Fame player for New York and San Francisco teams, but early in his career he had played a season (1951) with a minor league team, the Minneapolis Millers. A Minnesota woman, Toni Stone of St. Paul, was the first of three black women who, barred from the whites-only women's teams, played in the semipro and professional Negro Leagues with men; in the 1950s, she played second base for the Indianapolis Clowns and the Kansas City Monarchs.

In the later twentieth century, Minnesota produced two of the best black baseball players of all time: Kirby Puckett, who spent his entire career with the Minnesota Twins, and Dave Winfield, who played for the San Diego Padres but spent a season with the Twins at the end of his career.

As in many states, the black community in Minnesota, although small, nurtured a black musical tradition, beginning with the gospel and spirituals sung in black churches. Although other cities are considered the birthplaces of jazz, the blues, and rock and roll, Minneapolis also had a small role in the early days of jazz music. Musician and composer Wilbur Sweatman first recorded the ragtime records of Scott Joplin in Minneapolis. Sweatman later became wildly successful for his own Dixieland rag compositions and is considered one of the first black musicians to record the new jazz music in the 1910s.

Young black musicians in the 1960s and 1970s drew on the ragtime, jazz, gospel, and blues traditions to celebrate African American musical contributions. The Sounds of Blackness, organized in St. Paul around 1971, are a Grammy Award–winning group of singers and musicians who incorporate a variety of African American musical styles, including historical traditions of slave songs and spirituals. In the 1990s, the Sounds of Blackness were invited to play at events such as President Bill Clinton's inauguration and the 1996 Summer Olympics.

Black Minnesotans made a unique contribution to popular music as well in the 1980s and 1990s with the introduction of the "Minneapolis sound," pioneered by recording artist Prince. The Minneapolis sound combined the heavy guitar and dance rhythms of rock and roll and funk with elements of New Wave music such as synthesizers and electronic drums. This music was made hugely popular by Prince, and was adopted by other musical acts he nurtured and produced, including Morris Day (also a Minneapolis native and later leader of the band the Time), Sheila E., Vanity 6, and

Apollonia 6. Prince's style is evident as well in the hundreds of hit songs he wrote for other pop artists, including Sheila E. ("The Glamorous Life"), The Bangles ("Manic Monday"), and Sinead O'Connor ("Nothing Compares 2 U").

Bibliography

Fedo, Michael. *The Lynchings in Duluth*. Rev. ed. St. Paul: Minnesota Historical Society, 2000.

Green, William D. *A Peculiar Imbalance: The Fall and Rise of Racial Equality in Early Minnesota*. St. Paul: Minnesota Historical Society, 2007.

Hoffbeck, Steven R. *Swinging for the Fences: Black Baseball in Minnesota*. St. Paul: Minnesota Historical Society Press, 2005.

Lass, William E. *Minnesota: A History*. 2nd ed. New York: W. W. Norton, 2000.

Taylor, David Vassar. *African Americans in Minnesota*. St. Paul: Minnesota Historical Society, 2002.

MISSISSIPPI

Ben Wynne

Chronology

1717	The French begin importing African slaves into the Louisiana Colony.
1724	Jean Baptist de Bienville, a French governor, develops the Bienville Code, or the Black Code, to govern slaves.
1763	The British begin settlements in Mississippi, bringing slave laborers with them.
1806	Improvements in the cotton plant and growing use of the cotton gin increase the demand for slaves in Mississippi.
1817	Mississippi joins the Union as the 20th state.
1823	The Mississippi State legislature severely restricts grounds for freeing of slaves.
1830	Rose Hill Baptist Church, the state's oldest African American Baptist church, is founded in Natchez
1857	The Mississippi State legislature outlaws emancipation of slaves.
1861	(*January 9*) Mississippi becomes the second state to secede from the Union.
1861	(*July*) Federal forces capture Ship Island, which gives the Union control of Mississippi's Gulf Coast.
1862	(*May*) Corinth, in northern Mississippi, falls to Union forces; with the arrival of federal troops, an estimated 17,000 blacks slaves eventually join their ranks.
1863	(*January 1*) President Abraham Lincoln's Emancipation Proclamation takes effect, freeing all slaves in territory then in rebellion against the federal government.
1863	(*July 4*) After weeks of siege, Vicksburg on the Mississippi River, falls to Union forces under General Ulysses S. Grant.
1864	Mississippi's first African Methodist Episcopal church, Bethel AME, is established in Vicksburg.
1865	(*December 5*) Mississippi rejects the Thirteenth Amendment to the U.S. Constitution abolishing slavery in the United States.
1866	Rust College is established in Holly Springs as Shaw College, the first private liberal arts institution for freed slaves.
1867	The U.S. Congress rejects the reconstructed government of Mississippi and replaces it with a military government.
1867	African Americans vote for the first time in Mississippi.
1868	The so-called "Black and Tan Convention," a biracial constitutional convention, drafts a new state constitution that protects the rights of African Americans; voters reject the proposed constitution.

1869 Tougaloo College is founded north of Jackson.

1870 (*January 17*) Mississippi ratifies the Fourteenth Amendment to the U.S. Constitution extending citizenship to former slaves; the state's ratification comes a year and a half after the amendment was adopted.

1870 (*January 17*) As a requirement for sending representatives to Congress, Mississippi ratifies the Fifteenth Amendment to the U.S. Constitution, which protects the right of African American men to vote.

1870 (*February 23*) Mississippi is readmitted to the Union.

1870 Upon entering the U.S. Senate, Hiram R. Revels of Natchez becomes the first African American to sit in either house of the U.S. Congress.

1871 (*May 13*) Alcorn State University is created by the Mississippi legislature as the first land-grant school for African Americans in the United States.

1872 John R. Lynch becomes speaker of the Mississippi House of Representatives; Lynch is then elected to the U.S. House of Representatives from Mississippi.

1873 Thomas W. Stringer founds the Stringer Grand Lodge in Vicksburg, the first and largest African American Masonic Lodge in the state.

1875 Blanche K. Bruce is the first African American elected to the U.S. Senate.

1875 The "Mississippi Plan" is instituted by the state government to deter African American political participation.

1877 The Natchez Seminary for Black Ministers is founded in Natchez by the American Baptist Home Mission Society of New York.

1883 The Natchez Seminary for Black Ministers moves to Jackson and is renamed Jackson College, later becoming Jackson State University.

1887 Mound Bayou, the first Mississippi town founded by African Americans, is established.

1890 Isaiah Montgomery is the sole African American delegate at Mississippi's constitutional convention.

1890 The Second Mississippi Plan is written into the revised state constitution to circumvent the Fifteenth Amendment and thus constitutionally eliminate African Americans from state politics.

1894 Holy Family Catholic Church, the first African American Catholic church in the state, is built in Natchez.

1894 Smith Robertson opens as the first public African American school in Jackson, later becoming the Smith Robertson Museum.

1894 The Wechsler School becomes the first brick public school built for African Americans in Mississippi with funds from public school bonds.

1903	The State Federation of Colored Women's Clubs is founded.
1907	Dr. L. T. Miller opens the first sanitarium in the state for African Americans.
1908	The Farish Street District in Jackson grows to prominence.
1908	Richard Wright, a renowned author of the African American experience, is born near Natchez.
1909	Piney Woods Country Life School is founded 21 miles southeast of Jackson by Dr. Laurence Jones; the school provides vocational and secondary education for African American students.
1909	Zachery Taylor Hubert becomes the first African American president of Jackson State University.
1917	Civil rights activist Fannie Lou Hamer is born in Montgomery County.
1920	St. Augustine Church and Seminary, the oldest Roman Catholic Seminary in the state, is founded in Greenville.
1924	The Afro-American Sons and Daughters, a fraternal organization, is started by T. J. Huddleston Sr. in Yazoo City.
1925	*(July 2)* Medgar Wiley Evers, a leader in Mississippi's Civil Rights Movement, is born in Decatur.
1925	*(September 16)* Bluesman B. B. King is born in Itta Bena.
1927	*(February 10)* Opera star Leontyne Price is born in Laurel.
1928	T. J. Huddleston Sr. builds and operates the first hospital in the state owned and managed by African Americans.
1954	*(November 24)* Medgar Evers is appointed the National Association for the Advancement of Colored People (NAACP) field secretary for Mississippi.
1955	*(August 28)* Emmett Till, a black man from Chicago, is murdered in Money, a small town in the Delta region, supposedly for whistling at a white woman.
1960	The first African American protest in Mississippi in the civil rights era begins in Biloxi Beach, when blacks attempt to use a segregated beach.
1962	The desegregation of Mississippi schools and colleges begins when James Meredith becomes the first black registrant to be admitted to the University of Mississippi.
1962	*(December 20)* Mississippi rejects the Twenty-fourth Amendment to the U.S. Constitution, which abolishes the poll tax; Mississippi has never ratified this amendment, which took effect in January 1964.
1963	*(June12)* Medgar Evers, the NAACP field secretary for Mississippi, is assassinated in the driveway of his Jackson home.

1964 The Mississippi Freedom Democratic Party is founded to challenge the control of the whites-only regular Democratic Party in Mississippi.

1964 The Twenty-fourth Amendment to the U.S. Constitution is ratified, abolishing the poll tax, a major obstacle to African American voting.

1964 The Freedom Summer Program brings black and white college students, recruited and organized by civil rights groups, to come to Mississippi to lead voter registration efforts, fight illiteracy, and start "Freedom Schools."

1964 James Chaney, an African American man, and two white men, Michael Schwemer and Andrew Goodman, are murdered while investigating the burning of the Mt. Zion Methodist Church in Philadelphia, Mississippi.

1965 The Voting Rights Act becomes law.

1967 State Representative Robert G. Clark becomes the first African American to serve in the Mississippi legislature in the twentieth century.

1977 The first annual Delta Blues Festival is held in Clarksdale.

1978 The Mississippi Cultural Crossroads opens in Port Gibson.

1979 The first annual Farish Street Festival is held in Jackson.

1980 Bennie Thompson is elected to the Hinds County Board of Supervisors.

1984 Ruben Anderson from Jackson is elected as the first African American justice of the Mississippi Supreme Court.

1984 The Smith Robertson Museum and Cultural Center, focusing on the history of Mississippi's African Americans, opens in Jackson.

1985 The first permanent civil rights exhibit in the United States opens at the Old Capitol Museum in Jackson.

1986 Michael Espy is elected to the U.S. House of Representatives, becoming Mississippi's first African American congressman since Reconstruction.

1991 The Natchez Museum of African American History and Culture opens.

1993 Michael Espy of Mississippi is appointed U.S. secretary of agriculture by President Bill Clinton.

1993 Bennie Thompson is elected to succeed Mike Espy as representative of Mississippi's 2nd District in the U.S. House of Representatives.

1994 Byron de la Beckwith is convicted, after 31 years, of the 1963 assassination of civil rights leader Medgar Wiley Evers.

1995 (*March 16*) Mississippi ratifies the Thirteenth Amendment to the United States, 130 years after the amendment took effect.

1998 Sam Bowers, former head of the White Knights of the Ku Klux Klan in Mississippi, is convicted of the 1966 murder of civil rights activist Vernon Dahmer.

2005 Eighty-year-old Edgar Ray Killen is convicted of manslaughter in connection with the 1964 deaths of civil rights workers Michael Schwerner, James Chaney, and Andrew Goodman in Neshoba County.

2005 Representative Bennie Thompson of Mississippi becomes a leading Democrat on the new U.S. House Committee on Homeland Security.

Historical Overview

The Nineteenth Century

African Americans have lived on the land that is now the state of Mississippi for 300 years. The French were the first of the European powers to settle the region, establishing Fort Maurepas on the Gulf Coast in 1699 and Natchez on the Mississippi River in 1716. The French brought the first African slaves into Natchez in 1716 to serve as agricultural labor. For the rest of the eighteenth century, even as governance of the region passed from French into Spanish, British, and finally American hands, Natchez remained the center of economic activity in the area, and the highest concentration of slaves could be found along the Mississippi River in the Natchez vicinity. By the time the United States officially created the Mississippi Territory in 1798, Eli Whitney's invention of the cotton engine, or "gin," had made cotton profitable, and it quickly became the primary cash crop in the Natchez District. With statehood in 1817, Mississippi began to fill up with settlers and slaves, and while Natchez remained a center for the cotton trade in the state, the cotton kingdom began to expand into central Mississippi along the Pearl River and into the Yazoo and Tombigbee River valleys. As the cotton economy expanded in the state, so did the institution of slavery. When Mississippi seceded from the Union in 1861, more than 436,000 slaves resided within its borders, making up 55 percent of the state's total population.

During the course of the Civil War, around 17,000 former slaves from Mississippi served in the U.S. Army. Black soldiers in blue uniforms guarded federally-occupied cities and traversed Mississippi's roads as battle-ready infantry, cavalry, and artillery. From the time that the Union army first came to Mississippi, slaves flocked to the lines seeking freedom, and the federals set up contraband camps to meet the needs of the freedmen population. Once the U.S. government decided to use black troops in 1862, these contraband camps provided a pool of eager recruits, as did the ongoing flow of runaways into the federal lines. Former slaves did guard duty in Vicksburg and Natchez, and distinguished themselves in a number of engagements around the state.

Even though many former slaves enlisted in the Union army, and others were employed by the army to perform auxiliary functions, thousands were left with no means of support as U.S. forces occupied the state. After exploring a variety of options, federal authorities eventually organized "home farms" in some areas on which the freedmen could work for wages. These farms were located on plantations that had been seized by the army and leased, in many cases, to northern businessmen looking to make profits from cotton production. The system was ripe for abuse, and some northerners made large profits from the enterprise at the expense of the freedmen. Federal authorities also began distributing some lands to the freedmen themselves, though some of the land claims would be disputed in years to come.

Freedom Riders en route to Washington, D.C., from New York City hang signs from their bus windows to protest segregation. During the summer of 1961, hundreds of Freedom Riders rode in interstate buses into the prosegregationist South to test a U.S. Supreme Court decision that banned segregation of interstate transportation facilities. (Library of Congress)

At the end of the war, times were especially difficult for Mississippi's newly freed slaves. The war's outcome had given them their freedom but little else. Permanent equality for the former slaves never fully materialized and eventually gave way to social turmoil that would not be dealt with effectively for another century. Mississippi's freedmen owned no property and had few personal possessions, and slavery had scattered many of their families. After the war, many former slaves as quickly as possible tried to establish some sort of family life, and many freedmen wandered the roads of the state for months searching for lost relatives. Hundreds of slave marriages took place in the months immediately following the war, legally sanctioning unions that had not

been recognized during the antebellum period. The federal government created the Freedmen's Bureau to distribute supplies to the needy and settle other issues, but the agency was never large enough in scope to provide a long-range solution to Mississippi's (and the South's) many problems.

Even before the war ended Abraham Lincoln put in place a lenient plan for reconstructing both the southern states and the nation. His plan involved little more than most white southerners taking a loyalty oath to the Union and accepting emancipation. Upon Lincoln's death, the presidency passed to Andrew Johnson, who also advocated a lenient plan. While both plans were designed to bring the Union back together as quickly as possible, neither made any concrete provisions for civil rights for the newly freed slaves. Johnson, in fact, was at times openly hostile to the African American community. As a result, white political leaders in Mississippi, many of whom were Democrats and former Confederates, quickly began putting together state governments under what they considered favorable terms.

Andrew Johnson appointed a provisional governor in Mississippi who immediately called a constitutional convention that met in Jackson in August 1865. The convention produced a new constitution and elections were scheduled for state and local officials. Former Confederate General Benjamin G. Humphreys won the governor's seat and the elections also produced a state legislature firmly dedicated to turning back the clock and reestablishing white supremacy and the old social order. Once in office the newly elected legislature passed a series of laws collectively known as the Black Code. They were designed to regulate the activities of the newly freed slaves and keep the freedmen subordinate. Under the new laws freedmen could not rent or lease some rural land, they could not own firearms, and they had to have a special license to hold many jobs. The legislature also passed vagrancy laws under which former slaves could be arrested and, if they could not pay the required fine, farmed out to work for their former masters or other whites for no pay. During this initial phase of Reconstruction, federal troops were ordered to look out for the physical safety of the former slaves, but they were also told not to interfere to any great degree with Mississippi's civilian authorities. As a result, federal officials in Mississippi did little to counter the laws restricting freedmen.

Once Congress seized control of the Reconstruction process in 1868, the situation in Mississippi changed. Former Confederates were restricted from taking part in the formation of new state governments, and adult male freedmen were given the right to vote and hold office. As a result, the Republican Party governed Mississippi for several years, with the African American community constituting the party's largest voting bloc in the state. A new constitutional convention that included 16 African American delegates and 88 whites convened in Mississippi in January 1868. Despite the fact that there were relatively few African Americans at the convention, some conservative Democratic newspapers later disparaged the meeting as the "Black and Tan Convention" and downplayed its accomplishments. The 1868 Mississippi constitution that the convention produced was patterned after state constitutions in the North. Among other things, it declared that all persons residing in Mississippi who were citizens of the United States were citizens of the state and had equal civil and political rights. The constitution also provided for a system of free public education and for no discrimination in the use of public facilities. These provisions provoked bitter opposition from conservatives, and from many whites who soon regained their right to vote. Regardless, the constitution was ratified, new elections were held, and Mississippi officially reentered the Union in 1870 under Republican control.

The Republicans controlled Mississippi for about five years, during which time they repaired or rebuilt railroads, bridges, levees, and public buildings. The School Law of 1870 established Mississippi's first public school system and the legislature passed a Civil Rights Act prohibiting discrimination in public places and on public conveyances. While African American voters had influence, African Americans never dominated Mississippi's government during the period as some would later claim. No African American was ever elected governor, nor were African Americans ever a majority in the legislature. At the local level where the county sheriff was the most important elected office, only 12 of 74 counties ever had a black sheriff, this in a state where African Americans represented roughly half of the population and 70 to 80 percent of the population in some counties. Even though Mississippi's congressional delegation was always predominantly white, three African Americans briefly represented Mississippi in Washington during Reconstruction, Hiram R. Revels and Blanch K. Bruce in the U.S. Senate and John R. Lynch in the House of Representatives.

During the early 1870s, a significant backlash against Reconstruction policies in Mississippi developed among conservative whites whose goal was to reclaim the state for the Democratic Party and to put in place, in one form or another, the social structure of the antebellum period. Conservatives formed political "White Men's Clubs" to appeal to the white masses and "Taxpayer Leagues" to protest the Republicans' fiscal policies. These groups served two purposes. They unified many white voters based on race and they successfully circulated anti-Republican propaganda throughout the state. During the period, terror groups such as the Ku Klux Klan, the Knights of the White Camellia, and the Sons of Midnight harassed and sometimes killed black and white Republicans alike. During local elections in 1874 and the statewide legislative elections of 1875, violence prevailed as the Democrats implemented the "Mississippi Plan," which generally involved race-based appeals to white voters, stuffed ballot boxes, falsified election returns, and violence and intimidation designed to keep African Americans and white Republicans away from the polls. During the 1875 political season, serious race riots broke out at Water Valley, Louisville, Macon, Columbus, Vicksburg, and other places. In Clinton, more than 20 African Americans died during several days of rioting and many others were forced to flee the town. The statewide elections of 1875 represented a triumph for the Mississippi Plan. Widespread voter fraud and intimidation resulted in legislative victories for the Democrats in 62 of the state's 74 counties. Once seated, the new legislature impeached the Republican governor Adelbert Ames and forced other Republican politicians to give up their offices. Although the

disputed presidential election of 1876 and subsequent Compromise of 1877 that gave Rutherford Hayes the presidency marked the official end of Reconstruction in the South, the 1875 elections marked the end of Reconstruction in Mississippi and the beginning of a hundred years of Democratic dominance of the state.

The race-based Mississippi Plan became the blueprint used by other southern states to rid themselves of Republican rule. Meanwhile, the federal government did nothing to combat the abuses. By the mid-1870s, much of the northern public had grown tired of the Reconstruction debate, which, in turn, caused many northern politicians to lose interest. Civil rights for African Americans was not an issue that excited the northern electorate, and a financial panic in 1873 made economic concerns a priority in many circles. After four years of war, and several years of Reconstruction, the North was tired of fighting and gave the South back to the Democratic Party at the expense of the African American population. Soon African Americans in Mississippi, and in the rest of the South, would be excluded from the political system and legally segregated into a "separate but equal" world of their own.

Once national Reconstruction ended, the political leaders in the southern states were suddenly free to reconstruct their governments as they saw fit, which is exactly what happened in Mississippi. The Democratic Party, with a commitment to white supremacy as one of its central tenets, regained control of the state government and took steps to permanently keep the races separated. Without federal protection, African Americans in Mississippi were left at the mercy of the white establishment, and in the last decades of the nineteenth century, the state's leaders took steps to deny members of the black community their rights as citizens. Mississippi, along with other southern states, began implementing so-called Jim Crow laws, the goals of which were to keep the races separate, and to keep the African American population subordinate. These laws barred African Americans from most public accommodations frequented by whites such as hotels, theaters, restaurants, and public parks. They also called for separate railroad cars for whites and blacks, and for segregated schools. In 1890, Mississippi produced a new constitution that included Jim Crow laws as well as voting provisions that disfranchised many African Americans. A two-dollar poll tax was put in place, as was a literacy clause that required potential voters to read and interpret a section of the new constitution before they were allowed to cast their ballots. In 1892, less than 10,000 of the state's 186,000 eligible African American men were registered to vote. The U.S. Supreme Court upheld these constitutional provisions in 1898 in *William v. Mississippi* just two years after the landmark *Plessy v. Ferguson* case upheld the South's Jim Crow laws. In the decades after Reconstruction, most of Mississippi's African American population made their living on small farms, and regardless of how hard they worked, most remained poor. The sharecropping system that developed during the period was ripe for abuse by the relatively small group of major landowners in the state. It kept African Americans at the bottom of the economic ladder and was also used as a means of social control that effectively recreated the conditions of slavery in many parts of the state.

Civil Rights Era and Beyond

On May 17, 1954, the U.S. Supreme Court overturned the 1896 *Plessy* decision that had legalized segregation. In *Brown v. Board of Education*, a case dealing with the inequities of segregated schools, the justices ruled unanimously that separate educational facilities were inherently unequal. The ruling marked the beginning of the end of legal segregation in the South and was a bombshell in Mississippi. The state's stunned political establishment scrambled for a strategy to fight the decision and the editor of Mississippi's most influential

newspaper predicted bloodshed. The state's senior U.S. senator, James O. Eastland, publically declared that Mississippi and the rest of the South would never obey the ruling. Even the state's more moderate white voices pledged to fight desegregation by every means available. Among the first steps taken by the Mississippi legislature were bills abolishing compulsory school attendance and passage of a variety of resolutions lauding states' rights and condemning federal interference in state affairs. Throughout the state, threats increased against African Americans who were viewed as too outspoken on the issue of desegregation.

After the *Brown* decision, the Civil Rights Movement began in earnest, as did a period of turbulence in Mississippi the likes of which had not been seen since the Civil War. Mississippi's political and economic leaders pledged "massive resistance" to the movement, echoing the sentiments of their counterparts in other southern states. Several organizations, some private and others state-sponsored, were created to fight desegregation. In the Delta town of Indianola, farmer Robert Patterson organized local white business and community leaders into the state's first Citizens Council, a segregationist group. By November 1954, just six months after the *Brown* decision, over 100 council chapters were operating in the state and the movement claimed to have over 20,000 members. The Citizens Councils were made up primarily of upper- and middle-class whites who had the means to exert economic pressure on any African Americans who involved themselves in the Civil Rights Movement. Blacks who signed petitions supporting the *Brown* decision and calling for immediate school desegregation found themselves out of work, or unable to get credit at local banks. Those involved with the increasingly vocal National Association for the Advancement of Colored People (NAACP) might not have been able to purchase the necessities of life at white-owned stores. This

Emmett Till and his mother, Mamie Till Mobley. The 14-year-old Till was murdered by vigilantes in Mississippi in 1955. (Library of Congress)

type of pressure had an effect, successfully stifling the movement in many places, at least for a time. In 1956, the Mississippi legislature created the State Sovereignty Commission ostensibly to prevent encroachment upon the rights of the state by the federal government. The commission included state political and civic leaders, and employed private detectives to secretly investigate anyone associated with the Civil Rights Movement. Many of the commission's activities were coordinated with the Citizens Council.

Of course not all pressure was economic. The Civil Rights Movement in Mississippi also led to a great deal of violence. In some parts of the state, the Ku Klux Klan was revived to terrorize African Americans and harass any whites perceived as having sympathy for the movement. In Belzoni, Reverend George Lee, an NAACP leader, died in a car accident after his automobile was fired on. Lee's friend and fellow NAACP worker Gus Courts was shot and almost killed as he tended his grocery store. No one was ever charged in either crime. In Poplarville, Mack Charles Parker, an African American accused of assaulting a white woman, was dragged from a local jail and lynched by a group of white men, none of whom were ever held accountable for their actions.

Several race-related murders in Mississippi received major national attention during the Civil Rights era. In 1955, Emmett Till, a 14-year-old African American boy, came south from Chicago to visit relatives in Money, a small town in the predominantly black Delta region of the state. Till disappeared shortly after supposedly whistling at a white woman. His battered body, wrapped in barbed wire and weighted down, was later recovered from the Tallahatchie River.

Thousands attend a street rally in New York City on October 11, 1955, to protest the slaying of Emmett Till. The rally was jointly sponsored by the NAACP and District 65 of the Retail, Wholesale, and Department Store Workers Union. (Library of Congress)

Two men were acquitted of the murder but their trial focused major national attention on Mississippi's racial problems. During the late 1950s and early 1960s, World War II veteran Medgar Evers was Mississippi's NAACP field secretary, and as such was heavily involved in voter registration and various educational programs for African Americans in the state. On June 12, 1963, a sniper killed Evers with a single shot in the back from a high-powered rifle. The NAACP's chief representative in Mississippi fell in his driveway, having just arrived home after watching a televised address by President John F. Kennedy on racial justice. Evers' killer would not be forced to pay for his crime for more than a quarter century. A year after Evers' death, three civil rights

workers disappeared in Neshoba County as they drove back from investigating reports of an African American church burning. Their disappearance touched off a massive search and several weeks of national publicity before their bodies were finally found buried in an earthen dam. Several men with Ku Klux Klan ties, including local law enforcement officers, were implicated in their deaths.

Schwerner, Chaney, and Goodman were participating in a large project sponsored by the Council of Federated Organizations (COFO), a sometimes uneasy alliance of various civil rights groups including the NAACP, the Southern Christian Leadership Conference (SCLC), the Student Non-Violent Coordinating Committee

Medgar Evers, 1963. Evers was the National Association for the Advancement of Colored People field secretary for Mississippi. (AP/Wide World Photos)

(SNCC), and the Congress of Racial Equality (CORE). The effort, dubbed the Mississippi Summer Project of 1964, brought into the state hundreds of volunteers, both white and black, from around the country. Volunteers organized "freedom schools" to educate the African American community with regard to their rights as citizens, and lead voter registration drives. As a result, Klan activity increased and violence escalated. In addition to the Schwerner, Chaney, and Goodman murders, other civil rights workers—dubbed "outside agitators" by some Mississippi whites—were beaten, shot, or arrested, and dozens of churches and other buildings were bombed.

In 1962, one of the watershed events of the civil rights era in Mississippi took place as James Meredith, a 29-year-old African American Air Force veteran, prepared to enter the University of Mississippi (Ole Miss). Meredith had applied for admission the previous year, but he was rejected after the registrar's office discovered that he was not white. After a protracted legal battle, the Fifth Circuit Court of Appeals ruled that the university had engaged in a carefully calculated campaign of delay and harassment based of Meredith's race. The court also ordered Ole Miss to admit Meredith immediately. In response, Mississippi's segregationist governor Ross Barnett went on statewide television and vowed to resist the ruling.

On the afternoon of September 30, 1962, a crowd opposing Meredith's admission to the university gathered on campus and began harassing U.S. Marshals who had been brought in to keep order. Some members of the mob were from Mississippi, while many others were segregationists from neighboring states. They began throwing rocks and bottles, and overturning nearby cars and trucks and setting them on fire. As the sun set, events spiraled out of control and Marshals fired tear gas into the crowd. Bullets began to fly and a full-scale riot ensued, during which two people were killed and many others were hurt. One hundred and sixty Marshals were injured, including 28 who were shot during the fracas. Order was restored only after President John F. Kennedy nationalized the Mississippi National Guard and sent in an additional 20,000 federal troops. At 8:00 a.m., the morning after the riot, James Meredith officially broke the color barrier at the University of Mississippi by completing the registration process.

During the period, COFO workers also set up a political organization, the Mississippi Freedom Democratic Party (MFDP), to challenge Mississippi's political establishment. In August 1964, as the national Democratic Convention approached, traditional Mississippi Democrats made plans to send their all-white delegation to the gathering. In response, the MFDP protested and petitioned the credentials committee of the national Democratic Party, claiming that the

On October 8, 1962, James Meredith, the first African American to attend the University of Mississippi, leaves class during his second week at the school. An angry mob had tried to stop his entrance into the school, and federal troops were called in to stop the riot that ultimately left two dead, 28 wounded, and over 200 arrested. (Library of Congress)

delegation chosen by Mississippi Democrats did not accurately represent the people of the state because it did not include any African Americans. They argued that instead of seating the all-white group, the convention should seat a biracial coalition of MFDP members. The credentials committee refused to seat the integrated delegation but the national press covered the struggle, giving even more publicity to the state of political affairs in Mississippi, and in the South in general.

As the 1960s ended, the state of Mississippi began to achieve racial stability. The perseverance of those involved in the Civil Rights Movement, along with evolving attitudes among many whites, brought about change that would have seemed impossible to achieve just two decades earlier. Business leaders began to realize that racial strife retarded Mississippi's economic growth, and that it was difficult to attract industry to a state filled with so much turmoil. Most Mississippians, black and white, tired of conflict and an era of violence and uncertainty, gave way to an era of transition and relative peace. In 1967, two years after the passage of the federal Voting Rights Act, Robert G. Clark of Holmes County became the first African American of the modern era to serve in the state legislature, with other African Americans soon following him. Beginning with the 1969–1970 academic year, school desegregation took place across Mississippi with few incidents. While private all-white academies were established in some areas to circumvent desegregation, the vast majority of Mississippi's children began attending integrated public schools. At the university level James Meredith opened the door for other African Americans, and soon all of the state's institutions of higher learning were integrated. In 1976, popular Ole Miss football star Ben Williams, an African American, was elected by his fellow students as "Colonel Rebel," the most coveted social honor on the Ole Miss campus. Since then, African American students have served as president of the university's student body. In 1984, Ruben Anderson was elected as Mississippi's first African American Supreme Court justice, and two years later, Michael Espy became the first African American Mississippian elected to the U.S. House of Representatives since Reconstruction. In 1985, the first permanent civil rights exhibit opened at the state Mississippi History Museum in Jackson.

By the end of the twentieth century, the state of Mississippi had also taken steps to correct past injustices through an ongoing effort to bring to trial criminals from the civil rights era who had gone unpunished for decades. In 1994, after a highly publicized trial that drew national attention, a Mississippi jury convicted Byron de la Beckwith of the murder of Medgar Evers. Beckwith was given a life sentence and died in custody several years later. In 1998, Sam Bowers, former head of the White Knights of the Ku Klux Klan in Mississippi, was convicted of ordering the 1966 murder of civil rights activist Vernon Dahmer, who died from injuries sustained when his home was firebombed. Bowers also received a life sentence and died in prison. In 2005, 80-year-old Edgar Ray Killen was convicted of manslaughter in connection with the 1964 deaths of Michael Schwerner, James Chaney, and Andrew Goodman in Neshoba County. Due to Killen's advanced age and health, the 60-year sentence he received for the crime was effectively a life sentence.

Notable African Americans

Alexander, Margaret Walker (1915–1998)

The daughter of a minister and a teacher, author Margaret Walker was born in 1915 in Birmingham, Alabama. She was encouraged by her parents to excel and as a child read a great deal of poetry and philosophy. In 1935, she graduated from Northwestern University in Chicago with a degree in English and the following year joined the Federal Writers' Project, where she worked with other prominent writers, including Richard Wright, Frank Yerby, and Gwendolyn Brooks. In 1942, Walker earned a master's degree in creative writing from the University of Iowa, and later earned a Ph.D. in English from the university. She won the Yale Younger Poets Competition for her volume of poetry titled *For My People*.

After her marriage to Firnist James Alexander, Walker taught at Livingston College in North Carolina and at West Virginia State College before moving to Mississippi in 1949 to accept an English professorship at Jackson State College (later Jackson State University). In 1966, she completed her landmark novel *Jubilee*, which won the Houghton Mifflin Literary Fellowship Award and sparked renewed public interest in her work. In 1970 she produced *Prophets for a New Day* and, three years later, *October Journey*. Walker taught at Jackson State until 1979, after which she toured, lectured, and continued to write.

Hamer, Fannie Lou (1917–1977)

Born in 1917 as the youngest of 20 children in a Montgomery County, Mississippi, sharecropping family, Fannie Lou Hamer gained national attention as a civil rights activist during the 1960s. Hamer married in 1944 and moved to Ruleville, where she worked as a field hand on a local plantation. She was later promoted to timekeeper when it was discovered that she could read and write. In 1962, the Civil Rights Movement arrived in Ruleville, and Hamer immediately became involved, registering to vote and losing her job as a result. She worked tirelessly for the Student Non-Violent Coordinating Committee (SNCC) and was a founder of the Freedom Democratic Party. As the party challenged the state's regular Democratic delegation at the 1964 Democratic

Convention, Hamer went on television and told her story of the abuse she had suffered a year earlier at the hands of the police in Mississippi after she had tried to use a local bus station.

In her community she was a larger-than-life character and a tireless worker to improve conditions for Mississippi's impoverished. During the 1970s Ruleville held "Fannie Lou Hamer Day" in recognition of her work, and she also received honorary degrees from Tougaloo College, Shaw University, Morehouse College, Columbia College, and Howard University.

King, B. B. (1925–)

Born Riley B. King near Indianola in the Mississippi Delta, bluesman B. B. King received his first guitar at the age of nine from a relative. As a youngster he sang in church and later worked as a disc jockey in Greenville, Mississippi. After World War II, King moved to Memphis, where he began his career as a professional musician. He was one of the first blues artists to record in the city and through radio station WDIA, "Blues Boy" B. B. King became well known in the region. He moved to Los Angeles in the early 1950s, where he produced hit after hit, including "Everyday," "Sweet Little Angel," and "Three O'clock Blues." In 1969, he released one of his biggest commercial records, "The Thrill Is Gone." One of the most popular and high-profile blues artists ever, King has performed all over the world, earning the title "Ambassador of the Blues."

He continues to make television and concert appearances and garner awards for his talent and body of work. He has received numerous honorary degrees from prestigious institutions such as Yale University and the Berkeley School of Music and has earned more than a dozen Grammy Awards, including an award for lifetime achievement. He received the Kennedy Center Honors

and was one of the first performers inducted into the Rock and Roll Hall of Fame. In 2006, King was awarded the Presidential Medal of Freedom by President George W. Bush.

Price, Leontyne (1927–)

Born in Laurel, Mississippi, opera star Mary Violet Leontyne Price displayed her talents at an early age. Her formal music instruction began with piano lessons at age five, and she grew up using her extraordinary voice as part of her church choir. After graduating from Oak Park High School in 1944, and earning a B.A. at Wilberforce (Ohio) College in 1948, she attended Juilliard School of Music in New York on a full-tuition scholarship. While attending Juilliard, she appeared in a revival of Gershwin's *Porgy and Bess*, which toured the United States and Europe. In 1955, an appearance on the National Broadcasting Company's *Opera Theater* marked her professional debut in grand opera, and her first appearance in a major opera house took place two years later in San Francisco.

On January 27, 1961, Price made her Metropolitan Opera debut as Leonora in Verdi's *Il Trovatore* and later that year became the first African American to open a Metropolitan Opera season. These performances generated rave reviews and established her as a major star. Her reputation grew through the 1960s and 1970s as she played to packed houses and made recordings that earned her 18 Grammy Awards. Price also appeared on the cover of *Time*, was awarded the Presidential Freedom Award, and received numerous international accolades recognizing her talent. She retired after a final performance on January 3, 1985.

Revels, Hiram (1822–1901)

Hiram Rhodes Revels, the first African American to serve in the U.S. Senate, was born to free parents in North Carolina in 1822. As a young man he worked briefly as a barber before leaving North Carolina to pursue his education. Revels attended school in Indiana and Ohio before graduating from Knox College in Bloomington, Illinois. In 1845, Revels was ordained as a minister by the African Methodist Church and traveled extensively, ministering to African American congregations. He eventually settled in Baltimore, Maryland, where he became pastor of a local church and principal of a school for African American students. With the outbreak of the Civil War, he helped organize Maryland's first two African American regiments and eventually joined the Union army himself as a chaplain.

After the war, Revels settled in Natchez, Mississippi, where he involved himself in Republican politics. Taking a conciliatory attitude toward former Confederates, he served as an alderman in Natchez and as a state senator before the Mississippi legislature chose him as a U.S. senator. He served in Washington for just over a year, returning home in 1871 to become president of Alcorn College, now Alcorn State University, the first state-supported school for African Americans in Mississippi. He served in that position until 1873, and then again from 1876 to 1882. He later taught theology at Rust College while continuing his religious work. Revels died in 1901 while attending a church conference. Praised by whites and blacks alike, Hiram Rhodes Revels was buried in Holly Springs.

Wells, Ida B. (1862–1931)

Born to slave parents in Holly Springs, Mississippi, Ida B. Wells spent her adult life crusading for the rights of African Americans and women in the United States. After her parents died in a yellow fever epidemic, Wells raised her younger siblings while attending Rust College in Holly Springs. She later moved her family to Memphis where

she became a teacher, and eventually co-owner of a local black newspaper. She began her career as a journalist writing editorials promoting equal rights for African Americans and crusading against lynching. Forced to leave Memphis after her life was threatened, she moved to Chicago where she married Ferdinand Barnett, an attorney and editor of one of Chicago's early African American newspapers. Always outspoken, she continued her antilynching crusade and also took up the cause of women's suffrage. In 1906, she joined W. E. B. Du Bois as part of the Niagara Movement and three years later was among the founders of the National Association for the Advancement of Colored People (NAACP). She remained one of the African American community's strongest voices until her death in 1931.

Wright, Richard (1908–1960)

One of America's finest authors, Richard Wright was also one of the first African American writers to achieve widespread literary fame. Wright was born in 1908 near Natchez, the son of an illiterate sharecropper and an educated school teacher. After his father abandoned the family, Wright moved with his mother to Arkansas, Tennessee, and back to Mississippi. He spent his early life in poverty, working at menial jobs in the segregated South. In hopes of escaping the racism and limited opportunities that his region afforded African Americans, Wright moved to Chicago, and then to New York, where he found employment with the Federal Writers' Project.

His first novel, *Uncle Tom's Children*, was published in 1938, and the next year he received a Guggenheim Fellowship that allowed him to write *Native Son* (1940). The latter work was a great success and was translated into six languages. In 1945, Wright published an autobiographical novel, *Black Boy*, which further established his reputation in the literary world. The central theme of

A sketch showing Union troops and contrabands constructing a canal near Vicksburg, Mississippi, 1863. (Library of Congress)

Wright's early work was the struggle of an African American male against racial prejudice and the social environment that it spawned. Realizing that discrimination was not limited to the South, Wright became angry and disenchanted with the United States and subsequently moved to France in 1946. A year later he became a French citizen. Wright remained overseas for the rest of his life, dying in Paris in 1960.

Cultural Contributions

African American artists in Mississippi have for generations made significant contributions to popular music in the United States and elsewhere, with the Mississippi Delta region in the northwestern part of the state being recognized worldwide as the "cradle of the blues." The Delta stretches from Memphis, Tennessee, south to Vicksburg, Mississippi, and is framed by the

Mississippi River on the west and the Yazoo River on the east. After the Civil War and into the twentieth century, it was an area populated primarily by poverty-stricken African Americans who did agricultural labor, usually as tenants or sharecroppers on land owned by a minority of more affluent whites. The blues drew on a variety of influences including traditional work songs and "field hollers," religious music, nineteenth-century minstrel shows and strains of music later more identified with white country artists. During the first decades of the twentieth century, roaming blues musicians traveled through the Mississippi Delta playing in juke joints and at house parties, drawing crowds and expanding blues music's base in the region.

In the neverending quest for profits, early recording companies sought to create new market niches after World War I based on performers' regional appeal, ethnicity, or race. As a result, representatives from major labels as well as independent companies began scouring Mississippi and the rest of the South in search of inspired artists whose records could be marketed directly to African American audiences in northern cities and the southern countryside. One of the first, and most influential, Mississippi blues artists of the twentieth century was Charley Patton, who lived and performed in the Delta and made records for several years before his untimely death from heart disease in 1934 at the age of 42. Patton's flamboyant performing style won him fans throughout the region and influenced the bluesmen who followed him. Blues music's most legendary character, Robert Johnson, was born in 1911 in Hazlehurst, Mississippi, but spent much of his life traveling from place to place, supporting himself by playing guitar and singing at parties and in juke joints. He is also the central figure in one of the most lasting myths of American popular culture. As the story goes, Johnson sold his soul to the devil one night at a dark Delta crossroads in exchange for extraordinary musical talent. In 1936 and 1937, he recorded 29 songs that would prove to be his legacy. While still in his 20s, Johnson died after supposedly being poisoned in a juke joint by a jealous husband.

While Patton and Johnson died prematurely, other blues artists from Mississippi had much longer careers and cast their own long shadows over the history of American popular music. Born Chester Arthur Burnett near West Point, Mississippi, bluesman Howlin' Wolf possessed one of the most powerful and distinct voices ever recorded. Though he was never completely proficient on the guitar and could barely count to keep formal time, he gained worldwide fame as a blues pioneer whose gruff, gravely sound made a lasting impression on all who heard it. Wolf's early life was marked by poverty. In 1923 he moved with his family to Clarksdale, Mississippi, where he worked on a large plantation for years. He moved

to Memphis after World War II and found work as a disc jockey while also leading his own band at night. His radio show allowed him to acquire a significant following around the South, as did recordings he made for noted producer Sam Phillips in 1948. He eventually moved to Chicago after signing an exclusive contract to record with Chess Records, and he remained there for the rest of his life. Wolf continued making records until his death in 1976. Born McKinley Morganfield near Rolling Fork, Mississippi, Muddy Waters also went on to become a central figure in the history of blues music as one of the creators of the electric "Chicago" blues style. As a young man Waters drove a tractor on a cotton plantation during the day and played music at night in local clubs. He left the South in 1943, bound for Chicago, where his unique talent soon gained him a following in the city's black nightclubs. Always the innovator, he used an electric guitar and bottleneck to produce a gritty sound that came to the attention of Chess Records. Waters made a number of records for Chess and put together a band that included many of the greatest blues artists of the period. Waters gained international acclaim during the 1960s when British rock groups like the Rolling Stones, who took their name from a Waters song, exposed the American masses to blues music. As a result, he achieved his greatest commercial success during the later years of his life. Waters continued to tour America and Europe until his death in 1983.

Men like Patton, Johnson, Howlin' Wolf, and Waters remain cultural icons in the United States. Since the 1960s, blues music has been recognized around the globe as a uniquely American musical form that gave rise to other genres, most notably rock and roll. As a result, while the exact origins of the music remain shrouded in time, there is little doubt that the genesis of the blues as a worldwide phenomenon can be traced back to the Mississippi Delta.

Bibliography

Barnwell, Marion, ed. *A Place Called Mississippi: Collected Narratives*. Jackson: University Press of Mississippi, 1997.

Barry, John M. *Rising Tide: The Great Mississippi Flood of 1927 and How It Changed America*. New York: Simon and Schuster, 1998.

Bolton, Charles C. *The Hardest Deal of All: The Battle over School Integration in Mississippi, 1870–1980*. Jackson: University Press of Mississippi, 2005.

Bond, Bradley G. *Mississippi: A Documentary History*. Jackson: University Press of Mississippi, 2005.

Burner, Eric R. *And Gently He Shall Lead Them: Robert Parris Moses and Civil Rights in Mississippi*. New York: New York University Press, 1995.

Busby, Westley F., Jr. *Mississippi: A History*. Wheeling, IL: Harlan Davidson, Inc., 2006.

Cagin, Seth, and Philip Dray. *We Are Not Afraid: The Story of Goodman, Schwerner, and Chaney, and the Civil Rights Campaign for Mississippi*. New York: Nation Books, 2006.

Clark, Thomas D., and John D. W. Guice. *The Old Southwest, 1795–1830: Frontiers in Conflict*. Norman: University of Oklahoma Press, 1996.

Cobb, James C. *The Most Southern Place on Earth: The Mississippi Delta and the Roots of Regional Identity*. New York: Oxford University Press, 1992.

Cohn, Lawrence. *Nothing But the Blues: The Music and the Musicians*. New York: Abbeville, 1993.

Cooper, William J., Jr. *Liberty and Slavery: Southern Politics to 1860*. New York: Alfred A. Knopf, 1983.

Cresswell, Stephen. *Rednecks, Redeemers, and Race: Mississippi after Reconstruction, 1877–1917*. Jackson: University Press of Mississippi, 2006.

Doyle, William. *An American Insurrection: The Battle of Oxford, Mississippi, 1962*. New York: Doubleday, 2001.

Hendrickson, Paul. *Sons of Mississippi: A Story of Race and Its Legacy*. New York: Alfred A. Knopf, 2003.

Huie, William Bradford. *Three Lives in Mississippi*. Jackson: University Press of Mississippi, 2000.

Katagiri, Yasuhiro. *The Mississippi State Sovereignty Commission: Civil Rights and States' Rights*. Jackson: University Press of Mississippi, 2001.

Libby, David J. *Slavery and Frontier Mississippi, 1720–1830*. Jackson: University Press of Mississippi, 2004.

Loewen, James W., and Charles Sallis, eds. *Mississippi: Conflict and Change*. New York: Random House, Inc., 1974.

Lomax, Alan. *The Land Where the Blues Began*. Reprint ed. New York: Pantheon Books, 1993.

Mars, Florence. *Witness in Philadelphia*. Baton Rouge: Louisiana State University Press, 1989.

Marsh, Charles. *God's Long Summer: Stories of Faith and Civil Rights*. Princeton, NJ: Princeton University Press, 1997.

McCord, William Maxwell. *Mississippi: The Long Hot Summer*. New York: Norton, 1965.

McLemore, Richard Aubrey, ed. *A History of Mississippi*. 2 vols. Hattiesburg: University and College Press of Mississippi, 1973.

Minor, Bill. *Eyes on Mississippi: A Fifty Year Chronicle of Change*. Jackson, MS: J. Prichard Morris Books, 2001.

Moody, Anne, *Coming of Age in Mississippi*. New York: Dial Press, 1968.

Nossiter, Adam. *Of Long Memory: Mississippi and the Murder of Medgar Evers*. New York: Da Capo Press, 2002.

Palmer, Robert. *Deep Blues*. Reprint ed. New York: Penguin, 1981.

Pritchard, James. *In Search of Empire: The French in the Americas, 1670–1730*. Cambridge: Cambridge University Press, 2004.

Rhodes, Lelia G. *Jackson State University: The First Hundred Years, 1877–1977*. Jackson: University Press of Mississippi, 1979.

Sugarman, Tracy. *Strangers at the Gates: A Summer in Mississippi*. New York: Hill and Wang, 1966.

Taylor, William Banks. *Down on Parchman Farm: The Great Prison in the Mississippi Delta*. Columbus: Ohio State University Press, 1999.

Unser, Daniel H., Jr. *Indians, Settlers, and Slaves in a Frontier Exchange Economy: The Lower Mississippi Valley Before 1783*. Chapel Hill: University of North Carolina Press, 1992.

Wald, Elijah. *Escaping the Delta: Robert Johnson and the Invention of the Blues*. New York: Amistad, 2004.

Webb, Clive. *Fight Against Fear: Southern Jews and Black Civil Rights*. Athens: University of Georgia Press, 2001.

Willis, John C. *Forgotten Time: The Yazoo-Mississippi Delta after the Civil War*. Charlottesville: University Press of Virginia, 2000.

Wirt, Frederick M. *We Ain't What We Was: Civil Rights in the New South*. Durham, NC: Duke University Press, 1997.

Wynne, Ben. *Mississippi's Civil War: A Narrative History*. Macon, GA: Mercer University Press, 2006.

MISSOURI

Tiffany K. Wayne

Chronology

| 1720 | The first African American slaves are brought by the French to work in the lead mines of colonial Missouri. |

1720   The first African American slaves are brought by the French to work in the lead mines of colonial Missouri.

1724   King Louis XV of France issues an "Edict Concerning the Negro Slaves in Louisiana" as part of the *Code Noir*, or Black Code, regulating slavery in the French colonies.

1764   French fur traders establish a settlement at St. Louis, where the Mississippi and Missouri Rivers meet.

1769   Spain outlaws Indian slavery in the Upper Louisiana region, making African slaves the preferred labor source.

1787   Under the Northwest Ordinance, the U.S. Congress prohibits slavery in the new western territories.

1803   The Louisiana Purchase doubles the geographic size of the United States and includes what is now Missouri and 13 other states.

1804   Black Codes are established to regulate slavery in the new Louisiana Territory (including Missouri).

1820   Under the Missouri Compromise, Missouri is to be admitted as a slave state and Maine is to be admitted as a free state in an effort to maintain a balance between northern and southern political representation. The Missouri Compromise also establishes the 36°30′ line—the southern boundary of Missouri—as the dividing line between northern (free) and southern (slave) states.

1821   (*August 10*) Missouri enters the Union as the 24th state.

1824–29   In a series of cases, Missouri courts uphold the principle that blacks born or living in free territories remain free even if they later come to Missouri, thus following the Northwest Ordinance and establishing a "once free, always free" precedent for determining slave status.

1835   The Missouri General Assembly creates restrictions on free black citizens, including ordering that all free blacks have a "license" and that free blacks under the age of 21 be registered as apprentices or servants.

1846   Dred and Harriet Scott file a lawsuit in St. Louis claiming they are free citizens due to previous residence in a free territory; the state of Missouri denies their claim and the case eventually goes to the U.S. Supreme Court.

1847   The Missouri Legislature makes it illegal to teach any blacks, free or slave, to read or write.

1854   The Kansas-Nebraska Act allows slavery in the U.S. territories to be determined by the citizens through "popular sovereignty," thus nullifying the earlier Missouri Compromise and leading many proslavery whites from Missouri to cross into Kansas to vote illegally on the issue.

1857	In *Dred Scott v. Sandford*, the U.S. Supreme Court denies Dred Scott's claim to freedom based on state of residence; in addition to denying the constitutionality of the Missouri Compromise by declaring that each state may have its own laws regarding slavery, the Court also denies Scott's right to bring suit, declaring that no black person, slave or free, has the rights of U.S. citizenship.
1863	In St. Louis, more than 300 men volunteer for the First Regiment of Missouri Colored Infantry to fight in the Civil War.
1865	Slavery is abolished in the Missouri state Constitution, several months before the end of the Civil War and almost a year before the ratification of the Thirteenth Amendment to the U.S. Constitution ending slavery throughout the nation.
1865	The Missouri Equal Rights League is founded to promote the legal and civil rights of black Missourians.
1865	(*February 6*) Missouri ratifies the Thirteenth Amendment to the U.S. constitution abolishing slavery.
1866	The Missouri legislature orders that schools must be provided for black children, but allows separate schools for blacks and whites.
1866	The Lincoln Institute (later Lincoln University) is founded for African American students in Jefferson City.
1867	(*January 25*) Missouri ratifies the Fourteenth Amendment to the U.S. Constitution extending full citizenship rights to African Americans.
1870	(*January 7*) Missouri ratifies the Fifteenth Amendment guaranteeing African American men the right to vote.
1890	In *Lehew v. Brummell*, the Missouri Supreme Court upholds the legality of segregated schools.
1892	(*May 31*) Fifteen hundred people gather in St. Louis after black leaders call a national day of prayer and remembrance for victims of lynching in the United States.
1898	A black regiment of volunteers is raised in St. Louis for service in the Spanish-American War.
1906	Hundreds of African Americans flee Springfield after racial violence results in the lynching of three black men over Easter weekend.
1917	Hundreds of African Americans cross the Mississippi River into St. Louis to escape a race riot between black and white workers in East St. Louis, Illinois.
1920	Walthall Moore of St. Louis is the first African American elected to serve in the Missouri legislature.
1924	The Kansas City Monarchs beat the Hilldale Club of Pennsylvania in the first Negro World Series baseball game.

1938	In *Missouri ex rel. Gaines v. Canada, Registrar of the University, et al.*, the U.S. Supreme Court rules that the state violated equal protection laws by not admitting Lloyd Gaines to the University of Missouri Law School when no equal educational options existed for blacks within the state.
1941	In another challenge to segregation in higher education, the Missouri Supreme Court rules in *State ex rel. Bluford v. Canada* to allow the University of Missouri School of Journalism to deny admission to Lucile Bluford if another school is available for black students.
1942	The U.S. Department of Justice investigates the lynching of Cleo Wright in Sikeston, the first time the federal government intervenes in a local civil rights issue. Wright's murder is the last known lynching of an African American in Missouri.
1943	The National Park Service dedicates the Diamond, Missouri, farm of scientist and inventor George Washington Carver as a national monument, making it the first national monument recognizing an African American.
1948	In *Shelley v. Kraemer*, the U.S. Supreme Court overturns an earlier Missouri court decision allowing for state enforcement of racial covenants to prevent the sale or rental of real estate to African Americans.
1950	The first black students are admitted to the University of Missouri.
1957	The Missouri Commission on Human Rights is created as a state agency to address racial discrimination in employment, public accommodations, and housing.
1961	The Missouri State Legislature passes a Fair Employment Practices Act to outlaw employment discrimination.
1963	(*May 13*) Missouri ratifies the Twenty-fourth Amendment to the U.S. Constitution abolishing the poll tax.
1963	The Congress of Racial Equality (CORE) organizes a protest against Jefferson Bank in St. Louis for refusing to hire black tellers, thus inspiring boycotts of other businesses practicing employment discrimination.
1965	The state legislature passes the Missouri Public Accommodations Act to outlaw segregation and discrimination in public facilities.
1968	William L. Clay Sr. is elected Missouri's first African American U.S. congressman, representing the St. Louis district.
1969	The University of Missouri hires its first African American professor, historian Arvarh E. Strickland.
1972	The Missouri state legislature passes the Fair Housing Act.
1976	Twenty-four years after the U.S. Supreme Court decision in *Brown v. Board of Education*, the Missouri state constitution is amended to end segregation in Missouri's schools.

1991	Emanuel Cleaver II is elected the first African American mayor of Kansas City, Missouri.
1993	Freeman Bosley Jr. is elected as the first African American mayor of St. Louis.
1995	More than 40 years after the landmark *Brown v. Board of Education* case, the U.S. Supreme Court rules in *Missouri v. Jenkins* that the state cannot be required to fund special programs to address de facto racial segregation of schools.
2005	Emanuel Cleaver II is elected to the U.S. House of Representatives from Missouri.
2008	*(February 5)* Barack Obama, an African American senator from Illinois, wins the Missouri Democratic primary, narrowly defeating Senator Hillary Clinton of New York; as the Democratic nominee, Obama narrowly loses Missouri to Republican John McCain in the general election in November.

Historical Overview

Missouri is a midwestern state with 5.6 million residents according to the 2000 Census. The capital of Missouri is Jefferson City, but its largest cities are Kansas City, Springfield, and St. Louis. African Americans make up nearly 12 percent of the entire population of Missouri and are concentrated in these urban areas. A combination of urban and rural economies, Missouri is known for its industry and mining of coal and lead, as well as for its agricultural products, such as wheat, corn, and livestock. At times under French and Spanish colonial control, Missouri was part of the Louisiana Territory purchased by the United States in 1803, and was admitted as the 24th state in 1821.

Africans in Early Missouri

In the late 1600s, the French made their way to the Mississippi River valley via Canada. Unlike the English settlements with their plantation agriculture, the French were interested in fur trapping, trading, and silver and mineral mining. They also needed cheap labor, and like other Europeans, the French saw opportunity in the availability of African slaves. In 1719, the first black slaves were brought by the French into the Upper Lousiana area (which includes present-day Missouri). These slaves were most likely from French-controlled Haiti; in 1720, Phillippe Francois Renault, the French head of mining operations in the region, brought 500 slaves to work in the lead and salt mines. The first permanent white European settlement in Missouri was established at Ste. Genevieve around 1750. After 1750, more slaves were brought for agricultural and household labor and to work in the Mississippi River boat trades.

The French *Code Noir* (or Black Code) dated to 1685 and was the primary legal framework for the treatment of the colonial slave workforce in the Missouri region. The Code Noir protected slaves from enforced work on Sundays and stipulated that families could not be separated by sale; it even allowed for the recognition of slave marriages. But the laws also protected the rights of slave owners by allowing strict punishments, even death, for rebellious slaves. Although the Code Noir acknowledged that free black persons held "the same rights, privileges, and immunities" as white French citizens, this was contradicted by the fact that free blacks could be enslaved as punishment for crimes. As in other European-American colonial settlements, the existence of a free black population created anxiety among whites by undermining racial justifications for African slavery; and the colonial period saw increased regulation of the "free" black community, which remained small in Missouri before 1800.

Throughout the eighteenth century, the area that is now Missouri was part of a long power struggle between the French, Spanish, and British empires. The French were defeated by the English in the Seven Years' War (or French and Indian War, 1756–1763), and awarded the Louisiana Territory to their allies, the Spanish. To promote peace in the region, the Spanish abolished the use of Native Americans as slaves, making Africans the preferred source of unpaid labor. The Louisiana Territory reverted back to French rule in a treaty arranged by Napoleon Bonaparte in 1800.

Missouri and the New United States

After the French and Indian War, Britain sought to tax the colonists to pay for the war and also sought to restrict westward settlement in order to avoid further conflict with Native Americans and in order to keep colonial economic interests near the Atlantic coast. The colonists soon rebelled against British policy, declaring their independence in 1776. After defeating the British in the American Revolution, the 13 colonies formed a new United States. One of the first acts of the new Congress was to regulate settlement in the western territories, and the Northwest Ordinance of 1787 prohibited slavery between the Appalachian Mountains and the Mississippi River. The United States, however, was on the verge of pushing settlement beyond the Mississippi River and, after the slave revolt in Haiti in 1803, Napoleon was losing interest in his vision of a North American empire dependent upon colonial slave labor. President Jefferson seized the opportunity to negotiate the Louisiana Purchase, removing French competition, doubling the size of the nation, and suddenly incorporating many French, Spanish, Native American, and African slaves under the control of the United States.

The prohibition on slavery in the west under the Northwest Ordinance no longer applied and the new territorial government of Missouri drew up its own Black Codes, similar to the French Code Noir, but incorporating many of the particularly American precedents from Virginia as well. The existence of slavery in the territories was far from settled, however, and continued to pose a problem as new states were added to the union. The U.S. Constitution itself did not directly address slavery, only to the extent of including slaves themselves as private property to be protected and allowing the South to count three-fifths of the slave population for purposes of representation and taxation. When Missouri sought admission as a state in 1820, the territory included close to 10,000 African American slaves. The question of whether Missouri would be admitted as a slave state or a free state was a matter of great political significance since, at that time, there were an equal number of slave and free states in the Union and so there was a balance of power and representation in Congress. Sensing that the Missouri question was "like a fire bell in the night," an elderly Thomas Jefferson feared that the very future of the nation was at stake.

Congress settled the issue with the Missouri Compromise of 1820, which established the admittance of Missouri as a slave state, balanced by the admission of Maine as a free state. It also established the 36°30′ parallel of Missouri's southern border as a line extending westward through the territories to solve future issues of slavery, with the prohibition of slavery in regions north of the line, and allowing slavery south of it. This compromise addressed the issue of slavery in Missouri, but it did not address the issue of slavery's existence, which would continue to divide the nation.

The new Missouri state constitution once again revised the laws regarding slavery and the status and movement of free blacks, including statutes restricting the rights of free blacks from other states from settling in Missouri. As the abolitionist movement grew in the 1830s and 1840s, new and stricter legislation regarding runaway slaves was passed in Missouri, including offering rewards to white citizens who apprehended runaways and imposing strict fines on anyone harboring fugitive slaves. In 1837, the state assembly also passed an act prohibiting abolitionist literature or "doctrines" in the state, and, in 1847, made it illegal for anyone to teach any "negroes or mulattos," slave or free, to read or write, and for African Americans to hold their own religious services or meetings.

Several important "freedom" cases in nineteenth-century Missouri involved African Americans who were either physically abused or were, in fact, legally free blacks who had been wrongfully enslaved. In 1846, Dred and Harriet Scott filed a suit in St. Louis claiming they had lived in free territory before being brought to Missouri. Dred

Dred Scott, his daughters, and wife are depicted in this June 27, 1857, edition of *Frank Leslie's Illustrated Newspaper.* (Library of Congress)

Scott's case went all the way to the U.S. Supreme Court, which, in 1857, not only denied him his freedom, striking down the precedent of slave status based on residency, but also denied Scott's right to sue in the first place, declaring all blacks as noncitizens. Just a few years before the Dred Scott decision, another slave was in court in Missouri, fighting for her life, not her freedom. The case of *State of Missouri v. Celia* reveals the story of Celia, a young slave purchased as a domestic worker for a Missouri widower and his daughters. Celia was kept in a separate cabin from the owner's house, where she was sexually exploited for years and eventually rebelled by murdering the owner one night. The state of Missouri found Celia, a 19-year-old mother of two, guilty, and had her executed in December 1855.

Missouri Blacks in the Civil War

After the passage of the federal Fugitive Slave Law, Missouri (especially St. Louis) was an important stop on the Underground Railroad because it bordered several free states. Although slavery existed in Missouri, as a border state it was economically and socially tied to the North. When the Civil War broke out in April 1861, Missouri did not secede from the Union as did several other southern states. Although the Confederacy eventually claimed Missouri, like the other border states, Kentucky and Virginia, the Missouri government and the population itself were split between Union and Confederate sympathies. Missouri developed two state governments and sent representatives to both the U.S. and Confederate Congresses.

The question of whether Missouri's blacks should serve in the Union army was another challenge to the question of slavery in the state. In 1863, President Lincoln began allowing black men to enlist in the Union army, and Missouri blacks were recruited to serve in black regiments in other states, such as the 54th Massachusetts Regiment and the 1st Kansas Colored Volunteer

Infantry Regiment. In June 1863, the 1st Regiment of Missouri Colored Infantry was raised in St. Louis with more than 300 volunteers, and more troops were organized the following year. While thousands volunteered, some counties had to institute a draft of both white and black men to meet quotas. Many whites, slaveholding or not, resisted black enrollment for fear of arming blacks and inciting rebellion or encouraging fugitive slaves to join. Other whites, however, did not hide the fact that they were glad to have black men fill the armies and militia rather than sending their own brothers and sons to fight and die.

Despite their service to the Union, Missouri's slave population was not freed by Lincoln's Emancipation Proclamation in 1863, which applied only to slaves held in rebel states. However, the Missouri state constitutional convention freed the state's slaves in January 1865, prompting celebrations of freedom throughout Missouri many months before the end of the war and the ratification of the Thirteenth Amendment to the U.S. Constitution that ended slavery throughout the nation.

Reconstruction in Missouri

The end of the Civil War, and the beginning of federal Reconstruction throughout the South, brought increased racial hostility, segregation, and attacks on the black community, but also the opportunity for Missouri's black population to create its own schools, businesses, churches, banks, and cooperative, benevolent, and political organizations. Efforts at educating blacks in Missouri began before the Civil War. St. Louis had so many schools that a separate black board of education had been established and 600 students were enrolled before the end of the war in 1865. Lincoln Institute (later University) was founded in Jefferson City in 1866 as a black vocational training school, and in 1865, the Missouri Equal Rights League was established to lobby for the education of black children and the right of black men to vote

and hold office. These rights would not be secured at the state level, however, and only came through further amendments to the U.S. Constitution in 1868 and 1870. James Milton Turner was one of the most prominent black activists and political reformers in Missouri at this time, working with Radical Republicans in state government, with the federal Freedman's Bureau, and appointed as minister to Liberia by President Grant in 1871.

Throughout the 1870s and early 1880s, blacks in Missouri sought political representation, but were increasingly ignored by the Republican Party they had supported. In Kansas City and St. Louis, blacks were elected to city offices, but these were isolated victories in the era of segregation, lack of educational funding, and lynchings. Missouri had one of the worst lynching records in the nation. Between 1889 and 1918, 51 African Americans were lynched in Missouri, and in May 1892, black leaders called for a "lamentation day" in St. Louis to call attention to the mob violence against blacks that went unpunished. One of the greatest outbreaks of violence occurred in Springfield, where, not coincidentally, by the end of the century blacks had achieved some economic and political presence; in 1890, one-third of registered voters were black and three black men had served on the Springfield City Council. Before Easter in April 1906, a white woman claimed to have been raped by two black men in Springfield. Two suspects were arrested and a mob broke into the jail, removing not only the suspects but a third inmate in jail on unrelated charges. The men were killed, resulting in riots and many black families leaving the city for good. The mob leader was later acquitted of all charges.

Black Migrations

By 1870, a majority of blacks throughout the South remained employed in agricultural labor, mostly as sharecroppers. The need for new economic opportunities, combined with a new freedom of movement, led many blacks to leave the rural South in the decades after the Civil War. In the spring of 1879, thousands of southern blacks passed through St. Louis and Kansas City on a "great Exodus," headed to Kansas and other destinations. These "Exodusters" were extremely poor and many were stranded in Missouri's big cities, unable to finance their complete journeys. Whether they stayed or continued on, many were assisted by black churches and benevolent societies in St. Louis and Kansas City. Some found work in urban factories, others became entrepreneurs, and a small black urban middle class began to grow in the early decades of the twentieth century.

Again, the white community responded to the influx of black workers, and the small successes of the black community, with violence and intimidation. White factory owners often refused to hire or fairly pay black workers, and their white coworkers locked blacks out of the labor union and broke their strikes. A 1908 white newspaper in St. Louis reported, "The Negro Must Go, Is Cry: West End Citizens Bitterly Resent Invasion of Blacks." In July 1917, a violent riot broke out between black and white workers in East St. Louis, Illinois, forcing many black residents to flee to the Missouri side of the city.

Between the World Wars

The outbreak of World War I was another impetus for black movement to cities and into the industrial workforce. Labor needs increased as white men not only left for war, but the influx of European immigrants that had characterized the previous decades suddenly stopped. Once again, blacks living in rural areas moved to cities such as Kansas City and St Louis in search of jobs. Just as they had in the Civil War and the Spanish-American War (which saw 1,000 men join a black regiment out of St. Louis), African American men also enlisted to fight in World War I, this time joining a cause to combat inequality on a global scale, even as they faced racism at home. During World War I, more than 9,000 black soldiers from Missouri joined the war effort. Some ended up on the battlefront in France and Germany, while other African Americans supported the war from the homefront through the Missouri Negro Industrial Commission, founded to help black farmers in Missouri, which helped sell war bonds and promote wartime conservation. This was at a time when the Ku Klux Klan (organized during the Civil War) was still on the rise throughout the South; between 1900 and 1931, another 17 black men were lynched by mobs in Missouri alone.

The 1930s and 1940s brought continued economic and social struggles for blacks in Missouri, but also a flourishing of black culture and the beginning of efforts to strike the final blows against segregation. Two Missouri cases challenging segregation in higher education made it to the U.S. Supreme Court, although in both cases the University of Missouri (in Columbia) was able to avoid integration by the establishment of "separate but equal" institutions for black students. During World War II, the national effort behind the cause of fighting tyranny and oppression abroad focused attention on the injustices and violence at home. In 1942, a federal investigation followed the lynching of mill worker Cleo Wright in Sikeston, Missouri. Wright had been beaten and shot by police and was dragged, unconscious, through the streets and murdered by a lynch mob. The federal grand jury did not prosecute any members of the mob, claiming that Wright died from his previous injuries. Although individual acts of racial violence continued throughout the South, Wright's high-profile murder was the last lynching in Missouri. It is understandable, then, that African Americans who enlisted during World War II were said to be fighting a "Double-V" campaign, fighting for victory both at home and abroad. Once again, the 1940s were an era in which Missouri blacks joined the military and also migrated into cities to fill wartime industrial labor needs and opportunities.

Civil Rights Movement and Beyond

In 1950, the first African American students were admitted to the University of Missouri. The focus of the black Civil Rights Movement throughout the 1950s was on the integration of public facilities, transportation, and schools and colleges. In 1954, the U.S. Supreme Court finally ruled in *Brown v. Board of Education* that the "separate but equal" provisions were unconstitutional. Desegregation efforts in Missouri, however, would continue for decades, especially in urban areas such as Kansas City and St. Louis, with the large black population segregated into separate neighborhoods. Most neighborhood schools, therefore, were composed of all-black or all-white children not because of discrimination by the schools, but because of the segregation of society at large. Many families did not want (or could not afford) their children to be bused into predominantly white schools, and many districts did not want to pay for such efforts. Desegregation efforts in Missouri, therefore, resulted in logistical and legal challenges that continued into the 1990s.

The underlying problems of housing segregation, employment discrimination, and urban poverty also became the focus for black civil rights activists in Missouri in the 1960s and 1970s. In 1963, the St. Louis chapter of the national civil rights group, the Congress of Racial Equality (CORE), organized a protest and boycott of the Jefferson Bank for refusing to hire black tellers. Ivory Perry was among the more than 100 who gathered, many of them arrested and given punishments of jail sentences, up to one year, and large, unreasonable fines. The St. Louis CORE chapter went on to organize rallies and marches on city hall, and raised money to pay jail fines. In 1964, the bank hired its first black tellers, and other banks and businesses followed. In the coming months, empowered by the CORE campaign as well as by the national efforts of Martin Luther King Jr., protesters and students in St. Louis and other cities challenged the segregation of restaurants, hotels, and other facilities, culminating in the federal civil rights legislation of 1964 and 1965.

Despite legal and social gains at both the state and national levels, the Klan maintained a presence in Missouri through the 1970s and beyond. Black citizens worked independently, locally, and through state-level organizations such as the Missouri Commission on Human Rights to continue to challenge illegal segregation and the effects of racism in employment discrimination, unemployment, poverty, and substandard housing. The state government also created agencies and passed legislation to address these issues. Missouri sent its first black congressman to the U.S. House of Representatives in 1968 and African Americans increased their presence in city and state positions throughout the 1970s. By the 1980s and 1990s, poverty and discrimination and the segregation of neighborhoods continued to plague black communities, with the resulting problems of crime, gangs, poverty, health concerns, and access to services for black citizens. Missouri's urban population saw new hope, however, in the appointment of the first black police chief in St. Louis in 1991, Clarence Harmon, who in 1997 became the mayor of St. Louis. St. Louis had elected its first black mayor in 1993, and Kansas City's first black mayor was elected in 1991. In the twenty-first century, St. Louis and Kansas City remain among the most racially segregated cities in the United States.

Notable African Americans

Angelou, Maya (1928–)

Maya Angelou is an acclaimed writer and civil rights activist and one of the nation's most beloved poets. She is perhaps best known for her poem, "On the Pulse of Morning," delivered at the inauguration of President Bill Clinton in 1993. Born

Maya Angelou is one of the premier U.S. poets of the twentieth century. (National Archives)

Marguerite Ann Johnson in St. Louis, her childhood was split between living in Arkansas with her grandmother and living back in Missouri with her mother. Beginning with her 1970 memoir, *I Know Why the Caged Bird Sings*, Angelou's books and poetry have chronicled the struggles and spirit of black life in the south. Beginning in the 1960s, she became active in the Civil Rights Movement as a coordinator in Martin Luther King's Southern Christian Leadership Conference.

Baker, Josephine (1906–1975)

Josephine Baker (born Freda Josephine McDonald) was an internationally acclaimed singer, dancer, and entertainer. She was born into a poor family in St. Louis, Missouri. When she was just 13, she joined a touring vaudeville group and eventually moved to New York to dance in the musical review, *Shuffle Along*. In 1925, she traveled to France

as part of *La Revue Nègre*, where her risqué act launched her as one of the most popular and well-paid celebrities of the era. She never achieved the same level of success and recognition in the racially segregated United States as she did throughout Europe.

Basie, William "Count"(1904–1984)

William "Count" Basie was a jazz musician who is credited with creating the famous Kansas City style of big band jazz known as "swing." Born in New Jersey, Basie had practiced piano with "Fats" Waller in New York before moving to Kansas City in 1927. He played in local bands and clubs and was dubbed the "Count" by a local Kansas City radio announcer. The exposure led to a record contract and a move to New York City. In 1961, Basie performed for President John F. Kennedy's inaugural ball. The Count Basie Orchestra continues to perform today.

Bass, Tom (1859–1934)

Tom Bass was a famous equestrian who earned acclaim for training and riding show horses. Born a slave in Boone County, he later moved to the town of Mexico, Missouri, and then was invited to Kansas City to train horses of the city's elites. His skills earned him invitations to appear in parades, to compete in riding championships, and to represent Missouri at the Chicago World's Fair in 1893. He was involved in establishing the American Royal Horse Show, which is held in Kansas City, and he invented the "Bass bit" to protect horses' mouths during training.

Beckwourth, James (1798–1866)

James Pierson Beckwourth (sometimes Beckwith) was a black fur trapper and explorer. He was born a slave in Virginia, the son of a white Revolutionary War veteran. His family moved

Josephine Baker, a young dancer from New York City's Harlem neighborhood, was the star attraction in the 1920s at the Folies Bergères in Paris. (Library of Congress)

to the Louisiana Territory in 1809. His father sent him to St. Louis to be educated and later emancipated him so that he could learn a trade. In the 1820s, Beckwourth joined a fur-trapping expedition into the Rocky Mountains, where he lived with the Crow Indians. He led an expedition through the Sierra Nevada Mountains on what became known as the Beckwourth Pass, a popular trail for settlers into California.

Berry, Chuck (1926–)

Charles Edward Anderson "Chuck" Berry is a legendary rock-and-roll musician and songwriter.

Chuck Berry performing in 1965. (Library of Congress)

With his signature guitar style and showmanship, Berry is credited as one of the founders of rock-and-roll music in the 1950s with his hit songs such as "Roll over Beethoven," "Johnny B. Goode," and "Maybellene," which sold more than one million copies. Born in St. Louis, Missouri, Berry was heavily influenced by both rhythm and blues and white country-and-western music, both elements of which he incorporated into his new rock-and-roll style. In 1986, Berry was one of the first inductees into the new Rock and Roll Hall of Fame.

Bluford, Lucile (1911–2003)

Lucile H. Bluford was a journalist who fought to desegregate higher education in Missouri. Born in North Carolina, she moved to Kansas City as a young child and graduated from the University of Kansas. In 1939, Bluford was denied admission to the University of Missouri's graduate program in journalism. She sued the university but the court upheld the school's position, citing Lincoln University as a separate but equal educational facility available to blacks in the state. Bluford spent her entire career at the Kansas City paper, the *Call*, first as a journalist and then taking over as editor after the death of founder Chester Arthur Franklin in 1955.

Boone, John "Blind" (1864–1927)

John William "Blind" Boone was one of the most well-known ragtime musicians of the early twentieth century. Born in Miami, Missouri, to a contraband slave mother and a white cavalry bugler during the Civil War, his eyes were removed due to an illness when he was just an infant. He grew up in the town of Warrensburg, where friends and family recognized his musical talent and sponsored him to study piano at the St. Louis School for the Blind. He left school to return home and began playing with local musicians, launching his own career in ragtime and jazz music.

Brown, William Wells (c. 1814–1884)

William Wells Brown was an author who is credited with publication of both the first novel by an African American, *Clotel, or, the President's Daughter: a Narrative of Slave Life in the United States* (1853), and the first play by an African American, *The Escape; Or, a Leap for Freedom* (1858). Born a slave in Kentucky, Brown was moved to Missouri as a young child. He was sold many times before escaping to freedom in Ohio and becoming a prominent abolitionist, assisting many fugitive slaves on the Underground Railroad.

Bruce, Blanche K. (1841–1898)

Blanche Kelso Bruce was the first African American, and the only former slave, to serve a full term in the U.S. Senate, as a Republican representing Mississippi between 1875 and 1881. Born a slave in Virginia, Bruce spent most of his childhood in Missouri and was educated and eventually freed by his white father. After the Civil War he attended Oberlin College in Ohio before settling in Mississippi during the Reconstruction era. He held several county political positions before being elected to the state legislature and then U.S. Senate.

Carver, George Washington (c. 1865–1943)

George Washington Carver is one of the most renowned African American scientists and inventors. His discoveries helped improve crop production in the South, in particular by developing peanut farming as an alternative to cotton in the early twentieth century. Although his concern was that poor farmers grow a successful commercial crop that could also serve as food, as a chemist he also developed a variety of peanut-related products for household and farming use. Born in Diamond, Missouri, at the end of the Civil War, he later moved to Kansas in search of an education.

Cedric the Entertainer (1964–)

Cedric Antonio Kyles (stage name Cedric the Entertainer) is a comedian and actor who has appeared on *The Steve Harvey Show* and was one of four black comedians featured in Spike Lee's film, *The Original Kings of Comedy*. Born in Jefferson City, Missouri, Cedric attended Southeast Missouri State University and taught high school before turning to comedy full time. He broke out with his 1992 appearance on *It's Showtime at the Apollo*, and soon appeared in other national cable stand-up comedy shows. He was inducted into the St. Louis Walk of Fame in 2008 and provides scholarships to his former high school in Berkeley, Missouri.

Cheadle, Donald Frank (1964–)

Donald Frank Cheadle Jr. is an actor, film producer, and humanitarian well known for his television and film appearances. He received an Academy Award nomination for his role in the 2004 film, *Hotel Rwanda*. Born in Kansas City, Missouri, he was educated in Colorado and California, graduating from the California Institute of the Arts. His acting career began in the 1980s; he appeared in films such as *Traffic* and *Ocean's Eleven*, and was coproducer of *Crash*, which won the Academy Award for Best Picture in 2005. Cheadle has focused attention on the genocide in Darfur, Sudan, Africa, and has coauthored a book entitled *Not on Our Watch: The Mission to End Genocide in Darfur and Beyond.*

Foxx, Redd (1922–1991)

Redd Foxx was a comedian and actor best known for his character, Fred Sanford, in the

1970s television show *Sanford and Son*. Born John Elroy Sanford in St. Louis, he was raised in Chicago and later moved to New York City, where he worked as a dishwasher and performed as a comedian in nightclubs. Nicknamed "Chicago Red" due to his hair color, Sanford adopted the stage name of Redd Foxx after a favorite baseball player, Jimmie Foxx. He gained notoriety through recorded albums of his sometimes risqué comedy acts and appeared in a film, *Cotton Comes to Harlem*, before being offered the *Sanford and Son* sitcom, which ran between 1972 and 1977.

Franklin, Chester Arthur (1880–1955)

Chester Arthur Franklin founded and edited *The Call*, an African American newspaper in Kansas City. Franklin published the first issue in May 1919 and served as editor until his death in 1955. He focused the paper on serious political and social issues of concern to the African American community and hired many black journalists, including Lucile Bluford. Born in Texas, Franklin and his parents left the South in search of opportunities. He attended the University of Nebraska and lived in Denver, Colorado, where he published the newspaper, the *Star*, before moving to Kansas City in search of a larger black population and audience.

Giles, Gwen B. (1932–1986)

Gwen B. Giles was the first African American woman to serve in the Missouri State Senate, elected in 1977. Born in Atlanta, Georgia, Giles moved to St. Louis as a young child and attended St. Louis University. She held a variety of city positions and worked with the mayor of St. Louis on passage of a 1976 city civil rights bill. She later became the first black and first female city assessor of St. Louis, focusing on housing issues. As state senator, she supported the federal Equal Rights Amendment for gender equality and served on a federal women's task force under President Carter.

Hughes, Langston (1902–1967)

James Mercer Langston Hughes was one of the major figures of the Harlem Renaissance black literary movement of the 1920s. In works such as his first book of poetry, *The Weary Blues*, and the article, "The Negro Artist and the Racial Mountain" (both 1926), and his many novels, stories, and plays, Hughes captured the struggles and creative spirit of African Americans of his generation. Hughes was born in Joplin, Missouri, but moved throughout his childhood to Kansas, Illinois, and Ohio. In high school he was named class poet and later attended Columbia University in New York.

Joplin, Scott (1868–1917)

Scott Joplin was a musician and composer, considered the "King of Ragtime" music. He published dozens of songs, a ballet, and two operas, and his "Maple Leaf Rag" (1899) and "The Entertainer" (1902) are some of the most popular ragtime hits of all time. Born in Texas, Joplin attended college in Sedalia, Missouri, where he worked as a pianist at local clubs, and where the annual Scott Joplin Festival is still held. He also lived in St. Louis, where he performed at the 1904 World's Fair and collaborated with several other ragtime musicians of the era, such as Arthur Marshall.

Keckley, Elizabeth (1818–1907)

Elizabeth Hobbs Keckley (sometimes Keckly) was a former slave who served as dressmaker and personal assistant to First Lady Mary Todd Lincoln, experiences recounted in Keckley's 1868 autobiography, *Behind the Scenes Or, Thirty Years a Slave and Four Years in the White House*. Born a slave in Virginia, Keckley spent several years in St. Louis, Missouri, before moving to Washington, D.C., where she marketed her seamstress services to an elite government clientele that eventually included Mrs. Lincoln.

Malone, Annie (1869–1957)

Annie Malone was a successful entrepreneur who developed and sold hair care products for black women at the same time as her more well-known colleague and former salesperson, Madam C. J. Walker. Born in Illinois, Malone moved to St. Louis, Missouri, where she sold her "Poro" brand products door to door and used new sales and marketing techniques to build her empire. In 1917, Malone founded a beauty training school for African American women, Poro College in St. Louis. Malone was a philanthropist who gave much of her money to black schools and organizations.

Meachum, John Berry (1789–1854)

John Berry Meachum was a minister who founded the First African Baptist Church of St. Louis in 1825, one of the first all-black Protestant congregations. Born a slave in Virginia, he eventually purchased his own freedom and followed his enslaved wife's owner to St. Louis. He secretly taught black children to read and write at his church and opened a floating "freedom school" on a boat in the Mississippi River.

Nelly (1974–)

Cornell Haynes Jr. (stage name Nelly) is a Grammy Award–winning rapper and actor, considered one of the top musical artists of the early 2000s. Born in Austin, Texas, Nelly moved to University City, Missouri, as a teenager. In 1993, he joined the St. Louis hip-hop group, the St. Lunatics, and signed a record contract with Universal Records in 1999. In 2000, Nelly released his first solo album and has sold more than 20 million copies of his records, including *Country Grammar* (2000), *Nellyville* (2002), *Sweat* (2004), and *Suit* (2004). He has also had success as a businessman, developing clothing lines, and as an actor, starring with Adam Sandler and Chris Rock in the 2005 film *The Longest Yard*.

Paige, Satchel (1906–1982)

Leroy Robert "Satchel" Paige (formerly Page) was a renowned baseball player and was considered the best pitcher in the Negro Leagues. A contemporary of Jackie Robinson, Paige became the first black pitcher to play in the major leagues when he was signed by the Cleveland Indians in 1948. Born in Mobile, Alabama, he played for several minor and major league teams, including the St. Louis Browns and the Kansas City Athletics toward the end of his career in 1965. He eventually made his permanent home in Kansas City, Missouri.

Parker, Charlie "Bird" (1920–1955)

Charles Christopher Parker Jr. was creator of the "bebop" style of quick, improvised jazz. He was born in Kansas City, Kansas, but his family moved to Kansas City, Missouri, where he played saxophone in his school band. Largely self-taught, he played in local clubs before moving to New York City in 1939, joining with other beboppers such as Dizzy Gillespie and Thelonius Monk to create an alternative style to the big band jazz of fellow Kansas City bandleader Count Basie and others. Parker achieved immense mainstream popularity by the 1950s but, unfortunately, died at a young age after years of alcohol and drug addiction.

Perry, Ivory (1930–1989)

Ivory Perry was a prominent civil rights activist in St. Louis during the 1950s and 1960s. He participated in a number of boycotts and demonstrations against segregation and employment discrimination, including as a major figure in the Jefferson Bank boycotts of 1963 to protest the refusal of banks to hire black tellers. Born in Arkansas, he served in an all-black military unit during the Korean War and moved to St. Louis in 1954. Perry was the subject of a 2006 award-winning documentary on his campaign to raise awareness about lead poisoning in housing units in poor neighborhoods where African Americans predominated, resulting in anti-lead legislation in St. Louis in 1970.

Pruitt, Wendell (1920–1945)

Wendell Oliver Pruitt was a decorated World War II fighter pilot trained as one of the Tuskegee Airmen group of black pilots at a time when the U.S. military was still racially segregated. Born in St. Louis, Missouri, Pruitt attended Lincoln University before enlisting in the army and training in Tuskegee, Alabama. During the war he flew dozens of missions in Italy and received medals of honor for downing several enemy planes and a destroyer. He was killed in a training flight crash back in Alabama in 1945.

Smith, Ozzie (1954–)

Osborne Earl "Ozzie" Smith is a retired baseball player who played in three World Series with the St. Louis Cardinals. Born in Alabama, Smith grew up in California. After graduating from Cal Poly San Luis Obispo, he was recruited as a shortstop for the San Diego Padres. He was traded to the St. Louis Cardinals in 1982, taking the team to a World Series win that year. The Cardinals made it to the World Series again in 1987, losing to the Minnesota Twins. In 1987, the record-breaking Smith had a $2 million contract with the Cardinals, the largest for any player in the National League. Smith retired in 1996 but remains a national hero and prominent public figure in St. Louis.

Troupe, Quincy (1943–)

Quincy Thomas Troupe Jr. is an acclaimed poet and writer who wrote a biography of jazz musician Miles Davis and cowrote *The Pursuit of Happyness*, the 2006 memoir that inspired the film starring Will Smith. Born in St. Louis, the son of a Negro League catcher, Troupe attended Grambling State University in Louisiana intending to play baseball, but left school to join the army. He then pursued writing and held several teaching positions before joining the faculty at the University of California, San Diego. Troupe was named California's first poet laureate in 2002 but was forced to retire from UCSD when it was discovered that he had never earned a college degree as claimed.

Turner, Ike (1931–2007)

Ike Turner was a Grammy award–winning singer, musician, and record producer best known for his collaboration with Tina Turner in the 1960s and 1970s. Ike Turner is considered one of the pioneers of rock-and-roll music and was the first artist to record a guitar distortion effect. Born in Clarksdale, Mississippi, Turner worked at a local radio station before moving to St. Louis, where he met Anna Mae Bullock, who became a backup singer for his band. After their marriage in 1962, she changed her name and they formed the Ike & Tina Turner Revue. Both performers were inducted into the Rock and Roll Hall of Fame and the St. Louis Walk of Fame.

Turner, Tina (1939–)

Tina Turner (born Anna Mae Bullock) is a singer and actress who had a long collaboration with her former husband, Ike Turner, producing hit songs such as "River Deep, Mountain High" and "Proud Mary" in the 1960s and 1970s. Born in Tennessee, as a teenager Turner moved to St. Louis, where she met Ike Turner in a nightclub and joined his band as a backup vocalist. After their 15-year marriage ended, Tina Turner launched a solo career that included the Grammy Award–winning album *Private Dancer* (1984) and the popular single, "What's Love Got to Do with It?" She and Ike Turner were both inducted into the Rock and Roll Hall of Fame and the St. Louis Walk of Fame.

Walker, Madam C. J. (1867–1919)

Sarah Breedlove McWilliams Davis Walker was the creator of a line of hair care and beauty products for black women and the most successful female entrepreneur of her time. She was born in Louisiana to former slaves, and later lived in Mississippi and then St. Louis, Missouri, where she worked as a laundress and then selling beauty products for Annie Malone. Sarah moved to Colorado where, going by her married name, she created Madam Walker's Wonderful Hair Grower. She established company headquarters, and a training college, in Pittsburgh, Pennsylvania, before moving to an even larger factory in Indianapolis.

Wilson, Margaret Bush (1919–2009)

Margaret Bush Wilson was a civil rights activist and only the second woman to graduate from Lincoln University Law School, which had been established as a result of the Lloyd Gaines case requiring Missouri to offer legal education to blacks. A native of St. Louis, Wilson in 1943 became one of the state's first black lawyers. She fought for desegregated housing for black Missourians and was involved in a 1948 U.S. Supreme Court case, *Shelley v. Kraemer*, challenging racial covenants in real estate transactions. In 1962, she became president of the Missouri branch of the National Association for the Advancement of Colored People (NAACP) and served many years as the first female national chair.

Yates, Josephine (1852–1912)

Josephine Silone Yates was an educator and activist who taught at Lincoln University in Jefferson City, Missouri, and served as president of the National Association of Colored Women (NACW) between 1901 and 1906. Born in Long Island, New York, Yates was educated at a school for black children in Philadelphia and was the only black graduate in her high school class in Newport, Rhode Island. She moved to Missouri to teach science at Lincoln University and was active in local and national organizations for racial and social equality.

Young, Hiram (c. 1812–1882)

Hiram Young was a free black wagon maker in Independence, Missouri, who supplied many of the pioneers moving westward on the Santa Fe Trail through the Missouri-Kansas border. Born a slave in Tennessee, Young moved to Missouri where, after purchasing his freedom, he started a wagon-building business. By 1860, Young was one of the most successful black entrepreneurs in Missouri. He moved to Kansas during the Civil War to avoid local hostility against blacks in Missouri, finding his business destroyed upon his return and the peak of pioneer activity passed. He founded a school for black children in Independence.

Cultural Contributions

The contributions of black Missourians to music and literature have had an enormous impact on the cultural development of the region and on the nation. Out of the violent postslavery years of the late nineteenth century, a new generation of African American musicians and composers emerged who would bring ragtime piano music, the blues, and then jazz to audiences first in the nightclubs of St. Louis and Kansas City, and then to the nation as a whole, creating enduring American musical traditions that influenced later genres of rock and roll and hip-hop. John "Blind" Boone was one of the founders of ragtime piano music and a trio of popularizers of ragtime came out of Sedalia, Missouri, at the turn of the century: Scott Joplin, Scott Hayden, and Arthur Marshall. Kansas City is considered the birthplace of the blues, but W. C. Handy's "St. Louis Blue" (1914) became one of the most popular blues songs of all time. Female blues singers such as Mary Johnson and Alice Moore also made their mark on the St. Louis music scene in the 1920s and 1930s.

In the 1920s New York was the center of black cultural life with the Harlem Renaissance, but two of the era's biggest stars were born in Missouri, singer and dancer Josephine Baker and poet Langston Hughes. Missouri also remained at the forefront of musical experimentation, especially with the development of jazz. The most famous jazz musician of the era was "Count" Basie, who created a unique Kansas City style of bebop jazz. In the 1940s, Miles Davis got his start just across the border from St. Louis in East St. Louis, Illinois. Davis played with his idol, Charlie "Bird" Parker, before moving to New York and achieving immense success as one of the greatest jazz musicians of the twentieth century.

Black Missourians have also had a prominent role in the history of baseball, adding the Kansas City Monarchs and the St. Louis Stars to the Negro Leagues in the 1920s. The Kansas City Monarchs won the first Negro World Series game held in 1924, and both Satchel Paige and Jackie Robinson later played for the Monarchs

before moving on to the major leagues. The Negro Leagues Baseball Museum is housed in Kansas City. The major league team the St. Louis Cardinals did not have black players until 1954; in 1982, Ozzie Smith led the Cardinals to victory in the World Series. In 1981, the National Collegiate Athletic Association (NCAA) named its first black president, James Frank, a graduate of and former president of Lincoln University in Jefferson City, Missouri.

Bibliography

Greene, Lorenzo, Gary R. Kremer, and Antonio F. Holland. *Missouri's Black Heritage*. Revised ed. Columbia: University of Missouri Press, 1993.

Jack, Bryan M. *The St. Louis African American Community and the Exodusters*. Columbia: University of Missouri Press, 2008.

McLaurin, Melton. *Celia, a Slave*. Athens: University of Georgia Press, 1991.

"Missouri's African American History," Missouri State Archives. www.sos.mo.gov/archives/resources/africanamerican.

Nolen, Rose M. *Hoecakes, Hambone, and All That Jazz: African American Traditions in Missouri*. Columbia: University of Missouri Press, 2003.

MONTANA

William Gibbons and Gordon E. Thompson

Chronology

1803	The United States purchases the Louisiana Territory from the French; the new territory, which includes Montana, nearly doubles the size of the country.
1804–1806	The Lewis and Clark expedition explores newly purchased Louisiana Territory and the Pacific Northwest; an African American, York, is prominent in the expedition.
1806	Edward Rose travels up the Missouri River to the Rocky Mountains to become the first of dozens of African American fur trappers and traders in the region.
1825	James Beckwourth, an African American fur trapper and mountaineer, enters the Rocky Mountains as a wrangler of William Henry Ashley's fur-trapping expedition. Based in Montana, Beckwourth operates throughout much of the West.
1834	James Beckwourth achieves an unheard-of honor for any non-Indian, becoming "chief of chiefs" of the Crow Indian nation.
1856	James Beckwourth publishes his autobiography, *The Life and Adventures of James P. Beckwourth*, as told to Thomas Bonner, in which he recounted his experiences as a mountain man, trapper, scout, and honorary member of the Crow tribe. His autobiography was the first work in American literature to relay the story of an African American on the western frontier.
1861	*(April 12)* The Civil War begins with the Confederate bombardment of Fort Sumter in the harbor of Charleston, South Carolina.
1862	*(June)* Congress abolishes slavery in the western territories of the United States.
1862	African Americans are among the first settlers of Helena, which is established after a gold discovery.
1864	*(May 26)* Congress creates the Montana Territory.
1865	*(February 1)* President Abraham Lincoln signs the Thirteenth Amendment to the U.S. Constitution, which, upon its ratification in December, outlaws slavery throughout the United States.
1866	After the Civil War, Congress authorizes the creation of the all-black 9th and 10th Cavalry and 24th and 25th Infantry, which are led mostly by white officers. These men, eventually called buffalo soldiers, initiate the first period in U.S. history when African American soldiers are a permanent component of the U.S. military.
1866	Riding to Fort C. F. Smith in what is today Montana, James Beckwourth complains of headaches and nosebleeds. While in the camp of his old friends, the Crow, Beckwourth suffers symptoms of a stroke and dies at 67 or 68 years of age. He was buried on Crow land in what is today Montana near the present Bighorn Canyon National Recreation Area.
1867	*(January 10)* Congress passes the Territorial Suffrage Act, which allows African Americans in the western territories to vote. The act immediately enfranchises about 800

black male voters in those territories; 200 African American men cast ballots in the election of 1867, although not without challenge.

1867   Sammy Hays is killed by a gang of Irishmen in a violent post election riot in Helena.

1868   *(July 21)* The Fourteenth Amendment to the U.S. Constitution is ratified, granting citizenship to any person born or naturalized in the United States.

1868   *(Summer)* Beginning with the cattle drive of William G. Butler, African American cowboys will participate for the next two decades in cattle drives through the Montana territory.

1869   James Pratt, a former Union soldier, stakes a successful mining claim in Marysville until 1886, when he sells the mine and moves to Helena to operate a saloon.

1870   *(March 30)* The Fifteenth Amendment to the U.S. Constitution is ratified, guaranteeing African American males the right to vote.

1870   The U.S. Census documents 183 African Americans in the state, 71 of them residing in Helena.

1871   Joe Clark is a hunter assigned to the crew of the Ferdinand Hayden expedition that received funds from Congress to explore the Yellowstone area. Other nameless African Americans of the expedition supplied and maintained tents and firearms, tended to horses and livestock, and provided fresh meat.

1872   The Montana territorial legislature passes a law segregating African American children in public schools.

1876   *(June 25)* Isaiah Dorman, a guide, translator, and hero, perishes in a battle with Sioux Indians on the same day famed General George Armstrong Custer is killed at the Little Bighorn River.

1879   An African American fraternal order, the Lodge of the Good Templars, is organized in Helena by 20 African Americans.

1882   Protests, dwindling enrollment, and the increasing cost of maintaining segregated schools result in a successful referendum vote to prohibit racial segregation in Montana schools.

1885   Charles Porter Grove, a former slave, discovers gold in Broadwater County.

1885   Mary Fields arrives in Cascade to become a successful business owner, running a restaurant and laundry; she is also the second African American U.S. postal worker in Montana, driving a mail coach from Cascade to Fort Shaw and Simms until she is almost 70.

1888   Reverend James Hubbard establishes the St. James African Methodist Episcopal Church in Helena.

1888   The 25th Infantry—one of four African American regiments created after the Civil War—arrives at Fort Missoula.

1888	William C. Irvin is Helena's first African American policeman.
1889	(*November 8*) Montana enters the Union as the 41st state.
1890	Union Bethel African Methodist Episcopal (AME) Church is founded in Great Falls.
1892	George Williams is the first African American police officer in Great Falls.
1894	(*September 3*) Montana's first black newspaper, the *Helena Colored Citizen*, is founded by Ohio-born photographer J. P. Ball Jr.
1894	The 10th Cavalry transfers to Fort Assinniboine from Arizona, before being deployed to Cuba in 1898 to fight in the Spanish-American War.
1896	The James A. Moss group of the 25th Infantry Bicycle Corps from Fort Missoula, Montana, in Yellowstone National Park is assigned the task of testing bicycles as a means of military transportation; for a year, several groups start from the northern Rockies in Montana and tour southward, crossing Wyoming, Colorado, and New Mexico. The experiment is a failure but leaves intriguing photographs of African American troops.
1902	The Manhattan Social Club, a social organization in Helena, is founded; it boasts a reading room, billard parlor, and ping-pong room, private dining facilities, and a bar.
1902	(*May 2*) The *Butte New Age*, Montana's second African American newspaper, is published.
1906	(*March 16*) The first issue of the *Montana Plaindealer*, edited in Helena by Joseph B. Bass, is published and circulates until 1911.
1907	Joseph B. Bass helps organize a Helena chapter of Booker T. Washington's National Negro Business League, which includes dozens of businesses.
1908	The Afro-Amercan Building Association is established, a self-help group of African American real estate owners in Montana.
1909	Henry J. Baker, J. E. W. Clark, Joseph B. Bass, and others spearhead the Afro-American Protective League, an ambitious statewide organization that defends African Americans in Montana from racism.
1909	A miscegenation bill passes outlawing marriage between blacks and whites in Montana.
1920	(*August 26*) The Nineteenth Amendment to the U.S. Constitution is ratified, giving all women the right to vote. Black women already have the right to vote in Wyoming, Washington, Colorado, California, and other western states.
1921	(*August 3*) The first meeting of the Montana Federation of Negro Women's Club is held.
1922	The Great Falls chapter of the National Association for the Advancement of Colored People (NAACP) is established, but is defunct by 1930.

1948	*(July 26)* President Harry S. Truman issues Executive Order 9981 directing the desegregation of the armed forces.
1949	Arcella Hayes of Missoula initiates a successful campaign to repeal discriminatory statues and enact the Fair Employment Practices Law.
1957	Alma Jacobs of Lewistown becomes the first African American to be elected president of the Pacific Northwest Library Association.
1963	*(January 28)* Montana ratifies the Twenty-fourth Amendment to the U.S. constitution abolishing the poll tax.
1965	Black and white residents of Missoula and Billings hold marches and prayer services in reaction to the beating of black civil rights marchers in Selma, Alabama.
1968	Professor Ulysses Doss establishes a black studies program at the University of Montana; it is only the third such program in the country.
1969	Ophelia Fenter, who teaches home economics, becomes the first African American teacher at Butte High School.
1970	The U.S. Census counts 1,995 African Americans resident in Montana.
1972	Montana adopts a new state constitution with a strong civil rights statement.
1973	Alma Jacobs of Lewistown is appointed Montana state librarian.
1974	Great Falls librarian Geraldine Travis becomes the first African American elected to the Montana State Legislature.
1980	The U.S. Census counts 1,786 African Americans resident in Montana.
1990	The U.S. Census counts 2,381 African Americans resident in Montana.
1991	Montana declares the birthday of Dr. Martin Luther King Jr. a holiday, becoming the 48th state to do so.
1992	The Great Falls chapter of the reestablished NAACP holds a rally protesting the acquittal of the Los Angeles police officers accused of beating black motorist Rodney King.
2000	The U.S. Census documents 2,692 African Americans residing in the state, constituting just over 0.3 percent of the state's population.
2006	African Americans comprise 0.5 percent of Montana's total population.
2007	Johnnie Lockett Thomas of Miles City receives the Montana Governor's Humanities Award for his research and presentations on the history of African Americans in the state.
2009	*(November 1)* A Diversity March is held in Bozeman to protest attempts by a white supremacist group to establish a base of operations in the community.

Historical Overview

African American history has had its colorful moments in the thinly populated state of Montana. In 1804, the Lewis and Clark expedition brought Montana into the American consciousness. York, a slave, manservant, and guide, accompanied Lewis and Clark and befriended the natives who were fascinated by his black skin. This famous encounter has been painted by Russell Lewis and hangs in the Montana State House of Representatives. Among the early explorers to the area were a group of blacks who became fur trappers. In the 1860s, gold miners followed, among whom were the first permanent black settlers.

Montana became a state in 1889, but black males won the right to vote as early as 1867, after a tense challenge in Helena by pro-Democratic gangs said to be responsible for the death of Sammy Hays, a black male. Helena, the capital, once had the largest black community in Montana, though today many African Americans reside in Billings, Butte, and Great Falls. These cities, except Billings, lie in the most populated region of Montana, along or close to Highway 15, running from the south central city of Butte northward toward Helena, Cascade, and Great Falls.

Fort Shaw

Among Montana's more significant landmarks is Fort Shaw, an outpost on the Montana frontier just outside Great Falls. It was one of three posts Congress authorized to be built in 1865 and was completed in 1868. Opened in 1867, it was used by military personnel until 1891. The fort is located west of Great Falls in the Sun River Valley and was built of adobe and lumber by the 13th Infantry. It had a parade ground that was 400 feet long, and consisted of barracks for officers, a hospital, and a trading post and housing for 450 soldiers.

The all-black 25th Infantry Regiment, posted there, named the fort after Robert Gould Shaw to honor his leadership of the all-black 54th Infantry Regiment, one of the first all–African American

Buffalo soldiers of the 25th Infantry, some wearing the buffalo robes for which they were named, Fort Keogh, Montana. (Library of Congress)

regiments serving during the American Civil War, although it is doubtful Shaw ever stood on this site.

The town of Missoula, west of Helena, was populated with soldiers from the nearby fort alongside blacks who worked as servants in hotels, restaurants, homes, and clubs. Not to be forgotten were cowboys such as Bob Leavitt and Newt Clendennon, who worked the cattle ranches.

Fort Missoula

Fort Missoula was the true home of the 25th Infantry. Built in 1877, the 25th saw the uprising of Chief Joseph and his men and experimented with using bicycles in place of horses. The infantry also saw activity in the Spanish-American War of 1898. The other two posts in the Montana Territory were Camp Cooke on the Judith River and Fort C. F. Smith on the Bozeman Trail in south central Montana Territory.

Helena

The growth and development of Helena parallels the growth and development of the state and of the black community of Montana in general. In 1864, four prospectors found gold near Helena, calling this site Last Chance Gulch. It was later renamed Helena and became the state capital. While blacks resided in Helena's Prickly Pear Valley before it became a city, its small African American community peaked in 1910, reaching 420 inhabitants. As early as 1870, 71 blacks were reported to reside in Helena, among whom where black cowboys and soldiers. These men and some women worked as cooks, servants, and cowboys, but they also came as soldiers and as gold miners. From these beginnings, thriving businesses would develop that included everything from a beauty parlor to a laundry.

While Montana was still a territory, the area legislature passed a statute segregating the schools of Montana. As a consequence, the black community opened a separate school; but with no more

than 20 students, it was not financially sustainable and closed its doors in 1882. Despite the segregated school, most residential neighborhoods were modestly integrated as a factor of the relatively small size of the black population, offering an explanation, in addition, for relatively low levels of racial conflict in this city.

But the growth of a black church and a lodge, the Good Templars, reflected Helena's otherwise segregated black community. The most prominent black church in the area, St. James African Methodist Episcopal Church, grew out of a small religious society. In 1888, Reverend James Hubbard arrived from Kansas to launch a full-blown black congregation. As with black communities in the East, the black church was dynamic and central to community cohesion. Everyone of note associated with St. James Church to the extent that it was truly integral to the development of black Helena's social and political stability. As a consequence, the African American community was able to build an imposing frame structure in 1888 that supported a Sunday school, benevolent associations, a literary society, and other recreational and artistic groups. As a complement to the church, the St. James Literary Society, founded in 1906, had a large membership devoted to sponsoring poets, playwrights, writers and other artists and entertainers.

Personalities

Among the many black notables of Montana's past, one may include the ex-slave gold miners, Charles Porter Grove and Millie Ringgold, a woman who single-handedly opened a hotel and restaurant; another woman, Sara Bickford, constructed a reservoir and provided water for Virginia City residents; and William Bairpaugh became a rare African American homesteader who later operated one of Montana's largest farms dedicated to growing wheat. William C. Irvin became a successful businessman, owned his own home, and served proudly as a police officer in Helena though he started out as little more than a porter. Arriving from Missouri in 1891, Walter Dorsey rose from the position of steward at the Montana Club to become the proprietor of his own grocery and later the owner of an entire building. Prominent men and women such as these presented an imposing face of black Montanans to the outside world.

One of Montana's most colorful characters, however, was Mary Fields, known for her 200-pound weight, her pistol, and her charitable disposition. She resided in Cascade, Montana, and went by the cognomen of "Black Mary." Born a slave in Hickman County, Tennessee, about 1832, she made her way in part by steamboat to Toledo, Ohio, arriving in Cascade as the maid and friend of a nun, Mother Amadeus, who had taken ill. Widely admired, Mary Fields wore the hat and boots and other clothing associated with men, including a revolver stashed under her apron for good measure. She was said to drink and smoke cigars with men in the town's saloon. As tough as any man, she handled a stagecoach by herself, ferrying passengers from the town and the train station to the convent, giving her a second cognomen, "Stagecoach Mary."

The sisters relied on her, in addition, to wash their clothes, tend to a large brood of chickens, and do subsistence gardening. Once, they attempted to do her work for her while Fields was away. The sisters discovered how much they relied on her when some cartridges accidentally went off, luckily not wounding anyone. They were much relieved when Fields returned.

While she lived at the convent of St. Peters, she continued to drink, smoke, swear, and tell tall tales with her male bar mates. She also engaged in gun duels. This lasted for 10 years until someone alerted the bishop of Montana, who decided Fields could no longer live or work at the convent. As a result, Fields, newly housed in Cascade, was enlisted to take mail back and forth between the town and the convent, becoming only the second woman in the country, it is said, to serve in this capacity.

A while later, Mother Amadeus left for another post in Alaska, and Fields gave up her mail route, supporting herself by taking in the town's laundry, but she also attempted to open an eating establishment; it failed twice. As she moved further up in age, she took up babysitting and was wildly popular at this. Near death, she hid in the grass to avoid becoming a burden to the town. She was nursed by townspeople and given a heartfelt funeral by the entire town when she died a few days later.

The white population of Montana grew faster than the African American community so that the black population today is approximately 0.5 percent of a total population of 902,125, corresponding to about 4,470 residents. While Arcella Hayes spearheaded a successful effort to repeal the ban on interracial marriage enacted in 1909, by the 1940s, African Americans were still fighting for their civil rights. Today, while black incomes average somewhat less than the average income of the total population, blacks in Montana do not appear to fare any less well than other Montanans overall. According to the 2000 U.S. Census, 2,692 African Americans were residing in the state, constituting just over 0.3 percent of the state's population. Estimates for the 2010 Census put African Americans at about 0.5 percent of Montana's total population.

Notable African Americans

Beckwourth, James P. (1798–1866)

Mountaineer, scout, trapper, interpreter, and Indian Chief, James Beckwourth was a legend of the western frontier. A skilled outdoorsmen, he established trading posts, befriended and became a member of the Crow Indians, pioneered the Oregon Trail, and discovered a pass that bears his name in the Sierra Nevada Mountains. Beckwourth was born into slavery on April 26, 1798, in Frederick County, Virginia. His father Jennings Beckwourth was a slave owner and officer in the

James Beckwourth, African American Indian explorer, trapper, and trader (1798–1866). (Courtesy Mercaldo Archives)

Revolutionary War. Beckwourth's mother was a mulatto slave on the Beckwourth plantation. Relocating his family to St. Louis, Missouri, Jennings sent James to school at the age of 10 and later apprenticed him as a blacksmith. Drawn to the outdoor life, young Beckwourth abandoned the idea of becoming a blacksmith and joined General William H. Ashley's Rocky Mountains Fur Trading Company in 1825 as a wrangler and body servant. As a trapper, Beckwourth established himself among many of his contemporaries such as Jim Bridger, Edward Rose, and Hugh Glass.

Adventurous, Beckwourth roamed throughout the Great Plains and Northwest as an independent trapper, first visiting Montana in 1825. He lived twice with the Crow Indians in Montana and during that time took two Native American wives. In 1828, he was made a member of the Crow tribe. He lived with the Crow for

almost seven years. In 1834, Beckwourth became a chief of chiefs of the Crow Indian nation, an almost unheard-of honor for any non-Indian. In 1850, Beckwourth discovered a pass in the Sierra Nevada Mountains that allowed wagons and horses relatively easy access to the west, becoming known as the Beckwourth Pass. In later years, he opened a bar and other businesses in a small village that would become Denver, Colorado. His life's exploits are recorded in his autobiography, *The Life and Adventures of James Beckwourth*, as told to Thomas Bonner in 1856. Beckwourth died in Montana at the Bighorn River among the Crow Indians in 1866.

Dorman, Isaiah (c. 1820–1876)

Frontiersman, guide, interpreter, and soldier, Isaiah Dorman, a former slave who served as an interpreter and guide on various private military expeditions on the western frontier for the U.S. Army during the Indian Wars, was the only African American known to have been present during the Battle of the Little Bighorn. Dorman perished in a battle with the Sioux Indians the same day General George Armstrong Custer was killed at the Little Bighorn River just three miles away.

Known for his diligence, dependability, and courage, Dorman's early life is a mystery. There are no photographs of him known to exist. What little is known is derived from military records. Records suggest that he was probably born in slavery around the 1820s in Louisiana to the D'Orman family, and like others, he escaped and went out West. By 1850, he was living with the Lakota tribe as a trapper and trader. He eventually settled near Fort Rice in the Dakota Territory, near present-day Bismarck, North Dakota, and married a woman of Inkpaduta's band of the Santee Sioux. There he supported himself by cutting wood. In the early fall of 1865, he was hired by the trading firm of Durkee & Peck to cut wood. Written records indicate that he was so strong that he could cut a cord of wood faster than his helper could stack it. There is also a story that his wife was a goddaughter of Sitting Bull and that the two were friends. When military officers discovered Dorman's relationship with the Sioux and his vast knowledge of the land, he was hired as a guide and interpreter.

On November 11, 1865, Dorman was hired as a courier to carry mail between Fort Wadsworth and Fort Rice, Dakota Territory, a distance of 360 miles. It is said that he had no horse and walked the entire distance with his sleeping bag over his shoulder and the mail in a waterproof pouch. He did this for about two years. He was rehired in 1867 to do the same job because it was too dangerous for soldiers to carry the mail. At the time, his income averaged $50 to $60 per month, which was comparable to a lieutenant in the army.

As he established himself on the frontier, he served in various capacities for the army. In September 1871, he served as a guide and interpreter for a party of engineers making the Northern Pacific Railroad Survey. For his service he was paid $100 per month. A month later, in October 1871, Dorman was hired as an interpreter at Fort Rice. He was paid $75 per month for his service.

With a well-established reputation and ability to speak the Sioux language, Dorman was hired by General George Armstrong Custer as an interpreter for his expedition to the Little Bighorn country in the late spring of 1876. Custer himself issued a special order that Isaiah should be brought along as an interpreter. On June 25, 1876, he accompanied the detachment of Major Marcus Reno's battalion that Custer ordered to cross the Little Bighorn River and attack the Indian encampment from the south. This attack exposed the battalion to concentrated fire from the Indians forcing Major Reno's retreat, but not before Dorman received a fatal wound to the chest. Pinned under his horse and left behind when Major Reno retired across the river to high

bluffs, Dorman's body was found stripped of all clothing. There are two accounts of how his body was deposed. One account suggests that upon discovery of his body by the Sioux women, Sitting Bull intervened to prevent the customary ritual of mutilation—a custom designed to prevent the victim from passing into the spirit world as a "whole man." Sitting Bull, then, buried his friend Isaiah Dorman with honor.

At the time of Dorman's death, $102.50 was due to him for services rendered during the months of May and June. The money was never claimed. The irony in the story of Isaiah Dorman is the fact that he would have remained unknown if not for the accidental or incidental identification of Dorman by Major Reno in his report. Another account has his body being recovered and buried on the Reno battlefield and subsequently removed in 1877 and taken to the Little Bighorn National Cemetery.

Rose, Edward (c. 1780–c. 1834)

Mountaineer, guide, interpreter, and fur trapper, African American Ed Rose, one of the first trappers involved in the early ventures on the western frontier and chief of the Crow Indians, was a trailblazer during the early nineteenth century. Traveling with some of the most well-known trappers, Rose went up the Missouri River in 1807 with Manuel Lisa in the first large-scale trapping expedition. He traveled along the Yellowstone River in 1809 with Ezekiel Williams. He was an interpreter and guide at Fort Wilson with Price Hunt, who led the Astorians westward in 1811. In 1823, he joined the famous William Ashley Expedition. It is unknown where Rose was born or precisely when, where, or how he died. It was said he was born around 1780, a slave to a mixed blood Cherokee trapper and African-Cherokee women. No written word of Rose is preserved.

The earliest record of Rose is in 1806 in the company of other trappers on the Osage River.

Supposedly, Rose was raised near Louisville, Kentucky. His first biographer was Lieutenant Reuben Holmes, who was with the Atkinson-O'Fallon expedition of 1825. His work was published in 1828 in the *St. Louis Beacon*. Washington Irving wrote of Rose in *Astoria* and in the *Adventures of Captain Bonneville*. David H. Coyner wrote of him in *The Lost Trappers*, published in 1859. It is said that sometime around 1834, Rose was scalped and killed by a group of Arikara Indians. He was ambushed along with friend Hugh Glass traveling on foot along the Yellowstone River.

York (1770–1832)

Slave and manservant, York was a valuable member of the Lewis and Clark expedition. During the 28-month journey, York had been treated as an equal. He hunted on his own, carried a gun, and voted. York's contributions were invaluable to the expedition. On one occasion, York risked his own life to save William Clark in a flood on the Missouri River near Great Falls in present-day Montana. York, the son of slaves Rose and Old York, was born in Caroline County, Virginia, and raised on a Kentucky plantation near Louisville with Clark, who inherited York in 1799 as part of his father's estate. York's display of skills, strength, and popularity made him a valuable member of the expedition.

Standing well over six feet and weighing more than 200 pounds, with dark skin and kinky hair, York was a source of fascination for the Native American people. The tribes had never seen a man of his dark complexion before, and all flocked around York and examined him. On one occasion while traveling through Montana in 1805, York's color intrigued and occupied the attention of a band of Shoshone Indians.

After the Corps of Discovery returned, York apparently asked Clark for his freedom based upon his good services during the expedition. Clark, who had settled in St. Louis, refused York's request, claiming financial difficulties,

A painting of York, only identified as York, the only African American member of the Lewis and Clark expedition and William Clark's personal slave. (AP/Wide World Photos)

although he allowed York to return temporarily to Louisville to rejoin his wife. Clark may have set York free sometime after 1816 and set him up with a business in Tennessee and Kentucky. There are, however, some doubts about this story. At least one other account suggests he may have escaped to live on the frontier. While some historians believe York was eventually freed, it has never been documented. He died of cholera sometime between 1822 and 1832 in Tennessee.

Cultural Contributions

Montana's Black Newspapers

The *Colored Citizen* and the *Montana Plaindealer*, out of Helena, and the *New Age*, published in Butte, were the most influential newspapers in Montana from 1894 to 1911 at the height of the black population. The demise of these papers probably had as much to do with politics as with demographics.

Helena's black newspapermen were among its best-known civic personalities. Joseph B. Bass and J. P. Ball Jr. founded their respective papers, the *Montana Plaindealer* and the *Colored Citizen*, in 1894. Bass and Ball edited these civic organizations until the papers went out of business. Ball also served as his own photographer. J. P. Ball Jr. is remembered for his effort to urge black voters to weigh in on the issue of whether Anaconda or Helena would be designated as the state capital. It is arguable whether the black population of Helena actually tilted the scales in Helena's favor, but Ball is credited as having played a notable role in this decision, even though his paper lasted a scant two months.

Just as life went out of the *Colored Citizen* as a result of its successful campaign—along with the rest of Helena—against the Anaconda Copper Company and its bid to make its town the capital of the state, so did Butte's *New Age* lose purpose in its connection with the copper company's campaign. In fact, it is precisely because of the support by *New Age* for the Anaconda Copper Company, later known as the Amalgamated Copper Company, that it too went out of business when Amalgamated won the license to mine the mineral fields around Butte. But unlike the *Colored Citizen*, *New Age* supported the Democratic Party, evidence that at some point it became less an organ of the black community and little more than the handmaiden of Amalgamated, since blacks otherwise had almost nothing to do with the Democratic Party at that time.

As for Helena's second black paper, the *Montana Plaindealer*, the most successful black news organ, its editor, Joseph B. Bass, identified with the Republicans, the party of Lincoln. Hailing from Topeka, Kansas, Bass started the *Plaindealer* in 1894, and it became the main organ of the African American community. Besides Bass's progressive-sounding editorials, his paper

published news of note alongside a gossip column that played a major part in sustaining a cohesive black community. Bass' progressivism promoted Booker T. Washington–style self-help projects in Helena, featuring in the newspaper Washington's speeches and ideas. Bass is also instrumental in forming a branch of the Booker T. Washington National Negro Business League.

The *Plaindealer's* view on racial matters, however, upset some of its black and white readers when Bass' paper took up the issue of gambling dens owned by blacks in the city of Helena and miscegenation. The gambling issue was associated with the Zanzibar Saloon. Black businessman Lloyd V. Graye, while he owned stock in reputable businesses such as a cleaners and a shoe repair shop, also owned the notorious Zanzibar. The issue of the Zanzibar became known as the "tempest on Clore Street." Owned jointly by Graye and David Gordon, the Zanzibar Club was more than a saloon: it was also a gambling establishment and meeting place for prostitutes and their johns. It had been popular among the black soldiers housed at Fort Harrison, but it also attracted white and black civilians. Matters not directly related to it brought down the Zanzibar, however. While Helena's mayor wanted to run on a platform of cleaning up his town, two murders, one associated with the club, the other not, fueled the ill feelings of the citizens and made them strongly disposed to closing the establishment.

The controversy over the political and legal issues associated with Lewis and Clark County Attorney Leon LaCroix's attempt to close the Zanzibar brought Bass' paper considerable debate. In his attempt to put an end to this business, LaCroix raised the ire of Bass, who felt that LaCroix's actions were racially tinged. Since LaCroix was also running for reelection against a Republican candidate, Bass was urged on by the Republican establishment to cross LaCroix. Bass also had hopes, consequently, for a patronage job, but it was not given to him, wounding Bass' sense of party loyalty tremendously. He felt he had been used to exploit the black voters of Helena.

Yet he placed his hope in the Republicans again when a miscegenation bill came up in the Republican-dominated state Senate on February 6, 1909, and subsequently passed, outlawing marriage between blacks and whites. With bitter closure achieved on this controversy, the *Plaindealer* declined, going out of business two years later. It is also true that the black population of Helena declined precipitously between 1912 and 1920. In fact, in 1912, the last black soldiers to be housed at the nearby fort left, seriously eroding the newspaper's readership.

Bibliography

Burton, Art A. *Black, Buckskin, and Blue: African American Scouts and Soldiers on the Western Frontier.* Austin: Texas Eakin Press, 1999.

Felton, Harold W. *Edward Rose: Negro Trail Blazer.* New York: Dodd, Mead & Company, 1967.

Felton, Harold W. *Jim Beckwourth: Negro Mountain Man.* New York: Dodd, Mead & Company, 1966.

Katz, William Loren. *Black Pioneers: An Untold Story.* New York: Atheneum Books, 1999.

Lang, William L. "The Nearly Forgotten Negroes on the Last Chance Gulch." *Pacific Northwest Quarterly* 70 (1979).

Lang, William L. "Tempest on Clore Street: Race and Politics in Helena, Montana, 1906." *Scratchgravel Hills* 3 (1980).

McConnell, Roland C. "Isaiah Dorman and the Custer Expedition." *Journal of Negro History* 33, no. 3 (1948).

Myers, Rex C. "Montana's Negro Newspapers, 1894–1911." *Montana Journalism Review* 16 (1973).

Ravage, John W. *Black Pioneers: Images of the Black Experience on the North American Frontier.* Salt Lake City: The University of Utah Press, 1997.

Taylor, Quintard. "The Emergence of Afro-American Communities in the Pacific Northwest 1865–1910." *Journal of Negro History* 64 (1979).

Taylor, Quintard. *In Search of the Racial Frontier: African Americans in the West.* New York: W. W. Norton & Company, 1999.

Taylor, Quintard. "Montana." *The African American Encyclopedia.* Vol. 4. New York: Simon & Schuster, 1995, 1838–1840.